AN LEABHAR MÒR

THE GREAT BOOK *of* GAELIC

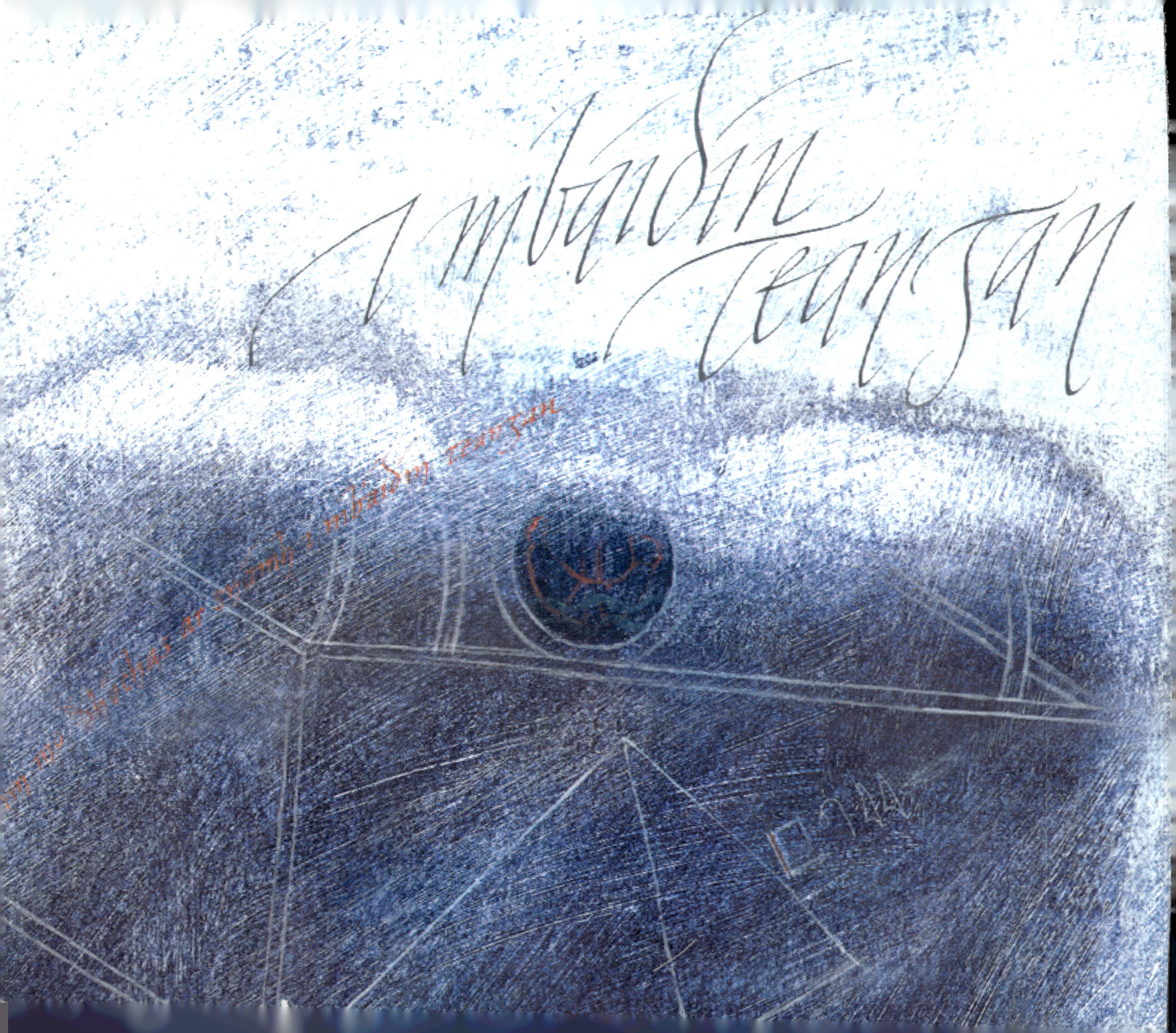
i mbáidín teangan
m mo dhóchas ar snámh i mbáidín teangan

AN LEABHAR MÒR

THE GREAT BOOK *of* GAELIC

Edited by
MALCOLM MACLEAN
and THEO DORGAN

Editorial Panel
Aodán Mac Póilín, Will Maclean, Iain MacDhòmhnaill, Aonghas Dubh MacNeacail,
Frances Breen, Marisa Macdonald, Arthur Watson, Mairi S. MacLeod

CANONGATE BOOKS

PROISEACT NAN EALAN
The Gaelic Arts Agency

First published in Great Britain in 2002
by Canongate Books,
14 High Street,
Edinburgh EH1 1TE

10 9 8 7 6 5 4 3 2 1

For details of copyright permissions, see page 310

British Library Cataloguing-in-Publication Data
A catalogue record for this book is available
on request from the British Library

The Gaelic Arts Agency, Proiseact nan Ealan,
gratefully acknowledges the financial support of the following funders:
Iomairt Cholm Cille; the Scottish Executive; Highlands and Islands Enterprise;
the Scottish Arts Council; the Arts Council of Northern Ireland; An Chomhairle Ealaion;
Comhairle nan Leabhraichean; Comataidh Craolaidh Gaidhlig; Comhairle nan Eilean Siar;
Glasgow City Council; the Esmee Fairbairn Foundation; the Millennium Festival
and the British Council

The publisher gratefully acknowledges the financial assistance of
the Scottish Arts Council in the publication of this volume

ISBN 1 84195 250 8

Design and art direction by James Hutcheson
Design and layout by Barrie Tullett
Set in Monotype Bembo and Trajan

Printed by Butler and Tanner,
Frome, Somerset

www.canongate.net
www.leabharmor.net
www.gaelic-arts.com

for Jo

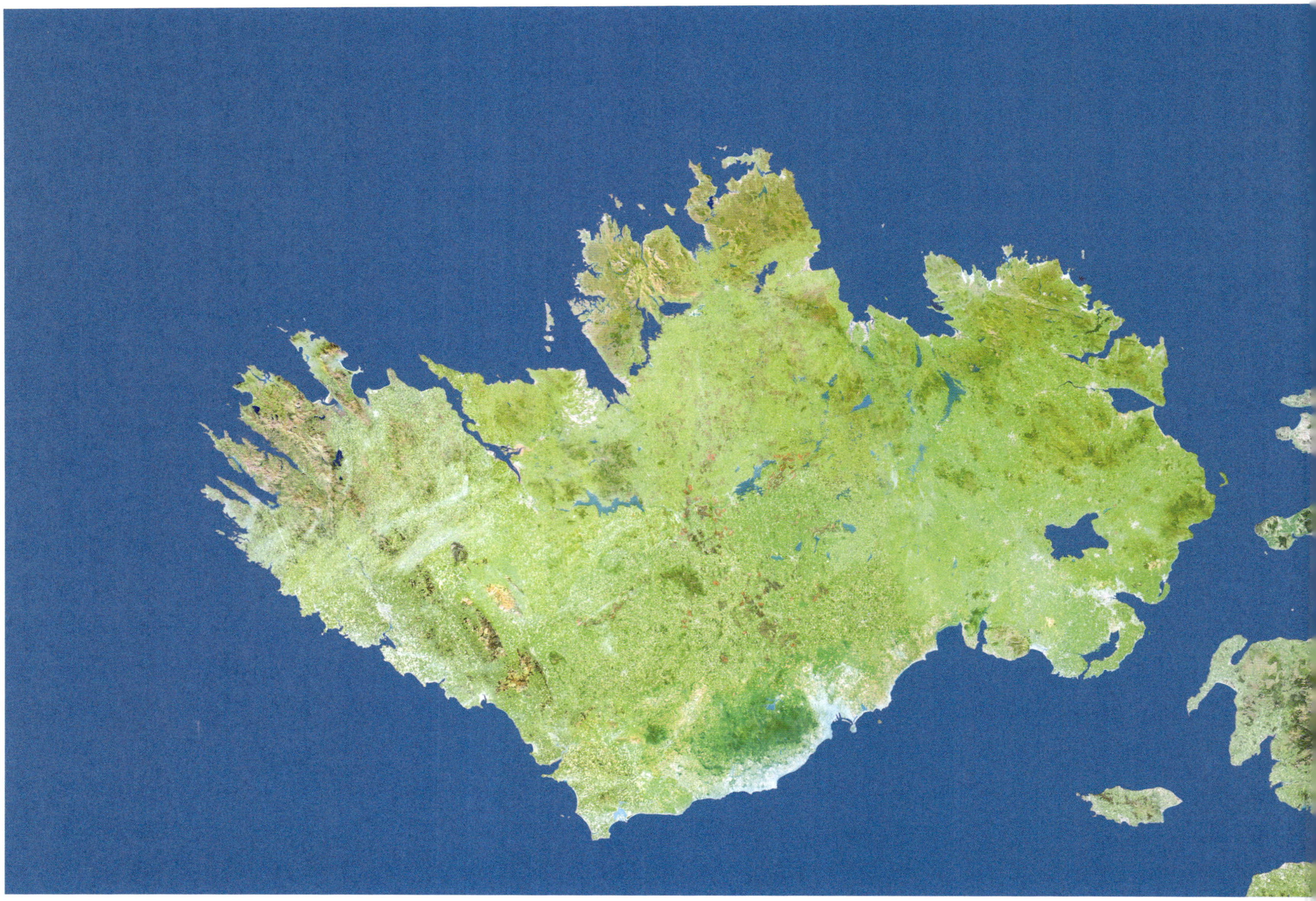

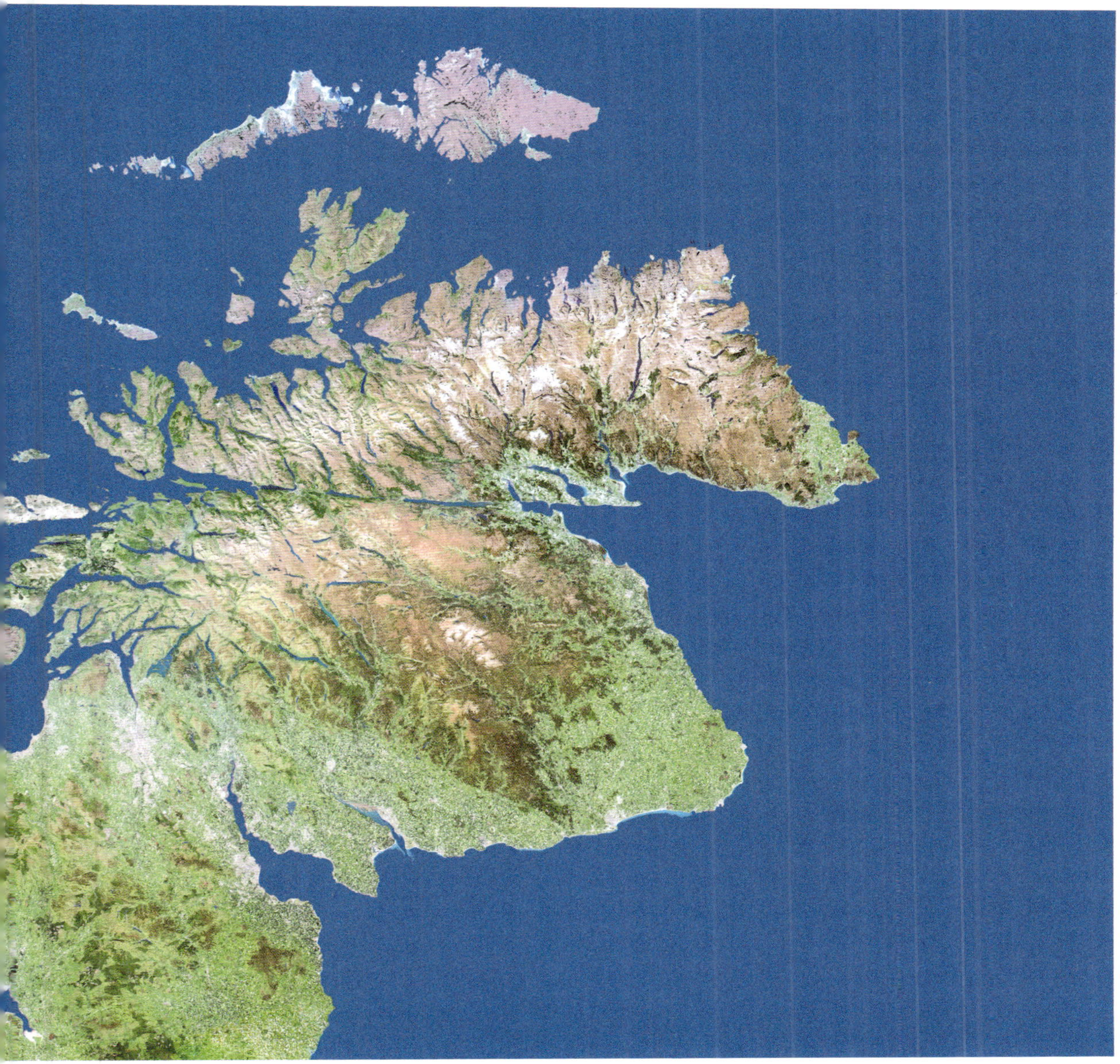

... an fhéile
Nach do reub an cuan,
Nach do mhill mìle bliadhna;
Buaidh a' Ghàidheil buan.

... the humanity
That the sea did not tear,
That a thousand years did not spoil:
The quality of the Gael permanent.

Somhairle MacGill-Eain
Sorley MacLean
1911–96

NUALA NÍ DHOMHNAILL

Ealaíontóir/Artist:
Will Maclean

Peannaire/Calligrapher:
Frances Breen

Aistritheoir/Translator:
Paul Muldoon

Ceist na Teangan
Nuala Ní Dhomhnaill

Cuirim mo dhóchas ar snámh
i mbáidín teangan
faoi mar a leagfá naíonán
i gcliabhán
a bheadh fite fuaite
de dhuilleoga feileastraim
is bitiúman agus pic
bheith cuimilte lena thóin

ansan é a leagadh síos
i measc na ngiolcach
is coigeal na mban sí
le taobh na habhann,
féachaint n'fheadaraís
cá dtabharfaidh an sruth é,
féachaint, dála Mhaoise,
an bhfóirfidh iníon Fharoinn?

The Language Issue
Paul Muldoon

I place my hope on the water
in this little boat
of the language, the way a body might
put
an infant

in a basket of intertwined
iris leaves,
its underside proofed
with bitumen and pitch,

then set the whole thing down amidst
the sedge
and bulrushes by the edge
of a river

only to have it borne hither and
thither,
not knowing where it might end up;
in the lap, perhaps,
of some Pharaoh's daughter.

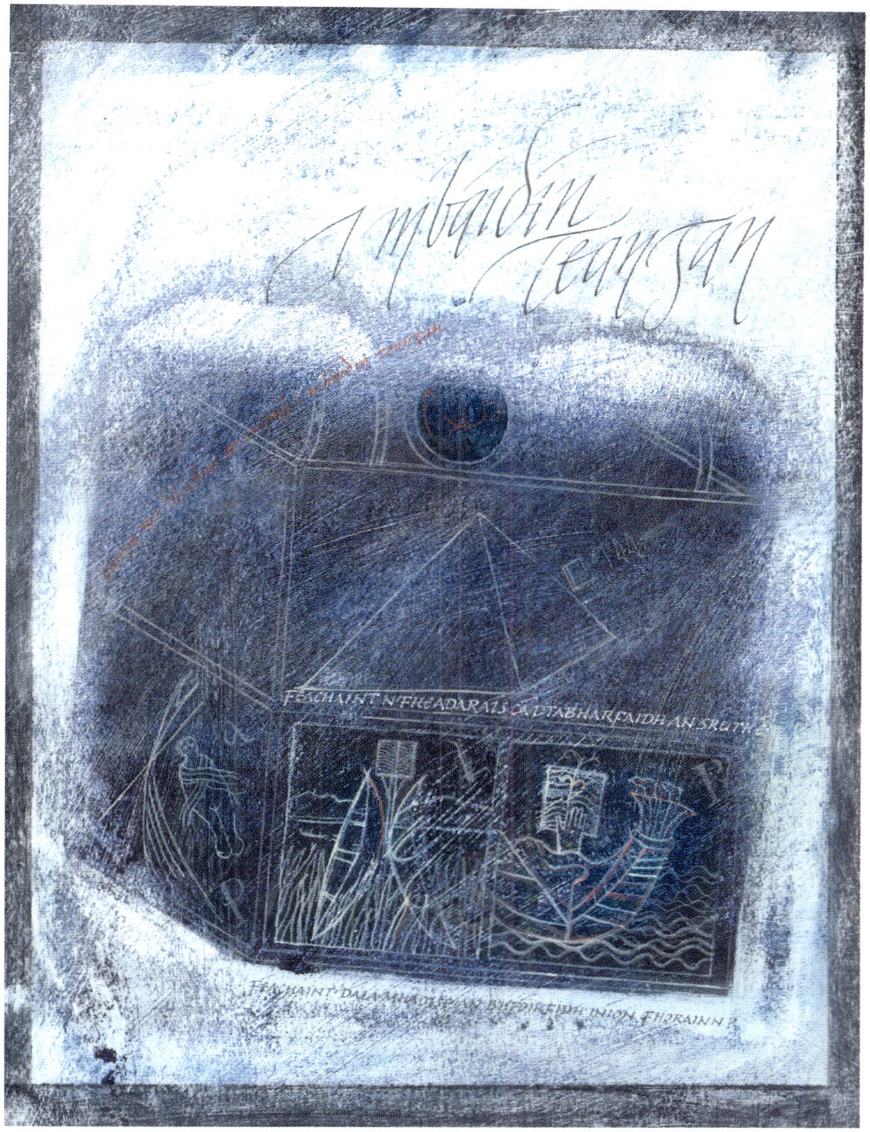
FEACHAINT N'FHEADARAIS CA DTABHARFAIDH AN SRUTH

CONTENTS

INTRODUCTIONS

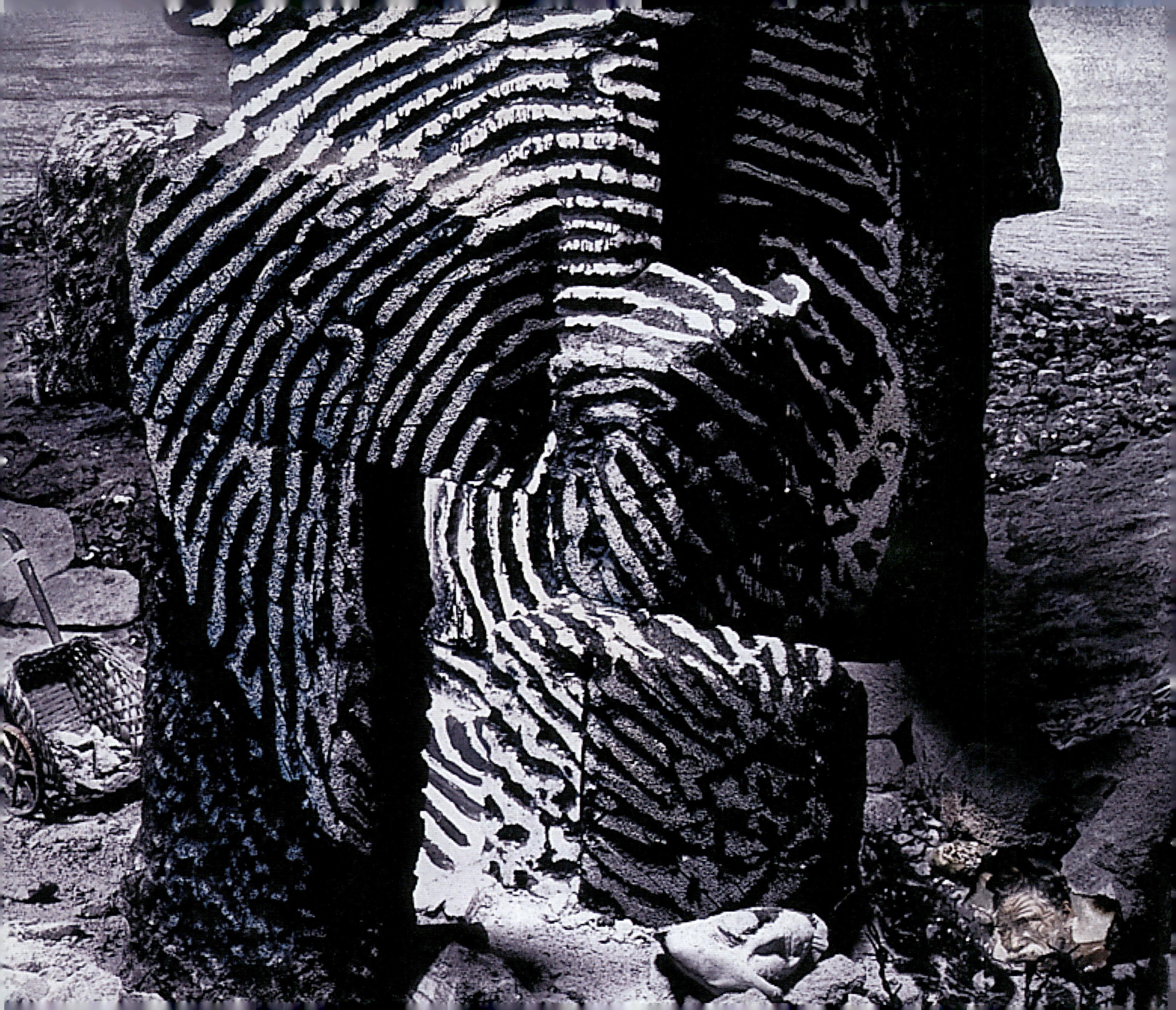

I

AN LEABHAR MÒR

General Introduction

Malcolm Maclean

'GOOD IDEAS DON'T MIND who has them.' On the other hand, Cholm Cille or St Columba, once wisely adjudicated a dispute with the resolution, 'to every cow its calf'. The *Leabhar Mòr* is the 'calf' of the Great Book of Ireland which is itself one of the many calves of the Book of Kells. Its genesis dates to a crisp and sunny winter's day in January 1997.

I had come to the home of Poetry Ireland in Dublin Castle to view the Great Book of Ireland and to meet its architect, the poet Theo Dorgan. Our conversation was lively and ranged from the European *Schottenklöster* and rock 'n' roll, to the fragile ceasefire in the North and Sorley MacLean. Latterly we talked about the continuing power of Gaelic poetry, despite centuries of division, to inspire and delight and to connect our countries. By the time we parted it seemed obvious to both of us that the time was right for a Great Book of Gaelic, a 21st-century *Leabhar Mòr,* that would celebrate 1,500 years of shared Gaelic heritage and embrace the poetry of both Scotland and Ireland.

The idea grew and I returned some months later with a proposal which mapped out how, if all went well, we could create a new book that built on Theo's experience in new ways. We agreed to take the leap together and he gifted me a book of his poems inscribed, 'For Malcolm, the day we decided to crucify ourselves with *Leabhar Mòr na Gaeilge/Gaidhlig. Ar aghaidh linn!*' The idea has continued to grow.

The first confirmation that the time was right came later that summer with President Mary Robinson's visit to Scotland and the announcement of the Columba Initiative, *Iomairt Chaluim Chille.* This important inter-governmental initiative, aiming to renew and redevelop the links between Gaelic Scotland and Ireland, became a key partner in progressing the *Leabhar Mòr.*

The time was also right in terms of Scottish and Irish constitutional change. By devolution in 1999, the Council of the Isles and the Northern Ireland peace process had created a new political context in which the idea of the *Leabhar Mòr* has flourished. In many ways the artists have anticipated or paralleled the best of the political process by working across old boundaries, seeking new perspectives, creating new relationships and reconciling history with the cutting edge of the here-and-now.

The key confirmation that the time was right, however, was the immediate enthusiasm of the great team of talents that collectively created this Great Book.

The idea of the *Leabhar Mòr* has generated a remarkable degree of goodwill from the hundreds of artists, poets and others who have contributed generously along the way. One American visitor heard a BBC radio programme about the *Leabhar Mòr* while caught up in London traffic, and was inspired to pop a £50 note into the post 'as a contribution to this wonderful project'.

Why the idea of the *Leabhar Mòr* has attracted such interest and support is beyond the scope of this brief introduction but three principle factors suggest themselves.

Firstly, ancient meets modern on a grand scale with 100 contemporary artists' perspectives on 1,500 years of Gaelic history and identity. Secondly, it also transcends academic and creative disciplines in its collaborative exploration of poetry and language through contemporary arts practice. Finally, perhaps the most important factor, is that it transcends political boundaries to celebrate the unity and diversity of Gaelic culture as an integral part of contemporary life in both countries.

A language map of Europe reflects cultural realities that bear little resemblance to political boundaries. This is particularly true of Gaelic Scotland and Ireland. There are no two countries in Europe with more in common. We share a mythology, three languages, a rich music tradition and some significant history, and yet a great deal of this enduring connection has been consistently glossed over or deliberately obscured.

It was the Irish Gaels, known as the Scoti, who migrated into Scotland from the 5th century and gave it its name. The most famous artefact from Ireland's golden age, the Book of Kells, originated on the Scottish Island of Iona. It was the Gaels who united Scotland in the 9th century and made Gaelic the language of the medieval court. The 'Irish' Gaelic culture in the Scottish Highlands survived that in Ireland by a century and a half. The Scots were 'planted' into Northern Ireland from the 17th century and hundreds of thousands of Irish people migrated to Scotland in the 19th and 20th centuries. It is less well known that the Hebrides were once mapped as the Irish Isles or that Michael Davitt was a leading figure in the Scottish Highland Land League.

The interwoven pattern of our separate histories continues and the Gaelic language remains our most potent living link. The models of modern Gaelic language development in Scotland, Northern Ireland and the Republic have all been different and there is everything to be gained from sharing experience and collaborating on future developments.

Scottish Gaelic, for example, has an unexpected resonance in Northern Ireland where Gaelic has become widely regarded as a badge of Catholic republicanism. The predominant protestantism of the Scots Gaels, and their habit of voting for all parties and for none, provides a healthy antidote to such stereotyping and opens up fresh perspectives on old issues of language and identity for both the unionist and the nationalist communities.

The Irish connection expands the horizons of the Scottish Gaidhealtachd following decades of contraction. It does so at a time when the Gaelic community looks hopefully to the new Scottish Parliament for a new recognition. Since the 1980s there have been important developments in Gaelic-medium education, broadcasting, the arts and the cultural economy, but Scotland's overall relationship with its Gaelic dimension remains ambivalent. The language has been reclaimed from the museums but remains poised between eclipse and rejuvenation.

This issue is not local but international. One of our planet's 6,500 languages becomes extinct every two weeks and the total number of languages is likely to halve in the coming century. Language death is now of global significance and sustaining language diversity will be one of the paramount cultural challenges of the 21st century. If more artists recognise this acceleration in language death as an appropriate subject for literature, drama, music, visual art and as yet uncategorised artforms, then the issue will come alive in the minds of the general public. The *Leabhar Mòr* is a modest, but significant and optimistic, step in that direction.

It falls to me to outline the practical process that, step by step, brought the *Leabhar Mòr* into existance. In planning the project we followed the advice of poet Michael Davitt to 'trust in God, but tie your camel'. We were able to learn from the experience of the making of the Great Book of Ireland and use that to create a very different kind of book. My own visual arts background meant a different perspective that inevitably shifted the emphasis.

Our decision to work with hand-made paper, as opposed to vellum, enhanced dramatically the scope for visual arts experimentation. The selection process for poets and artists would be different. We would work with a team of ten calligraphers/typographers instead of a single individual. Each page would be framed as a discrete artwork and all would be toured as an art exhibition prior to their binding into a permanent book form. The artworks would not be illustrations but creative responses to the poetry. The artists' visual translations would be intensely personal reflections emanating from a poem or theme.

The potential for synergy would be maximised by means of a touring exhibition, publication of a book, development of a website, production of a BBC radio series, television documentary and an education pack. The concept was clarified and budgeted in 1998 and we began to raise the necessary funding.

At the first meeting of the full editorial team at the Glasgow home of MP Brian Wilson in June 1999, the selection process for both the poets and the artists was hammered out. The literary panel aimed to select 25 Scottish and 25 Irish poets, and to invite them to provide one poem of their own and to nominate one other, giving – in all – 100 poems. Following extensive discussion, however, it was finally decided that 15 Scots and 15 Irish poets would each provide one poem of their own and nominate two others, giving a total of 50 poems. The remaining ten poems were nominated by other writers with an intimate knowledge of Gaelic poetry. They were all asked to nominate their preferred translation.

Consequently, the *Leabhar Mòr* is not a conventional anthology, with all the gravitas that that implies, but a collection of favourite poems that inevitably omits some important poets. The *Leabhar Mòr* makes no pretence of being comprehensive or balanced, but offers a poet's and artist's insight into Gaelic poetry, and so may be more human, more inclusive and more unpredictable. Each poet is represented once and the 100 poems come from almost every century between the 6th and the 21st. An impossible feat for most other European languages, including English.

The visual artists were selected on the basis of 50 per cent by nomination and 50 per cent by open submission. Key individuals with a knowledge of the visual arts and of the Gaelic communities were asked to propose artists on the understanding that at least two of their nominations would be invited to contribute. Advertisements placed in the arts and Gaelic press in both countries invited open-entry submissions from artists interested in the project. The difficult task of selecting the final 100 artists took place in the Chester Beatty Library in Dublin and in a hotel ballroom in the Western Isles in early 2001. The consistently high quality of the finished artwork confirms the good judgement of our Scots and Irish visual arts panels.

Representatives from both the literary and visual arts panels met in Newman House in Dublin for the pairing of poets and artists. Each artist's work was shown and discussed as the panels sought five poems that might suit the artist's interests. Every artist was offered a poem by a living and a deceased Scottish poet, a poem by a living and a deceased Irish poet, plus one 'wild card' poem. The artists indicated their choices of poem in order of preference.

The poems were finally allocated on a first-come, first-served basis as an incentive to the artists to choose and respond promptly. Eventually 75 per cent of the artists were allocated either their first or second choice of poem and the remaining 25 per cent were dealt with on a one-to-one basis until we matched all 100 poems to all 100 artists.

The ten-strong calligraphy team was assembled and led by Frances Breen, and included typographer Don Addison. They first met in the Writers' Centre in Dublin at the time of the Irish press launch on *Latha Brìde*, February 2001, traditionally known as Poets' Day. Forty artists, calligraphers and a support team met in the Belfast College of Art later that month.

The Visual Research Centre in Dundee, led by Arthur Watson and supported by Paul Harrison, was commissioned to provide all technical, printmaking and other support for the artists and calligraphers throughout the artwork production period. They also supervised the production and distribution of the hand-made paper.

The process has been as important as the product throughout the making of the *Leabhar Mòr*. Simply bringing together substantial numbers of poets, artists, calligraphers, academics, arts workers, film makers, publishers, designers and others has had its own intrinsic value. Effecting introductions across artforms, borders and languages has initiated new understandings and dialogues and some lasting relationships.

The process of 'translation', characterised by one artist as 'a letting go', has also been central. Not only the translation from the original Gaelic text into English, but the translation from text to artist's image, the calligraphers' squaring of the circle and the subsequent translation of the *Leabhar Mòr* into other media such as this book, the film, the BBC radio series and the website. These multiple translations enable the *Leabhar Mòr* to be experienced in several ways simultaneously and offer a rich compound value.

The following introductory texts provide background information on the Irish and Scottish Gaelic poetry, both ancient and modern, and on the artworks. professor Colm Ó Baoill outlines the historical development of Irish and Scottish Gaelic poetry over 1,400 years from the time of Cholm Cille to the 20th century. Theo Dorgan and Ronald Black focus on the 20th-century poets and Professor Duncan Macmillan provides expert commentary on the visual artworks.

It has been my privilege to work with all of the remarkable team of talents that has created the *Leabhar Mòr* and given new shapes and forms to the Gaelic language. Every picture carries the story of its making, of those who made it and the innumerable creative interactions, decisions and discoveries that have brought it into being. Different readers will seek, and find, different things within its pages. It is already something more than the sum of its parts. Maybe it represents a small punctuation mark in the Gaelic story. Time will tell if it marks an ending or a beginning – or simply a great, illuminated question mark.

Dhòmhsa dheth, thàinig seo uile a-mach à gaol mòr eadar mi fhìn agus tè shònraichte bho eilean Eireann.

Malcolm Maclean
August 2002

EXPLANATORY NOTES

Poetry and artwork pages:
The pre-20th-century poems are generally, but not exclusively, sequenced in chronological order. Each poetry page gives the poet's dates, the original Gaelic text of the poem and its English language translation plus the names of the poet, artist, calligrapher, translator and nominator of the poem.

Key poetry lines:
The lines of text indicated in bold are those featured by the artist and calligrapher in the artwork.

Translations:
The English versions of the poems are generally the choice of those who nominated the Gaelic texts. They range from literal prose translations to free interpretations of the originals.

Supplementary Texts:
Where poems have been too long to include in their entireity on the one page edited excerpts are continued in the Supplementary Texts section that begins on page 233.

Alternative Sources:
A few of the poems run to several hundred lines and have been too long for inclusion in even the supplementary texts. The Alternative Sources section on page 265 suggests publications where these poems are available in their entireity.

Biographies:
Brief biographies of all of the poets, artists, calligraphers, nominators and other key contributors are provided in Gaelic and English on page 267. The individual biographies are grouped around the particular poems with which they were involved. Each biography is given only once so where calligraphers and nominators have been involved in more than one collaboration they are identified by name only in the subsequent biography listings. Further information on individual contributors is available on the *Leabhar Mòr* website at www.leabharmor.net

Artists' Media:
The listing on page 307 gives a note of the diverse media used by the visual artists in the production of their artworks. Where the artists have worked with a printmaker whose name is known to us they have also been credited in the listing. We apologise for any omissions.

Bibliography:
The bibliography on page 311 offers some further reading from a range of other publications on Irish and Scottish Gaelic poetry, Irish and Scottish visual arts, calligraphy and the language question.

II

SCOTTISH AND IRISH VISUAL ART

Duncan MacMillan

Leabhar Mòr, The Great Book of Gaelic, celebrates the reconnection of Gaelic Ireland and Gaelic Scotland after nearly five centuries of religious and political division imposed by forces of history far beyond the control of the people of either country. When peace finally came to Northern Ireland, or at least when a process began which it is hoped will lead to real peace in that troubled province, it was the fading of the last aftershock of the Reformation. The fault-line from that cataclysm generating these aftershocks is not unique in Europe, but uniquely it has remained tragically active till now, and it is this that has split Ireland from Scotland. One side was predominantly Protestant, the other predominantly Catholic, and so, once united by language, they were divided by faith. The consequence of this espousal of the two opposing sides in the religious divide was that, although in so many ways the positions of Scotland and Ireland were similar and their common history so important, that similarity and those links were obscured by religious difference and it was difficult, or even impossible, for the two sibling nations to make common cause as so often they might have done.

The impact on Gaelic culture was profound; all the more so as in both Ireland and Scotland the fault-line coincided pretty much with the linguistic frontier and for much of the time the Gaels found themselves on the losing side politically. What was until the Reformation a single culture, or at least one in two closely allied parts, has since then been decisively split. If the loss of most of its medieval heritage of religious art and architecture is the most conspicuous consequence of the Reformation in Scotland, breaking the connection of the Gaelic part of the country with Ireland was surely as disastrous. Now, with the onset of peace in Northern Ireland, it has at last been possible to reunite the two divided halves of Gaeldom.

As *An Leabhar Mòr* celebrates the restoration of these vital links between Scottish and Irish Gaelic, so too, however, by uniting that ambition with a major project in the visual arts in specific and intimate relationship with the great, shared tradition of Gaelic poetry, it takes on both sides of the loss that stemmed from the Reformation: the divided language and the lost art. The Book of Kells is the grandest symbol of this ancient common culture. Preserved for more than a thousand years in Ireland, it was written in St Columba's abbey on Iona at a time when the waters of the Irish Sea did not divide Scotland and Ireland but united them. Written in a monastic scriptorium, it was the product, we can only suppose, of a great cooperative effort. So too is *An Leabhar Mòr* and it is also intended that its pages will eventually be bound into a great book as its name implies. But there, nevertheless, the similarity ends. Instead of the unity of the Book of Kells, we have the diversity of a work created by a hundred modern artists, all as highly individual as we expect our artists to be. In the result there are as many different approaches as there are artists and their contributions are every bit as diverse, both in form and in medium, as the modern stress on individualism necessarily entails. In form alone the contributions vary widely. There are paintings, collages, photographs and prints of many kinds. Joanne Breen has even made a miniature tapestry. Mhairi Killin has used copper wire. Alastair MacLennan's contribution was in origin a performance.

We would be profoundly disappointed were there to be any less variety. But then, to add to this complexity, in addition to the one hundred artists there are the calligraphers whose brilliant contribution is so important here. In many cases they have worked independently of the artists, adding their work to the finished art work and so contributing another vector of individuality to the whole. Then there are the poets who range from anonymous authors contemporary with the Book of Kells itself to writers of today. In addition to them, however, there are also the poets involved in the selection of the poetry, fifteen each from Ireland and Scotland. The poetry they have chosen ranges from the incidental to the tragic.

There is great love poetry that speaks of the universals of human experience. There is poetry of loss and poetry of hope. But then on top of all this there is the lottery of the distribution of these diverse chosen texts to the individual artists. Finally, all this has been brought together and wrought into a single entity with great skill at Dundee Visual Research Centre with the employment of the latest high-tech printmaking equipment.

The whole thing in all its dizzying complexity is definitively a product of the fragmented aesthetics of the modern world. But microcosmic chaos can produce macrocosmic order. In a stormy sea, the disorder of the restless surface does not diminish the grand unity of the whole and there are themes and continuities that come through the total work in spite of its diversity. Kate Whiteford and Sean Hillen, for instance, both touch directly on the rejoining that is central to the project. Illustrating the MacKenzie woman's seventeenth-century poem of love surviving the violence of a bitter feud, Sean Hillen takes the image of a handshake against the landscape of Kosovo, but Ann Bowen's vivid, joyous calligraphy lifts it above cliché to make this gesture a celebration. Kate Whiteford illustrates, albeit very loosely, Murchadh MacPhàrlain's poem 'I Saw at a Distance the Hill'. The hill of the first line appears as a schematic form in her print, but the main part of her image is nevertheless very telling as it bears on the whole book. It is taken from a piece of waste tweed created at the junction on the loom between two different lengths as the weaver has moved from one to the next without cutting warp. The two joined halves in the original piece are in red and blue. In the print, this is rendered in monochrome, but the interweaving of the two different patterns to make one is clearly legible and, reduced to a single colour, the continuity between the two parts is even clearer, but the image of shears also reminds us that each piece has its own identity.

This is a good epitome of the whole project, but the process of reunification that it renders so beautifully also reaches more deeply into our common culture and provides a theme for the book that is appropriately broader than the circumstances of its creation. For if *An Leabhar Mòr* celebrates the transcendence at last of the religious fault-lines of the Reformation which have perpetuated ancient schisms of politics and religion at the expense of the integrity of Gaelic culture, it also addresses another more general fault-line, the dualism that runs through the whole of Western culture.

Some of the images here work superbly as illustration at the level of visual equivalence. There is Simon Fraser's medieval scholar with his magician's coat, dancing with his feline companion, Pangur the cat; and Neil MacPherson's mountaineer striding through the clouds. Frances Breen's script flies like the author's embattled aircraft through the flak rendered by Fionnuala Ní Chiosáin as delicate blobs of ink in her response to the poem 'D-Day' by Pól Ó Muirí. Stan Clementsmith and Réiltín Murphy have created speaking trees reminiscent of Arthur Rackham, one of the greatest illustrators of fairy tales. Caitlín Gallagher captures the furtiveness of secret love in her response to Niall Mór Mac Muireadhaigh's poem, her image beautifully matched by David McGrail's calligraphy. Catherine Harper's gloriously wanton woman in her unlaced corset responds enthusiastically to the bawdy female voice in the poem by the fifteenth-century poet Iseabal Ní Mhic Cailéin. John Bellany finds a match for his own personal imagery in Alan Titley's poem, 'The Ship Sailing'.

Indeed illustration is not really the word to describe such partnerships, and in the illuminated books of Europe before the advent of printing and the Reformation that it in part precipitated, that was how the relationship of text and picture worked. It really was a partnership. In the result, word and image are indivisible. They project unity, not duality. In the Book of Kells the mystery enshrined in the words of the Gospel is expressed in the decorations; or better, the illuminations that adorn the page do literally light up the text, give substance to the light that the devout monks who made the book saw shining from the words that they transcribed, make divinity immanent. This is a difficult concept nowadays, perhaps, for words for us are mundane things, transparent vehicles, invisible servants not jewels that illuminate. The form of our alphabet helps this illusion. In China or Japan, the pictograms of the Kanji alphabet still keep their character as pictures needing interpretation. They take their place on the page alongside a painted image and the two are visibly one, parallel manifestations of the same imaginative energy enshrined indifferently in poem or picture. Instead in the West we have letters that are as neutral as counters, and so the written word stands in danger of losing its transparency and vitality to seem as inert as a coin or a brick. Instead of building windows with words to let light in, we build walls with them to keep it out and so imprison thought.

The dangers in this approach to the written language have been the preoccupation of many modern thinkers, but long before Derrida or Foucault, William Blake understood that there was a perilous gulf between the rational word and the imaginative freedom embodied in poetry and picture. He saw this gulf as exemplifying the triumph of reason over the imagination. The imagination which, as the fount of sympathy, is the source of our moral natures and so the principal means by which we understand our unity with our fellow creatures and all the world around us. It must be free, but he saw it imprisoned by cold reason. This he thought was the real nature of the Fall. By objectifying the word, we objectify the world itself, and so in dualism we detach ourselves from it with consequences that we now know are potentially disastrous.

Where the rational word is dominant, the potentially imaginative image is reduced to illustration. Its power is limited and as a subservient reflection of the meaning inherent in the words, it is no longer able to enhance them. To overcome this, imitating the great illuminated books of the Middle Ages, Blake sought to recombine word and image, even devising his own method of relief etching so that they would literally be one as they were printed, and so he might recapture the imaginative potential of their union. In his books the images do not merely translate the burden of the words into a different medium. They embody the imaginative energy enshrined in them, liberate them and restore their power. And that of course is what we have so often here: artist and calligrapher cooperating and their work so entwined as to be indivisible.

In this the role of the calligraphers has been crucial, for they have woven the texts with immense skill into the images to make something that really is indivisible. Often too they have given power and mystery back to the word by transcribing, not the whole text, but only a fragment of it, a few lines, or even a single word picked out like a talisman. Take the spectacular fireworks of Ann Bowen's calligraphy running across Mary Avril Gillan's painting to capture the image in the poem by Tomás Mac Síomóin where 'waves may sing beneath the sun'; or the whirling wind of many coloured words in the slipstream of John Byrne's image of himself and his wife, Tilda Swinton, riding naked on a motorbike, for all the world as though Tam O' Shanter had joined Cutty Sark on her broomstick. Frances Breen has echoed the curling lines of the waves in Dòmhnall MacIomhair's poem, 'The Sea's Lofty Roar' in her calligraphy to Clare Langan's images of the sea; while David McGrail's calligraphy blends with Eileen Ferguson's landscape like the boom of the bittern's voice in the mist in Cathal Buí Mac Giolla Ghunna's 'The Yellow Bittern'. Likewise Réiltín Murphy's text merges with the waves of Fiona Hutchison's sea. One of the most beautiful pages is by Deirdre O'Mahony and Réiltín Murphy, again illustrating the tender elegy to his dead wife by the thirteenth-century poet, Muireadhach Albanach. The text is written in grand monumental script as though on a grave slab over the impression of a prostrate body, the colour of cold clay.

Oona Hyland in her lovely etching has taken as her inspiration the lines of Cairistìona NicFhearghais's poem, 'Though I were left all alone/with not a thing but a shift,/my fair young love'. She has created her etching from an impression of an actual shift onto which she has painstakingly embroidered words in the calligraphy of Donald Murray. The embroidered shift has itself then been passed through the etching press and the result is the absolute integration of word and image just as Blake sought to achieve it in his own process of relief etching. Frances Hegarty and Frances Breen have achieved the same thing working in black on black. The calligrapher's text is only differentiated from the artist's sooty black image by its reflective, shiny surface. Thus it renders brilliantly the utter blackness of Nuala Ní Dhomhnaill's poem called simply 'Dubh' – 'Black'. Then in contrast there is the simple joyfulness of Michael Kane's painting and Frances Breen's calligraphy in Antoin Ó Raifteirí's poem, 'The Lass from Bally-na-Lee', a spirited lass to match the spirited writing. Louise Donaldson's calligraphy is carried in a simple gold band in Kevin MacLean's rendering of the image of a gold-banded hat in the poem in praise of her handsome lover by Eibhlín Dhubh Ní Chonaill, 'How well your hat suited you,/ Bright, gold-banded'.

These poems have been given a vivid imaginative life in their new visual form. One of the finest examples of this is Alastair MacLennan's contribution, a response to Anne C. Frater's poem about the terrible sinking of the *Iolaire*, the *Eagle*, returning to Stornoway with two hundred demobbed soldiers and sailors on New Year's night, 1919. With special cruelty, fate decreed that they should survive the horrors of the Western Front only to drown within sight of home. The basis of the image is a manipulated photograph, a bird's eye view – an eagle's?– of the artist himself immersed in water. This was the performance. Frances Breen's transcription of the poem floats on the surface of the water like flowers, wreaths of words thrown into the sea in memory of the lost. It is a moving and beautiful equivalent to the poem and to the tragic impact of the event it records.

In literary terms one of the key works in the collection is Sorley MacLean's poem 'Hallaig'. In response to the tragic emptiness of the once populous place that the poet describes so movingly in such lines as 'The window is nailed and boarded/through which I saw the west . . .', Donald Urquhart has provided an image of mute pathos, a simple wash of grey painted with water from the burn at Hallaig. But it would be only mute if it were not for the dense dark script in which Louise Donaldson has transcribed the poem alongside, a pibroch in calligraphy sounding across the silence that artist and poet evoke. Perhaps the most eloquent and apposite expression of the significance of this integration of word and image, however, comes from Remco de Fouw and Réiltín Murphy taking an image from the poem by Kevin MacNeil of a poetic oar, like a 'huge broken pen'. The oar is a line of beautiful writing dipped in the rippling surface of the water, itself captured by the artist with immense difficulty – he has painted it with light. He used a light-sensitive emulsion on paper, immersed in the water of Cork harbour on a moonless night, to capture the delicate, restless pattern of ripples in the water's surface. This is illumination indeed and it is a wonderful metaphor for the way in which this intimate collaboration of text and image can reveal the aura of poetry.

In this of course, *An Leabhar Mòr* is in the great tradition of the artist's book. This goes back more than a hundred years to the work of William Morris and Walter Crane and beyond them to Blake himself, and has engaged the talents of some of the greatest modern artists. Picasso, Matisse, Braque, Kandinsky, Paolozzi and many others have all made such books. In parallel to this, but closely linked to it, there is also the use of text as an aspect of the image which began with the invention of collage by Braque and Picasso. In his 'Calligrammes' Apollinaire sought to turn this into an actual poetic form with a symbiosis between the words and their form on the page and, following his initiative, texts used as images assumed an almost mystic power with the Surrealists. One of the most striking examples is the work of Miró, in whose hands letters become animated things endowed with their own mysterious energy. Alan Davie follows in this tradition. He regularly incorporates texts into his work. Sometimes the texts he uses are in languages which, like Gaelic, he does not understand. These texts then work like incantations. Here his image is beautifully balanced with Louise Donaldson's transcription of a few lines of the ancient Gaelic poem, 'Scél Lem Dúib'. For many of the artists, the texts in Gaelic are as mysterious as they are for Alan Davie, but as he shows us, this is also a way of restoring to writing its magical power. In her illustration to an anonymous ninth-century hymn, Olwen Shone has a photograph of a printed book decomposing back into mystery, its printed text contrasted to Frances Breen's lively calligraphy; whereas by using the letter groupings of a code in a brutally modern environment, Doug Cocker asserts the enduring power of this kind of mystery.

This book will, therefore, take its place alongside the great books in the modernist tradition, but it differs in one vital respect. It is rooted in Gaelic culture, and in this it achieves another great reunion. In the early medieval period, as the carved stones and crosses of Scotland and Ireland and the illuminated books whose forms they echo bear eloquent witness, the Celtic world had a visual tradition that was second to none. It was not exclusively religious, but the changes and upheavals consequent on the Reformation nevertheless brought it to an end. Since that time, in northern Europe at least, visual art has been largely a product of the urban economy, its consumers mainly the urban bourgeoisie. When so many of the Gaelic-speaking people of Ireland and Scotland were urbanised in the nineteenth century, it was as the proletariat in an English-speaking world. If some among them did join the bourgeoisie, it was by becoming anglicised. Even in this adversity there was no overall cultural deficit in the Gaelic-speaking world, but the will to celebrate life through the making of art found expression more readily in the forms that were quite independent of the urban economy, poetry, music and dance - all three of them at one time social, both the latter of course social still.

But there was a deficit in the visual arts, all the same, and in filling that deficit, the experience of the Scottish and Irish Gaels has been rather different. In Ireland, where Gaelic is the national language, there is not the same association with place that so clearly marks the Scottish Gàidhealtachd. The experience is more diffuse. The sense of a landscape inhabited by memory that is too often tragically a memory of loss and displacement, so powerfully evoked by Sorley MacLean in 'Hallaig', has not been so much part of the Irish tradition, not that there is any lack of tragic memory, but perhaps there was not the same artistic and poetic investment in the landscape. On the other hand, in Ireland the history of violent trouble is so much closer than it now is in Gaelic Scotland. Thus Conor McFeeley takes as his image of an empty house described in Maoilios Caimbeul's poem, not an abandoned croft house beside the sea, but an urban block, while Mick O'Kelly, Sean Hillen and Anthony Haughey take the injustices of the modern world and comment on the human condition by making the association with the Irish story. But this is not exclusive. Scottish artist John McNaught, for instance, renders the experience of a nineteenth-century Highlander in industrial Glasgow in a simple woodcut. Moira Scott has been as topical as any of her Irish contemporaries, recognising the timelessness and tragically current relevance of fourteenth-century poet Gofraidh Fionn Ó Dálaigh's poem about a child born in prison. Meanwhile, too, with the Irish artists landscape is not entirely banished either. Oliver Comerford reflects the casual voyage described in the poem by Tormod Caimbeul with a coastal scene and a lighthouse. The sailors in the poem are not completely lost. Helen O'Leary invokes the ancient field patterns of Ireland and Donald Murray builds stone dykes of words in their joint response to Louis de Paor's poem of place. Rita Duffy takes the imagery in a poetic lament for three fallen Jacobites of Clanranald to create an image of a man as a tree rooted in blood and soil and so in landscape; and in a simple landscape Bridget Flannery paints the bright island of Colm Breathnach's poem above a blue sea.

In Scotland, the creation of a modern iconography that could reflect even indirectly the experience of the Gaels really began from outside the country in the eighteenth century, with the dramatic emergence onto the modern political stage of the Highland soldiers in the Jacobite armies, followed immediately by the extraordinary success and influence, first of Macpherson's *Ossian* and then of Scott's poetry and his Waverley novels. The image of the Scottish Gaels projected in this way, however imaginary, became the model for the creation of national iconographies throughout Europe, from Wagner's *Ring Cycle* to Axelei Galen-Kalela's painting of the Finnish national myth, the Kalevala, that helped secure Finland's independence from Russia at the beginning of the last century. In Ireland too at the end of the nineteenth century, this was reflected in the art produced with consciously Irish forms and themes under the inspiration of the Arts and Crafts movement and in the circle of Yeats, which also, incidentally, had close links to Scotland through Patrick Geddes. Indeed one of the leading artists in Geddes's circle in Edinburgh was Irish-born Phoebe Traquair and appropriately a series of illuminated books inspired by Blake is among her most beautiful productions.

Two artists, Elizabeth Ogilvie and Calum Colvin, touch obliquely on the power of the Romantic image of the Scottish Gael. Elizabeth Ogilvie's image of a stick in a pool invokes the ripples of influence that, whether true or false, spread throughout the world. Calum Colvin gives us a megalithic monument bearing the giant fingerprint of myth and history. Perhaps, too, Steve Dilworth's mysterious – but actual – rocking stone with its runic inscription is also an image of the enduring poetic power of myth, whatever its origin either in fiction or historic truth.

There was, however, another potent myth promoted by Macpherson and Walter Scott which has been even more enduring, perhaps because in the Scottish experience, it really is valid. This is the proposal that there is a symbiotic relationship between poetry and landscape, not at the level of inspiration or description, but in a more profound way, as though poetry were itself a product of wild nature in us. Given the wonderful tradition of nature poetry in Gaelic and its role in the development of both modern landscape poetry in English and the great tradition of British landscape painting through the example of James Thomson, who first rendered it in English, this was not completely off the point, but its legacy was to make landscape for many years the definitive image of Gaelic Scotland. In Scotland too, as it happened, one of the very few Gaelic-speaking artists to achieve distinction was also one of the greatest landscape painters, William McTaggart, whose magnificent 'Sailing of the Emigrant Ship' is iconic in the history of Scottish art. But, seeing it from the real perspective of the Gaels, he completely transcends the conventional romantic 'Highland' image to create a tragic picture of a world in fragmentation under pressure of forces beyond its control.

As landscape remains an important part of the modern response to the need for an iconography, perhaps because of the continuing importance of place, others have followed McTaggart in this. Norman Shaw's dense, black etching is the dark landscape of exile invoked in Iain MacGillEathain's poem composed in Canada. Marian Leven's abstract painting is also clearly a landscape. Jake Harvey's black shield or breastplate with light above dark renders a blackbird's song over a loch. Eddie Summerton neatly unites landscape and the passage of time with his image of footsteps, a journey in time and space. Eileen Coates, too, has a pattern of footsteps. While Frances Walker gives us an image of the graveyard at Aignis on Lewis stripped of any sentimental burden, but presented as beautiful, stern and real. The human presence in the group of men among the gravestones described in Iain Crichton Smith's poem as gathered there to mourn, like the shortness of human life, is dwarfed by the grand curve of the earth. The isthmus Walker describes in the picture is the site now of Will Maclean's Aignis monument, one of three memorials that he has created to the Lewis land raiders who, by their resistance, reversed the long history of the Clearances' forced depopulation.

For Calum Angus Mackay, Craig Mackay and Gus Wylie, this Highland landscape is still inhabited by intensely felt memories of these events. Calum Angus MacKay paints Ben Dobhrain in photographic emulsion and so uses time and the transience of light itself to suggest memory and look back to the world of Donnchadh Bàn's poem composed in the eighteenth century. Using old photographs, Craig Mackay creates a collage of memories of people and places, of gravestones and landscapes, to match Séamas Dall Mac Cuarta's lament in a modern idiom that speaks not just of individual loss, but of the loss of a people invoked by the single word 'Exodus' on the collaged page of a bible. Gus Wylie epitomises this approach, shared by so many Scottish artists in different ways, in his beautiful image of a landscape in sharp focus where the human presence, a girl, a lover, or the ghost of a whole people, is blurred and ephemeral.

This preoccupation with time and memory links these artists to Will Maclean, who has been a leader in this move to find a way of making visible the experience of the Scottish Gaels, not just as a documentary record of the past, but at the level of imaginative commitment that will reclaim the past and make it a still vital part of the present, the objective of this whole project, perhaps. Maclean's image of three hide boats is beautifully enhanced by Frances Breen's calligraphy. These are like the boats in which St Brendan went on his voyage of white martyrdom and her script is like the surface of the water on which they float, pilgrims adrift on the sea of memory, coracles carrying the mystery of the past and the seeds of the future as we carry memory collectively. As the poet Aonghas Dubh MacNeacail puts it: 'every current will carry a vessel/put a seed like memory into the vessel/like the breath of a people/in the vessel'. There could be no more suitable epigraph to this whole project than these lines.

There is much else here to celebrate. George Wyllie sums up the history of division, responding to four lines of a ninth-century poem in a single graphic image of the Irish Sea as a channel of blue filled with weapons of all eras. At a quite different level in a delightful image, Helen MacAlister offers a personal gloss on the freshness of the waterfall described by Crìsdean Whyte by tucking a tiny picture of it into the neckline of a vest with a flower growing out of the armpit as testimony to its concomitant freshness. Silvana McLean answers the riddle in Dáibhí Ó Bruadair's poem with the single word 'warmth' embossed in the page and Alasdair Gray, for whom text and image are always closely linked, has, inimitably, illuminated his own page in the manner of the great originals of a thousand years ago. But these are just a few. Altogether there is far more in number and diversity than there is room to comment on here.

Malcolm Maclean and others with him, notably Arthur Watson and Paul Harrison at VRC, Dundee, must be congratulated for bringing such an ambitious and complex project to fruition. This is the third such project in which Malcolm Maclean has been closely involved and that has set out deliberately to tackle this deficit in order to create a visible and meaningful presence for the experience of the Scottish Gaels. First there were the two touring exhibitions originated at An Lanntair, 'As an Fhearann' and 'Calanais'. The first ranged from documentary to the work of contemporary artists in exploring the representation of life in the Highlands The second did as the present project has done and concentrated on the work of living artists. The exhibition invited the response of an international group of artists to one of the greatest and most ancient monuments of the Western Isles, the stones of Calanais. In *An Leabhar Mòr* the ambition is still the same, bringing the response of Irish and Scottish artists to an identifiable common heritage and so bringing fresh thought and diversity of approach to fulfilling this admirable ambition.

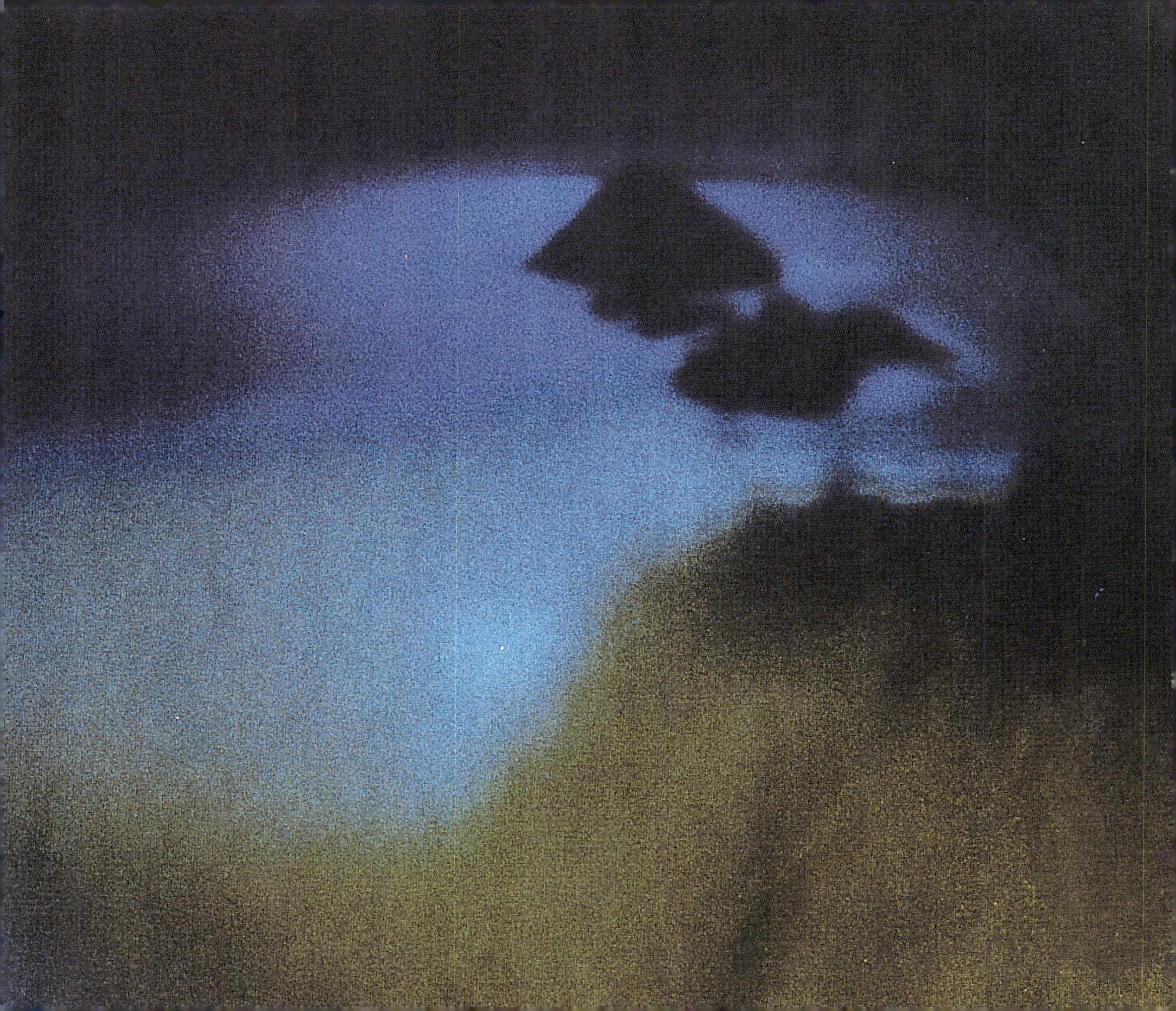

III

EARLY IRISH AND SCOTTISH GAELIC POETRY

Colm Ó Baoill

IT CANNOT BE EMPHASISED too strongly that the early Gaelic literary, linguistic and cultural world was a single unit: the modern division into three distinct Gaelic languages (if that is what they are) is not visible much before the sixteenth century. And so the early poetry, unless we really know where it was composed, should not be labelled Irish or Scottish or Manx but simply Gaelic. We can never say when poetry was first composed in Gaelic, but it has long been widely held that 'Amra Choluim Chille', the large-scale heroic lament on the death of Calum Cille in 597, is the earliest Gaelic poem which survives in more or less the form in which it was composed. Perhaps the exigencies of metre and rhyme have preserved in it forms and spellings which (in prose) might be expected to have changed over the centuries. But scholars are less certain nowadays that we have here a genuine sixth-century composition, for the study necessary to prove that point remains to be carried out.

The early Gaelic church, centred so much on monasteries, has had the crucial role in giving us our first great flowering of lyric poetry, in the centuries following 800, most of it joy-filled and Christ-focused, a large part of it describing and delighting in nature. Much nonsense has been written about these early monks and their closeness to nature: the authors of these early nature poems have been seen as hermits, living and writing outdoors among the trees and animals, in weather conditions which are gloriously inconsistent with Scottish, Irish and Manx reality. It is more than likely, for instance, that the precise and 'minimalist' 'An Lon Dubh', which observes nature so beautifully, was written inside the relatively cosy monastery of Bangor, Co. Down, and that 'Scél Lem Dúib', evokes a beautiful winter scene from the cheerful viewpoint of one who does not have to endure all winter's rigours.

'Pangur Bán' and 'Is Scíth Mo Chrob ón Scríbainn', are also clearly the products of monasteries, the latter having even been ascribed to Colum Cille, despite the fact that its language betrays its date as around 1100. 'Is Acher in Gaoth Anocht', gives expression to a fear of Viking raiding which was doubtless common to monks as to everyone else in the ninth century. And we probably must ascribe to the monasteries the religious poems of the time, like 'Rop Tú Mo Baile', which made its way into English-language hymn-books as 'Be Thou My Vision'.

When the king of Scots, Maol Cholaim, married the Saxon Saint Margaret around 1070, the way was open for a fast slide from Gaelic rule to Norman-French rule. By the middle of the twelfth century the old Gaelic form of church organisation, of which the monasteries were an important part, had given way to the continental system both in Scotland and in Ireland, and in 1169 the Normans began to arrive in force in Ireland to take over control and rule, especially in the east. So the Gaelic literary world could no longer be centred on its church, and a major revolution, the details of which may never be fully known, took place in the Gaelic political and cultural leadership around 1200. They were deprived now of the wealthier lands of eastern Ireland and a new social system developed whereby political leadership and poetic wisdom became interdependent in a new Gaelic world: the hereditary local *rí*, or petty king or chief, maintained a hereditary dynasty of poets, providing land and property in return for political guidance, which might be expressed in praise poetry. The professional poet in this system, called *file* in Gaelic, received years of rigorous technical training in all branches of Gaelic learning, including enormously complex metrical systems, and the technical perfection required of his output was enough to stop any untrained amateur from straying into this lucrative profession. Great learned families emerged and were engaged as poets for centuries, including the Ó Dálaigh family in Ireland and its Scottish offshoot, the MacMhuirich family.

Professional poetry, composed in praise of the ruler who is paying for it, is inevitably predictable in content and likely, however brilliant its construction technically, to bore the modern reader. But where the poet felt called upon to compose without his eye on payment – to compose, for instance, a poem of personal love or lament or a poem of praise to God or Mary – the full panoply of brilliant verbal ornamentation is brought to bear on the expression of feeling in a way that approaches the love or grief of a modern lyric, but on a much larger scale. Thus 'M'anam do Sgar Riomsa A-raoir' and 'A Phaidrín do dhúisg mo Dhéar', are works of heart-rending grief at the loss of a spouse, both taken from the early-sixteenth-century Scottish manuscript known as *The Book of the Dean of Lismore*, the first attributed to Muireadhach Albanach Ó Dálaigh, the thirteenth-century eponym of the MacMhuirich family, the second to the desolated wife of a fifteenth-century MacNeill chief. Similarly in 'Bean Torrach, fa Tuar Broide', Gofraidh Fionn Ó Dálaigh (d.1387) presents a neatly-argued Christian moral in perfect syllabic poetry; and in 'Soraidh Slán don Oidhche A-réir' Niall Mòr MacMhuirich celebrates the flowing alcohol at an aristocratic wedding in Dunvegan, probably in 1613.

A little closer to the usual theme of this professional verse is 'Fúar Leam an Oidhche-se dh'Aodh', where his *file* fears for the life of Hugh Maguire of Fermanagh in 1600, and paints a startlingly Macphersonesque picture of fearsome weather, floods, blasts and lightning, doubtless as metaphors for the horror of the war which killed Maguire. The English translation by James Clarence Mangan (who knew no Gaelic at all) has been much criticised.

But amateurs did make a little headway in verse during that period (c.1200–c.1650) of classical Gaelic syllabic verse. The continental tradition of *amour courtois*, and of the troubadours who sang its lovesongs, came into the Gaelic tradition through the Normans, and some of the Gaelic aristocracy ventured to express ideas of free love for the unattainably married, as well as naughtier ideas, using the learned metres of the professional *file* in simplified forms the upper class could handle. One such poet was Iseabail Ní Mheic Cailéin, identified as 'Countess of Argyll' and probably living in the fifteenth century, who in 'Éistibh, a Luchd an Tighe-se' expatiates on the size of a priest's penis.

The old Gaelic way of life was swept away in Ireland when the last of the independent Gaelic leaders were defeated by the English in a series of battles and campaigns between 1601 and 1690. With no chiefs to support them and their learned poetry, the poets found themselves unemployed and their training schools were closed; much of the poetry of seventeenth-century Ireland gives vent to outraged surprise at the low regard in which poets are now held. The last major Irish poet of the old learned tradition was Dáibhí Ó Bruadair (c.1625–98), who lived in Munster. In 'Is mairg nár chrean le maitheas saoghalta' he bemoans the fact that he is now (in 1674) reduced to hard physical labour; but he does it in the new rhythmical forms which were replacing the old syllabic verse throughout Gaeldom, as does another Munster poet, Aogán Ó Rathaille, lamenting great social changes at the end of that century in 'Is Fada Liom Oíche Fhírfhliuch'.

Ireland and Scotland go their different literary ways in the seventeenth century, having now lost the strong adhesive of the old learned tradition. The last great poet of the MacMhuirich family died in 1726, but a century earlier we can see the growth of a significant body of Gaelic song in Scotland. Ireland too had her songs at that time, of course, but few of these are today identifiable, with their tunes, as belonging to that century. The Scottish seventeenth century is marked, Professor Derick S. Thomson has pointed out, by its songs of clan and politics, the work of songmakers who maintain much of the social and political function of the learned poetic families. These songs are less learned, of course, than the older professional poetry, and they belong essentially to a non-literate tradition. Many survived for one hundred years or more in the oral tradition, and most of those we have were first written down in the aftermath of the 1745 rising, when devoted clergymen noted them from their singers. Clan songs of the seventeenth century include 'Clann Ghriogair air Fògradh' (on the MacGregors) and 'Oran do MhacLeòid Dhùn Bheagain' and 'Crònan an Taibh', both to MacLeod chiefs, the former a biting satire of about 1694 addressed to a chief who favoured too many Lowland luxuries.

Praise songs to the chief continued to be composed in the eighteenth century ('Alasdair à Gleanna Garadh' is a famous lament for a chief who died in 1721), but that century also sees a great broadening of the range of themes in Highland verse as well as an increase in literacy, learning and the use of print, especially in the case of Alasdair Mac Mhaighstir Alasdair (c.1690–c.1770), the great MacDonald poet of nature, love and Jacobite politics, and of much else. Here he is represented by his ambitious heroic sea-faring narrative, 'Birlinn Chlann Raghnaill', published in his son's 1776 collection, while the love poetry of the eighteenth century is represented by Uilleam Ros and Rob Donn in 'Feasgar Luain' and 'Is Trom Leam an Airigh'. Love and grief and politics are mixed in the exquisite song 'Mo Rùn Geal Òg' and nature poetry is represented by Donnchadh Bàn's 'Cead Deireannach nam Beann' composed in 1802.

The eighteenth century in Ireland was different: there the Gaels have been defeated and left powerless, and their poets see only the Stuarts as possible saviours. Life and poetry must go on, however, and it is likely that many well-known Irish traditional songs, especially love-songs, were composed in that century or earlier, though precise dating is usually impossible. Among these are 'Dónall Óg', a wonderful love-song which has verses in common with a Scottish love-song and must therefore surely be old, 'An Draighneán Donn' and 'Tá Mé i Mo Shuí'. A new experimental verse form, known as *trí rainn agus amhrán* and based on the English sonnet, arose in Ireland late in the seventeenth century and remained popular till the nineteenth century: 'An Lon Dubh Báite' is an attractive northern example, possibly from the early eighteenth century (the ascription to Séamas Dall is questionable). Two ambitious large-scale works, from the south of the country and from the later eighteenth century, are represented here by sizeable excerpts: Art Ó Leary, who was killed in 1773, is mourned on an epic scale by his widow, exploiting all the traditional ideas and forms of Gaelic lament ('Caoineadh Airt Uí Laoghaire'); and in 'Cúirt an Mheán Oíche' Brian Merriman (?1749-1803) satirises the social and sexual mores of the Irish of his time.

In both Ireland and Scotland the nineteenth century gets a fairly bad press in the matter of Gaelic poetry, being widely regarded as devoid of anything new or adventurous, or too much in the grip of cultural depression resulting from the decline of the language. Especially with the disastrous famine of 1846-9, the Irish language and its culture did suffer grievously: perhaps its finest songs are to be sought in the pre-famine period, when 'Máire Ní Eidhin' and 'Cath Chéim an Fhiadh' were made, the first a fine love-song from the west, the second a heroic political song from the south sung to a majestic tune but, as often happens, dealing with political events of little importance.

In Highland Scotland too the century opened to disasters related to the land and its ownership - the Clearances and the resultant large-scale emigration, and the same famine as in Ireland, though on a lesser scale. But here the Gaels fought back and were able to establish some rights for themselves, and their poetry comes to reflect something of a new confidence. While the reality of exile in Canada is awesome to the author of 'Am Bàrd an Canada' early in the century, Iain MacGillEathain later came to write of the pleasanter side of that new Gaelic world. Niall MacLeòid (1843-1913), a master of sentimentality, has been widely and unfairly seen as typical of his time, but other poets could be much more positive and critical, especially Màiri Mhòr (1821-98), who campaigned in her songs for her people's rights. However, nostalgia for Skye in her youth is the theme of 'Nuair Bha Mi Òg'.

Much more realistic comment marks 'Spiorad a' Charthannais' and 'Fios thun a' Bhàird'. The former, by John Smith or Seonaidh Phàdraig (1848-81) in Lewis, piously proclaims the importance of Christian 'kindliness', and the latter, by Uilleam MacDhunLèibhe (1808-70), opens lyrically about the beauty of his native Islay; but then both switch effortlessly to swingeing attacks on the tyranny of landholders and their agents, who lack 'kindliness' as Islay now lacks people.

IV

TWENTIETH-CENTURY SCOTTISH GAELIC POETRY

Ronald Black

THE CENTURY WAS USHERED in by two folklorists. Fr Allan McDonald (1859–1905) blended secular and sacred in 'An t-Eòintein' to express the love of God in metaphors as brilliantly chiselled as those used by Sorley MacLean three decades later to express love for a woman. Fr Allan also operated across the whole spectrum of satire from corrective to invective, and by the end of his short life his literary talents were bubbling and steaming strongly enough to lift the lid off the sacerdotal pot. Unfortunately that part of his work which was published in his lifetime - his many hymns and his song on Eriskay of 1904, 'Eilein na h-Òige - was outstanding only in ways which threatened no conventions.

On the other hand Alexander Carmichael (1832–1912) exemplified in *Carmina Gadelica* of 1900 an idyllic view of the Highlands and Islands which was smashed by the realism of the First World War. Even in 1938, however, the century's leading poet, Sorley MacLean from Raasay (1911–96), identified the exponents of the kind of romanticism which Carmichael had provoked as the most prominent figures in the Gaelic poetry of the century so far.

The Lewisman John Munro (1889–1918) fell after three-and-a-half years at the front, leaving his thoughts on his fallen comrades in tortured free verse full of reminiscence-of-rhyme; forty more years were to pass before free verse became widespread. However, the outstanding Gaelic poet of the trenches was Dòmhnall Ruadh Chorùna from North Uist (Donald Macdonald, 1887–1967), who described in a remarkable sequence of poems what it looked, felt, sounded and even smelled like to march up to the front, lie awake on the eve of battle, go over the top, be gassed, wear a mask, and be surrounded by the dead and dying remains of Gaelic-speaking comrades.

In 1921 Thomas MacDonald from Appin (1864–1937) published a long poem, 'An Déidh a' Chogaidh', glued together by passages of lyric power, which looked beyond the mountains to survey the condition of humanity in other countries. The idea was soon taken up by MacLean in 'An Cuilithionn'. Another elderly poet of the period was Donald MacCallum (1849–1929), from Craignish, a Church of Scotland minister who had made his name as an orator in the cause of land reform. MacLean called him 'not much of a poet', but he deserves to be remembered as the most brilliant exponent of anti-landlordism in Gaelic verse. His principal achievement was the long poem 'Domhnullan' of 1925.

Throughout the first half of the century An Comunn Gaidhealach – founded in 1892 to run an annual festival called the Mod – made prodigious efforts to nurture Gaelic verse, and in 1923 its poetry competitions were amalgamated into a single contest for a Bardic Crown. The aims were to rehearse and preserve the riches of Gaelic vocabulary and idiom, and to search for a new medium that could be as faithful to the needs and rhythms of Gaelic as free verse was to those of English. Entrepreneurial Gaelic publishing largely collapsed after the War, however, and until the Second World War the collections of Gaelic verse that received the lion's share of public attention were those which harked back to the nineteenth century and beyond. A great deal of what was published during the first half of the century was not very good, and a great deal of what was very good was not yet published.

The most outstanding victim of this was Donald Macintyre (Dòmhnall Ruadh Phàislig, 1889–1964), a South Uist man who lived in Paisley and worked as a brick-layer. His work, finally published as *Sporan Dhòmhnaill* in 1968, amounts to over ten thousand lines. He displays a huge and limpid vocabulary, and that uncanny facility of expression which has now died with the monoglot Gaelic world. His instincts are rooted in the seventeenth century, and he describes a Glasgow pub in 'Bùth Dhòmhnaill 'IcLeòid' as if he had just fallen through a time warp. Far from preventing him being the Gaelic voice of Red Clydeside in the ghastly era of the Depression, however, this historical consciousness lends his political satires huge authority. They are executed with subtlety, a big-hearted sense of humour, and an innovative literary sensibility.

The publication of MacLean's *Dàin do Eimhir* in 1943 marked a watershed. The elements that formed his poetry are love, a strong and radical traditional background, the intellectual stimulation of Edinburgh, the cataclysmic political events of the time, and the innovative trends set in motion by An Comunn Gaidhealach, MacDonald and MacCallum. Out of the rich vocabulary of the early poetry, the terse but passionate eloquence of popular song and the subtle abstractions of Presbyterian religious terminology - traditional metres, traditional vocabulary, traditional symbols - MacLean created a breathtakingly new and exciting instrument of poetic expression. He was the first Gaelic poet whose subjects and attitudes were totally 'modern', but his success lay in the fact that he was steeped in the old.

To the extent that MacLean's poetry radiates from the Highlands to take in the entire globe, he was representative of his generation. The twentieth-century Highlander's knowledge of the world, through war, migration, or a life on the high seas, was considerable. Murdo MacFarlane (1901–82) returned to Lewis from the prairies of Manitoba, as he put it himself, 'nearly as poor as I left, but a little wiser'. He went on to gain a reputation as 'the Cole Porter of Gaeldom' from his ability to set his material to original airs; the label does little justice to his formidable intellect, and the fresh wind of his imagination barks through his songs.

The most remarkable of the emigrant poets was perhaps Duncan Livingstone (1877–1964), a stonemason from Mull who went to live in South Africa after the Boer War. He experimented with free verse and other forms, and in a series of mould-breaking works savaged imperialism and surveyed its legacy throughout the world. Following the Sharpeville Massacre of 1960 he put the words of a black woman mourning her husband who had been killed by the police into a very traditional Gaelic verse-form to warn his readers of the dangers of racism. A deeply religious man, he recognised apartheid at work in Christ's birth in a stable. Well over a hundred of his earlier poems lie in a manuscript in Cape Town, while his later ones are scattered through journals published in South Africa, Scotland and Canada.

It is a short step from Livingstone to George Campbell Hay (1915–84), who was brought up in Kintyre but spent the Second World War in North Africa, Italy and Greece, then endured a long twilight life of mental illness. For thirty years our judgement of his work was based on his collections *Fuaran Sléibh* (1947) and *O na Ceithir Àirdean* (1952), and for many that judgement was of a brilliant virtuoso: one who loved ideas well, but words more. However, when *Mochtàr is Dùghall* appeared belatedly in 1982 the judgement had to be reversed, for this long North African poem is one of the great sustained achievements of Gaelic literature. It has philosophical depth, music, humour, atmosphere, colour, excitement, and a conceptual richness that takes the breath away. *Mochtàr is Dùghall* permanently broadened the range of Gaelic verse - after that any kind of subject-matter was possible, and in this respect the line of poetic succession passed to Christopher Whyte (b. 1952), whose 'Bho Leabhar-Latha Maria Malibran (1996) is a hugely successful attempt to write poetry in Gaelic without a trace of Gaelic convention.

MacLean and Hay were being seen as 'the last gleam of the Gaelic sky', so what happened after 1952 fully deserves the title of renaissance. That was the *annus mirabilis* in which the quarterly *Gairm* was founded by Derick Thomson and Finlay J. Macdonald; before it was out they had already published poems whose status is now iconic, such as Iain Crichton Smith's 'Tha Thu air Aigeann m' Inntinn' and Thomson's own 'Na Cailleachan'.

Born in Lewis in 1921, Thomson is the island's greatest poet ever, in precisely the way that Hay is the bard of Algeria rather than of Kintyre, for he celebrates not the island's landscape or her seascape but her people. Although he works almost entirely in free verse, his ability to paint a clear picture with a few deft strokes puts him in the mainstream tradition of 'Eilein na h-Òige'. In his best poem, 'Àirc a' Choimhcheangail' (1982), he explores religious doubt and prays that he be not found praying, while putting beyond doubt that his was the major voice of Gaelic poetry in the second half of the century.

The other defining poet of the period was Iain Crichton Smith (1928–98). In a sense he was the Betjeman of Gaelic verse. Ordinary people and everyday objects flit in and out of his work. He watches television, goes to see *The Sound of Music* at the pictures.

He makes much use of platitudes and commonplaces, but his work is never dull. He fires poems like machine-guns, spraying symbols and images manically. His work stands out for its stylistic sharpness, its questioning intelligence, its easy-going biculturalism, and its wit.

During the quarter-century between the founding of *Gairm* and the appearance of Thomson's fourth collection *Saorsa agus an Iolaire* in 1977 a holy war was fought between traditionalists and innovators for the soul of Gaelic poetry. In the words of Donald MacAulay from Lewis (b. 1930), the traditionalists were 'the ones who have chosen/deafness and blindness - and are facing dumbness'. The principal battle-grounds (apart from the obvious one of fixed metres *v.* free verse) were religion and the homeland. It was difficult to stand simultaneously on traditional ground with regard to belief and on modern ground with regard to the means of expression: an anonymous contributor to *Gairm* in 1966 hammered home the message that 'Gaelic will not live without Bible' ('Cha bhi Gàidhlig beò gun Bhìobull') in rhyme, but showed willingness to experiment when dealing with purely moral themes.

It became a characteristic innovative trend to point out that Calvinism is an aberration in Gaelic culture. MacAulay's 'Soisgeul 1955' finds a psalm-tune as mysterious as the voyage of Maol Dùin, a prayer as his people's access to poetry, but a sermon so vicious, alien and embarrassing that he gets pins and needles. Thomson's 'Am Bodach-Ròcais' tells how the scarecrow of the title came into the ceilidh-house with Middle-Eastern tales and Genevan philosophy, sweeping the fire from the middle of the floor and putting a 'bonfire in our breasts', while in Smith's 'Coinnichidh Sinn' a pious man's view of an innocent heaven sounds to the woman like a frozen one and her bosom goes cold. Strong as it may seem, this was tame stuff compared to some of the spiritual verse of the century, in which terrified sinners poured out intense love for God on their deathbeds, thanks were expressed for conversion experiences in unlikely-sounding locations, the graphic teachings of inspired preachers were recounted, women strove to reconcile their feelings for the crucified Christ with more earthly emotions, and ordained ministers expressed the anguish of doubt.

The 'homeland' issue was best put into perspective, I think, by Donald John MacLeod (b. 1943), a Marxist from Harris who in 'Ràithean na Bliadhna' turned a simple aphorism into a torrent of prose castigating his forefathers for knuckling under to capitalism, and finished with the ultimate heresy: 'An eilean mo luaidh, is fuath leam eilean mo ghràidh'. ('In the isle of my heart, I hate the isle of my love').

The holy war had come to an end by the late 1970s, when MacAulay's important anthology *Nua-Bhàrdachd Ghàidhlig* and MacLean's retrospective *Reothairt is Contraigh* appeared in quick succession – both containing parallel translation. None of Thomson's four collections down to that point had included parallel translation; all his three subsequent collections did so. This shows that the market for Gaelic was now mainly outside Gaelic society, which, with the passing of the traditionalists, scarcely existed any longer; from here on Gaelic was the one sector of poetry publishing in Scotland that made money. What is more, since 1971

Gaelic poets had been joining others on the public stage in venues in Scotland, Ireland and abroad, and this led to a lightening of tone - innovative poets were beginning to create work for public performance, just as traditionalists had always done. The old term of opprobrium *bàrd baile* must now be reassessed or ditched: innovators were *bàird baile* too, whether their *baile* was Glasgow or the global village.

In the final quarter of the century we must note the presence of one representative voice maintained through several collections, that of Myles Campbell from Skye (b. 1944), and of three trends - a return to mythology, best seen in the highly innovative work of Aonghas Dubh MacNeacail (b.1942); the refeminisation of verse through the reappearance of women poets such as Mary Montgomery from Lewis (b. 1955) and the reapplication of female qualities (it was the authority of this centuries-old voice that Livingstone had evoked in his Sharpeville poem); and the arrival of learners such as Fearghas MacFhionnlaigh (b. 1948), an explosively good poet with a unique high-tech voice. Tradition now came to mean the expression of a Gaelic literary sensibility, innovation its replacement by other sensibilities; the 'guru' of innovation in the third quarter, MacAulay, thus found himself championing tradition in the fourth.

There were more Gaelic poets in the single island of Tiree in 1900 than in the whole of Scotland in 2000. In 1985 the Scottish Poetry Library counted forty living poets writing in Gaelic; the full total was, and is, more like double this, but probably not over a hundred. Many of the hundred have developed poetic voices which are extremely clear and distinctive; those who find the tools to win the battle, as did MacLean, can yet become giants in the new millennium.

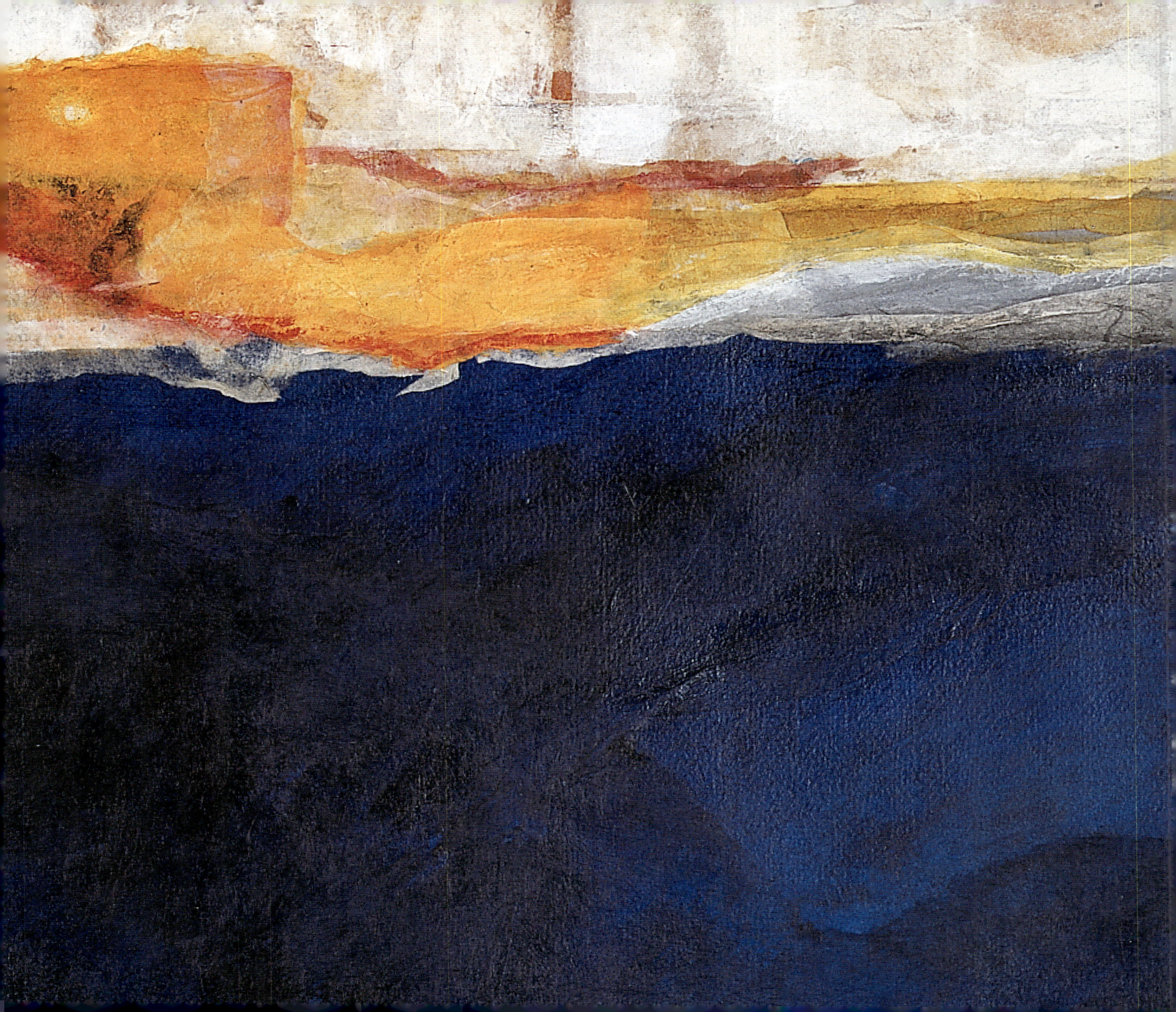

V

TWENTIETH-CENTURY IRISH-LANGUAGE POETRY

Theo Dorgan

AT THE DAWN OF the twentieth century, borne up on the rising tide of national feeling, nurtured by the Gaelic League's recuperative work on the poetry of the past, an Irish-speaking optimist might have predicted a flood of new poetry in the language as a feature of the coming times. He, or she, would have been both incautious and destined to be disappointed. The first Gaelic poet of serious achievement in the new century, Máirtín Ó Direáin, would not even begin to think of writing poetry in Irish until 1938, and would say at the outset 'Níor chabhair mhór d'éinne againn san aois seo aon uaill ná mac alla ó na filí a chuaigh romhainn inár dteanga féin' – ('No cry or echo from the poets who went before us in our own tongue would be of help to any of us in this time').

Apart from Ó Direáin, no poetry of true value would appear in the Irish language until Seán Ó Ríordáin published *Eireaball Spideoige* in 1952. Consumptive, lonely and disillusioned, Ó Ríordáin was a kind of alienated pietist whose work strikes the first truly modern note in Gaelic poetry. Refusing the succour of sentimental loyalty to the forms and tropes of the high Gaelic tradition, his agonised soul-searching is a local version of the doubt and existential anguish which now seems so characteristic of the European mid-century. But Ó Direáin's reluctant, even angry abandoning of the Arcadian peasant dream does not quite make him modern, in the sense that Eoghan Ó Tuairisc, say, writing self-consciously under the shadow of the Bomb, is modern. Paradoxically, Máire Mhac an tSaoi, immersed as she is in the poet-scholar tradition, becomes modern precisely because of her ability to play off a distinctly independent and contemporary sensibility against the structures and strictures of inherited traditions. Seán Ó Tuama, with his Corkman's ancestral yearning for the Mediterranean, and Pearse Hutchinson, drawn to Galicia and Catalonia, find distinctive contemporary voices in Irish outside the sway of world-girdling English; one might say the same of Tomás Mac Síomóin, heavily and productively indebted to a Continental sensibility which owes more to Pasolini than to Pearse.

Caitlín Maude, who died tragically young, and Micheal Ó hAirtnéide (Michael Hartnett), to whom we will return, both born in 1941, carry the mid-century: the former as a feminist *avant la lettre*, the latter as a gifted poet in both Irish and English, translator of *Ó Bruadair*, eidetic companion to the present generation even in death. Maude and Ó hAirtnéide, as with the generation following swiftly on their heels, were more of the present moment than of Ireland, in the important sense that the Gaelic world was for them a repository of enormous resource for the living of a life, far more than it was a heavy and inescapable ancestral burden. They and their successors are of post-Catholic, post-nationalist Ireland, the Ireland that was beginning to struggle to its feet at about the time they began publishing their youthful verses.

If the Gaelic League had, as it were, an afterlife following the establishment of the Irish Free State, it was not vivifying, but the reverse. We can see it now as an admirable project of recovery and recuperation which carried within itself the metal fatigue of Victorian sentimentalism. The lost Gaelic order towards which it flung out a bridge was aristocratic, disdainful, Catholic and doomed. Apt in and for its time, the poetry of that order was spectacularly ill-suited to the grubby, dour, post-colonial truth of the infant Republic which would seize on it as the epitome of native high culture and, by force-feeding it in the schools, rob it of its political charge while unconsciously undermining its power as art. The insular, primitive nationalism of the new ruling class seized on the rich poetry of the seventeenth and eighteenth centuries as a shining string of baubles, the pathetic jewels of the poor who do not recognise their own poverty nor understand where their true wealth is to be found. By resolutely closing out the modern in favour of an idealised and unreal nexus of virtuous peasant and cultured Lord, the State, through its 'education' system, made the disjunction between a glorious poetry of the past and a possible poetry of the present both absolute and prescriptive. Seeking, for perhaps the best motives, to celebrate the high poetry of a comparatively recent past, it silenced the present.

There were, to be sure, disruptions. Frank O'Connor, no cherished treasure of the State, published a muscular translation of *Cúirt an Mheán-Oíche* (*The Midnight Court*) in 1945, followed by *Kings, Lords and Commons* and *A Golden Treasury of Irish Poetry 600–1200* (with David Greene), both in 1959. These books, paradoxically, awakened his English language readers to the intrinsic riches of the Gaelic poetic tradition, and helped make it possible to see in a positive context work which, unfortunately, the State had helped stigmatise as backward and unworthy of serious attention.

There were disruptions, and there was also a nourishing silence. Away from the eyes of the State and the new professional class of *Gaeilgeoirí*, in 'unforgiven places' as Tony Curtis puts it, Irish continued to be spoken as a living, adaptive and ambitious language. On building sites in Coventry as much as in the botháns of Kerry and the fire stations of Boston and Chicago, with neither fuss nor fanfare, the language endured and mutated, as all living languages do, out of sight and out of mind. There is nobody more secretively rebellious than a man or woman who is assured by the well-off that poverty is an admirable thing; nothing is better suited to the life of a language than the secrecy of the poor; and nothing more appeals to a rebel than a language in which to access simultaneously both a hidden past and an unborn future. The rebels, as it happens, were waiting in the wings.

When Nuala Ní Dhomhnaill and Michael Davitt, Gabriel Rosenstock and Liam Ó Muirthile arrived in University College Cork, they were coming to themselves as poets in what Che Guevara, in a different context but at more or less the same time, described as 'an objectively revolutionary situation'. They would found, and be published in, a radical journal, *INNTI*.

The power of the State to contain reality had withered. The electronic age and the first world generation were upon us, rock and roll had thundered out across the world and the short-lived counter culture, for a dizzy moment, held the commanding heights. The first transnational generation had arrived to claim its place in the sun, and considerably to the surprise of the tweeds and Fáinne brigade this brash and exuberant generation of poets was as unremarkably at home in the *Gaeltachts* as in the hip, wide world.

Nuala Ní Dhomhnaill, born in Lancashire, brought up in Nenagh and in the *Gaeltacht* of Corca Dhuibhne, was a natural rebel with a profound sense of the riches of the folk tradition, as source both of story and syntax. Michael Davitt, son of a CIE worker, and Liam Ó Muirthile from the heart of Cork City found themselves wildly at home in the *Gaeltachts* of Corcha Dhuibhne and Cúil Aodha, party and privy to a racy reality the pietists of the language had ignored or tried to forget. There was a true exuberance in the air, perhaps more soberly shared by Gréagóir Ó Dúill and Micheal O' Siadhail (his own preferred spelling) in other places, a sense that, as John Montague put it, old moulds are broken and that a new world, a new language, was both possible and necessary. An Irish language, to put it this way, that could contain LSD and Gabriel Rosenstock's abiding faith in the wisdom-literature of the East.

The wily and sceptical Seán Ó Tuama offered a bracing counterpoint to their wilder enthusiasms, perhaps, as Seán Ó Riada brought a demonic precision to the music he did so much to uncover and make new again, in the same place and at the same time. But for all that, the *INNTI* poets were essentially unruly and individual as much as they were ever a school. Their education helped shape but does not explain them.

They were excoriated as shallow barbarians, dabblers in the language, polluters of the unsullied, sex-free, drug-free paradise of the Gael. Contemptuous of the carefully-nurtured and comfortable state-within-a-state which the professional *Gaeilgeoirí* had so profitably and quietly nurtured, they earned, in some quarters, genuine, spitting hatred. It is true that their focus was on the immediate, the lyric instant of the body present to itself, the street as theatre of the present moment, the exalted state of mind as both norm and normative. In that sense they were very much of their time, in fact so much of their time that, disconcertingly, they were of the *avant-garde* in a way that few of their English-language contemporaries were. Formally and thematically, they were ripping through received forms and received wisdom in unprecedented ways; perhaps only Paul Durcan, at that time, was doing in English what these poets were doing in Irish. This cleavage with the past, especially with the immediate past, was so shocking that, in effect, the shock anaesthetised itself. They were out and through into a new, unexpected reappropriation of the past almost before they themselves realised what was going on.

It should be noted that the rising generation of poets was both heartened and inspired to a more capacious sense of their inheritance by the visits to Ireland of Scottish Gaelic poets, singers and musicians organised by Colonel Eoghan Ó Néill, and by the reciprocal visits to Scotland which would enter into the folklore as well as the poetry. The sense of a cognate tradition and of a comradeship in struggle became and remains an amplification and a quickening of commitment to the language; to a life in the language.

We live in a changed landscape now. Biddy Jenkinson can forge, as she has done, a lapidary and rigorous language of her own, steeped in the cold water of the language, and be and feel free to do so. Áine Ní Ghlinn can dare her poems to the edge of cold prose, write of the most painful things, and occasion no reproach that she lacks the classical frame of reference. Cathal Ó Searcaigh, whose beginning was in Kerouac, whose delight is in an unabashed gay sensibility, can write of Nepal and Gort a' Choirce and sex satisfactory and unsatisfactory and know he will be read and heard as a poet of the living moment. These things are true, and remarkable. Louis de Paor and Colm Breathnach are the first of the post-*INNTI* generations, each a true and individual poet, both of them born into a new kind of liberty.

The cleavage is absolute between our now and our past, insofar as that past was constructed as an ideal reservation without whose walls there could be no salvation. The cleavage is, also, an illusion: language comes down to us as a living stream, defying all efforts to shape and contain its course. It is literally not possible to engage with the present of a language, to write in a language, without being informed by the past of that language. What is different is that the poet today can pick and choose where to immerse herself in the past, can come to the past as part of the project of making his own, unique existential self as a poet. There is an essential freedom in this relationship to the past, a freedom which is at base a kind of absolute humility and without which there can be no genuine respect for the life and work of those who have gone before us.

When Michael Hartnett came 'with meagre gifts to court the language of my people', when he turned from English to Irish, to his own immediate present as well as the living present of Ó Bruadair and Ó Rathaille, it was a gesture read in one of two ways: it was quixotic and arbitrary, or it was a choice made in the face of forces, ahistorical powers, he was helpless to resist. With the passage of time, and following his uncriticised and civilly-received return to English, it is possible now to see that Hartnett's choice was made in response to a simple imperative: the words sought him out, and the words were in Irish.

And this, I think, is where we are now. When poets now living make their poems in Irish, they are making poems, not obeisances, not signs made in the name of a tradition but the elements themselves of a free, living tradition. Poems. In Irish. No more, and no less.

THE POEMS AND ARTWORKS

I

DALLÁN FORGAILL

c.600

Ealaíontóir/Artist:
William Crozier

Peannaire/Calligrapher:
Donald Murray

Aistritheoir/Translator:
Prof. P. L. Henry

Ainmníodh ag/Nominator:
Biddy Jenkinson

Amra Choluim Chille (sliocht)

Dé Dé da-rrogus ré tés ine gnúis
Culu tré néit,
Dé nime ním-reilge i lurgu i n-égthiar,
ar múich dia méit,
Dé már mo anacul di múr theintidiu,
Diuderc ndér,
Dé firián firfocus chluines mo donóll
Di niméth nél.

Ni díscéoil due Néill,
Ni huchtat óenmaige,
Mór mairg, mór deilm,
Dífhulaing riss ré aisneid
Colum cen beith cen chill.
Co-india duí dó – sceo Nera!
In fáith Dé de déis Sion suidiath
Is nú nad mair;
Ni marthar lenn,
Ni less anma ar suí;
Ar-don condiath con-roeter biu -bath,
Ar-don-bath ba ar n-airchenn adlicen,
Ar-don-bath ba ar fiadait foídiam,
Ar-nin-fissid fris-bered omnu húain,
Ar-nin-tathrith do-sluinned focul fir,
Ar-nin-forcetlaid for-canad túatha Toí,
Huile bith ba h-ae h-é;
Is crot cen chéis, is cell cen abbaid . . .

(Archaic Irish version of lines 1–26, normalised to standard of c. 600 ad, by P. L. Henry)

Amra Choluim Chille

Guionn Dallán Dia

Dia, Dia a ghuífinn sula dtéim ina dháil
Trí charbaid ghleo.
Nár lige Dia neimhe i mbuíonta an éimh mé,
Ar mhéad a ndobróin.
Go saora Dia ar an múr tine mé,
Ar bhuanpholl na ndeor!
Dia fíréan fiorchóngarach a chluineann mo nuallghol
Ó Pharthas an cheo.

Colum: Scéala agus Méala a Bháis

Ní díscéil teach Néill,
Ní mion-osna aon-mhá:
Mór an mhairg, mór an chreach,
Dífhulaing a fhaisnéis
Nach maireann Colum ina chill.
Conas a léireoidh daoi é – go fiú Néra féin:
– Fáidh Dé de dhíorma na suadh i Síon
Anois beag a d'éag?
Ní mhaireann sé linn,
Ní leas anma dúinn ár saoi;
Ár ndídean a chaomhnaigh na beo, atá marbh.
D'éag orainn ár n-urra, taca na mbocht.
D'éag orainn ár dtaidhleoir don Tiarna.
Mar ní farainn atá an saoi a scaipeadh uainn imeagla;
Mar nach dtiocfaidh arís chugainn an té a labhraíodh focal fíor;
Mar nach maireann an t-oide a mhúineadh tuatha Toí.
An saol go léir – ba leis é;
– Is cruit gan chéis anois, is cill gan abb.

Dallán's Elegy for Columba (excerpt)

The blind poet Dallán invokes God

God, my God I will entreat ere I come before Him
Through the war chariots of Satan.
May God of Heaven not leave me
On the tracks of the anguished
In great desolation.
May the great God save me from the fiery wall,
From the long-lasting pit of tears.
The just God is near me
And hears my sad cry
From the cloudland of Heaven.

The News of Colum's Death

Not without tidings is the House of Niall,
Not the sighing of a single plain
But a great grief, a woe
Painful to relate:
Colum no longer lives.
How shall a fool declare it – even Nera?
God's prophet from the elect of Sion
Has just passed away.
No longer with us,
Our sage will no more salve our soul,
Our protector who shielded the living has died,
Our leader, support of the poor.
We have no-one now to speak for us to the Lord.
Gone is the noble one who banished our fear,
He who spoke truth will not return to us –
The master who once taught the tribes of Tay.
The whole world was his,
Now the harp has no key, the church no abbot.

We have only been able to give an excerpt from this poem. For an alternative source of the full text see the listing on page 265

(continued on page 233)

Las an Tuaisceart
Gur ghealaigh an tIarthar
Is gur bhladhm an tOirthear
De dheasca na gcléireach diantréanach
Ba thaibhseach a bhás

Donald Murray

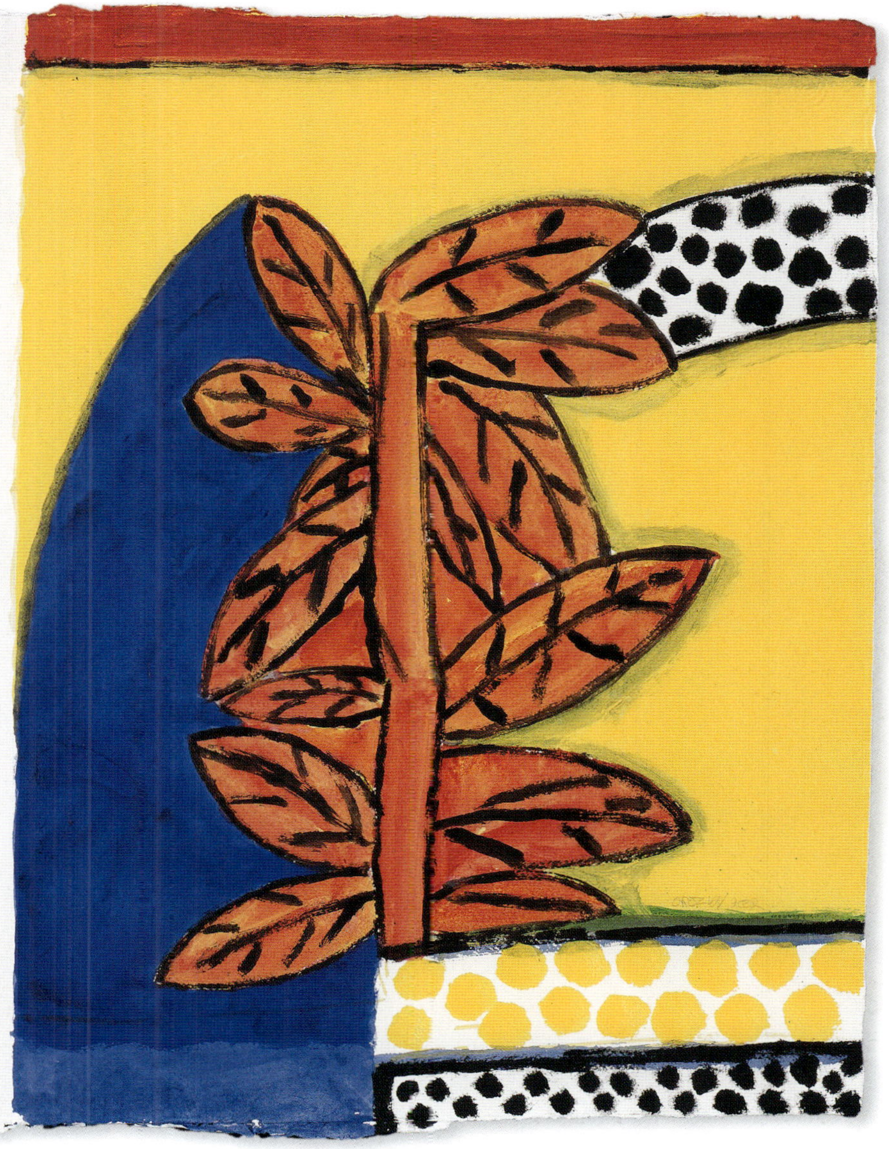

2

GAN AINM

ANON

c.900

Ealaíontóir/Artist:
Sonja Stringer

Peannaire/Calligrapher:
Réiltín Murphy

Aistritheoir/Translator:
Gabriel Rosenstock

Ainmníodh ag/Nominator:
Gabriel Rosenstock

A Bé Find

A Bé find, in rega lim
I tír n-ingnad hi fil rind?
  Is barr sobairche folt and,
  Is dath snechtai corp co ind.

Is and nád bí muí ná taí,
Gela dét and, dubai braí,
  Is lí súla lín ar slúag,
  Is dath sion and cech grúad.

Is corcur maige cach muin
Is lí súla ugae luin,
  Cid caín déicsiu Maige Fáil
  Annam íar ngnáis Maige máir.

Cid mesc lib coirm Inse Fáil
Is mescu coirm Tíre Máir,
  Amra tíre tír as-biur,
  Ní tét oac and ré siun.

Srotha téithmilsi tar tír,
Rogu de mid ocus fin
  Doíni delgnaidi cen on,
  Combart cen peccad, cen chol.

Ad-chiam cách for cach leth
Ocus níconn-acci nech;
  Teimil imorbais Ádaim
  Dodon-aircheil ar áraim.

A ben, día rís mo thúaith tind
Is barr óir bias fort chind,
  Muc úr, laith, lemnacht la lind
  Rot-bía lim and, a Bé Find.

Lovely Lady *(Mír's Wooing of Éadaoin)*

Lovely lady, will you go
To that kingdom where stars glow?
  Primrose there the colour of hair,
  Snow-white each body fair.

'Yours' and 'mine' are words not known yet,
Ivory teeth and brows of pure jet;
  Foxglove the colour of every cheek,
  The whole company radiant and sleek.

Every plain of purple hue,
The blackbird's eggs flecked with blue,
  The plains of Ireland will seem bare
  After you have lingered there.

For Ireland's beer you will not long,
The Great Land's beer is twice as strong!
  It is a land of purest gold,
  The young don't die before the old.

All round gentle streams entwine,
Mead is drunk, the best of wine,
  The people have not learned to hate,
  It's not a sin to copulate!

We see all on every side,
Though none sees us – we do not hide
  But Adam's sin has caused a cloak
  Between us and ordinary folk.

Woman, if you come with me,
On your head a crown will be,
  Fresh pork, milk, the finest ale
  Await us now beyond the pale

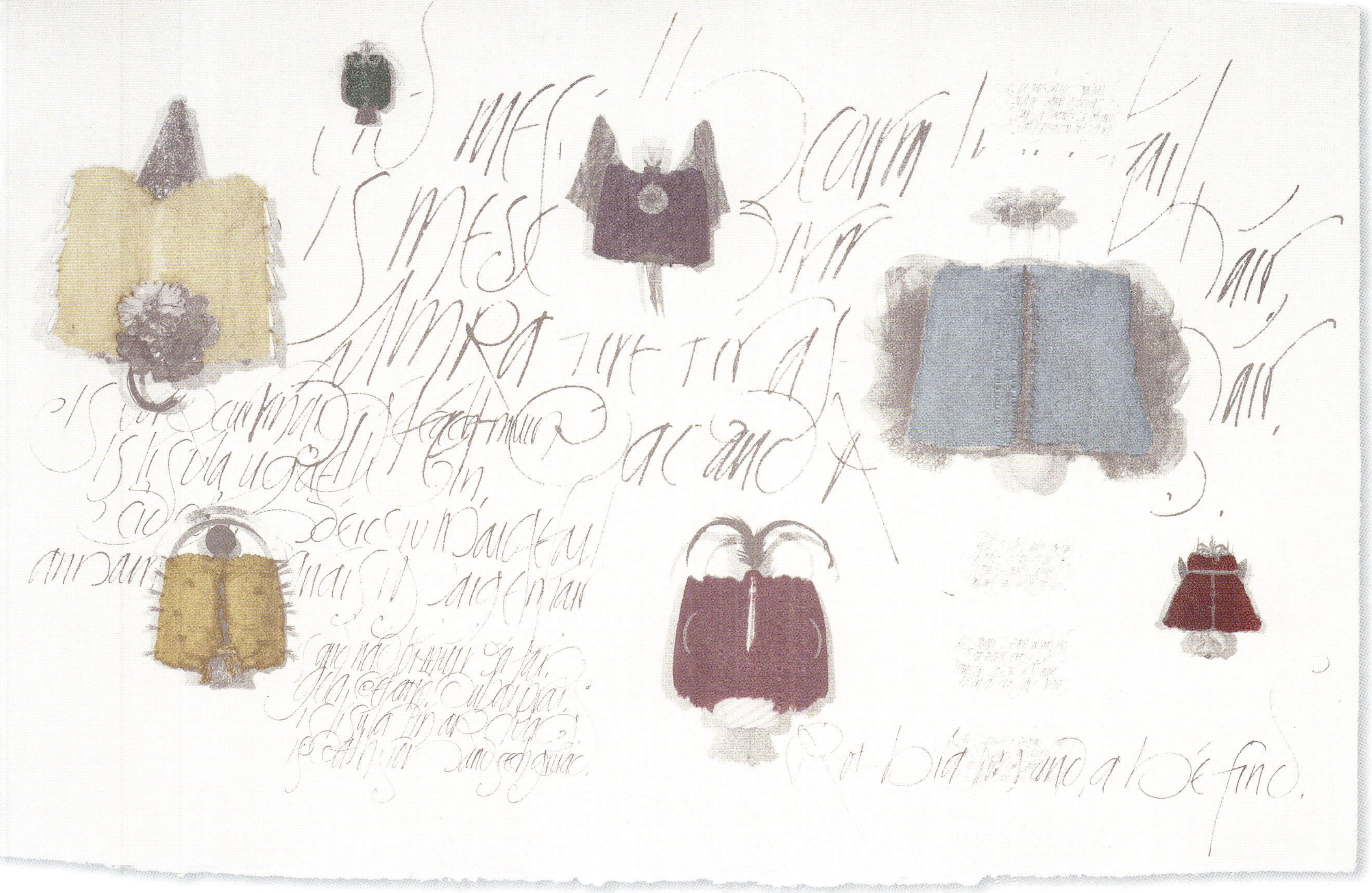

3

GAN AINM

ANON

c.800

Ealaíontóir/Artist:
Jake Harvey

Peannaire/Calligrapher:
Donald Murray

Aistritheoir/Translators:
David Greene, Frank O'Connor

Ainmníodh ag/Nominator:
Tomás Mac Símáin

An Lon Dubh

Int én bec
ro léic feit
do rind guip
glanbuidi;
fo-cheird faíd
os Loch Laíg
lon do chraíb
charnbuidi.

Blackbird at Belfast Lough

The little bird has whistled from the tip of his bright yellow beak; the blackbird from a bough laden with yellow blossom has tossed a cry over Belfast Lough.

Int én bec

The wee bird

Ro léic feit

has let out a whistle

Do rinn guip

from the point of a beak

glanbuidi

bright yellow

fo-ceird faíd

it sends out a call

ós Loch Laíg

above Loch Laig

lon do chraíb

a blackbird from a branch

charnbuidi

yellow-heaped

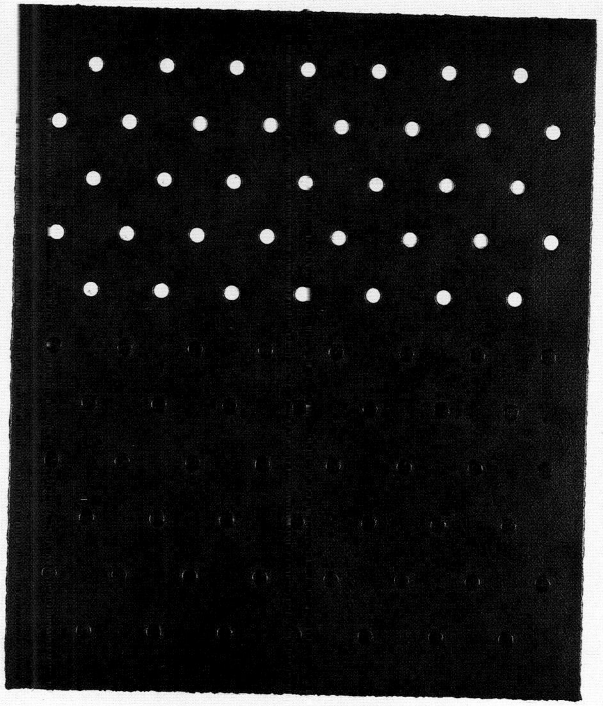

4

GAN AINM

ANON

c.900-1000

Ealaíontóir/Artist:
Alan Davie

Peannaire/Calligrapher:
Louise Donaldson

Aistritheoir/Translator:
Fearghas MacFhionnlaigh

Ainmníodh ag/Nominator:
Fearghas MacFhionnlaigh

Scél Lem Dúib

Scél lem dúib:
dordaid dam;
snigid gaim;
ro-fáith sam;

Gáeth ard úar;
ísel grían;
gair a rrith;
ruirthech rían;

Rorúad rath;
ro cleth cruth;
ro gab gnáth
giugrann guth.

Ro gab úacht
etti én;
aigre ré –
é mo scél.

Brief Account

Brief account:
Stag's complaint.
Cold front.
Summer's spent.

High cold blow.
Sun holds low.
Short the day.
Sea just spray.

Bracken brown,
Broken down.
Geese all mouth,
Heading south.

Chilled each quill.
Feathers' flurry.
Weather's hoary.
End of story!

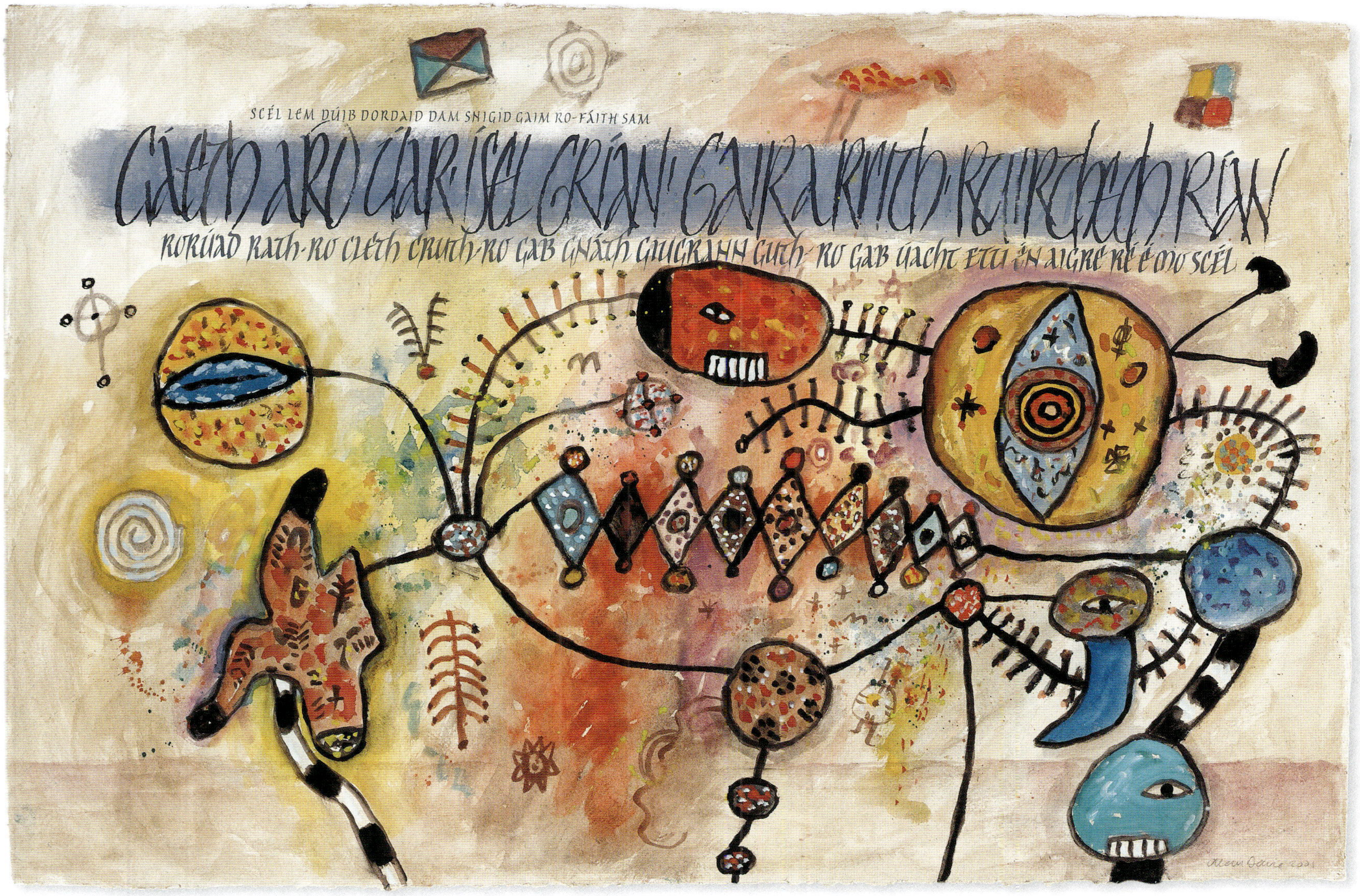
SCÉL LEM DÚIB DORDAID DAM SNIGID GAIM RO-FÁITH SAM
RORÚAD RATH · RO CLETH CRUTH · RO GAB GNÁTH GIUGRANN GUTH · RO GAB ÚACHT ETTI ÉN AIGRE RÉ É MO SCÉL

5

GAN AINM

ANON

c.900-1000

Ealaíontóir/Artist:
George Wyllie

Peannaire/Calligrapher:
Tim O'Neill

Aistritheoir/Translators:
David Greene, Frank O'Connor

Ainmníodh ag/Nominator:
Rody Gorman

Is Acher in Gaith In-Nocht

**Is acher in gaith in-nocht,
Fo-fúasna fairrge findfholt;
Ní águsr réimm mora mind
Dond laechraid lainn ó Lothlind.**

Is Athghéar an Ghaoth Anocht

Is athghéar an ghaoth anocht;
Croitear fionnfholt na farraige.
Ní heagal teacht thar mhuir mhín
Laochra fiáine Lochlainne.

Gaoth Àrd ann A-Nochd

Agus gaoth àrd
Ann a-nochd

Agus druim bàn a' chuain
Fo chuthach,

Chan eagal dhomh
Gràisg ifrinn

A' tighinn tarsainn
Air Muir Mheann.

Since Tonight the Wind is High

Since tonight the wind is high,
The sea's white mane a fury,
I need not fear the hordes of Hell
Coursing the Irish Channel.

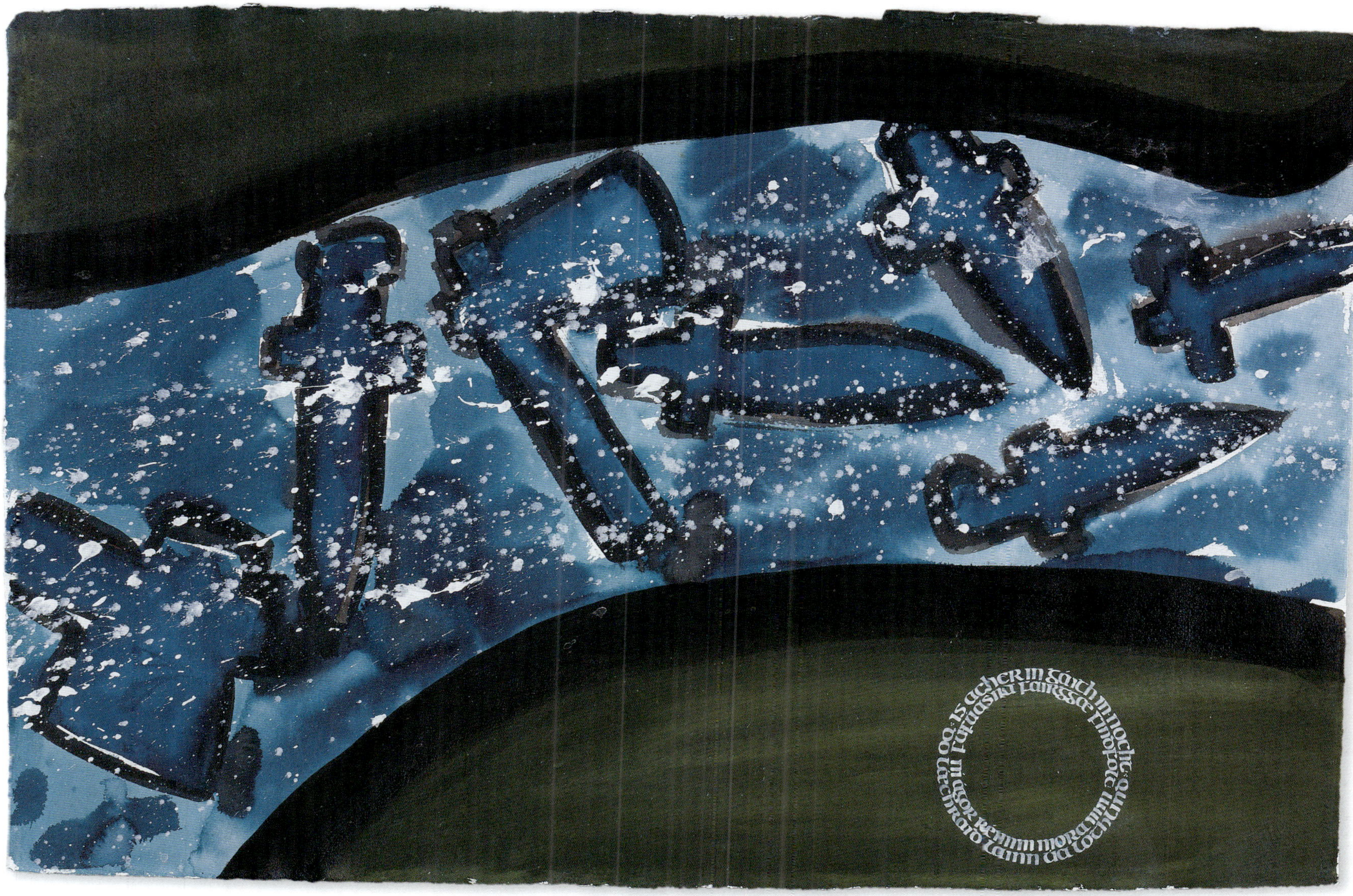

Is acher in gáith in-nocht
fu-fuasna fairggae findfolt
ni ágor réimm mora minn
dond láechraid lainn ua Lothlind

6

GAN AINM

ANON

c.900

Ealaíontóir/Artist:
Bernadette Cotter

Peannaire/Calligrapher:
David McGrail

Aistritheoir/Translator:
Donncha Ó hAodha

Ainmníodh ag/Nominator:
Biddy Jenkinson

Aithbe Damsa Bés Mara (sliocht)

Aithbe damsa bés mara;
sentu fom-dera croan;
toirsi oca ce do-gnéo,
sona do-táet a loan.

Is mé Caillech Bérre Buí,
do-meilinn léne mbithnuí;
indíu táthum dom shémi
ná melainn cid athléni.

It moíni
charthar lib, nidat doíni;
ind inbaid i mmarsamar
batar doíni carsamar.

Batar inmaini doíni
ata maige mad-ríadam;
ba maith no meilmis leo,
ba bec no moítis íaram.

Indíu trá caín-timgarat,
ocus ní mór nond-oídet;
cíasu bec do-n-idnaiget,
is mór a mét no-moídet.

Carpait lúaith
ocus eich do-beirtis búaid,
ro boí, denus, tuile díb:
bennacht ar ríg roda-úaid.

Tocair mo chorp co n-aichri
dochum adba díar aichni;
tan bas mithig la Mac nDé
do-té do breith a aithni.

The Lament of the Old Woman of Beare (excerpt)

Ebb-tide to me as to the sea; old age causes me to be sallow; although I may grieve thereat, it comes to its food joyfully.

I am the Old Woman of Beare, from Dursey; I used to wear a smock that was always new. Today I am become so thin that I would not wear out even a cast-off smock.

It is riches you love, and not people; when we were alive, it was people we loved.

Beloved were the people whose lands we happily traversed; well did we fare among them, and it was little they boasted afterwards.

Today indeed they are good at claiming, and they are not lavish in granting the claim; although they bestow little, great is the extent to which they boast of it.

Swift chariots and steeds that took the prize, for a time there was an abundance of them: a blessing on the king who gave them.

Bitterly does my body seek to go to a dwelling where it is known; when the Son of God deems it time, let him come to carry off His deposit.

We have only been able to give an excerpt from this poem.
For an alternative source of the full text see the listing on page 265

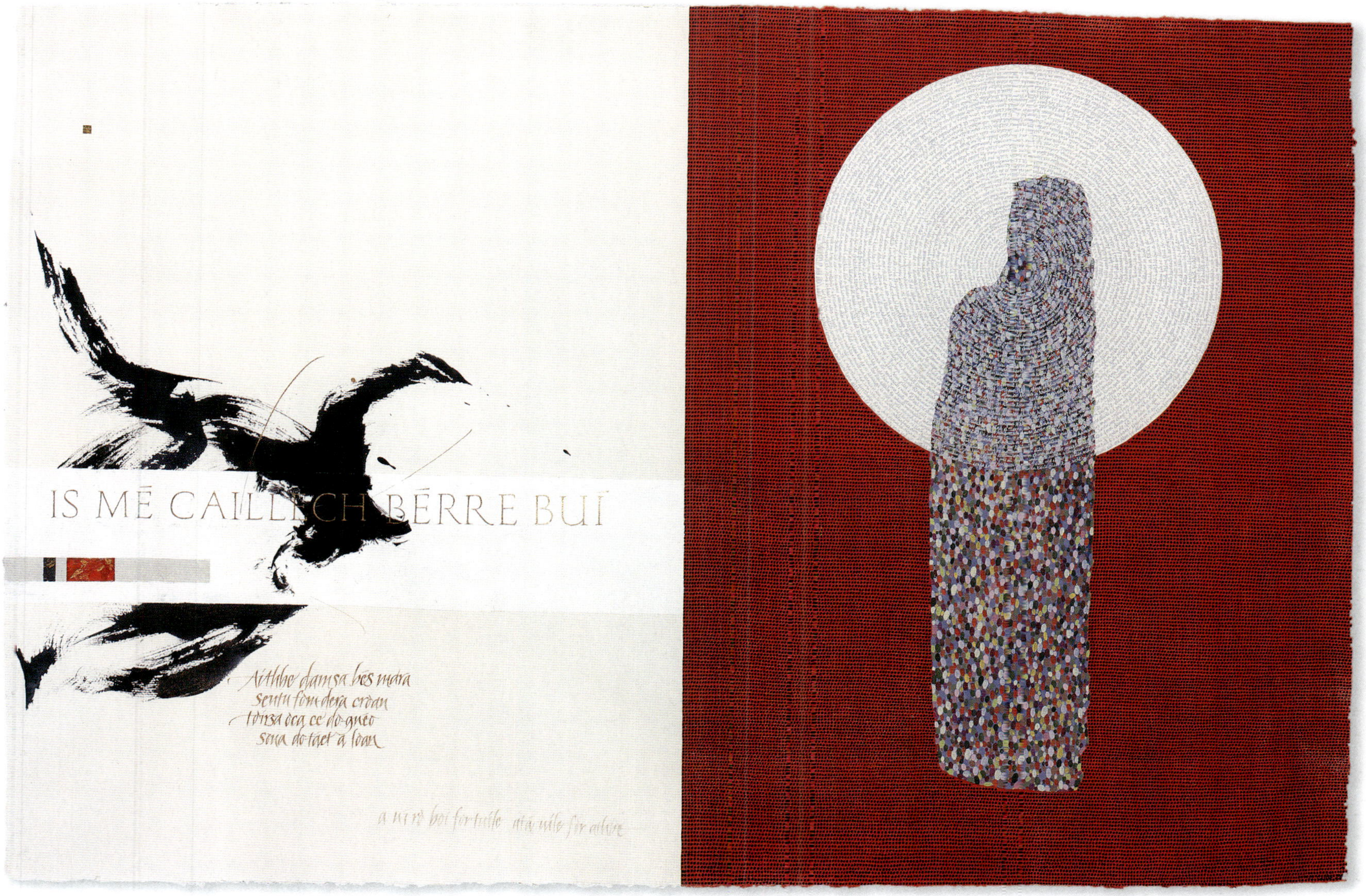
IS MĒ CAILLECH BĒRRE BUĪ
Aithbe damsa bés mara
sentu fom-dera croan
toirsa oca ce do-gneo
sona do-taet a loan

7

GAN AINM

ANON

c.900

Ealaíontóir/Artist:
Simon Fraser

Peannaire/Calligrapher:
Frances Breen

Aistritheoir/Translator:
Gerard Murphy

Ainmníodh ag/Nominator:
Seamus Heaney

Pangur Bán

Messe ocus Pangur bán,
cechtar nathar fria shaindán:
bíth a menmasam fri seilgg,
mu menma céin im shaincheirdd.

Caraimse fos, ferr cach clú,
oc mu lebrán, léir ingnu;
ní foirmtech frimm Pangur bán:
caraid cesin a maccdán.

Ó ru biam, scél cen scís,
innar tegdais, ar n-óendís,
táithiunn, díchríchide clius,
ní fris tarddam ar n-áthius.

Gnáth, húaraib, ar gressaib gal
glenaid luch inna línsam;
os mé, du-fuit im lín chéin
dliged ndoraid cu ndronchéill.

Fúachaidsem fri frega fál
a rosc, a nglése comlán;
fúachimm chéin fri fégi fis
mu rosc réil, cesu imdis.

Fáelidsem cu ndéne dul
hi nglen luch inna gérchrub;
hi tucu cheist ndoraid ndil
os mé chene am fáelid.

Cia beimmi a-min nach ré
ní derban cách a chéle:
maith la cechtar nár a dán;
subaigthius a óenurán.

The Scholar and his Cat

I and white Pangur practise each of us his special art: his mind is set on hunting, my mind on my special craft.

I love – it is better than all fame – to be quiet beside my book, diligently pursuing knowledge. White Pangur does not envy me: he loves his childish craft.

When the two of us – this tale never wearies us – are alone together in our house, we have something to which we may apply our skill, an endless sport.

It is usual, at times, for a mouse to stick in his net, as a result of warlike battlings. For my part, into my net falls some difficult rule of hard meaning.

He directs his bright perfect eye against an enclosing wall. Though my clear eye is very weak, I direct it against keenness of knowledge.

He is joyful with swift movement when a mouse sticks in his sharp paw. I too am joyful when I understand a dearly loved difficult problem.

Though we be thus at any time, neither of us hinders the other: each of us likes his craft, severally rejoicing in them.

(Continued on page 233)

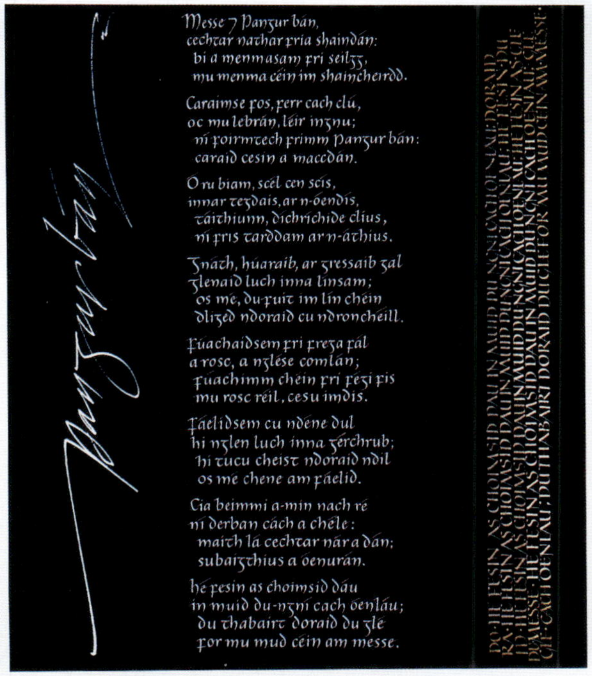
Pangur bán
Messe 7 Pangur bán,
cechtar nathar fria shaindán:
bi a menmasam fri seilgg,
mu menma céin im shaincheirdd.
Caraimse fos, ferr cach clú,
oc mu lebrán, léir ingnu;
ní foirmtech frimm Pangur bán:
caraid cesin a maccdán.
Ó ru biam, scél cen scís,
innar tegdais, ar n-óendís,
táithiunn, dichríchide clius,
ní fris tarddam ar n-áthius.
Gnáth, húaraib, ar gressaib gal
glenaid luch inna línsam;
os me, du-fuit im lín chéin
dliged ndoraid cu ndronchéill.
Fúachaidsem fri frega fál
a rosc, a nglése comlán;
fúachimm chéin fri fegi fis
mu rosc réil, cesu imdis.
Fáelidsem cu ndéne dul
hi nglen luch inna gérchrub;
hi tucu cheist ndoraid ndil
os me chene am fáelid.
Cia beimmi a-min nach ré
ni derban cách a chéle:
maith lá cechtar nár a dán;
subaigthius a óenurán.
Hé fesin as choimsid dáu
in muid du-ngní cach óenláu;
du thabairt doraid du glé
for mu mud céin am messe.

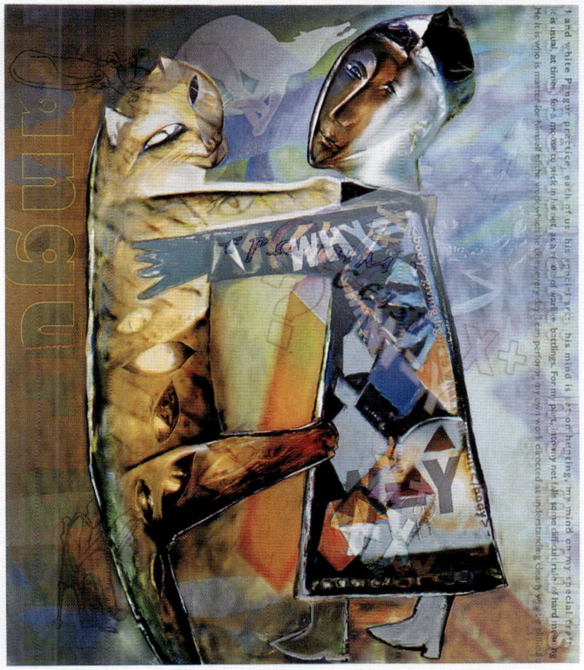

8

GAN AINM

ANON

c. 1000

Ealaíontóir/Artist:
Olwen Shone

Peannaire/Calligrapher:
Frances Breen

Aistritheoir/Translator:
Fearghas MacFhionnlaigh

Ainmníodh ag/Nominator:
Fearghas MacFhionnlaigh

Rop Tú Mo Baile

Rop tú mo baile,
a Choimdiu cride;
ní ní nech aile
acht Rí secht nime.

Rop tú mo scrútain
i lló 's i n-aidche;
rop tú ad-chear
im chotlud caidche.

Rop tú mo labra,
rop tú mo thuicsiu;
rop tussu damsa,
rop misse duitsiu.

Rop tussu m'athair,
rop mé do macsu;
rop tussu lemsa,
rop misse latsu.

Rop tú mo chathscíath,
rop tú mo chlaideb;
rop tussu m'ordan,
rop tussu m'airer.

Rop tú mo dítiu,
rop tú mo daingen;
rop tú nom-thocba
i n-áentaid n-aingel.

Rop tú cech maithius
dom churp, dom anmain;
rop tú mo fhlaithius
i nnim 's i talmain.

Fill My Horizon

Fill my horizon,
Lord of love.
Still my eyes
On the King above.

Be my thought
By day and night.
When eyelids shut,
Yet stay in sight.

Be my speech.
Be my IQ.
You for me.
I for You.

Be my Father.
I Your Son.
We together,
Kith and kin.

Be my battleshield.
Be my sword.
Be my dignity.
Be my reward.

Be my safehouse,
My basecamp strong.
Be my air-lift
With angel throng!

My body's balm,
My spirit's health,
Be my regime
In heaven and earth.

(Continued on page 233)

Ron tussu t'aenur
sainshere mo chride;
ni ron neach aile
acht Ainbi nime.
Co talla forum
re ndul it tama:
mo chuit mo chotlud
ar meit do grada.
Ron tussu t'aenur
sainshere mo chride;
ni ron neach aile
acht Ainbi nime.
Co talla forum
re ndul it tama:
mo chuit mo chotlud
ar meit do grada

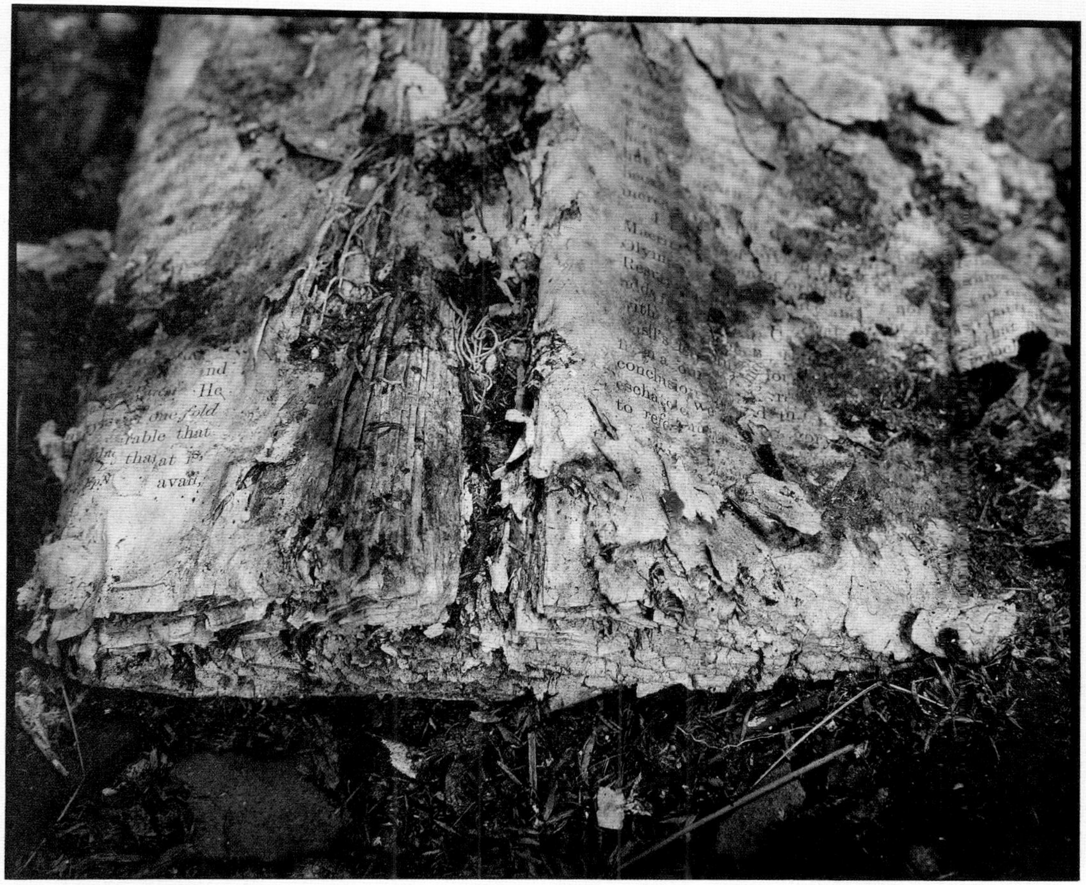

9

GAN AINM

ANON

c.1200

Ealaíontóir/Artist:
Alasdair Gray

Peannaire/Calligrapher:
The Artist

Aistritheoir/Translator:
Kuno Meyer

Ainmníodh ag/Nominator:
Nuala Ní Dhomhnaill

Is Scíth Mo Chrob ón Scríbainn

Is scíth mo chrob ón scríbainn;
Ní dígainn mo glés géroll;
Sceithid penn – gulban caelda
Dig ndaelda do dub glégorm.

Bruinnid srúaim n-ecna ndedairn
As mo láim degduinn desmais;
Doirtid a dig for duilinn
Do dub in chuilinn chnesglais.

Sínim mo phenn mbec mbraenach
Tar aenach lebar lígoll
Cen scor fri selba ségonn,
Dían scíth mo chrob ón scríbonn.

My Hand is Weary with Writing

My hand is weary with writing,
My sharp quill is not steady,
My slender-beaked pen jets forth
A black draught of shining dark-blue ink.

A stream of wisdom of blessèd God
Springs from my fair-brown shapely hand:
On the page it squirts its draught
Of ink of the green-skinned holly.

My little dripping pen travels
Across the plain of shining books,
Without ceasing for the wealth of the great –
Whence my hand is weary with writing.

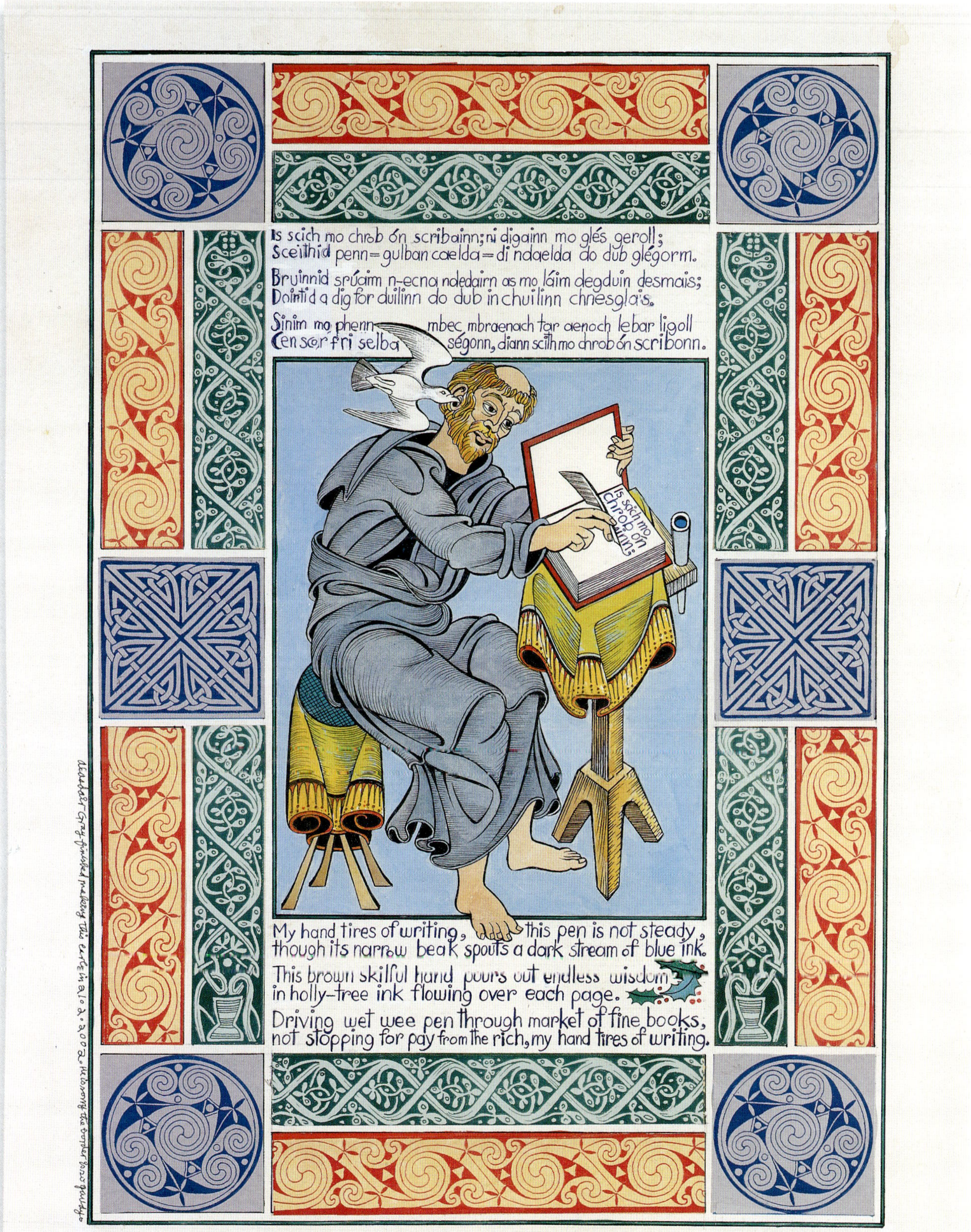
Is scích mo chrob ón scríbainn; ní digainn mo glés geroll;
Sceithid penn=gulban caelda=di ndaelda do dub glégorm.
Bruinnid srúaim n-ecna ndedairn as mo láim degduin desmais;
Dointid a dig for duilinn do dub in chuilinn chnesglais.
Sínim mo phenn mbec mbraenach tar aenoch lebar ligoll
Cen scor fri selba ségonn, dianid scíth mo chrob ón scribonn.
Is scích mo chrob ón ...inn:
My hand tires of writing, this pen is not steady,
though its narrow beak spouts a dark stream of blue ink.
This brown skilful hand pours out endless wisdom
in holly-tree ink flowing over each page.
Driving wet wee pen through market of fine books,
not stopping for pay from the rich, my hand tires of writing.

10

MUIREADHACH ALBANACH

c. 1300

Ealaíontóir/Artist:
Deirdre O'Mahony

Peannaire/Calligrapher:
Réiltín Murphy

Aistritheoir/Translator:
Frank O'Connor

Ainmníodh ag/Nominator:
Biddy Jenkinson

M'anam do Sgar Riomsa A-raoir

M'anam do sgar riomsa a-raoir,
calann ghlan dob ionnsa i n-uaigh;
rugadh bruinne maordha mín
is aonbhla lín uime uainn.

Do tógbhadh sgath aobhdha fhionn
a-mach ar an bhfaongha bhfann:
laogh mo chridhise do chrom,
craobh throm an tighise thall.

M'aonar a-nocht damhsa, a Dhé,
olc an saoghal camsa ad-chí;
dob álainn trom an taoibh naoi
do bhaoi sonn a-raoir, a Rí.

Truagh leam an leabasa thiar,
mo pheall seadasa dhá snámh;
tárramair corp seada saor
is folt claon, a leaba, id lár.

Do bhí duine go ndreich moill
ina luighe ar leith mo phill;
gan bharamhail acht bláth cuill
don sgáth duinn bhanamhail bhinn.

Maol Mheadha na malach ndonn
mo dhabhach mheadha a-raon rom;
mo chridhe an sgáth do sgar riom,
bláth mhionn arna car do chrom.

Táinig an chlí as ar gcuing,
agus dí ráinig mar roinn:
corp idir dá aisil inn
ar dtocht don fhinn mhaisigh mhoill.

On the Death of his Wife

I parted from my life last night,
A woman's body sunk in clay:
The tender bosom that I loved
Wrapped in a sheet they took away.

The heavy blossom that had lit
The ancient boughs is tossed and blown;
Hers was the burden of delight
That long had weighed the old tree down.

And I am left alone tonight
And desolate is the world I see,
For lovely was that woman's weight
That even last night had lain on me.

Weeping I look upon the place
Where she used to rest her head,
For yesterday her body's length
Reposed upon you too, my bed.

Yesterday that smiling face
Upon one side of you was laid
That could match the hazel bloom
In its dark delicate sweet shade.

Maelva of the shadowy brows
Was the mead-cask at my side;
Fairest of all flowers that grow
Was the beauty that has died.

My body's self deserts me now,
The half of me that was her own,
Since all I knew of brightness died
Half of me lingers, half is gone.

(Continued on page 234)

11

GOFRAIDH FIONN Ó DÁLAIGH

c. 1400

Ealaíontóir / Artist:
Moira Scott

Peannaire / Calligrapher:
Réiltín Murphy

Aistritheoir / Translator:
Thomas Kinsella

Ainmníodh ag / Nominator:
Thomas Kinsella

Bean Torrach, fa Tuar Broide

Bean torrach, fa tuar broide,
do bhí i bpríosún pheannaide,
berar dho chead Dé na ndúl,
lé leanabh beag sa bhríosún.

Ar n-a bhreith do bhí an macámh
ag fás mar gach bhfochlocán,
dá fhiadhnaibh mar budh each dhún,
seal do bhliadhnaibh sa bhríosun.

An inghean d'fhagháil bhroise -
meanma an leinbh níor lughaide,
sí dhá réir gé dho bhaoi i mbroid,
mar mhnaoi gan phéin gan pheannaid.

Do shoillse an laoi níor léir dhóibh
acht a bhfaicdís – fáth dobróin! –
do dhruim iodhan an achaidh
tré ionadh thuill tarathair.

Mun n-orchra níorbh ionann dál
dá mháthair is don mhacámh;
do aithrigh dealbh dá dreich gil
is an leanbh ag breith bhisigh.

An leanbh dá oileamhain ann
dob fheirrde aige an fhulang,
níor léir don bharrthais óg úr
nárbh fhód Parrthais an priosún.

Seisean ag breith ruag reabhraidh,
sise ag dul i ndoimheanmain;
mairg, thrá, nach tiobhradh dá aoidh
ionnramh na mná 'sa macaoimh.

A Child Born in Prison

A pregnant woman (sorrow's sign)
once there was, in painful prison.
The God of Elements let her bear
in prison there a little child.

The little boy, when he was born,
grew up like any other child
(plain as we could see him there)
for a space of years, in prison.

That the woman was a prisoner
did not lower the baby's spirits.
She minded him, though in prison,
like one without punishment or pain.

Nothing of the light of day
(O misery!) could they see
but the bright ridge of a field
through a hole someone had made.

Yet the loss was not the same
for the son as for the mother:
her fair face failed in form
while the baby gained in health.

The child, raised where he was,
grew better by his bondage,
not knowing in his fresh frail limbs
but prison was ground of Paradise.

He made little playful runs
while her spirits only deepened.
(Mark well, lest you regret,
these deeds of son and mother.)

(Continued on page 235)

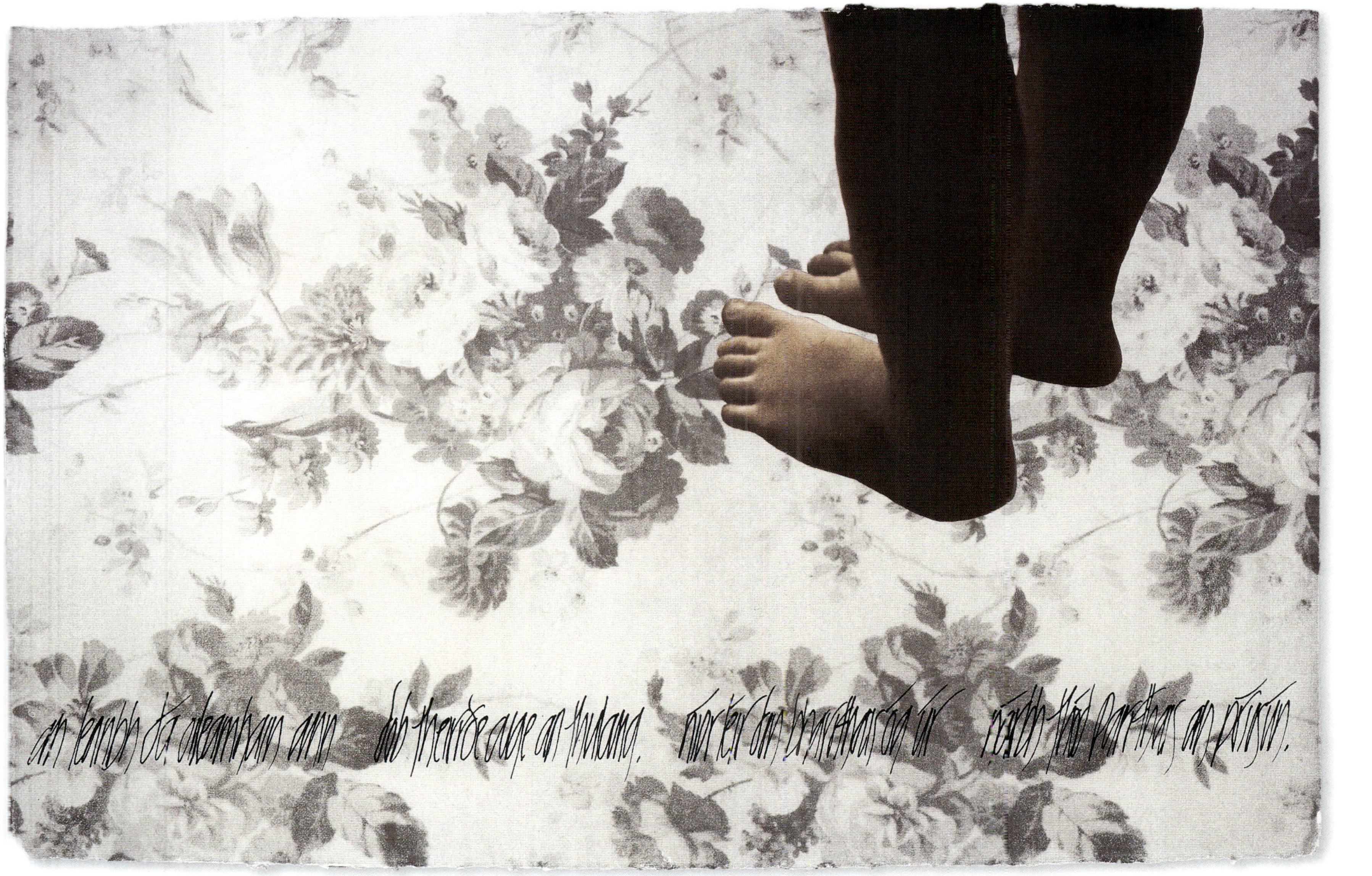

12

ISEABAIL NÍ MHEIC CAILÉIN

c.1500

Ealaíontóir/Artist:
Catherine Harper

Peannaire/Calligrapher:
Réiltín Murphy

Aistritheoir/Translator:
Anne C. Frater

Ainmníodh ag/Nominator:
Aonghas MacNeacail

Éistibh, a Luchd an Tighe-se

Éistibh a luchd an tighe-se
re scél na mbod bríoghmhar
do shanntaich mo chridhe-sa
cuid dana scéalaibh do sgríobhadh.

Cé líonmhor bod bréagh-bhileach
do bhí san aimsir romhainn
tá aig fear an úird chrábhaidh seo
bod as cho mór righinn.

Bod mo shagairt thuarasdail
cé tá cho fada seasmhach
o tha céin ní chualabhair
an reabh atá ina mhacan.

Atá a riabh ro-reamhar
an sin 's ní h-é scéal bréagach
nocha [chuala] cho-reamhar
mhotha bhod arís. Éistibh.

Listen, People of this House

Listen, people of this house,
to the tale of the powerful penis
which has made my heart greedy.
I will write some of the tale.

Although many beautiful tree-like penises
have been in the time before,
this man of the religious order
has a penis so big and rigid.

The penis of my household priest,
although it is so long and firm,
the thickness of his manhood
has not been heard of for a long time.

That thick drill of his,
and it is no word of a lie,
never has its thickness been heard of
or a larger penis.

Estuf, a lucht in ti so.
reskail ma bod breouir.
dy hanluth mochiessa
cuf dane skallou dy screff.

Gaileneour bod braw lucht
dy yu sin amsur roun.
tak far la nvird crawe so
bod is caf mor rotinge.

Bod mo haaavd, horistil
aa tu ao fad sessouil.
otha keuinn an quha lavir
in reuf ata na vackans.

Ata reuf roiravur
an sin she skail brea.
nocha chojai chourauur
vaa vod arris es. Estuve.

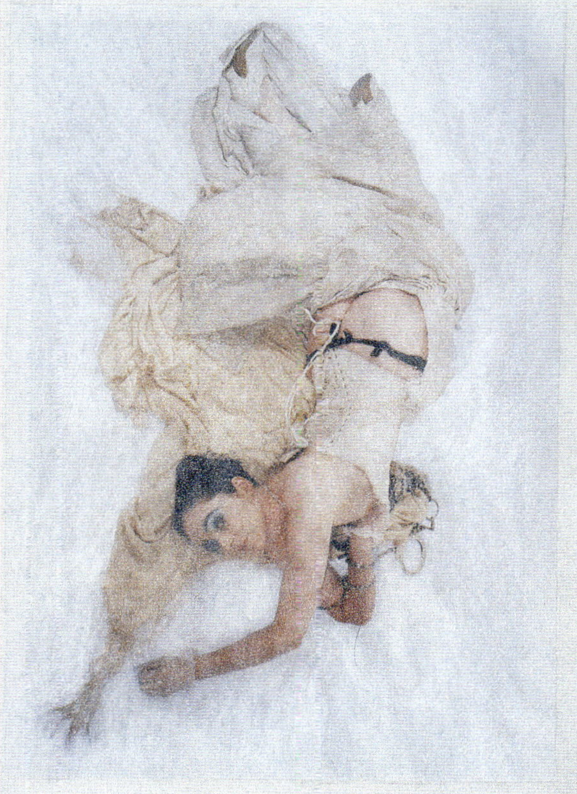

13

AITHBHREAC INGHEAN COIRCEADAIL

c. 1500

Neach-ealain / Artist:
Kathleen O'Donnell

Snas-sgrìobhadair / Calligrapher:
Tim O'Neill

Eadar-theangaichte aig / Translator:
William J. Watson

Roghainn / Nominator:
Anne C. Frater

A Phaidrín do Dhúisg Mo Dhéar

A Phaidrín do dhúisg mo dhéar,
ionmhain méar do bhitheadh ort;
ionmhain cridhe fáilteach fial
'ga raibhe riamh gus a-nocht.

Dá éag is túirseach atáim,
an lámh má mbitheá gach n-uair,
nach cluinim a beith a gclí
agus nach bhfaicim í uaim.

Mo chridhe-se is tinn atá
ó theacht go crích an lá dhúinn,
ba ghoirid do éist ré ghlóir,
ré h-agallaimh an óig úir.

Béal asa ndob aobhdha glór,
dhéantaidhe a ghlór is gach tír;
leómhan Muile na múr ngeal,
seabhag Íle na magh mín.

Fear ba ghéar meabhair air dhán,
ó nach deachaidh dámh gan díol,
taoiseach deigh-einigh suairc séimh,
agá bhfaighthí méin mheic ríogh.

Dámh ag teacht ó Dhún an Óir
is dámh ón Bhóinn go a fholt fhiar:
minic thánaig iad fá theist,
ní mionca ná leis a riar.

Seabhag seangglan Sléibhe Gaoil,
fear do chuir a chaoin ré cléir;
dreagan Leódhus na learg ngeal,
éigne Sanais na sreabh séimh.

Thou Rosary That Has Waked My Tear

Thou rosary that has waked my tear, dear the finger that was wont to be on thee; dear the heart, hospitable and generous, which owned thee ever until tonight.

Sad am I for his death, he whose hand thou didst each hour encircle, sad that I hear not that that hand is in life, and that I see it not before me.

Sick is my heart since the day's close is come to us; all too short a time it listened to his speech, to the converse of the goodly youth.

A mouth whose winning speech would wile the hearts of all in every land; lion of white-walled Mull, hawk of Islay of smooth plains.

The man whose memory for song was keen, from whom no poet-band went without reward; a chief nobly generous, courteous and calm, with whom was found a prince's mind.

Poets came from Dún an Óir, poets too from the Boyne to seek his curling hair; oft did they come drawn by his fame, not more often than they got from him all their wish.

Slim bright hawk of Sliabh Gaoil, a man who showed kindness to the Church; dragon of Lewis of bright slopes, salmon of Sanas of quiet streams.

(Continued on page 236)

A phaidrín do dhúisg mo dhéar:
ionmhain méar do bhitheadh ort;
ionmhain cridhe fáilteach fial
'ga raibhe riamh gus anocht.
Dá éag is tuirseach atáim,
an lámh má mbithea gach n-uair
nach cluinim a beith a gclí
agus nach bhfaicim í uaim.

Gan duine ris' dtig mo mhiann
ar sliocht nan Niall ó Niall óg
gan mhuirn gan mheadhair ag mnáibh
gan aoibhneas an dáin im dhóigh.

Is briste mo chridhe im chlí,
agus bidh nó go dtí m'éag,
ar éis an abhradh dhuibh úir:
a phaidrín do dhúisg mo dhéar:
a phaidrín.
Muire mháthair-muime an Ríogh.
go robh 'gam dhíon ar gach séad,
is a mac do chruthuigh gach dúil:
a phaidrín do dhúisg mo dhéar:
a phaidrín.

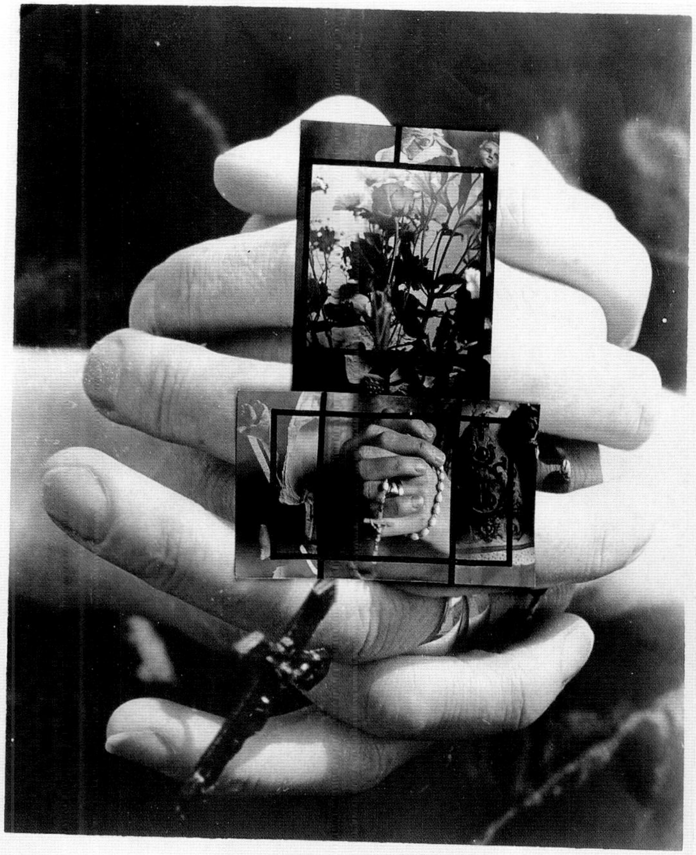

14

DÒMHNALL MAC FHIONNLAIGH NAN DÀN

c. 1540 - 1610

Neach-ealain / Artist:
Diarmuid Delargy

Snas-sgrìobhadair / Calligrapher:
Donald Murray

Eadar-theangaichte aig / Translator:
John MacKechnie

Roghainn / Nominator:
Myles Campbell

A' Chomhachag (earrann)

Aoibhinn an obair an t-sealg,
Aoibhinn a meanmna 's a beachd:
Is mòr gum b' annsa leam a fonn
Na long is i dol fo bheairt.

Fad a bhithinn beò no maireann,
Deò den anail ann am chorp,
Dh'fhanainn am fochair an fhèidh –
Sin an sprèidh an robh mo thoirt.

Ceòl as binne de gach ceòl
Guth a' ghadhair mhòir 's e teachd;
Damh na shìomanaich le gleann,
Mìolchoin a bhith ann is às.

'S truagh an-diugh nach beò an fheadhainn,
Gun ann ach an ceò den bhuidhinn
Leis 'm bu mhiannach glòir nan gadhar –
Gun mheadhair, gun òl, gun bhruidhinn.

Cead as truaighe ghabhas riamh:
Don fhiadhach bu mhòr mo thoil;
Chan fhalbh mi le bogha fom sgèith
'S gu là bhràth cha leig mi coin.

Mise is tusa, ghadhair bhàin,
Is tùirseach ar turas don eilean;
Chaill sinn an tabhann 's an dàn,
Ged bha sinn grathann ri ceanal.

Thug a' choille dhìots' an earb,
Thug an t-àrd dhìomsa na fèidh:
Chan eil nàire dhuinn, a laoich,
On laigh an aois oirnn le chèil'.

The Owl of Strone (excerpt)

It is a pleasant work, the hunting: pleasant is its spirit, and the recollection of it: much more I preferred its bustle to a ship getting under sail.

As long as I should live or last with a breath of the spirit in my body, I would live near the deer – that is the herd wherein my profit lay.

Music sweeter than all music is the voice of the great hound as he comes: a stag curving his way down a glen, hunting-dogs attacking him and escaping.

It is a pity those folks are not alive today, that nothing but the shade of the company is left who wished for the crying of the hounds, without memory, without drinking, without speaking.

As sad a farewell as ever was taken: in the hunting my delight was great: I will not go with a bow under my arm and till Doomsday I will not slip hounds.

You and I, O white hound, sad is our journey to the island: we have lost the barking and the singing, although we were cheerful for a time.

The forest has taken the roe from you: the peak has taken the deer from me: it is no disgrace for us, my hero, for age has fallen on us together.

We have only been able to give an excerpt from this text.
For an alternative source of the full text see the listing on page 265.

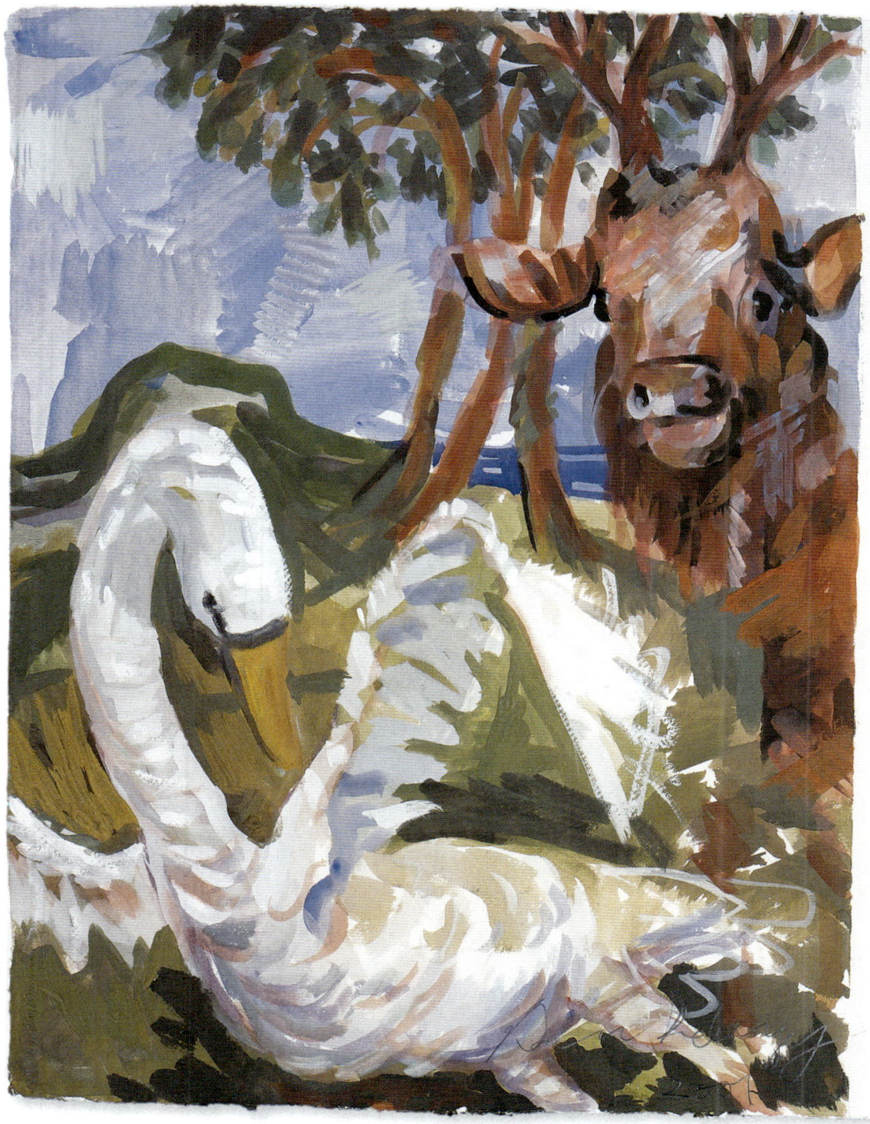

Aoibhinn an
obair an t-sealg
Aoibhinn
a meanmna 'sa
beachd
Is mòr gum
b'annsa leam
a fonn
Na long is i dol
fo bheairt

15

NIGHEAN FHIR NA RÈILIG

THE DAUGHTER OF THE TACKSMAN OF REELIG

c. 1700

Neach-ealain / Artist:
Alice McCartney

Snas-sgrìobhadair / Calligrapher:
Donald Murray

Eadar-theangaichte aig / Translators:
Morag MacLeod, John MacInnes

Roghainn / Nominator:
John Murray

Thig Trì Nithean gun Iarraidh

Thig trì nithean gun iarraidh,
An t-eagal, an t-iadach 's an gaol,
'S gur beag a' chùis mhaslaidh
Ged ghlacadh leo mis' air a h-aon,
'S a liuthad bean-uasal
A fhuaradh sa chiont an robh mi,
A thug an gaol fuadain
Air ro bheagan duaise ga chionn.

Sèist
Air failirinn, illirinn,
Uilirinn, ò horo laoidh,
'S cruaidh-fhortan gun fhios
A chuir mise fo chuing do ghaoil.

Fhir a dhìreas am bealach,
Beir soraidh don ghleannan fo thuath,
Is innis dom leannan
Gur maireann mo ghaol 's gur buan:
Fear eile cha ghabh mi
'S chan fhuiling mi idir a luaidh -
Gus an dèan thu, ghaoil, m' àicheadh,
Cha chreid mi bho chàch gur fuath.

Fhir nan gorm-shùilean meallach,
On ghleannan dem bitheadh an smùid,
Gam bheil a' chaoin-mhala
Mar chanach an t-slèibh' fo dhriùchd,
Nuair readh tu air t' uilinn,
Bhiodh fuil air fear dhìreadh nan stùc,
'S nam biodh tu, ghaoil, mar rium,
Cha b' fhanaid an cèile leam thu.

Three Things Come Without Asking

Three things come without asking:
fear, jealousy and love;
and it is no cause of shame
though I have been caught by them too,
seeing how many ladies
have been found guilty like me –
who gave clandestine love
with little profit because of it.

Refrain
.... it was a cruel fate that came unaware
and left me under the yoke of your love.

You who climb the hill pass,
bear this greeting to the little glen in the north,
and tell my lover
that my love remains and will endure.
I will take no other man,
I cannot bear to have it spoken of,
and until you deny me, my love,
I will not believe that you are hostile.

Man of the beguiling blue eyes
from the glen of the mist,
whose slender brows
are like bog cotton with dew:
when you'd take aim,
he who climbs the peaks [the stag] would be bloodied –
if you were with me, love,
you would not as companion be scorned.

(Continued on page 236)

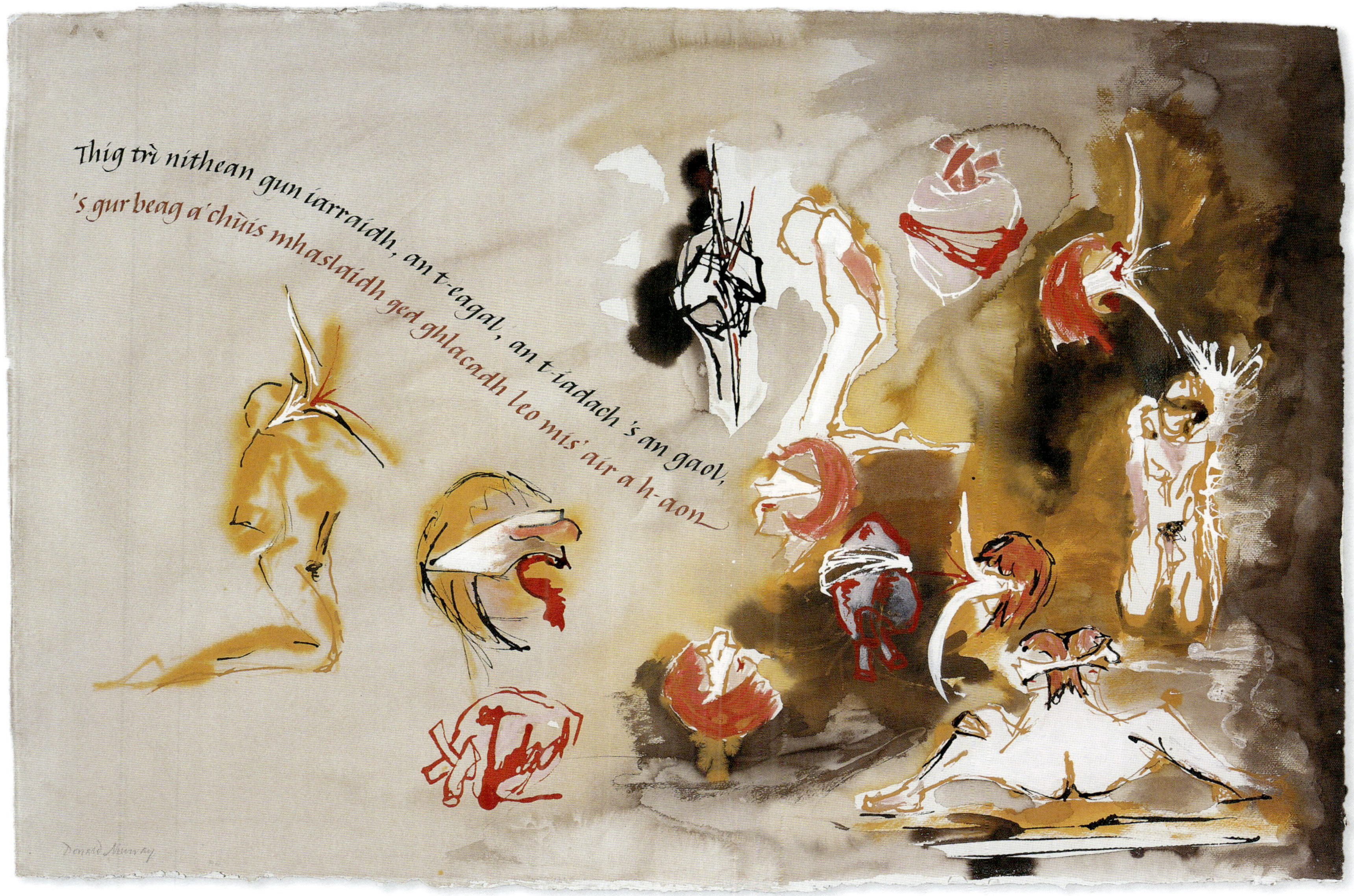
Thig trì nithean gun iarraidh, an t-eagal, an t-iadach 's an gaol,
's gur beag a' chùis mhaslaidh ged ghlacadh leo mis' air a h-aon

16

EOCHAIDH Ó HEOGHASA

c. 1560–1612

Ealaíontóir/Artist:
Ian Charles Scott

Peannaire/Calligrapher:
Susan Leiper

Aistritheoir/Translator:
James Clarence Mangan

Ainmníodh ag/Nominator:
Louis de Paor

Fuar Leam an Oidhche-se dh'Aodh

Fuar leam an oidhche-se dh'Aodh!
Cúis toirse truime a ciothbhraon,
Mo thruaighe sein dár seise
Neimh fhuaire na hoidhcheise.

Anocht, is neimh rem chridhe,
Fearthar frasa teintidhe,
I gcomhdháil na gclá seacdha
Mar tá is orghráin aigeanta.

Do hosgladh ós octaibh néal
Doirse uisgidhe an aiér,
Tug sé minlinnte 'na muir,
Do sgé fhirminnte a hurbhuidh.

Gémadh fiaidhmhíol i bhfiodhbhaidh,
Gémadh éigne ar inbhiormhuir,
Gémadh ealta, is doiligh dhi
Soighidh ar eachtra an uairsi.

Saoth leamsa Aodh Mag Uidhir
Anocht i gcrích comhuighidh,
Fá ghrís ndeirg gcaorshoighnéan gceath
Re feirg bhfaobhoirnéal bhfuighleach.

I gcóigeadh chloinne Dáire
Dursan linn dar leannáinne
Idir dhorchladh bhfuairfhliuch bhfeóir
Is confadh uaibhreach an aeóir.

Fuar leam dá leacain shubhaigh
Fraoch na n-iodhlann n-earrchumhail
Ag séideadh síonghaoth na reann
Fá ríoghlaoch ngéigeal nGaileang.

Ode to the Maguire

Where is my Chief, my master, this bleak night, *mavrone!*
O cold, cold, miserably cold is this bleak night for Hugh,
Its showery, arrowy, speary sleet pierceth one through and through –
Pierceth one to the very bone!

Rolls real thunder? Or was that red, livid light
Only a meteor? I scarce know; but through the midnight dim
That pitiless ice-wind streams. Except the hate that persecutes *him,*
Nothing hath crueller venomy might.

An awful, a tremendous night is this, meseems!
The flood-gates of the rivers of heaven, I think, have been burst wide –
Down from the overcharged clouds, like unto headlong ocean's tide,
Descends grey rain in roaring streams.

Though he were even a wolf ranging the round green woods,
Though he were even a pleasant salmon in the unchainable sea,
Though he were a wild mountain eagle, he could scarce bear, he,
This sharp, sore sleet, these howling floods.

O mournful is my soul this night for Hugh Maguire!
Darkly, as in a dream, he strays! Before him and behind
Triumphs the tyrannous anger of the wounding wind,
The wounding wind, that burns as fire!

It is my bitter grief – it cuts me to the heart –
That in the country of Clan Darry this should be his fate!
O, woe is me, where is he? Wandering, houseless, desolate,
Alone, without or guide or chart!

Medreams I see just now his face, the strawberry bright,
Uplifted to the blackened heavens, while the tempestuous winds
Blow fiercely over and round him, and the smiting sleet-shower blinds
The hero of Galang tonight!

(Continued on page 237)

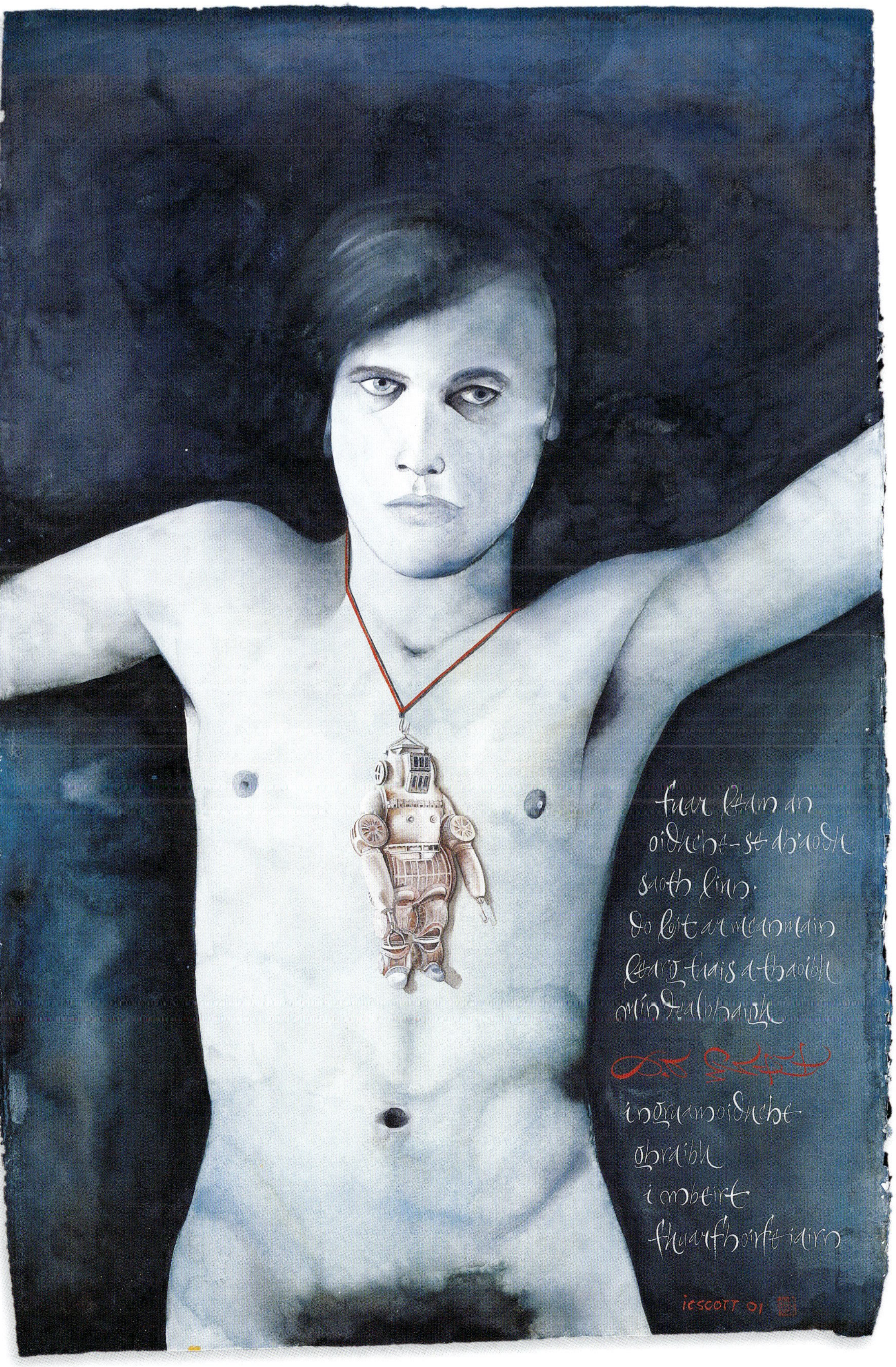
fuar leam an
oidhche-se dh'aodh
saoth linn.
do loit ar meanmain
learg tuais a thaoibh
mín dealbhaigh
in gruamoidhche
ghraibh
i mbeirt
fhuarfhoirfe iairn
icscott 01

17

TÈ DE CHLOINN 'ICCOINNICH

ANON MACKENZIE WOMAN

c.1700

Neach-ealain/Artist:
Sean Hillen

Snas-sgrìobhadair/Calligrapher:
Ann Bowen

Eadar-theangaichte aig/Translator:
Meg Bateman

Roghainn/Nominator:
Meg Bateman

Ailean Dubh à Lòchaidh

'S toigh leam Ailean Dubh à Lòchaidh,
Mo ghaol Ailean donn a' chòta;
'S toigh leam Ailean Dubh à Lòchaidh.

Ailein, Ailein, 's ait leam beò thu:
Sguab thu mo sprèidh bhàrr na mòintich,
Loisg thu m' iodhlann choirce 's eòrna,
Mharbh thu mo thriùir bhràithrean òga,
Mharbh thu m' athair is m' fhear-pòsta;
'S ged rinn thu siud, 's ait leam beò thu.

Ailean Dubh from Lochy

I like Ailean Dubh from Lochy,
I love brown Ailean of the trim coat,
I like Ailean Dubh from Lochy.

Ailean, Ailean, I'm pleased you're living.
You swept my cattle from the moorland,
you burnt my stackyard of oats and barley,
you killed my three youthful brothers,
you killed my father and my husband.
Though you did that, I'm pleased you're living.

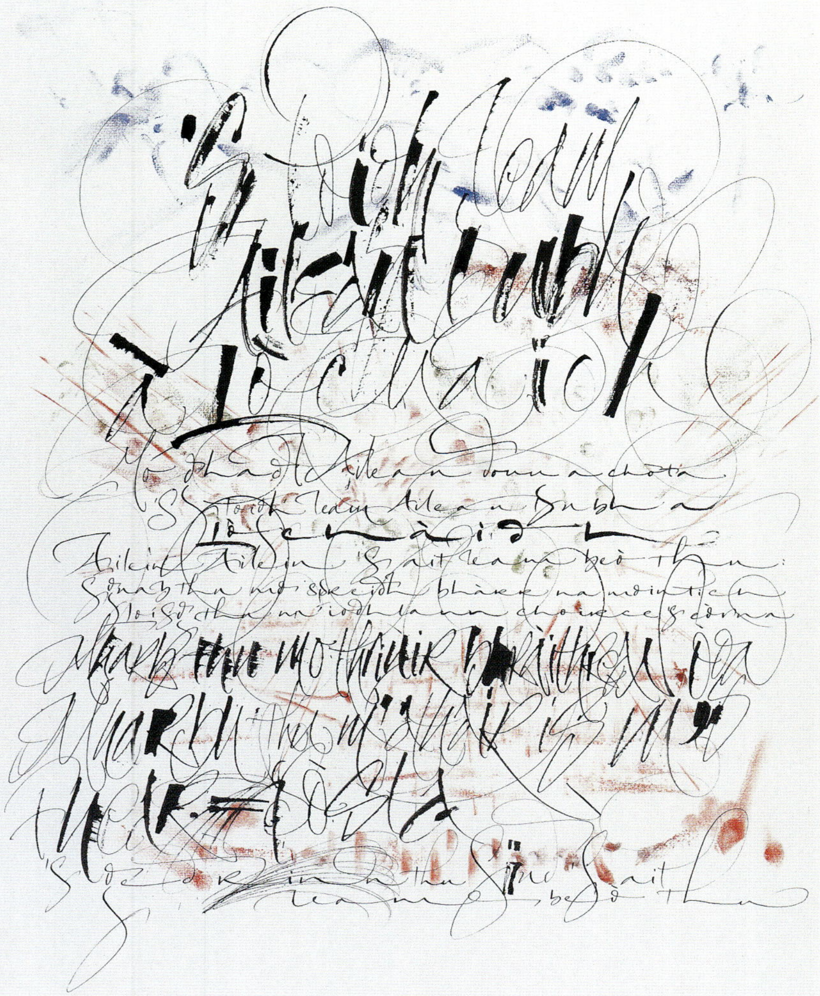

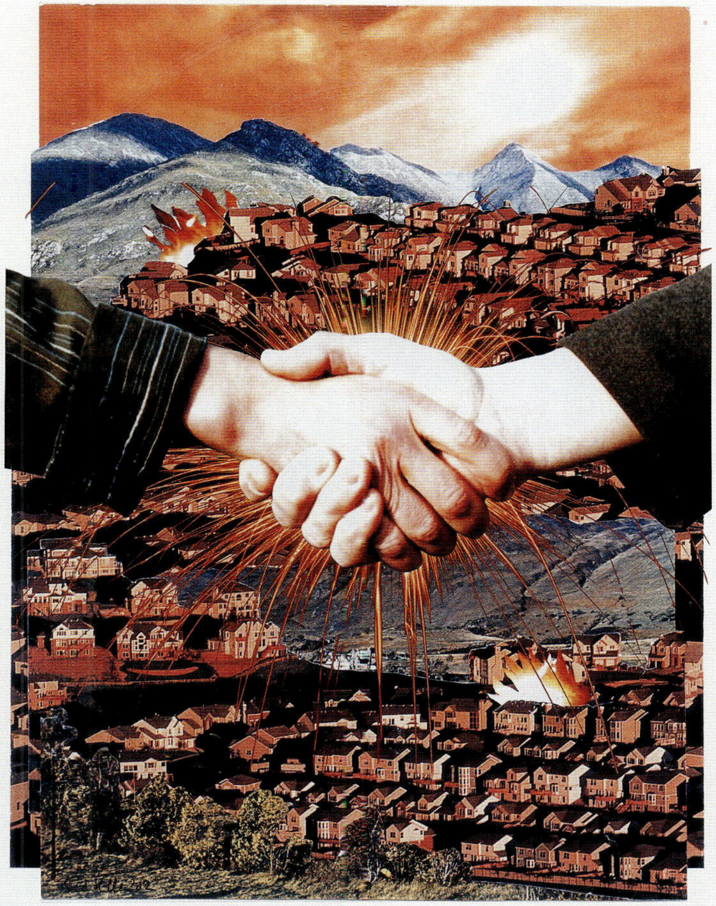

18

MÀIRI CHAMSHRON

MARY CAMERON

c.1700

Neach-ealain/Artist:
Mary Kelly

Snas-sgrìobhadair/Calligrapher:
Susan Leiper

Eadar-theangaichte aig/Translator:
Anne C. Frater

Roghainn/Nominator:
Anne C. Frater

A Mhic Dhonnchaidh Inbhir Abha

A Mhic Dhonnchaidh Inbhir Abha,
Is coimheach a ghabhas tu 'n rathad,
Ged tha Màiri Chamshron romhad;
'S òg a chaill mi riut mo ghnothach.

Eudail a dh'fhearaibh na Dàlach,
Thug thu mach à taigh na plàigh mi,
Far an robh m' athair 's mo mhàthair,
Mo phiuthar ghaoil 's mo chòignear bhràithrean.

Eudail a dh'fhearaibh na grèine,
Thog thu taigh dhomh 'n coill nan geugan,
'S bu shunndach ann mo laighe 's m' èirigh;
Cha b' iongnadh siud, oir b' ùr mo chèile.

M' eudail, m' aighear is m' annsachd,
'S ann ad thaigh nach biodh a' ghainntir;
Gheibhte sitheann ghlas nam beanntan
'S na geala-bhradain a bu reamhra.

Rìgh, gur mis' a th' air mo sgaradh,
Bhith dol le fear eil' a laighe
Is m' fhear fèin air cùl an taighe,
Sealgair nan damh donn 's nan aighean.

Saoil nach mise th' air mo sgaradh -
'S ioma rud a rinn mi fhaicinn;
Chunna mi bhith roinn do bhreacain,
A' tiodhlacadh do ghunna glaice.

Fhuair mi dusan ded chrodh-bainne
'S ceud no dhà ded chaoraich gheala,
Ach ged fhuair, chan fhada mhaireas -
Thèid mi leat gun dàil fon talamh.

Son of Duncan of Inverawe

Son of Duncan of Inverawe
bitter how you go on your way
although Mairi Cameron is before you
I was young when I lost my heart to you.

Beloved of the men of Dalach
you took me out of the house of plague
where my father and my mother were
my beloved sister and my five brothers.

Beloved of men under the sun
you built a house for me in the branched woods
and happy there my sleeping and waking,
and little wonder, with my new husband.

My beloved, my joy and my happiness
in your house there would be no lack
there would be game from the mountains
and the plumpest shiny salmon.

Lord, I am torn apart
having to lie with another
while my own love lies behind the house
hunter of the brown stags and hinds.

How could I not be torn apart
many a thing have I seen
I saw your plaid being parted
burying your fowling-piece.

I got a dozen of your milch cows
and a hundred or two of white sheep
but although I got these it will not last long
I will join you in the ground before long.

(Continued on page 238)

Rìgh, cuir mis' a thàir mo sgaradh

a mhic dhomhnaill inbhir aibhe

thèid mi leat gun dàil fon talamh

bhith
dol
dh
fhear
eil' a
laighe
is
m' fhear
fèin
air
cùl
an
laighe.
seat air
nan
damh
donn 's
nan
aighean

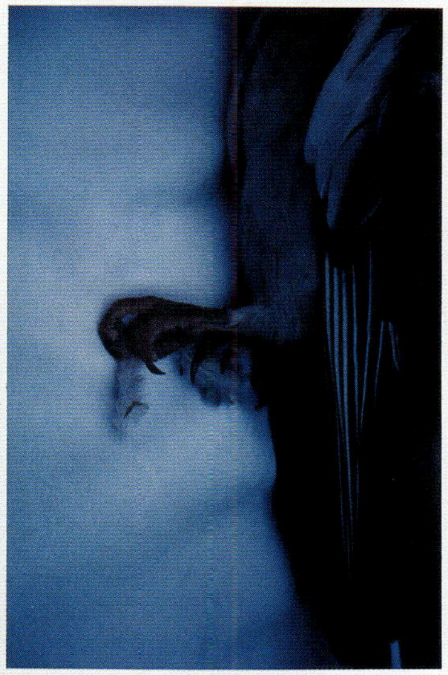

19

GUN URRAINN

ANON

c.1700

Neach-ealain/Artist:
Anthony Haughey

Clò-bhuailtear/Typographer:
Donald Addison

Eadar-theangaichte aig/Translator:
Derick S. Thomson

Roghainn/Nominator:
Derick S. Thomson

Clann Ghriogair air Fògradh

Is mi suidhe 'n seo am ònar
Air còmhnard an rathaid,

Dh'fheuch am faic mi fear-fuadain
Tighinn o Chruachan a' cheathaich

Bheir dhomh sgeul air Clann Ghriogair
No fios cia an do ghabh iad.

Cha d'fhuair mi dan sgeulaibh
Ach iad bhith 'n-dè air na Sraithibh;

Thall 's a-bhos mu Loch Fìne,
Masa fìor mo luchd-bratha;

Ann an Clachan an Dìseirt
Ag òl fìon air na maithibh.

Bha Griogair mòr ruadh ann,
Làmh chruaidh air chùl claidhimh;

Agus Griogair mòr meadhrach,
Ceann-feadhn' ar luchd-taighe.

Mhic an fhir à Srath h-Ardail,
Bhiodh na bàird ort a' tathaich;

'S a bheireadh greis air a' chlàrsaich
'S air an tàileasg gu h-aighear;

Is a sheinneadh an fhidheall,
Chuireadh fioghair fo mhnathaibh.

Pursuit of Clan Gregor

I sit here alone by the level roadway,
hoping to see, coming from Cruachan of the Mist, a fugitive
who will give me news of Clan Gregor, or of where they have gone.
I have had no news of them but that they were in Strath Fillan yesterday,
that they were here and there about Loch Fyne, if my informants spoke true,
and in Dalmally, drinking wine to the health of the gentles.
Great red-haired Gregor was there, whose hand was hard behind his sword,
and great mirthful Gregor, the chief of our household.
O son of the laird of Strathardle, the bards used to visit you,
and you would play the harp, and play backgammon willingly,
and you would make the fiddle sing, inciting women to dance.

(Continued on page 238)

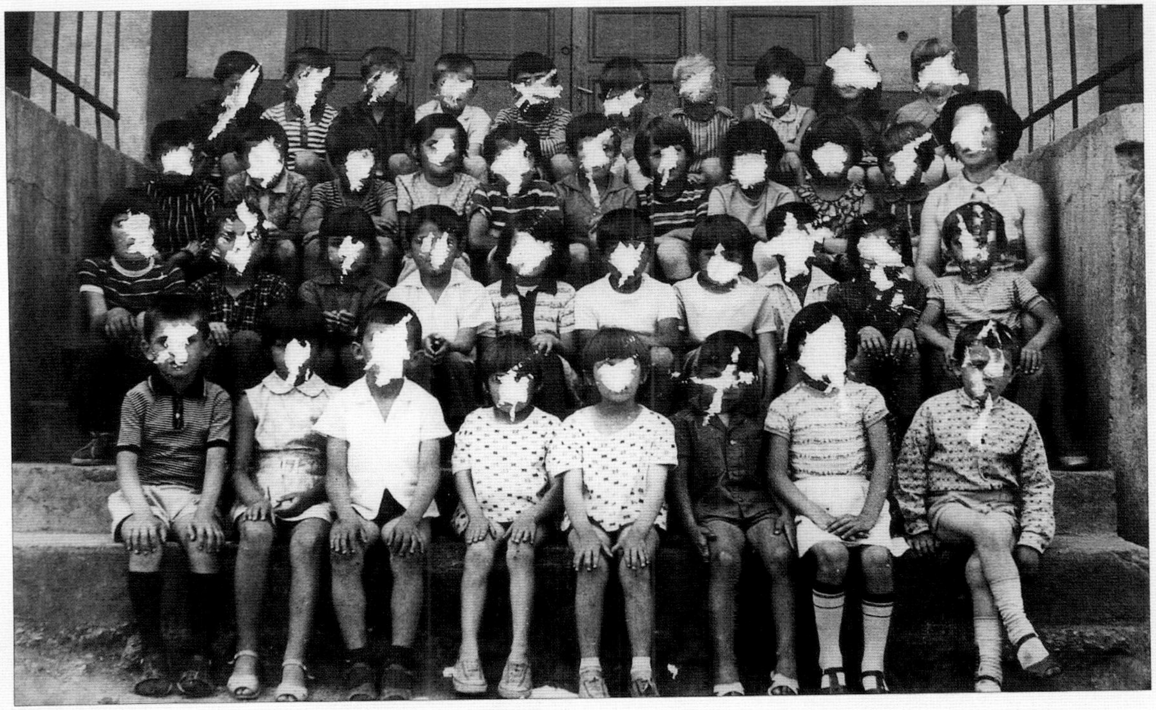

Class of '73

VASO PASHE PRIMARY SCHOOL, PEJE, KOSOVA

Clann Ghriogair air Fògradh

'S ann bha bhuidheann gun chòmhradh
Didòmhnaich 'm bràighe bhaile;

Is cha dèan mi gàir èibhinn
An àm èirigh no laighe.

'S beag an t-iongnadh dhomh f'in siud
'S mi bhith 'n dèidh mo luchd-taighe.

1 - *Identity & fate unknown*
2 Mehmet Gorani living in Kosova
3 - *Identity & fate unknown*
4 Dukagoin Lika living in Kosova
5 - *Identity & fate unknown*
6 - *Identity & fate unknown*
7 Ardita Rusta living in Norway
8 Ifakete Harbuzi living in Kosova
9 - *Identity & fate unknown*
10 - *Identity & fate unknown*
11 - *Identity & fate unknown*
12 - *Identity & fate unknown*
13 - *Identity & fate unknown*
14 Mithat Haxhibasani living in Kosova
15 Remzie Krasniqi living in Kosova
16 - *Identity & fate unknown*
17 - *Identity & fate unknown*
18 Agime Gjakova living in Kosova
19 - *Identity & fate unknown*
20 Basshkim Kastrati living in Kosova
21 Sajde Kelmendi, retired schoolteacher, living in Kosova
22 Nazlie Kelmendi living in Kosova
23 - *Identity & fate unknown*
24 Eshira Muhaghri living in Kosova
25 - *Identity & fate unknown*
26 Linje Avdimetaj living in Kosova
27 - *Identity & fate unknown*
28 - *Identity & fate unknown*
29 - *Identity & fate unknown*
30 Nasire Shabani living in Kosova
31 - *Identity & fate unknown*
32 Naxhie Bardhi living in Kosova
33 Bujar Kastrati living in Belgium
34 Suzana Neshiqi living in Germany
35 - *Identity & fate unknown*
36 - *Identity & fate unknown*
37 - *Identity & fate unknown*
38 Besin Turjaka living in Kosova
39 - *Identity & fate unknown*

20

AOGÁN Ó RATHAILLE

c. 1670–1729

Ealaíontóir/Artist:
Calum Colvin

Peannaire/Calligrapher:
Réiltín Murphy

Aistritheoir/Translator:
Thomas Kinsella

Ainmníodh ag/Nominator:
Michael Davitt

Is Fada Liom Oíche Fhírfhliuch

Is fada liom oíche fhírfhliuch gan suan, gan srann,
gan ceathra, gan maoin caoire ná buaibh na mbeann;
anfa ar toinn taoibh liom do bhuair mo cheann,
's nár chleachtas im naíon fiogaigh ná ruacain abhann.

Dá maireadh an rí díomhair ó bhruach na Leamhan
's an ghasra do bhí ag roinn leis lér thrua mo chall
i gceannas na gcríoch gcaoin gcluthar gcuanach gcam,
go dealbh í dtír Dhuibhneach níor bhuan mo chlann.

An Carathach groí fiochmhar lér fuadh an mheang
is Carathach Laoi i ndaoirse gan fuascladh fann;
Carathach, rí Chinn Toirc, in uaigh 's a chlann,
's is atuirse tríom chroí gan a dtuairisc ann.

Do shearg mo chroí im chlíteach, do bhuair mo leann,
na seabhaic nár fríth cinnte, agár dhual an eang
ó Chaiseal go Toinn Chlíona 's go Tuamhain thall,
a mbailte 's a dtír díthchreachta ag sluaghaibh Gall.

A thonnsa thíos is airde géim go hard,
meabhair mo chinnse cloíte ód bhéiceach tá;
cabhair dá dtíodh arís ar Éirinn bhán,
do ghlam nach binn do dhingfinn féin id bhráid.

The Drenching Night Drags On

The drenching night drags on: no sleep or snore,
no stock, no wealth of sheep, no horned cows.
This storm on the waves nearby has harrowed my head
– I who ate no winkles or dogfish in my youth!

If that guardian King from the bank of the Leamhan lived on,
with all who shared his fate (and would pity my plight)
to rule that soft, snug region, bayed and harboured,
my people would not stay poor in Duibhne country.

Great Carthy, fierce and fine, who loathed deceit;
with Carthy of the Laoi, in yoke unyielding, faint;
and Carthy King of Ceann Toirc with his children, buried;
it is bitterness through my heart they have left no trace.

My heart has dried in my ribs, my humours soured,
that those never-niggardly lords, whose holdings ranged
from Caiseal to Clíona's Wave and out to Thomond,
are savaged by alien hordes in land and townland.

You wave down there, lifting your loudest roar,
the wits in my head are worsted by your wails.
If help ever came to lovely Ireland again,
I'd wedge your ugly howling down your throat!

is fada liom oíche
fhírfhliuch
gan suan,
gan srann,
gan ceathra,
gan maoin caoire
ná buaibh
na mbeann

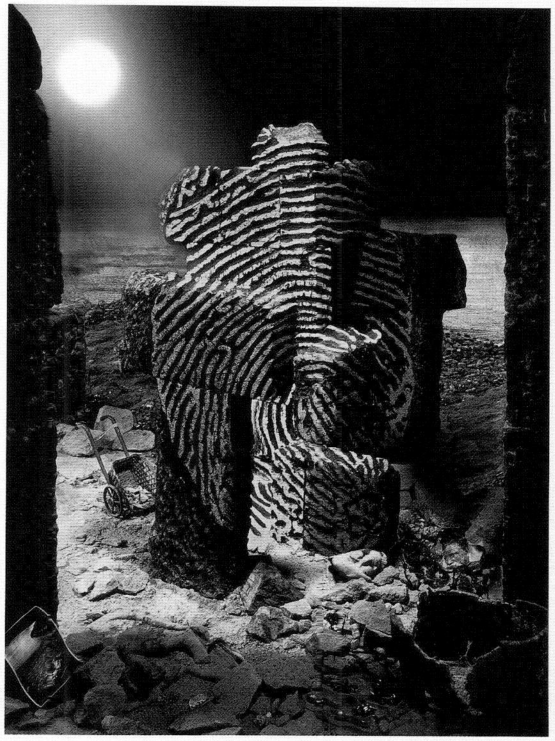

21

DÁIBHÍ Ó BRUADAIR

c. 1625-1698

Ealaíontóir/Artist:
Silvana McLean

Peannaire/Calligrapher:
Frances Breen

Aistritheoir/Translator:
Thomas Kinsella

Ainmníodh ag/Nominator:
Liam Ó Muirthile

Is Mairg nár Chrean le Maitheas Saoghalta

Is mairg nár chrean le maitheas saoghalta
do cheangal ar gad sul ndeacha in éagantacht,
's an ainnise im theach ó las an chéadluisne
nach meastar gur fhan an dadamh céille agam.

An tamall im ghlaic do mhair an ghléphingin,
ba geanamhail gart dar leat mo thréithe-se -
do labhrainn Laidean ghasta is Béarla glic
's do tharraingínn dais ba cleas ar chléireachaibh.

Do bheannachadh dhamh an bhean 's a céile cnis,
an bhanaltra mhaith 's a mac ar céadlongadh;
dá ngairminn baile is leath a ngréithe-sean,
ba deacair 'na measc go mbainfeadh éara dhom.

Do ghabhainn isteach 's amach gan éad i dtigh
is níor aistear uim aitreabh teacht aréir 's aniogh;
dob aitheasc a searc fá seach le chéile againn
'Achainghim, ceadaigh blaiseadh ár béile-ne'.

D'athraigh 'na ndearcaibh dath mo néimhe anois
ar aiste nach aithnidh ceart im chéimeannaibh;
ó shearg mo lacht le hais na caomhdhroinge,
d'aithle mo cheana is marcach mé dem chois.

Is annamh an tansa neach dom éileamhsa
is dá n-agrainn fear ba falamh a éiricsin;
ní fhaiceann mo thaise an chara chéibheann chlis
dar gheallamhain seal 'Is leat a bhféadaimse'.

Gé fada le sail mo sheasamh tréithchuisleach
ó mhaidin go feascar seasc gan bhéilfhliuchadh,
dá dtairginn banna sleamhain séalaithe
ar chnagaire leanna, a casc ní bhéarainn sin.

Woe to that Man who Leaves on his Vagaries

Woe to that man who leaves on his vagaries
without busying himself tying up some worldly goods.
There is misery in my house from the first dawn-light,
and no-one believes I've got one tatter of sense.

For as long as the shining penny was in my fist
my ways were charming and cheerful, you would think.
My speech was fluent Latin and cunning English!
I could describe a flourish to dazzle the scribes!

Wives and the mates of their flesh saluted me
and mothers and their boys before their breakfast.
If I were to ask for a village, with half its contents,
I'd find it hard to get a refusal among them.

I could enter and leave a house, and no complaint;
turn up at the same house night and day – it was nothing.
Jointly and several, the burthen of their love
was: 'Deign, I implore you, to take a taste of our meal!'

But I've taken a different colour now in their eyes,
so that they see no right in my procedures.
To judge by this gentry now, my milk has turned
and after my time of respect I must ride on foot.

It is seldom anyone seeks my services,
while if I press them on people the pay is poor.
I find no more that cunning and sweet companion
who promised me once: 'All I can do, it is yours.'

I could stand at the counter long and wearily
from morn till night – arid, with unwet lips –
and not if I offered a surety sealed and shining
for a naggin of beer, could I lure it out of the cask.

(Continued on page 239)

Is mairg nár chrean le maitheas saoghalta
do cheangal ar gad sul ndeacha in éagantacht,
's an ainnise im theach ó las an chéadluisne
nach meastar gur fhan an dadamh céille agam.

A Athair na bhfeart do cheap na céidnithe,
talamh is neamh is reanna is réithleanna,
earrach is teaspach, tartha is teachtuisce;
t'fheargain cas is freagair m'eagnachsa.

IS MAIRG NÁR CHREAN LE MAITHEAS SAOGHALTA
DO CHEANGAL AR GAD SUL NDEACHA IN ÉAGANTACHT
'S AN AINNISE IM THEACH Ó LAS AN CHÉADLUISNE
NACH MEASTAR GUR FHAN AN DADAMH CÉILLE AGAM.

D'ATHRAIGH NA NDEARGAIBH DATH MO NÉIMHE ANOIS
AR AISTE NACH AITHNIDH CEART IM CHÉIMEANNAIBH;
Ó SHEARG MO TACHT LE HAIS NA CAOMHDHROINGE
D'AITHLE MO CHEANA IS MARCACH MÉ DEM CHOIS.

A ATHAIR NA BHFEART DO CHEAP NA CÉIDNITHE
TALAMH IS NEAMH IS REANNA IS RÉITHLEANNA
EARRACH IS TEASPACH TARTHA IS TEACHTUISCE
T'FHEARGAIN CAS IS FREAGAIR M'EAGNACHSA.

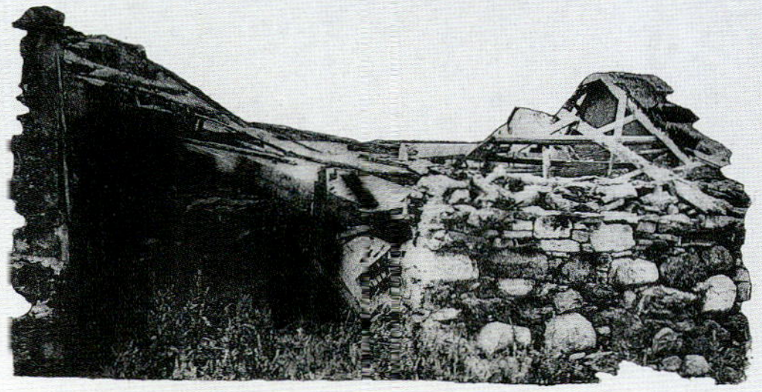

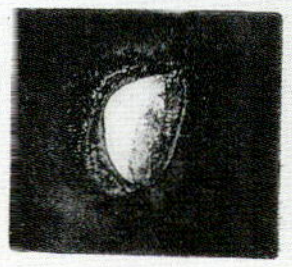

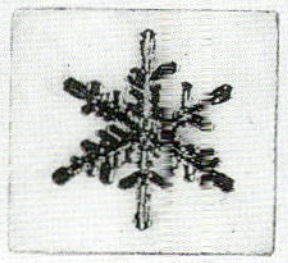

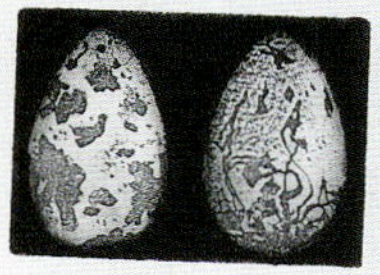

13/13

Silvana McLean 01

22

GAN AINM

ANON

c.1700

Ealaíontóir/Artist: David Quinn

Peannaire/Calligrapher: Frances Breen

Aistritheoir/Translator: Louis de Paor

Ainmníodh ag/Nominator: Louis de Paor

Dónall Óg

A Dhónaill Óig, má théir thar farraige,
Beir mé féin leat, as ná déan mo dhearmad;
As beidh agat féirín lá aonaigh is margaidh,
Is iníon rí Gréige mar chéile leapa agat.

Má théir-se anonn, tá comhartha agam ort:
Tá cúl fionn agus dhá shúil ghlasa agat,
Dhá chocán déag i do chúl buí bachallach,
Mar bheadh béal na bó nó rós i ngarraithe.

Is déanach aréir do labhair an gadhar ort,
Do labhair an naoscach sa churraichín doimhin ort,
Is tú id chaonaí aonair ar fud na gcoillte,
Is go rabhair gan chéile go héag go bhfaghair me!

Do gheallais domh-sa, agus d'innsis bréag dom,
Go mbeitheá romham-sa ag cró na gcaorach;
Do leigeas fead agus trí chéad ghlaoch chút,
Is ní bhfuaras ann ach uan ag méiligh.

Do gheallais domh-sa ní ba dheacair duit:
Loingeas óir fá chrann seoil airgid,
Dhá bhaile dhéag de bhailtibh margaidh,
Is cúirt bhreágh aolga cois taobh na farraige.

Do gheallais domh-sa ní nár bhféidir,
Go dtabharfá lámhainne de chroiceann éisc dom,
Go dtabharfá bróga de chroiceann éan dom,
Is culaith den tsíoda ba dhaoire in Éirinn.

A Dhónaill Óig, b'fhearr duit mise agat
Ná bean uasal uaibhreach iomarcach;
Do chrúfainn bó is do dhéanfainn cuigeann duit,
Is dá mba chruaidh é bhuailfinn buille leat.

Dónal Óg

Dónal Óg, if you cross the sea,
take me with you and don't forget,
I'll be your toy, brought home from market,
a Greek king's daughter beside you in bed.

I'd know you anywhere, if you cross the ocean,
your hair is blond, your eyes grey,
there are twelve curls in your branching yellow hair
like cowslip or a rose in a garden.

The dog gave you away late last night,
the snipe betrayed you far out in the wet bog
as you moved like a woodkern through the woods –
may you never have a woman till you find me again.

You promised me something you knew was a lie,
that you'd wait for me by the sheepfold;
I whistled, and called you three hundred times
and got no answer, only the bleat of a lamb.

You promised me something that was hard to give,
golden ships with silver masts,
twelve towns with a fair in each one
and a limewhite palace beside the sea.

You promised me something that was impossible,
gloves that were made from the skins of fish,
birdskin shoes and a suit
of the dearest silk in Ireland.

Dónal Óg, better you had me
than some proud wealthy gentlewoman;
I'd milk a cow and churn the cream for you
and I'd fight beside you when the blows were struck.

(Continued on page 239)

DO BHANAIS SOIR DHIOM
IS DO BHANAIS SIAR DHIOM

DO BHANAIS ROMHAM IS
DO BHANAIS IM DHIAIDH DHIOM

DO BHANAIS GEALACH IS
DO BHANAIS GRIAN DHIOM

'S IS RÓ-MHÓR M'EAGLA
GUR BHANAIS DIA DHIOM

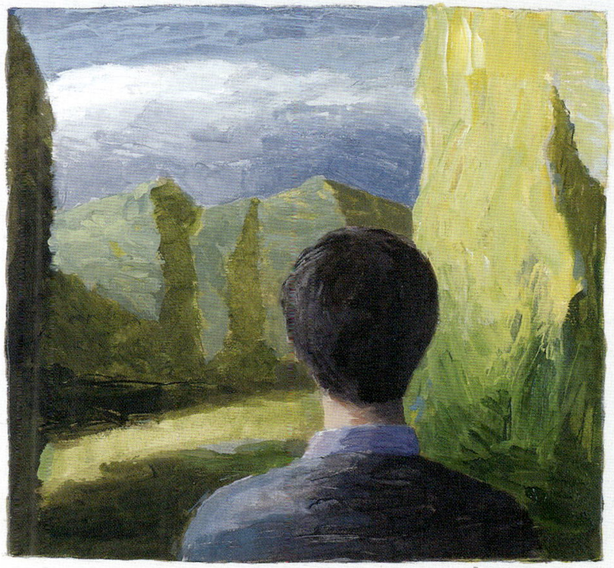

DAVID QUINN.

23

ALASDAIR MAC MHAIGHSTIR ALASDAIR

c. 1698-1770

Neach-ealain / Artist:
Anna MacLeod

Snas-sgrìobhadair / Calligrapher:
Frances Breen

Eadar-theangaichte aig / Translator:
Hugh MacDiarmid

Roghainn / Nominator:
Ronald Black

Birlinn Chlann Raghnaill (earrann)

Ghairm an fhairge sìoth-shaimh rinne
Air crois Chaol Ile;
Gun d'fhuair a' garbh-ghaoth shearbh-
ghlòireach
Ordugh sìnidh.

Thog i uainn do dh'ionadaibh
Uachdrach an adhair,
'S chinn i dhuinn na clàr rèidh mìn-gheal
An deidh a tabhainn.

Thug sinn buidheachas don Ard-Rìgh
Chùm na dùilean
Deagh Chlann Raghnaill a bhith sàbhailt'
O bhàs brùideil.

An sin bheum sinn na siùil thana,
Bhallach, thùilinn,
'S leag sinn a croinn mhìn-dearg, ghasd'
Air fad a h-ùrlair.

Chuir sinn a-mach ràimh chaol
bhaisgeant'
Dhathte, mhìne
Den ghiuthas a bhuain MacBharrais
An Eilein Fhìonain.

Rinn sinn an t-iomradh rèidh tulganach,
Gun dearmad,
'S ghabh sinn deagh longphort aig
barraibh
Charraig Fhearghais.

Thilg sinn acraichean gu socair
Anns an ròd sin;
Ghabh sinn biadh is deoch gun airceas
'S rinn sinn còmhnaidh.

The Birlinn of Clanranald (excerpt)

The sea proclaimed peace with us
At the fork of Islay Sound
And the hostile barking wind
Was ordered off the ground.

It went to the upper places of the air
And became a quiet
Glossy-white surface to us there
After all its riot,

And to God we made thanksgiving
That good Clanranald
Was spared the brutal death for which
The elements had wrangled.

Then we pulled down the speckled canvas
And lowered
The sleek red masts and along her bottom
Safely stored,

And put out the slender well-wrought oars
Coloured, and smooth to the hand,
Made of the pine cut by MacBharais
In Finnan's Island,

And set up the right-royal, rocking, rowing,
Deft and timeous,
And made good harbour there at the top
Of Carrickfergus.

We threw out anchors peacefully
In that roadstead.
We took food and drink unstinting
And there we stayed.

For an alternative source of the full text see page 265.

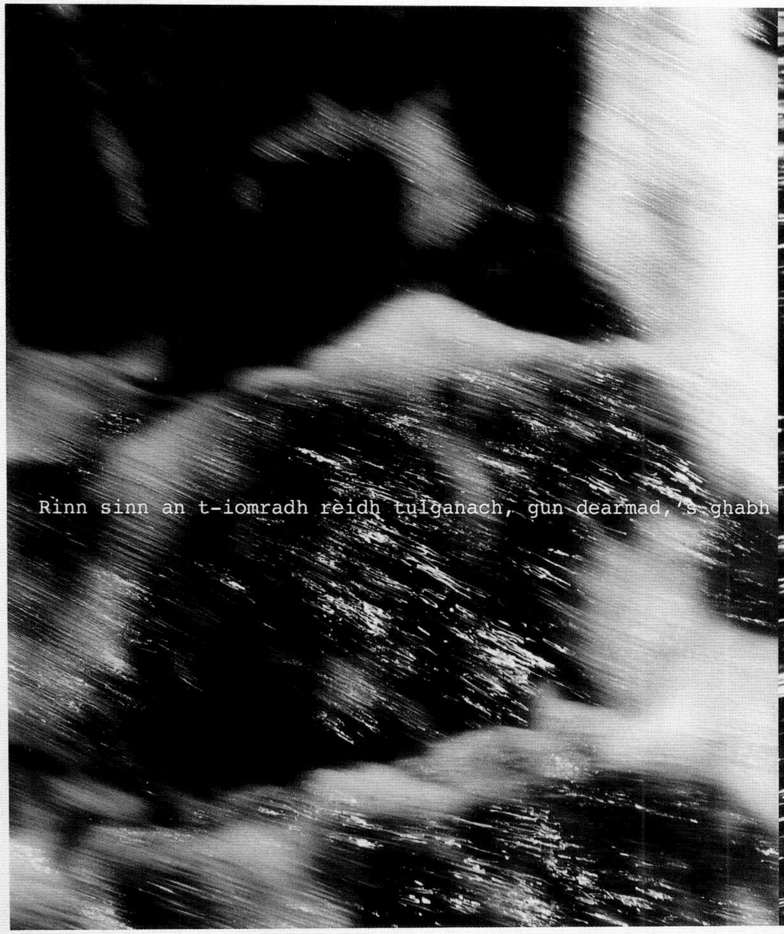
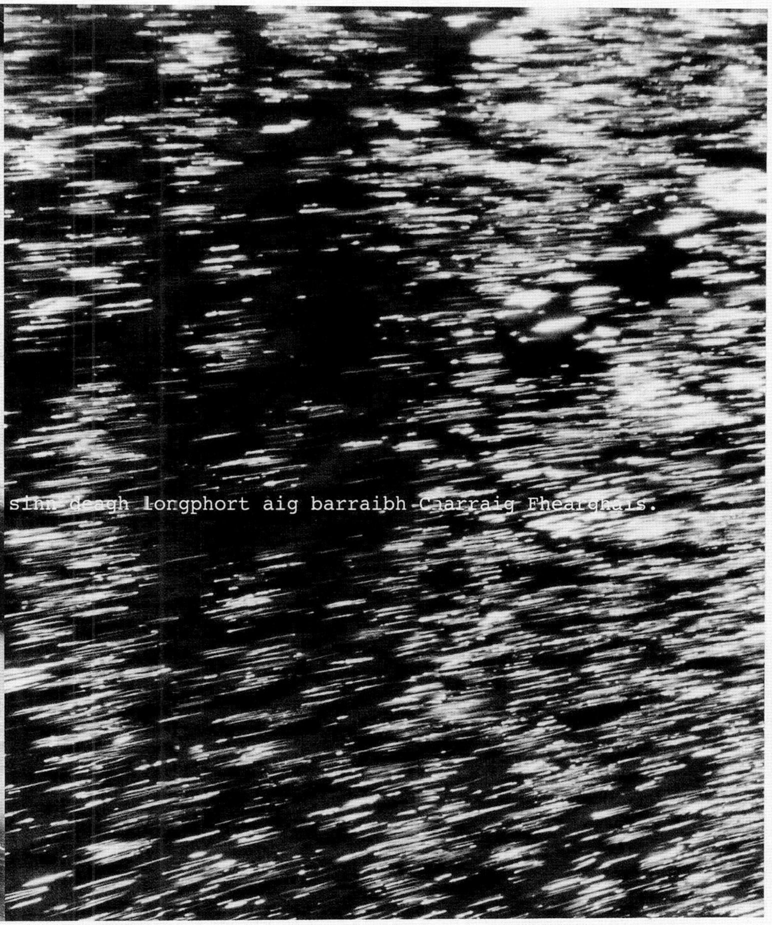

Rinn sinn an t-iomradh reidh tulganach, gun dearmad, 's ghabh sinn deagh longphort aig barraibh Carraig Fhearghais.

24

SÉAMAS DALL MAC CUARTA

c. 1650–1733

Ealaíontóir/Artist:
Craig Mackay

Peannaire/Calligrapher:
Réiltín Murphy

Aistritheoir/Translator:
Thomas Kinsella

Ainmníodh ag/Nominator:
Gréagóir Ó Dúill

An Lon Dubh Báite

A iníon álainn Choinn Uí Néill,
is fada do shuan tar éis d'áir;
is nach gcluin uaisle do chine féin
tú ag caoineadh do spré tar éis a bháis.

Ceiliúr an éin lúfair luaith
theastaigh uait, a fhaoileann bhán;
cha bhíonn tubaiste ach mar mbíonn spré,
is déansa foighid ó ghreadadh lámh.

Ó ghreadadh lámh is ó shileadh rosc,
glacsa tost, a fhaoileann úr;
a iníon álainn Choinn Uí Néill,
fá bhás an éin ná fliuch do shúil.

A fhaoileann a d'fhás ó ardrí Uladh na rí,
fuirigh mar tá, is fearr é nó imeacht le baois;
fá d'éan beag a b'áille gáire ar imeall na gcraobh,
chan ceist duit a bhás go brách is é nite le haol.

The Drowned Blackbird

Lovely daughter of Conn Ó Néill,
sleep long after your great loss.
Don't let your noble kinsmen hear you
weeping after your treasure's death.

The song of that swift, nimble bird
is gone for good, my beauty pale.
But where's the treasure brings no trouble?
Hold a while, don't beat your hands.

Not beaten hands and streaming eyes
but silence, my noble beauty.
Lovely daughter of Conn Ó Néill,
the bird is dead, don't wet your eyes.

O beauty, grown from kings of royal Ulster,
be steady now; it is better than raving wild.
Your small bird laughing loveliest on the bough-tips,
fret no more for his death: he is washed in lime.

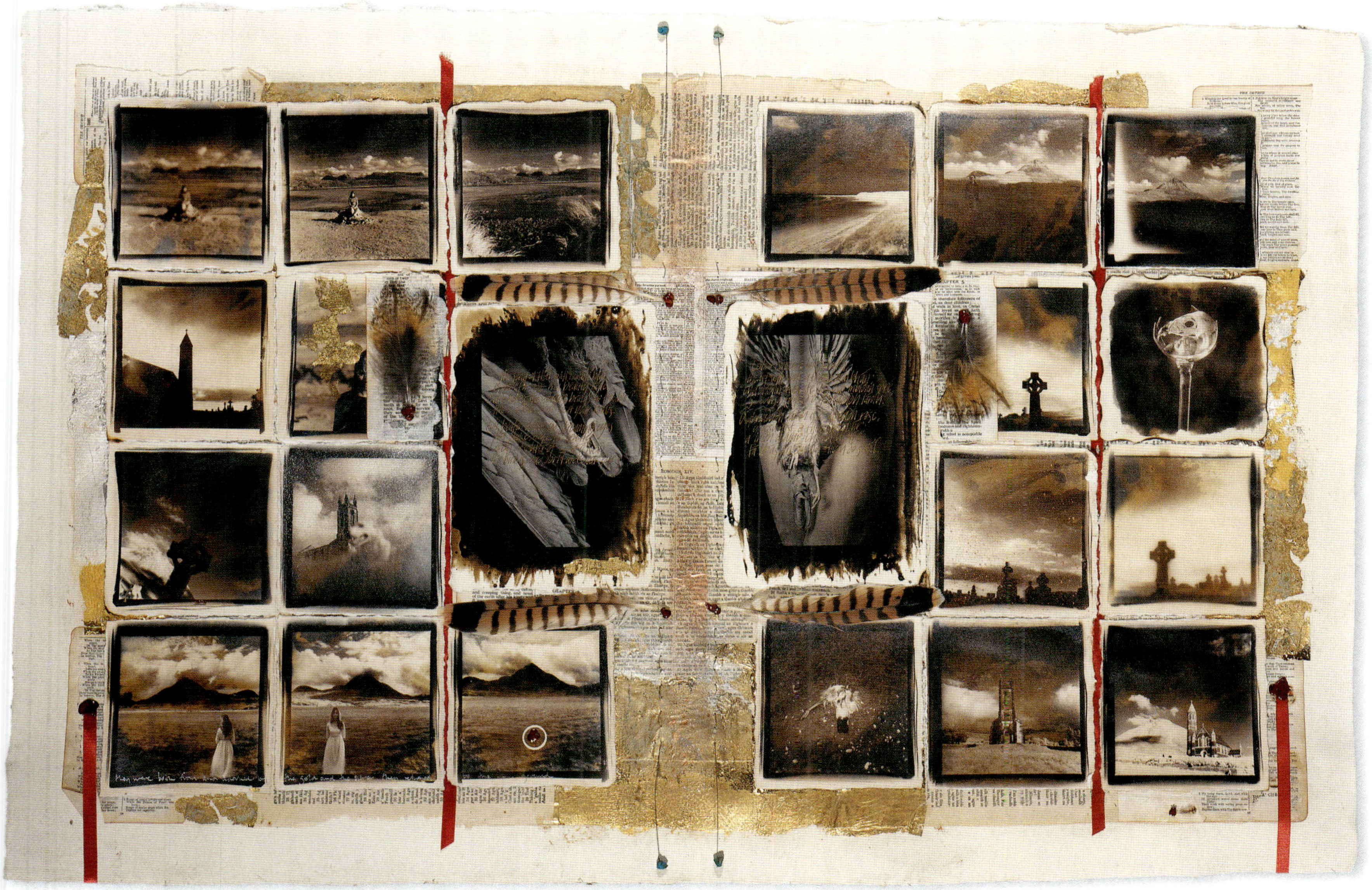

25

SÌLEAS NA CEAPAICH

c. 1660-1729

Neach-ealain / Artist:
Rita Duffy

Snas-sgrìobhadair / Calligrapher:
Donald Murray

Eadar-theangaichte aig / Translator:
Colm Ó Baoill

Roghainn / Nominator:
Morag Montgomery

Alasdair à Gleanna Garadh

Alasdair à Gleanna Garadh,
Thug thu 'n-diugh gal air mo shùilibh;
'S beag ioghnadh mi bhith fo
chreuchdaibh,
'S gur tric gan reubadh às ùr iad;
'S beag ioghnadh mi bhith trom-osnach,
'S meud an dosgaidh th' air mo chàirdibh;
Gur tric an t-eug uainn a' gearradh
Rogha nan darag as àirde.

Chaill sinn ionann agus còmhla
Sir Dòmhnall 's a mhac 's a bhràthair;
Ciod e 'n stà dhuinn bhith gan gearan?
Thuit Mac Mhic Ailein sa bhlàr uainn;
Chaill sinn darag làidir liath-ghlas
A chumadh dìon air ar càirdean,
Capall-coille bhàrr na giùthsaich,
Seabhag sùil-ghorm lùthmhor làidir.

Bu tu ceann air cèill 's air comhairl'
Anns gach gnothach am biodh cùram,
Aghaidh shoilleir sholta thlachdmhor,
Cridhe fial farsaing mun chùinneadh;
Bu tu roghainn nan sàr-ghaisgeach,
Ar guala thaice, 's tu b' fhiùghail;
Leòmhann smiorail fearail feumail,
Ceann-feachda chaill Seumas Stiùbhart.

Alasdair of Glengarry

Alasdair of Glengarry, you have caused me to shed tears today. Small wonder that I am covered with wounds and that they are repeatedly being burst open; small wonder that I am filled with deep sighing, considering all the misfortune that has befallen my friends. Death is constantly cutting off from us the best of the tallest oaks.

We lost, almost at the same time, Sir Donald, his son and his brother. What use is it for us to complain over them? - Clanranald fell from us on the battle-field. We have lost a strong grey oak-tree which sheltered our friends, a wood-grouse from the pine-wood, a blue-eyed hawk, vigorous and strong.

You were the leader in wisdom and counsel in every activity where responsibility was concerned; bright, pleasant and handsome face, heart generous and liberal with money. You were the choice of excellent warriors, a shoulder to support us, as you were worthy to be; a courageous, manly and effective lion, a leader whom James Stuart has lost.

(Continued on page 240)

Bu tu'n iubhar thar gach coillidh
Bu tu'n darach daingeann làidir
Bu tu'n cuileann 's bu tu'n draigheann
Bu tu'n t-abhall molach blàthmhor
Cha robh do dhàimh ris a' chritheann
Na do dhligheadh ris an fheàrna
Cha robh bheag ionnad den leamhan
Bu tu leannan nam ban àlainn

Guidheam t'anam a bhith sàbhailt'
On a chàireadh anns an ùir thu
Guidheam sonas air na dh'fhàg thu
Ann ad àros 's ann ad dhùthaich
Gum faic mi do mhac ad àite
Ann an saidhbhreas 's ann an cùram
Alasdair à Gleanna Garadh
Thug thu 'n-diugh gal air mo shùilibh

Donald Murray

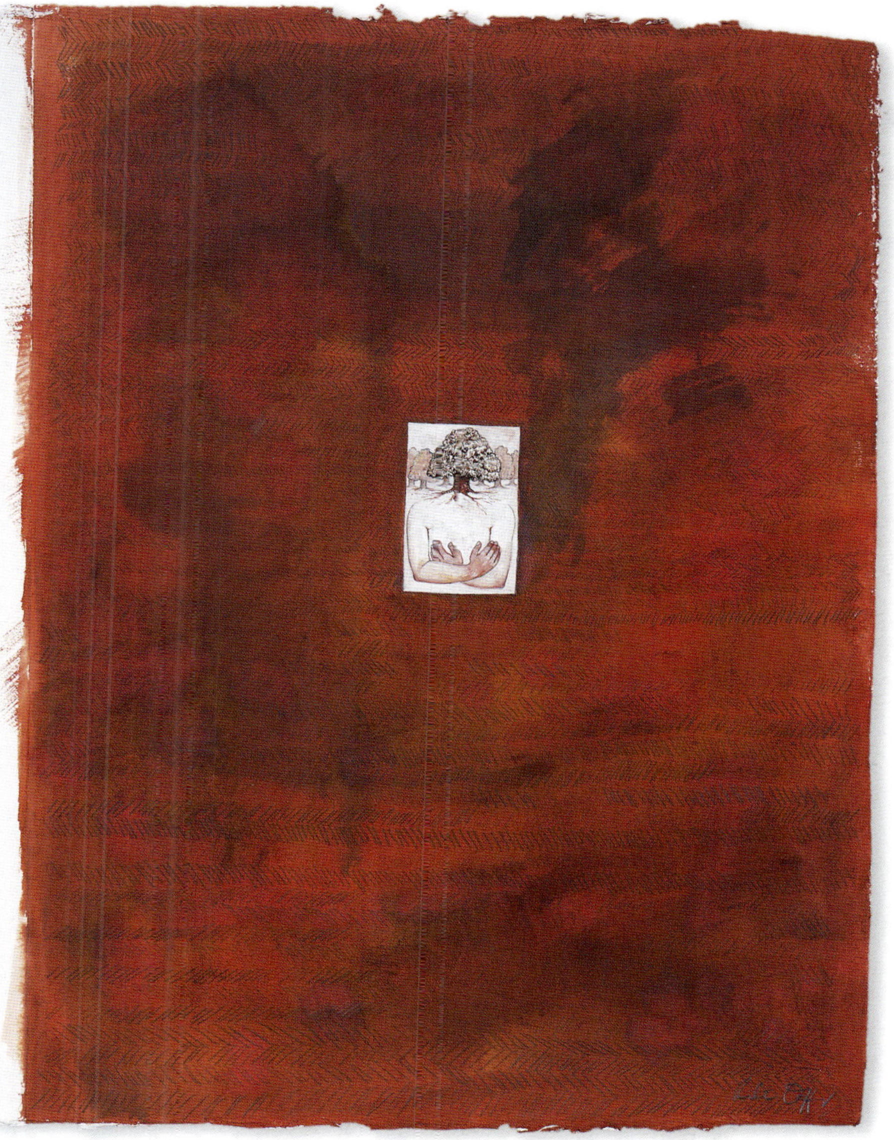

26

CAIRISTÌONA NICFHEARGHAIS

CHRISTIANA FERGUSSON

c. 1750

Neach-ealain / Artist:
Oona Hyland

Snas-sgrìobhadair / Calligrapher:
Donald Murray

Eadar-theangaichte aig / Translator:
Derick S. Thomson

Roghainn / Nominator:
Morag Montgomery

Mo Rùn Geal Òg

Och, a Theàrlaich òig Stiùbhairt,
'S e do chùis rinn mo lèireadh:
Thug thu bhuam gach nì bh' agam
Ann an cogadh nad adhbhar;
Cha chrodh is cha chaoraich
Tha mi caoidh ach mo chèile,
Ged a dh'fhàgte mi 'm aonar
Gun sìon san t-saoghal ach lèine:
  Mo rùn geal òg.

Cò nis thogas an claidheamh
No nì 'chathair a lìonadh?
'S gann gur h-e tha air m' aire,
O nach maireann mo chiad ghràdh.
Ach ciamar gheibhinn om nàdar
A bhith 'g àicheadh na 's miann leam,
Is mo thogradh cho làidir
Thoirt gu 'àite, mo rìgh math?
  Mo rùn geal òg.

Bu tu 'm fear mòr bu mhath cumadh
Od mhullach gud bhrògan;
Bha do shlios mar an eala
'S blas na meal' air do phògan;
T' fhalt dualach, donn, lurach
Mu do mhuineal an òrdugh,
'S e gu camalubach, cuimir,
'S gach aon toirt urram da bhòidhchead:
  Mo rùn geal òg.

My Fair Young Love

O young Charles Stuart,
it's your cause that has grieved me,
you took everything from me
in this war in your interest;
it's not sheep, it's not cattle
that I miss, but my first-love,
though I were left all alone
with not a thing but a shift,
my fair young love.

Who now will lift up the sword
or cause the throne to be filled?
All that hardly concerns me
since my first-love's not living.
Yet how can my nature
disavow what I long for,
since my own strong desire
is the king's restoration,
my fair young love?

You were big, you were shapely
from your head to your feet,
your side like the swan
and like honey your kisses,
curly brown bonny hair
draped over your shoulders,
intertwining so neatly,
and all praised its beauty,
my fair young love.

(Continued on page 241)

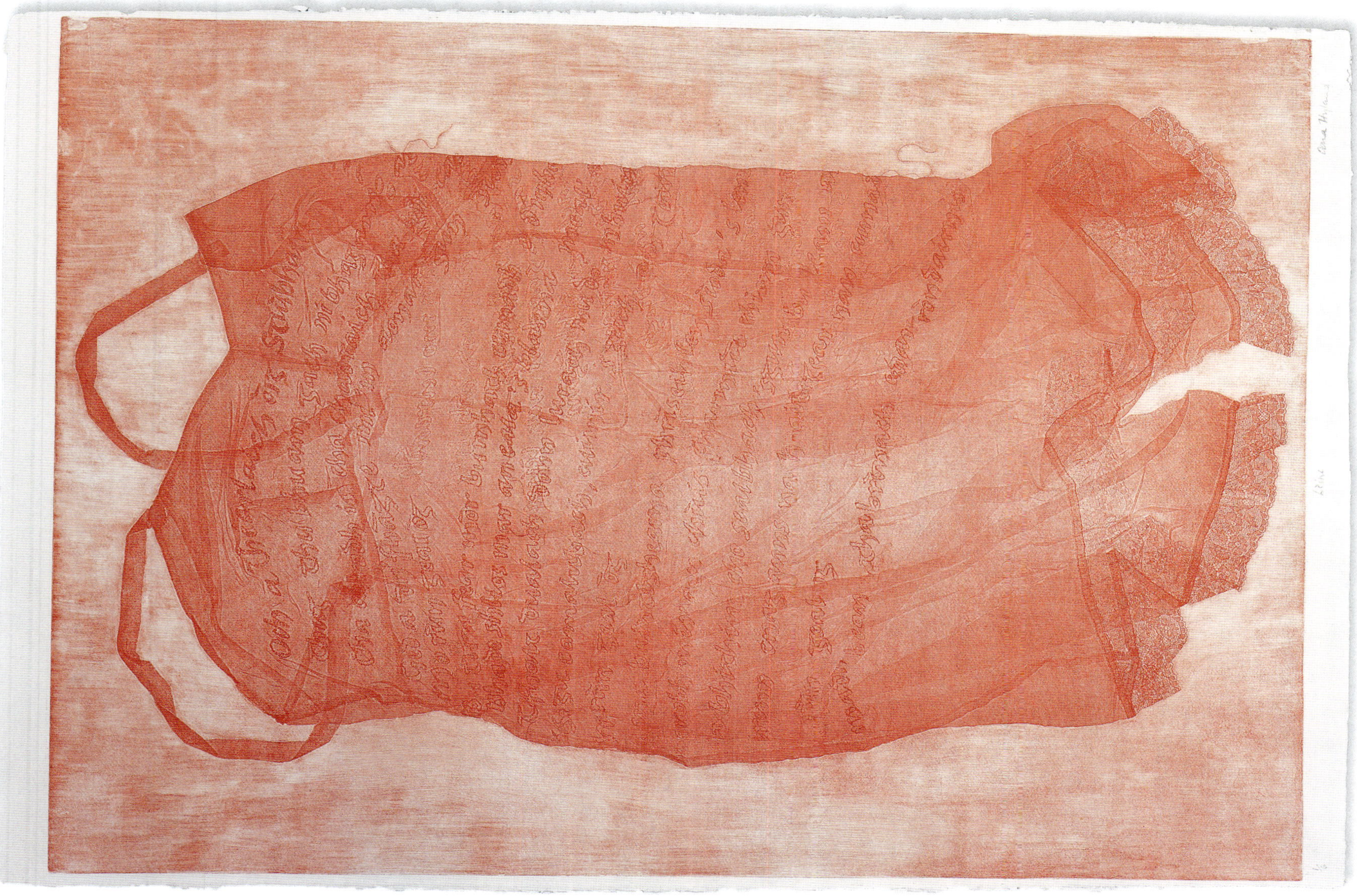

27

RUAIRIDH MACMHUIRICH (AN CLÀRSAIR DALL)

RODERICK MORISON

c. 1656–1713/14

Neach-ealain/Artist:
George A. Macpherson

Snas-sgrìobhadair/Calligrapher:
Ann Bowen

Eadar-theangaichte aig/Translator:
Meg Bateman

Roghainn/Nominator:
The Editorial Panel

Oran do MhacLeòid Dhùn Bheagain (earrann)

'An àm èirigh gu moch
Ann an teaghlach gun sprochd, gun ghruaim,
Chluinnte gleadhraich nan dos,
   Is an cèil' air a cois on t-suain;
An tràth ghabhadh i làn,
   'S i chuireadh os àird na fhuair
Le meòir chionalta ghnìomhach
   Dhrithleannach dhìonach luath.

'Bhiodh an rianadair fèin
   Cur a dh'fhiachaibh gur h-e bhiodh ann,
E 'g èirigh nam measg,
   'S an èighe gu tric na cheann;
Cha bu truagh leinn an glaodh
   Nuair a thuairgneadh se i gu teann,
Cur a thagradh an cruas
   Le h-aideachadh luath is mall.

'An tràth chuirte na tàmh i
   Le furtachd na fàrdaich fèin,
Dhomhsa b' fhurast' a ràdh
   Gum bu chuireideach gàir nan teud,
Le h-iomairt dhà làmh
   Cur am binneis do chàch an cèill –
Rìgh, bu shiùbhlach rim chluais
   An lùthadh le luasgan mheur.

'Anns an fheasgar na dhèidh,
   An àm teasdadh don ghrèin tràth-nòn',
Fir a' cnapraich mun chlàr
   Is cath air a ghnàth chur leò;

A Song to MacLeod of Dunvegan (excerpt)

'When it was time to rise
   there was heard in that house without gloom
the skirl of the drones
   with their spouse afoot after sleep;
when she had taken her fill,
   she gave out all she had got,
with agile fingers, kind,
   sparkling, nimble and fleet.

'The player himself
   asserting that he was there,
rising in their midst,
   their calls resounding in his head;
we pitied not their cries
   when he tightly squeezed the bag,
setting out his theme
   with a response quick then slow.

'When she was laid to rest,
   relieved in her own place,
I could say with ease
   how frisky the cry of the strings,
under the play of two hands
   drawing out their sweetness for all:
God, rippling in my ears
   their variation by fingers swift.

'In the evening after that
   when the afternoon sun would expire,
men shaking dice at the board,
   waging battle as was their wont;

We have only been able to give an excerpt from this poem. *For an alternative source of the full text see the listing on page 265.*

ÒRAN DO MHACLEÒID DHÙN BHEAGAIN

'AN ÀM ÈIRIGH GU MOCH:
ANN AN TÈAGHLACH GUN SPROCHD GUN GHRUAIM:
CHLUINNTE GLEADHRAICH NAN DOS:
IS AN CÈIL' AIR A COIS ON T-SUAIN:
AN TRÀTH GHABHADH I LÀN:
IS I CHUIREADH OS ÀIRD NA FHUAIR
LE MEÒIR CHIONALTA GHNÌOMHACH
DHRITHLEANNACH DHIONACH LUATH.

"BHIODH AN RIANADAIR FÈIN
CUR A DH'FHIACHAIBH GUR H-E BHIODH ANN:
E'G ÈIRIGH NAM MEASG:
'S AN EIGHE GU TRIC NA CHEANN:
CHA BU TRUAGH LEINN AN GLAODH
NUAIR A THUAIRGNEADH SE I GU TEANN
CUR A THAGRADH AN CRIAS
LE H-AIDEACHADH LUATH IS MALL".

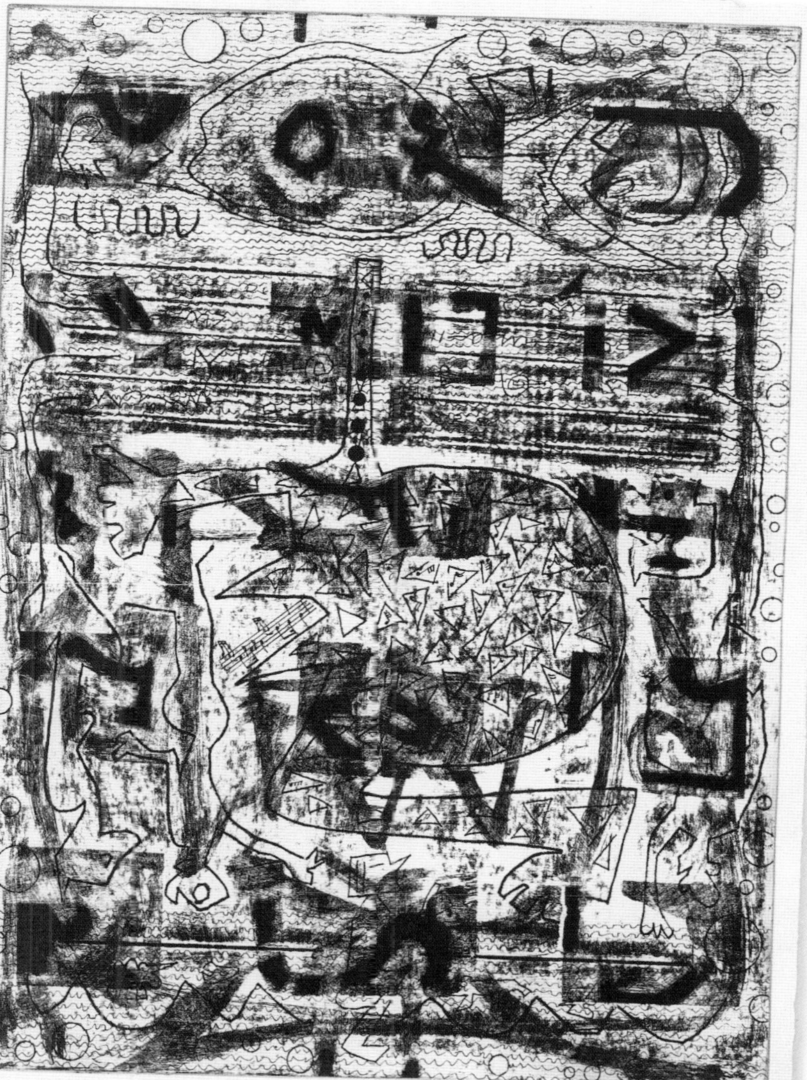

28

MÀIRI NIGHEAN ALASDAIR RUAIDH

MARY MACLEOD

c. 1615-1707

Neach-ealain/Artist:
Elizabeth Ogilvie

Clò-bhuailtear/Typographer:
Donald Addison

Eadar-theangaichte aig/Translator:
James Carmichael Watson

Roghainn/Nominator:
Aonghas Dubh MacNeacail

Crònan an Taibh (earrann)

Ri fuaim an taibh
Is uaigneach mo ghean;
Bha mis' uair nach b' e siud m'àbhaist.

Ach pìob nuallanach mhòr
Bheireadh buaidh air gach ceòl,
An uair a ghluaist' i le meòir Phàdraig ...

Thoir an t-soraidh seo bhuam
Gu talla nan cuach,
Far 'm biodh tathaich nan truagh
dàimheil ...

Chun an taighe nach gann
Fon an leathad ud thall,
Far bheil aighear is ceann mo mhànrain.

Sir Tormod mo rùin,
Olgharach thu,
Foirmeil o thùs t' àbhaist.

A thasgaidh's a chiall,
'S e bu chleachdamh dut riamh
Teach farsaing 's e fial fàilteach.

Bhiodh teanal nan cliar
Rè tamaill is cian,
Dh'fhios a' bhaile 'm biodh triall
chàirdean.

Nàile, chunnaic mi uair
'S glan an lasadh bha 'd ghruaidh
Fo ghruaig chleachdaich nan dual àr-
bhuidh'.

The Ocean-Croon (excerpt)

At the ocean's sound my mood is forlorn – time was that
such was not my wont to hear,

But the great shrill-voiced pipe, all music surpassing
when Patrick's fingers stirred it ...

Bear this greeting from me to the hall of wine-cups,
haunt of kinsmen in distress ...

To the dwelling that is not scanty, over yonder beneath
the slope, where is the joy and the theme of my melody.

Sir Norman of my love, one of Olgar's race art thou,
stately from of old thy custom.

Thou treasure beloved, this was ever thy wont: a wide
house liberal and welcoming.

For many a day poet-bands would gather towards the
homestead whereunto friends would fare.

Lo, I have seen the day when bright shone thy cheek,
under the gold-yellow ringlets of thy head;

We have only been able to give an excerpt from this poem.
For an alternative source of the full text see the listing on page 265.

RI FUAIM AN TAIBH

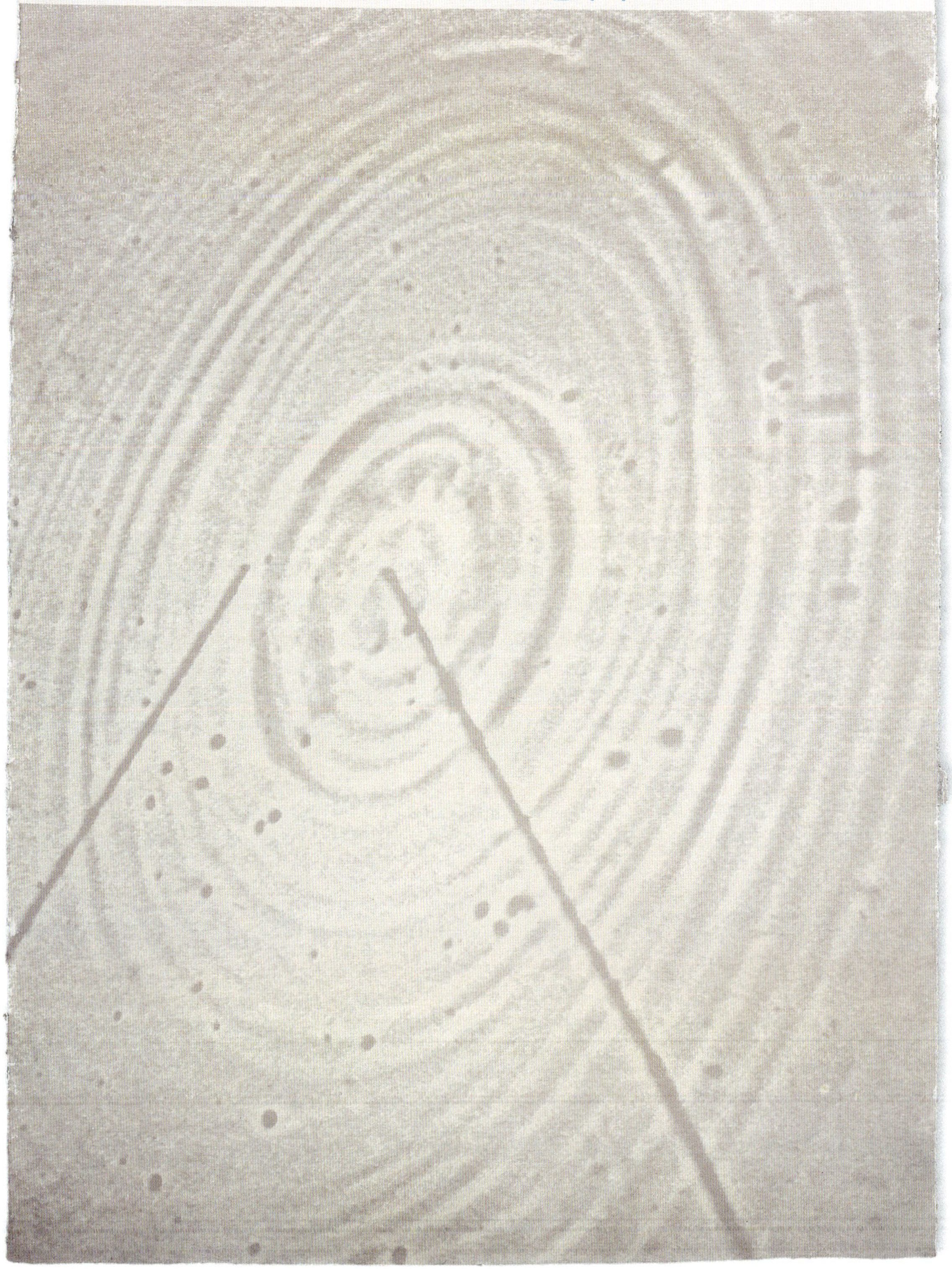

29

DONNCHADH BÀN MAC AN T-SAOIR

DUNCAN BAN MACINTYRE

1724-1812

Neach-ealain/Artist:
Calum Angus Mackay

Snas-sgrìobhadair/Calligrapher:
Susan Leiper

Eadar-theangaichte aig/Translator:
Angus MacLeod

Roghainn/Nominator:
William Neill

Cead Deireannach nam Beann

Bha mi 'n-dè 'm Beinn Dòbhrain,
'S na còir cha robh mi aineolach;
Chunna mi na gleanntan
'S na beanntaichean a b' aithne dhomh;
B 'e sin an sealladh èibhinn,
Bhith 'g imeachd air na slèibhtean
Nuair bhiodh a' ghrian ag èirigh
'S a bhiodh na fèidh a' langanaich.

'S aobhach a' ghreigh uallach
Nuair ghluaiseadh iad gu faramach;
'S na h-èildean air an fhuaran,
Bu chuannar na laoigh bhallach ann;
Na maoislichean 's na ruadh-bhuic,
Na coilich dhubha 's ruadha -
'S e 'n ceòl bu bhinne chualas
Nuair chluinnt' am fuaim sa chamhanaich.

'S togarrach a dh'fhalbhainn
Gu sealgaireachd nam bealaichean,
Dol mach a dhìreadh garbhlaich,
'S gum b' anmoch tighinn gu baile mi;
An t-uisge glan 's am fàile
Th' air mullach nam beann àrda,
Chuidich e gu fàs mi,
'S e rinn domh slàint' is fallaineachd.

Final Farewell to the Bens

I was on Ben Dobhrain yesterday,
no stranger in her bounds was I;
I looked upon the glens
and the bens that I had known so well;
this was a happy picture –
to be tramping on the hillsides
at the hour the sun was rising
and the deer would be a-bellowing.

The gallant herd is joyous,
as they moved off with noisy stir;
the hinds are by the spring,
and the speckled calves looked bonny there;
then the does and roe-bucks,
the black-cocks and the grouse cocks –
the sweetest music ever heard
was their sound when heard at dawn of day.

Blithely would I set out
for stalking on the hill passes,
away to climb rough country,
and late would I be coming home;
the clean rain and the air
on the peaks of the high mountains
helped me to grow, and gave me
robustness and vitality.

(Continued on p. 241)

Bha mi 'n-dè san aonach
'S bha smaointean mòr air m' aire-sa:
Nach robh 'n luchd-gaoil a b' àbhaist
Bhith siubhal fàsaich mar rium ann;
'S a' bheinn as beag a shaoil mi
Gun dèanadh i-se caochladh,
On tha i nis fo chaoraibh,
'S ann thug an saoghal car asam.

Nuair sheall mi air gach taobh dhiom,
Chan fhaodainn gun bhith smalanach,
On theirig coill is fraoch ann,
'S na daoine bh' ann, cha mhaireann iad;
Chan eil fiadh ra shealg ann,
Chan eil eun no earb ann,
An beagan nach eil marbh dhiubh,
'S e rinn iad falbh gu baileach às.

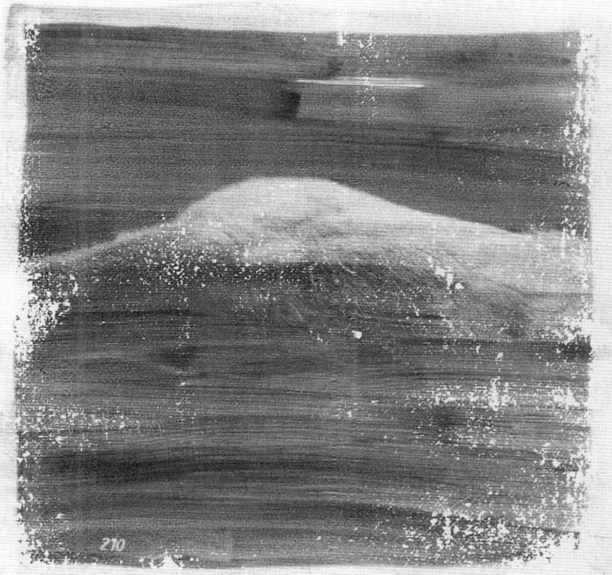

Mo shoraidh leis na frìthean,
O 's mìorbhaileach na beanntan iad,
Le biolair uaine 's fìor-uisg',
Deoch uasal rìomhach cheanalta,
Na blàran a tha prìseil
'S na fàsaichean tha lìonmhor.
O 's àit a leig mi dhìom iad,
Gu bràth mo mhìle beannachd leò.

Cead
deireannach
nam
beann

30

GAN AINM

ANON

c.1800

Ealaíontóir/Artist:
Joyce W. Cairns

Peannaire/Calligrapher:
Donald Murray

Aistritheoir/Translator:
Eamonn Ó Bróithe

Ainmníodh ag/Nominator:
Gearóid Mac Lochlainn

An Draighneán Donn

Fuaireas féirín lá aonaigh ó bhuachaill deas
Agus céad póg an lá ina dhiaidh sin ó leon na bhfear,
Scalladh cléibh ar an té a déarfadh nach tú mo shearc,
A bhuachaill ghléigil is breáth' in Éirinn is go n-éalóinnse leat.

Agus síleann céad fear gur leo féin mé nuair a ólaim leann;
Ní airím iad nuair a smaoiním ar a gcomhrá liom.
A choim is míne ná an síoda atá air Shliabh na mBan Fionn,
Is tá mo ghrása, ó, mar bhláth na n-airní ar an draighneán donn.

Is más ag imeacht taoi, beir mo bheannacht leat is go dté tú slán,
Mar nár imís nó gur bhrisis an croí seo i mo lár.
Níl coite agam go leanainn tú, long nó bád,
Is go bhfuil an fharraige ina tonnta eadrainn is ní heol dom snámh.

Agus a Dhé dhíl, cad a dhéanfad má imíonn tú uaim?
Cé a bhéarfaidh eolas chun do thí dhom má thagaim ar cuairt?
Sneachta síolmhar a bheith dá shíorchur agus mise faoi ghruaim,
Mná na hÉireann ag déanamh géim díom is mo ghrá i bhfad uaim.

Ó is mairg a théann ag allagar le crann mór ard
Nuair a d'fhág sé crann íseal a shroichfeadh a lámh,
Mar dá mb'airde é an crann caorthainn bíonn sé searbh ina lár,
Agus fásann úlla agus géaga cumhra ar an chrann is ísle bláth.

The Blackthorn Bush

I received a present from a fine lad on a market day
And the next day a hundred kisses from a lion among men.
A heart-scald on all who deny that you are my love,
My bright boy, Ireland's best, I would run away with you.

And when I drink ale a hundred men think I am theirs alone;
But I don't heed them when I recall how they spoke to me.
Your skin is finer than the silk on Sliabh na mBan Fionn,
And my love is like the sloe-blossom on the bare blackthorn.

If leave you must, take my blessing and may you always thrive,
Though you did not go before breaking the heart in my breast.
I have no skiff to follow you, neither ship nor boat,
The waves of the sea are between us and I cannot swim.

O loving God, what will I do if you abandon me?
Who will lead me to your house if I come to see you?
The driven snow falls ever more heavily and I am sick at heart,
The women of Ireland mock me and my love is far away.

Why contend foolishly with the great high tree
And neglect that which is within your reach.
However tall the rowan may be, its fruit is bitter,
But apples and fragrant blossoms grow on the lowly bough.

(Continued on page 242)

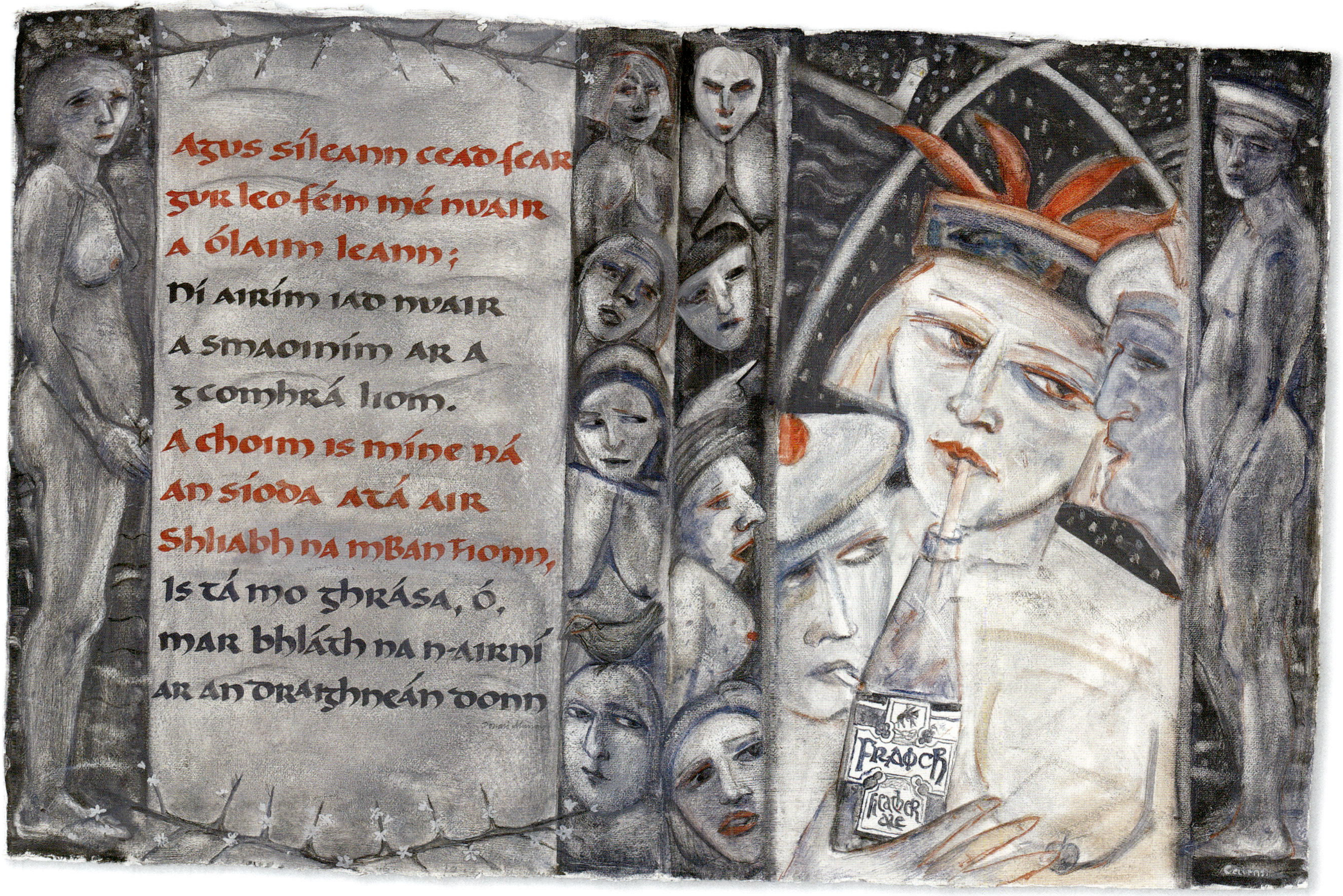
Agus síleann cead fear
gur leo féin mé nuair
a ólaim leann;
Ní airím iad nuair
a smaoiním ar a
gcomhrá liom.
A choim is míne ná
an síoda atá air
Shliabh na mBan Fionn,
Is tá mo ghrása, ó,
mar bhláth na h-airní
ar an draighneán donn
FRAOCH
Heather Ale

31

CATHAL BUÍ MAC GIOLLA GHUNNA

c.1680-1756

Ealaíontóir/Artist:
Eileen Ferguson

Peannaire/Calligrapher:
David McGrail

Aistritheoir/Translator:
Thomas MacDonagh

Ainmníodh ag/Nominator:
Nuala Ní Dhomhnaill

An Bonnán Buí

A bhonnáin bhuí, is é mo chrá do luí
   is do chnámha críon tar éis a gcreim,
is chan díobháil bídh ach easpa dí
   d'fhág tú 'do luí ar chúl do chinn;
is measa liom féin ná scrios na Traí
   thú bheith sínte ar leacaibh lom,
is nach ndearna tú díth ná dolaidh is tír
   is nárbh fhearr leat fíon ná uisce poill.

Is a bhonnáin álainn, mo mhíle crá
   do chúl ar lár amuigh insa tslí,
is gur moch gach lá a chluininn do ghráig
   ar an láib agus tú ag ól na dí;
is é an ní adeir cách le do dheartháir Cathal
   go bhfaighidh mé bás mar súd, más fíor;
ní hamhlaidh atá – súd an préachán breá
   chuaigh a dh'éag ar ball, gan aon bhraon dí.

A bhonnáin óig, is é mo mhíle brón
   thú bheith romham i measc na dtom,
is na lucha móra ag triall chun do thórraimh
   ag déanamh spóirt is pléisiúir ann;
dá gcuirfeá scéala in am fá mo dhéinse
   go raibh tú i ngéibheann nó i mbroid fá dheoch,
do bhrisfinn béim ar an loch sin Vesey
   a fhliuchfadh do bhéal is do chorp isteach.

Ní hé bhur n-éanlaith atá mise ag éagnach,
   an lon, an smaolach, ná an chorr ghlas -
ach mo bhonnán buí a bhí lán den chroí,
   is gur cosúil liom féin é ina ghné is a dhath;

The Yellow Bittern

The yellow bittern that never broke out
   In a drinking bout might as well have drunk;
His bones are thrown on a naked stone
   Where he lived alone like a hermit monk.
O yellow bittern! I pity your lot,
   Though they say that a sot like myself is curst –
I was sober a while, but I'll drink and be wise,
   For I fear I should die in the end of thirst.

It's not for the common birds that I'd mourn,
   The blackbird, the corncrake, or the crane,
But for the bittern that's shy and apart
   And drinks in the marsh from the lone bog-drain.
Oh! If I had known you were near your death,
   While my breath held out I'd have run to you,
Till a splash from the Lake of the Son of the Bird
   Your soul would have stirred and waked anew.

My darling told me to drink no more
   Or my life would be o'er in a little short while;
But I told her 'tis drink gives me health and strength
   And will lengthen my road by many a mile.
You see how the bird of the long smooth neck
   Could get his death from the thirst at last –
Come, son of my soul, and drain your cup,
   You'll get no sup when your life is past.

In a wintering island by Constantine's halls
   A bittern calls from a wineless place,
And tells me that hither he cannot come
   Till summer is here and the sunny days.

(Continued on page 242)

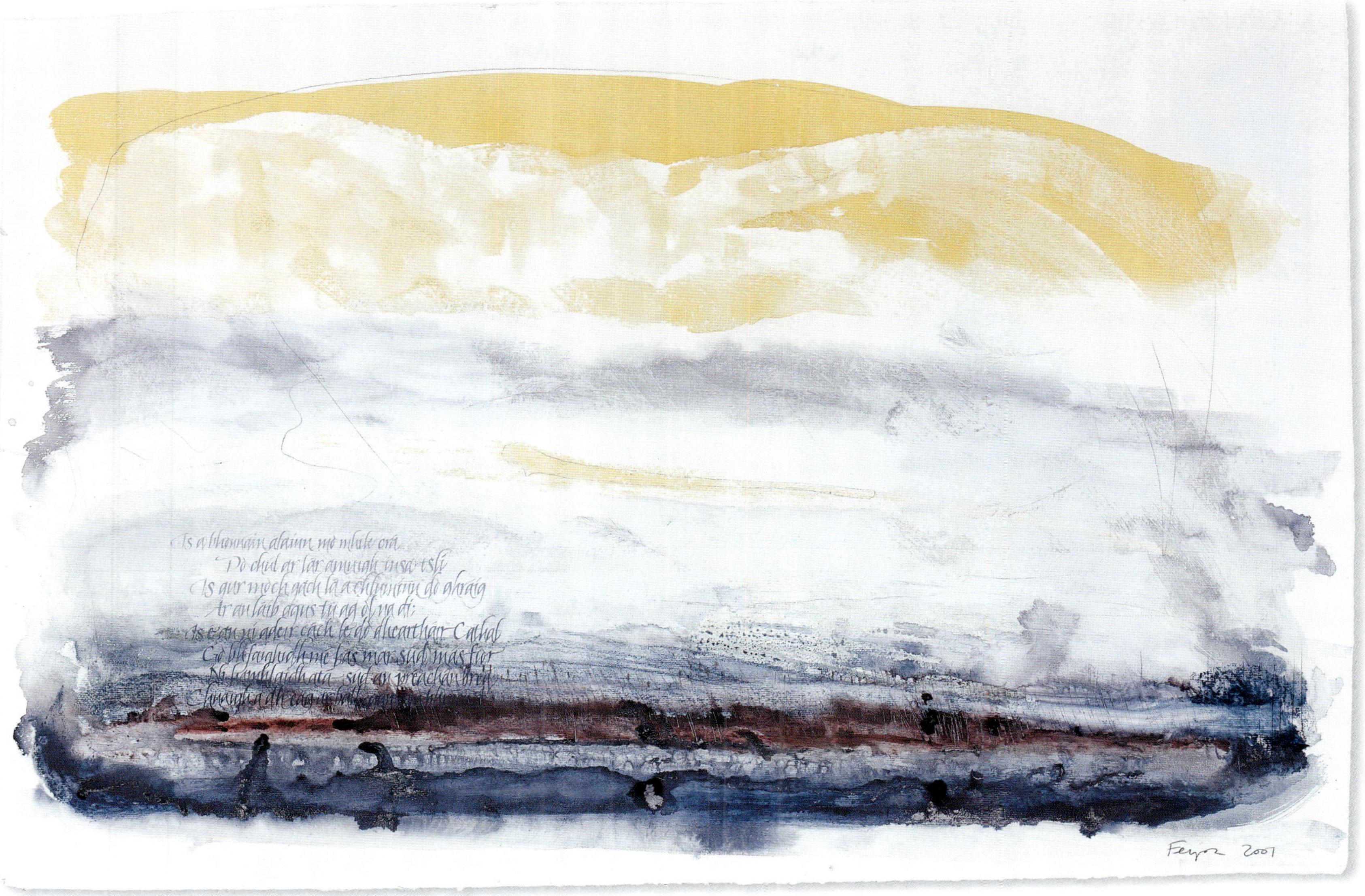
Is a bhonnáin álainn mo mhíle crá
Do chuil ar lár amuigh insa tslí
Is gur moch gach lá a chluininn do ghráig
Ar an láib agus tú ag ól na dí;
Is é an ní adeir cách le do dhearthair Cathal
Go bhfaighidh mé bás mar súd más fíor

32

GUN ARRAINN

ANON

c.1800

Neach-ealain / Artist:
Cóilín Murray

Snas-sgrìobhadair / Calligrapher:
Frances Breen

Eadar-theangaichte aig / Translator:
Màiri Sìne Campbell

Roghainn / Nominator:
Norman Campbell

Bothan Airigh am Bràigh Raithneach

Gur h-e m' anam is m' eudail
A bha 'n-dè 'n Gleanna Garadh,

Fear na gruaige mar òr
Is nam pòg air bhlas meala.

O hì ò o hù ò
O hì ò o hù ò
Hìriri oho èileadh
O hìri riri o gheallaibh o.

Fear na gruaige mar òr
Is nam pòg air bhlas meala.

'S tu as fheàrr dhan tig deise
Dha na sheas air an talamh;

'S tu as fheàrr dhan tig culaidh
Dha na chunna mi dh'fhearaibh.

'S tu as fheàrr dhan tig osan
'S bròg shocrach nam barrall;

Còta Lunnainneach dùbhghorm,
'S bidh na crùintean ga cheannach;

'S math thig triubhais on iarann
Air sliasaid a' ghallain;

'S math thig bonaid le fàbhar
Air fear àrd a' chùil chlannaich.

An uair a ruigeadh tu 'n fhèill,
'S e mo ghèar-sa thig dhachaigh:

A Shieling in Brae Rannoch

It was my love and my darling
Who was yesterday in Glen Garry,

He of the hair like gold
And kisses sweet as honey:

He of the hair like gold
And kisses sweet as honey:

You carry your clothes best
Of any who have stood on the earth.

You carry your gear best
Of all the men I have ever seen.

You suit your hose best
And the well-fitting shoe with the laces,

A dark blue coat from London
That costs crowns to buy;

Well do trews fresh from the iron look
On the thigh of the gallant;

Well does a bonnet with a cockade look
On the tall man with the curly hair.

When you would arrive at the fair,
This is the gear you would bring home to me:

(Continued on page 242)

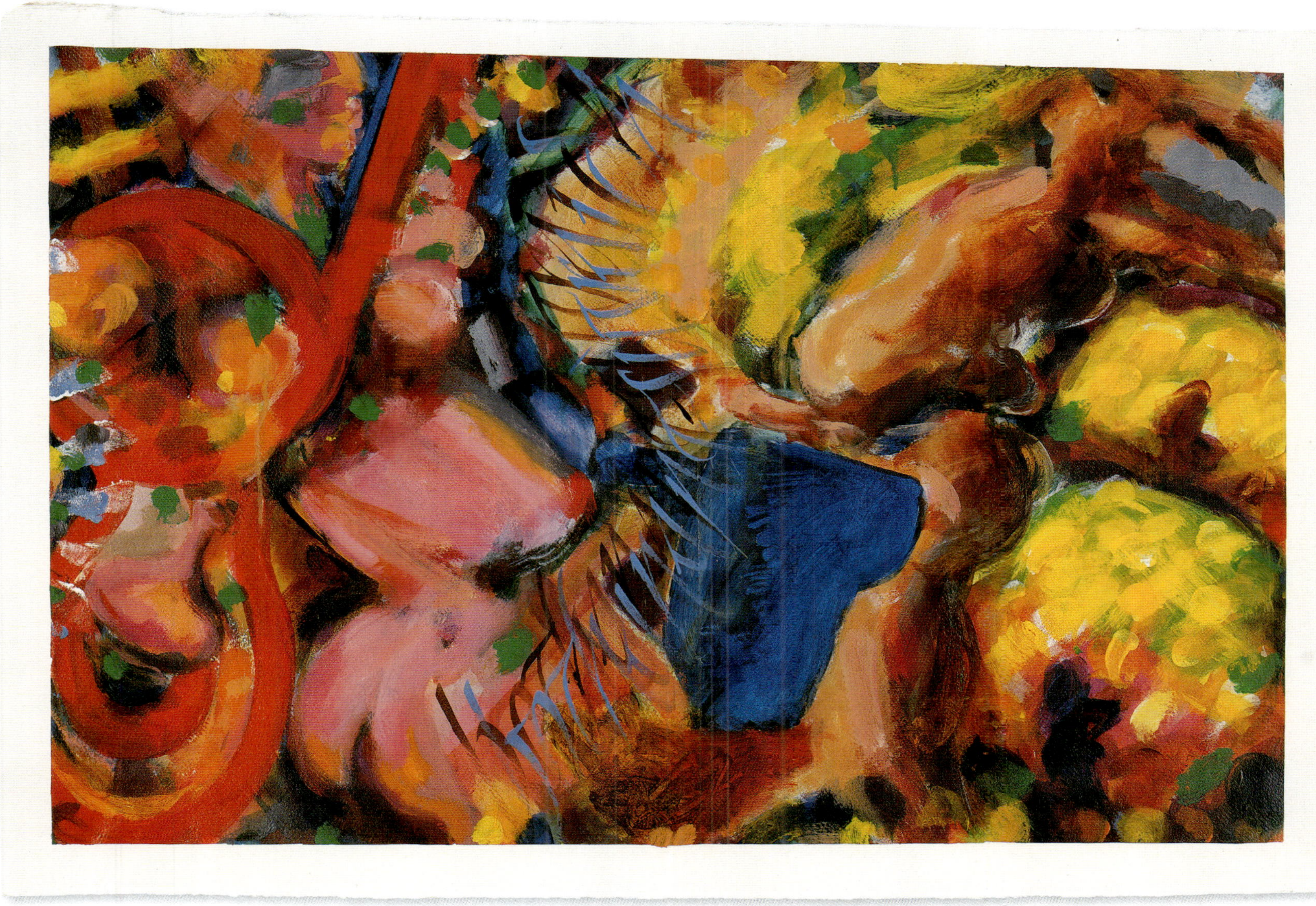

33

NIALL MÓR MAC MUIREADHAIGH

c. 1550–1613

Neach-ealain / Artist:
Caitlín Gallagher

Snas-sgrìobhadair / Calligrapher:
David McGrail

Eadar-theangaichte aig / Translator:
Unknown

Roghainn / Nominator:
Anne C. Frater

Soraidh Slán don Oidhche A-Réir

Soraidh slán don oidhche a-réir,
fada géar a dul ar gcúl;
dá ndáiltí mo chur i gcroich,
is truagh nach í a-nocht a tús.

Atáid dias is tigh-se a-nocht
ar nách ceileann rosg a rún;
gion go bhfuilid béal ri béal,
is géar géar silleadh a súl.

Tocht an ní chuireas an chiall
ar shilleadh siubhlach na súl.
Cá feirrde an tocht do-ní an béal
sgéal do-ní an rosg ar a rún?

Uch, ni léigid lucht na mbréag
smid tar mo bhéal, a rosg mhall;
tuig an ní-se adeir mo shúil,
agus tú insan chúil úd thall.

'Cuinnibh dhúinn an oidhche a-nocht,
truagh gan sinn mar so go brách;
ná léig an mhaidean is-teach,
éirigh 's cuir a-mach an lá!'

Uch, a Mhuire, a bhuime sheang,
ós tú is ceann ar gach cléir,
tárthaigh agus gabh mo lámh –
soraidh slán don oidhche a-réir!

Farewell Forever to Last Night

Farewell forever to last night,
the memory of it will be piercing and long-lasting;
though it were ordained that I should be hung,
it is a pity that it does not begin again tonight.

There are two in this house tonight
from whom the eye does not hide their secret;
though they are not lip to lip,
keen, keen is the glancing of their eyes.

Silence is the thing that puts meaning
into the fervent glancing of the eyes.
How is the silence that the mouths make
the better than the tale the eyes tell of their secret?

Alas, the people who carry lies do not allow
a single syllable to pass my lips, o languid eye,
understand this that my eye says
and you in yonder corner.

'Hoard up for us this night,
it is sad that we are not thus forever;
do not let the morning in,
rise up and drive out the day!'

Ah, Mary, lithe foster-mother,
since you are at the head of all poet-bands,
go near and take my hand –
farewell forever to last night.

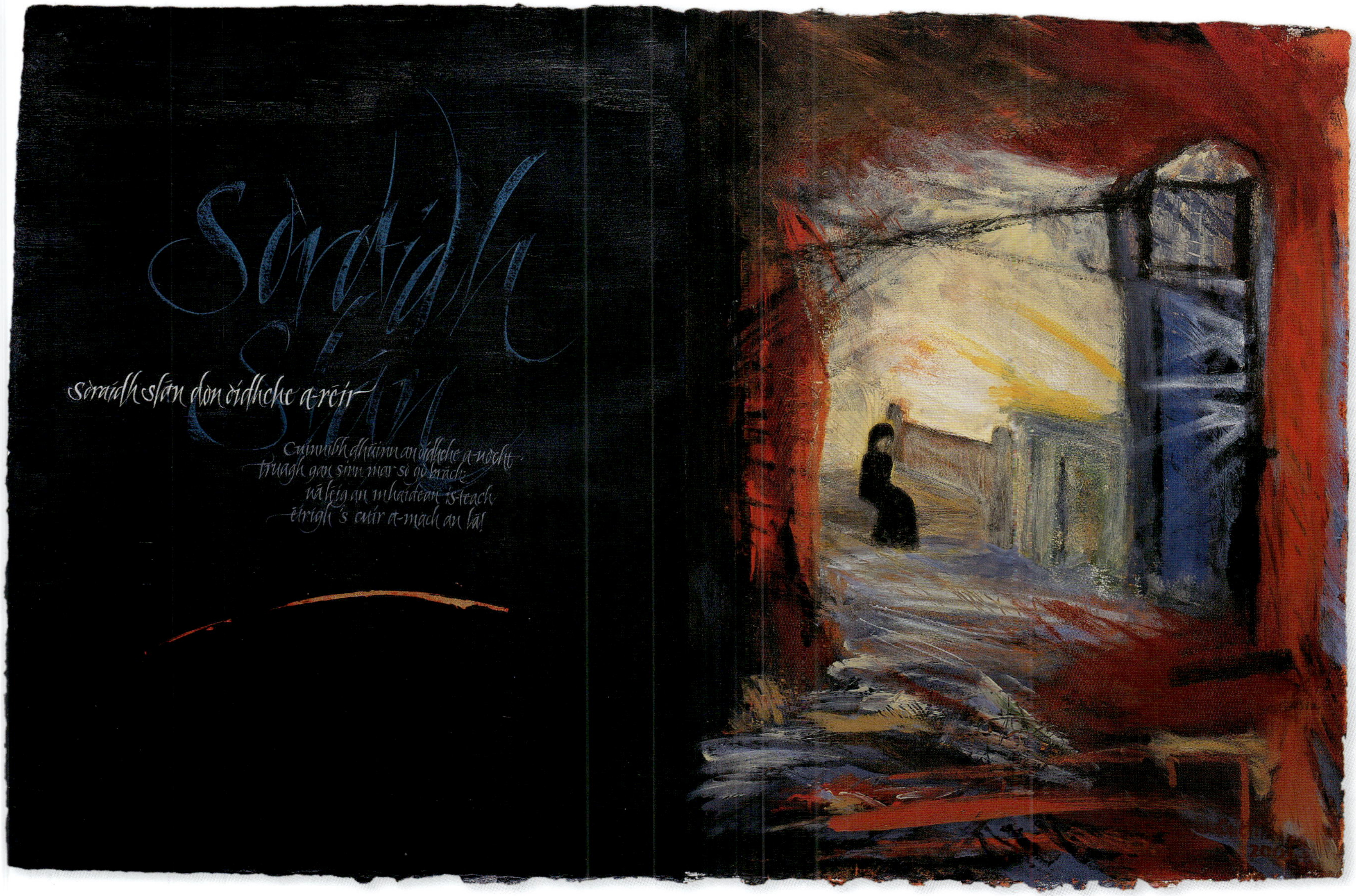
Soraidh Slàn
Sòraidh slàn don òidhche a-rèir
Cuimnibh dhùinn an òidhche a-nocht
truagh gan sinn mar sò go bràch
nà lèig an mhaidean is-teach
ēirigh 's cuir a-mach an là!

34

UILLEAM ROS

WILLIAM ROSS

c. 1762–1791

Neach-ealain / Artist:
Joseph Urie

Snas-sgrìobhadair / Calligrapher:
Ann Bowen

Eadar-theangaichte aig / Translator:
Derick S. Thomson

Roghainn / Nominator:
Catriona Montgomery

Feasgar Luain

… Chaidh mi steach an ceann na còisridh,
An robh òl is ceòl is danns,
Rìbhinnean is fleasgaich òga
'S iad an òrdugh grinn gun mheang …
'S ghlacadh mo chridhe 's mo shùil cò-luath
'S rinn an gaol mo leòn air ball.

Dhiùchd mar aingeal mu mo choinneamh
'N ainnir òg bu ghrinne snuadh:
Seang-shlios fallain air bhlàth canaich
No mar eala air a' chuan;
Sùil ghorm mheallach fo chaoil-mhala
'S caoin' a sheallas 'g amharc uath';
Beul tlàth, tairis gun ghnè smalain,
Dhan gnàth carthannachd gun uaill.

'S bachlach, dualach, cas-bhuidh', cuachach
Càradh suaineis gruag do chinn,
Gu h-àlainn, bòidheach, fàinneach, òr-bhuidh',
An caraibh seòighn 's an òrdugh grinn;
Gun chron a' fàs riut a dh'fheudt' àireamh
O do bhàrr gu sàil do bhuinn –
Dhiùchd na buaidhean, òigh, mun cuairt dut,
Gu meudachdainn t' uaill 's gach puing.

Bu leigheas eucail, slàn on eug,
Do dh'fhear a dh'fheudadh bhith mud chòir;
B' fheàrr na cadal bhith nad fhagaisg,
'G èisdeachd agallaidh do bheòil.
Cha robh Bheunas am measg leugaibh,
Dh'aindeoin feucantachd, cho bòidh'ch
Ri Mòir, nighean mhìn a leòn mo chrìdh'
Le buaidhean, 's mi ga dìth rim bheò.

Monday Evening

… I went in and joined the crowd
where there was music, drink and dance,
maidens there and young gallants,
ranged in order, flawless, neat …
and my heart and my eye were transfixed
and love pierced me on the spot.

There appeared, like an angel, before me
the young maid of finest mien:
lithe, healthy form, with skin as white
as cotton-grass or swan on sea;
blue eyes enticing, pencil brows,
yet kindly as they looked at me;
warm, gentle lips, no sign of gloom,
nor pride, their nature always kind.

In pleats and ringlets, yellow, curled
in careful order is your hair,
all lovely, beautiful, curled, golden,
in shapes so rare, yet ordered well;
with no fault that can be found
from top of head to sole and heel;
you were surrounded quite by grace,
a cause of pride at every point.

Disease's healing, death's respite
it were to one to be with you;
better than sleep to be near you,
listening to the words you speak.
Venus, surrounded by jewels,
with peacock's preen, was not so fair
as gentle Mòr, whose virtues left
my heart wounded, quite lost to me.

'S rinn an gaol mo leòn air ball.

Dh'fhiùcha mar aingeal mu mo choinneamh
'n ainnir òg bu ghrinne snuadh;
Seang-shlios fallain air bhlàth canaich
no mar an eal' air a' chuan;
Sùil ghorm mheallach fo chaoil-mhala
'S caoin' a sheallas' 's g' amharc uath';
Beul blàth: tairis gun ghnè smalain:
Dhan gnàth carthannachd gun uaill.

'S bachlach: dualach; cas-bhuidh' cuachach
Càradh suaineis gruaig a cinn;
Gu h-àlainn bòidheach fàinneach òr-bhuidh'
an caraibh seòighn 's an dualach grinn;
Gun chron a' fàs riutha a dh'fhuadach airtnimh
o do bhàrr gu sàil do bhuinn.
Dh'fhiùcha na buaidhean, òigh, mun cuairt dut,
Gu meudaicheadh d' uaill 's gach puing;

Bu lus-thèas eucail: slàn on eug;
Do 'n fhear a dh'fheudadh bhith mud chòir;
B' fhearr na càdal bhith na d' fhagaisg;
'G èisdeachd agallaidh do bheòil;
Cha robh bheunas am measg leugaibh;
Dh'aindeoin feucantachd: cho bòidh'ch
Ri m' òir nighean mhìn a leòn mo chridh'
Le buaidhean 's mi ga àiteamh rim bheò.

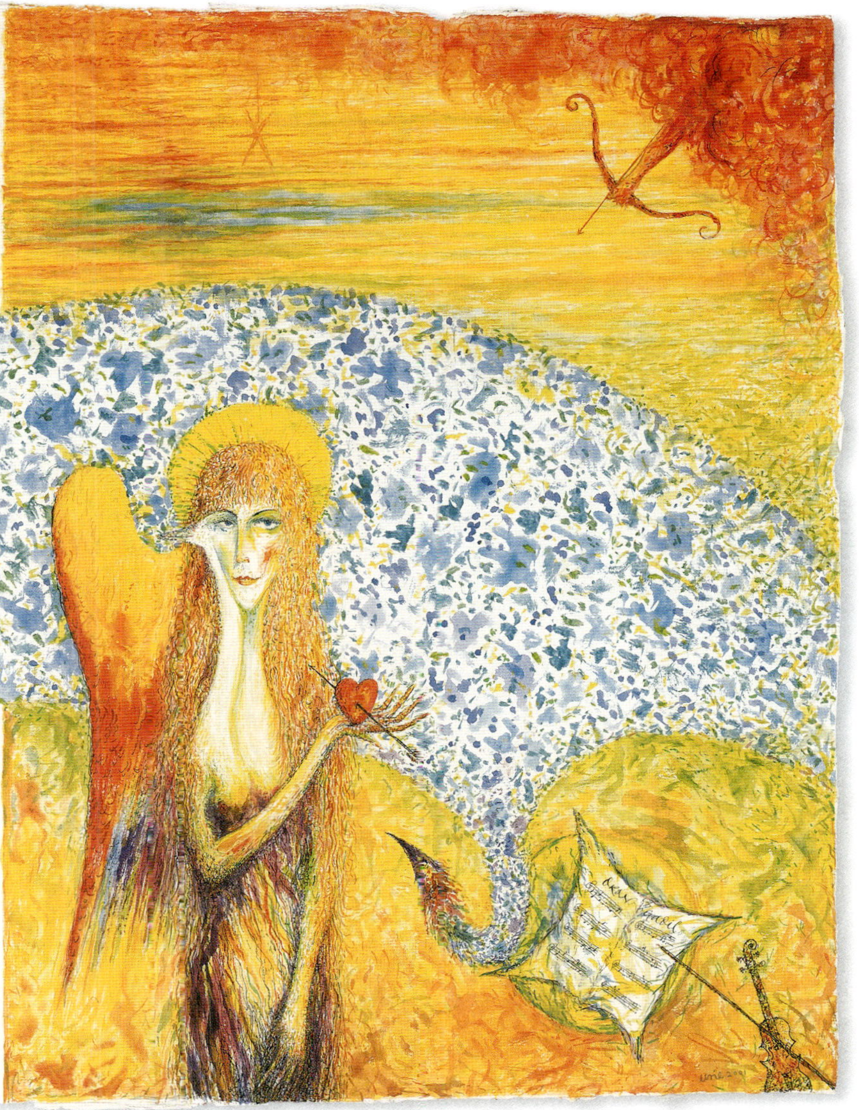

35

ROB DONN MACAOIDH

ROB DONN MACKAY

1714-1778

Neach-ealain/Artist:
Abigail O'Brien

Snas-sgrìobhadair/Calligrapher:
Susan Leiper

Eadar-theangaichte aig/Translator:
Ian Grimble

Roghainn/Nominator:
Catriona Montgomery

Is Trom Leam an Airigh

Is trom leam an àirigh, 's a' ghàir' seo a th' innt',
Gun a' phàirtidh a dh'fhàg mi bhith 'n tràth s' air mo chinn –
Anna chaol-mhalach, chìoch-chorrach, shlìob-cheannach, chruinn
Is Iseabail a' bheòil mhilis, mhànranaich, bhinn.
Heich! Mar a bha, air mo chinn,
A dh'fhàg mi cho cràiteach, 's nach stàth dhomh bhith 'g inns'.

Shiubhail mis' a' bhuaile 's a-suas feadh nan craobh
'S gach àit' anns am b' àbhaist bhith pàgadh mo ghaoil;
Nuair chunnaic mi 'm fear bàn ud, 's e mànran ra mhnaoi,
B' fheàrr leam nach tiginn idir làmh riu no 'n gaoith.
'S e mar a bha, air mo chinn,
A dh'fhàg air bheag tàth mi, ge nàr e ri sheinn.

Ach, Anna bhuidh Dhòmhnaill, nam b' eòl dhut mo nì,
'S e do ghràdh gun bhith pàight' leag a-bhàn uam mo chlì;
Tha e dhomh à t' fhianais cho gnìomhach 's nuair chì,
A' diogalladh 's a' smùsach, 's gur ciùrrt thu mo chrìdh'.
Ach, ma tha mi ga do dhìth,
Gum b' fheàirrde mi pàg uat mus fàgainn an tìr.

On chualas gun gluaiseadh tu uam leis an t-saor,
Tha mo shuain air a buaireadh le bruadraichean faoin:
Dhen chàirdeas a bha siud chan fhàir mi bhith saor –
Gun bhàirnigeadh làmh riut, tha 'n gràdh dhomh na mhaor
Air gach tràth, 's mi ann an strì
A' feuchainn ra àicheadh, 's e fàs rium mar chraoibh.

The Shieling is a Sad Place for Me

The shieling is a sad place for me, when the present company in it –
Rather than the company who used to be there – are near to me –
Anna of the pointed breasts, finely-arched brows, shining hair, full figure
And honey-mouthed Isabel, melodious, sweet.
Alas for things as they were close to me –
I have grown so bereft, there is no point in talking about it.

I wandered across the fold and up into the woods
And everywhere I used to kiss my love.
When I saw that fair fellow courting his wife,
I wish I had not come near them or beside them.
That's how it was, close to me,
What has made me so dispirited – it's no good talking about it.

Fair Anna, Donald's daughter, if you knew my condition,
It is unrequited love for you that deprived me of my strength.
It remains as lively with me as in your presence,
Teasing and provoking, wounding me to the heart.
Now, if I am to lose you,
I would be the better of a kiss from you, before I leave the country.

Since it was rumoured that you would forsake me for the carpenter,
My sleep is disturbed with dreams of love.
Of the affection that was between us I cannot break free:
When I am not beside you, love is like a bailiff to me.
At every hour I am in turmoil,
Trying to deny it, while it grows in me like a tree.

(Continued on page 243)

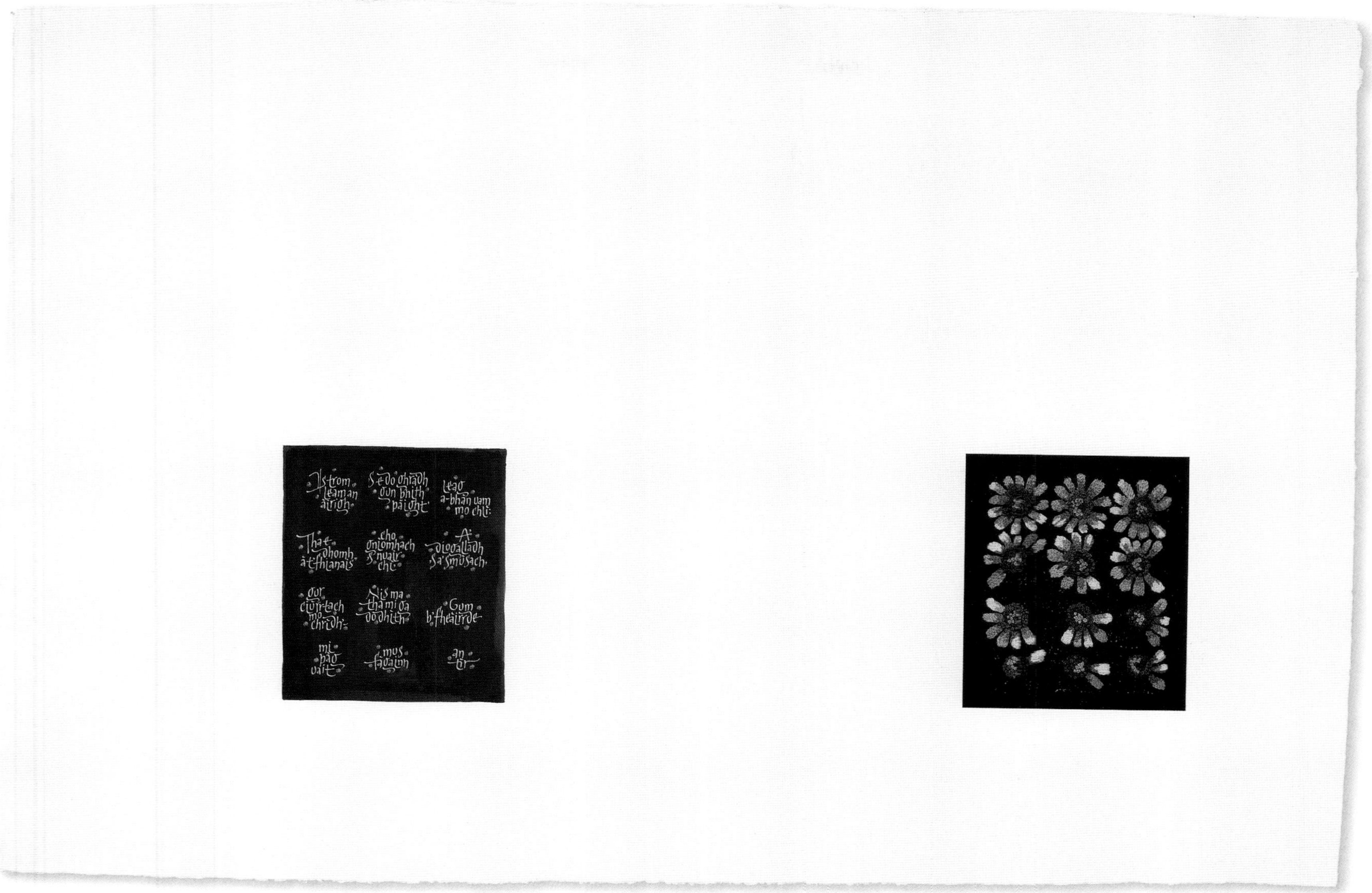
Is trom leam an àirigh
'S e do ghràdh gun bhith pàight'
Leag a-bhàn uam mo chlì;
Tha e dhomh à t'fhianais
cho gnìomhach 's nuair chì
A' diogalladh sa' smùsach
gur ciùrrtach mo chridh':
Nis ma tha mi ga do dhìth
Gum b'fheàirrde
mi bàs uait
mus fàgainn
an tìr

36

GAN AINM

ANON

c. 1800

Ealaíontóir/Artist:
Andrew McMorrine

Peannaire/Calligrapher:
David McGrail

Aistritheoir/Translator:
Theo Dorgan

Ainmníodh ag/Nominator:
Cathal Ó Searcaigh

Tá Mé i Mo Shuí

Tá mé i mo shuí ó d'éirigh an ghealach aréir,
Ag cur tine síos go buan is á fadú go géar;
Tá bunadh an tí ina luí is tá mise liom féin,
Tá an coileach ag glaoch is tá an saol ina gcodladh ach mé.

'Sheacht mh'anam déag, do bhéal, do mhalaí is do ghrua,
Do shúil ghorm ghlé faoinar thréig mise aiteas is suairc,
Le cumha i do dhéidh ní léir dom an bealach a shiúl,
Is, a chara mo chléibh, tá an saol ag dul idir mé is tú.

'S é deir lucht léinn gur cloíte an galar an grá:
Char admhaigh mé féin é go ndearna sé mo chroí istigh a chrá;
Aicíd ró-ghéar, faraoir nár sheachain mé í,
Chuir sí arraing is céad go géar trí cheartlár mo chroí.

Casadh bean sí dom thíos ag lios Bhéal an Átha,
D'fhiafraigh mé díthe an scaoilfeadh glas ar bith grá;
Labhair sí os íseal i mbriathra soineanta sámha,
"An grá a théid fán chroí, cha scaoiltear as é go brách."

Up All Night

Since moonrise last evening I'm here like a fool sitting up,
Feeding the fire and stoking the embers and coals,
The house is asleep and I'm here on my own all the night,
Here's the cock crowing and everyone snoring but me.

All I can see is your mouth, your brow and your cheek,
Your burning blue eye that robbed me of quiet and peace,
Lonely without you I can't find a path for my feet,
Friend of my heart, there are mountains between me and you.

The learned men say that love is a killing disease,
I wouldn't believe them until it had scalded my heart,
The acid is eating me I'd have done better to shun,
Stabbing like splinters of lightning tonight in my chest.

I met a wise woman below at the mouth of the ford,
I asked if she knew of a herb that might ease love's pain,
Her voice when she answered was soft, regretful and low:
When it goes to the heart it will never come out again.

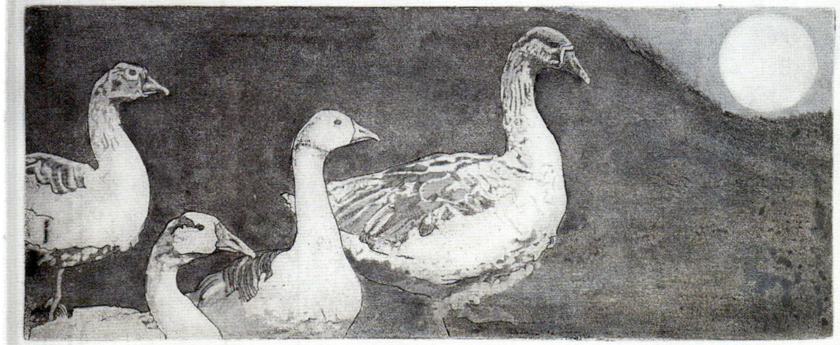

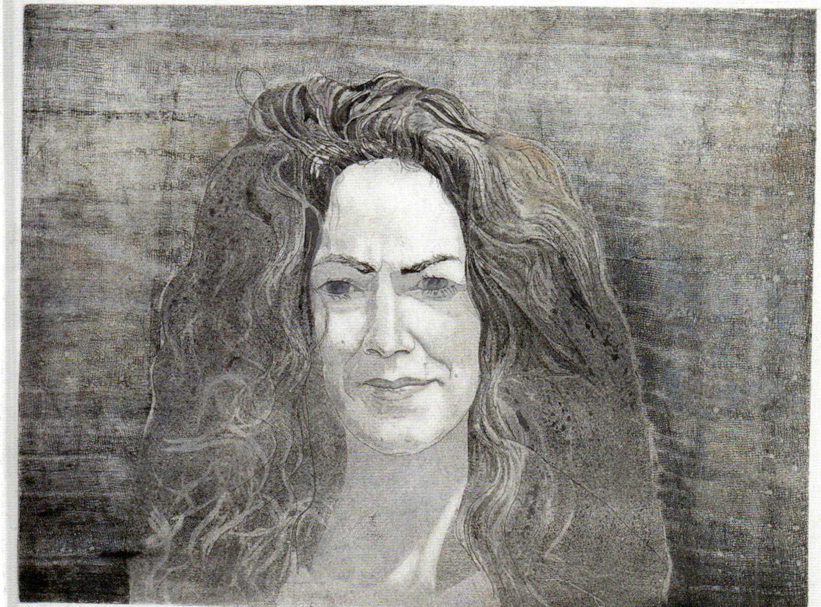

Tá mé i mo shuí ó d'éirigh an ghealach aréir,
Ag cur tine síos go buan is á fadú go géar;
Tá bunadh an tí ina luí is tá mise liom féin,
Tá an coileach ag glaoch is tá an saol ina gcodladh ach mé

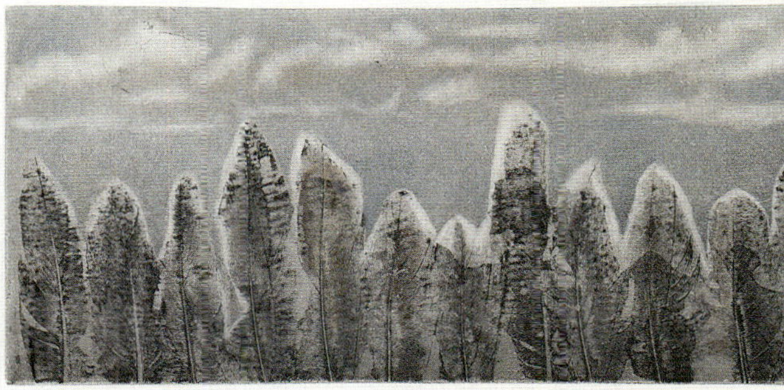

Andrew McMorrine

37

EOGHAN RUA Ó SUILEABHÁIN

OWEN ROE O'SULLIVAN

c. 1748-1784

Ealaíontóir/Artist:
Steven Campbell

Peannaire/Calligrapher:
Réiltín Murphy

Aistritheoir/Translator:
Aodán Mac Póilín

Ainmníodh ag/Nominator:
The Editorial Panel

Suantraí dá Mhac Tabhartha

Seóthó, a thoil, ná goil go fóill,
Do gheobhair gan dearmad taisce gach seoid
Do bhí ag do shinsear ríoga romhat
In Éirinn liath-ghlas Choinn is Eoghain.
Seóthó, a thoil, ná goil go fóill,
Seóthó, a thoil, ná goil aon deoir,
Seóthó, a linbh, a chumainn 's a stóir,
Tú ag sileadh na súl is do chom gan lón.

Ar dtúis nuair chonac an fhinne-bhean óg,
A súil ba ghlaise is bhí luisne 'na snó,
Níor dhiúltaigh mise nuair dhruideas 'na treo,
Is mo chumha, níor thuigeas an tuirse a bhí romham.
Seóthó, srl

A súil chum toirmisc cliste go leor,
Cúileann d'imreadh cluiche na n-óg,
Is í d'fhúig mise fá iomarca bróin,
Ag luascadh linbh is ag sileadh na ndeor.
Seóthó, srl

Do gheobhair ar dtúis an t-úll id' dhóid
Do bhí ag an dtriúr i gclúid id' chomhair,
An staf bhí ag Pan - ba ghreanta an tseoid –
'S an tslat bhí ag Maois ghníodh díon is treoir.
Seóthó srl

Do gheobhair 'na bhfochair sin lomra an óir
Thug Jason tréan don Ghréig ar bord,
'S an tréan-each cuthaigh mear cumasach óg
Do bhí ag Coin Chulainn, ceann urraidh na sló.
Seóthó, srl

Lullaby to his Illegitimate Son

Hush, my love, don't cry a while.
You will have jewels in store without fail,
All that was owned by your royal line
In the green-clad Ireland of Conn and Eoghan.
Hush, my love, don't cry a while,
Hush, my love, don't cry a tear,
Hush, my child, my treasure, my dear,
Your belly is empty and you're crying sore.

When first I saw the fair young woman
With the greenest eyes, and a glowing complexion,
My advances she did not reject
But little I thought of the sorrowful ending.
Hush, my love, etc.

She had an eye that was made for trouble,
This beauty could play the games of the young
And leave me here in deepest dejection,
Rocking a child and heavily weeping.
Hush, my love, etc.

First you shall get in your fist the apple
Put aside for you by the three Graces,
The staff of Pan – a notable treasure –
And the rod of Moses which guided and protected him.
Hush, my love, etc.

You shall get as well the golden fleece
Which great Jason brought on the sea to Greece
And the swift, sturdy, mettlesome horse
Which belonged to Cuchulainn, leader of hosts.
Hush, my love, etc

(Continued on page 243)

seóthó, a thoil, ná goil go fóill,
do gheobhair gan dearmad taisce gach seoid
do bhí ag do shinsear ríoga romhat
in Éirinn liath-ghlas Chuinn is Eoghain.

seóthó, a thoil, ná goil go fóill,
seóthó, a thoil, ná goil aon deoir,
seóthó, a linbh, a chumainn 's a stóir
tú ag sileadh na súl is do chom gan lón.

Ar dtúis nuair chonac an fhinne-bhean óg,
a súil ba ghlaise is bhí luisne 'na snó,
níor dhiúltaigh mise nuair dhruideas 'na treo,
is mo chumha, níor thuigeas an tuirse bhí romham.

seóthó, a thoil, ná goil go fóill,
seóthó, a thoil, ná goil aon deoir,
seóthó, a linbh, a chumainn 's a stóir
tú ag sileadh na súl is do chom gan lón.

A súil chum tairmisc cliste go leor,
cúileann d'imreadh cluiche na n-óg,
is í d'fhuig mise fá iomcara bróin,
ag luascadh linbh is ag sileadh na ndeor.

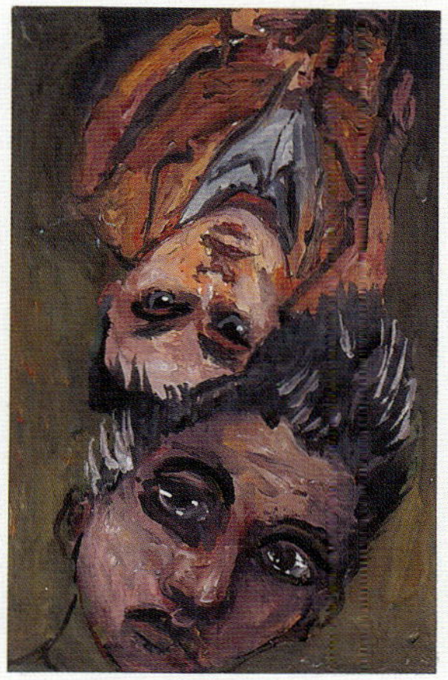

38

BRIAN MERRIMAN

c. 1745-1805

Ealaíontóir/Artist:
Shane Cullen

Peannaire/Calligrapher:
Frances Breen

Aistritheoir/Translator:
Frank O'Connor

Ainmníodh ag/Nominator:
The Editorial Panel

Cúirt an Mheán Oíche (sliocht)

Ní fiú liom freagra freastail a thabhairt ort,
A shnámhaire galair nach aiteas do labhartha!
Ach 'neosad feasta do mhaithe na cúirte
An nós 'nar cailleadh an ainnir nárbh fhiú thú.
Do bhí sí lag, gan ba gan púntaibh,
Bhí sí i bhfad gan teas gan clúdadh,
Cortha dá saol, ar strae á seoladh
Ó phosta go p'léar gan ghaol gan chóngas,
Gan scíth gan spás de lá ná d'oíche
Ag stríocadh an aráin ó mhná nár chuí léi.
Do gheall an fear so dreas sócúil di,
Gheall an spreas di teas is clúdadh,
Cothrom glan is ba le crú dhi
Is codladh fada ar leabain chlúimh dhi,
Teallaí teo is móin a daoithin,
Ballaí fód gan leoithne gaoithe,
Fothain is díon ón síon 's ón spéir dhi
Is olann is líon le sníomh chun éadaigh.
Dob fheasach don tsaol 's don phéist seo láithreach
Nach taitneamh ná téamh ná aonphioc grá dho
Cheangail an péarla maorga mná so
Ach easnamh go léir - ba déirc léi an tsástacht!
Ba dubhach an fuadar suairceas oíche:
Smúid is ualach, duais is líonadh,
Lúithní lua' is guaillí caola
Is glúine crua chomh fuar le hoighre,
Cosa feoite dóite ón ngríosaigh
Is colainn bhreoite dhreoite chríonna!

The Midnight Court (excerpt)

'I'd honour you much if I gave the lie
To an impudent speech that needs no reply;
'Tis enough if I tell the sort of life
You led your unfortunate, decent wife.

'This girl was poor, she hadn't a home,
Or a single thing she could call her own,
Drifting about in the saddest of lives,
Doing odd jobs for other men's wives,
As if for drudgery created,
Begging a crust from women she hated.
He pretended her troubles were over;
Married to him she'd live in clover;
The cows she milked would be her own,
The feather bed and a decent home,
The stack of turf, the lamp to light,
The good earth wall of a winter's night,
Flax and wool to weave and wind,
The womanly things for which she pined.
Even his friends could not have said
That his looks were such that she lost her head.
How else would he come by such a wife
But that ease was the alms she asked of life?
What possible use could she have at night
For dourness, dropsy, bother and blight,
A basket of bones with thighs of lead,
Knees absconded from the dead,
Fire-speckled shanks and temples whitening,
Looking like one that was struck by lightning?

We have only been able to give an excerpt from this poem. For an alternative source of the full text see the listing on page 265.

(Continued on page 234)

Mediae Noctis Consilium An File: Ar cheangal mo shúl go dlúth le chéile greamaithe dúnta i ndúghlas néallta,
is magaidh agam poitiche ó chuilibh go sásta i dtaibhreamh d'fhuiling mé an chuilithe chráite,
do chorraigh, do lom, do pholl go haé mé, im chodladh go trom, gan mheabhair gan éirim
An Spéirbhean: 'Múscail, corraigh, a chodlataigh ghránna! Is dubhach do shlí bheith sínte id shleasta
is cúirt 'na suí 's na mílte ag triall ann...cuirt na dtrua, na mbua is na mbeithe...!'
Bean Óg: 'Is dearfa bhím am shíorthaspánadh ar mhachaire mhín gach fíoriomána, ag rince, báire,
rás is radaireacht, tinte cnámh is rapla is ragairne, aonach, margadh is Aifreann Domhnaigh
ag éileamh breathnaithe, ag amharc 's ag togha fir. Chaitheas mo chiall le fiach gan éifeacht,
dhalladar riamh mé, is d'iadar m'ae ionnam, t'réis mo chumainn, mo tharraing 's mo ghrá dhóibh,
t'réis ar fhulaing mé d'iomada cránais, t'réis ar chaitheas le caitheamh na scalaí, beithe baltha, is
cailleacha cártaí. Níl cleas dá mbeidir léamh ná trácht air le teacht na ré nó t'réis bheith lán dí,
um Inid, um Shamhain, ná ar shiúl na bliana ná tuigim gur leamhas bheith ag súil le ciall as!
Níorbh áil liom codladh go socair aon uair díobh gan lán mo stoca de thorthaibh fém chluasa,
is deimhin nárbh obair liom troscadh le cráifeacht, is greim ná blogam ní shlogainn trí trátha;
in aghaidh na srotha do thomainn mo léine ag súil trím chodladh le cogar óm chéile;
'S é fáth mo scéil go léir 's a bhrí dhuit — táim gan chéile t'réis mo dhíchill,
fáth mo sheanchais fhada, mo phian-chreach! Táim in achrann daingean na mblianta,
ag tarraing go tréan ar laethaibh liatha, is eagal liom éag gan cinnea'om iarraidh...!'
Preabann anuas go fuadrach fíochmhar seanduine suarach is fuadach nimhe fé:
'Nach mór an tobhacht 's an gleo i measc daoine tuta nire det short, gan bhó gan chaora,
búclaí id bhróga is clóicín síoda ort, ciarsúir póca ag góil na gaoithe!
Dallair an saol go léir led thaibhse — is aithnid dom féin thú ar dtaobh do chaidhpse;
is deacair dom labhairt, do lom is léir dom, is fada do dhrom gan chabhair ón léine...'
Bean Óg: Ní fiú liom freagra freastail a thabhairt ort a shnamhaire galair nach aiteas do labhartha!
Ach neosad feasta do mhaithe na cúirte an nós 'nár cailleadh an ainnir nárbh fhiú thú.
Do bhí sí lag, gan ba gan púntaibh, bhí sí i bhfad gan teas gan cludach
cortha dá saol, ar strae á seoladh ó phosta go piléar gan ghaol gan chongas,
gan scíth gan spás de ló ná d'oíche ag scríobadh an aráin ó mhná nár chuí léi.
Do gheall an fear so dreas sóúil di, gheall an spreas di teas is cludach, cothrom glan is ba le crú dhi
is codladh fada ar leabain chlúimh dhi, teallaí teo is móin a daorthim ballaí fód gan leoithne gaoithe,
fothain is díon ón sion 's ón spéir dhi is olann is líon le sníomh chun éadaigh.
Dob fhéasach don tsaol 's don phéist seo laithreach nach taitneamh ná téamh ná aonphioc grá dho
cheangail an péarla maorga mná so ach easnamh go léir — ba deire léi an tsástacht!
Ba dubhach an fuadar suairceas oíche smúid is ualach, duais is líonadh, luithní lua is guaillí caola
is glúine crua chomh fuar le hoighre, cosa feoite doite ón ngríosaigh is colainn bhreoite dhreoite chríonna!
An bhfuil stuaire beo ná feofadh liath ag cuail dá short bheith pósta riamh,
nár chuardaigh fós fá dhó le bliain cé buachaill óg í, feoil, nó iasc?
's an feoiteach fuar so suas léi sínte dreoite duairc, gan bhua gan bhíogadh.
O! Cár mhuar di bualadh bríomhar ar nós an diabhail dhá uair gach oíche!
Ní dóch go dtuigir gurb ise bu chiontach ná fós go gclisfeadh ar laige le tamhandacht
an maighre mascalach carthanach cuimtais — is doimhin go bhfaca sí a mhalairt de mhúineadh!
Ní labharfadh focal dá mb'obair an oíche is thabharfadh cothrom do stollaire bríomhar,
go brách ar siúl nár dhiúltaigh riamh é ar cnámh a cúl 's a súile iata.
Ní thabharfadh preab le stailc mhíchumasach, fogha mar chat ná sraic ná scríob air,
acht í go léir ina slaod comh-sínte, taobh ar thaobh 's a géag ina thimpeall,
ó scéal go scéal ag breagadh a smaointe, béal ar bhéal 's ag méaraíocht síos air.
Is minic a chuir sí a cos taobh 'nonn de is chuimil a brush ó chrios go glún de,
sciobadh an phluid 's an chuilt dá ghúnga ag sprionga ag suite le moirt gan súchas.
Níor chabhair dhi cigilt ná cuimilt ná fáscadh, fogha dá huillinn, dá hingin ná a sála;
is nár dom aithris mar chaitheadh sí an oíche ag fáscadh an chnaiste 's ag searradh 's ag síneadh,
ag feacadh na ngéag 's an t-éadach fuithi, a ballaibh go léir 's a déid ar luthchrith,
go loinnir an lae gan néall do dhubhadh uirthi ag imirt ó thaobh go taobh 's ag iompaíre.
Aoibheall: 'Achtaímid mar dhlí do bhéithe an seacht fá thrí gan chuibhreach céile...
Is ciallmhar ceart an t-Acht é, silim, bliain an Achta so is ceart é scríobh dúinn; (1780)
An File: 'Glacann sí an peann, is mo cheannsa snaite ar eagla m'fheannta is scanradh an bhuailte;
an aga do bhí sí ag scríobh an dáta is maithibh an tí aici suite ar garda ann,
scaras lem néall, do réidheas mo shúile is phreabas de léim ón bpéin im dhúiseacht!

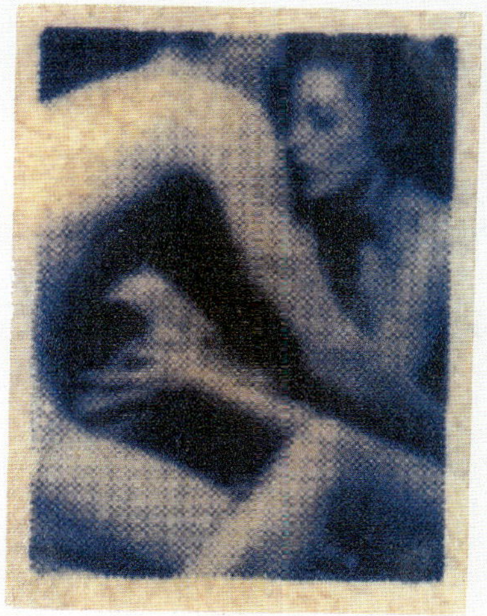

39

EIBHLÍN DHUBH NÍ CHONAILL

c. 1743–1800

Ealaíontóir/Artist:
Kevin MacLean

Peannaire/Calligrapher:
Louise Donaldson

Aistritheoirí/Translators:
Eilís Dillon, John Montague

Ainmníodh ag/Nominator:
John Montague

Caoineadh Airt Uí Laoghaire (sliocht)

Mo ghrá go daingean tu!
Lá dá bhfaca thu
ag ceann tí an mhargaidh,
thug mo shúil aire dhuit,
thug mo chroí taitneamh duit,
d'éalaíos óm charaid leat
i bhfad ó bhaile leat.

Is domhsa nárbh aithreach:
chuiris parlús á ghealadh dhom,
rúmanna á mbreacadh dhom,
bácús á dheargadh dhom,
brící á gceapadh dhom,
rósta ar bhearaibh dom,
mairt á leagadh dhom;
codladh i gclúmh lachan dom
go dtíodh an t-eadartha
nó thairis dá dtaitneadh liom.

Mo chara go daingean tu!
Is cuimhin lem aigne
an lá breá earraigh úd,
gur bhreá thíodh hata dhuit
faoi bhanda óir tarraingthe;
claíomh cinn airgid,
lámh dheas chalma,
rompsáil bhagarthach –
fír-chritheagla
ar námhaid chealgach –
tú i gcóir chun falaracht
is each caol ceannann fút.

Lament for Art O'Leary (excerpt)

My love forever!
The day I first saw you
At the end of the market-house,
My eye observed you,
My heart approved you,
I fled from my father with you,
Far from my home with you.

I never repented it:
You whitened a parlour for me,
Painted rooms for me,
Reddened ovens for me,
Baked fine bread for me,
Basted meat for me,
Slaughtered beasts for me;
I slept in ducks' feathers
Till midday milking-time
Or more if it pleased me.

My friend forever!
My mind remembers
That fine spring day
How well your hat suited you,
Bright gold-banded,
Sword silver-hilted –
Right hand steady –
Threatening aspect –
Trembling terror
On treacherous enemy –
You poised for a canter
On your slender bay horse.

We have only been able to give an excerpt from this poem. For an alternative source of the full text see the listing on page 265.

Mo ghrá go daingean tú!

Lá dá bhfaca thú ag ceann tí an mhargaidh thug mo shúil aire dhuit thug mo chroí taitneamh duit, d'éalaíos ón charaid leat.

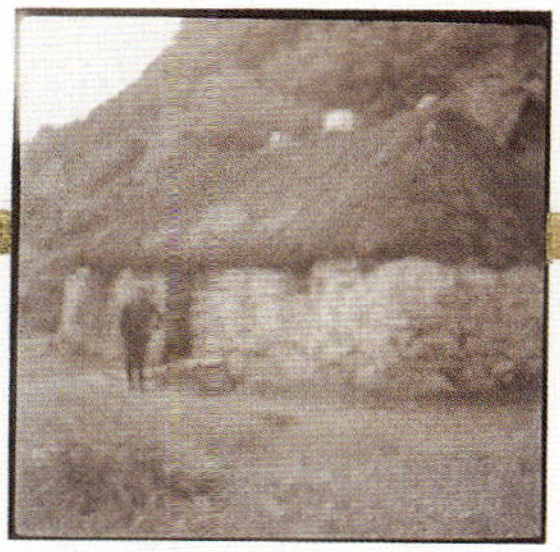

i bhfad ó bhaile leat

IAIN MACGILLEATHAIN

JOHN MACLEAN

c. 1787-1848

Neach-ealain / Artist:
Norman Shaw

Snas-sgrìobhadair / Calligrapher:
Réiltín Murphy

Eadar-theangaichte aig / Translator:
William Neill

Roghainn / Nominator:
Alastair MacLeod

Am Bàrd an Canada (earrann)

'A' Choille Ghruamach'

Gu bheil mi 'm ònrachd sa choille ghruamaich,
Mo smaointean luaineach, cha tog mi fonn:
Fhuair mi 'n t-àite seo 'n aghaidh nàdair –
Gun d' thrèig gach tàlanta bha nam cheann.
Cha dèan mi òran a chur air dòigh ann –
Nuair nì mi tòiseachadh bidh mi trom:
Chaill mi a' Ghàidhlig seach mar a b' àbhaist dhomh
An uair a bha mi san dùthaich thall.

Chan fhaigh mi m' inntinn leam ann an òrdugh,
Ged bha mi eòlach air dèanamh rann;
'S e mheudaich bròn dhomh 's a lùghdaich sòlas
Gun duine còmhla rium nì rium cainnt.
Gach là is oidhche 's gach car a nì mi,
Gum bi mi cuimhneachadh anns gach àm
An tìr a dh'fhàg mi tha 'n taic an t-sàile,
Ged tha mi 'n dràst ann am bràighe ghleann.

Chan iongnadh dhòmhsa ged tha mi brònach,
'S ann tha mo chòmhnaidh air cùl nam beann,
Am meadhan fàsaich air Abhainn Bhàrnaidh,
Gun dad as fheàrr na buntàta lom;
Mun dèan mi àiteach 's mun tog mi bàrr ann,
'S a' choille ghàbhaidh chur as a bonn
Le neart mo ghàirdein, gum bi mi sàraichte
'S treis' air fàillinn mum fàs a' chlann.

'S i seo an dùthaich sa bheil an cruadal,
Gun fhios don t-sluagh a tha tighinn a-nall;
Gur h-olc a fhuaras oirnn luchd a' bhuairidh
A rinn len tuairisgeul ar toirt ann;

The Poet in Canada (excerpt)

Also known as 'The Gloomy Woodland'

I'm all alone in this gloomy woodland,
my mind is troubled, I sing no song:
against all nature I took this place here
and native wit from my mind has gone.
I have no spirit to polish poems,
my will to start them is dulled by care;
I lose the Gaelic that was my custom
in yon far country over there.

I cannot muster my thoughts in order
though making songs was my great delight;
there's little joy comes to smoor my sadness
with no companion to ease my plight;
each night and day, in each task I turn to,
the ache of memory grows more and more;
I left my dear land beside the ocean
and now no sea laps my dwelling's shore.

It is no wonder I should be grieving
behind these hills in a desert bare,
in this hard country of Barney's River;
a few potatoes my only fare;
I must keep digging to win bare living
to hold these wild threatening woods at bay;
my strength alone serves till sons reach manhood
and I may fail long before that day.

This is a country that's hard and cruel,
they do not know it who journey still;
evil the yarns of the smooth-tongued coaxers
who brought us hither against our will;

We have only been able to give an excerpt from this poem. For an alternative source of the full text see the listing on page 265.

gu bheil mi 'm ònrachd sa choille ghruamaich, mo smaointean luaineach, dha tag mi fonn:
fhuair mi an t-àit seo an aghaidh nàdair, gun thrèig gach tàlant a bha nam cheann.

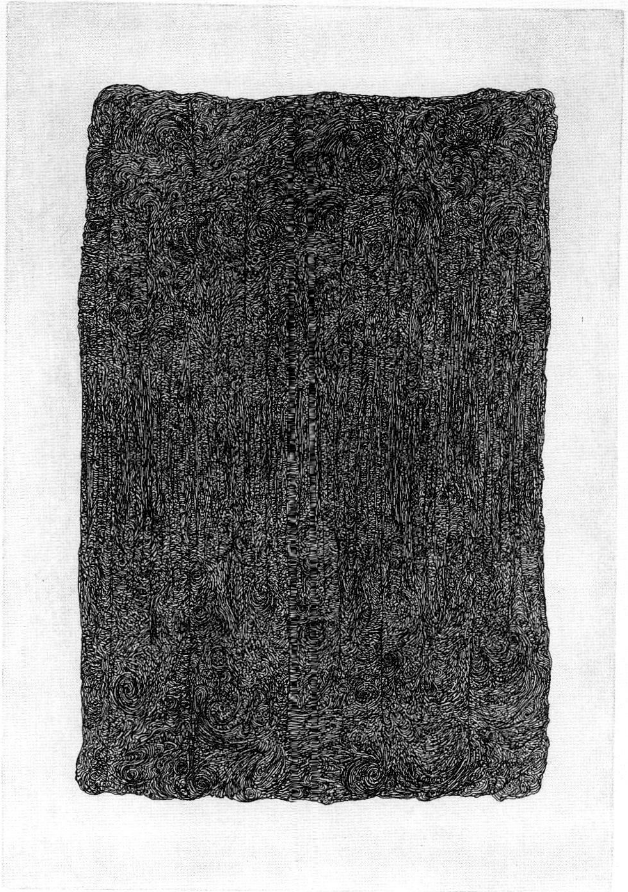

41

NIALL MACLEÒID

c. 1843-1924

Neach-ealain / Artist:
John McNaught

Snas-sgrìobhadair / Calligrapher:
Louise Donaldson

Eadar-theangaichte aig / Translator:
Unknown

Roghainn / Nominator:
Mary Montgomery

Turas Dhòmhnaill do Ghlaschu (earrann)

Thuirt i rium gum bu chòir dhuinn
Dol do sheòmar nan uinneag –
Gu robh cluich agus ceòl ann,
Gu robh òl ann is iomairt,
Gu robh maighdeannan òg ann
Dhe gach seòrs' agus cinneadh,
Agus taghadh nan òigfhear,
''S bidh tu, Dhòmhnaill, air mhire
Mun tig thu às!'

Nuair a ràinig mi 'n cala,
Cha b' e talla nan uaislean –
Bha aon chòig no sia bhalaich
Agus caile thiugh ruadh ann;
Iad ri mionnan 's ri bòilich
Agus còmhradh gun tuaiream –
Bheirinn fàsgadh air sgòrnan
Na tè neònaich thug suas mi,
Nam biodh i mach.

Chuirinn impidh gun sòradh
Air gach Dòmhnall sa bhaile
Gun e lùbadh le gòraig
A bhiodh bòidheach na shealladh;
Ged as milis an còmhradh,
Tha ceud fòtas fon earradh –
'S math tha fios aig mo phòca,
'S far 'n do sgròb iad mo mhala,
Gu bheil sin ceart.

Donald's Trip to Glasgow (excerpt)

She said we should go to
the room with the windows,
there'd be games there and music,
there'd be drink there and frolics,
and my choice of young maidens
of every kind and colour,
and the best of the young men,
'And you'll be in your element
before you leave'.

When I got to that harbour,
it was no great lords' castle –
there were five or six lads there
and a stout red-haired lassie;
they were cursing and bawling,
their talk was aimless:
I'd wring the neck of
the strange one who enticed me
were she about.

I'd beg with no hesitation
every Donald in the city
not to be swayed by a silly girl
who looks pretty to his eyes;
although her speech may be sweet,
her dress conceals a hundred blemishes,
and well my pocket knows,
and my brow where they scratched me,
that that's correct.

We have only been able to give an excerpt from this poem. For an alternative source of the full text see the listing on page 265.

Chuirinn impidh gun sòradh Air gach Dòmhnall sa bhaile
Gun e lùbadh le gòraig A bhiodh bòidheach na shèalladh;
Ged as milis an còmhradh, Tha ceud fòtas fon earradh -
'S math tha fios aig mo phòca, 'S far 'n do sgròb iad mo mhala,
Gu bheil sin ceart.

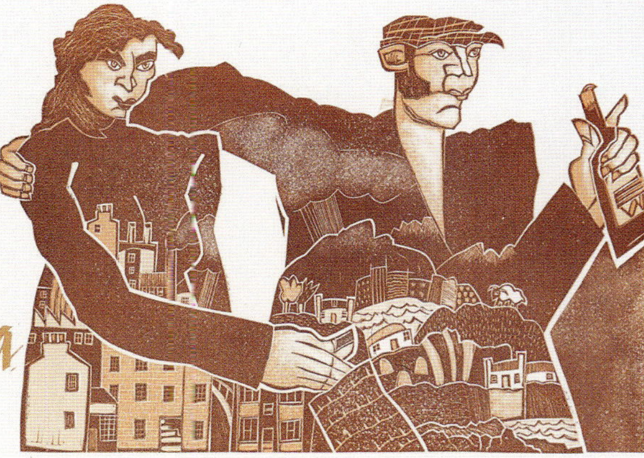

A/P I

TOUGHER

42

MÀIRI MHÒR NAN ÒRAN

MARY MACPHERSON

c. 1821-1898

Neach-ealain/Artist:
Stephen Lawson

Snas-sgrìobhadair/Calligrapher:
Donald Murray

Eadar-theangaichte aig/Translator:
Aonghas Dubh MacNeacail

Roghainn/Nominator:
Aonghas Dubh MacNeacail

Nuair Bha Mi Òg

Moch 's mi 'g èirigh air bheagan èislein
Air madainn Chèitein 's mi ann an Os,
Bha sprèidh a' geumnaich an ceann a chèile,
'S a' ghrian ag èirigh air Leac an Stòrr;
Bha gath a' boillsgeadh air slios nam beanntan,
Cur tuar na h-oidhche na dheann fo sgòd,
Is os mo chionn sheinn an uiseag ghreannmhor,
Toirt na mo chuimhne nuair bha mi òg.

Toirt na mo chuimhne le bròn is aoibhneas
Nach fhaigh mi cainnt gus a chur air dòigh
Gach car is tionndadh an corp 's an inntinn
Bhon dh'fhàg mi 'n gleann 'n robh na suinn gun ghò;
Bha sruth na h-aibhne dol sìos cho tàimhidh
Is toirm nan allt freagairt cainnt mo bheòil,
'S an smeòrach bhinn suidhe seinn air meanglan,
Toirt na mo chuimhne nuair bha mi òg.

Nuair bha mi gòrach a' siubhal mòintich
'S am fraoch a' stròiceadh mo chòta bàn,
Feadh thoman còinnich gun snàthainn a bhrògan
'S an eigh na còsan air lochan tàimh;
A' falbh an aonaich ag iarraidh chaorach
'S mi cheart cho aotrom ri naosg air lòn -
Gach bota 's poll agus talamh-toll
Toirt na mo chuimhne nuair bha mi òg.

Toirt na mo chuimhn' iomadh nì a rinn mi,
Nach faigh mi 'm bann gu ceann thall mo sgeòil -
A' falbh sa gheamhradh gu luaidh is bainnsean
Gun solas lainnteir ach ceann an fhòid;

When I Was Young

In early rising, I'm free of sorrow
on this May morning and I in Os,
one to another the cows are calling,
the sun is rising above the Storr;
a spear of sunlight upon the mountains
saw the last shadow of darkness gone,
the blithesome lark high above me singing
brought back to mind days when I was young.

Brought back to mind with both joy and sadness,
beyond my power to put in words,
each twist and turn felt by mind and body,
since I left the glen where we'd known no guile;
the river rippling so gently seawards,
my own speech echoed in the streamlet's flow,
sweet sang the mavis in budding branches,
brought back to mind days when I was young.

In careless joy I would roam the moorland,
the heather tips brushing my white dress,
through mossy knowes without help of footwear,
or when ice formed ridges on silent lochs;
or on the high moors in search of sheep flocks
light as the snipe over meadow grass,
each mound and pool and rolling hollow
brought back to mind days when I was young.

Brought back to mind all the things I did there,
that will not fade till my story's done,
going in winter to waulkings, wedding,
my only lantern a peat in hand;

(Continued on page 244)

Moch 's mi 'g èirigh air bheagan èislein air madainn Chèitein 's mi ann an Os,
Bha sprèidh a' geumnaich an ceann a chèile, 's a ghrian ag èirigh air Leac an Stòrr;
Bha gath a' boillsgeadh air slios nam beanntan, cur tuar na h-oidhche na dheann fo sgòd
Is os mo chionn sheinn an uiseag ghreannmhor toirt na mo chuimhne nuair bha mi òg.

I early arose one May morning, untroubled by care, while I was in Ose – the cattle lowing, the rising sun on the Storr Rock its rays lighting up the mountain-sides and banishing the shades of night; above me the skylark – reminded me of the days when I was young –

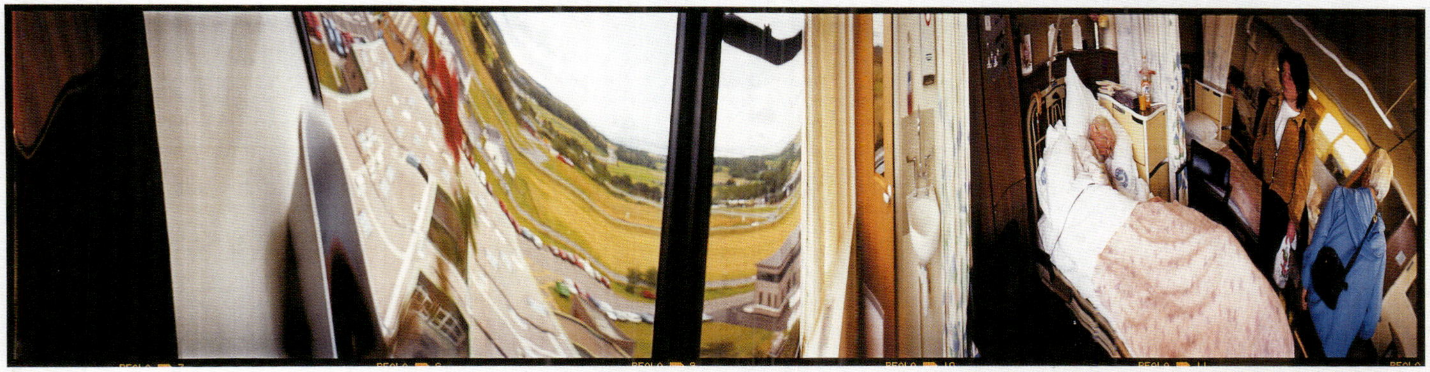

When I turned away from the sweet island, aboard the vessel without sail sounding her note of parting and taking a course away from the land of mist, heartbroken, I was going to a land without joy or music, without thistle or daisy, heather or rush on brae or marsh

Nuair chuir mi cùl ris an eilean chùbhraidh, 's a ghabh mi iùbhrach na smùid gun seòl
Nuair shèid i 'n dùdach 's a shìn an ùspairt, 's a thog i cùrsa o Thìr a' Cheò –
Mo chridhe brùite 's na deòir lem shùilean a' falbh gu dùthaich gun sùrd gun cheòl
Far nach faic mi cluaran no neòinean guanach no fraoch no luachair air bruaich no lòn

43

IAIN MAC A' GHOBHAINN

JOHN SMITH

c. 1848-1881

Neach-ealain/Artist:
Hughie O'Donoghue

Snas-sgrìobhadair/Calligrapher:
Louise Donaldson

Eadar-theangaichte aig/Translator:
Donald E. Meek

Roghainn/Nominator:
Donald MacAulay

Spiorad a' Charthannais (earrann)

O, criothnaich measg do shòlasan,
Fhir-fhòirneirt làidir chruaidh!
Dè 'm bàs no 'm pian a dhòirtear ort
Airson do leòn air sluagh?
'S e osnaich bhròin nam bantraichean
Tha sèid do shaidhbhreis suas;
Gach cupan fìon a dh'òlas tu,
'S e deòir nan ainnis truagh.

Ged thachradh oighreachd mhòr agad
'S ged ghèill na slòigh fod smachd,
Tha 'm bàs is laghan geur aige,
'S gu feum thu gèill da reachd;
Siud uachdaran a dh'òrdaicheas
Co-ionnan còir gach neach,
'S mar oighreachd bheir e lèine dhut
'S dà cheum de thalamh glas.

'S e siud as deireadh suarach dhut,
Thus', fhir an uabhair mhòir,
Led shumanan 's led bhàirlinnean
A' cumail chàich fo bhròn;
Nuair gheibh thu 'n oighreachd shàmhach ud,
Bidh d'àrdan beag gu leòr;
Cha chluinnear trod a' bhàillidh ann
'S cha chuir maor grànd' air ròig.

'N sin molaidh a' chnuimh shnàigeach thu,
Cho tàirceach 's a bhios d'fheòil,
Nuair gheibh i air do chàradh thu
Gu sàmhach air a bòrd;
Their i, ''S e fear mèath tha 'n seo
Tha math do bhiast nan còs,
On rinn e caol na ceudan
Gus e fhèin a bhiathadh dhòmhs'.'

The Spirit of Kindliness (excerpt)

O tremble midst your pleasures,
you oppressor, hard and strong!
What pain or death can justly be
your reward for people's wrongs?
The sorrowful sighs of widows
are what inflates your wealth;
every cup of wine you drink
is the tears of each poor wretch.

Though your estate should be so vast,
and hosts should yield to you,
death has the very strictest laws,
and you must obey its rule.
That's the lord who will ordain
an equal share for all;
he'll grant a shroud as your estate,
and two paces of green sward.

That will be your lowly end,
you man of haughtiest ways,
with your notices and summonses,
keeping others in their pain;
when you receive that quiet estate,
your pride will be cut down;
no factor there will make a row,
nor will a vile officer frown.

Then the crawling worm will praise you,
for the tastiness of your flesh,
when it finds you stretched straight out
on its board without a breath;
it will say, 'This one is plump,
just right for crevice beast,
since he made many hundreds thin
to make for me a feast!'

We have only been able to give an excerpt from this poem. For an alternative source of the full text see the listing on page 265.

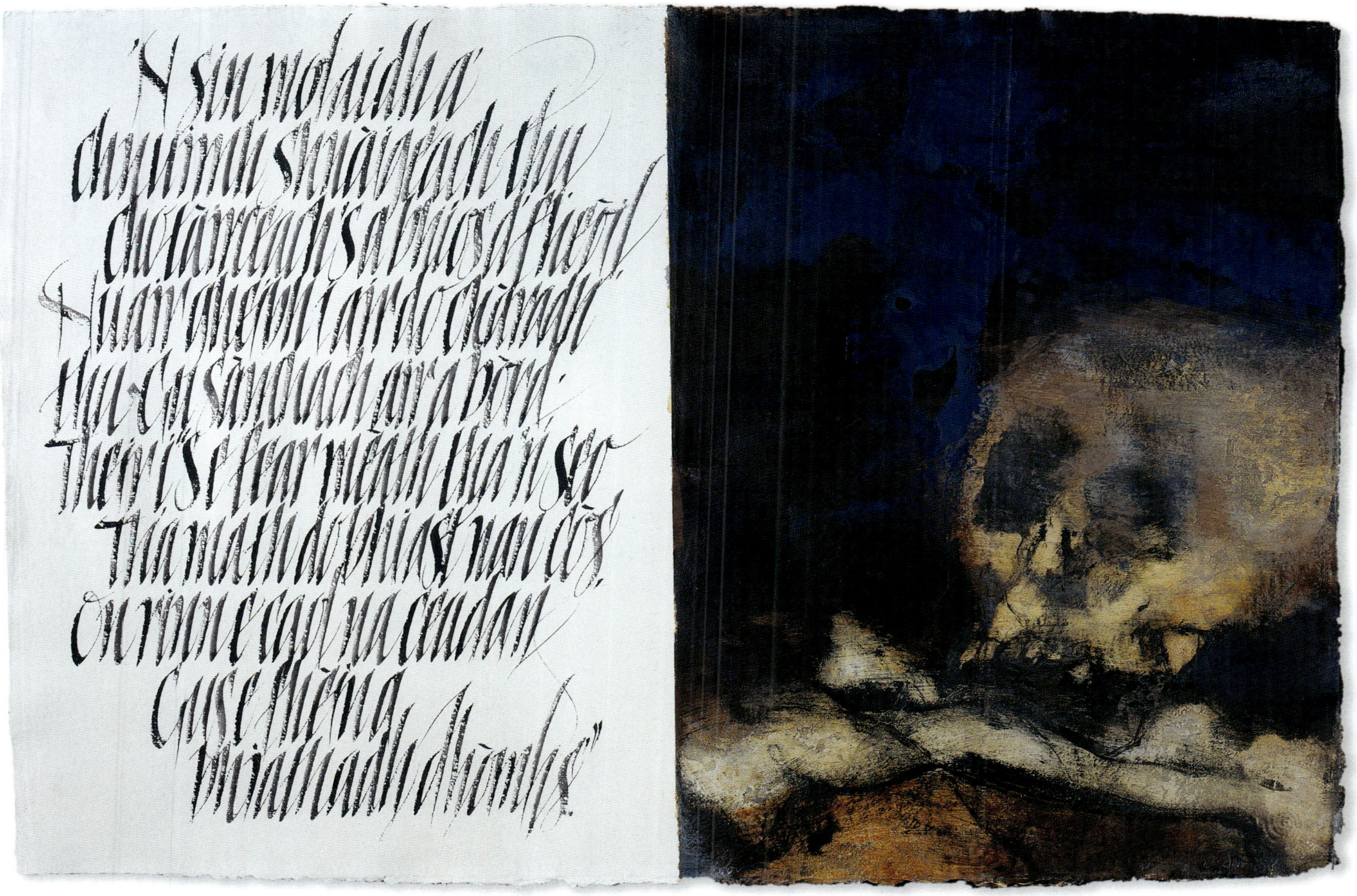

44

DÒMHNALL MAC A' GHOBHAINN

DONALD SMITH

1786-1862

Neach-ealain/Artist:
Noel Sheridan

Snas-sgrìobhadair/Calligrapher:
Ann Bowen

Eadar-theangaichte aig/Translators:
Morag MacLeod, William Matheson

Roghainn/Nominator:
John Murray

Trì Fichead Bliadhna 's a Trì

Trì fichead bliadhna 's a trì, b'e sin an aois mun an robh thu –
cha mhòr tuilleadh a shaoghal tha cuid a dhaoine ri faighinn –
nuair a dh'fhàg thu do dhìlsean, 's b'fhaoin an nì dha do leithid,
gu dhol a ghearradh nan craobhan, och, gus an seann duine chaitheamh.

Bha do cheann 's e air liathadh, bha do chiabhan air glasadh –
obair duine gun chiall a dhol a dh'iarraidh a' bheartais
far nach fhaic thu luchd-eòlais a nì còmhradh le tlachd riut
no nì faighneachd dè 's beo dhut, no bheir lòn dhut an asgaidh.

Cha b'ionnan dhuit fuireach sna Dailean 'g àiteach fearann a' chòmhnaird,
far an itheadh tu 'n t-aran 's far an garadh a' mhòin' thu,
seach a dhol a dh'fhàgail na tìre san d'fhuair do shinnsearan beòshlaint,
far nach goideadh mathan ort caora measg an fhraoich air a' mhòintich.

Bu tu buachaill nan caorach, cas a dhìreadh nam mullach,
's cha bu mhiosa là buain thu togail sguab air an iomair:
'S e sin dh'fhàg mise fo ghruaimean nuair thèid mi suas dhan a' mhuilinn,
's mi faicinn thobhtaichean fàsa far am b'àbhaist dhut fuireach.

Nuair a thigeadh tu 'n bhaile dh'aithnichinn sadadh do làimhe;
nuair a bhitheadh tu cainnt rium, gheibhinn d'inntinn cho làidir:
's e sin dh'fhàg mise gun mhisneachd an uair nach tuigte le càch mi,
's gun fhios o Ailean no Dhòmhnall a bheil thu beò no 'n do bhàsaich.

'S ann agad tha 'n naidheachd ma tha do là air a shìneadh
mun an eaglais a dh'fhàg thu gun nì ach càradh ort d'aodaich,
far an cluinneadh tu briathran o bheul nach fiaradh an fhìrinn,
's tu 'n-diugh measg fhineachan fiadhaich nach cuala diadhachd on sinnsear.

Chan e do bhòidhchead no d'àilleachd a tha mi 'n dràsta ri facain
ach nach fhaic mi gu bràth thu latha Sàbaid no seachdain –
sinn cho fada bho chèile 's tha 'n cruinne-cè 's e cho farsaing,
sinn gun sgrìobhadh gun leughadh, och, gu sgeul a thoir ead'rainn.

Sixty-Three Years

Sixty-three years, that was about your age – some people do not live much longer – when you left your friends (what a foolish thing for someone like you) to go lumberjacking, och, to finish off the old man.

Your head had gone grey, your locks silvered. It was a senseless idea to go looking for wealth where you will see no acquaintances to converse pleasantly with you, or to ask how you are, or to give you food for nothing.

How different if you had stayed in the Dells cultivating the land on the level where you could eat bread, and where the peat would warm you, rather than leave the land where your ancestors got their livelihood – where no bear could steal your sheep, among the heather on the moor.

You were a good shepherd, good at climbing the hills, and you were just as good on a harvest day lifting sheaves in the field. That is why I feel so sad when I go up to the mill to see deserted ruins where you used to live.

When you came to the township I knew the swing of your arm. When you spoke to me I found your mind so made up. That is why I feel so distressed – and no-one else understands it – when there's no word from Alan and Donald whether you are alive or dead.

What a tale you have to tell, if you have enjoyed length of days, about the church you left just to get yourself ready, where you would hear words from a mouth that would not twist the truth. And now you are amongst savage tribes who have not learned Godliness from their forebears.

It is not your handsomeness or your beauty that I lament, but that I shall never see you again on Sabbath or weekday. We are as far apart as the world is wide; we cannot write nor read, oh, to give each other news.

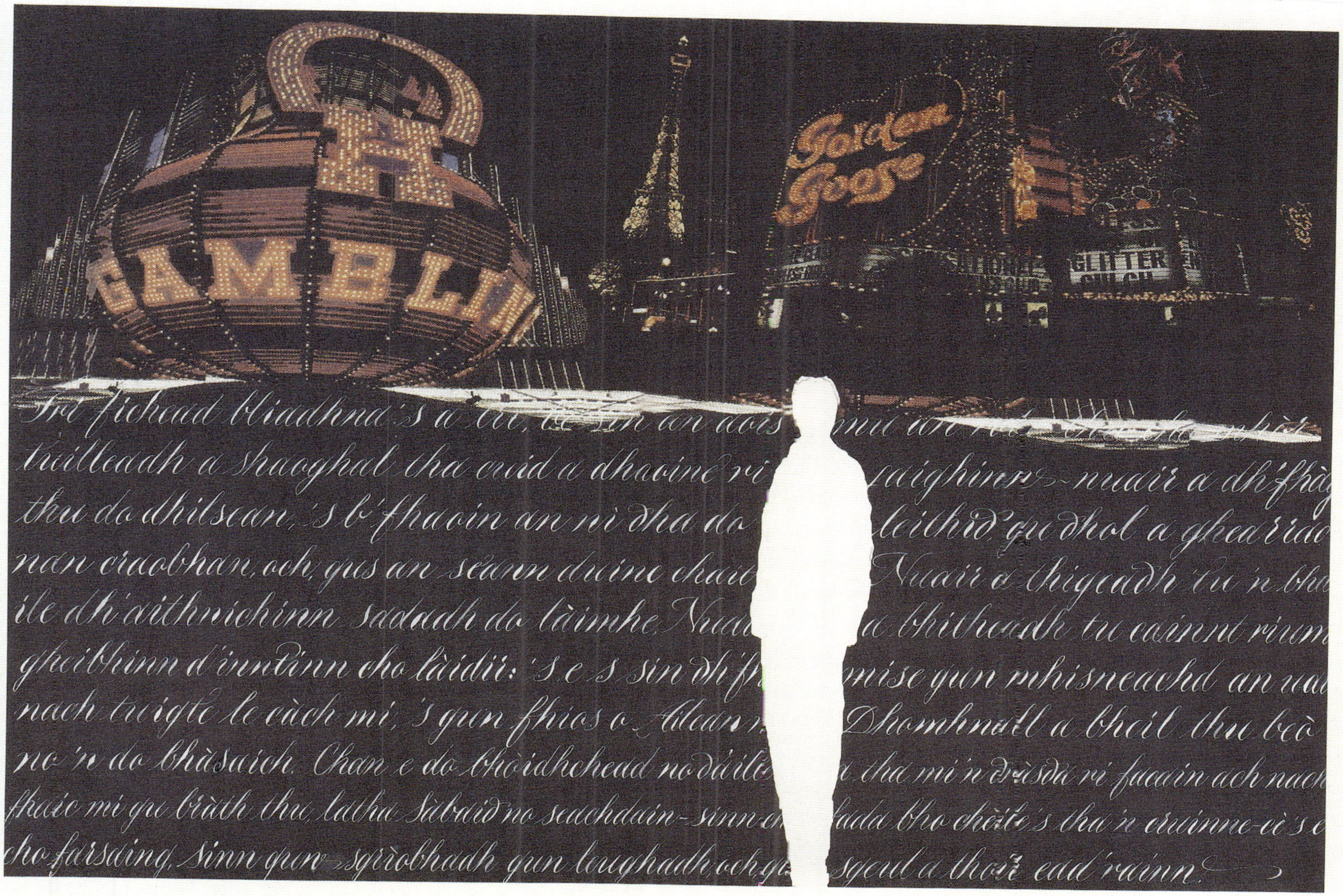
GAMBLIN
Golden Goose
GLITTER GULCH
Trì fichead bliadhna 's a trì, 's e sin an aois
tràilleadh a shaoghal tha cuid a dhaoine ri … faighinn - nuair a dh'fhàg
thu do dhilsean, 's b' fhaoin an nì dha do … leithid' gu dhol a ghearradh
nan craobhan, och, gus an seann duine chaidh … Nuair a thigeadh tu 'n bhad
ile dh'aithnichinn sadadh do làimhe, Nuair … a bhitheadh tu cainnt rium
gheibhinn d' inntinn cho làidir: 'S e 's sin dh'fh… mise gun mhisneachd an uair
nach tuigte le càch mi, 's gun fhios o Ailean m… Dhomhnaill a bheil thu beò
no 'n do bhàsaich. Chan e do bhòidhchead no d'àille … tha mi 'n dràsda ri faicinn ach nach
fhaic mi gu bràth thu, latha Sàbaid no seachdain - sinn … fada bho chèile 's tha 'n cruinne-cè 's e
cho farsaing. Sinn gun sgrìobhadh gun leughadh, och gu … sgeul a thoirt eadarainn.

45

UILLEAM MACDHUNLÈIBHE

WILLIAM LIVINGSTONE

c. 1808-1870

Neach-ealain / Artist:
Anna Davis

Snas-sgrìobhadair / Calligrapher:
Louise Donaldson

Eadar-theangaichte aig / Translator:
Henry Whyte

Roghainn / Nominator:
Christopher Whyte

Fios thun a' Bhàird (earrann)

Tha taighean-seilbh na dh'fhàg sinn
Feadh an fhuinn nan càrnan fuar –
Dh'fhalbh 's cha till na Gàidheil,
Stad an t-àiteach, cur is buain;
Tha stèidh nan làrach tiamhaidh
A' toirt fianais air 's ag ràdh:
Mar a fhuair 's a chunnaic mise,
Thoir am fios seo thun a' Bhàird.

Thoir am fios seo thun a' Bhàird,
Thoir am fios seo thun a' Bhàird;
Mar a fhuair 's a chunnaic mise,
Thoir am fios seo thun a' Bhàird.

Chan fhaigh an dèirceach fasgadh
No 'm fear-astair fois o sgìths,
No soisgeulach luchd-èisdeachd –
Bhuadhaich eucoir, Goill is cìs;
Tha 'n nathair bhreac na lùban
Air na h-ùrlair far an d' fhàs
Na fir mhòra chunnaic mise:
Thoir am fios seo thun a' Bhàird.

Lomadh ceàrn na h-O,
An Lanndaidh bhòidheach 's Roinn MhicAoidh;
Tha 'n Learga ghlacach ghrianach
'S fuidheall cianail air a taobh;
Tha 'n gleann na fhiathair uaine,
Aig luchd-fuath gun tuath, gun bhàrr:
Mar a fhuair 's a chunnaic mise,
Thoir am fios seo thun a' Bhàird.

Tidings to the Bard (excerpt)

Their old, abandoned steadings
Like cold cairns mark the land;
Oh, the Gael are gone for ever,
And their farm-work's at a stand;
Their lonely ruins mouldering
Ever claim our fond regard –
What I hear and see around me
Bring as tidings to the Bard.

Tell the tidings to the Bard;
Tell the tidings to the Bard
All I hear and see around me
Bring as tidings to the Bard.

The needy finds no shelter,
Nor the weary rest at eve;
The preacher finds no people
His glad message to receive.
The spotted snake is twining
On the hearth round which was heard
The stirring tales of heroes –
Bring these tidings to the Bard.

Stripped is the area of Oa,
The Rhinns and lovely Lanndaidh too;
The Learga's sunny hollows
Home to a miserable few;
Green, overgrown the glen is,
No folk, no crops, a hostile guard –
What I hear and see around me
Bring as tidings to the Bard.

We have only been able to give an excerpt from this poem. For an alternative source of the full text see the listing on page 265.

Chan fhaigh an dèirceach fasgadh
No'm fear-astair fois o sgìths,
No soisgeulach luchd-èisdeachd—
Bhuadhaich eucoir, Goill is cìs;
Tha'n nathair bhreac na lùban
Air na h-ùrlair far an d'fhàs
Na fir mhòra chunnaic mise:
Thoir am fios seo thun a' Bhàird.

Lomadh ceàrn na h—o,
An Lanndaidh bhòidheach 's Roinn Mhic Aoidh;
Tha'n Learga ghlacach ghrianach
'S fuidheall cianail air a taobh;
Tha'n gleann na fhiathair uaine,
Aig luchd-fuath gun tuath, gun bhàrr:
Mar a fhuair 's a chunnaic mise,
Thoir am fios seo thun a' Bhàird.

Thoir am fios seo thun a' Bhàird.

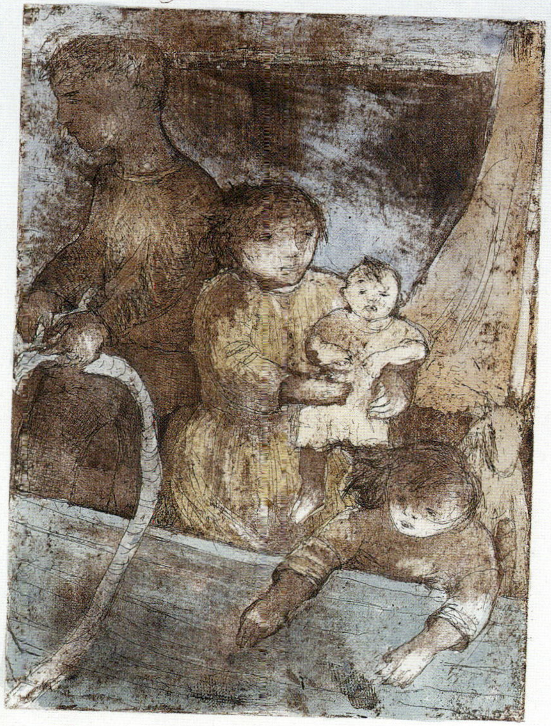

Thoir am fios seo thun a' Bhàird;
Mar a fhuair 's chunnaic mise,
Thoir am fios seo thun a' Bhàird.

46

ANTOIN Ó RAIFTEIRÍ

ANTHONY RAFTERY

c.1779-1835

Ealaíontóir/Artist:
Michael Kane

Peannaire/Calligrapher:
Frances Breen

Aistritheoir/Translator:
Desmond O'Grady

Ainmníodh ag/Nominator:
The Editorial Panel

Máire Ní Eidhin

Ar mo dhul chuig an Aifreann le toil na ngrásta,

Bhí an lá ag cur báistí is d'ardaigh gaoth,

Casadh an ainnir liom le taobh Chill Tartain

Is thit mé láithreach i ngrá le mnaoi.

Labhair mé léi go múinte mánla,

Is de réir a cáilíochta d'fhreagair sí,

'Sé dúirt sí - "Raifteirí, tá m'intinn sásta,

Agus gluais go lá liom go Baile Uí Laí."

Nuair a fuair mé an tairscint níor lig mé ar cairde í,

Rinne mé gáire agus gheit mo chroí,

Ní raibh le dul againn ach trasna páirce

Agus thug sin slán sinn go tóin an tí.

Leagadh chughainn bord a raibh gloine is cárta air,

Is bhí an chúileann fáinneach le m'ais ina suí,

'Sé dúirt sí - "Raifteirí, bí ag ól is céad fáilte,

Tá an siléar láidir i mBaile Uí Laí."

The Lass from Bally-na-Lee

On my way to Mass
To say a prayer,
The wind was high
Sowing rain,
I met a maid
With wind-wild hair
And madly fell
In love again.
I spoke with learning,
Charm and pride
And, as was fitting,
Answered she:
'My mind is now
well satisfied,
So walk with me
To Bally-na-Lee.'
Given the offer,
I didn't delay,
And blowing a laugh
At this willing young lass,
I swung with her over
The fields through the day
Till shortly we reached
The rump of the house.

A table with glasses
And drink was set
And then says the lassie,
Turning to me:
'You are welcome, Raftery,
So drink a wet
To love's demands
In Bally-na-Lee.'

(*Continued on page 245*)

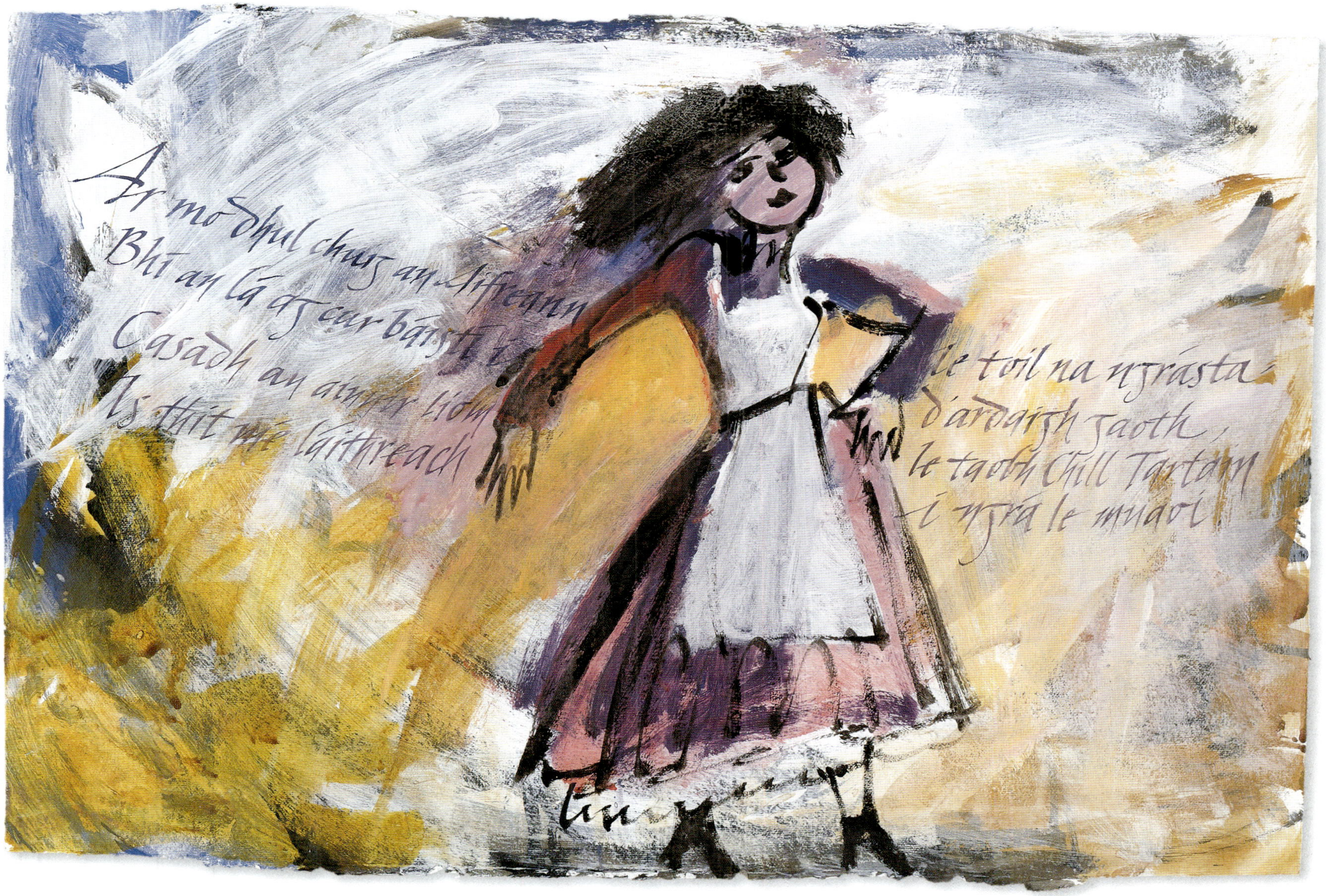
Ar mo dhul chuig an Aifreann
Bhí an lá ag cur báistí
Casadh an ainnir liom
Is thit mé láithreach
le toil na ngrásta
d'ardaigh gaoth,
le taobh Chill Tartain
i ngrá le mnaoi.

47

MÁIRE BHUÍ NÍ LAOIRE

c. 1774-1849

Ealaíontóir/Artist:
Tom Fitzgerald

Peannaire/Calligrapher:
David McGrail

Aistritheoir/Translator:
Colm Breathnach

Ainmníodh ag/Nominator:
Colm Breathnach

Cath Chéim an Fhiadh

Cois abhann Ghleanna an Chéama i nUíbh Laoghaire seadh bhím-se
Mar a dtéigheann an fiadh san oidhche chun síor-chodladh soghail,
Ag machtnamh seal díom féinig ag déanamh mo smaointe
Ag éisteacht i gcoilltibh le binn-ghuth na n-eon;
Nuair a chuala an cath ag teacht aniar,
Glór na n-each ag teacht le sians
Le fuaim an airm do chrith an sliabh
Is níor bhinn linn an glór:
Thánadar go námhadmhar mar a thiocfadh garda de chonaibh nimhe
Is mo chumha-sa na sáirfhir do fágadh fí bhrón.

Níor fhan bean ná páiste i mbun aitribh na tighe aca
Ach na gártha do bhí aca agus mílte ologón,
Ag féachaint ar an ngarda ag teacht láidir 'na dtimcheall
Ag lámhach is ag líonadh is ag scaoileadh 'na dtreo;
An liú gur lean abhfad i gcian,
Sé dubhairt gach flaith gur mhaith leis triall:
'Gluaisidh mear, tá an cath dhá rian
Agus téighmis 'na chomhair';
Thánadar na sáirfhir i gcuim áthais le clannaibh Gaoidheal
Is chomáineadar na páinthigh le fánaidh ar seol.

Is gairid dúinn go dtáinig lámh láidir ár dtimcheall
Do sheol amach ar ndaoine go fíor-mhoch fí'n gceo:
An Barrach 'na bhumbáille, Barnet agus Beecher,
Hedges agus Faoitigh is na mílte eile leo;
Rí na bhfeart go lagaidh iad,
Gan chlú, gan mheas, gan rath, gan séan
I dteinte teasa ameasc na bpian
Gan faeseamh go deo!
Céad moladh mór le hÍosa nár dhíolamair as an dtóir
Ach bheith ag déanamh grinn de is á innsint ar sógh.

The Battle of Keimaneigh

In the valley below Keimaneigh
By the river that flows through Ivleary
Where at night the deer goes
To sleep in pleasant repose
I like to think things out in my head
To sit a while and meditate
Listening to the sweet birds
All singing in the woods
When I heard the soldiers coming
Their horse hooves were drumming
And their noise shook the mountains
A sound grating to the marrow
They came with vicious intent like a pack of venomous hounds from hell
And I pity the fine men they left stretched in sorrow.

No woman or child bided by home or house
But all were out with wails and piteous shouts
Watching the yeomen surrounding them in force
Firing at them as fast as they could reload;
The cry went far and wide for help
They are princes all who answered the call and said
'Get a move on, the battle's under way.
Let's all hurry to the fray.'
There they came those men so brave
Exulting with the great pride of their race
And they drove that paunchy bunch downwards and away.

It wasn't long before a large force had us in a fix
Sending our people out early in the mist.
Barry the bumbailiff, Barnet and Beecher
Hedges and the Whites and a thousand other such creatures
May the God of wonders reduce them
Without fame or standing, prosperity or fortune
In the fires of hell stew them
And without cease abuse them
A thousand thanks to the Son of Man that we escaped the reckoning
And can laugh about that day's rout with each humorous retelling.

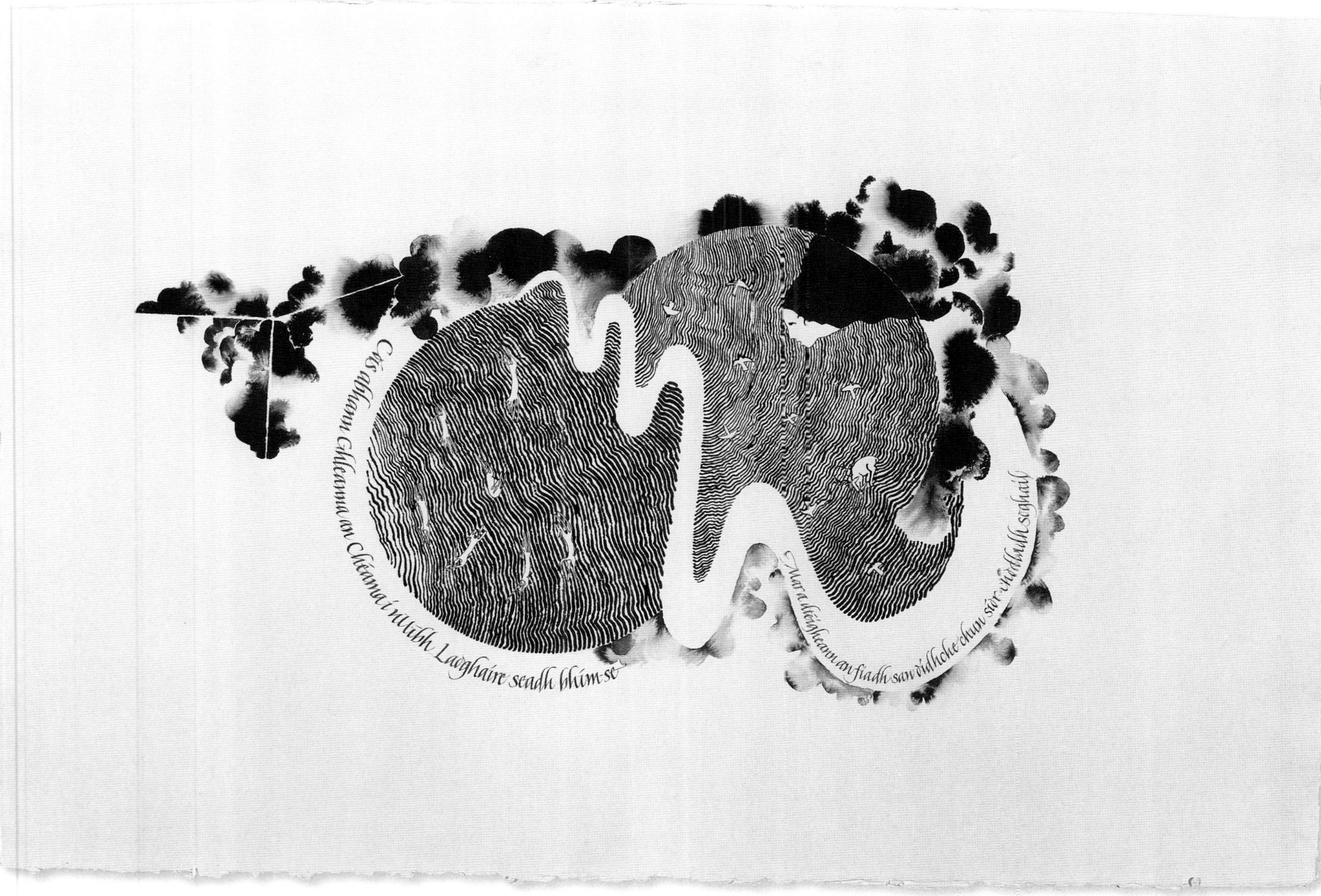
Cois abhann Ghleanna an Chéama i nUíbh Laoghaire seadh bhím-se
Mar a dtéigheann an fiadh san oidhche chun síor-chodladh soghail

48

EOIN MAC AMBRÓIS

JOHN MCCAMBRIDGE

c. 1793-1873

Ealaíontóir/Artist:
Brian Connolly

Peannaire/Calligrapher:
Tim O'Neill

Aistritheoir/Translator:
Aodán Mac Póilín

Ainmníodh ag/Nominator:
The Editorial Panel

Ard a' Chuain

'Á mbeinn phéin in Ard a' Chuain
In aice an tsléibhe úd atá i bhfad bhuam,
A Rí! gurbh aighearach mo chuairt
Go Gleann na gCuach Dé Domhnaigh.

Loinneog ***Agus och, och éirí 'lig is ó***
Éirí lionndubh is ó
'Sé mo chroí atá trom is é leonta.

Is ioma' Nollaig a bhí agam péin
I mBun Abhann Doinne is mé gan chéill,
Ag iomáin ar an tráigh bhán,
Mo chamán bán in mo dhorn liom.

Loinneog

Nach tuirseach mise anseo liom péin,
Nach n-airím guth coiligh, londuibh nó traon',
Gealbhan, smólach, naoscach phéin,
Is chan aithním péin an Domhnach.

Loinneog

Is ioma' amharc a bhí agam péin
Ó Shrón Ghearráin go dtí an Mhaoil
Ar loingeas mór ag cáith ar ghaoith,
Agus cabhlach an Rí Seorlaí.

Loinneog

'Á mbeinn phéin i mBun Abhann Doinne,
Far a bhfuil mo chairdean uile,
Gheobhainn ceol ann, ól is imirt,
Is chan fhaighinn bás in uaigneas.

Loinneog

Mo sheacht mallacht ar an tsaol,
Is caraí é go mór ná an t-éag;
Mheall sé mé ó mo mhuintir phéin,
Mar mheallfaí an t-uan bhón chaora.

Loinneog

'Á mbeadh agam péin ach coit' is rámh,
Ná go n-iomairinn ar dhroim an tsnáimh,
Ag dúil as Dia go ruiginn slán
Is go bhfaighinn bás in Éirinn.

Loinneog

If Only I Were in Articoan

If only I were in Articoan,
Near that mountain that is far away,
O King! my visit would be light-hearted
To the Cuckoos' Glen on Sunday.

Agus och, och éirí 'lig is ó
Éirí lionndubh is ó
My heart is heavy and wounded.

Many's a Christmas I would be,
In Cushendun when [young and] foolish,
Hurling on the white strand,
My white hurl in my hand.

Agus och, etc.

Am I not miserable here by myself,
Not hearing the voice of cock, blackbird or corncrake,
Sparrow, thrush, or even the snipe,
And I do not even recognise Sundays.

Agus och, etc.

Many's the sight that I saw
From Garron Point to the Moyle,
A great fleet driven by the wind;
And King Charlie's armada.

Agus och, etc.

If I were in Cushendun,
Where all my friends are,
I would find music there, drink and games,
And I would not die alone.

Agus och, etc.

My seven curses on the world,
It is more treacherous than death;
It lured me from my own people,
As the lamb would be lured from the sheep.

Agus och, etc.

If only I had a skiff and oar,
I would row upon the flood-tide,
Hoping to God to arrive safely,
So that I will be in Ireland when I die.

Agus och, etc.

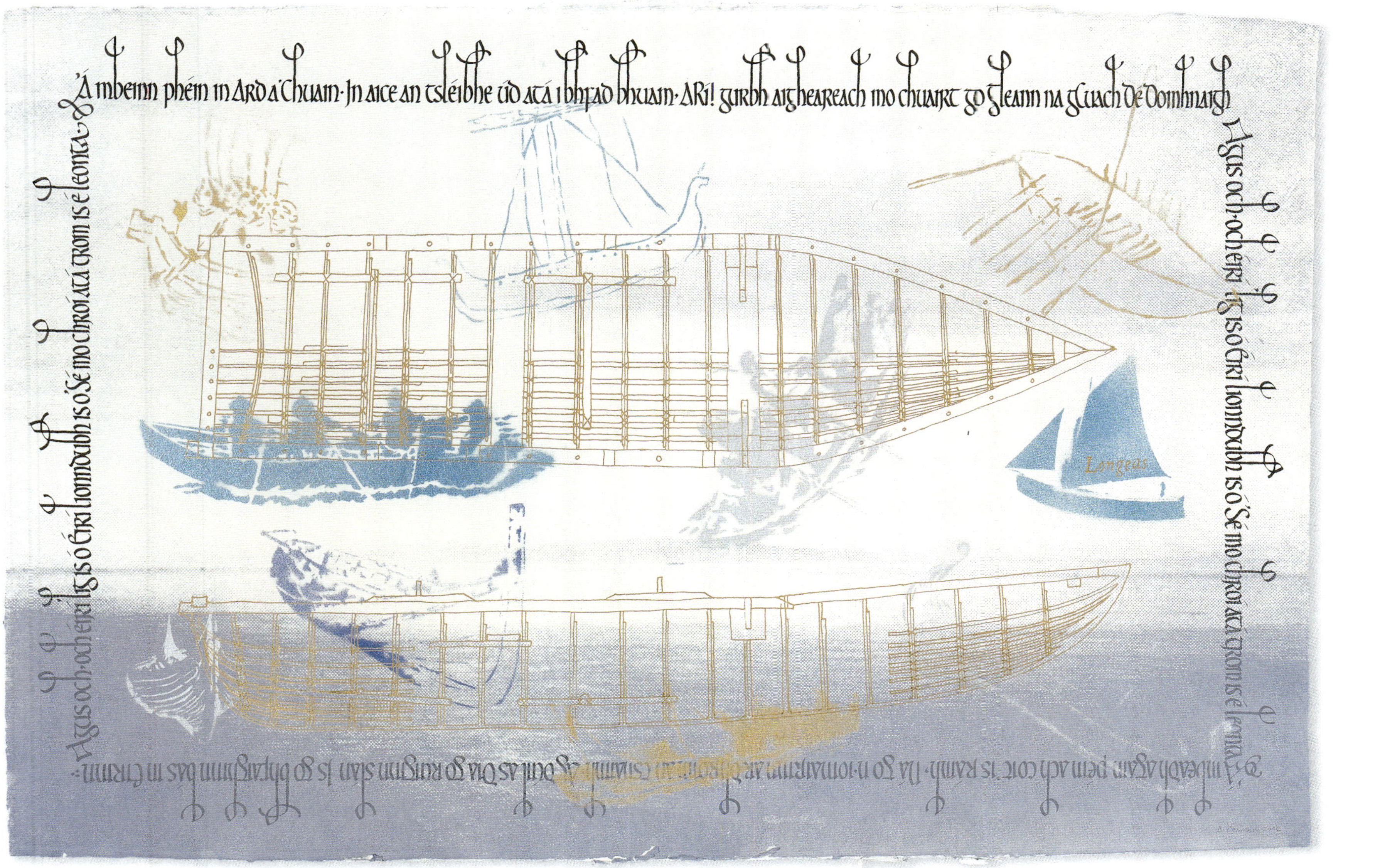
Á mbeinn phéin in Ard a'Chuain · In aice an tsléibhe úd atá i bhfad bhuain · A Rí! gurbh aighearach mo chuairt go Gleann na gCuach Dé Domhnaigh
Longeas

49

DONNCHADH MACDHUNLÈIBHE

DUNCAN LIVINGSTONE

1877-1964

Neach-ealain / Artist:
Mick O'Kelly

Snas-sgrìobhadair / Calligrapher:
The Artist

Eadar-theangaichte aig / Translator:
Ronald Black

Roghainn / Nominator:
Myles Campbell

Bean Dubh a' Caoidh a Fir a Chaidh a Mharbhadh leis a' Phoileas

Baba Inkòsi Sikelele, Baba Inkòsi Sikelele.*
Carson, a Dhè a tha sa chathair,
Carson an-diugh a rinn Thu 'n latha?
  Baba Inkòsi Sikelele, Baba Inkòsi Sikelele.

Mo-nuar gum faca mi a shoillse
Ach a bhith gu bràth san oidhche.
  Baba Inkòsi Sikelele, Baba Inkòsi Sikelele.

Och, mo chràdh, mo chràdh 's mo lèireadh,
An latha thug iad uam mo cheud-ghràdh.
  Baba Inkòsi Sikelele, Baba Inkòsi Sikelele.

Do chorp donn an sin na laighe,
Toll air tholl a' sileadh fala.
  Baba Inkòsi Sikelele, Baba Inkòsi Sikelele.

Am fear bòidheach laigh rim thaobh-sa
An sin 's a mhionach às a' slaodadh.
  Baba Inkòsi Sikelele, Baba Inkòsi Sikelele.

Aichbheil, aichbheil, sgrios is lèireadh
Air an luchd a rinn mo cheusadh.
  Baba Inkòsi Sikelele, Baba Inkòsi Sikelele.

Eisd rim ghuidhean, Rìgh nan Dùilean,
Eisd rim athchuinge 's rim ùrnaigh.
  Baba Inkòsi Sikelele, Baba Inkòsi Sikelele.

Tha 'n luchd bàn an-diugh làn aigheir
'S tha mo phàistean-sa gun athair.
  Baba Inkòsi Sikelele, Baba Inkòsi Sikelele.

Is tha mo bheatha-sa nis falamh -
Ach ceadaich dhomh, mum fàg mi 'n talamh,
  Baba Inkòsi Sikelele, Baba Inkòsi Sikelele.

**Athair, a Thighearna, tèarainn sinn*

A Black Woman Mourns her Husband Killed by the Police

Baba Inkòsi Sikelele, Baba Inkòsi Sikelele.*
Why, O God upon the throne,
Why did you make the day today?
  Baba Inkòsi Sikelele, Baba Inkòsi Sikelele.

Alas that I ever saw its brightness,
I'd rather it were night forever.
  Baba Inkòsi Sikelele, Baba Inkòsi Sikelele.

Oh, my pain, my pain, my torment's
The day they took my first love from me.
  Baba Inkòsi Sikelele, Baba Inkòsi Sikelele.

Your brown body lying before me,
Blood pouring out from wound on wound.
  Baba Inkòsi Sikelele, Baba Inkòsi Sikelele.

The handsome man who lay beside me
There with his intestines trailing loose.
  Baba Inkòsi Sikelele, Baba Inkòsi Sikelele.

Vengeance, vengeance, grief, destruction
On the people who've had me crucified.
  Baba Inkòsi Sikelele, Baba Inkòsi Sikelele.

King of the Elements, hear my oaths,
Listen to my petition and my prayer.
  Baba Inkòsi Sikelele, Baba Inkòsi Sikelele.

Today the whites are full of gladness
And my children have no father.
  Baba Inkòsi Sikelele, Baba Inkòsi Sikelele.

And my life is empty now -
But grant me, while I'm still on earth,
  Baba Inkòsi Sikelele, Baba Inkòsi Sikelele.

**Father, O Lord, save us*

(Continued on page 246)

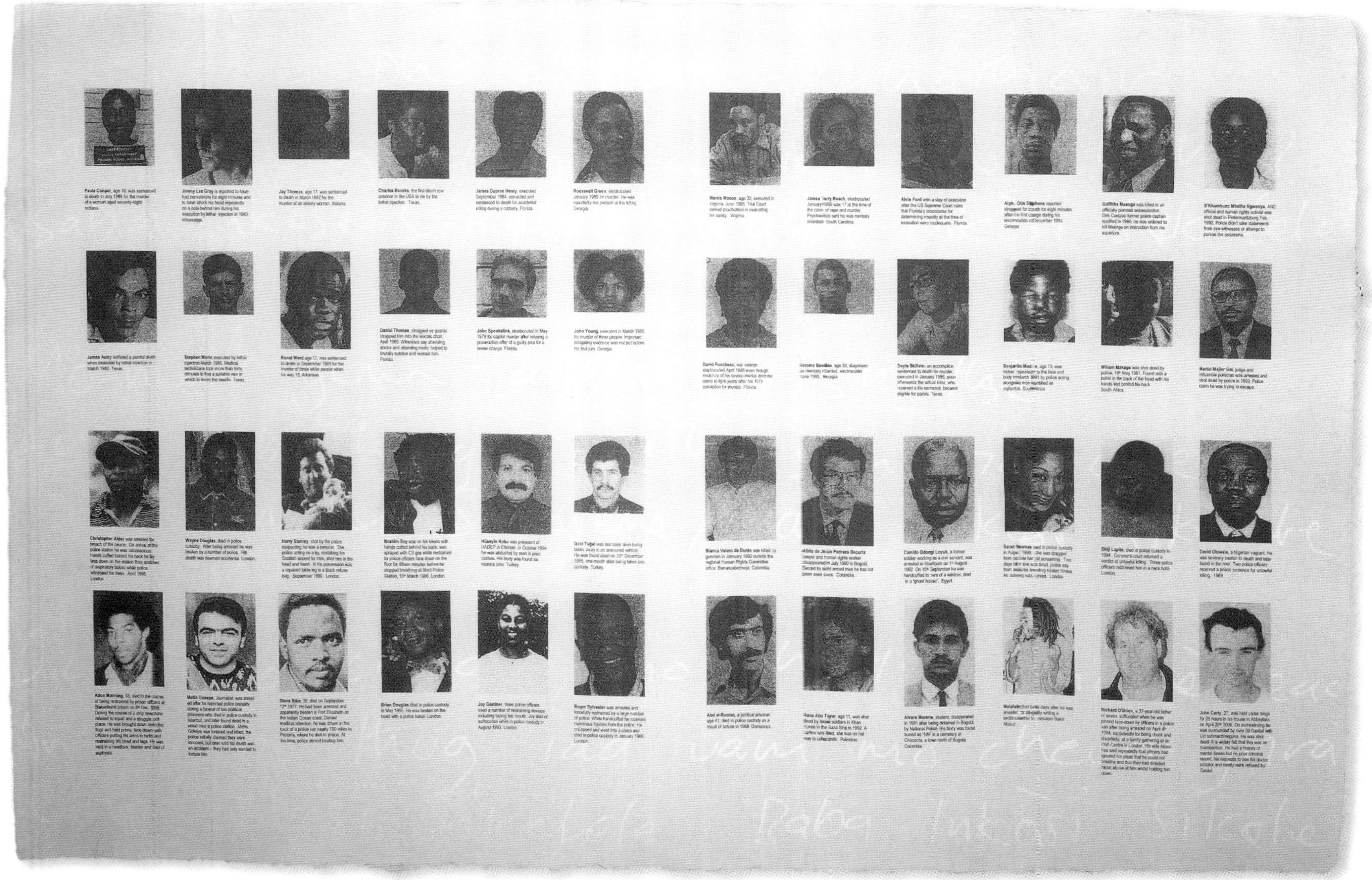

50

MÀIRI NICGUMARAID

MARY MONTGOMERY

b. 1955

Neach-ealain / Artist:
Joanne Breen

Snas-sgrìobhadair / Calligrapher:
Frances Breen

Eadar-theangaichte aig / Translator:
The Author

Roghainn / Nominator:
The Author

Aois Leòdhais

Anns an talamh luasgadh gaoithe
Anns a' ghaoith fasgadh iarmailt
Anns an iarmailt faileas thonn
Anns na tuinn toraidheachd

Thuit do bhruthach dhan allt
Thuit an t-allt dhan abhainn
Ruith an abhainn ris a' bheinn
'S chaill a' bheinn a creag-cridhe

Bha do shamhradh mar do ghlòir
'S bha do dhùthaich na grinneas
Bha do shluagh a' gabhail na grèine
Bu mhath nam maireadh, ma mhaireas idir

'S bu mhath nan seasadh, ma sheasas idir

Agus seasaidh
Seasaidh Leòdhas
Seasaidh Leòdhas ri cearcall beatha
Ged a bhiodh na tuinn a' toradh feòir
'S an t-iasg a' snàmh air na feannagan

The Age of Lewis

In the ground the swelling wind
In the wind the sheltered sky
In the sky the shadowed waves
In the waves fertility

Your bank fell in the stream
The stream fell in the river
The river ran down the mountain
And the mountain lost its heartstone

Your summer was like your glory
And your countryside was green
Your people bathed in sunshine
It would do well to last, if well it lasts

And it would do well to stand, if well it stands

And it will stand
Lewis will
Lewis will stand its life cycle
Though the waves would yield up grass
And the fish swim through the ground

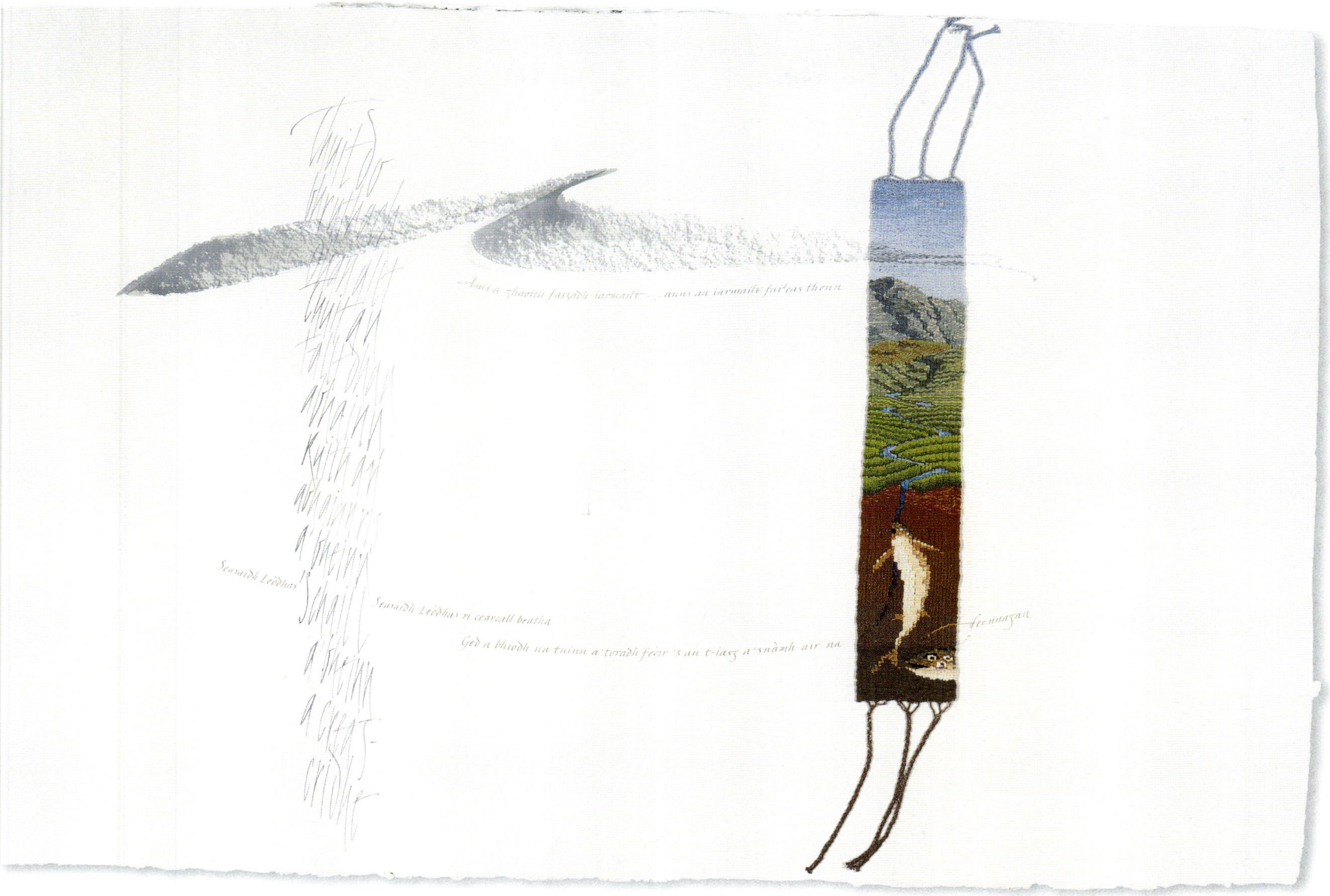
Seasaidh Leòdhas
Seasaidh Leòdhas ri cearcall beatha
Ged a bhiodh na tuinn a' toradh feòir 's an t-iasg a' snàmh air na
feannagan

51

MÒRAG NICGUMARAID

MORAG MONTGOMERY

b. 1950

Neach-ealain / Artist:
Eileen Coates

Snas-sgrìobhadair / Calligrapher:
Réiltín Murphy

Eadar-theangaichte aig / Translator:
The Author

Roghainn / Nominator:
The Author

Coimhead Iad

Coimhead iad
fhathast a' tighinn
ceum air cheum
le eagal nan crìdh'
's iad nan leth-chadal
ach fhathast ag èisdeachd
mar gum bu chòir don
ghaoth tuiteam
agus faclan a ràdh
ann an cogar.

Cha leig an t-eagal leotha tilleadh –
iadsan a tha a' sabaid airson Beatha,
iadsan a tha a' cosg èibhleag an teine
aig an crìdh'.
Rugadh iad don ghrèin
's sheòl iad greiseag ga h-ionnsaigh,
fear an dèidh fir,
ceum air cheum.
'S cha bhi air fhàgail
ach an onair
air a sgrìobhadh
air oiteig gaoithe.

Watch Them

Watch them still returning
one after the other
step by step
with fear in their hearts
but half asleep
yet listening
as though the wind should drop
and speak in a whisper.

Fear won't let them return –
those who are fighting for life,
those who wear the cinder of fire
at their hearts.
They were born to the sun,
and sailed a while towards her,
and will continue towards her,
one after the other –
step by step.
And only their honour is left –
written on a breath of wind.

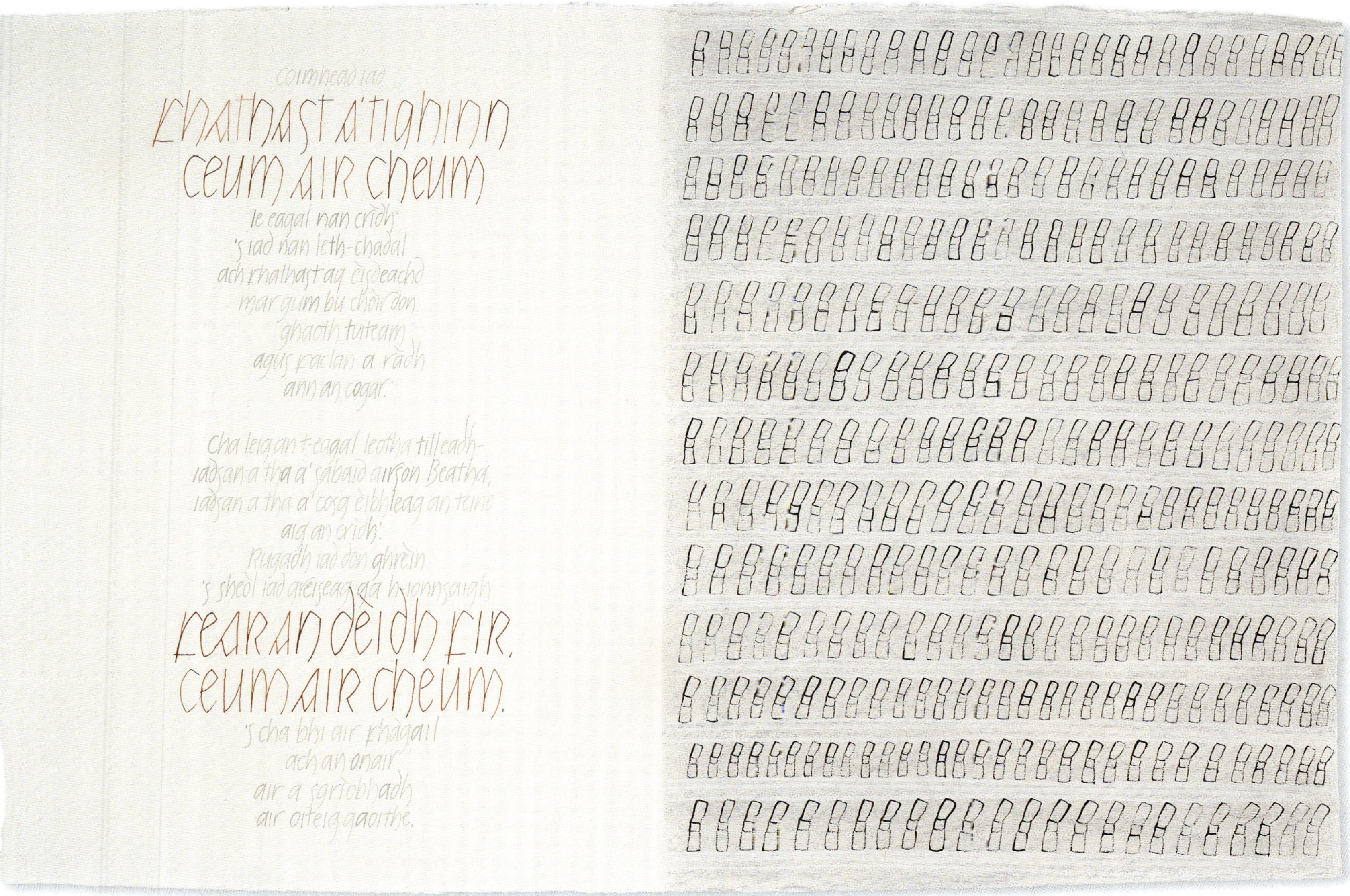
coimhead iad
fhathast a' tighinn
ceum air cheum
le eagal nan cridh'
's iad nan leth-chadal
ach fhathast ag èisdeachd
mar gum bu chòir don
ghaoth tuiteam
agus faclan a ràdh
ann an cogar.
Cha leig an t-eagal leotha tilleadh-
iadsan a tha a' sabaid airson Beatha,
iadsan a tha a' cosg èibhleag an teine
aig an cridh'.
Rugadh iad don ghrèin
's sheòl iad greiseag ga h-ionnsaigh.
fear an dèidh fir,
ceum air cheum.
's cha bhi air fhàgail
ach an onair
air a sgrìobhadh
air oiteag gaoithe.

52

DOMHNALL MACAMHLAIGH

DONALD MACAULAY

b. 1930

Neach-ealain / Artist:
Neil MacPherson

Snas-sgrìobhadair / Calligrapher:
Réiltín Murphy

Eadar-theangaichte aig / Translator:
The Author

Roghainn / Nominator:
The Author

Circeabost: An Ceann a Deas 2000

Shiubhail mi a-raoir as mo chadal
eadar Rubha Taigh Phàil is a' Charadh
is shaothraich mi an t-slighe mhara
air ais mu ghob an Rubha Chaoil,
a' ruith ro ghaoth is sruth carach,
le dìosgail air acfhainn,
dà cheann anns an t-seòl;
ràmh ri taobh an fhasgaidh
a' fannadh a-steach gu caladh
air a' Phort Mhòr …

Is choisich mi an t-suan-shlighe eadar
a' Ghamhnach is Creag a' Bhainne;
lean blas an fhìr-uisg air mo theanga
san direadh chas bho bhun an uillte;
tarsainn air làrach nam muilnean,
air athadach nan taighean –
Tobhta Chaluim Fìdhleir 's Tobhta a' Bhàird
an tasgaidh Cnoc a' Charmaig –
seachad air athadach nan leasan,
air Iodhlainn Chruinn na h-Athadh,
suas gu ruige an t-òs.

'S a-mach air uachdair Loch Mharcoil,
am fasgadh Cnoc a' Chàrnan 's a' Chnuic Mhòir,
a' chuimhne le ceum-neog a' sgaoileadh
a h-àl de chearcaill fhabhdach,
a' turracail seòlaid na h-eala 's na faoileig
's a' togail saoghal na crannlach
is gobha-dubh an uisge mu bhòrd …

Kirkibost: The South End 2000

Last night I made the journey in my sleep
between Paul's House Point and the Weir,
and I worked the sea-passage
back around the tip of the Narrow Point,
running before a veering wind and current,
with creaking of rigging,
the sail two points shortened;
a supporting oar to leeward
inching in to land
in the Broad Haven.

And I walked the sleep-road between
the Milch-Cow and the Milking Rock;
the taste of the fresh water stayed on my tongue
on the steep climb from the outlet of the stream;
over the ruins of the mills
and the remains of the houses –
Calum the Fiddler's site and the Bard's
in Carmaig Hill's safekeeping –
past the ruins of the gardens
and the Circular Cornyard of the Kiln,
up to the stream's outlet.

And out on the surface of Marcol Loch,
sheltered between the Hill of the Cairn and the High Hill,
memory like a skimming-stone spreading
its brood of random waves,
rocking the waterway of the swan and the seagull,
and making contact with the world of the teal
and of the water ousel along its shores.

(Continued on page 246)

is choisich mi
an t-suan-shlighe eadar
a' Ghamhnach
is Creag a' Bhainne;
lean blas an fhìr-uisg
air mo theanga
san dìreadh chas
bho bhun an uillte;

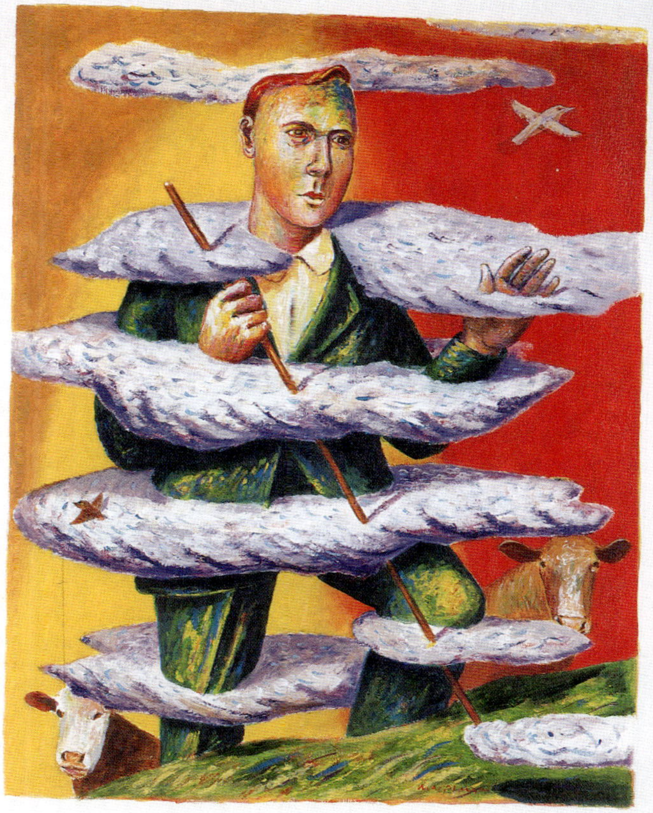

53

IAIN MAC A' GHOBHAINN

IAIN CRICHTON SMITH

1928-1998

Neach-ealain/Artist:
Frances Walker

Clò-bhuailtear/Typographer:
Donald Addison

Eadar-theangaichte aig/Translator:
The Author

Roghainn/Nominator:
Donald MacAulay

Aig a' Chladh

Chunna mi aig a' chladh an-dè iad,
Le adan dubh orr', 's grian ag èirigh,
Deàrrsadh dhìtheanan mun casan,
Is fear a' caitheamh searbh-lèine.

Lasair an adhair, cuan a' seinn,
Dòrtadh fheur, is seasmhachd bheann,
Còmhradh bàsmhor adan dorcha,
Bàrdachd samhraidh bun-os-cionn.

Latha farsaing fad' air fàire,
Bìoball a' losgadh ann an làmhan
Gaoithe 's grèine, 's cuan a' tuiteam
Mar dheise fhalamh air an tràigh ud.

'S tha esan a-nise far a bheil e,
Mo nàbaidh na laighe fon t-seillean
A' crònan am measg dhìthean milis.
B' e 'm bàs a thug bàs dha 's cha b' e 'm peileir.

Is grian a' dòrtadh, cuan a' dòrtadh,
Adan dubh' gu dorch a' seòladh
Air cuan ròsan mar a dh'fhalbhas
Facail bhochd air làn na ceòlraidh.

At the Cemetery

I saw them yesterday at the cemetery
Wearing black hats, while a sun was rising,
A glowing of flowers about their feet
And one wearing a salt shirt.

Glitter of the sky, sea singing,
Pouring of grass, steadiness of mountains,
Mortal conversation of black hats,
Poetry of summer topsy-turvy.

A long wide day on the horizon,
A Bible burning in the hands
Of wind and sun, and a sea falling
Like an empty dress on that shore.

But he is now where he is,
My neighbour lying under the bee
That is humming among sweet flowers.
It was death that killed him and not the bullet.

Sun pouring, sea pouring,
Black hats darkly sailing
On a sea of roses as there sail
Poor words on a full tide of music.

IAIN MAC A' GHOBHAINN

Aig a' Chladh

Chunna mi aig a' chladh an-dè iad,
Le adan dubh orr', 's grian ag èirigh,
Deàrrsadh dhìtheanan mun casan,
Is fear a' caitheamh searbh-lèine.

Lasair an adhair, cuan a' seinn,
Dòrtadh fheur, is seasmhachd bheann,
Còmhradh bàsmhor adan dorcha,
Bàrdachd samhraidh bun-os-cionn.

Latha farsaing fad' air fàire,
Bìoball a' losgadh ann an làmhan
Gaoithe 's grèine, 's cuan a' tuiteam
Mar dheise fhalamh air an tràigh ud.

'S tha esan a-nise far a bheil e,
Mo nàbaidh na laighe fon t-seillean
A' crònan am measg dhìthean milis.
B 'e 'm bàs a thug bàs dha 's cha b 'e 'm peileir.

Is grian a' dòrtadh, cuan a' dòrtadh,
Adan dubh' gu dorch a' seòladh
Air cuan ròsan mar a dh'fhalbhas
Facail bhochd air làn na ceòlraidh.

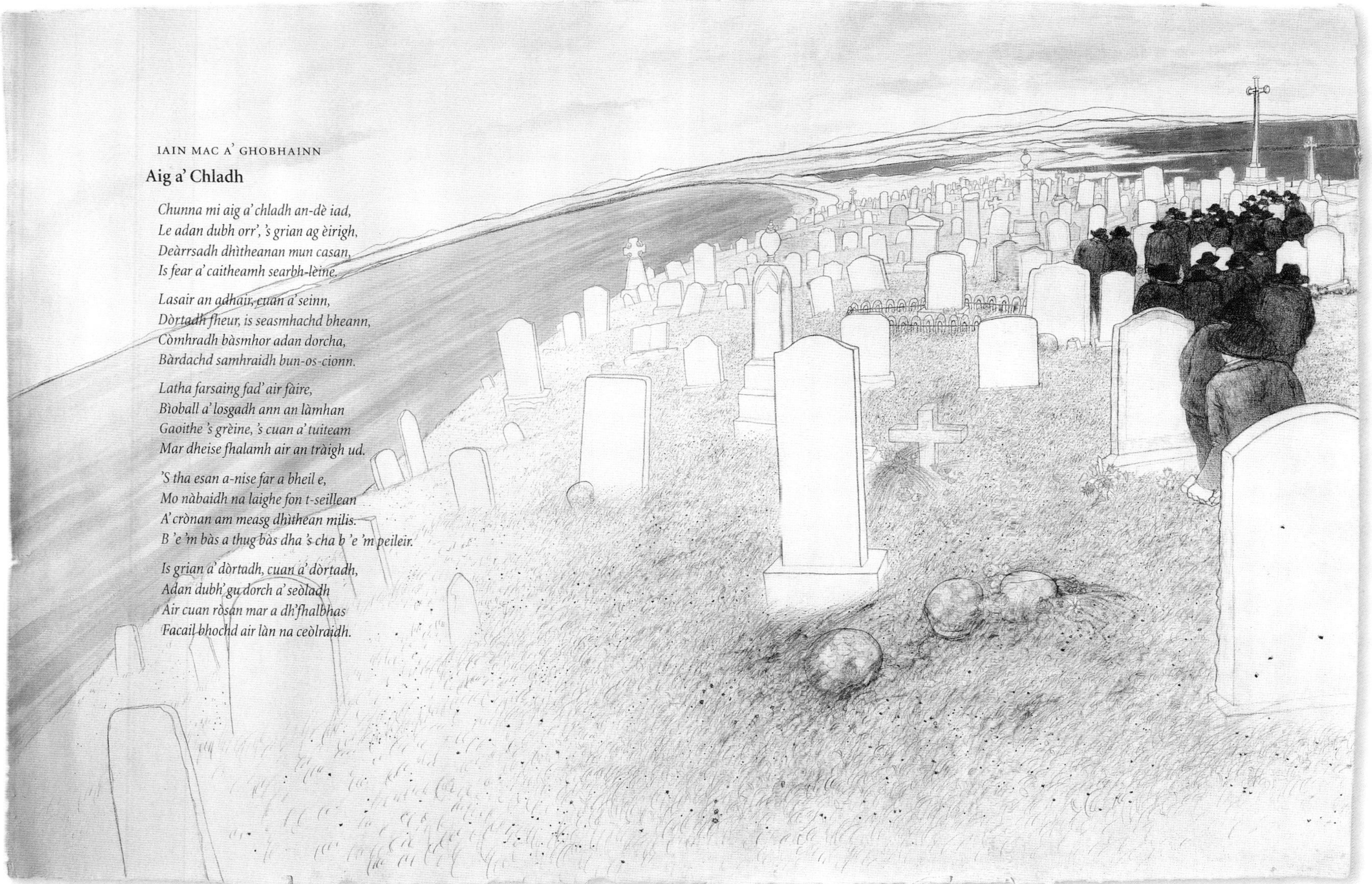

54

FEARGHAS MACFHIONNLAIGH

b. 1948

Neach-ealain / Artist:
Katherine Boucher-Beug

Snas-sgrìobhadair / Calligrapher:
Donald Murray

Eadar-theangaichte aig / Translator:
The Author

Roghainn / Nominator:
The Author

An Tuagh

thàinig e oirbh mar shròn-adharcach na dheann
is sibh a' feitheamh
mar Shùlu le sleagh

thàinig e oirbh mar tharbh
is sibh a' feitheamh
mar mhatador le claidheamh

thàinig e oirbh mar thanca
is sibh a' feitheamh
mar shaighdear le greinèid

thàinig e oirbh mar dhràgon
is sibh a' feitheamh (gu h-ìoranta, tha fhios)
mar an Naomh Seòras

thàinig e oirbh le ulfhartaich chon is Talai-hò
ach bu sionnach sibh
nach teicheadh

thàinig e oirbh mar dhìneosor
ach b'ainmhidh ùr sibh
le Einstein nur ceann

thàinig e oirbh mar locomòtaibh fo smùid
is sibh mar dhrochaid
an impis èirigh

thàinig e oirbh
le àrdan Napoleon,
le gaoir-chatha Genghis Khan
le tàir-chainnt Hiotlair fhèin
le an-iochd Stailinn
le ìmpireachas Shasainn
le bodhaig de Bohuin

The Axe

he came at you like an angry rhino
and you waiting
like a Zulu with a spear

he came at you like a bull
and you waiting
like a matador with a sword

he came at you like a tank
and you waiting
like a soldier with a grenade

he came at you like a dragon
and you waiting (ironically of course)
like Saint George

he came at you with a baying of hounds and Tally-ho
but you were a fox
that would not run

he came at you like a dinosaur
but you were a subtle creature
with Einstein in your brain

he came at you like a locomotive under steam
and you like a bridge
about to rise

he came at you
with the hauteur of Napoleon
with the battle-cry of Genghis Khan
with the vituperation of Hitler himself
with the brutality of Stalin
with the imperialism of England
with the body of de Bohun

(Continued on page 247)

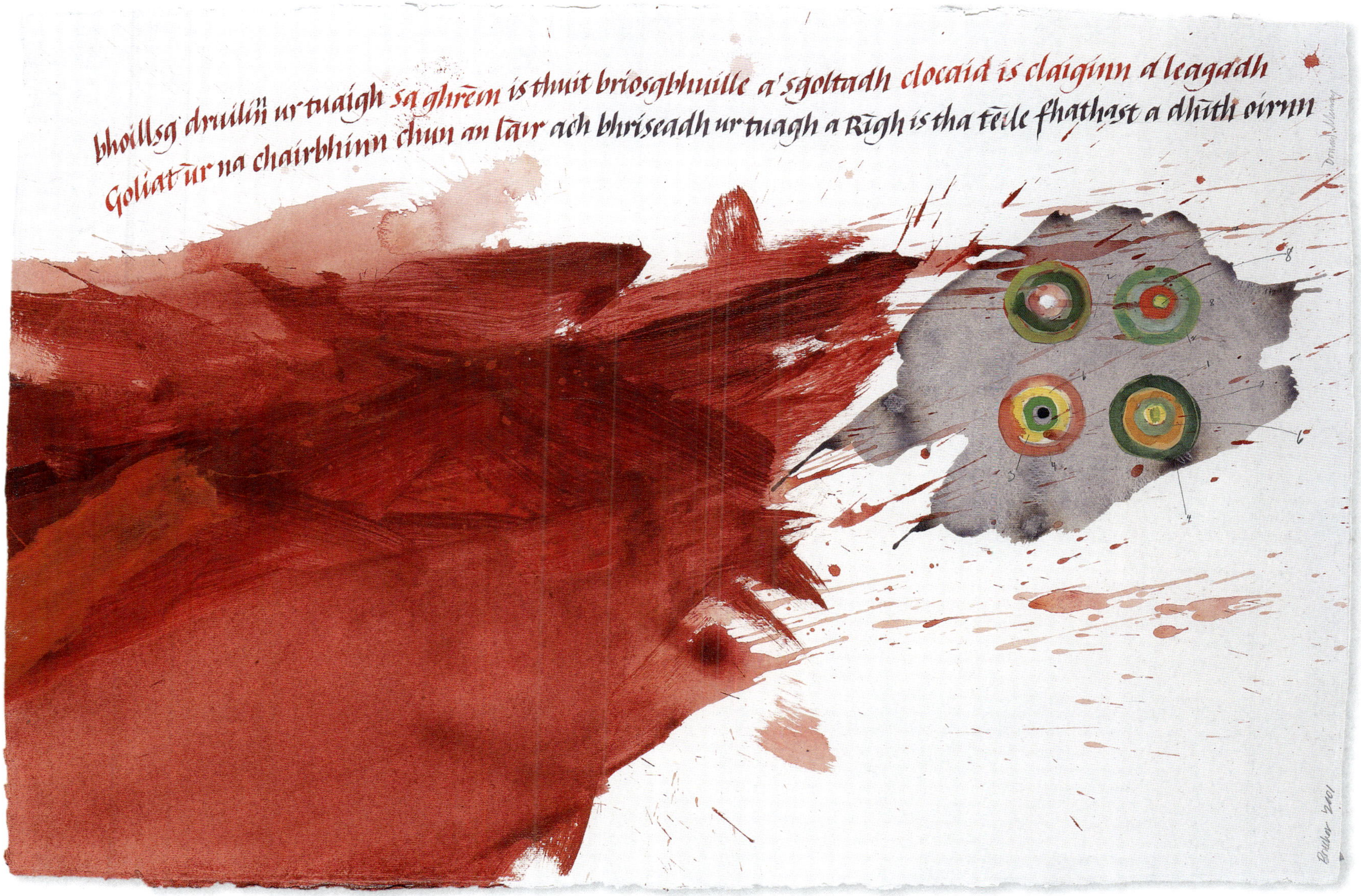
bhoillsg druilinn ur tuaigh sa ghrēim is thuit briosgbhuille a' sgoltadh clocaid is claiginn a leagadh
Goliat ūr na chairbhinn chun an lāir ach bhriseadh ur tuagh a Rīgh is tha tēile fhathast a dhūth oirnn

55

AONGHAS DUBH MACNEACAIL

b. 1942

Neach-ealain / Artist:
Will Maclean

Snas-sgrìobhadair / Calligrapher:
Frances Breen

Eadar-theangaichte aig / Translator:
The Author

Roghainn / Nominator:
The Author

na thàinig anns a' churach ud

caith a h-uile clach gu làr,
leig leis an luibhe fàs –
tha anail fhathast san fhonn

mùch an teanga le smachd,
cùm an aigne fo dheachd –
srad dùbhlain fhathast sa chom

chan fhaighear sruth
nach giùlain soitheach

cuir pòr, mar chuimhne,
anns an t-soitheach

mar anail sluaighe
anns an t-soitheach

a' giùlain dachaigh
anns an t-soitheach

à doire àrd
nan darach ruighinn
thàinig coinneal sìl
sa churach sheang

bu cholum soitheach
dhan an t-sìol
a thàinig thar
na maoile nall

bhrùchd an sìol a-mach
air leathad 's lios
na dhuilleach gorm,
mar dhannsair dàn

bu siud an sruth
a sgaoil tron tìr

chaidh cainnt na tuath
air feadh na tìr

all that came in that one coracle

cast every stone to the ground,
let the weeds grow wild –
there's a breath remains in the earth

still the tongue with force,
keep the mind oppressed –
the body will not be a corpse

every current
will carry a vessel

put a seed, like memory,
into the vessel

like the breath of a people
in the vessel

carrying a home
in the vessel

from high derry
of tenacious oaks
a seed-candle came
in the slender coracle

a dove was vessel
for the seed
that came across
the bald-browed sea

that seed burst out
on slope and lawn,
its green green leaves
like a dancer, bold

that was the stream
spread through the land

a people's words
went through the land

(Continued on page 247)

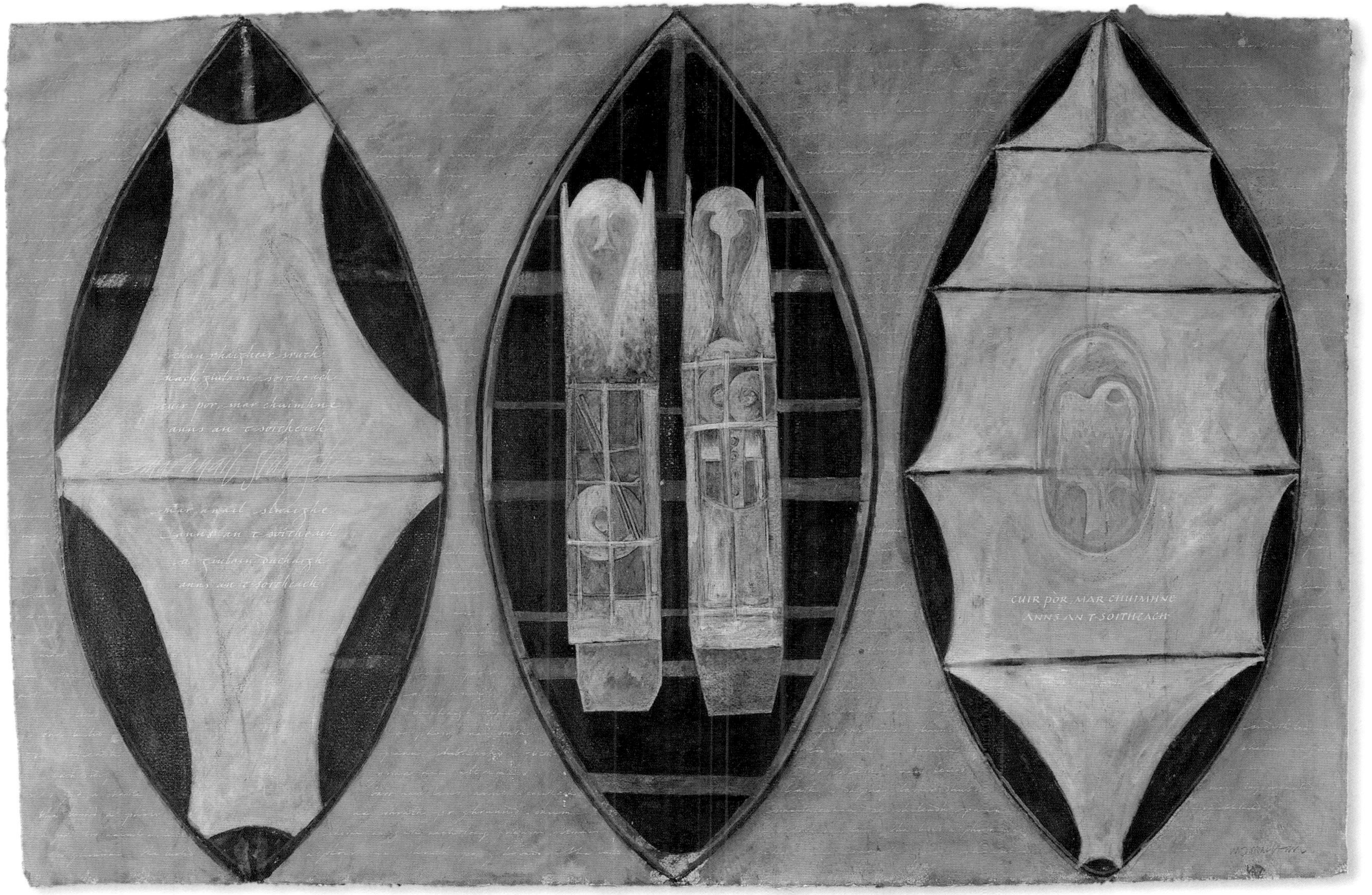
CUIR POR MAR CHUIMHNE
ANNS AN T-SOITHEACH

56

UILLEAM NÈILL

WILLIAM NEILL

b. 1922

Neach-ealain / Artist:
Stan Clementsmith

Snas-sgrìobhadair / Calligrapher:
Réiltín Murphy

Eadar-theangaichte aig / Translator:
The Author

Roghainn / Nominator:
The Author

Dè a Thug Ort Sgrìobhadh sa Ghàidhlig?

Theirinn gum bu dual domh sin –
dòch' gur h-e Bhaltair Mòr as coireach,
sgeadaichte gu lèir sa bhreacan
ged nach bu spìocach e mu bhriogais;
b' e *gluntow wi giltin hippis,*
ag èigheach 'Suas leis a' Ghàidhlig'
mus robh an Comunn idir againn
's a' Bheurla mhòr a' tighinn don fhasan
an Cathair cheòthaich mhòir Dhùn Eideann –
bu chaomh le Uilleam an t-àite sin
is e ag ràdh *ane lawland ers*
wad mak a better noyis, ma-tha.

Greitand doun in Gallowa
mar bu dual don *gallow breid*
a' dranndail is a' canntaireachd
le *my trechour tung*, gun teagamh
that *hes taen ane heland strynd.*

A' siùbhal dùthaich Chinneide
bho 'Carrick tae the Cruives o Cree',
mur eil luchd-labhairt eile ann,
O, horò, nach bithinn sùgrach
bruidhinn ris gach craoibh a th' innte.

Nach b' fheàrr dhomh mo neart a chur
gu sgrìobhadh Beurla Lunnainn shlàn,
's gum faighinn leabhar bàrdachd beag
is e le còmhdach cruaidh glan
na bhith a' toirt *the Carrick clay*
to Edinburgh Cors, a ghràidh.

What Compelled You to Write in Gaelic?

I would say that was my right,
likely Walter Mor's to blame,
dressed up in the Gaelic fashion,
though not mean about the breeches;
he went bare-kneed with saffron hippings
shouting 'Up with the Gaelic'
before An Comunn was with us at all,
and posh English coming into fashion
in the big smoky city of Edinburgh,
a place that Will (Dunbar) much liked
and he saying that *one Lowland arse*
would make a better noise indeed.

Grumbling down in Galloway
the habit of yon gallows breed,
muttering and deedling
with my traitor tongue, doubtless,
that has taken a Highland twist.

Travelling in Kennedie's country
from 'Carrick to the Cruives of Cree',
if I find no other speakers (of Gaelic)
O horo won't I be joyful
speaking to each tree that's there.

Would it not have been better to spend my powers
writing faultless London English,
so I could get a little poetry book
with clean hard covers on it,
than that I bring the Carrick clay
to Edinburgh Cross, my dear.

(Continued on page 248)

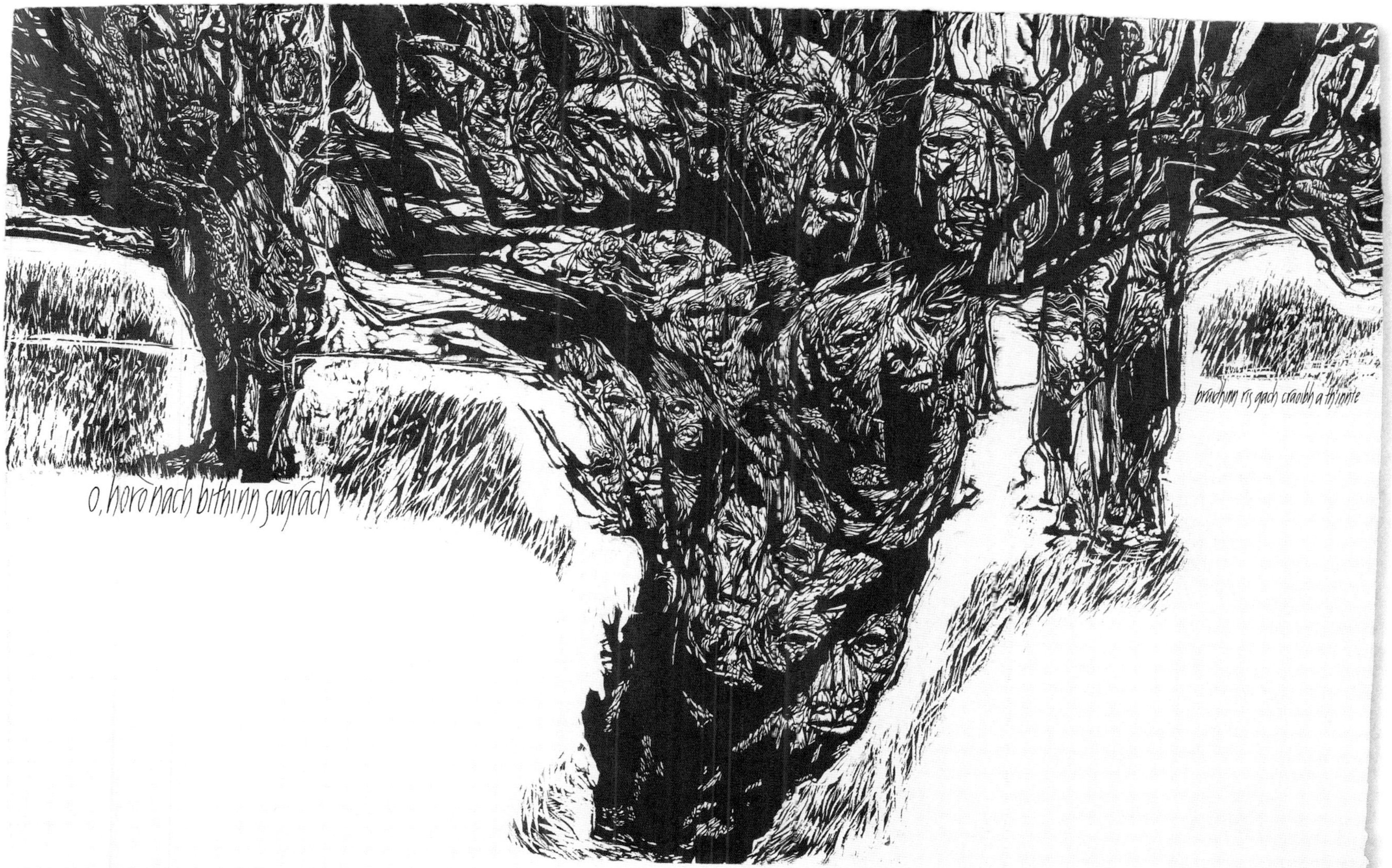
bruidhinn ris gach craoibh a th'innte
o, horò nach bithinn sugrach

57

RUARAIDH MACTHÒMAIS

DERICK S. THOMSON

b. 1921

Neach-ealain/Artist:
Flòraidh MacKenzie

Snas-sgrìobhadair/Calligrapher:
The Artist

Eadar-theangaichte aig/Translator:
The Author

Roghainn/Nominator:
The Author

An Turas

Ann an doras a' *Chaley*
thachair E rium
's dh'fhaighnich E dhiom
a robh mi ag iarraidh slàinte.
Bhà, iomadach slàinte.

Agus ann an doras a' *Chrown*
chuala mi 'n Nàmhaid aig mo ghualainn
ag ràdh "Seachainn seo,"
ach cha do dh'èisd mi ris an Nàmhaid.

Ann an doras a' *Star*
chunna mi sealladh de Bhetlehem
's dhùin mi mo shùilean.

Ann an doras a' *Charlton*
cha d'rinn mi àicheadh air mo ghràdh dhut

Ann an doras a' *Chlub*.

An oidhch' ud ann an Ibrox,
an solas a' ciar-bhuidheadh air a staidhre,
an aol gun tiormachadh,
's na taighean-seinns' air sgaoileadh,
chuimhnich mi air tè dha m' fheadhainn
ann a Singapore
nach bu bhuidhe dhomh.

Dearg, dearg tha fuil mo bheatha,
sin an fhuil anns a bheil slàint,
nuair a laigheas làn a' bhotail
air mo sgòrnan anns a' mhadainn
tha e mar gun d'fhuair mi gràs,
dearg, dearg tha fuil a' bhotail
air mo chuisle, fuil mo ghràidh.

The Journey

At the door of the *Caley*
He met me
and asked me
if I was seeking for health.
Yes, many healths.

And at the door of the *Crown*
I heard the Devil at my shoulder
saying 'Pass this by',
but I did not listen to the Devil.

At the door of the *Star*
I saw a vision of Bethlehem
and I closed my eyes.

At the door of the *Carlton*
I did not deny my love for you

At the door of the *Club*.

That night in Ibrox,
the lights dun-yellow on the stair,
the pipe-clay not quite dry,
after the pubs had skailed
I remembered a girl I had
in Singapore –
she wasn't a lucky omen.

Red, red is my life's blood,
that's the blood that's full of health,
when the brimming bottle lies
on my gullet in the morning
then I feel I've found grace,
red, red is the bottle's blood
on my veins, the blood I love.

(Continued on page 249)

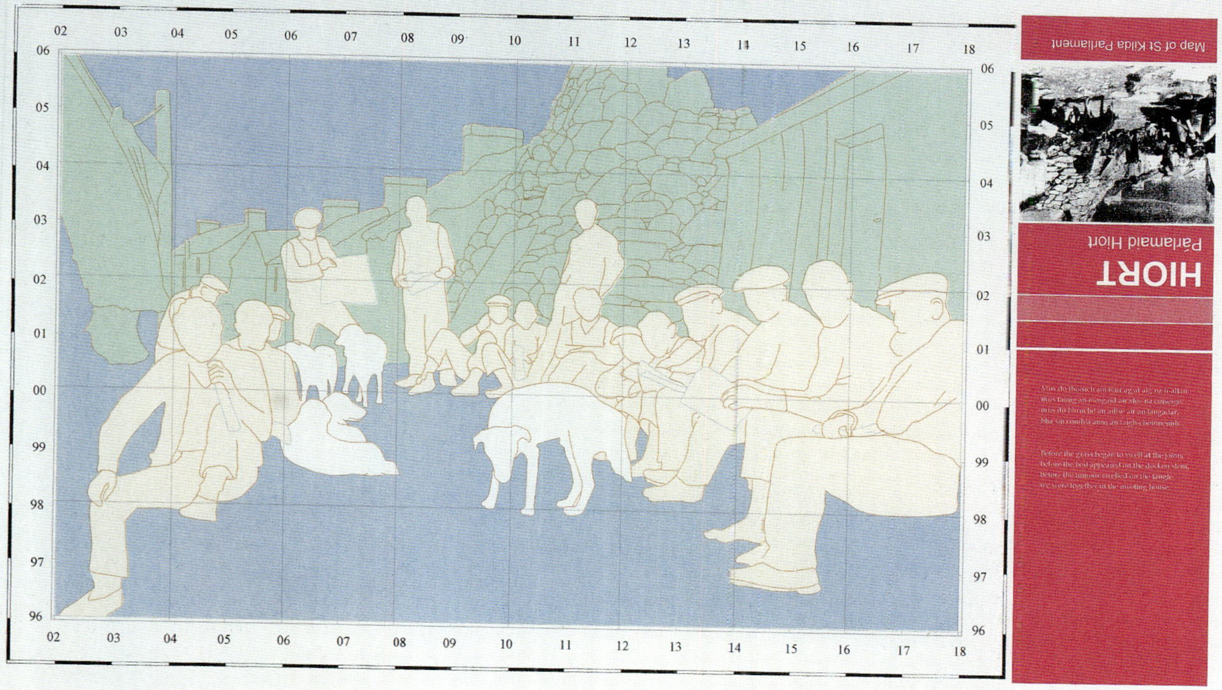
Map of St Kilda Parliament
HIORT
Párlamaid Hiort

58

DEÒRSA MAC IAIN DEÒRSA

GEORGE CAMPBELL HAY

1915-1984

Neach-ealain/Artist:
Iain McCulloch

Clò-bhuailtear/Typographer:
Donald Addison

Eadar-theangaichte aig/Translator:
The Author

Roghainn/Nominator:
Derick S. Thomson

Bisearta

Chì mi rè geard na h-oidhche
Dreòs air chrith 'na fhroidhneas thall air fàire,
A' clapail le a sgiathaibh,
A' sgapadh 's a' ciaradh rionnagan na h-àird' ud.

Shaoileadh tu gun cluinnte,
Ge cian, o 'bhuillsgein ochanaich no caoineadh,
Ràn corraich no gàir fuatha,
Comhart chon cuthaich uaith' no ulfhairt fhaolchon,
Gun ruigeadh drannd an fhòirneirt
On fhùirneis òmair iomall fhèin an t-saoghail.
Ach siud a' dol an leud e
Ri oir an speur an tostachd olc is aognaidh.

C' ainm nochd a th' orra,
Na sràidean bochda anns an sgeith gach uinneag
A lasraichean 's a deatach,
A sradagan is sgreadail a luchd-thuinidh,
Is taigh air thaigh ga reubadh,
Am broinn a chèile am brùchdadh toit' a' tuiteam?
Is cò a-nochd tha 'g atach
Am bàs a theachd gu grad 'nan cainntibh uile,
No a' spàirn measg chlach is shailthean,
Air bhainidh a' gairm air cobhair, is nach cluinnear?
Cò a-nochd a phàigheas
Seann chìs àbhaisteach na fala cumant'?

Uair dearg mar lod na h-àraich,
Uair bàn mar ghile thràighte an eagail èitigh,
A' dìreadh 's uair a' teàrnadh,
A' sìneadh le sitheadh àrd 's a' call a mheudachd,
A' fannachadh car aitil
'S ag at mar anail dhiabhail air dhèinead,

Bizerta

I see during the night guard
A blaze flickering, fringing the skyline over yonder,
Beating with its wings,
and scattering and dimming the stars of that airt.

You would think that there would be heard
From its midst, though far away, wailing and lamentation,
The roar of rage and the yell of hate,
The barking of the dogs from it or the howling of wolves,
That the snarl of violence would reach
From yon amber furnace the very edge of the world;
But yonder it spreads
Along the rim of the sky in evil ghastly silence.

What is their name tonight,
The poor streets where every window spews
Its flame and smoke,
Its sparks and the screaming of its inmates,
While house upon house is rent
And collapses in a gust of smoke?
And who tonight are beseeching
Death to come quickly in all their tongues,
Or are struggling among stones and beams,
Crying in frenzy for help, and are not heard?
Who tonight is paying
The old accustomed tax of common blood?

Now red like a battlefield puddle,
Now pale like the drained whiteness of foul fear,
Climbing and sinking,
Reaching and darting up and shrinking in size,
Growing faint for a moment
And swelling like the breath of a devil in intensity,

(Continued on page 252)

Deòrsa Caimbeul Hay

BISEARTA

CHÌ MI RÈ GEARD NA H-OIDHCHE
DREÒS AIR CHRITH 'NA FHROIDHNEAS THALL AIR FÀIRE,
A' CLAPAIL LE A SGIATHAIBH,
A' SGAPADH 'S A' CIARADH RIONNAGAN NA H-ÀIRD' UD.

SHAOILEADH TU GUN CLUINNTE,
GE CIAN, O 'BHUILLSGEIN OCHANAICH NO CAOINEADH,
RÀN CORRAICH NO GÀIR FUATHA,
COMHART CHON CUTHAICH UAITH' NO ULFHAIRT FHAOLCHON,
GUN RUIGEADH DRANND AN FHÒIRNEIRT
ON FHÙIRNEIS ÒMAIR IOMALL FHÈIN AN T-SAOGHAIL.
ACH SIUD A' DOL AN LEUD E
RI OIR AN SPEUR AN TOSTACHD OLC IS AOGNAIDH.

C' AINM NOCHD A TH' ORRA,
NA SRÀIDEAN BOCHDA ANNS AN SGEITH GACH UINNEAG
A LASRAICHEAN 'S A DEATACH,
A SRADAGAN IS SGREADAIL A LUCHD-THUINIDH,
IS TAIGH AIR THAIGH GA REUBADH,
AM BROINN A CHÈILE AM BRÙCHDADH TOIT' A' TUITEAM?
IS CÒ A-NOCHD THA 'G ATACH
AM BÀS A THEACHD GU GRAD 'NAN CAINNTIBH UILE,
NO A' SPÀIRN MEASG CHLACH IS SHAILTHEAN
AIR BHAINIDH A' GAIRM AIR COBHAIR, IS NACH CLUINNEAR?
CÒ A-NOCHD A PHÀIGHEAS
SEANN CHÌS ABHAISTEACH NA FALA CUMANT'?
UAIR DEARG MAR LOD NA H-ARAICH,
UAIR BÀN MAR GHILE THRÀIGHTE AN EAGAIL ÈITIGH,
A' DÌREADH 'S UAIR A' TEÀRNADH,
A' SÌNEADH LE SITHEADH ÀRD 'S A' CALL A MHEUDACHD,
A' FANNACHADH CAR AITIL
'S AG AT MAR ANAIL DHIABHAIL AIR DHÈINEAD,
AN T-OLC 'NA CHRIDHE 'S 'NA CHUISLE,
CHÌ MI 'NA BHUILLEAN A' SÌOLADH 'S A' LEUM E.
THA 'N DREÒS 'NA OILLT AIR FÀIRE,
'NA FHÀINNE RÒIS IS ÒIR AM BUN NAN SPEURAN,
A' BREUGNACHADH 'S AG ÀICHEADH
LE 'SHOILLSE SÈIMHE ÀRSAIDH ÀRD NAN REULTAN.

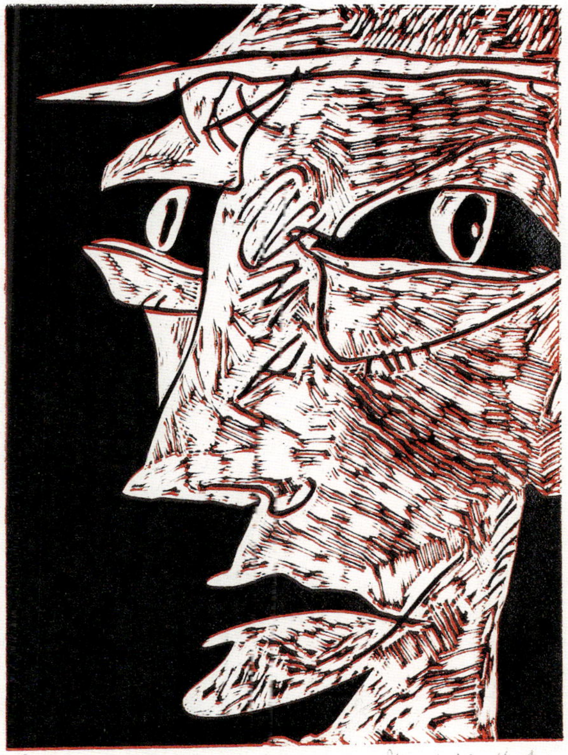

59

MURCHADH MACILLEMHOIRE

MURDO MORRISON

1884-1965

Neach-ealain/Artist:
Gus Wylie

Snas-sgrìobhadair/Calligrapher:
Susan Leiper

Eadar-theangaichte aig/Translator:
John Murray

Roghainn/Nominator:
John Murray

Nuair Dh'iathas Ceò an Fheasgair Dlùth

Nuair dh'iathas ceò an fheasgair dlùth,
Cur smùid air bhàrr nam beann,
'S an crodh bhon innis cnàmh an cìr
Cho sgìth a' tighinn don ghleann;
Nuair bhios a' bhanachag 'm beul na h-oidhch'
Do na laoigh toirt deoch le meòir,
Coinnichidh mi an gleann an fhraoich
Mo ghaol, mo rìbhinn òg.

Nuair bhios a' ghrian san àird an iar
Dol sìos aig crìoch an lò,
'S a' cur a soills air feadh nan sliabh,
'S a sgiamh air dhreach an òir,
'S nuair bhios na caoraich leis na h-uain
Cho suaimhneach aig a' chrò,
Coinnichidh mi an gleann an fhraoich
Mo ghaol, mo rìbhinn òg.

An uair bhios coileach ruadh an t-slèibh
Measg gheugan leum cho beò,
'S a' gogail shuas mu bhil na fèith,
'S a chèile fèin na chòir,
'S gach creutair beag mu sgàil nam bruach
Nan suain len àl gun treòir,
Coinnichidh mi an gleann an fhraoich
Mo ghaol, mo rìbhinn òg.

'S ged bhitheadh air an fheasgar gruaim
'S an t-slighe buan gu leòr,
Is tuinn nan loch a' flodraich fuar
Lem fuaim am measg nan còs,
Gun dèan na thug mi dhut de luaidh
An ruaig chur air gach bròn;
Coinnichidh mi an gleann an fhraoich
Mo ghaol, mo rìbhinn òg.

When the Evening Mist Surrounds Us

When the evening mist surrounds us, draping mist over the mountain tops, and the cattle chew the cud as they return to the glen; when the milkmaid at dusk offers a drink to the calves from her hand, I shall meet in the heather glen my love, my young maiden.

When the setting sun in the west at day's end casts a golden light on the moor and the sheep rest contented with their lambs in the pen, I shall meet in the heather glen my love, my young maiden.

When the frisky russet moorcock jumps in the heather branches and cackles at the edge of the hollow beside his mate, and little creatures sleep in the shade of the banks with their feeble brood, I shall meet in the heather glen my love, my young maiden.

Even if the evening is surly, the journey very long, and the cold loch waves beat noisily amongst the crevices, my love for you will vanquish all sorrow and I shall meet in the heather glen my love, my young maiden.

(Continued on page 252)

Nuair dh'iathas ceò an fheasgair dlùth
Car smùid air bhàrr nam beann,
'S an crodh bhon innis a' tàmh an cèir,
Cho sèimh a' tighinn don ghleann,
Nuair bhios a' bhanachag
'm beul na h-oidhche
Dol a laoigh leis deoch le còrn...

Nuair bhios a' ghrian san àird an iar
Dol sìos aig crìoch an là,
Le 'cur a soills air feadh nan sliabh,
'S a sgiamh air dhreach an òir,
'S nuair bhios na caoraich leis na h-uain
Cho suaimhneach aig a' chrò...

Coinnichidh mi an gleann an fhraoich
Mo ghaol, mo ribhinn òg

A nuair bhios coileach ruadh an t-slèibh
Measg chuachan leum cho beò,
'S a' gogail shuas na bhil na feith,
'S a chèile fèin na chòir,
'S gach creutair beag na sgàil nam bruach
Nan suain le'n àl gun treòir...

'S gach bith eadh air an fheasgar ghruaim
'S an t-sliabh cho buan gu leòr,
Is fuinn nan loch a' flodraich fuar
Le'm fuaim an measg nan eòs,
Gun dèan na thug mi dhut de luaidh
A ruaig chur air gach bròn...

Bheil cuimhn' agad nuair bha sinn saor
'S air feadh nan raon gun leòn,
A' buachailleachd a' chruidh 's nan laogh,
Gun smaoin air maoin no stòr?
Tha cuimhneachan air àm a dh'aom
Gam dhèanamh aotrom beò...

Tha bàt' na smùid don chala dlùth
'S gach ròp is stiùir air dòigh,
'S nuair ruigeas i leam tìr mo rùin
San robh mi 'n tùs mo lò,
San am ochi chiùin nuair bhios gach flùr
'S an earach ùr nan glòir...

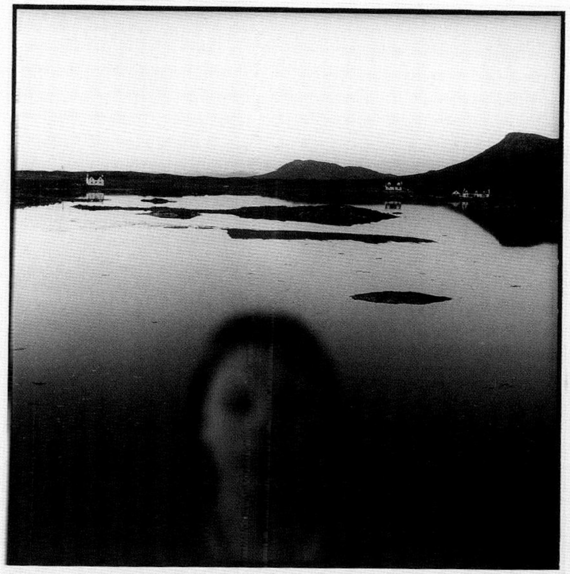

60

COLM BREATHNACH

b. 1961

Ealaíontóir/Artist:
Bridget Flannery

Peannaire/Calligrapher:
Réiltín Murphy

Aistritheoir/Translator:
The Author

Ainmníodh ag/Nominator:
The Author

CoDán do Scáthach

an t-oileán glé úd gurb é tusa é
tá sé fairsing sléibhtiúil
ceilteach agus oscailte
is nuair a bhogann néalta
trasna na spéire os do chionn
léirítear ailteanna is machairí

seangacht agus méithe in éineacht
agus scáth ar scáth ag leanúint a chéile
timpeall ar do cholainn bhán go léir

tráth gur shínis amach
ar an dtocht lomnocht
sa tseomra dorcha
os cionn na mara
bhí caille ar d'éadan
a d'fholaigh do cheannaithe
do shúile fiú
nuair ba léir iad faoin bhfial
bhí mar a bheadh scim orthu

do bheanna mórtasacha
ag éirí is ag ísliú
gile fhíochmhar do chnis
ina hoileán i lár an dorchadais
shnámhas go dtí tú
m'fheargacht go léir ar crith
le tnúth agus le heagla
do lámha anall tharam is mé ag dul isteach ort

A Poem to Scáthach

you are a bright island
hilly and wide

reserved and open
as clouds drift over you
across the sky
plains and ravines are revealed

swelling and slender together
as shadow follows shadow
around about your white body

when you stretched
naked on the bed
in the dark chamber
above the sea
the veil on your face
concealing your features
even your eyes
when seen
seemed hazed

your proud peaks
rising and falling
the fierce splendour of your skin
an island in the midst of dark
toward you I swam
my manliness trembling
with longing and fear

your arms around me as I reached your land

(Continued on page 252)

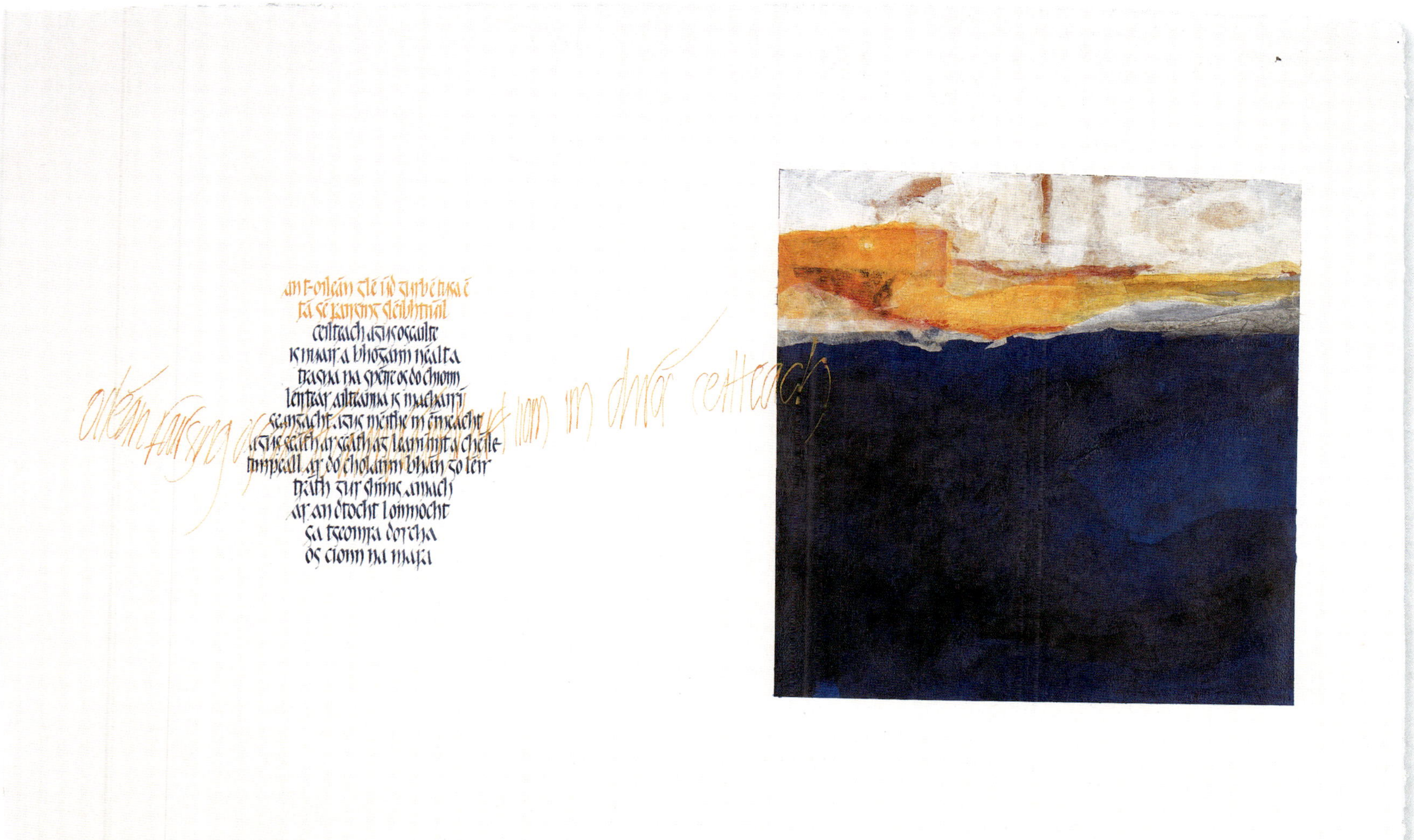
an t-oileán eile úd gurb é tusa é
ceilteach agus oscailte
is iomaí a bhogann néalta
trasna na spéire os do chionn
léirítear aillteanna is machairí
seargacht agus méithe in éineacht
agus scáth ar scáth ag leanúint a chéile
timpeall ar do cholainn bhán go léir
tráth gur shíneas amach
ar an dtocht lomnocht
sa tseomra dorcha
os cionn na mara
oileán fairsing

61

MÁIRTÍN Ó DIREÁIN

1910-1988

Ealaíontóir/Artist:
Scott Kilgour

Peannaire/Calligrapher:
David McGrail

Aistritheoir/Translator:
Colm Breathnach

Ainmníodh ag/Nominator:
Colm Breathnach

Bí i do Chrann

Coigil do bhrí,
A fhir an dáin,
Coigil faoi thrí,
Bí i do chrann.

Coigil gach ní,
A fhir an dáin,
Ná bog ná lúb
Roimh anfa an cháis.

Fan socair,
Fan teann,
Is fair an uain
Go dtaga do lá.

Corraíodh an ghaoth,
A fhir na laoithe,
Gach duille ort thuas;
Do stoc bíodh buan.

Uaigneach crann
I lár na coille,
Uaigneach file
Thar gach duine.

Daingean crann
I dtalamh suite,
Cosa i dtaca
Cuir, a fhile!

Coigil do chlí,
Coigil d' aird,
Coigil gach slí
I gcomhair an dáin.

Tá do leath baineann,
A fhir an dáin,
Bí fireann, bí slán,
Bí i do chrann.

Be as a Tree

Man who makes poems,
Keep back their true import,
Conceal by three,
Be as a tree.

Gather in all that's known,
Man who makes poems,
Don't stir, don't bend
Before this present tempest.

Stay steady,
Unswaying,
Watching the weather
Until the right day.

Let the wind disarray,
Maker of lays,
All your outer foliage;
Your trunk don't budge.

A tree is alone
In the wood's midst,
Among people a poet
Above all is loneliest.

A tree is steadfast
In its portion of land,
Poet, set yourself, man,
Take a stand!

Save your frame,
Gather your knowing,
Focus in every way
Prepared for the poem.

Maker of poems,
You are half womanly,
Be male, be whole,
Be as a tree.

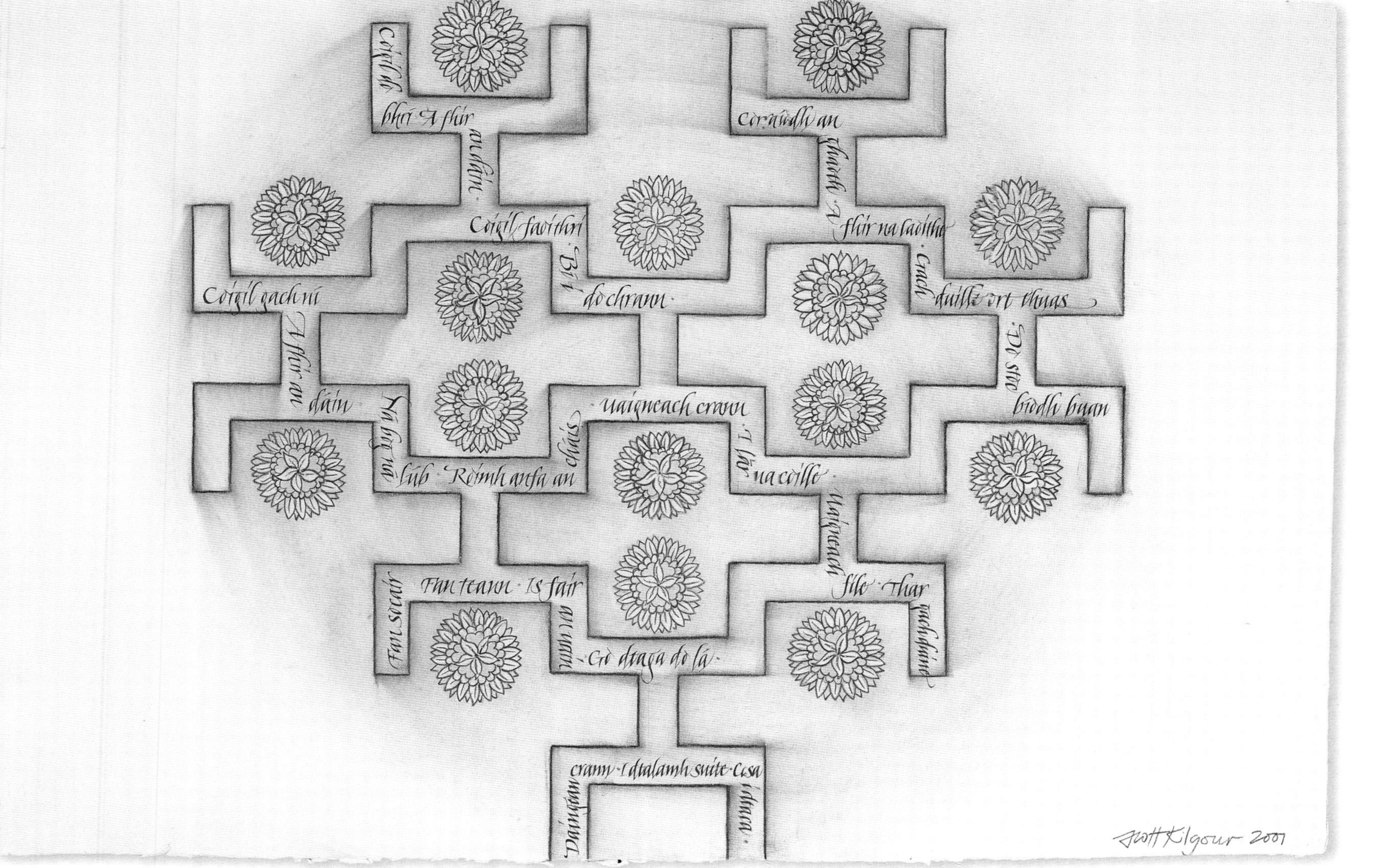
Coigil gach ní
A fhir an dáin
uaigneach crann
I lár na coille
Uaigneach file
Thar gach dáin
Gé daga do lá
crann i dtalamh suite
Scott Kilgour 2001

62

LOUIS DE PAOR

b. 1961

Ealaíontóir/Artist:
Helen O'Leary

Peannaire/Calligrapher:
Donald Murray

Aistritheoir/Translator:
The Author

Ainmníodh ag/Nominator:
The Author

Focaldeoch
I gcuimhne Iain Mhic a' Ghobhainn

Bhíos ag cur síos dó ar fhear Inis Cara
a chuir saothar seanBhíobla ar fhocail,
a chuir turraing aibhléise
le huisinn na teanga
nó gur labhair an eitinn
is an Uimhir Dhé
ar leathscamhóg as béal a chéile.

Bhí babhlaí briste is conamar cainte
scaipthe romhainn sa tslí
ó Mhaigh Cuilinn go Ros Cathail,
gléas ón ngrian ar chlogad a chinn
is a bhlaosc chomh maol le muga cré
i suíochán an bháis lem ais.

Bhí an t-am ag scinneadh tharainn
ar luas gluaisteáin ón tSeapáin,
fallaí fuara scoite aige cheana ina cheann
dom thabhairt leis siar
leathchéad bliain go dtí Oileán Leodhais
mar ar bhrúigh béal na baintrí
lus mínáireach an chromchinn faoi chois
chomh diongbháilte le téacs seanTiomna.

Chuir sí de gheasa air, dá mhéid a íota,
gan deoir a bhlaiseadh i gcroit ná i mbothán
mar a raibh fríd an ghalair á cuisniú
ag miasa is mugaí scoilte,
tinneas ina ráfla mailíseach á scaipeadh
chomh huilechumhachtach dofheicthe
le trócaire Dé ar thairseach an tsaoil.

Gospel
I.M. Iain Crichton Smith

I was telling him about the man in Inis Cara
who made words work hard as an old Bible,
who sent electric shocks
through the temples of language
until tuberculosis and the binary number
spoke as one voice with damaged breath.

Broken bowls and shards of talk
were scattered before us on the road
from Moycullen to Roscahill,
the sun glinting on the helmet of his head
bare as a cup
in the death-seat beside me.

Time skidded past us
like a Japanese car and already
he was clearing stone walls in his head
taking me with him
fifty years back to the Isle of Lewis
where the widow's words
trampled the shameless daffodil
with the certainty of a lesson from the Old Testament.

She made him promise,
whatever his thirst, not to touch
a drop in any croft or cottage
where a hint of disease might have lodged
in cracked mugs or dishes,
as sickness spread like a vicious rumour
all-powerful and invisible
as God's mercy on the threshold of the world.

(Continued on page 252)

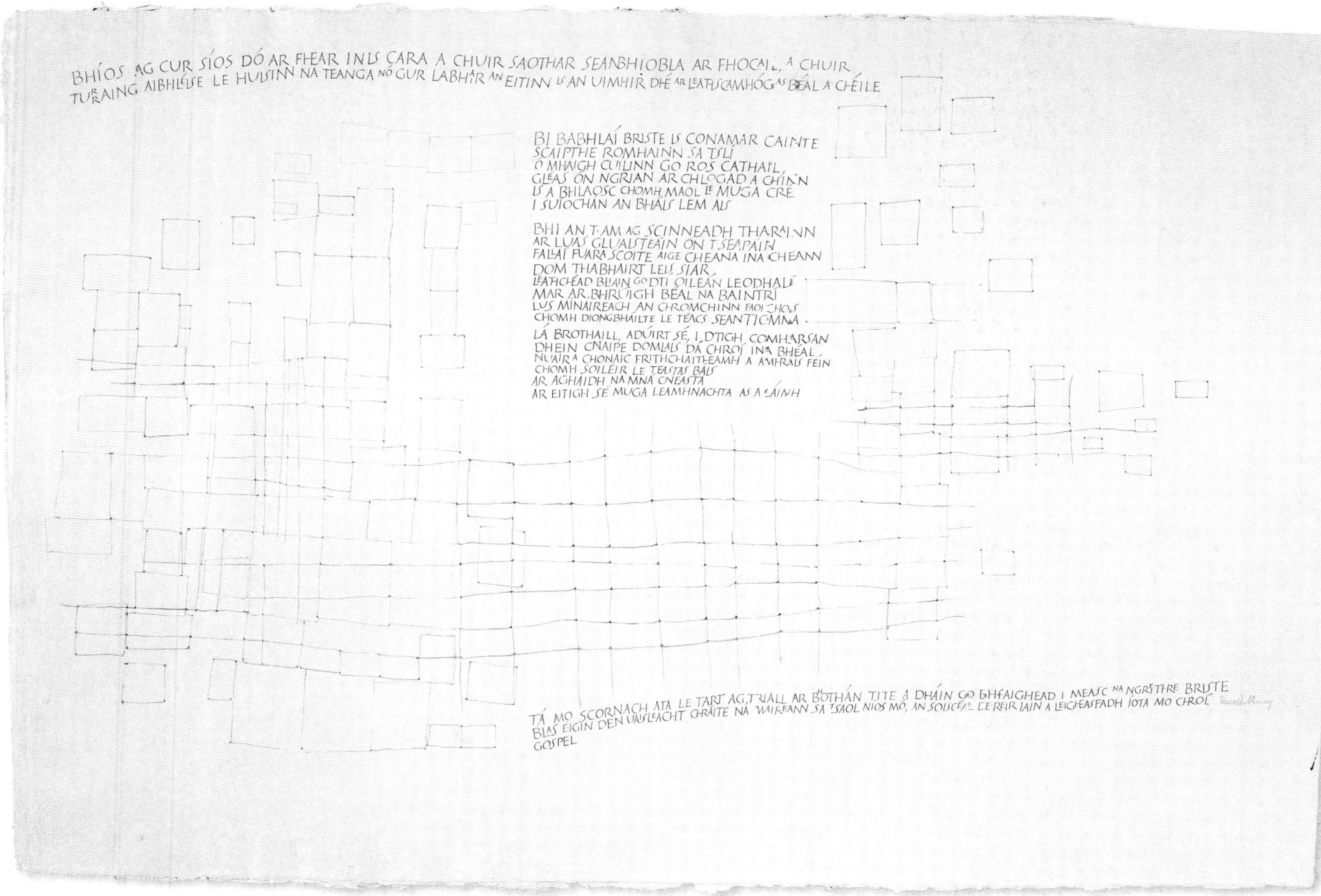
BHÍOS AG CUR SÍOS DÓ AR FHEAR INIS CARA A CHUIR SAOTHAR SEANBHIOBLA AR FHOCAIL, A CHUIR
TURRAING AIBHLÉISE LE HUISINN NA TEANGA NÓ GUR LABHAIR AN EITINN IS AN UIMHIR DHÉ AR LEATHSCAMHÓG AS BÉAL A CHÉILE
BÍ BABHLAÍ BRISTE IS CONAMAR CAINTE
SCAIPTHE ROMHAINN SA TSLÍ
Ó MHAIGH CUILINN GO ROS CATHAIL,
GLEAS ÓN NGRIAN AR CHLOGAD A CHINN
IS A BHLAOSC CHOMH MAOL LE MUGA CRÉ
I SUÍOCHÁN AN BHÁIS LEM AIS
BHÍ AN T-AM AG SCINNEADH THARAINN
AR LUAS GLUAISTEÁIN ÓN TSEAPÁIN
FALLAÍ FUARA SCOITE AIGE CHEANA INA CHEANN
DOM THABHAIRT LEIS SIAR
LEATHCHÉAD BLIAIN GO DTÍ OILEÁN LEODHAIS
MAR AR BHRÚIGH BÉAL NA BAINTRÍ
LUS MINAIREACH AN CHROMCHINN FAOI CHOS
CHOMH DIONGBHÁILTE LE TÉACS SEANTIOMNA.
LÁ BROTHAILL, ADÚIRT SÉ, I DTIGH COMHARSAN
DHEIN CNAIPE DOMLAIS DÁ CHROÍ INA BHÉAL
NUAIR A CHONAIC FRITHCHAITHEAMH A AMHRAIS FÉIN
CHOMH SOILÉIR LE TEASTAS BÁIS
AR AGHAIDH NA MNÁ CNEASTA
AR EITIGH SÉ MUGA LEAMHNACHTA AS A LÁIMH
TÁ MO SCORNACH ATA LE TART AG TRIALL AR BHOTHÁN TÍTE Á DHÁIN GO BHFAIGHEAD I MEASC NA NGRÉITHRE BRISTE
BLAS ÉIGIN DEN UAISLEACHT CHRÁITE NÁ HAIFREANN SA TSAOL NÍOS MÓ, AN SOISCÉAL DE RÉIR IAIN A LEIGHEASFADH ÍOTA MO CHROÍ.
GOSPEL

63

SOMHAIRLE MACGILL-EAIN

SORLEY MACLEAN

1911-1996

Neach-ealain / Artist:
Donald Urquhart

Snas-sgrìobhadair / Calligrapher:
Louise Donaldson

Eadar-theangaichte aig / Translator:
The Author

Roghainn / Nominator:
Hamish Henderson, Louis de Paor

Hallaig

'Tha tìm, am fiadh, an Coille Hallaig.'

Tha bùird is tàirnean air an uinneig
trom faca mi an Aird an Iar
's tha mo ghaol aig Allt Hallaig
'na craoibh bheithe, 's bha i riamh

eadar an t-Inbhir 's Poll a' Bhainne,
thall 's a-bhos mu Bhaile Chùirn:
tha i 'na beithe, 'na calltainn,
'na caorann dhìreach sheang ùir.

Ann an Sgreapadal mo chinnidh,
far robh Tarmad 's Eachann Mòr,
tha 'n nigheanan 's am mic 'nan coille
a' gabhail suas ri taobh an lòin.

Uaibhreach a-nochd na coilich ghiuthais
a' gairm air mullach Cnoc an Rà,
dìreach an druim ris a' ghealaich –
chan iadsan coille mo ghràidh.

Fuirichidh mi ris a' bheithe
gus an tig i mach an Càrn,
gus am bi am bearradh uile
o Bheinn na Lice fa sgàil.

Mura tig 's ann theàrnas mi a Hallaig,
a dh'ionnsaigh sàbaid nam marbh,
far a bheil an sluagh a' tathaich,
gach aon ghinealach a dh'fhalbh.

Tha iad fhathast ann a Hallaig,
Clann Ghill-Eain 's Clann MhicLeòid,
na bh' ann ri linn Mhic Ghille Chaluim:
chunnacas na mairbh beò –

Hallaig

'Time, the deer, is in the Wood of Hallaig.'

The window is nailed and boarded
through which I saw the West
and my love is at the Burn of Hallaig,
a birch tree, and she has always been

between Inver and Milk Hollow,
here and there about Baile-chuirn:
she is a birch, a hazel,
a straight slender young rowan.

In Screapadal of my people,
where Norman and Big Hector were,
their daughters and their sons are a wood
going up beside the stream.

Proud tonight the pine cocks
crowing on the top of Cnoc an Ra,
straight their backs in the moonlight –
they are not the wood I love.

I will wait for the birch wood
until it comes up by the Cairn,
until the whole ridge from Beinn na Lice
will be under its shade.

If it does not, I will go down to Hallaig,
to the sabbath of the dead,
where the people are frequenting,
every single generation gone.

They are still in Hallaig,
MacLeans and MacLeods,
all who were there in the time of Mac Gille Chaluim:
the dead have been seen alive –

(Continued on page 253)

Uisge-dhathach deante le uisge on eas, An Steall, Hallaig, air an 27mh dhen t-Sultain 2001
Watercolour made with water collected from the waterfall, An Steall, at Hallaig, on 27th September 2001

64

MÁIRE MHAC AN T-SAOI

b. 1922

Ealaíontóir/Artist:
Patricia Looby

Peannaire/Calligrapher:
Frances Breen

Aistritheoir/Translator:
The Author

Ainmníodh ag/Nominator:
The Author

Maireann an t-Seanmhuintir

Thaithin leo an t-éadan ard ar mhnaoi –
Faisean an ghlibe ar bhaineannach ní bhfuair cion –
Agus scaradh leathan na súl
Agus an séanas mealltach chun tosaigh sa chár gléigeal:
Canóin na háilleachta 'ceapadh roimh theacht do Chríost …
Agus shamhlaíos dom féin go mbreacfainn a dtuairisc,
Mar, nuair nach ann dár nglúin-ne,
Cé bhlaisfidh a séimhe siúd 'bhéascna?

Tharla mé ag múineadh scoile thiar ag an am san,
Agus ansan ar an mbinse leanbh mar lile:
Coimheascar na rós ar a leacain
Is a cúl dob' órbhuí,
Gorm a rosca agus mall,
Caoincheart a braoithe,
Agus a béilin úr mar shú na gcraobh insa Mheitheamh.
Aon bhliain déag do chláraigh
Is splanc ní raibh ina cloigeann,
Ná í in aon chor 'na thinneas,
Ba leor bheith ann is bheith amhlaidh.

Tháinig an focal 'bé' i dtreis le linn teagaisc;
'Sin focal ná beidh agaibh,' do ráidh an mháistreás leo.
Phreab an lámh bheag in airde:
'Thá sé agamsa'…
Íoróin throm an mhúinteora scaoileas den éill léi:
'Inis má sea don rang é, a Treas, a' stór do chuid eolais.'
Dána is teann as a gleoiteacht do raid sí an freagra:
'Bean gan aon éadach uirthi!'…
Do gháir Eoghan Rua.

The Old Live On

They liked a high forehead on a woman –
The fashion for fringes on females was not prized –
And the broad separation of the eyes,
And the charming gap between the very white front teeth:
The canon of beauty laid down before the coming of Christ …
And I thought I would jot down their tidings,
For, when our generation is no more,
Who will taste the gentleness of their conventions?

I happened to be teaching school at that time in the West,
And there on the bench [sat] a child like a lily,
A conflict of roses on her cheeks
And her head of hair golden-yellow,
Her eyes blue and slow-moving,
Her brows precisely drawn,
And her small fresh mouth like raspberries in June.
She registered eleven years
And there wasn't a spark of sense in her head,
Nor was she at all worried by that,
It was enough to be there and be thus.

The word for 'muse' cropped up during teaching;
'That is a word you won't know,' the mistress declared to them.
The little hand shot up:
'I know it …'
I unleashed the teacher's heavy irony at her:
'Tell it then to the class, Teresa, from the store of your knowledge.'
Bold and confident in her loveliness, she shot back the answer:
'A woman with no clothes on!'…
Eoghan Rua laughed.

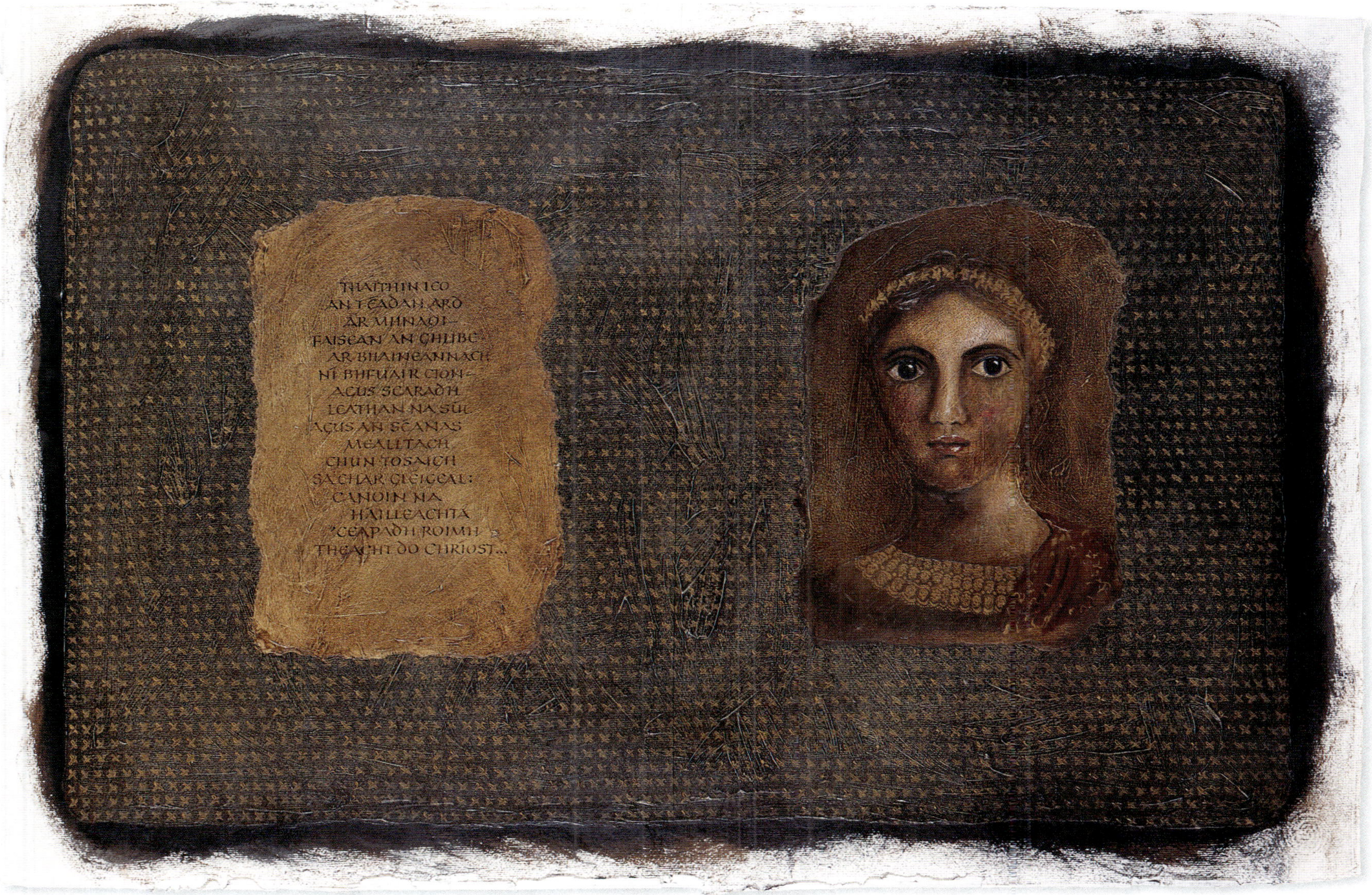
THAITHIN LEO
AN TÉADAN ARD
AR MHNAOI–
FAISEAN AN CHLIBE–
AR BHAINEANNACH
NÍ BHFUAIR CION–
AGUS SCARADH
LEATHAN NA SÚL
AGUS AN SCANAS
MEALLTACH
CHUN TOSAIGH
SA CHAR GLEIGEAL:
CANOIN NA
HÁILLEACHTA
'CEAPADH ROIMH
THEACHT DO CHRIOST...

65

GRÉAGÓIR Ó DÚILL

b. 1946

Ealaíontóir/Artist:
Ronnie Hughes

Peannaire/Calligrapher:
Donald Murray

Aistritheoir/Translator:
The Author

Ainmníodh ag/Nominator:
The Author

An Frog Sa Bhucaeid

Tá frog sa bhucaeid.
Cá fhad anois ansin é? Is ar éigean beo:
Ní bhogann an scórnach,
Tá mogall ar na súile,
Tá an craiceann iomlán tirim,
É ina ghlóthach seirgthe,
É ar dhath luaithreach na móna thart air,
É ina chac tirim caora ag an mhóin,
Ina chamal caillte sa ghaineamhlach shinciarainn.

Tiontaigh an bucaeid bun os cionn,
Nó ní cónra mhiotail é dá leithéid shoineanta
Nár thuill an cillín buí.
Amharc air. Bogann sé, suíonn ceart,
Droim íota le spéir, géaga le sráid,
Súile leat. Ní iarrann. Fanann.

Buacaire an chlóis taobh leat, ní haon rud mór
Boiseog a shilt anuas air, braon ar bhraon.
Amharc a dhroim, dathanna ag filleadh ar an chraiceann
leis an bhaisteadh.
Tógann sé a dhá lámh mar chosaint ar a shúile,
Nó malaí agus fabhraí níor bronnadh air san ubh.

Agus imigh leat, anois, do ghnósa déanta.
Cead amhairc i gcionn leathuaire agat - ní bheidh sé ann.

The Frog in the Bucket

There's a frog in the bucket.
How long's he been there? He is hardly alive.
His throat is still, his eyes are hooded,
His skin is wholly dry.
He is withered spawn,
His colour the yellow of the turf ash about him.
He's a sheep turd dried out by the turf,
A camel lost in a galvanised desert.

Upend the bucket.
His innocence does not deserve a metal coffin
Or shite-coloured cell walls.
Look at him. He moves, sits upright,
His parched back to the sky, his feet planted firm,
His eye on yours. He does not ask. He waits.

The outside water-tap is close. It's nothing to you
To drip a palmful, drop by drop, down on him.
See his back, as rain returns the colours.
He raises his hands to his eyes, complaining
That no brows nor eyelashes came to him from the egg.

You may go now, your part in this is finished.
Check again in half an hour, and he'll be gone.

Tá frog sa bhucaeid.
Cá fhad anois ansin é? Is ar éigean beo:
Ní bhogann an scórnach,
Tá mogall ar na súile,
Tá an craiceann iomlán tirim,
É ina ghlóthach seirgthe,
É ar dhath luaithreach na móna thart air
É ina chac tirim caora ag an mhóin
Ina chamal caillte sa ghaineamhlach shinciarainn

Tiontaigh an bucaeid bun os cionn,
Nó ní cónra mhiotail é dá leithéid shoineanta
Nár thuill an cillín buí.
Amharc air. Bogann sé, suíonn ceart,
Droim iota le spéir, géaga le sráid,
Súile leat. Ní iarrann. Fanann.

Buacaire an chlóis taobh leat, ní haon rud mór
Boiseog a shilt anuas air, braon ar bhraon.
Amharc a dhroim, dathanna ag filleadh ar an chraiceann leis an bhaisteadh.
Tógann sé a dhá lámh mar chosaint ar a shúile,
Nó malaí agus fabhraí níor bronnadh air san ubh.

Agus imigh leat, anois, do ghnósa déanta.
Cead amhairc i gcionn leathuaire agad—ní bheidh sé ann.

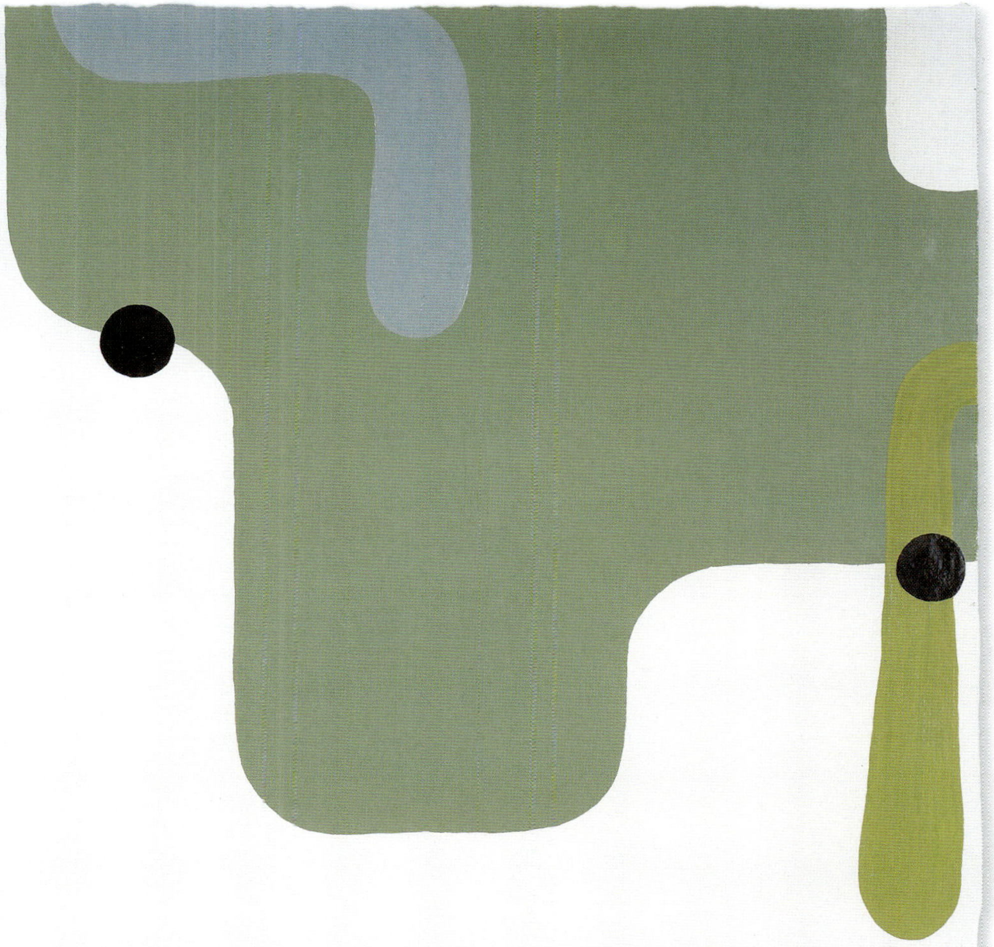

66

DIARMAID Ó DOIBHLIN

b. 1942

Ealaíontóir / Artist:
Marian Leven

Clóghrafóir / Typographer:
Donald Addison

Aistritheoir / Translator:
The Author

Ainmníodh ag / Nominator:
Gréagóir Ó Dúill

Loch na Craoibhe

Tá dreach na tíre seo againn breac le mionlocha ciúine,
Iad faoi cheilt, faoi rúin, d'fhéadfá a rá,
Ag cnocáin mhaola agus ag sceacha cumhra.
Ní mór duit dul sa tóir orthu,
An carr a pháirceáil cois an bhealaigh mhóir
Agus cead a iarraidh ar an scológ choimhthíoch,
An geata meirgeach a scaoileadh,
Móinéar agus páirc a shiúl,
Agus fiastalach na tíre faoi do chosa,
Nó go nochtann chugat de phlimp
Gealscillingí na staire.
Ní thuigeann ach na sceacha sin a mhalairt.

Agus tá scéal mo mhuintire breac leis na mionlocha seo,
Agus leis an tom chrannógach udaí,
Amuigh ar an oileán chraobhach sin.
Ionad foscaidh ag Gaeil, port aireachais na muintire,
Tráth a mhair siad agus a gceart acu.
Loch Inse Uí Fhloinn, Loch líofa Ruacháin,
Loch Luca Ghleann Chon Cadhain, agus Loch seo na
Craoibhe –
Ní sceitheann siad a rún:
Cad a sheol Aodh Mór an bealach aistearach seo
Ar a thuras léanmhar?
Cad a spreag Tarlach Gruama gur chuir a dhóchas
I ngarbhsceacha Ruacháin?
Ní thuigeann ach na sceacha féin agus slaparnach an uisce,
Agus tá Loch Luca ina sheascann críon
Agus is bogach inniu Loch Inse Uí Fhloinn.

Crew Lough

The face of this country of ours is dotted with little loughs
Hidden as they are at the foot of sloping hills mid fragrant
whitethorn
You must seek them out
Park there by the roadside
And nod to planter's writ and whim.
Then follow field and fallow
The coarse grass of the land bristling at your feet
Then suddenly they are there before you
The bright shillings of our story.
Only the whitethorns understand the difference.

And my people's story is dotted with these little loughs
And with the bushy dwelling on these leafy islands.
The harbour of the Gael, our sanctuary once
When we held sway.
And had our way and presence here.
Loughinsholin and smooth Roughan
And this lough here at Crew.
They keep their secrets well.
What brought the Great Ó Neill this way
On his fateful journey? I ask.
And Tarlach Gruama – why put your trust
In those rough thorns at Roughan?

Only the thorns now know,
And the silent waters.
And Lough Lug today is but a wizened fen,
And Loughinsholin a tired bog.

(Continued on page 254)

LOCH NA CRAOIBHE

TÁ DREACH NA TÍRE SEO AGAINN BREAC LE MIONLOCHA CIÚINE,
IAD FAOI CHEILT, FAOI RÚIN, D'FHÉADFÁ A RÁ,
AG CNOCÁIN MHAOLA AGUS AG SCEACHA CUMHRA.
NÍ MÓR DUIT DUL SA TÓIR ORTHU,
AN CARR A PHÁIRCEÁIL COIS AN BHEALAIGH MHÓIR
AGUS CEAD A IARRAIDH AR AN SCOLÓG CHOIMHTHÍOCH,
AN GEATA MEIRGEACH A SCAOILEADH,
MÓINÉAR AGUS PÁIRC A SHIÚL,
AGUS FIASTALACH NA TÍRE FAOI DO CHOSA,
NÓ GO NOCHTANN CHUGAT DE PHLIMP
GEALSCILLINGÍ NA STAIRE.
NÍ THUIGEANN ACH NA SCEACHA SIN A MHALAIRT.

AGUS TÁ SCÉAL MO MHUINTIRE BREAC LEIS NA MIONLOCHA SEO,
AGUS LEIS AN TOM CHRANNÓGACH UDAÍ,
AMUIGH AR AN OILEÁN CHRAOBHACH SIN.
IONAD FOSCAIDH AG GAEIL, PORT AIREACHAIS NA MUINTIRE,
TRÁTH A MHAIR SIAD AGUS A GCEART ACU.
LOCH INSE UÍ FHLOINN, LOCH LÍOFA RUACHÁIN,
LOCH LUCA GHLEANN CHON CADHAIN, AGUS LOCH SEO NA CRAOIBHE –
NÍ SCEITHEANN SIAD A RÚN:
CAD A SHEOL AODH MÓR AN BEALACH AISTEARACH SEO
AR A THURAS LÉANMHAR?
CAD A SPREAG TARLACH GRUAMA GUR CHUIR A DHÓCHAS
I NGARBHSCEACHA RUACHÁIN?
NÍ THUIGEANN ACH NA SCEACHA FÉIN AGUS SLAPARNACH AN UISCE,
AGUS TÁ LOCH LUCA INA SHEASCANN CRÍON
AGUS IS BOGACH INNIU LOCH INSE UÍ FHLOINN.

NÍL FEIDHM LEO FEASTA MAR IONAID
NÍL FEIDHM ACH MAR ÁBHAR MACHNAIMH
MAR SHAMHAILT DON TÉ ISTIGH COIS TINE OÍCHE GHEIMHRIDH
AG IOMPÚ LEATHANAIGH A CHINE
AGUS STOIRM NA TÍRE AG RIASTRADH TAOBH AMUIGH.
FÁG IAD MAR ATÁ, IMPÍM ORT,
FÁG FAOI NA SCOLÓGA COIMHTHÍOCHA
NACH BHFEICEANN CHOÍCHE MARCLAIGH NÁ SLUA,
NACH GCLUINEANN CHOÍCHE CLAISCEADAL NA DTÉAD ÚR,
NACH MBRAITHEANN CHOÍCHE UAIGNEAS SAN FHUARLACH SEO.

FÁG IAD MAR ATÁ,
NÍL ANN ACH SCÉAL AG SEANMHNÁ,
GO MBÍONN A GCUID FÉIN AG LOCHA.

DIARMAID Ó DOIBHLIN

67

GABRIEL ROSENSTOCK

b. 1949

Ealaíontóir / Artist:
William Brotherston

Peannaire / Calligrapher:
Donald Murray

Aistritheoir / Translator:
Paddy Bushe

Ainmníodh ag / Nominator:
The Author

Liadhain

Liadhain ...
Bhí fios agam di.
Mé Cuirithir.
Le Dia a leath dhíom
le Liadhain an leath eile.

An leath dhíom ar le Dia í
is seasc, marbh

An leath dhíom ar le Liadhain í
is bruithneach

I ndoire sea luíomar le chéile.
Ba gheall le cnó á oscailt é
is á chur im béal
ag crobh cailce dofheicthe

Siolla níor labhair sí
ach nuair a dhún sí a súile
ba léir di an sú
ag éirí sna crainn
Gur chuala sásamh ársa na gcraobh

Nuair a théann sí i bhfolach orm
chím gach áit í

Leanaim scáth an fhia
is an tseabhaic
Líontar an doire lena héagmais

Nuair a dhúisíonn sí ar maidin
féachaim go domhain sna súile aici

Is tobar í
ina bhfeicim mé féin

Ólaim asam féin

Liadhain

Liadhain ...
Knowledge flowed between us.
I am Cuirithir.
God goes halves in me
with Liadhain.

God's share
is sterile, lifeless,

Liadhain's
boils me alive.

We lay together among oaks.
It was like a nut being shelled
and placed in my mouth
by a creamy, invisible hand.

She said nothing at all
but when she closed her eyes
she could see the sap
rising in trees,
hear the old fulfilment of branches.

When she hides from me
I see her everywhere.

I follow the deer's shadow
And the hawk's.
Her absence flits among the oaks.

When she wakes in the morning
I look deep into her eyes.

She is a well
that reflects me.

I drink of myself.

(Continued on page 254)

Liathain . . . . .
Bhí fios agam di
Mé Cuirithir
Le Dia a leath dhíom
le Liathain an leath eile—

I ndoire sea luíomar le chéile
Ba gheall le cnó á oscailt é
is á chur im béal
ag crobh cailce dofheicthe

A Dhé! Tabhair le chéile arís sinn
Naisc sinn—achainím ort—
ar feadh aon oíche amháin
I bParthas róshoiseach na naomh

Donald Murray

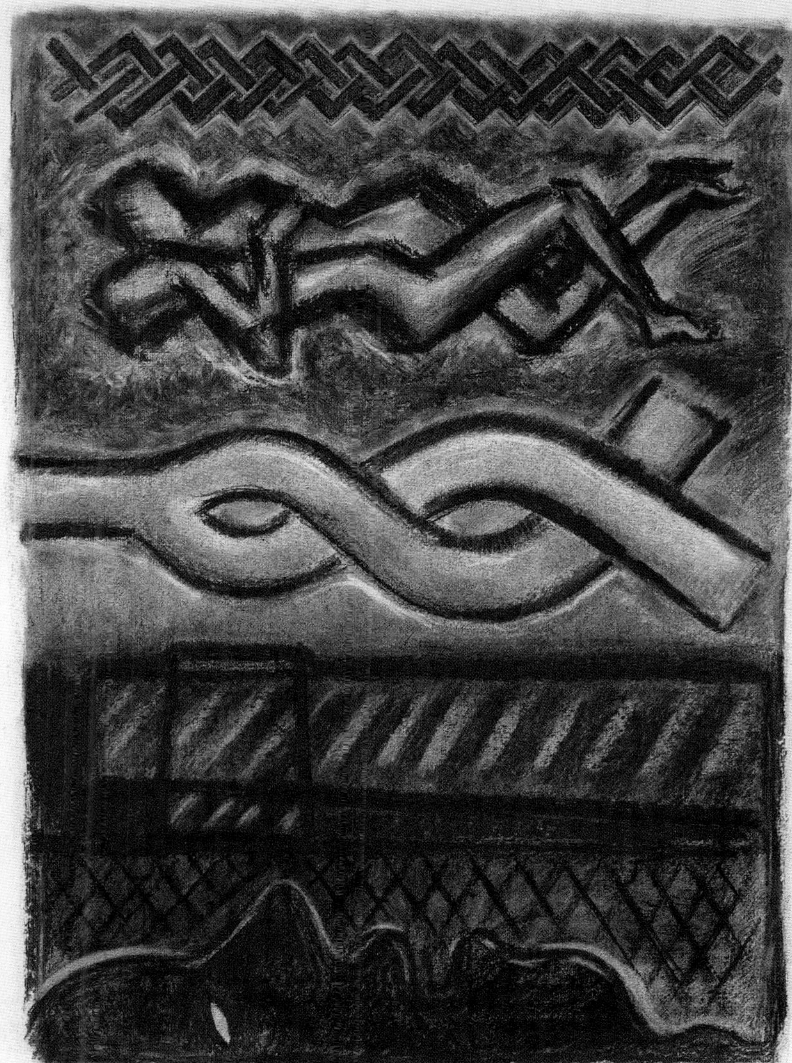

68

SEÁN Ó CURRAOIN

Ealaíontóir/Artist:
Edward Summerton

Peannaire/Calligrapher:
Louise Donaldson

Aistritheoir/Translator:
The Author

Ainmníodh ag/Nominator:
The Author

Mo Shinsear

Chuir mo shinsear an súil ribe
Agus rinne siad an fiach.
Leag siad an cliabhán éanachaí
San áit a raibh an bearradh fial.
D'aimsigh siad an leaba dhearg
Sa luachair mhaoth bhog thais,
Is mharaigh an míol istigh inti
Le buille den mhaide droighin.
Leag siad na constaicí
Is chart siad an chré.
D'fhág scéim ina ndiaidh
Nach rachaidh in éag.

Lá saoire níorbh áil leo
Ach ag biorrú is ag tógáil leo
Claidheachaí arda eagair,
Le foirmlí chomh sean leis an gceo.

A oidí mo mhúinte,
Is le ceo cumha
A chuimhním anois oraibh,
A d'íoc bhur ndeachúna
Ar bhóithre crua deacra,
Ag déanamh míorúiltí beaga
Le bhur lámha ildánacha,
Nuair a bhuaileadh an ragús oibre sibh,
Ag glanadh na talún ón mháthair ghoir
Chuir sibh an báire ar thalamh is ar muir.
Níorbh aon ribín réidh sin
Is an saol mar a bhí
Lán cruatain is olc.

My Ancestors

My ancestors set the snare
And went hunting.
They laid the bird-trap
In the most advantageous place.
They found the animal's lair
In the damp soft moist rushes
And killed the animal there
With a blow of the blackthorn stick.
They knocked down the obstacles
And dug the earth.
They left a plan behind them
That will not die.
They did not wish to take a holiday
But pointing and building away
High arranged stonewalls
With formulas as old as the hills.
O teachers who have taught me,
I remember you now with great longing
Who paid your tithes on roads full of hardship and difficulty
Performing little miracles
With your hands skilled in various arts
When a working-fit came,

Clearing the earth from its blemishes,
You got the better of land and sea.
It was not easy to do this
Because life then was full of hardship and evil.

(NB - 'animal' refers to hare or rabbit)

Chuir mo shinsear an súil ribe
Agus rinne siad an fiach
Leag siad an cliabhán éanachai
San áit a raibh an bearradh fial

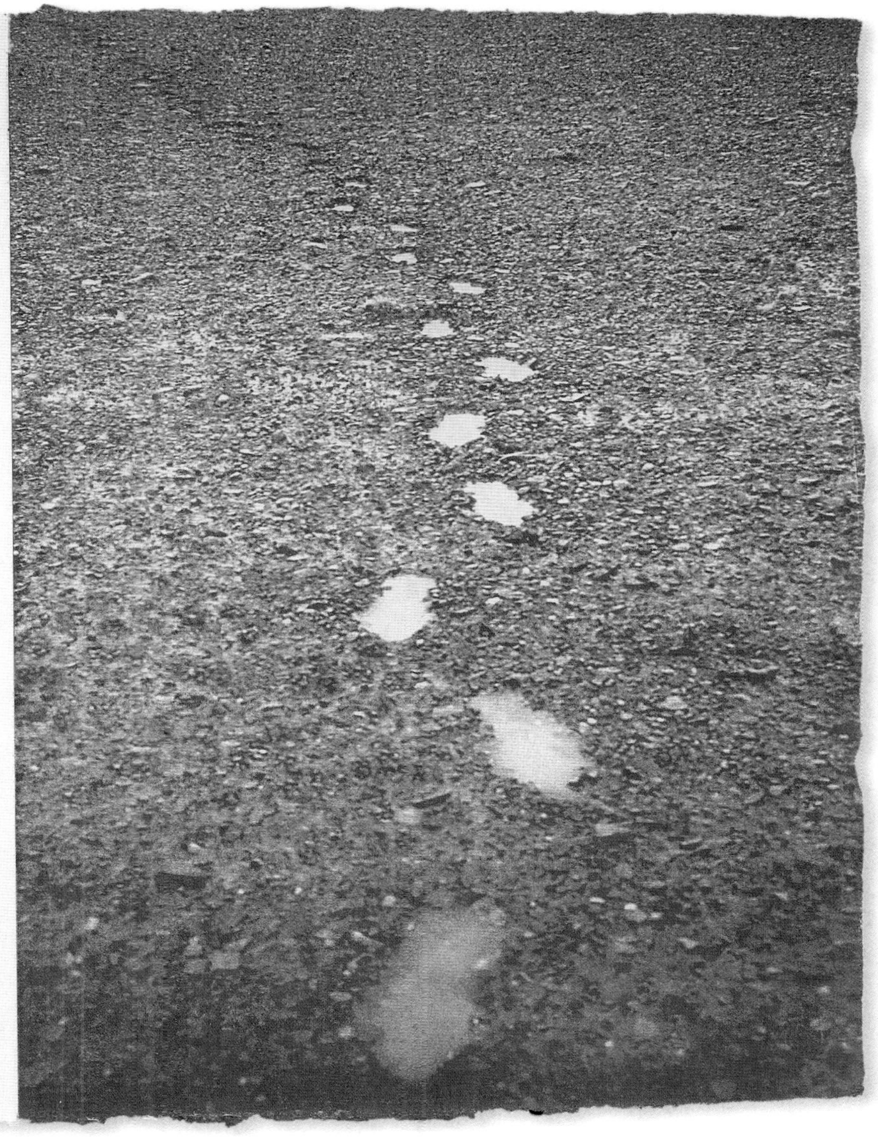

69

PADRAIG DE BRÚN

1889-1960

Ealaíontóir/Artist:
Tadhg McSweeney

Peannaire/Calligrapher:
Frances Breen

Aistritheoir/Translator:
Seán Ó Curraoin

Ainmníodh ag/Nominator:
Seán Ó Curraoin

Valparaiso

Fá thuairim Bhéarla Oilifĕir Shinseoin Uí Ghógartaigh

Tháinig long ó Valparaiso,
Scaoileadh téad a seol sa chuan,
Chuir a hainm dom i gcuimhne
Ríocht na gréine, tír na mbua.

'Gluais,' ar sí, 'ar thuras fada
Liom ó scamall is ó cheo;
Tá fé shleasa gorm-Ándes
Cathair scáfar, glé mar sheod.'

Ach bhíos óg is ní imeoinnse,
Am an dóchais, tús mo shaoil,
Chreideas fós go raibh i ndán dom
Iontaisí na ndán is na scéal.

Ghluais an long thar linnte mara
Fad ó shin is a crann mar ór,
Scríobh a scéal ar phár na hoíche,
Ard i rian na réiltean mór.

Fillfidh sí arís chugam, áfach,
Chífead cathair bhán fén sléibh
Le hais Mara na Síochána,
Creidim fós, beagnach, a Dhé.

Valparaiso

A ship from Valparaiso came
And in the bay her sails were furled.
Her name reminded me of a sunny clime,
A land of opportunity.

'Come travel with me,' she said
'From gloom and wet;
You will find beneath the Andes blue
A sheltered city, bright as a jewel.'

But I was young and would not go,
A time of hope, the beginning of my life.
I still believed that the wonders
Of song and story were still in store for me.

The ship sailed over the wide ocean
Long since and her mast glittered like gold.
She traced her story on the night's scroll,
High in the track of the great stars.

She will return to me, however,
I shall see a fair city at the foot of the mountain
Beside the Pacific Ocean –
By God, I still believe it yet.

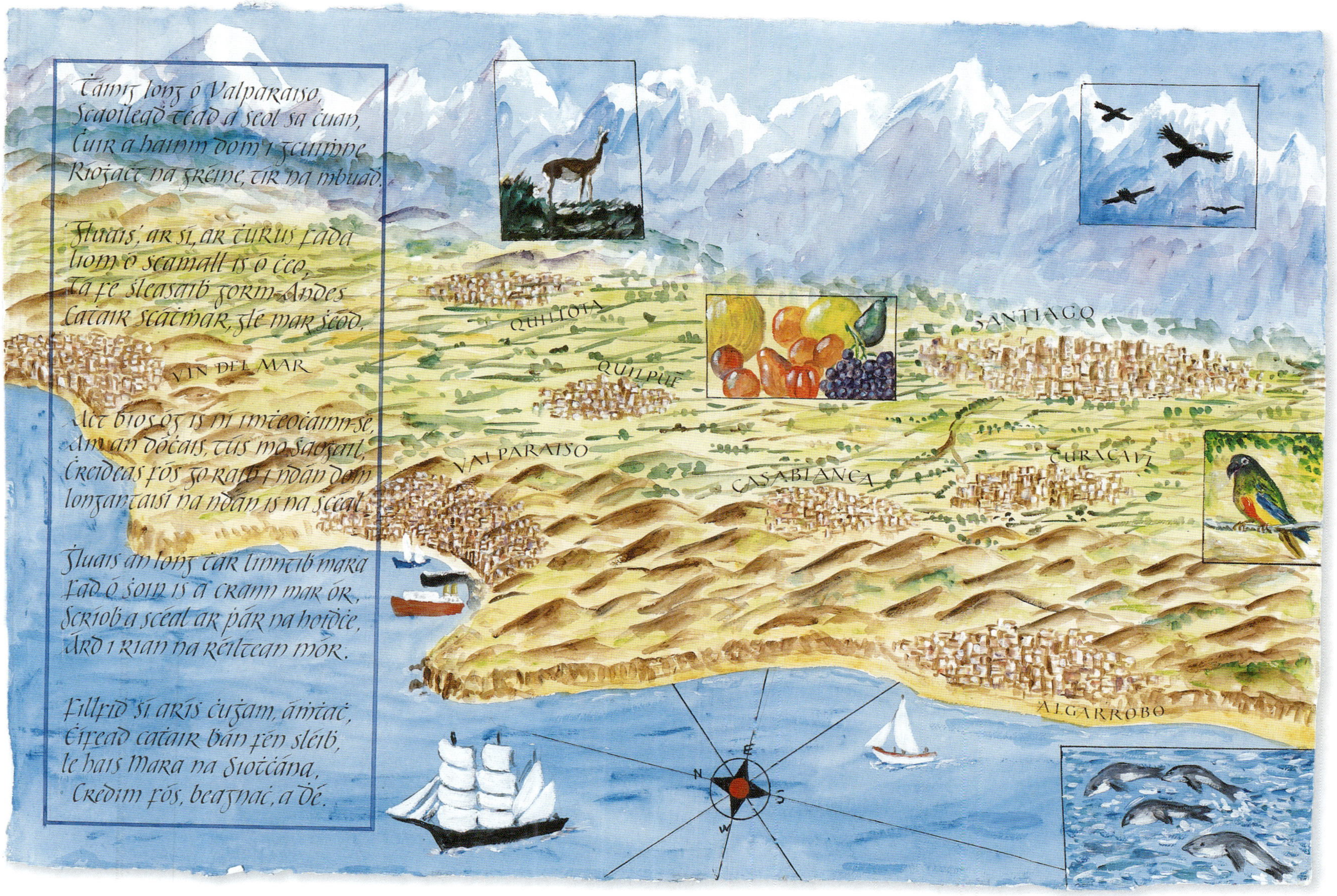
Ṫáinig long ó Valparaiso,
Scaoileaḋ téad a seol sa ċuan,
Ċuir a hainm dom i gcuiṁne
Ríoġacht na gréine, tír na mbuaḋ.

'Gluais,' ar sí, 'ar ṫuras fada
liom ó scamall is ó ċeo,
Tá fé ṡleasaiḃ gorm-Andes
Caṫair scáṫmar, glé mar ṡeod.

Ach bíos óg is ní imṫeoċainn-se,
Am an dóċais, tús mo ṡaoġail,
Ċreideas fós go raiḃ i ndán dom
Iongantaisí na ndán is na scéal.

Ġluais an long tar linntiḃ mara
Fad ó ṡoin is a crann mar ór,
Scríoḃ a scéal ar pár na hoiḋċe,
Árd i rian na réiltean mór.

Fillfiḋ sí arís ċuġam, ániṫaċ,
Ċífead caṫair bán fén sléiḃ,
le hais Mara na Síoṫċána,
Creidim fós, beagnaċ, a Ḋé.
QUILLOTA
SANTIAGO
VIN DEL MAR
QUILPUÉ
VALPARAISO
CASABLANCA
CURACAVI
ALGARROBO
N
E
S
W

70

GEARÓID MAC LOCHLAINN

b. 1966

Ealaíontóir/Artist:
Brian Maguire

Peannaire/Calligrapher:
Réiltín Murphy

Aistritheoir/Translator:
The Author

Ainmníodh ag/Nominator:
The Author

Paddy

(i ndil chuimhne)

'Did ya hear about Donal's wee brother?'
a scairt Chips liom thar longbhá an tábla, callán an ghrúpa.
Trí fhaobhair bhána *feedback* ón *Fender.* An t-inneal toite is an smúit.
Mé ar seachrán, ag mairnéalach,
smaointí mistiúrtha faoi lán seoil,
ag bádóireacht ar thonnta chordaí is *riff*eanna,
as mo cheann ar *Bush* is raithneach,
ag gig éigean, víbeanna ag bleaisteáil.
Is chuala me do scéal, a Phadaí óig,
thaibhsigh tú i gcuan cáiteach mo chuimhne
an oíche ólta sin
le d'fholt dubh, tiubh, slíoctha,
cíortha siar ó d'éadan muscach
inar neadaigh lonta dubha do chuid súl.
Padaí óg na *good looks*.
Gléasta i do chulaith fhaiseanta nua néata gan smál
a chuir poll i do phóca.
Wee Paddy a thug muid ort is tú thar sé throigh
nuair a lean tú lorg do dheartháireacha ba shine,
cárta bréagach aitheantais i do ghlac,
do phas go Kelly's, Lavery's, Robinson's,
le bheith ag guaillíocht leis na meisceoirí eile,
caillte i gcathair ghríobháin round síoraí.
Sa deireadh go Londain thall,
ar lorg luach do shaothair.
Pubanna is clubanna a d'oirfeadh do chulaith is úire,
d'acmhainn
– gone where the sun is shining thru the pourin' rain
where the weather suits my clothes

Paddy

'Did ya hear about Donal's wee brother?'
cried Chips through the din of mates
manning the shipwreck-table,
the white noise of the band,
his mouthed words parrying blades
of cranked up *Fender* amp feedback,
cutting through the smoke
and fog machines.

We had spliced the mainbrace
and become unmoored with Bush and grass,
drifting over looped chords and sinnets of riffs.
It was some gig or other,
good vibes crackling through
the valves and leads.

And as I heard your story, Paddy,
you ghosted into the squally harbour of memory,
sleek dark hair combed off a dusky forehead
where your blackbird-eyes nested,
dressed in your latest slick-cut suit
that burned a hole in your pocket.

We called you wee Paddy
though you were over six feet
when you trailed us,
flashing phoney ID to the monkeys
on the door of Kelly's, Lavery's, Robinson's,
where you'd go to rub shoulders with other mates
lost in the submarine labyrinth of an eternal round
and finally, fed up with it all,
to London.

(Continued on page 255)

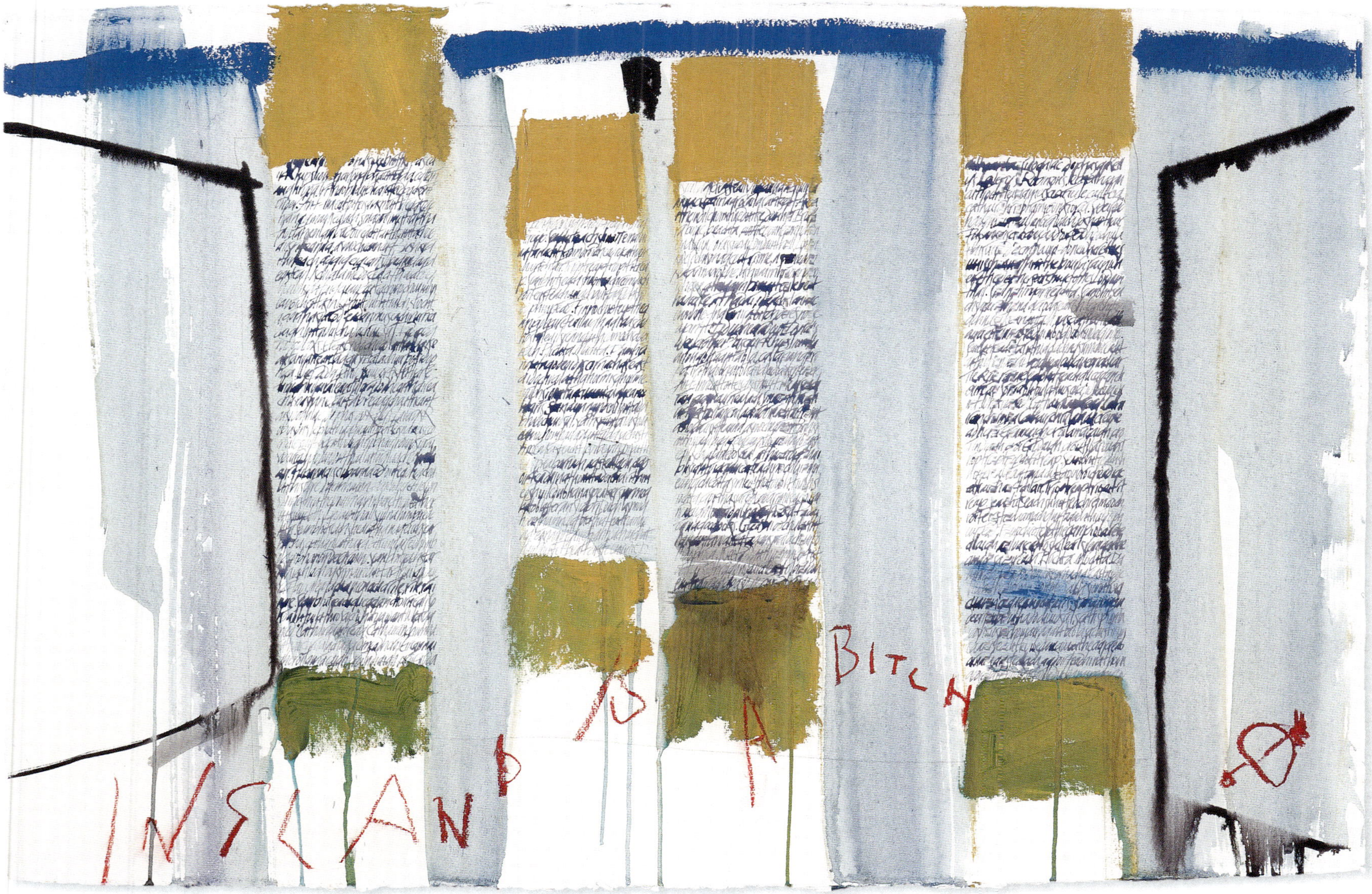
IRELAND IS A BITCH

71

NUALA NÍ DHOMHNAILL

b. 1952

Ealaíontóir/Artist:
Frances Hegarty

Peannaire/Calligrapher:
Frances Breen

Aistritheoir/Translator:
Paul Muldoon

Ainmníodh ag/Nominator:
The Author

Dubh

ar thitim Shrebenice, 11ú Iúil, 1995

Is lá dubh é seo,
Tá an spéir dubh.
Tá an fharraige dubh.
Tá na gáirdíní dubh.

Tá na crainn dubh.
Tá na cnoic dubh.
Tá na busanna dubh.
Tá na carranna a thugann na páistí ar scoil
ar maidin dubh.

Tá na siopaí dubh.
Tá a bhfuinneoga dubh.
Tá na sráideanna dubh (is ní le daoine é).

Tá na nuachtáin a dhíolann an cailín dubh
go bhfuil an folt láidir dubh uirthi
dubh dubh dubh.

Tá an damh dubh.
Tá na gadhair dubh.
Tá capall úd Uíbh Ráthaigh dubh.
Tá gach corr-éan a scinneann amach as an
ealta dubh.
An chaoire dhubh a sheasann amach de
ghnáth i lár an tréada
ní heisceacht í níos mó mar tá na caoirigh
ar fad dubh.

Tá na prátaí dubh.
Tá na turnapaí dubh.
Tá gach bileog cabáiste a chuirfeá síos i
dtóin corcáin dubh.

Tá na Caitlicigh dubh.
Tá na Protastúnaigh dubh.
Tá na Seirbigh is na Cróátaigh dubh.
Tá gach uile chine a shiúlann ar dhromchla
na cruinne
an mhaidin dhubh seo samhraidh dubh.

Black

on the fall of Srebenica, 11th July, 1995

A black day this,
The sky is black.
The sea is black.
The gardens are black.

The trees are black
The hills are black.
The buses are black.
The cars bringing the kids to school are black.

The shops are black.
Their windows are black.
The streets are black (and I don't mean with people).

The newspapers sold by the dark girl with the great head of dark hair
Are black, black, black.

The ox is black.
The hound is black.
The very horse from Iveragh is black.
The bird suddenly out of sync with the flock is black.
The black sheep that stood out from the ordinary run of sheep no longer stands out,
For all the sheep are black.

The spuds are black.
The turnips are black.
Every last leaf of cabbage in the pot is black.

The saucepan is black.
The kettle is black.
The bottom of every pot from here to the crack of doom is black.

The Catholics are black.
The Protestants are black.
The Serbs and the Croatians are black.
Every tribe on the face of the earth this blackest of black mornings black.

(Continued on page 256)

72

BIDDY JENKINSON

Ealaíontóir/Artist:
Geraldine O'Reilly

Peannaire/Calligrapher:
Frances Breen

Aistritheoir/Translator:
Theo Dorgan

Ainmníodh ag/Nominator:
The Author

Amhrán Mhis ag Grianstad an Gheimhridh

Oícheanta seaca
i mbile cille
mar éan i ngreim i nglae
lem chleití flichreocha
síos liom in aon bhrat oighir,
an dá chois crochta asam
mar phrátaí seaca
ag ceangal
de ghasa fada feoite,
chanainn
caintic na maidine,
imní ag giollaíocht
ar mo sheamsán dóchais
is reo na maidine ag athreo,
mo chuisle ceoil
ag cuisniú
is ag titim
ina gháire dóite.

Is bheinnse imithe ar eadarbhuas
ar bhaothréim siúil
ag lingeadh léimeanna
ó leamhan go hiubhar
mo chíoradh féin ar dheilgní an droighin
im ghealt
mar shíleadar,
murach
istigh im shlaod smeara
san idirfhásach
idir ghealtacht geilte
is gealtacht duine
cuimhne ag goradh
is ag spriúchadh teasa ...

Song of Mis at the Winter Solstice

Nights of hard frost
in the holy tree
trapped like a bird
with wet frozen feathers
I'd lay myself down in a sheet of ice
my feet sticking out,
frost potatoes
clinging
to long withered stalks,
and sing morning's canticle;
hagridden, trembling
on the drone of hope,
frost of morning hardening again,
my pulse of song
freezing
and falling
into bitter laughter.

I'd be away in a dizzy flight
in mad career
in springing leaps
from elm to yew
harrowing myself on spines of blackthorn,
half-crazy
the people thought,
only that
deep in my marrow,
deep between marrow and bone,
between the lunatic madness
and the madness of a sane woman
memory was nesting, brooding,
sputtering with damp heat . . .

(Continued on page 257)

Oícheanta seaca
 i mbile cille
mar éan i ngreim i nglae
 lem chleití flichreocha
síos liom in aon bhrat oighir,
 an dá chois crochta asam
mar phrátaí seaca
 ag ceangal
de ghasa fada feoite,
 chanainn
caintic na maidine,
 imní ag giollaíocht
ar mo sheamsán dóchais
 is reo na maidine ag athreo,
mo chuisle ceoil
 ag cuisniú
is ag titim
 ina gháire dóite.

Maidin in ainnise in iubhar na cille
 bláth seaca ar mo shúile
stualeirg mo dhroma
 ar cnagadh
ar an stoc reoite,
 mo mhásaí maoldearga
ag táth fúthu
 in uanán buinní biolair.
chasas soir
 is phóg gealán mo shúile
ag leá oighir iontu.
Ligh méar fhada gréine cuar mo bhéil
 is shlíoc mo ghruanna,
neadaigh im leicne.

Bhraitheas an dúléan ag leá im chroí
 an gile ag nochtadh cneá isteach go braon
 is an dubh ag rith uaim.
Shíneas uaim mo lámha chuig an ngrian
 a dheargaigh néalta
 a thug suntas
do gach lóipín sneachta gur las sé,
 gur tháth tír is aer in aon mhuir solais
mar ar chuir mo chroí chun cuain.

Amhrán Mhis ag Grianstad an Gheimhridh

Is bheinnse imithe ar eadarbhuas
 ar bhaothréim siúil
ag lingeadh léimeanna
 ó leamhán go hiubhar
mo chíoradh féin ar dheilgní an droighin
 im ghealt
mar shíleadar,
 murach
istigh im shlaod smeara
 san idirfhásach
idir ghealtacht geilte
 is gealtacht duine
cuimhne ag goradh
 is ag spriúchadh teasa...

Sa dúluachair,
 i bputóga dubha gach bliana,
mar chuiteamh comaoine,
 ceapaim an ghrian
i gcuaschomhlaí mo chroí
 is teilgim í sna harda
le hurchar ceoil
 de bheala éin an earraigh.

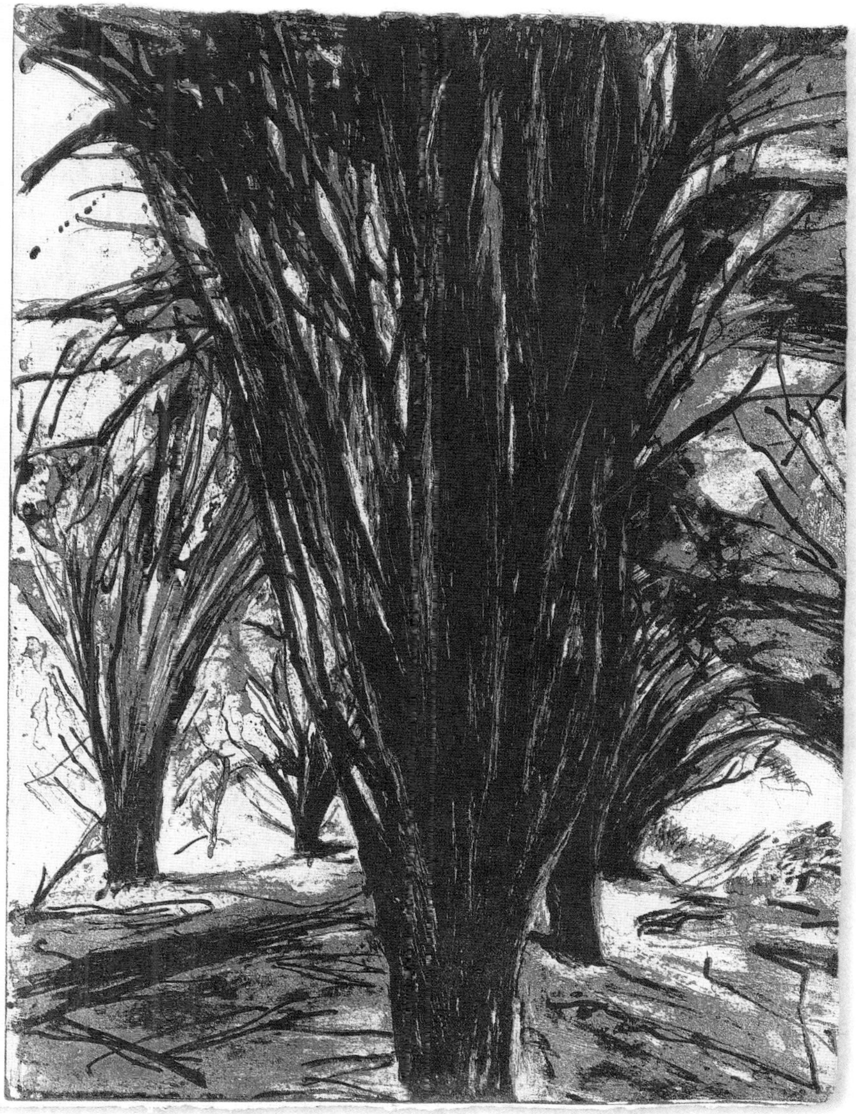

73

MICHAEL DAVITT

b. 1950

Ealaíontóir/Artist:
Andrew Folan

Peannaire/Calligrapher:
Réiltín Murphy

Aistritheoir/Translator:
Paul Muldoon

Ainmníodh ag/Nominator:
The Author

An Scáthán

i gcuimhne m' athar

Níorbh é m'athair níos mó é
ach ba mise a mhacsan;
paradacsa fuar a d'fháisceas,
dealbh i gculaith Dhomhnaigh
a cuireadh an lá dár gcionn.

Dhein sé an-lá deora, seirí,
fuiscí, ceapairí feola is tae.
Bhí seanchara leis ag eachtraí
faoi sciuird lae a thugadar
ar Eochaill sna triochaidí
is gurbh é a chéad pháirtí é
i seirbhís Chorcaí/An Sciobairín
amach sna daicheadaí.
Bhí dornán cártaí Aifrinn
ar mhatal an tseomra suí
ina gcorrán thart ar vás gloine,
a bhronntanas scoir ó CIE.

Níorbh eol dom go ceann dhá lá
gurbh é an scáthán a mharaigh é.

An seanscáthán ollmhór Victeoiriach
leis an bhfráma ornáideach bréagórga
a bhí romhainn sa tigh trí stór
nuair a bhogamar isteach ón tuath.
Bhinn scanraithe roimhe: go sciorrfadh
anuas den bhfalla is go slogfadh mé
d'aon tromanáil i lár na hoiche.

The Mirror

in memory of my father

He was no longer my father
but I was still his son;
I would get to grips with that cold paradox,
the remote figure in his Sunday best
who was buried the next day.

A great day for tears, snifters of sherry,
whiskey, beef sandwiches, tea.
An old mate of his was recounting
their day excursion
to Youghal in the Thirties,
how he was his first partner
on the Cork/Skibbereen route
in the late Forties.
There was a splay of Mass cards
on the sitting-room mantelpiece
which formed a crescent round a glass vase,
his retirement present from CIE.

I didn't realise until two days later
it was the mirror took his breath away.

The monstrous old Victorian mirror
with the ornate gilt frame
we had found in the three-storey house
when we moved in from the country.
I was afraid that it would sneak
down from the wall and swallow me up
in one gulp in the middle of the night.

(Continued on page 257)

an seanscáthán ollmhór victeoiriach
leis an bhfráma ornáideach breágorga
a bhí romhainn sa tigh trí stór
nuair a bhogamar isteach ón tuath,
bhínn scanraithe roimhe: go sciorrfadh
anuas den bhfalla is go slogfadh mé
d'aon-tromanáil i lár na hoíche.
ag maisiú an tseomra chodlata dó
d'ardaigh sé an scáthán anuas
gan lámh chúnta a iarraidh;
ar ball d'iompaigh dath na cré air.
an oíche sin phléasc a chroí.

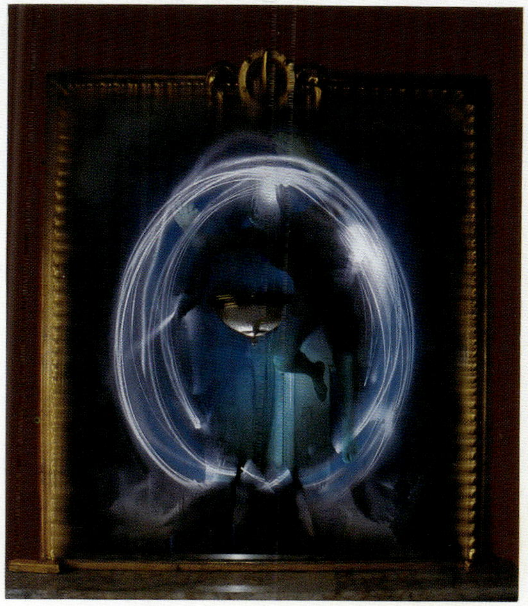

74

ALAN TITLEY

b.1957

Ealaíontóir/Artist:
John Bellany

Clóghrafóir/Typographer:
Donald Addison

Aistritheoir/Translator:
The Author

Ainmníodh ag/Nominator:
Michael Davitt

An Loingeas (sliocht)

Maidir lem iomthúsa idir Éirinn agus Albainn ní fiú mórán a aithris.

Lí na farraige go láidir fúinn, gile mara faoinár rámha. Shín uainn glas is buí. Tonntracha ag síorshnoí an talaimh i bhfad i gcéin.

Inis i gcónai ar íor ár súile agus rith fionn lena taobh gheal. Ghairm an fharraige síthshámh linn fan an bhealaigh. Lúcháir radhairc dúinn na bradáin bhreaca ag léim as broinn faoinár siúl ar an mhuir fhionn.

Luigh na gaotha síos is d'fhan go socair uainn in ionaid uachtracha an aeir, is shocraigh an mhuir ina clár réidh míngheal gan ghlam, gan tafann.

Daoine eile a ghabh an ród seo romham á n-iompar agam ar mo dhroim. Mic Uisleann nach raibh in Éirinn rí nach gcuirfeadh fáilte rompu. Colm Cille a raibh cumha ar éanacha agus ar ainmhithe éigiallda ina dhiaidh. Bhí sé i ndán dó siúd go síolfadh sé creideamh agus cráifeacht. Bhí mo chuidse cinniúna romham amach chomh dall leis an ghealach.

The Ship Sailing (excerpt)

About my goings from Ireland to Scotland there is not much to relate.

The slap of the sea strongly beneath us, the bright brine urged by our oars.

Always an isle on our eyes' edge, brushed with white billows. The saltsud sea beckoned us onwards. Joyjumps to our sight were the spotted salmon leaping from the waves on our white way.

The winds lay down and hid sweetly in the upper nooks of the air, and the sea settled to a quiet quilt without growl or glower.

Others before me who had passed this way I carried on my back. The sons of Uisneach whom no king in Ireland would not have given welcome. Colm Cille for whom the birds and the wild beasts pined. It was his fate to seed faith and fealty. My fate before me as blind as the moon.

This is an excerpt from the novel An Fear Dána, *which is an imaginative reconstruction of the life and times of the Irish-Scottish poet Muireadhach Albanach Ó Dalaigh (c.1180-1230). He had to flee Ireland after he murdered a steward of Domhnall Mór Ó Domhnaill who had insulted him, and spent several years as professional bard to the Earls of Lennox. He later went on a pilgrimage to the Holy Land, possibly on the coat-tails of the Crusades, and returned to Ireland to try to regain a poetic position and to make peace with his accusers. It is likely that this was unsuccessful and that he returned to Scotland, where he died. This piece describes his sea-journey from Ireland to Scotland while he was going into exile. (Alan Titley)*

We have only been able to give an excerpt from this text. For an alternative source of the full text see the listing on page 265.

(Continued on page 258)

An Loingeas

ALAN TITLEY

MAIDIR lem iomthúsa idir Éirinn agus Albainn ní fiú mórán a aithris.

Lí na farraige go láidir fúinn, gile mara faoinár rámha. Shín uainn glas is buí. Tonntracha ag síorshnoí an talaimh i bhfad i gcéin.

Inis i gcónai ar íor ár súile agus rith fionn lena taobh gheal. Ghairm an fharraige síthshámh linn fan an bhealaigh. Lúcháir radhairc dúinn na bradáin bhreaca ag léim as broinn faoinár siúl ar an mhuir fhionn.

Luigh na gaotha síos is d'fhan go socair uainn in ionaid uachtracha an aeir, is shocraigh an mhuir ina clár réidh míngheal gan ghlam, gan tafann.

Daoine eile a ghabh an ród seo romham á n-iompar agam ar mo dhroim. Mic Uisleann nach raibh in Éirinn rí nach gcuirfeadh fáilte rompu. Colm Cille a raibh cumha ar éanacha agus ar ainmhithe éigiallda ina dhiaidh. Bhí sé i ndán dó siúd go síolfadh sé creideamh agus cráifeacht. Bhí mo chuidse cinniúna romham amach chomh dall leis an ghealach.

Ba mhór eadrainne agus Fearghus Mór mac Eirc a shín a radharc thar sáile óna dhún suáilceach gur tháinig a ríocht i dtír lastoir de chaolas Íle. Chonaic sé uaidh a fhlaitheas gan chrích a raibh na lasracha uaidh ag lonradh ina aigne. Maidir liomsa, bhí an phian ag screadach trín pholl i mo chroí agus mé ag tabhairt cúl le hÉirinn.

Suibhne ina shuí thuas ar Charraig Alastair, áitreabh d'fhaoileáin, fuar dá haíonna. Fliuch ár leabana, beag a shíleamar gur charraig nó gur aistear naofa a bhí fúinn. Trua ár gcoinne-ne, dís chorr chrualoirgneacha, gealt ar eite agus file ar a theicheadh. Trua ár dturas-sa, cian ónár n-eolas-sa an chrioch gur ránamar.

Deatach ar chósta Chinn Tíre uainn ag scríobh ar an spéir. Bhéim sinn na seolta tana ballacha aoibhne agus leag sinn na crainn mhíndearga ghasta ar fud an urláir.

A mhalairt d'aistear aduaidh a chuir Labhán Draoi de in aimsir Dhiarmada mhic Cearúil a bheith i bhflaitheas Éireann. Maith a thuigeas a aois dhána. Lánmhar é ó bhród a cheirde. Chuala trácht ar oineach Eochaidh Aontsúla, sinsear síl Shúilleabháin.

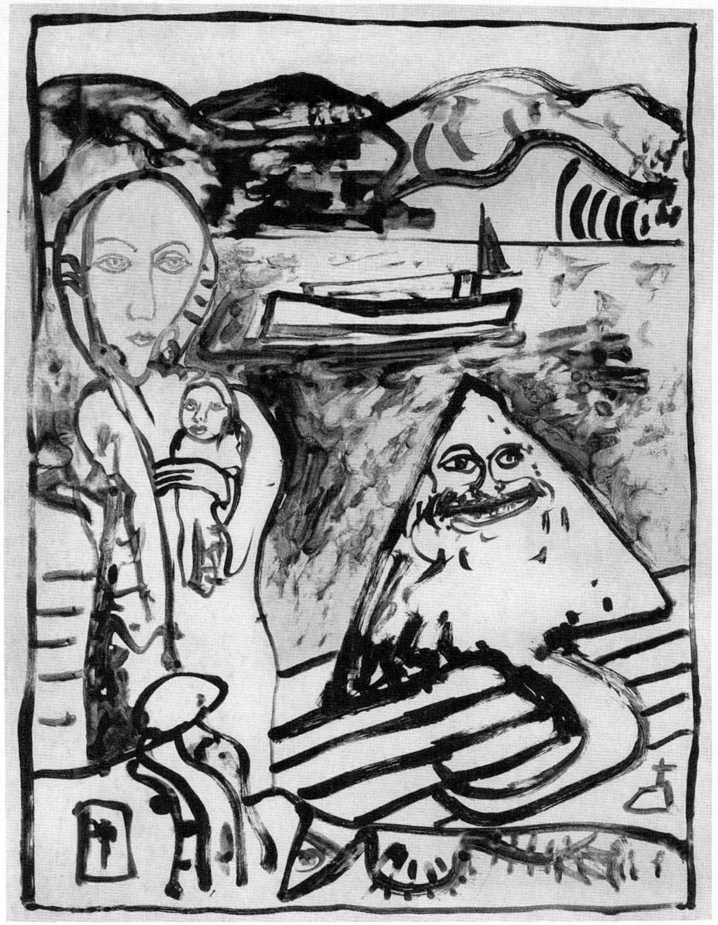

75

ÁINE NÍ GHLINN

b. 1955

Ealaíontóir/Artist:
Pauline Cummins

Peannaire/Calligrapher:
Louise Donaldson

Aistritheoir/Translator:
The Author

Ainmníodh ag/Nominator:
The Author

Cuair

Ó ghoid máinlia
a banúlacht uaithi
bíonn sí de shíor
ag stánadh
ar éirí na gréine
ar chomhchruinneas na gcnoc.
Ar pháipéar déanann
stuanna ciorcail
ceann i ndiaidh a chéile.
Ó fágadh coilm sceana
mar a mbíodh a brollach
tá sí ciaptha ag cuair.

Curves

She stares
at the rising sun,
rests her eyes
on the roundness of hills.
On paper
she draws circles,
arcs of circles,
circle after circle.
Since a surgeon
scalpelled out
her femininity,
she is haunted by curves.

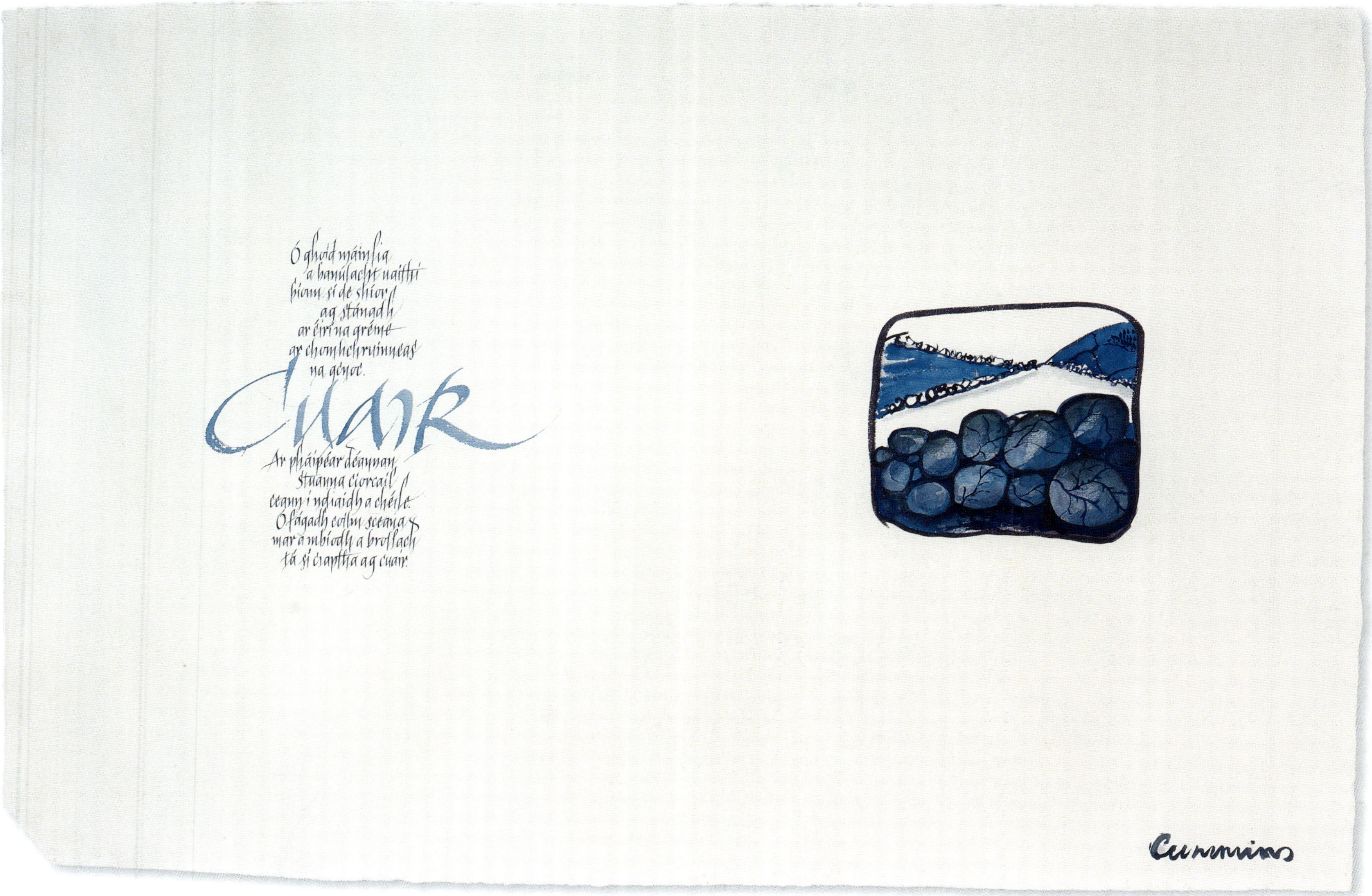
Ó ghoid máinlia
a banúlacht uaithi
bíonn sí de shíor
ag stánadh
ar éirí na gréine
ar chomhchruinneas
na gcnoc.
CUAIR
Ar pháipéar déanann
stuanna ciorcail
ceann i ndiaidh a chéile.
Ó fágadh coilm sceana
mar a mbíodh a brollach
tá sí craptha ag cuair.
Cummins

PÓL Ó MUIRÍ

b. 1965

Ealaíontóir/Artist:
Fionnuala Ní Chiosáin

Peannaire/Calligrapher:
Frances Breen

Aistritheoir/Translator:
The Author

Ainmníodh ag/Nominator:
The Author

D-Day

"Liberator" a thugtar ar an eitleán seo
Atá ag guairdeall i spéartha
snagscamallacha briste na Normáine.
Ina shoc, ar crith, bodhar ag dordán
piachánach na n-inneall,
Tá Marvin, ag guí Dé go ligfeadh sé
thairis an chailís seo.
I bpóca a léine taise tá pictiúr de Mary
McDonald, Bóthar na bhFál,
A teachtaireacht bheag de
ghlanmheabhair aige: Tar ar ais
chugam.
Amuigh fríd néalta colgacha an flak,
cluineann sé feothan tirim
An tSamhraidh ag bogadh thar mhachairí
torthúla Minnesota,
Siosarnach thostach thaibhsí na Sioux, a
deireadh na seanfhondúirí.

D-Day

This plane, hovering in the cloudy, broken skies
Of Normandy, is called a Liberator.
In its nose, shaking, deafened by the throaty droning
Of the engines, is Marvin, praying to God
To let this chalice pass. In the damp pocket of his shirt
A picture of Mary McDonald, Falls Road,
Her simple message learnt by heart: Come back to me.
Outside, through the waspish clouds of flak,
He hears the dry summer breeze moving
Over Minnesota's fruitful plains - the quiet whispering
Of the ghosts of the Sioux, the old ones used to say.

D.Day

"Liberator" a thugtar ar an eitleán seo

Atá ag guairdeall i spéartha snagscamallacha briste na Normáine.

Ina shuí, ar crith, bodhar ag dordán piachánach na n-inneall,

Tá Marvin, ag guí Dé go ligfeadh sé thairis an chailís seo.

I bpóca a léine taise tá pictiúr de Mary McDonald, Bóthar na bhFál,

a teachtaireacht bheag de ghlanmheabhair aige: Tar ar ais chugam.

Amuigh fríd néalta colgacha an flak, cluineann sé feothan tirim

an tSamhraidh ag bogadh thar mhachairí torthúla Minnesota,

siosarnach thostach thaibhsí na Sioux, a deireadh na seanfhondúirí.

77

LIAM Ó MUIRTHILE

b. 1950

Ealaíontóir / Artist:
Doug Cocker

Clóghrafóir / Typographer:
Donald Addison

Aistritheoir / Translator:
Greg Delanty

Ainmníodh ag / Nominator:
The Author

Tairseacha

Éinne amuigh thar tairseacha?
Aon tiompán ar crith
ar mhinicíocht ar bith
tríd an siosadh statach?

Táim ar an raon inchloiste is ísle
ard-dílse cogarnaíle daonna,
mar a thugaimidne domhandaigh
ar ár mbeo pláinéadach,
is gur sásamh é focail a chumadh
is a dhíchumadh go harmónach
le casúirín ar inneoin na héisteachta.

Táim ar an amhaire is ísle brí,
aimpligh mo ghuí ascalach,
amhastrach eachtardhomhanda
mhadra ultrasonach HMV
mar a bhí fadó, mar atá fós,
ar a chorraghiob buanmhaighnéadach
i mbéal chlosmhinicíocht an challaire.

Tabhair dúinn léas bíogtha
tríd an gceo leictreonach
is saor sinn ó gach olc
mo chogarnaíl íos-déine dB,
deonaigh dúinn nach macallaí
fuaimthoinne amháin ár nguí
ag luasghéarú trí shaol na saol
ar ais amach i gcrith mo scairte.

Thresholds

Anybody out there beyond the thresholds?
Any ear-drum reverberating
on any heavenly frequency
thru the hissing static?

I'm on the lowest high-fidelity
whispering range of humans,
which is what we terrestrials dub ourselves
in this sublunar life,
composing words with such satisfaction,
harmonically distorting them,
hammering on the anvil of the tympanum.

I'm on the lowest strength woofer;
amplify my oscillating prayer,
the extraterrestrial barking
of the HMV ultrasonic dog
as he was in the beginning and is still
on his permanently magnetized haunches
in the audible mouth of the speaker.

Grant us one answering ultra wave
of light back
thru the electronic fog
and deliver us from all evil.
Answer my low level dB mumbling.
Grant that our prayers
are not simply the echoes
of mere trembling sound waves,
riffing back and forth
from my midriff for ever and for ever.

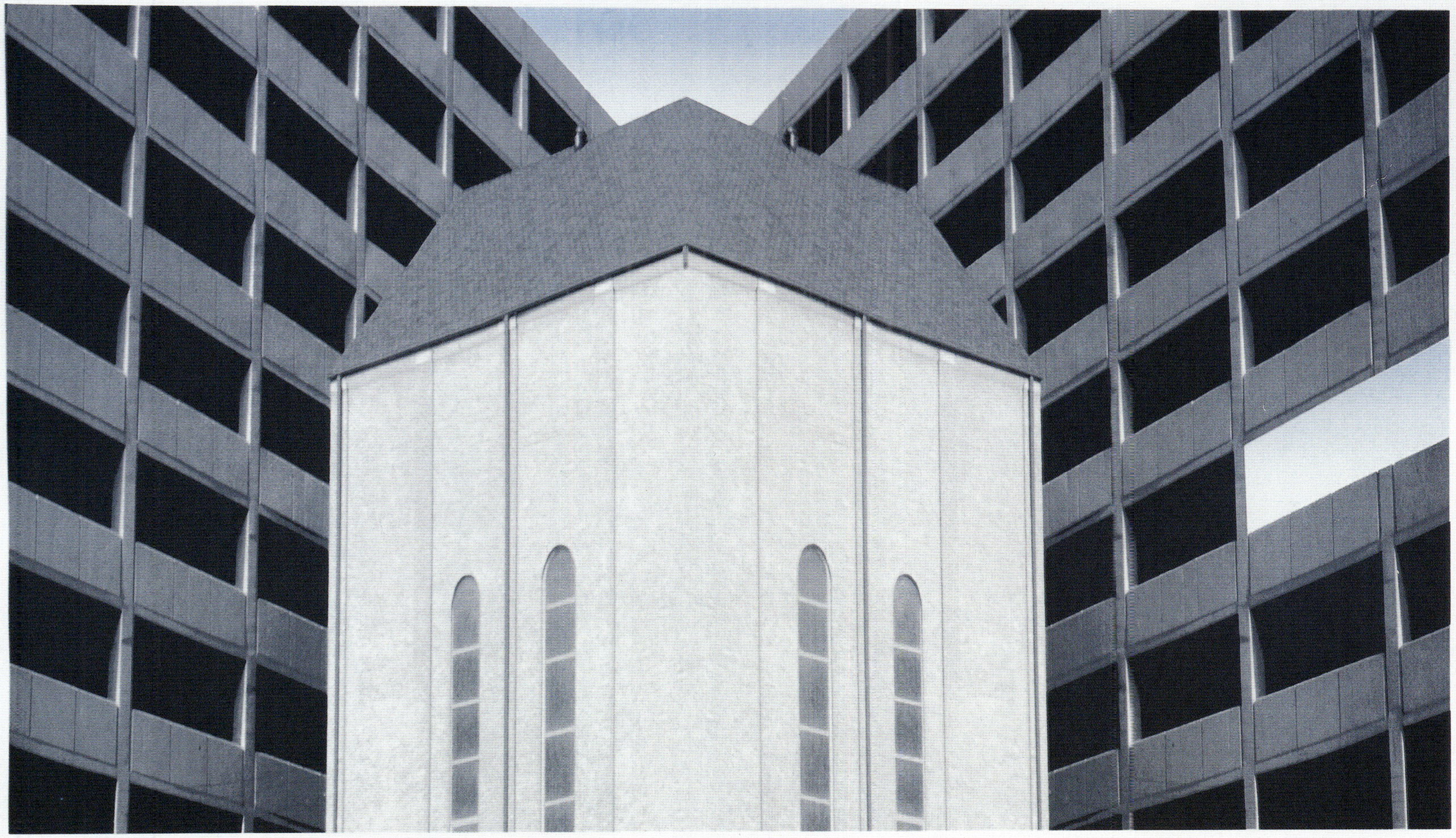

/// EINNE · XAMUI · GHXTH · ARX**TA · IRSEA · CHA**?X · XAONX · TIOMP · ANXAR · XCRIT · HXXAR · XMHIN · ICIOC · HTXAR · XBITH · XXTRI · DXANX · SIOSA · DH?XX ///

78

SEÁN Ó RÍORDÁIN

1917-1977

Ealaíontóir/Artist:
Aisling Ó Beirn

Peannaire/Calligrapher:
The Artist

Aistritheoir/Translator:
Greg Delanty

Ainmníodh ag/Nominator:
Liam Ó Muirthile

Fiabhras

Tá sléibhte na leapa mós ard,
Tá breoiteacht 'na brothall 'na lár,
Is fada an t-aistear urlár,
  Is na mílte is na mílte i gcéin
  Tá suí agus seasamh sa saol.

Atáimid i gceantar bráillín,
Ar éigean más cuimhin linn cathaoir,
  Ach bhí tráth sar ba mhachaire sinn,
  In aimsir choisíochta fadó,
  Go mbímis chomh hard le fuinneog.

Tá pictiúir ar an bhfalla ag at,
Tá an fráma imithe ina lacht,
Ceal creidimh ní féidir é bhac,
  Tá nithe ag druidim fém dhéin,
  Is braithim ag titim an saol.

Tá ceantar ag taisteal ón spéir,
Tá comharsanacht suite ar mo mhéar,
Dob fhuirist dom breith ar shéipéal,
  Tá ba ar an mbóthar ó thuaidh,
  Is níl ba na síoraíochta chomh ciúin.

Fever

The mountainous climb out of the bed,
Its sickly sweltering core
Is a long way from the floor.
  Miles and miles away
  People still sit and stand.

We're here in the locality of sheets.
We can barely recall a chair.
  Once we stood sound on level ground,
  In a time of walking, long ago.
  We were as tall as the window.

A picture swells off the wall.
The frame melts into a haze.
A lack of faith can't halt it.
  Things close in around me,
  The world comes apart.

A locality is forming in the ether,
A neighbourhood perches on my finger.
I could easily pluck off a chapel.
  There are cows on the road to the north.
  The cows of eternity are not as quiet.

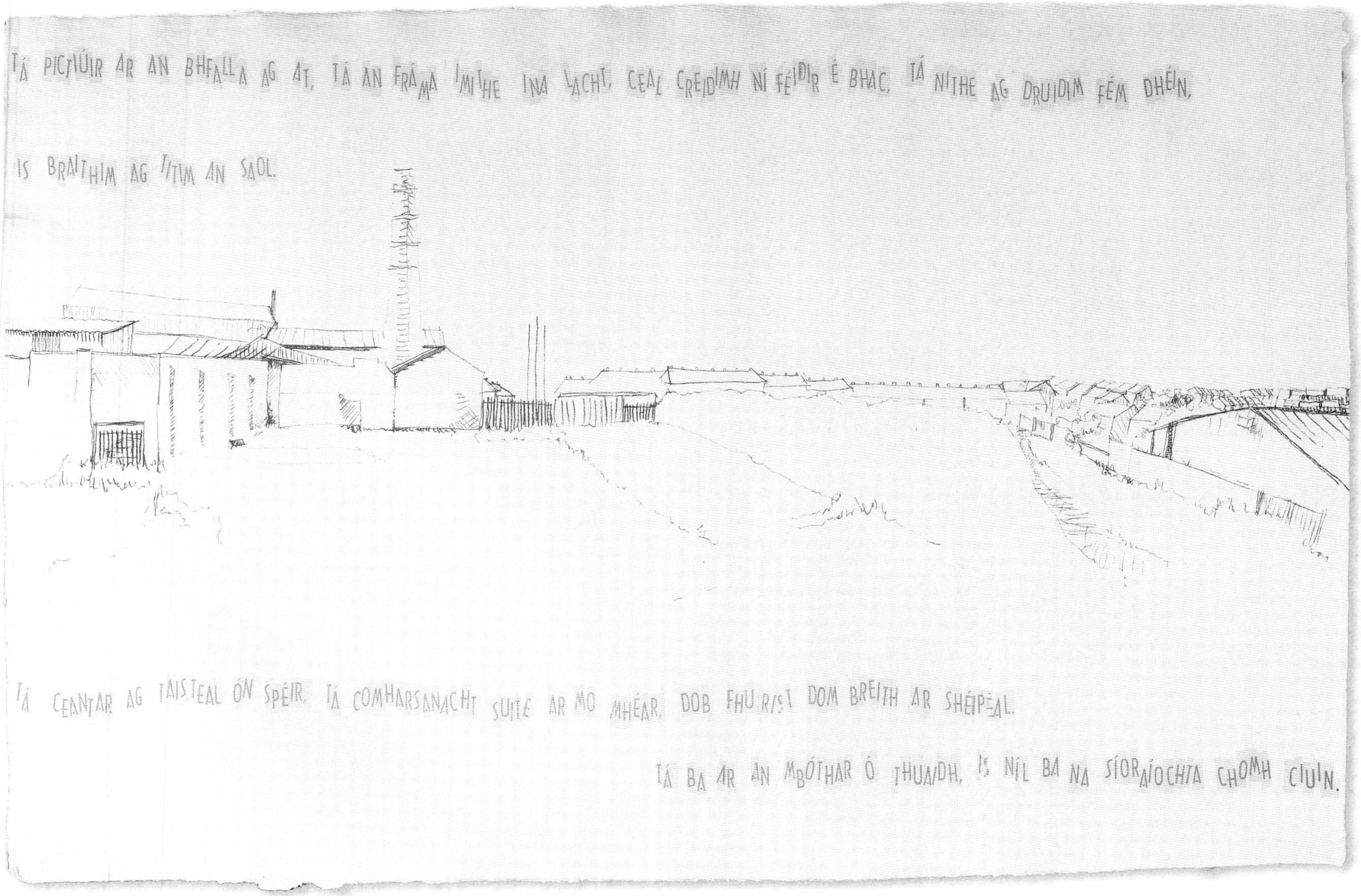
TÁ PICTIÚIR AR AN BHFALLA AG AT, TÁ AN FRÁMA IMITHE INA LACHT, CEAL CREIDIMH NÍ FÉIDIR É BHAC, TÁ NITHE AG DRUIDIM FÉM DHÉIN,
IS BRAITHIM AG TITIM AN SAOL.
TÁ CEANTAR AG TAISTEAL ÓN SPÉIR. TÁ COMHARSANACHT SUITE AR MO MHÉAR. DOB FHURIST DOM BREITH AR SHÉIPEAL.
TÁ BA AR AN MBÓTHAR Ó THUAIDH, IS NÍL BA NA SÍORAÍOCHTA CHOMH CIUIN.

79

CATHAL Ó SEARCAIGH

b. 1956

Ealaíontóir/Artist:
Ian Joyce

Peannaire/Calligrapher:
Réiltín Murphy

Aistritheoir/Translator:
Frank Sewell

Ainmníodh ag/Nominator:
The Author

Claochló

Tá mé ag ullmhú le bheith i mo chrann
agus chan de bharr go bhfuil dia ar bith
mo sheilg gan trua, é sa tóir orm go teann,
mé ag ealú óna **chaithréim spéire, mo chroí ag rith**
ina sceith sceoine, roimh bhuaile a **dhúile**.

D' aonghnó tiocfaidh **claochló aoibhinn ar mo chló**.
As mo cholainn daonna dhéanfar stoc darach.
Tiontóidh **craiceann ina choirt chranrach**; gan stró,
athróidh an **sruth fola ina shú**, an gheir ina smúsach:
fásaidh duilleoga ar mo **ghéaga cnámhacha**.

Cheana féin tá mo chuid ladhra ag síneadh,
ag géagú amach ina bhfréamhacha feitheogacha,
ag buanú sa chréafóg, ag taisceadh is ag teannadh.
Mothaím mé féin ag imeacht **le craobhacha**
nuair a **shéideann bogleoithne fríd mo ghéaga.**

Inniu chan ag análú atá mé ach ag siosarnach
agus mé mo sheasamh caol díreach gan bogadh;
éanacha na spéire ag ceiliúr ionam go haerach.
As an tsolas diamhair seo atá mo spreagadh
go dil, **cruthóidh mé clóraifil; mo ghlasdán . . .**

Transfigured

I am getting ready to become a tree,
not because some god is after me,
bearing down with his aerial authority,
my heart bolting from the thrust of his need.

My figure will be transfigured, in one go;
my human shell turned to the trunk of an oak,
my skin twisted to gnarled bark, my blood-flow
to sap. Out of my branch-bones leaves will grow.

Already, my fingers and toes are stretching out,
elongating into sinewy roots,
tucking themselves tightly into the ground;
and when a breeze blows my branches round,
I feel as if I'm going nuts, or out

of my tree. Today I stand tall and straight,
not breathing but rustling; birds congregate
in me, warbling airs while I create
chlorophyll, inspired by unfathomable light
to fulfil my destiny, synthesise my fate.

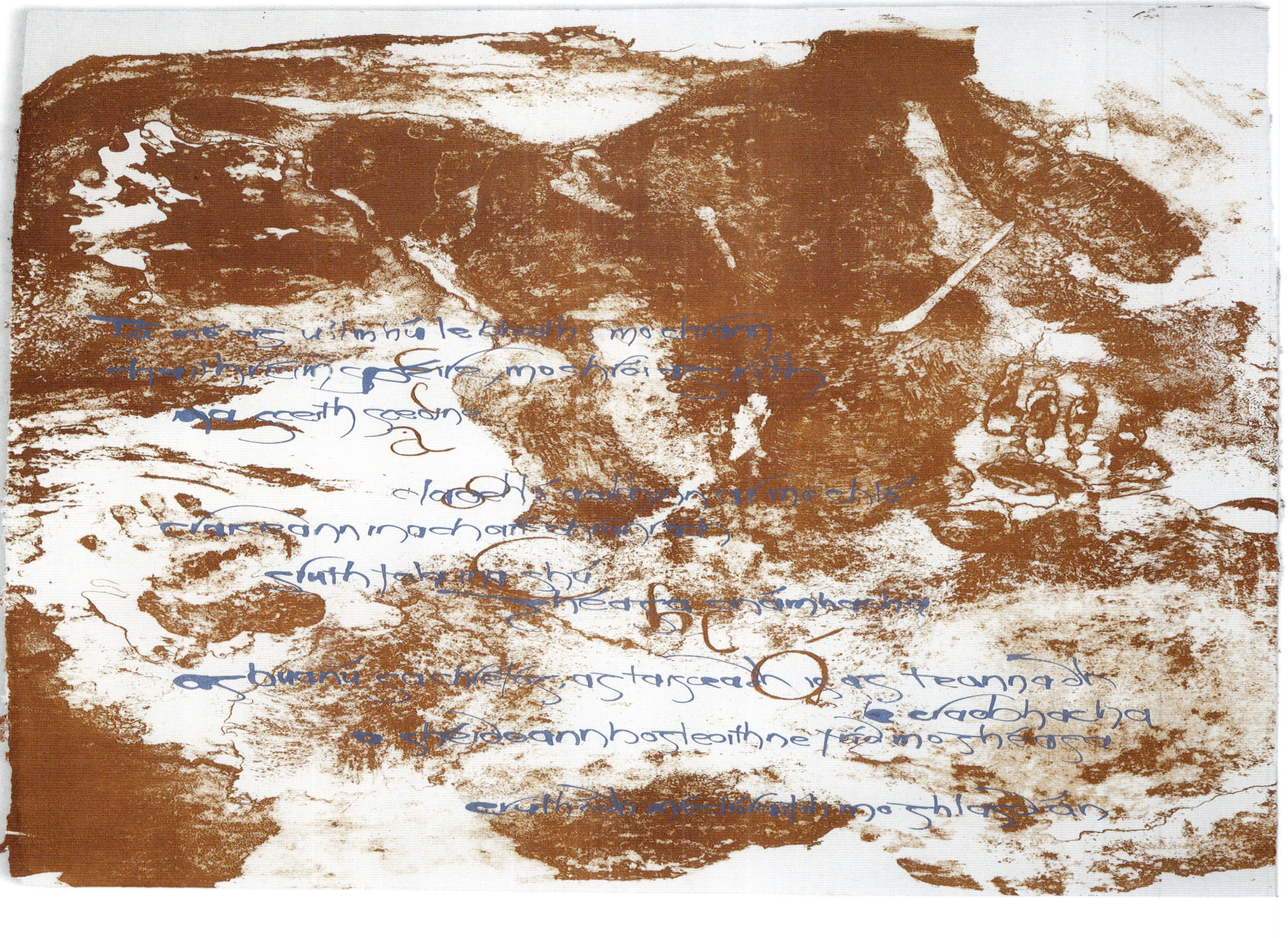
le craobhacha
trí mo ghéaga
mo ghlasán

80

MÍCHEÁL Ó CONGHAILE

b. 1962

Ealaíontóir/Artist:
Steve Dilworth

Peannaire/Calligrapher:
Susan Leiper

Aistritheoir/Translator:
Frank Sewell

Ainmníodh ag/Nominator:
Cathal Ó Searcaigh

An Charraig (sliocht)

Déarfá gurbh ann ariamh di. Í ina carraig chomh storrúil damanta mór . . . Mór millteach. Agus téagarach. Charnódh a ceathrú fiú na céadta tonna meáchain ar aon scála ar domhan. Go dimhin, ní carraig ach oílcharraig. Fathach-charraig. Dia-charraig . . . Í sáilbháite go leisciúil i sméar mhullaigh an chnoic - go sócúil compordach cheapfá, mar a sciorrrfadh go ceanúil d'ainsiléad Dé. Í ina máistir. Ina máistir feiceálach. Ina hardmháistír ceannasach, cumasach. Thar a bheith ceannasach cumasach ag breathnú - fiú más i ngan fhios agus dá hainneoin féin é. I ansiúd ag bearnú na mílte amharc i bhfáithim dhraíochtúil ildathach na spéartha. Níor ghéill an charraig ariamh d'aon tsúil ná sleasamharc dá ghéire, dá láidre, dá impíche. Rinne sclábhaithe feacúla adhrúla díobh dá mbuíochas ag urá a n-amharc. A cos i dtaca, sheas an fód go huasal dalba. Tostach. Marbhthostach. Tost críonna brionglóideach na haoise: na n-aoiseanna. A cruth sainiúil tostach féin aici ón uile mhíle uillinn sleasach. Síorathrú ar a síorchruth dá corp rocach carraigeach - na céadta leiceann uirthi: na céadta glúin: na céadta colpa: na céadta cluas: na céadta boiric: na céadta clár éadain: na céadta faithne: na céadta goirín: na céadta at: na céadta súil: na céadta gearradh drúichtín: na mílte céadta . . .

The Rock (excerpt)

You could say it had always been there. An enormous rock. Damned strong. And bulky. Even a quarter of it would weigh hundreds of tonnes on any scale. I'm telling you, it wasn't a rock but the mother of all rocks. A giant of a rock. A god among rocks . . . Stationed, at ease, on the top part of the hill - all comfy and cosy, you'd think, like it was tipped lovingly into place by the hand of God. It was like a Lord. An eminent Lord. A powerful, commanding Lord. Looking just the part, either despite itself or without knowing it. Interrupting thousands of glances at the magic, multi-coloured hem of the sky. The rock gave way to no-one's eye or side-glance, no matter how keen, strong or imploring. It made them submissive, bent-necked slaves for their trouble, eclipsing their view. Planted there, it stood its ground with daunting authority. Silent. Deadly silent. An ancient, dreamy silence that was timeless. Its own silent shape from a thousand different angles. Forever changing the look of its wrinkled, rocky body's eternal shape - with hundreds of cheeky slopes, knee-like steps, calf-shaped collops, ear-like edges, sticky out bits, brows, warts, pimples, lumps, hundreds of eye-shaped features, hard skin, split ends, trillions of things.

We have only been able to give an excerpt from this text. For an alternative source of the full text see the listing on page 265.

(Continued on page 258)

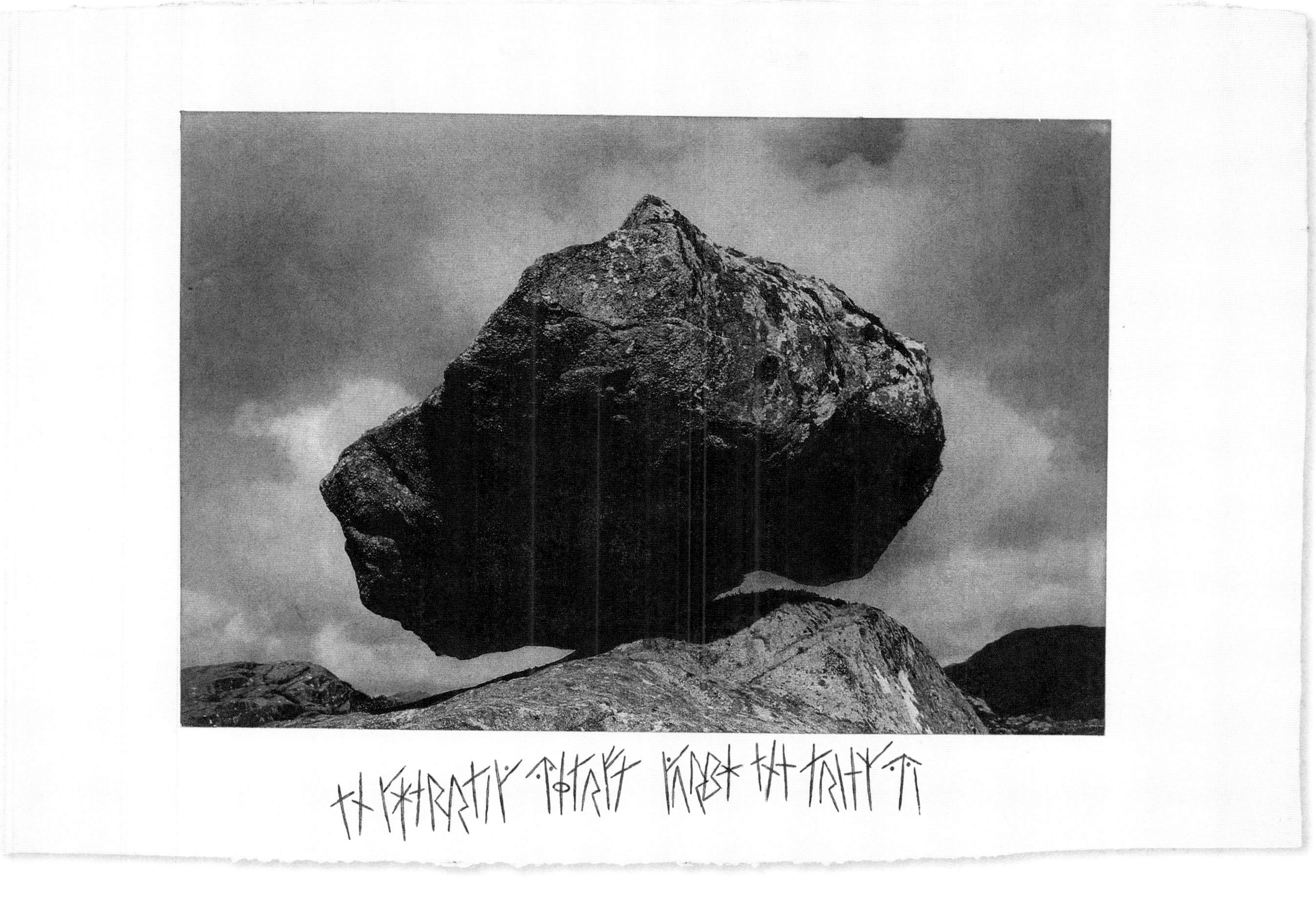

81

TOMÁS MAC SÍOMÓIN

b. 1938

Ealaíontóir/Artist:
Mary Avril Gillan

Peannaire/Calligrapher:
Ann Bowen

Aistritheoir/Translator:
Aodán Mac Póilín

Ainmníodh ag/Nominator:
The Author

Mairbhní ar Oileán Tréigthe

Is mé ar mo mharana ag faire,
Leabhar Uí Chriomhthainn im láimh,
Ar rince Mhanannáin ilsúiligh
Um chríocha an oileáin –

Tír ghorm ghainéad is ghuairdeall
Go faillte Uíbh Ráthaigh ag síneadh
Is an Cnoc Mór mar chloch chinn
Ar phaidrín mo bhalla críche …

'A nae seisean nochtóidh noiméad ar bith,'
Bhí an Tomás seo ag machnamh,
'Is fillfidh an Tomás eile aneas
Ar a róda goitre ón gCathar.'

Ach má gháireann cuan faoi aoibh na gréine,
Ceann Sreatha is Binn Dhiarmada,
Tá fothrach sramach taobh thíos ag feo
Is níl gáir i gcoileach na muintire;

Tá Tost ina Rí ar gach maoileann abhus
Is tá ceol na ndaoine go follas ar iarraidh;
An gadaí gan ghéim, nár fhan, mo léan,
Ina pholl taobh thiar den Tiaracht,

A réab gan taise thar chuan isteach,
A shealbhaigh gort an bhaile seo,
A strap anuas trí shúil gach dín
Gur shuigh isteach cois teallaigh …

Tá sé ag fuireach abhus ó shin;
Chím a scáth faoi scáth gach balla,
Is an chloch á baint ón gcloch aige,
An fhuaim ó gach macalla ...

Meditation on a Deserted Island

As I ponder, watching
– O'Crohan's book in my hand –
The dance of the many-eyed sea-god
Around the island rim,

Blue haunts of gannet and petrel
Stretch to Iveragh's cliffs;
Knockmore – the final bead –
Defines my rosary's limits.

His boat will appear any moment now,
This Tomás was thinking,
And that other Tomás will return again
Along the salt road from Cahirciveen.

Waves may sing beneath the sun,
Ceann Sreatha and Binn Dhiarmada,
But that dank ruin decays below,
The village rooster is silent.

Death is King of each mountain ridge,
The people's song is stilled
Since that robber left his den
In the seas to the west of Tiaracht.

He swept in here across the bay
And seized the village lands,
Climbed down every chimney-hole,
Sat mute at every hearth.

He has ruled here ever since
– A shadow in each wall's shadow –
Tumbling stones down from stones,
Stealing sound from echoes.

(Continued on p. 258)

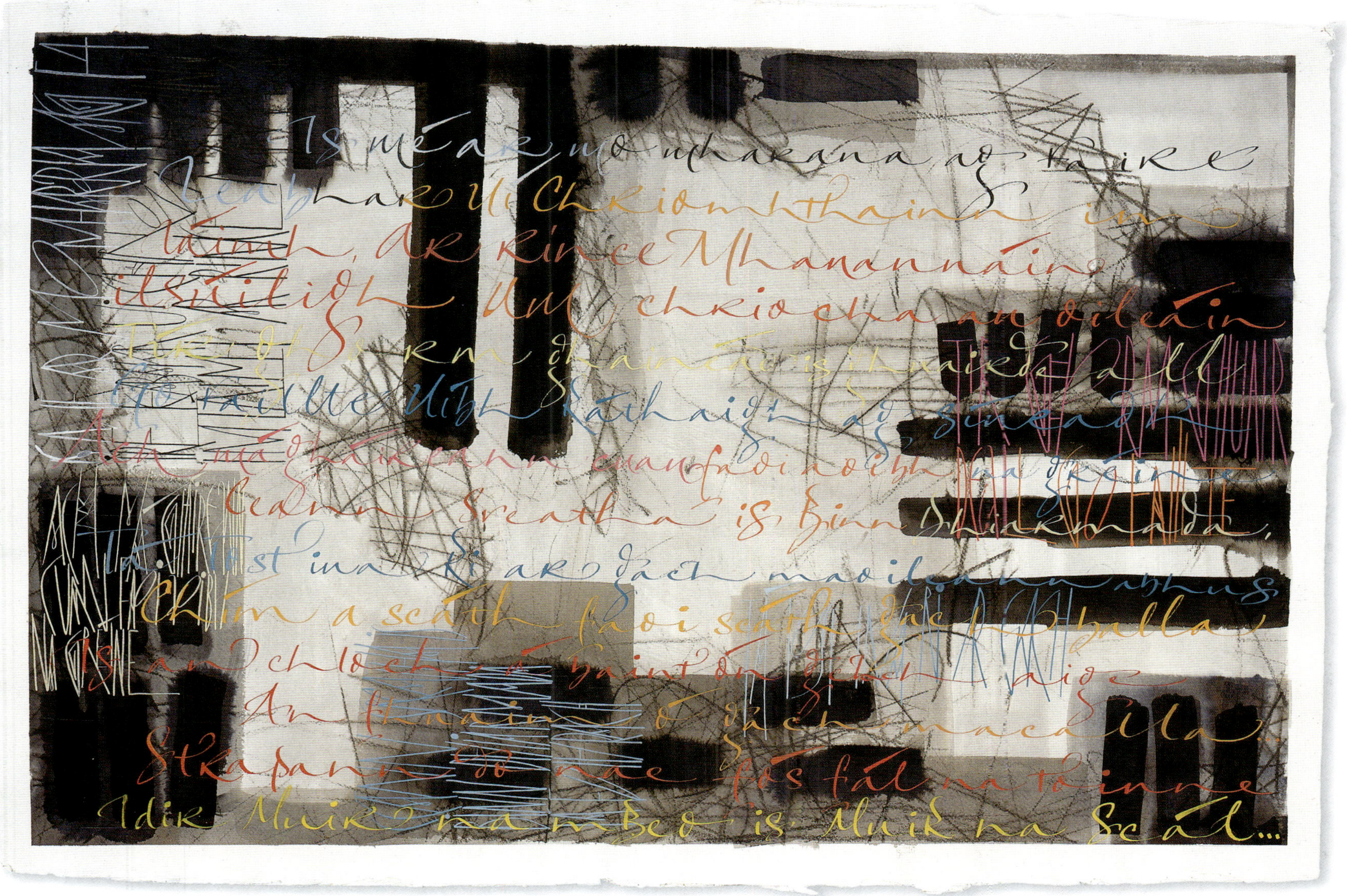

82

CAITLÍN MAUDE

1941-1982

Ealaíontóir/Artist:
Daphne Wright

Peannaire/Calligrapher:
Réiltín Murphy

Aistritheoir/Translator:
Aodán Mac Póilín

Ainmníodh ag/Nominator:
Tomás Mac Síomóin

Oilithreacht

Cleachtadh na ndeasgnáth
déan
an ceann crom
an croí trom

Saothraíodh an t-anam
an gaineamhlach tur

Cáilithe faoi dheoidh
don stuaim is don mheas
i dteach leathscoite deas

go n-éalaíonn peaca beag ciúin isteach
mar ghadaí san oích'

Ansin tagann clocha faoi bhláth
lasann an tír máguaird
siúlann an t-anam an téad mhín
idir 'sea' agus 'ní hea'.

Pilgrimage

The ceremonial rites
perform
the bowed head
the heavy heart

Let the soul cultivate
the arid desert

Eligible at last
for a prudent respectably
nice little semi

till a furtive little sin steals in
like a thief in the night

Then stones blossom
the land about ignites
the soul treads a fine line
between 'yes' and 'no'.

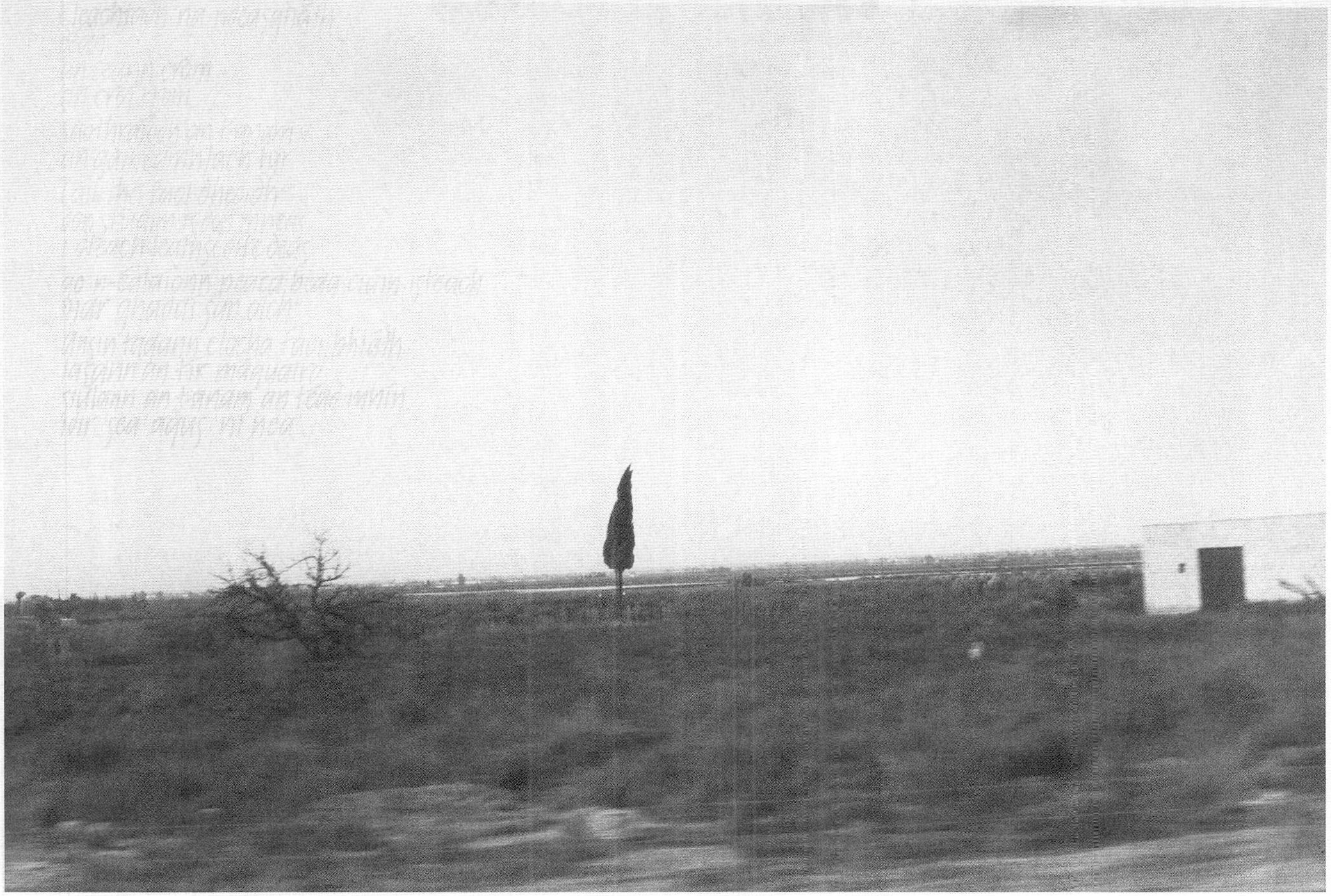

83

PEARSE HUTCHINSON

b. 1927

Ealaíontóir/Artist:
John Byrne

Peannaire/Calligrapher:
The Artist

Aistritheoir/Translator:
The Author

Ainmníodh ag/Nominator:
Tomás Mac Síomóin

Nár Mhéanar É

Mise 'mo shuí taobh thiar díot,
mo dhá láimh anall ort go dlúth,
an gluais-rothar ag imeacht ar luas,
abair céad míle san uair,
trí Pháirc an Fhíonuisce,
níos mire ná na fianna,
níos suaimhní ná an buar,
le breacadh lae nó um nóin,
gan duine ar bith eile ann
ar fud na páirce móire,
an bheirt againn geal-nocht,
's an rothar ag gluaiseacht go mear
fé ghrian na gcrann os ár gcionn,
gan fothram dá laghad ón inneall –
ach fuaim bheag anála na beirte.

Wouldn't It Be Lovely

Me on the pillion behind you,
my two arms tight around you,
the motor-bike going fast,
a hundred miles an hour, say,
right through the Phoenix Park,
swifter than deer,
more canty than kine,
at break-of-day or at noon,
with nobody else there
in the whole vast park,
the pair of us bright-naked,
and the bike moving fast
under the light of the sun
in the trees over our heads,
no noise at all from the engine –
only the small sound
of you and me breathing.

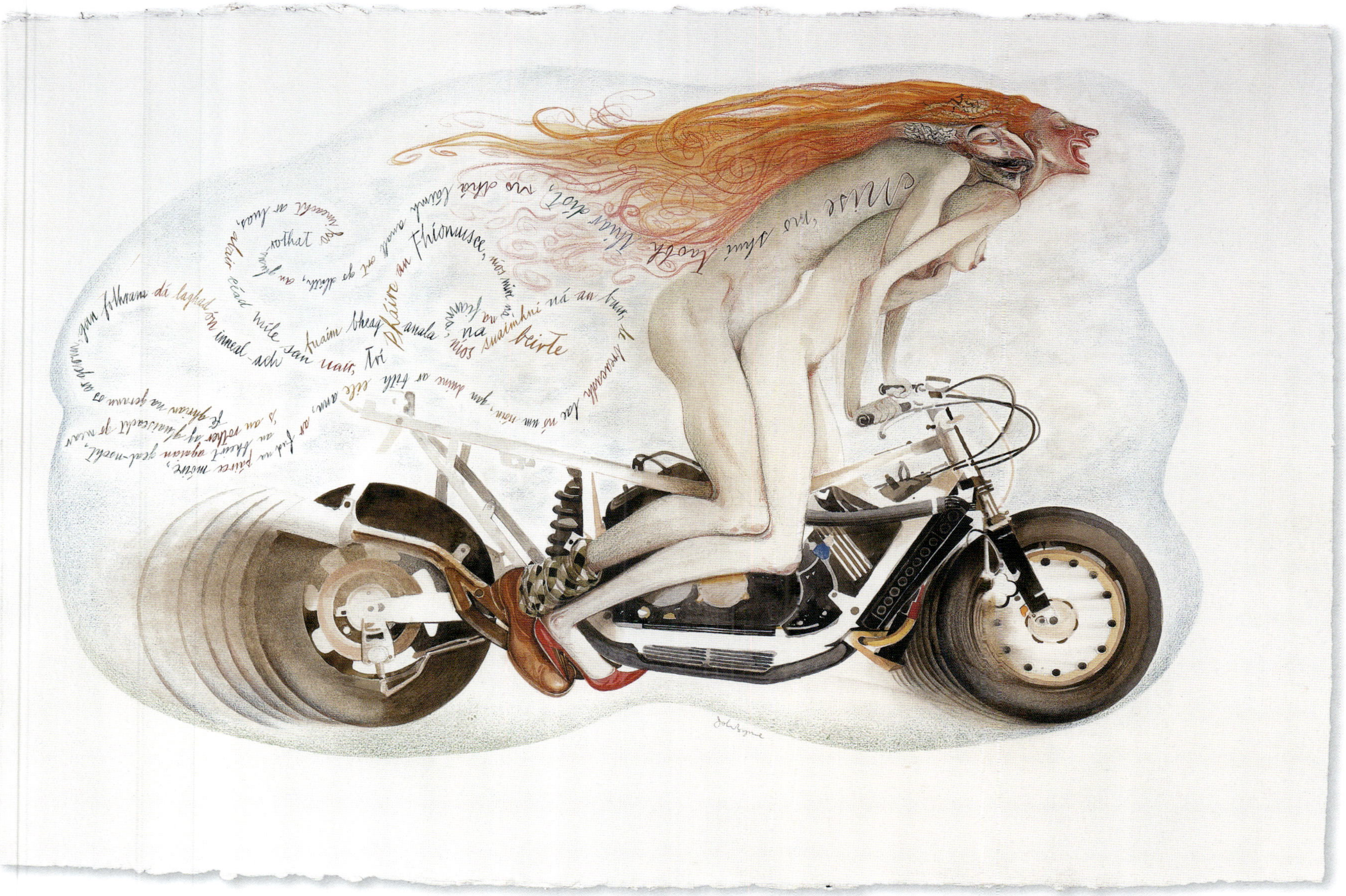

84

MEG BATEMAN

b. 1959

Neach-ealain / Artist:
Mhairi Killin

Snas-sgrìobhadair / Calligrapher:
Frances Breen

Eadar-theangaichte aig / Translator:
The Author

Roghainn / Nominator:
The Author

Naomh
Le taing do Tim Robinson

Sheall an duine Tobar Choluim Chille
dhan eòlaiche shìos air a' chladach,
is dh'fhaighnich e gu dè,
na bharail-san, am ball-acfhainn
a bha an Naomh air a chleachdadh
gus a cladhach cho domhainn is cho rèidh
san aol-chloich chruaidh.

Mhìnich an t-eòlaiche
mar a b' e dòirneag bu choireach,
a bha glacte san t-sloc iomadh bliadhna,
is mar a shnaidheadh i an toll
le gach làn-mara
's i a' bleith na creige
ann an sluaisreadh an t-sàil.

Cha bu dad nas lugha
urram an duine dhan Naomh,
oir bha fianais aige a-nist
air fhoighidinn is air fhàisneachd,
is air meud a chuid tròcair
leis an do cheannsaich e an cuan
gus uisge-leighis a ghleidheadh dha threud.

Saint
With thanks to Tim Robinson

The man showed the geologist
St Columba's Well on the shore,
and asked him his opinion
of the sort of tool
the saint might have used
to have bored the hole
so deep and smooth.

The geologist explained
it was made by a pebble
trapped in a hollow through the ages;
how it had rounded the basin
at every high-water,
grinding the rock down
in the swirling brine.

No less then the devotion
of the man to the saint,
for now he had evidence
of his patience and prescience,
and of the magnitude of his mercy
by which he had constrained the ocean
to safeguard healing-water for his flock.

Sheall an duine Tobar Choluim Chille
dhan eòlaiche shìos air a' chladach,
is dh'fhaighnich e gu dè,
na bharail-san, am ball-acfhainn
a bha an Naomh air a chleachdadh
gus a cladhach cho domhainn is cho rèidh
san aol-chloich chruaidh.

Mhìnich an t-eòlaiche
mar a b' e dòirneag bu choireach,
a bha glacte san t-sloc iomadh bliadhna,
is mar a shnaidheadh i an toll
le gach làn-mara
's i a' bleith na creige
ann an sluaisreadh an t-sàil.

Cha bu dad nas lugha
urram an duine dhan Naomh,
oir bha fianais aige a-nist
air fhoighidinn is air fhàisneachd,
is air meud a chuid tròcair
leis an do cheannsaich e an cuan
gus uisge-leighis a ghleidheadh dha threud.

NAOMH

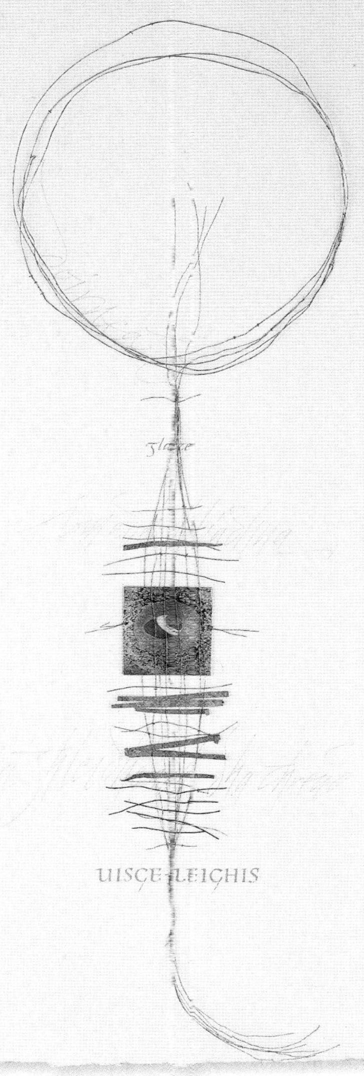

85

CEABHAN MACNÈILL

KEVIN MACNEIL

b. 1972

Neach-ealain / Artist:
Remco de Fouw

Snas-sgrìobhadair / Calligrapher:
Réiltín Murphy

Eadar-theangaichte aig / Translator:
The Author

Roghainn / Nominator:
Meg Bateman

o ghrunnd na mara / from the oceanfloor

acras ga shlacadh fhèin
air an dubhan

acras ga shlacadh fhèin
air an acair

*

hunger thrashing
on the fish-hook

hunger thrashing
on the anchor

*

ràmh
peann mòr briste
a chuidich iad a' dèanamh
iorraim, a bha dannsadh
uaireigin
ann am bàrdachd fheumail

*

oar
a huge broken pen
which helped them compose
rowing songs, which once
danced
in a useful poetry

*

's math dh' fhaodte g' eil do chnàmhan
faisg air alba nuadh
's math dh' fhaodte gu bheil pìos dhìot
ann an iasg air
nach cuala mi riamh

*

it's possible your bones lie
near nova scotia
it's possible a piece of you
is in a fish
i've never heard of

*

latha brèagha air
choreigin, ithidh am muir
mi. cuibhlidh sinn fad
grunnd na mara
man dà smuain
dìochuimhnichte

*

one day the sea will
swallow me. we shall
bump along the sea floor
like two forgotten thoughts

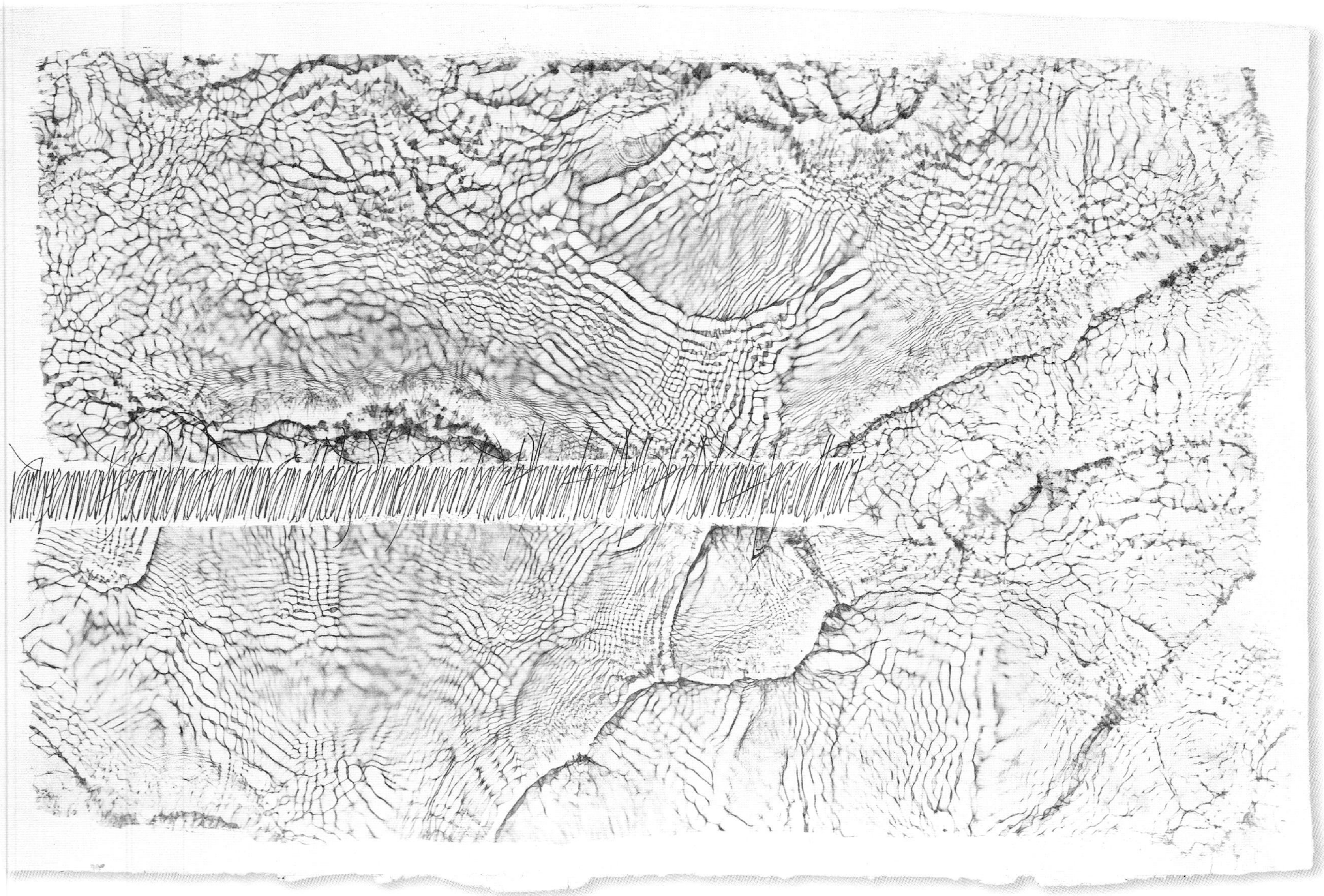

MAOILIOS M. CAIMBEUL

MYLES M. CAMPBELL

b. 1944

Neach-ealain / Artist:
Conor McFeely

Snas-sgrìobhadair / Calligrapher:
Réiltín Murphy

Eadar-theangaichte aig / Translator:
The Author

Roghainn / Nominator:
The Author

Dha Pàdraig, Bràthair Mo Mhàthar

Ged a tha mi an seo, chan eil mi an seo,
chaidh m' anam a dhèanamh
ann an àite eile, ann an aman eile.
Ceithir fichead bliadhna
o mo bhreith gus an t-àm seo
agus a-nise chan eil ann
ach coimhead air ais –
agus a bhith feitheamh.

Chan eil 'na ar beatha ach turas
eadar dà shian.
Tha an taigh falamh
ged a bhitheas a' ghaoth
a' crathadh nan sglèat.
Ruairidh, tha esan ann an Sairteal
ann an cur na bruaich
agus nì an ròs dubh iolach.
Tha Màiri a bhean ri thaobh
agus ar màthair 's ar n-athair,
anns an aiseirigh bidh sinn còmhla.
Chan fhaod an ròs dearg caoidh.

Cò a chruthaich na cnuic?
Bha E ealanta.
Tha iad a' fàs ann an cùil bheag.
Cò a rinn am feur agus an t-uisge,
a' mhuir agus Eilean Fhlòdagaraidh,
Grianan nam Maighdeann agus Beinn Eadarra fhèin?
Bha E ealanta.
Tha iad a' fàs ann an cùil bheag.

Uncle Peter

Although here, I am not here,
my soul was made
in another place, in another time.
Eighty years
since my birth
and now there is only
the backward look –
and the waiting.

Our life is but a journey
between storm-showers.
The house is empty
although the wind
rattles the slates.
Roddy, he is in Sartle,
in the weft of the bank,
and the black rose will rejoice.
Mary his wife beside him
and our father and mother,
in the resurrection we will be united.
The red rose must not weep.

Who created the hills?
He was skilful.
They flourish in a cul-de-sac.
Who made the grass and the water,
the sea and Flodigarry Isle,
Grianan nam Maighdeann and Ben Eadarra itself?
He was skilful.
They grow in a cul-de-sac.

(Continued on page 259)

87

TORMOD CAIMBEUL

NORMAN CAMPBELL

b. 1942

Neach-ealain / Artist:
Oliver Comerford

Clò-bhuailtear / Typographer:
Donald Addison

Eadar-theangaichte aig / Translator:
The Author

Roghainn / Nominator:
The Author

Tioram air Tìr

Mar Chuimhneachan air Murchadh Chaluim

Chuir Dòmhnall Bàn agus Tòrman
gu muir i a-raoir.
Chunnacas i stealladh
aig briseadh na faire,
an uiseag a' seinn!

Lorg Coinneach muir domhainn
am beul dubh na h-oidhch';
thug e greis air na sgeirean
ach tharraing iad às e
eadar dà lunn.

'S chan eil fhios a'm dè 'n cùrs
a ghabh balaich na h-Aird,
ach gun bhuail iad gu cala
fichead mìle bhon dachaigh
am baile nan sràid.

Na Moirich 's na Leòdaich,
's ann orra bha fonn
nuair a sgaoil an dubh-cheò ud
's a chunnaic iad Tòlas
a' riaghladh nan dram.

O, bha dalladh air òrain
's bha dalladh air leann;
's chan fhacas an Steòrnabhagh
– fiù 's air an Dròbha –
samhail nan sonn.

Back on Dry Land

In memory of Murchadh Chaluim

Dòmhnall Bàn and Torman put to sea last night.
She was seen breaking through the waves at dawn, the lark singing.

Coinneach searched out deep water in the early black hours
of the night. He spent some time on the reefs, but they
pulled him off between two swells.

And I don't know what course the Aird boys took, except
that they struck harbour twenty miles from home in the town of paved
streets.

The Murrays and the MacLeods were all in fine form
when that black mist dispersed and they saw Tòlas*
selling the drams.

Oh, they set to on songs and they set to on beer, and
there was never seen in Stornoway – even on the day of the Drove –
their like.

* *Tòlas – a bootlegger*

(Continued on p. 260)

TORMOD CAIMBEUL

Tioram air Tir

1

Mar Chuimhneachan air Murchadh Chaluim

Chuir Dòmhnall Bàn agus Tòrman
gu muir i a-raoir.
Chunnacas i stealladh
aig briseadh na faire,
an uiseag a' seinn!

Lorg Coinneach muir domhainn
am beul dubh na h-oidhch';
thug e greis air na sgeirean
ach tharraing iad às e
eadar dà unn.

'S chan eil fhios a'm dè 'n cùrs
a ghabh talaich na h-Aird,
ach gun bhuail iad gu cala
fichead mìle bhon dachaigh
am baile nan sràid.

Na Moirich 's na Leòdaich,
's ann orra bha fonn
nuair a sgaoil an dubh-cheò ud
's a chunnaic iad Tòlas
a' riaghladh nan dram.

O, bha dalladh air òrain
's bha dalladh air leann;
's chan fhacas an Steòrnabhagh
– fiù 's air an Dròbha –
samhail nan sonn.

An e làraidh no bhana
a thill leoth' a-null?
'S dòch' gur e Seòras
no carbaid le Ròigean –
dè 'n còrr a bhiodh ann?

Ach bhuannaich iad baile
dh'aindeoin ùpraid cinn!
Aig àm dol a chadal,
am fear nach d'fhuair leabaidh,
bu mhath leis a' bheing.

O, fàg iad nan cadal
's thoir maitheanas dhaibh –
feuch gun taisg thu an teine,
dùin gu socrach an doras,
tha na gaisgich fo rùm.

2

Dha Alasdair

Woill, 's fheudar dhomh togail orm.
'S mura dean mi monadh,
nì mi cladach dheth.
'S chan eil fhios nach tig iad
air curaigh Eòghainn
a-null mu Rubha Robhanais,
Calum Modo air a stiùir
's an t-Uibhisteach san toiseach aic'.

Fada dhan an oidhche gheal
na h-òrain a' dol le faram,
fada dhan an oidhche mhòr
fear nan stòp
a' tràghadh shearrag!

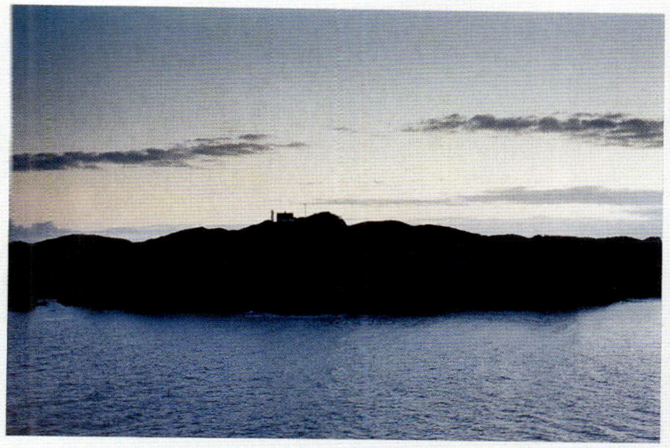

88

DÒMHNALL MACIOMHAIR

DONALD MACIVER

1857–1935

Neach-ealain / Artist:
Clare Langan

Snas-sgrìobhadair / Calligrapher:
Frances Breen

Eadar-theangaichte aig / Translator:
Ronald Black

Roghainn / Nominator:
Norman Campbell

An Ataireachd Ard

An ataireachd bhuan,
Cluinn fuaim na h-ataireachd àird:
Tha torran a' chuain
Mar chualas leams' e nam phàist' –
Gun mhùthadh, gun truas,
A' sluaisreadh gaineamh na tràgh'd;
An ataireachd bhuan,
Cluinn fuaim na h-ataireachd àird.

**Gach làd le a stuadh,
Cho luaisgeach, faramach, bàn,
Na chabhaig gu cruaidh,
'S e gruamach, dosrach gun sgàth;
Ach strìochdaidh a luaths
Aig bruaich na h-uidhe bh' aig càch,
Mar chaochail an sluagh
Bha uair sa bhaile sa tàmh.**

Sna coilltean a siar
Chan iarrainn fuireach gu bràth –
Bha m' inntinn 's mo mhiann
A-riamh air lagan a' bhàigh,
Ach iadsan bha fial
An gnìomh, an caidreabh 's an àgh
Air sgapadh gun dìon,
Mar thriallas ealtainn ro nàmh.

Seileach is luachair,
Cluaran, muran is stàrr
Air tachdadh nam fuaran
'N d' fhuair mi iomadh deoch-phàit';
Na tobhtaichean fuar
Le buathallan 's cuiseag gum bàrr
'S an deanntagach ruadh
Fàs suas sa chagailt bha blàth.

The Sea's Lofty Roar

Endless surge of the sea,
Hear the sound of the sea's lofty roar,
The thundering swell
That I heard as a child long ago –
Without change or compassion
Dragging the sand of the shore:
Endless surge of the sea,
Hear the sound of the sea's lofty roar.

All the waves crashing down
Are trembling, loud-sounding and white,
So hurried and cruel,
Grim and spuming without taking fright;
But their speed falls away
At the same destination each time
As the people have perished
Who once dwelt in this village of mine.

In the forests of the west
I've never wanted to stay,
My mind and ambition
Set firm on the hollow of the bay;
But those who were generous
In effort, in friendship and fame
Are scattered defenceless
Like birds in their enemy's way.

Rushes and willow,
And thistle, and marram and grass,
Have choked up the springs
Where I'd find many thirst-quenching draughts;
The ruins are so cold,
With ragwort and dockens growing high,
While the red nettle swarms
Where warm is the ghost of the hearth.

(Continued on p. 260)

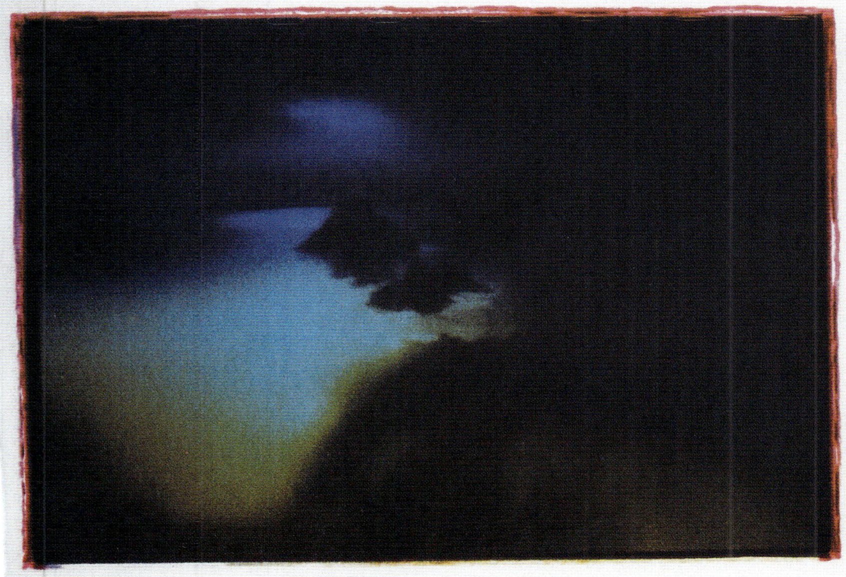 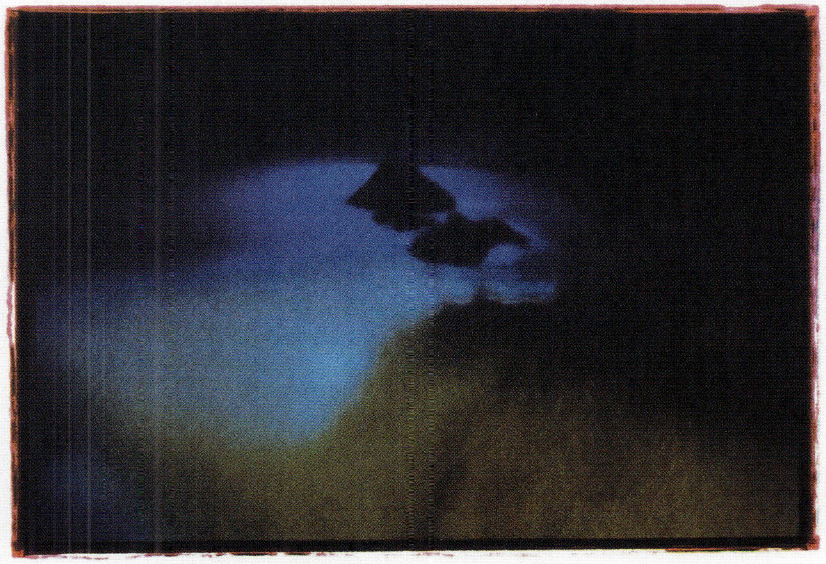

Gach là le a stuadh
cho luaisgeach farsaing bàn
'na chathair gu cruaidh
's e gruamach, dorach gun sgàth.
Ach striochdaidh a luathas
aig bruaich na h-oidhche bhàigh cach
mar chaochail an sluagh.
tha nair-sa bhàite 'sa tàmh.

89

DÒMHNALL RUADH CHORÙNA

DONALD MACDONALD

1887-1967

Neach-ealain / Artist:
Fiona R. Hutchison

Snas-sgrìobhadair / Calligrapher:
Réiltín Murphy

Eadar-theangaichte aig / Translator:
Ronald Black

Roghainn / Nominator:
Norman Campbell

Motor-Boat Heidhsgeir

Soraidh leis a' bhàta a dh'fhàg leinn Port Ròigh
'S a chaidh leinn gu Màisgeir sàbhailte tron cheò;
Faoileag gheal an t-sàile fàlaireachd ma sròin,
Pliuthannan dhen phràisich oirre 'n àite sheòl.

A' dol seachad Stocaigh, cop oirre le spàirn,
Hìobhairean ag osnaich 's iad gun fhois gun tàmh,
Suaile trom gu socair leigeil roc am bàrr
'S nuallan aig gach oitir roladh moil 's ga chnàmh.

Dol timcheall na h-Easgainn feasgar greannach fuar,
'S ann leam fhìn bu leisg e dol a shreap ri stuaigh;
Marannan a' cleasachd, tighinn on deas gu tuath,
Sùil airson na h-Eiste, 's eagal oirnn ro gruaim.

Sruth is gaoth a' còimhstri sa chòmhrag ri chèil' -
Cha robh 'n coltas bòidheach dol gam pògadh fhèin;
Clann Dòmhnaill mo luaidh ann ri guaillibh a chèil',
Bristeadh geal ma sròin ga còmhdach às a dèidh.

Ghabh i ris an fhuaradh, bhuail i ann le spàirn,
Gun d' sgoilt i le a gualainn rathad fuar fon t-sàl;
Dh'èirich i mar fhaoileag air a faobhar àrd,
Cuideam air a sliasaid, fiaradh air a sàil.

Seonaidh Mòr ga stiùireadh, 's gu robh shùil cho geur
Ri caiptean air criùsair dol a dh'ionnsaigh euchd;
Bha mise 's mi crùbadh ann an cùil leam fhèin,
'S an crodh ris an taobh-stoc air an taodadh rèidh.

Chan eil gheat no crùsair no tè-shiùil fon ghrèin
Gheibh nad uisge stiùrach 's tu fo shùrd do cheum;
Bidh iad dèanamh cùrs' ort, 'n dùil gum bi sibh rèidh –
Fàgaidh tu gun diù iad 's siùbhlaidh tu leat fhèin.

The Heisgeir Motor-Boat

Farewell to the boat that left Port Ròigh with us
And went with us to Màisgeir safely through the mist;
The white crest of the ocean dancing round her prow,
With flippers of brass on her instead of sails.

Going past Stocaigh, foam on her with effort,
Heaving combers moaning, restless on the move,
A heavy swell gently bringing tangle to the surface
With all the shallows howling, rolling shingle and grinding it.

Going round the 'Eel' on a cold surly evening,
It's I who was reluctant to face up to its waves,
Seas wrestling with each other, coming south to north,
Looking out for the Eist, we were afraid of its menace.

Wind and current wrestling in combat with each other -
They looked far from pretty moving in for the kiss;
My darling MacDonalds standing shoulder to shoulder,
White breakers at her bow raining down further aft.

She drove on to windward, struck with all her might,
Split with her forebreast a cold path through the brine;
She soared up like a seagull with her bow held high,
With her weight to one side, and her keel at a slant.

Big John steered her, and his eye was as sharp
As a cruiser captain's when sailing into battle;
I was crouched in a corner all by myself
With the cattle at the gunwale tethered neatly in line.

No yacht nor cruiser nor sailing-boat exists
Which can catch your rudder-wake when you're well under way;
They'll set a course for you, assuming you'll be easy –
But you'll leave them looking silly and press on by yourself.

(Continued on p. 261)

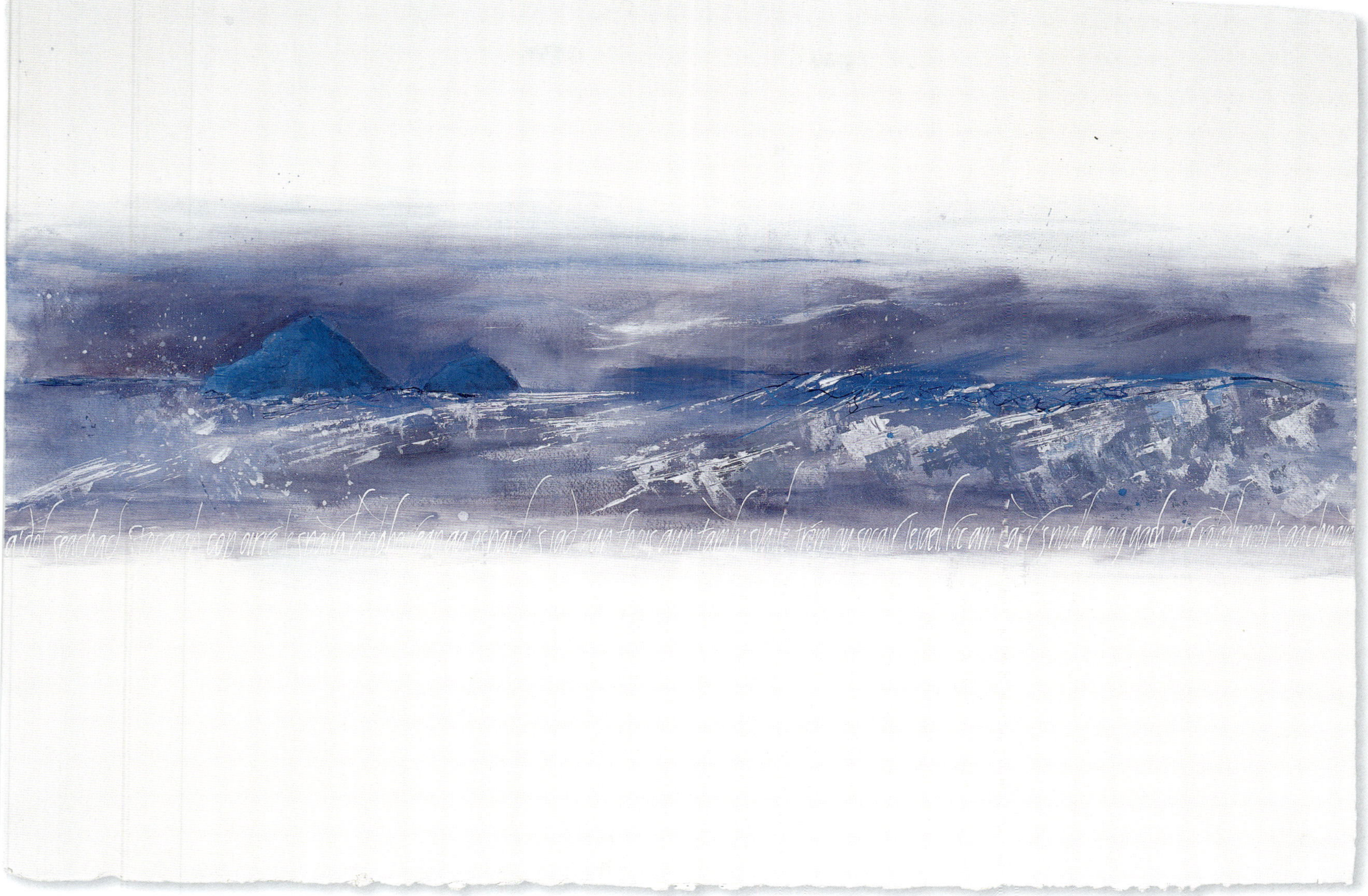

90

RODY GORMAN

b. 1960

Neach-ealain / Artist:
Alfred Graf

Clò-bhuailtear / Typographer:
Donald Addison

Eadar-theangaichte aig / Translator:
The Author

Roghainn / Nominator:
The Author

Boy John

Bidh am bodach,
Seadh, am braisiche,
A' falbh 's a' dèanamh suidhe
Thall ri taobh na h-uinneige
Ri beul na h-oidhche
Imíonn sé féin taobh leis féin
Go suíonn síos ar a thóin
Thiar le hais na fuinneoige
Le béal na hoíche
the bodach goes off, alone,
to sit
by the window after his dinner

'S a' sealltainn
A-mach air *Boy John* air chruaidh
Is go bhféachann sé leis ar an taobh thall
Agus ar *Boy John*
Amuigh léi féin sa ngóilín
and looks out
on Boy John *out at anchor*

Is, air a chùlaibh,
Air a' bhaile-shamhraidh
'S e a' dol air ais na bheinn
Agus, ar a chúl,
Ar bhaile fearainn an tsamhraidh
Ag imeacht ar ais ina shliabh
and, beyond,
on the summer village
going back to moorland.

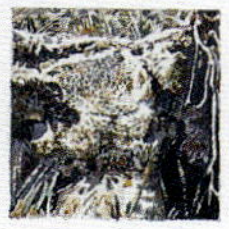

BOY JOHN

B ____
S ____
A' ____

I ____
G ____

TO SIT

THE BODACH GOES OFF, ALONE,

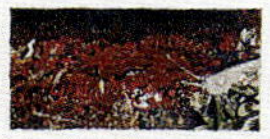

T ____
R ____

T ____
L ____

BY THE WINDOW AFTER HIS DINNER

'S ____

Á ____

AND LOOKS OUT

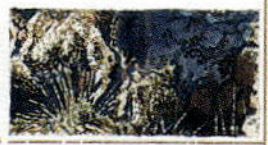

A ____

A ____
A ____

ON *BOY JOHN* OUT AT ANCHOR

'S ____

A ____

AND, BEYOND,

A ____

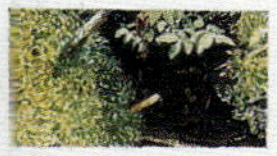

A ____

ON THE SUMMER VILLAGE

'S ____

A ____

GOING BACK TO MOORLAND.

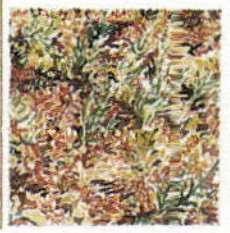

POET: RODY GORMAN
ARTIST: ALFRED GRAF

91

ANNA C. FRATER

ANNE C. FRATER

b. 1967

Neach-ealain / Artist:
Alastair MacLennan

Snas-sgrìobhadair / Calligrapher:
Frances Breen

Eadar-theangaichte aig / Translator:
The Author

Roghainn / Nominator:
The Author

Màiri Iain Mhurch' Chaluim
Mo sheanmhair, a chaill a h-athair air an Iolaire*,*
oidhche na Bliadhn' Uir, 1919

Tha mi nam shuidhe ag èisdeachd ribh
agus tha mo chridh' a' tuigsinn
barrachd na mo chlaisneachd;
's mo shùilean a' toirt a-steach
barrachd na mo chluasan.

Ur guth sèimh, ur cainnt
ag èirigh 's a' tuiteam mar thonn
air aghaidh fhuar a' chuain
's an dràst' 's a-rithist a' briseadh
air creag bhiorach cuimhne;
's an sàl a' tighinn gu bàrr
ann an glas-chuan ur sùilean.

'Bha e air an ròp
an uair a bhris e ... '

Agus bhris ur cridhe cuideachd
le call an ròpa chalma
air an robh grèim gràidheil agaibh
fhad' 's a bha sibh a' sreap suas
nur leanabh.

Agus, aig aois deich bliadhna,
cha robh agaibh ach cuimhne air a' chreig
a bhiodh gur cumail còmhnard;
's gach dòchas a bha nur sùilean
air a bhàthadh tron oidhch' ud,
's tro gach Bliadhn' Ur a lean.

Mairi Iain Mhurch' Chaluim
My grandmother, who lost her father on the Iolaire*,*
New Year's night, 1919

I sit listening to you
and my heart understands
more than my hearing;
and my eyes absorb
more than my ears.

Your soft voice, your speech
rising and falling like waves
on the cold surface of the sea,
and now and again breaking
on the sharp rock of memory;
and the brine rises up
in the grey seas of your eyes.

'He was on the rope
when it broke ... '

And your heart also broke
with the loss of the sturdy rope
which you had clung to lovingly
while you were growing up
as a child.

And, at ten years of age,
you had only a memory of the rock
that used to keep you straight;
and every hope that was in your eyes
was drowned on that night
and through each New Year that followed.

(Continued on p. 261)

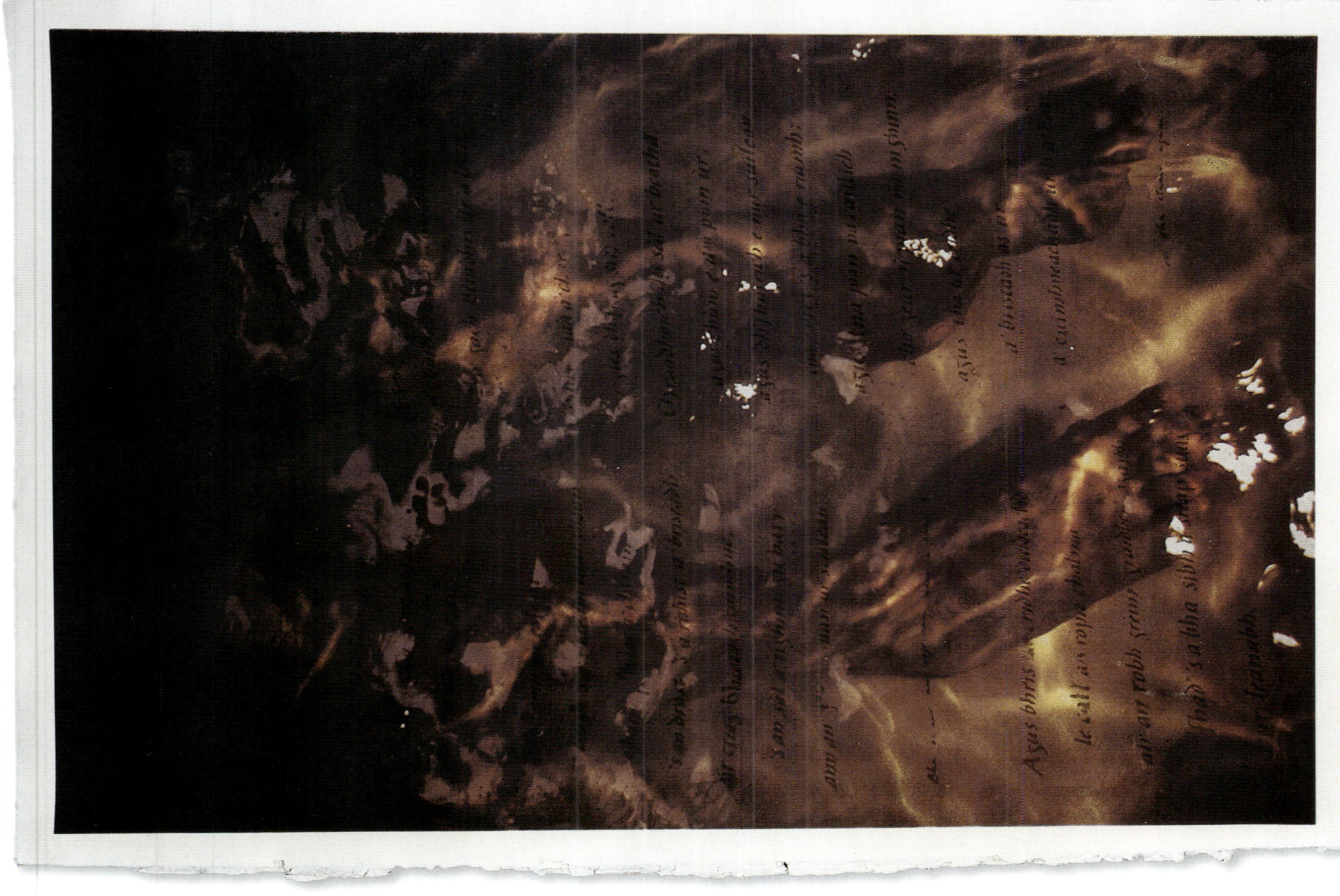

92

CATRÌONA NICGUMARAID

CATRIONA MONTGOMERY

b. 1947

Neach-ealain / Artist:
James Morrison

Snas-sgrìobhadair / Calligrapher:
Donald Murray

Eadar-theangaichte aig / Translator:
The Author

Roghainn / Nominator:
The Author

Cearcall mun Ghealaich

Bliadhna mhòr na stoirme
chunnaic mi cearcall mun ghealaich
's dh'fhalbh na h-adagan eòrna
nan sruth sìos chun a' chladaich,
is sheas sinn nar triùir ann
(mi fhèin, mo phiuthar is m' athair)
a' faicinn obair ar làimhe
na deann-ruith à sealladh.

Is chunnaic mi uair eile
cearcall mun ghealaich –
aig deireadh samhraidh sgiamhach
chaidh gaol às mo shealladh.
Bu riaslach an tìm ud
gu 'n tàinig leigheas an earraich,
ach thàinig le tìde
àm grianach gum aire.

Ach a-nis, aig deireadh samhraidh,
chì mi cearcall mun ghealaich
is tusa a' falbh bhuam
gu baile an Sasainn,
's mo chridhe cho sgaoilte,
na raon mòr fada farsaing
gun adagan ar gaoil ann
fon d'fhuair mi fasgadh bha abaich –
's ma dh'fhalbhas tu,
cha till grian bhrèagha an earraich.

Circle about the Moon

The year of the big storm
I saw a circle about the moon
and the stocks of barley streamed to the sea –
my father, sister and I stood
watching the work of our hands
rush from sight.

At another time
I saw a circle about the moon,
at the end of the summer
when love disappeared from sight,
a restless season till
the healing spring,
but through time
I noticed the sun.

But now at the end of a summer
I see a circle about the moon
and you going from me
to an English city;
my heart is desolate,
a wide swept open field
without the stooks of our love,
their ripe shelter
– should you not return,
neither will the spring sun.

CEARCALL MUN GHEALAICH

Bliadhna mhòr na stoirme
chunnaic mi cearcall mun ghealaich
's dh'fhalbh na h-adagan eòrna
nan sruth sìos chun a' chladaich
is sheas sinn nar triùir ann —
(mi fhèin, mo phiuthar is m'athair)
a' faicinn obair ar làimhe
na deann-ruith à sealladh.

Is chunnaic mi uair eile
cearcall mun ghealaich —
aig deireadh samhraidh sgiamhach
chaidh gaol às mo shealladh.
Bu riaslach an tìm ud
gu'n tàinig leigheas an earraich,
ach thàinig le tìde
àm grianach gum aire.

Ach a-nis, aig deireadh samhraidh,
chì mi cearcall mun ghealaich
is tusa a' falbh bhuam
gu baile an Sasainn —
's mo chridhe cho sgaoilte
na raon mòr fada farsaing
gun adagan ar gaoil ann
fon d'fhuair mi fasgadh bha abaich —
's ma dh'fhalbhas tu,
cha till grian bhrèagha an earraich.

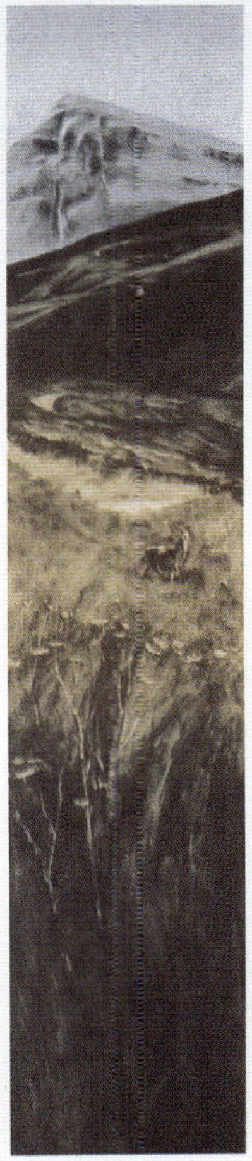

93

CRÌSDEAN WHYTE

CHRISTOPHER WHYTE

b. 1952

Neach-ealain / Artist:
Helen MacAlister

Clò-bhuailtear / Typographer:
Donald Addison

Eadar-theangaichte aig / Translator:
Michel Byrne

Roghainn / Nominator:
The Author

Aig Abhainn Chille Mhàrtainn

Dh'iarrainn-sa gnè na h-aibhne a bhith agam,
ruitheas gu soilleir glan fo Chille Mhàrtainn.

Chì thu i siubhal luath fon drochaid stàilinn
a thèid sràid an taigh-òsda thairis oirre.

Theireadh neach a bhiodh gad fhaicinn crom,
's tus' a' geur-amharc air na h-uisgeachan,

gur sgàthan e a bha thu sealltainn ann.
Ach cha ghlacar leat ìomhaigh sam bith,

chan fhaicear leat ach dian-atharrachadh
susbaint na h-aibhn', no fantainn ball-chritheach

nan iasg a tha mar chombaistean, a' toirt
fios air aomadh a ruith. Ge mòr an tlachd

a ghabhas iad san fhionnarachd do-thraoghadh,
ged a bu chaomh leam fhìn a bhith nam iasg,

dh'iarrainn, nam b' urrainn dhòmhs', a bhith nam abhainn,
gun fhios dè bhiodh na fhìor-bhrìgh dom bhith,

ioma-chaochlachd shìorraidh m' uisgeachan no mo dhà
bhruaich, a' toirt dhomh riochd is cruth

At Kilmartin River

I would like to have the nature of the river
that runs clear and unsullied by Kilmartin.

You see it coursing fast under the steel bridge
the road to the hotel runs across.

Anyone who saw you leaning over,
gazing intently at the waters, would say

it was a mirror you were looking into.
But you will catch no reflection at all,

all you can see are crazy permutations
of the river's essence, the shimmering suspension

of the fish, indicating like compasses
the direction of the flow. Though great the pleasure

they take in its inexhaustible freshness,
though I myself would love to be a fish,

if I could, I would choose to be the river,
blithely unaware where my true meaning lay,

in the multiple metamorphoses of my waters
or my two banks, giving me shape and form.

DH'IARRAINN-SA GNÈ NA H-AIBHNE A BHITH AGAM,
RUITHEAS GU SOILLEIR GLAN FO CHILLE MHÀRTAINN.
I WOULD LIKE TO HAVE THE NATURE OF THE RIVER
THAT RUNS CLEAR AND UNSULLIED BY KILMARTIN
Achlasan Chaluim-Chille
I will pluck my armpit-package

94

AONGHAS CAIMBEUL

ANGUS CAMPBELL

1903-1982

Neach-ealain/Artist:
Donald Smith

Snas-sgrìobhadair/Calligrapher:
Louise Donaldson

Eadar-theangaichte aig/Translator:
Norman Campbell

Roghainn/Nominator:
The Editorial Panel

Coinneach Nèill (earrann)

à Suathadh ri Iomadh Rubha

'S e a phiuthar, Màiri, a bha sealltainn às a dhèidh. Bha i oidhche Sàbaid san eaglais agus nach ann a chaidh Coinneach a shealltainn air seann bhean a bha air an leabaidh. Chaith i an ùine ag innse dha mu Eliah, am fàidh. Nuair a thill Coinneach dhachaigh, thuirt e ri Màiri gur ann comhla ri tè a phrìosanaich an dòchais a chaith e an oidhche. Thòisich e sin ag aithris seanchas na caillich mun 'an cèineach ud a chaidh a thogail bodily suas a nèamh'. Nuair a chrìochnaich e, cha b' urrainn e gun a chuid fhèin a chur ris, agus seo agaibh e: 'Agus 's e càil a b' ioghantaich gu lèir, an ceann dà latha, thuit a' bhriogais aige nuas agus an drathars na broinn.'

Coinneach Nèill (excerpt)

from Suathadh ri Iomadh Rubha

His sister Mary looked after him. One Sunday evening she was in church and Coinneach went to visit an old woman, who was bed-ridden. She spent time telling him about the prophet Elijah.*

When Coinneach returned home, he told Mary that he'd spent the evening with one of the 'prisoners of Hope.'** And he began to recite the old woman's story about 'that character who was lifted bodily up to heaven'. When he'd finished, he couldn't resist adding his own bit to it. Here it is.

'And the most amazing thing of all was that, two days later, his trousers - with his drawers in them - fell down to earth.'

* Kings II, 2

**Bunyan, *The Pilgrim's Progress*

We have only been able to give an excerpt from this text. For an alternative source of the full text see the listing on page 265.

COINNEACH NÈILL

'S e a phiuthar Màiri a bha sealltainn às a dèidh. Bha i oidhche Sàbaid san eaglais agus nach ann a chaidh Coinneach a shealltainn air seann bhean a bha air an leabaidh. Chaith i an ùine ag innse dha mu Eliah am fàidh. Nuair a thill Coinneach dhachaigh thuirt e ri Màiri gur ann comhla ri tè a phrìosanaich an dòchais a chaith e an oidhche. Thòisich e sin ag aithris seanchas na cailliche mun "an cèineach ud a chaidh a thogail bodily suas a nèamh." Nuair a chrìochnaich e, cha b' urrainn e gun a chuid fhèin a chur ris, agus seo agaibh e:

"AGUS 'S E CÀIL A B' IOGHANTAICH GU LÈIR, AN CEANN DÀ LATHA
THUIT A' BHRIOGAIS AIGE NUAS AGUS AN DRATHARS NA BROINN"

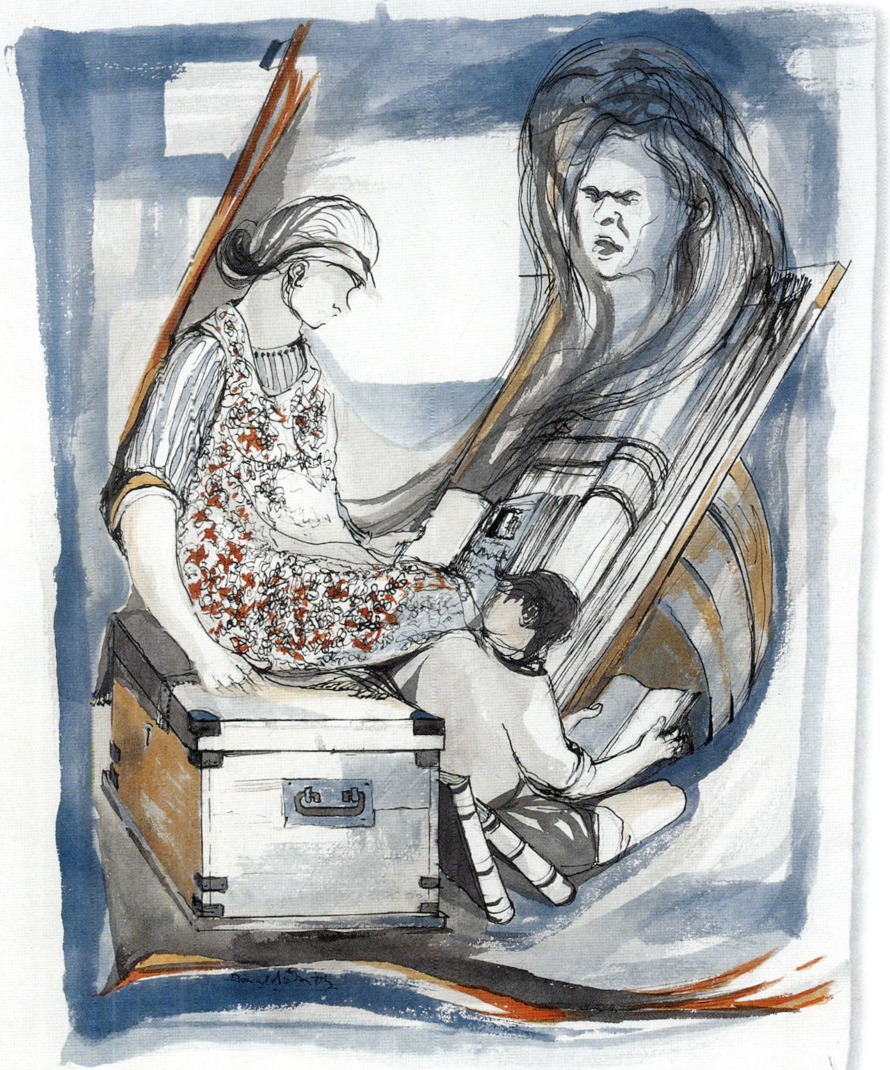

95

MURCHADH MACPHÀRLAIN

MURDO MACFARLANE

1901-1982

Neach-ealain / Artist:
Kate Whiteford

Clò-bhuailtear / Typographer:
Donald Addison

Eadar-theangaichte aig / Translator:
Nan S. MacLeod

Roghainn / Nominators:
The Editorial Panel

Chunnaic Mi Uam a' Bheinn

Chunnaic mi uam a' bheinn
'S mi siubhal air astar speur,
'S an aois a mhallachadh rinn,
Oir mhiannaich mi rithist bhith òg,
Sa bheinn gun bhonaid, gun bhròg -
Miann riamh nach do shealbhaich mac mnaoi,
'S oirnn fear-trusaidh gach linn an tòir.

Chunnaic mi uam a' bheinn
Air latha geal grinn is grèin',
'S mar dhùisgeas an doineann na tuinn
Nan suain air aghaidh a' chuain,
'S amhlaidh a dhùisgeadh mo smuain
'S a dhùisg à dùsal a' chuimhn'
Air bhith trusadh chaorach is uan;

'S a bhith togail o bhaile nan treud
Mu mheadhan bog-bhlàth-mhìos na Màigh.
An là ud dan sgoil sinn cha tèid,
'S bidh balaich is coin air an dòigh,
'S nuair ruigear na Beannaibh fa-dheòidh,
Sinn suidhidh air tom 's ithidh grèim -
Aran coirc' no eòrn' às ar dòirn.

Shaoil leam gum faicinn a' bheinn,
Suinn a bhuineadh do linn nach beò,
Le lùthag fon ghlùin 's orra sgoinn
A' dìreadh 's a' feannadh an t-slèibh,
'S gun cluinninn am fead is an èigh
Ri coin toirt na sprèidhe cruinn,
'S na deimhisean geur' dol gu feum.

I Saw at a Distance the Hill

I saw at a distance the hill
And I travelling by air,
And old age I cursed;
For I desired to be young again,
On the hill without cap or shoe,
A desire never granted to son of woman
And the Gatherer of each generation seeking us.

I saw at a distance the hill
On a white beautiful day of sun;
And as the tempests awaken the waves
Slumbering on the face of the ocean,
So my thoughts were awakened
And there awoke from slumber the memory
Of gathering sheep and lambs.

Of collecting flocks from the villages
About the middle of the soft warm month of May -
That day to school we did not go -
And boys and dogs were happy,
And when the Beannaibh* were reached at last,
Of sitting on a hillock and eating
Oatcake or barley scone from our fist.

It seemed to me that I could see on the hill
Champions of a generation not living,
With a band beneath their knee and they hurrying,
Climbing and descending the slope;
And that I could hear the whistle and the shout
To dogs to collect the flocks,
And the sharp shears at work.

**Na Baennaibh: these are a group of four hills – Beinn Bharabhais; Beinn Mholach; Beinn Bheàrnach; Beinn a Sgridhe – to which the village of Melbost, which was Murdo MacFarlane's home, took their sheep for grazing and later shearing. Murdo wrote this poem after seeing them from the plane coming into Stornoway airport.*

(Continued on page 261)

Chunnaic mi uam a' bheinn
Air latha geal grinn is grèin',
'S mar dhùisgeas an doineann na tuinn
Nan suain air aghaidh a' chuain,
'S amhlaidh a dhùisgeadh mo smuain
'S a dhùisg à dùsal a' chuimhn'
Air bhith trusadh chaorach is uan;
Shaoil leam gum faicinn a' bheinn,
Suinn a bhuineadh do linn nach beò,
Le lùthag fon ghlùin 's orra sgoinn
A' dìreadh 's a' feannadh an t-slèibh,
'S gun cluinninn am fead is an èigh
Ri coin toirt na sprèidhe cruinn,
'S na deimhisean geur' dol gu feum.

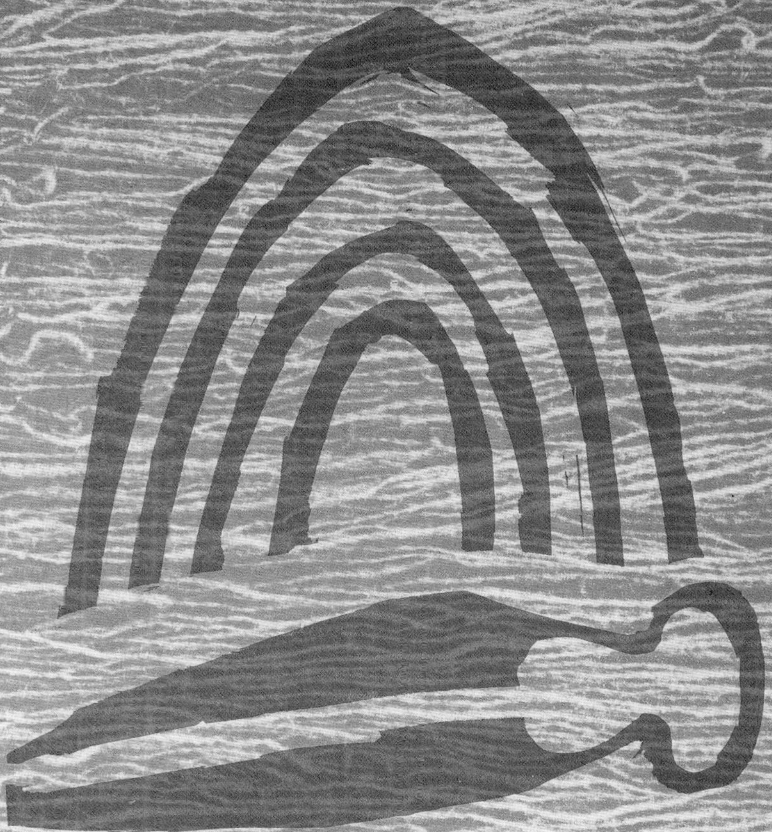

96

SEÁN Ó TUAMA

b. 1926

Ealaíontóir/Artist:
Robert Ballagh

Peannaire/Calligrapher:
Frances Breen

Aistritheoir/Translator:
The Author

Ainmníodh ag/Nominator:
The Editorial Panel

Christy Ring

Do thriail sé an ní dodhéanta
formhór gach Domhnach ar an bpáirc,
is uaireanta rith leis.

Ar leathghlúin dó
teanntaithe i gcúinne
nuair las a shúil -
réamhchríostaí, leictreonach -
's gur dhiúraic an liathróid uaidh
thar trasnán,
chrith an t-aer le hiontas.

Nuair thug gan coinne
aon ráig ghlan fiain
trí bhulc na bhfear
's gur phléasc an sliotar
faoi smidiríní solais
sa líontán,
do liúigh an laoch
san uile dhuine.

Aon neomat buile amháin
in earr a ré
is é Cúchulainn
bhí 'na ionad
ar an bpáirc -
d'at a chabhail
i radharc na sluaite,
do bholgaigh súil
's do rinc ar mire ...

Christy Ring*

He aimed at the impossible
each Sunday on the pitch;
sometimes he succeeded.

Down on one knee,
trapped in the corner of a field,
when his prechristian electronic eye
lit up in combat,
and the ball, a missile,
sped from him straight above the bar,
the air shook in awe.

When a driving lunge
brought him clear beyond
the ruck of men,
and the ball, propelled,
self-destructed in the net
to smithereens of light,
our cheering became a battle cry.

In one moment of raw frenzy
as his playing days ran out,
he summoned Cú Chulainn
to aid him on the pitch:
his trunk swelled up
in sight of thousands,
one eye bulged
and danced, demented ...

* Christy Ring was the Babe Ruth of hurling

(Continued on page 262)

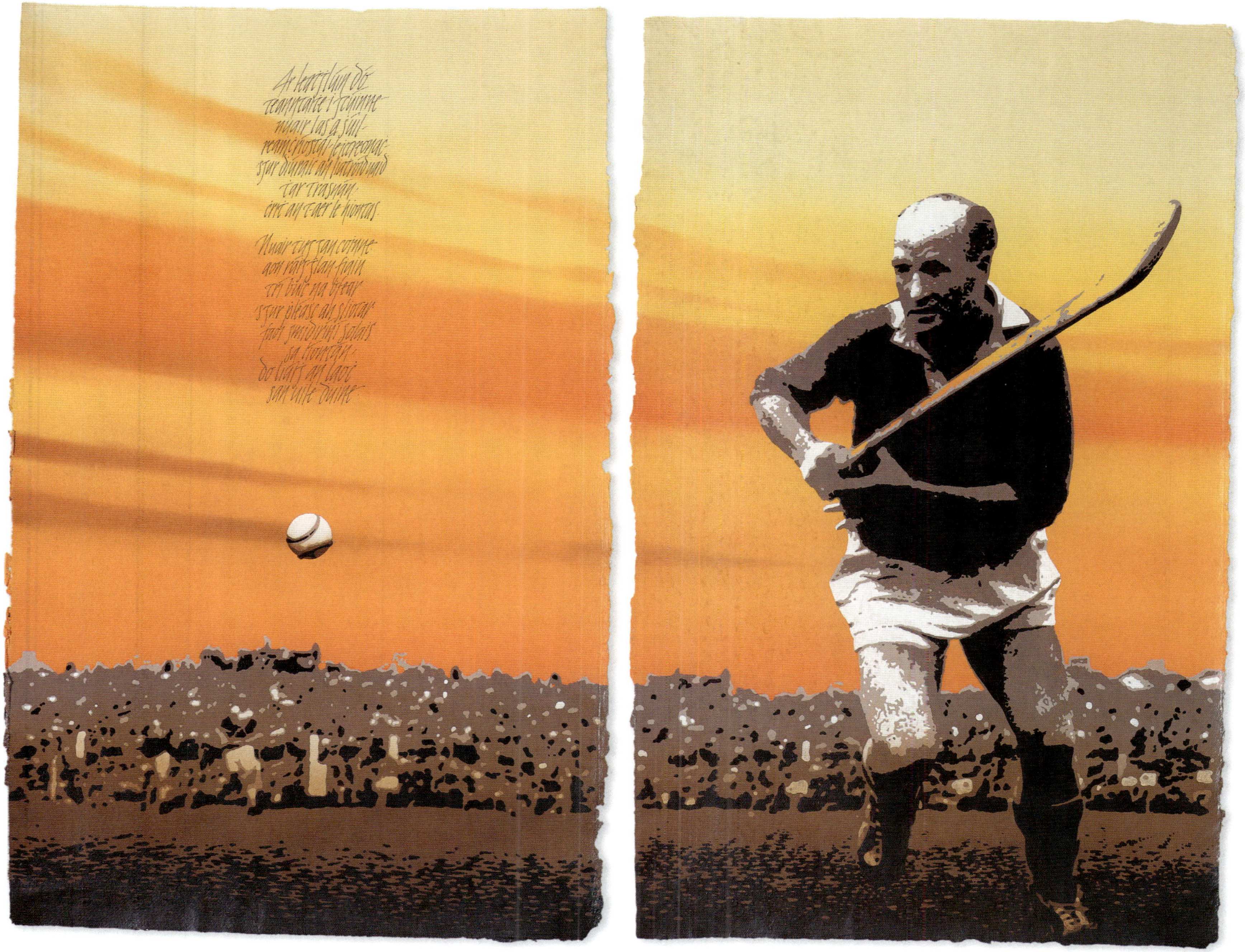

97

MÁIRTIN Ó CADHAIN

1906-1970

Ealaíontóir/Artist:
Ian Brady

Peannaire/Calligrapher:
Louise Donaldson

Aistritheoirí/Translators
Eibhlín Ní Allúráin, Maitin Ó Néill

Ainmníodh ag/Nominator:
The Editorial Panel

Cré na Cille (sliocht)

Ní mé an ar Áit an Phuint nó na Cúig Déag atá mé curtha? D'imigh an diabhal orthu dhá mba in Áit na Leathghine a chaithfidís mé, th'éis ar chuir mé d'fhainiceachaí orthu! Maidin an lae ar bhásaigh mé ghlaoigh mé aníos ón gcisteanach ar Phádraig: 'Achuiní agam ort a Phádraig a leanbh,' adeirimse. 'Cuir ar Áit an Phuint mé. Ar Áit Phuint. Tá cuid againn curtha ar Áit na Leathghine, ach má tá fhéin ... '

Dúirt mé leo an chónra a bfhearr tigh Thaidhg a fháil. Cónra mhaith dharaí í ar chaoi ar bith . . . Tá brat na scaball orm. Agus an bhráithlín bharróige. Bhí siad sin faoi réir agam fhéin . . . Tá spota ar an scaoilteoig seo. Is geall le práib shúí é. Ní hea. Lorg méire. Bean mo mhic go siúráilte. Is cosúil len a cuid pruisliocht é. Má chonnaic Neil é! Is dóigh go raibh sí ann. Ní bheadh dar fia dhá mbeadh aon neart agamsa air . . .

Is mí-stuama a ghearr Cáit bheag na gairéadaigh. Dúirt mé ariamh fhéin nár cheart aon deor len ól a thabhairt di féin ná do Bhid Shorcha nó go mbeadh an corp dealaithe den tsráid. Chuir mé fainic ar Phádraig dhá mbeadh ól déanta acu gan ligean dóibh na gairéadaigh a ghearradh. Ach ní féidir Cáit Bheag a choinneál ó choirp. Ba é a buac chuile lá ariamh marbhán a bheith in áit ar bith ar an dá bhaile. Dhá mbeadh na seacht sraith ar an iomaire d'fhanfaidís ar an iomaire, ach í ag fáil bonn coirp . . .

Cré na Cille (excerpt)

Now I wonder is it in the pound plot or in the fifteen shilling plot they have me buried. They went to the devil entirely if it's in the ten shilling place they threw me after all the warnings I gave them. The morning of the day I died I called Padraig up from the kitchen. 'Will you do me a favour, Padraig, *astore,*'* says I. 'Bury me in the pound plot. The pound plot. Some of us are laid in the ten shilling part, but if they are itself . . .'

I told them to get the best coffin there was in Tadhg's shop. It's a fine oak coffin in any case ... The brown habit is on me. And the winding sheet ... I had these ready myself ... There's a spot on this sheet. It's like a plaster of soot. No, it isn't. The mark of a finger. My son's wife for sure. It's like her handiwork. If Nell saw it! I suppose she was there. By gor, she wouldn't be there if I could help it ...

Kateen did a clumsy job of the binding strips. I always said neither herself or Bid Sorcha should get a drop of drink until the corpse would be left the street. I warned Padraig not to let them cut the binding strips if they had drink taken. But you couldn't keep that Kateen away from a corpse. She was never happy unless there was a corpse somewhere in the neighbourhood. The place could be on fire for all she cared once she got the smell of a corpse . . .

**dear one*

Note: Máirtín Ó Cadhain's experimental novel Cré na Cille *(1949) is the undisputed masterpiece of twentieth-century Irish prose. It consists almost entirely of dialogue, a continuous babble of simultaneous conversations between dozens of corpses in a graveyard in Connemara. The dead continue their above-ground feuds and obsessions in this strange setting, and even maintain the brutal snobbery of tiny class distinctions, in which status is measured by their being buried in plots costing ten shillings, fifteen shillings or a pound, the possession of a headstone, and the number of mourners at their funeral.*

Caitríona Phaudeen, the central character, is driven by hatred of her sister Nell, who in the distant past had married the man Caitríona loved. This bitter experience turned her into a savage-tongued virago whose loathing rippled out to include most of the living and the dead. The novel can be read as an exercise in social satire, but is much more than that; it is written in language of astonishing vitality, range and power, and is a work of sustained comic genius.

We have only been able to give an excerpt from this text. *For an alternative source of the full text see the listing on page 265.*

Ní mé an ar Áit an Phuint nó na Cúig Déag atá mé curtha? D'imigh an diabhal orthu dhá mba in Áit na Leathghine a chaithfidís mé, th'éis ar chuir mé d'fhainiceachaí orthu! Maidin an lae ar bhásaigh mé ghlaoigh me ghlaoigh mé aníos ón gcisteanach ar Phádraig: "Achuiní agam ort a Phádraig a leanbh," adeirimse. Cuir ar Áit an Phuint mé. Ar Áit Phuint. Tá cuid againn curtha ar Áit na Leathghine, ach má tá fhéin..."
Dúirt mé leo an chónra a b'fhearr tigh Thaidhg a fháil. Cónra mhaith dharaí í ar chaoi ar bith... Tá brat na scaball orm. Agus an bhráithlín bharróige. Bhí said sin faoi réir agam fhéin... Tá spota ar an scaoilteoig seo. Is geall le práib shúí é. Ní hea. Lorg méire. Bean mo mhic go siúráilte. Is cosúil len a cuid pruislíocht é. Ma chonnaic Neil é! Is dóigh go raibh sí ann. Ní bheadh dar fia dhá mbeadh aon neart agamsa air...

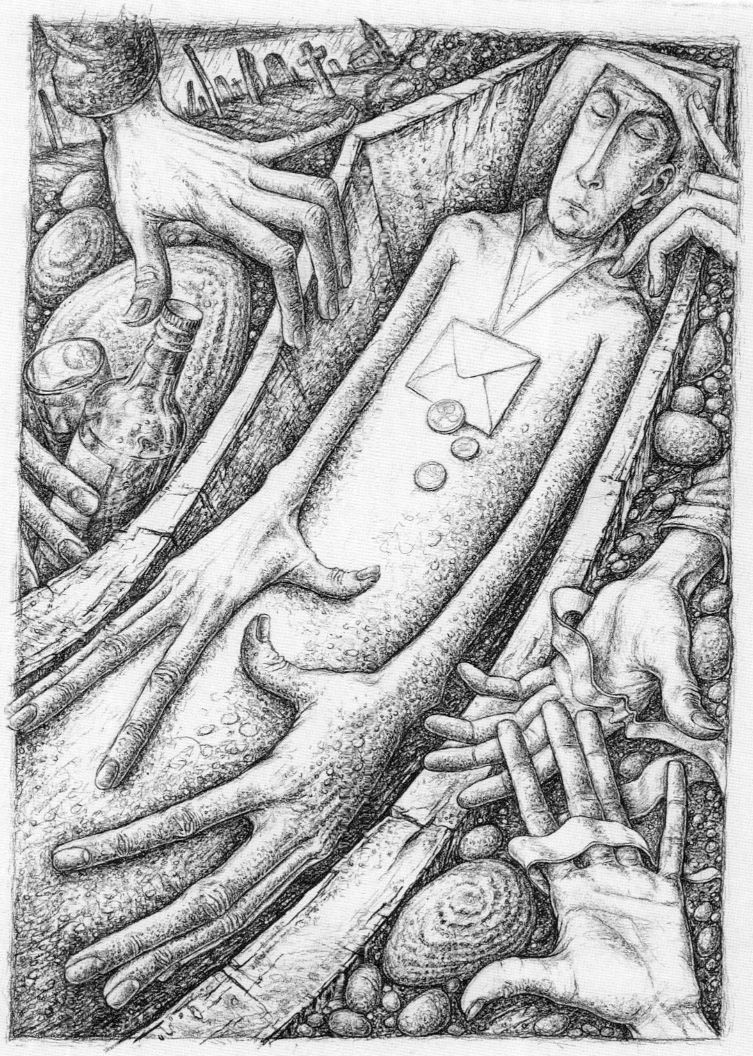

98

DÒMHNALL MAC AN T-SAOIR

DONALD MACINTYRE

1889-1964

Neach-ealain / Artist:
David Faithfull

Snas-sgrìobhadair / Calligrapher:
The Artist

Eadar-theangaichte aig / Translator:
Ronald Black

Roghainn / Nominator:
John MacInnes

Bùth Dhòmhnaill 'IcLeòid (earrann)

. . . 'Cuir a-nuas leth-tè chruaidh,' thuirt fear shuas mun cheann àrd,
'Glainne fìon,' thuirt fear shìos air bheil fìor choltas ceàird;
'Happy Day, come away,' labhair tè chamach bhàn
A bha bhlàth air a sròin gun do thòisich i tràth
   Ann am bùth Dhòmhnaill 'IcLeòid.

Chì thu deòraidheach ruadh agus spuic air a mhaol
'N dèidh bhith Dòmhnach gu Luan glaiste suas aig na maoir;
Dh'fhalbh e 's dh'òl e tè chruaidh 's ghabh an truaghan an caoch,
'S chuir e eòlas an uair sin g' eil smuais anns gach braon
   Th' ann am bùth Dhòmhnaill 'IcLeòid.

Nì sinn cinnteach mum falbh sinn à balgam no dhà
Thig à Ile thar fairg' air eil dealbh an Eich Bhàin;
Toradh brìgheil an arbhair as ainmeile gràn –
Cha bhi rìoghachd na h-Alba neo-shealbhach gu bràth
   Fhad 's a dh'fhàsas innt' eòrn'.

Their na làithean a dh'aom orm caoineadh nan deur –
Tha a bhlàth air an t-saoghal g' eil saorsa dol sìos
Nuair tha 'm bàrd 's e Dihaoine gun bhraon thèid 'na bheul,
'S e air fhàgail cho daor aig na daoine gun chiall,
   An luchd-riaghlaidh a th' oirnn.

Anns an aimsir a dh'fhalbh thug iad Albainn fo chìs,
Rinn iad ìocshlaint nam buadh a chur suas ann am prìs
Gus na gheàrr iad on t-sluagh e, mo thruaighe ri inns' –
Gun do thràigh iad am fuaran bu dualach dhan tìr
   Bha na mìltean ag òl.

Thràigh iad fuaran nam buadh, dh'fhàg iad sluagh ann an càs,
Tha na ceàrnachan tuath 's iad air thuar a bhith fàs;
Tha na fàrdaichean fuar a bha uaireigin blàth,
'S chan eil àbhachd aig cluais mur eil fuaim a' mhuir-làin,
   Far am b' àbhaisteach ceòl.

Donald MacLeod's Pub (excerpt)

. . . 'Send over a small whisky,' said a man up at the high end,
'Glass of wine,' said a man down here with a real tinker's look on him;
'Happy Day, come away,' said a talkative blonde
Who made clear by her nose that she started early
   In Donald MacLeod's pub.

You'll see a red-haired vagrant with a bruise on his forehead
Who'd been from Sunday to Monday locked up in a cell;
He went off and had a whisky and the wretch went crazy
And discovered then there's a punch in each drop
   That's in Donald MacLeod's pub.

We'll be sure before leaving to have a mouthful or two
That's crossed the sea from Islay under the White Horse label;
The substantial product of the corn whose grain is most famous –
The kingdom of Scotland will prosper forever
   As long as her barley grows.

Bygone days make me weep tears –
It seems from the world that freedom's on the decline
When the poet on a Friday puts not a drop in his mouth,
For it's been made so expensive by senseless people,
   Those who rule over us.

In times gone by they brought Scotland under tribute,
They raised the price of the magic elixir
Till they took it from the people, I'm sorry to say,
And dried up the well that was traditional to the land
   And that thousands drank.

They dried up the magic well, they left folk in a strait,
The northern districts are almost deserted;
The dwellings are cold that were formerly warm
And no ear has good cheer but the incoming tide
   Where once there was music.

We have only been able to give an excerpt from this poem. For an alternative source of the full text see the listing on page 265.

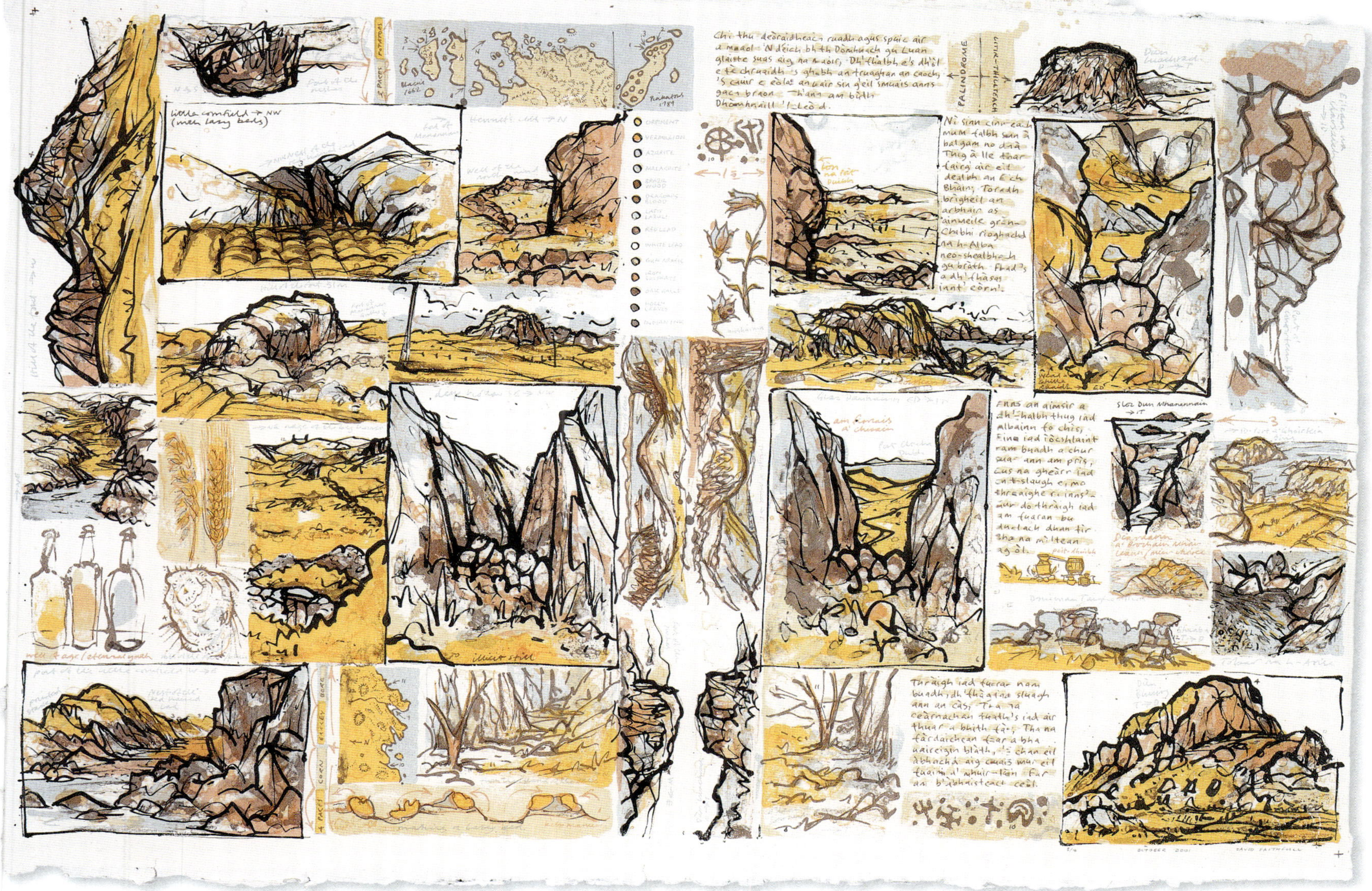

little cornfield → NW
(men lazy beds)
Blaeu 1662
Pinkerton's 1789
PALINDROME
illicit still
October 2001
David Faithfull

99

IAIN MOIREACH

JOHN MURRAY

b. 1938

Neach-ealain/Artist:
Sigrid Shone

Snas-sgrìobhadair/Calligrapher:
Réiltín Murphy

Eadar-theangaichte aig/Translator:
The Author

Roghainn/Nominator:
The Author

Turas an Asainte

Gàire tro Ghleann Lèireag,
seanachas sa Chaolas Chumhang,
dà cheud ràith a' tuiteam dhìot;
beòthail faileas d' òige
ait am measg thaibhsean
air gainmheach Sgobharaidh;
nad leum thar nan crìochan
ghlac creathaill mo làimhe
eòin chlis do chuimhne.

Reoth sùil na h-èilde
air sliabh Chuinneig,
shearg a' chnò challtainn
an clais mo theanga,
Loch Asainte air traoghadh
gun fhios dhomh,
cnàmhan donn na cuimhne
nan slèibhtrich
air grunnd tioram.

Anns an eadar-thràth
eadar an dà anail
eadar Asainte is Leòdhas
Sgobharaidh is Diluain
shiubhail thu
tro bheàrnan mo mheòir
nad ghainmheach
mhìn bhlàth
gu luath.

Once in Assynt

Laughter through Glen Leireag,
story-telling across Kylesku,
two hundred seasons falling off you;
lively the shadow of your youth
joyful amongst ghosts
on the sand in Scourie;
in your leap over the boundaries
the cradle of my hand caught
your memory's darting birds.

The hind's eye froze
on the slope of Quinag,
the hazelnut withered
in the hollow of my tongue,
Loch Assynt drained empty
unknown to me,
the brown bones of memory
lay strewn
on a dry bed.

In the interval
between the two breaths
between Assynt and Lewis
Scourie and Monday
you sped
through gaps in my fingers
as fine warm
sand
to ashes.

100

MICHEÀL Ó HAIRTNÉIDE

MICHAEL HARTNETT

1941-1999

Ealaíontóir/Artist:
Alanna O'Kelly

Peannaire/Calligrapher:
Réiltín Murphy

Aistritheoir/Translator:
The Author

Aimníodh ag/Nominator:
Aine Ní Ghlinn

Dán do Lara, 10

Fuinseog trí thine
gruaig do chinn
ag mealladh fuiseoige
le do ghlór binn
i bhféar glas,
is scata nóiníní
ag súgradh leat
is scata coiníní
ag damhsa leat
an lon dubh
is a órghob
mar sheoid leat
lasair choille
is a binneas
mar cheol leat.
Is cumhrach tusa,
is mil, is sú talún:
ceapann an beach féin
gur bláth sa pháirc thú.
A bhanríon óg thír na leabhar,
go raibh tú mar seo go deo
go raibh tú saor i gcónaí
ó shiabhra an bhróin.

Seo mo bheannacht ort, a chailín,
is is tábhachtach mar bheannú é
go raibh áilleacht anama do mháthar
leat is áilleacht a gné.

Poem for Lara, 10

An ashtree on fire
the hair of your head
coaxing larks
with your sweet voice
in the green grass,
a crowd of daisies
playing with you
a crowd of rabbits
dancing with you
the blackbird
with its gold bill
is a jewel for you
the goldfinch
with its sweetness
is your music.
You are perfume,
you are honey,
a wild strawberry:
even the bees think you
a flower in the field.
Little queen of the land of books,
may you always be thus
may you ever be free
from sorrow-chains.

Here's my blessing for you, girl,
and it is no petty grace –
may you have the beauty of your mother's soul
and the beauty of her face.

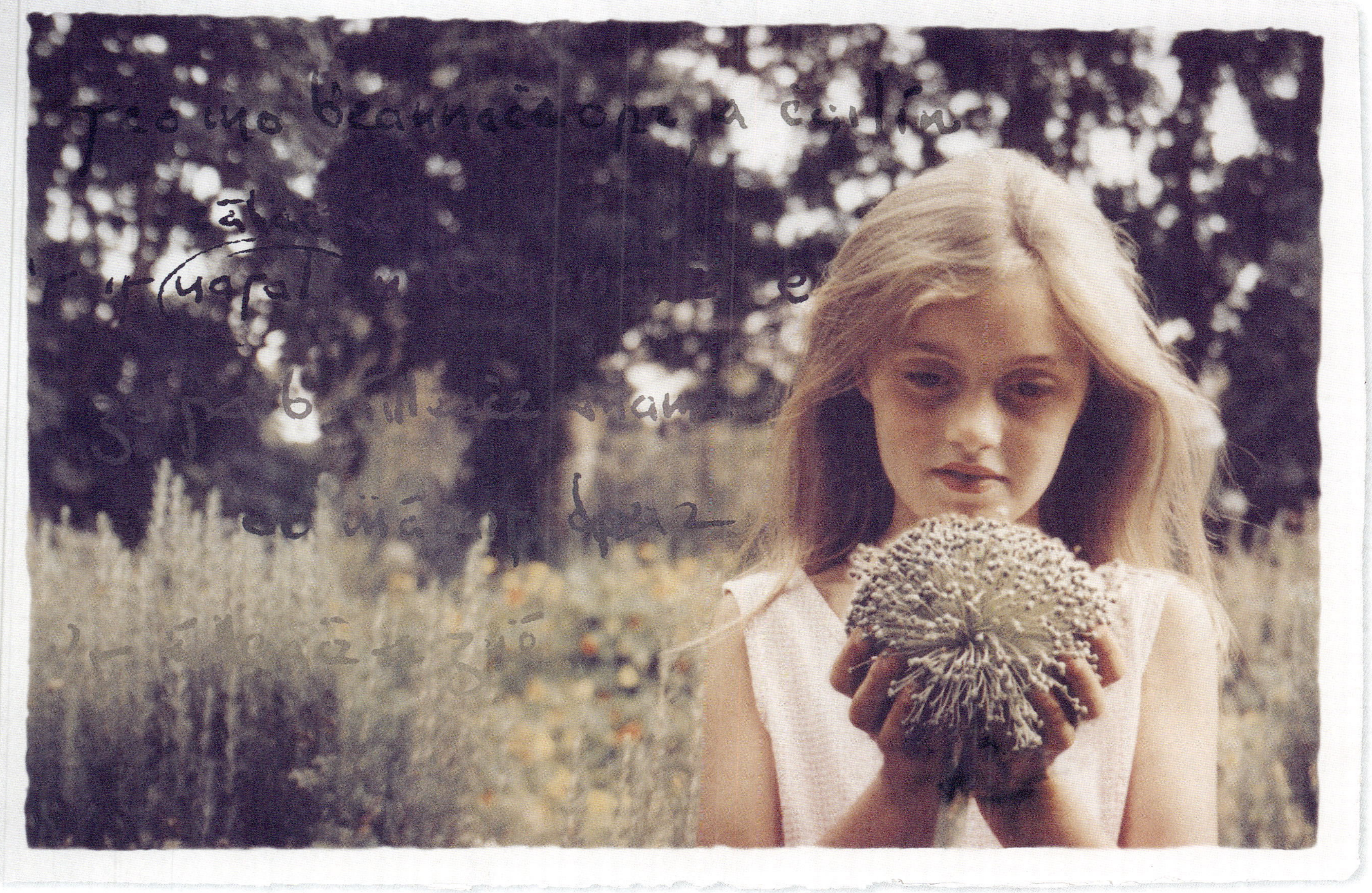

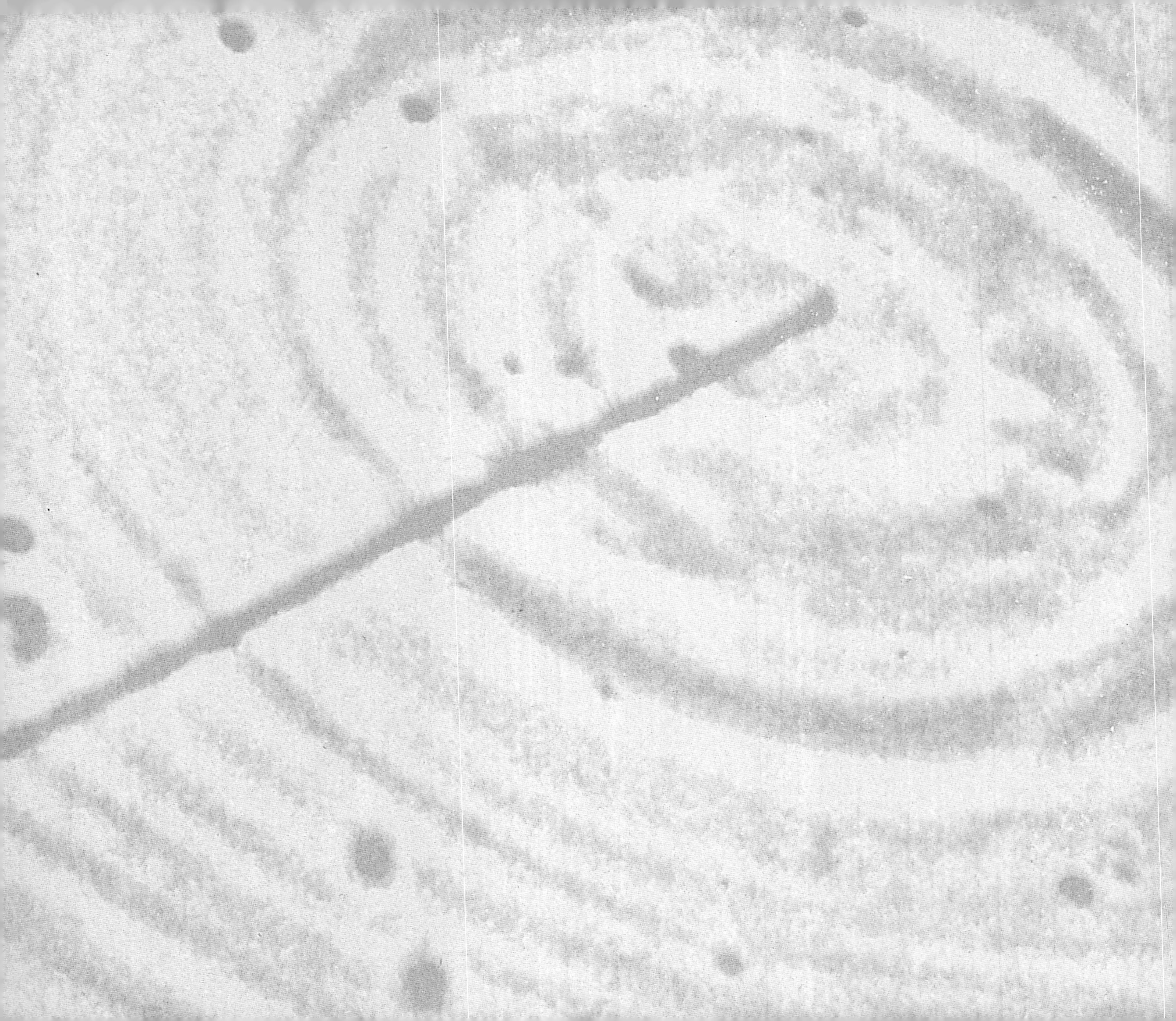

SUPPLEMENTARY TEXTS

The English versions of the works in this publication were generally the choice of those who nominated the Gaelic texts. They range from literal prose translations to free interpretations of the originals.

1 Amra Choluim Chille

Dallán Forgaill (c.600)

III A Dheascabháil ar Neamh

Éiríonn Colum in ard neimhe ar theacht chuige aingil Dé
– An freastal aoibhgheal.
Dhein sé a bhigil lena bheo;
Ba ghearr a ré;
Ba shuarach a sháith;
Ba shaoi sa Dinnsheanchas é;
B'údar i leabhar docht an dlí.
Las an Tuaisceart,
Gur ghealaigh an tIarthar,
Is gur bhladhm an tOirthear
De dheasca na gcléireach diantréanach.
Ba thaibhseach a bhás:
Aingil Dé ar a cheann ar éirí dó.

IV Na Flaithis agus a Muintir

Ráinig sé na hAspail is sluaite na nArdaingeal;
Ráinig tír nach bhfeictear inti oíche;
Ráinig tír Mhaoise, mar a dhealraímid;
Ráinig gan mhoill críocha an cheoil nach ngintear,
Nach n-éagann saoithe;
Rí na sagart a scar dá shaotha.

V Anró agus Suáilcí Choluim

Tamall á chrá dó roimh bhua,
Líon dá ghráin an diabhal
Is é i sáinn ag an Aifreann.
Ba thréan an té a chaomhnaigh an reacht
Trí chumhacht a cheirde;
Bhí aithne ar a mhainistir agus ar a Chathaoir aba;
Tugtaí dó léargas ar dhiagacht;
Is deimhin: ba mhaith é a bhás;
Bhí aithne aige ar aspail is aingil,
Bhain sé leas as breithiúntais Bhasil:
Choisc léiriú na nduan do mhórdhronga

Dallán's Elegy for Columba

III Colum Ascends to Heaven

Colum rises to high Heaven
When the angels of God come to him
– A radiant visitation.
While he lived he kept vigil;
His time was short,
His portion scant.
He was learned in the lore of places,
An authority on the difficult book of the law.
From the austere clerics of God
The North took fire,
The West lit up
And the East blazed.
Splendid was his death,
Angels of God before him as he rose to Heaven.

IV Heaven Described

He has reached the Apostles and the hosts of Archangels,
He has reached the land where night is not seen,
The land of Moses, as it seems;
Straight to the sphere of heavenly music he came,
Where sages do not die.
The king of clerics has parted from distress.

V Colum's struggles against the Devil and his life of virtue

Before his triumph for a time he was in torment;
The Devil, full of hate for him, was fettered by the Mass.
Strong was he who preserved the law
Through the power of his priesthood;
His monastery and abbacy were known far and wide.
Knowledge of the divinity was granted to him:
His death was indeed holy;
He was familiar with apostles and angels;
He applied the judgements of Basil
And forbade the chanting of songs at large meetings.

7 Pangur Bán

Gan Ainm (c.900)

Hé fesin as choimsid dáu
in muid du-ngní cach óenláu;
du thabairt doraid du glé
for mu mud céin am messe.

The Scholar and his Cat

He it is who is master for himself of the work which he does every day. I can perform my own work directed at understanding clearly what is difficult.

8 Rop Tú Mo Baile

Gan Ainm (c.1000)

Rop tussu t' aenur
sainsherc mo chride;
ní rop nech aile
acht Airdrí nime.

Co talla forum,
ré ndul it lámа,

mo chuit, mo chotlud,
ar méit do gráda.

Rop tussu t'áenur
m'urrann úais amra:
ní chuinngim daíne
ná maíne marba.

Rop amlaid dínsiur
cech sel, cech ságul,
mar marb oc brénad,
ar t'fhégad t'áenur.

Do sherc im anmain,
do grád im chride,
tabair dam amlaid,
a Rí secht nime.

Tabair dam amlaid,
a Rí secht nime,
do sherc im anmain,
do grád im chride.

Go Ríg na n-uile
rís íar mbúaid léire;
ro béo i flaith nime
i ngile gréine.

A Athair inmain,
cluinte mo núallsa:
mithig (mo-núarán!)
lasin trúagán trúagsa.

A Chríst mo chride,
cip ed dom-aire,
a Fhlaith na n-uile,
rop tú mo baile.

Fill My Horizon

Unto You alone
My heart shall cling.
None can dethrone
Heaven's High King.

Before You request,
Let me donate
My food, my rest –
Your care is so great.

Of all I savour
Be supreme –
Above intimate favour,
Inanimate gleam.

Let me rue the day,
The lifetime too,
As a corpse in decay,
If You're not in view.

In my soul Your touch,
In my heart Your love,
Bestow on me such,
King of heaven above.

Bestow on me such,
King of heaven above,
In my soul Your touch,
In my heart Your love.

With the King of All,
Tour of duty done,
Under heaven's rule,
Under dazzling sun.

Dear Father, please,
(My SOS to You!)
This wretch's release
Is now overdue!

Christ bless the days
Which face me still
Lord of earth and skies,
My horizon fill.

10 M'anam do Sgar Riomsa A-raoir

Muireadhach Albanach (c. 1300)

Leath mo throigheadh, leath mo thaobh,
a dreach mar an droighean bán,
níor dhísle neach dhí ná dhún,
leath mo shúl í, leath mo lámh.

Leath mo chuirp an choinneal naoi;
's guirt riom do roinneadh, a Rí;
agá labhra is meirtneach mé –
dob é ceirtleath m'anma í.

Mo chéadghrádh a dearc mhall mhór,
déadbhán agus cam a cliabh:
nochar bhean a colann caomh
ná a taobh ré fear romham riamh.

Fiche bliadhna inne ar-aon,
fá binne gach bliadhna ar nglór,
go rug éinleanabh déag dhún,
an ghéag úr mhéirleabhar mhór.

Gé tú, nocha n-oilim ann,
ó do thoirinn ar gcnú chorr;
ar sgaradh dár roghrádh rom,
falamh lom an domhnán donn.

Ón ló do sáidheadh cleath corr
im theach nochar ráidheadh rum –
ní thug aoighe d'ortha ann
dá barr naoidhe dhorcha dhunn.

A dhaoine, ná coisgidh damh;
faoidhe ré cloistin ní col;
táinig luinnchreach lom 'nar dteagh –
an bhruithneach gheal donn ar ndol.

Is é rug uan í 'na ghrúg,
Rí na sluagh is Rí na ród;
beag an cion do chúl na ngéag
a héag ó a fior go húr óg.

Ionmhain lámh bhog do bhí sonn,
   a Rí na gclog is na gceall:
ach! an lámh nachar logh mionn,
   crádh liom gan a cor fám cheann.

On the Death of his Wife

The face that was like hawthorn bloom
Was my right foot and my right side;
And my right hand and right eye
Were no more than hers who died.

Poor is the share of me that's left
Since half of me died with my wife;
I shudder at the words I speak;
Dear God, that girl was half my life.

And our first look was her first love;
No man had fondled ere I came
The little breasts so small and firm
And the long body like a flame.

For twenty years we shared a home,
Our converse milder with each year;
Eleven children in its time
Did that tall stately body bear.

It was the King of hosts and roads
Who snatched her from me in her prime:
Little she wished to leave alone
The man she loved before her time.

Now King of churches and of bells,
Though never raised to pledge a lie
That woman's hand – can it be true? –
No more beneath my head will lie.

11 Bean Torrach, fa Tuar Broide

Gofraidh Fionn Ó Dálaigh (c.1400)

Ar bhfaicsin déar ré dreich ngil,
ráidhis an leanbh lá éigin:
ó tharla a fhuidheall ar mh'óidh,
cluineam damhna do dhobhróin.

Neimhiongnadh gé dho-neinn maoith,
ar sise, a leinibh lánbhaoith;
is rian cumhang nár dhleacht dún,
teacht d'fhulang pian i bpríosún.

An bhfuil, ar sé, sódh eile,
is aoibhne ná ar n-innmhine,
nó an bhfuil ní as soillse ná so,
ó dho-ní an toirse tromsa?

Dar linn, ar an leanabh óg,
gé taoi brónach, a bheanód,
is léir dhúin ar ndíol soillse,
ná bíodh ar th'uidh attuirse.

A n-abrae ní hiongnadh dheit,
ar an inghean, a óigmheic;
dáigh treibhe an teagh do thoghais –
treabh eile ní fhacadhais.

Dá bhfaictheá a bhfacaidh meise,
ré dteacht don treibh dhoircheisi,
do bhiadh doimheanma ort ann,
do phort oileamhna, a anam.

Os agadsa is fhearr a dhearbh,
a inghean, ar an t-óigleanbh,
ná ceil foirn fionnachtain de,
do mhoirn d'iomarcaidh oirne.

Loise an tsaoghail mhóir amuigh,
is eadh tháirreas ó thosaigh;
mé i dtigh dhorcha 'na dheaghaidh,
a fhir chomtha, is cinneamhain.

Le cleachtadh deacrachta dhe,
's nach fuair sé sódh is aoibhne,
níor cheis a ghruadh ghríosúr ghlan
ar an bpríosún bhfuar bhfolamh.

Baramhail do-bearthar dún –
an dream do bhí sa bhríosún:
lucht an bheatha gé an cúpla,
a ré is beatha bhríosúnta.

Ag féachain meadhrach Mheic Dé,
flaitheas aga bhfuil buainré,
cúis bhróin beatha gach dúnaidh,
slóigh an bheatha is bríosúnaigh.

A Child Born in Prison

He said one day, beholding
a tear on her lovely face:
'I see the signs of sadness;
now let me hear the cause.'

'No wonder that I mourn,
my foolish child,' said she.
'This cramped place is not our lot,
and suffering pain in prison.'

'Is there another place,' he said,
'lovelier than ours?
Is there a brighter light than this
that your grief grows so heavy?'

'For I believe,' the young child said,
'mother, although you mourn,
we have our share of light.
Don't waste your thoughts in sorrow.'

'I do not wonder at what you say,
young son,' the girl replied.
'You think this is a hopeful place
because you have seen no other.

'If you knew what I have seen
before this dismal place
you would be downcast also
in your nursery here, my soul.'

'Since it is you know best, lady,'
the little child replied,
'hide from me no longer
what more it was you had.'

'A great outer world in glory
formerly was mine.
After that, beloved boy,
my fate is a darkened house.'

At home in all his hardships,
not knowing a happier state,
fresh-cheeked and bright, he did not grudge
the cold and desolate prison.

And so is the moral given:
the couple there in prison
are the people of this world,
imprisoned life their span.

Compared with joy in the Son of God
in His everlasting realm
an earthly mansion is only grief,
prisoners all the living.

13 A Phaidrín do Dhúisg Mo Dhéar

Aithbhreac Inghean Coirceadail (c. 1500)

A h-éagmhais aon duine a-mháin
im aonar atáim dá éis,
gan chluiche, gan chomhrádh caoin,
gan ábhacht, gan aoibh i gcéill.

**Gan duine ris' dtig mo mhiann
ar sliocht nan Niall ó Niall óg;
gan mhuirn gan mheadhair ag mnáibh,
gan aoibhneas an dáin im dhóigh.**

Mar thá Giodha an fhuinn mhín,
Dún Suibhne do-chím gan cheól,
faithche longphuirt na bhfear bhfial:
aithmhéala na Niall a n-eól.

Cúis ar lúthgháire má seach,
gusa mbímis ag teacht mall:
's nach fuilngim a-nois, mo nuar,
a fhaicinn uam ar gach ard.

Má bhrisis, a Mheic Dhé bhí,
ar bagaide na dtrí gcnó,
fa fior do ghabhais ar ngiall:
do bhainis an trian ba mhó.

Cnú mhullaigh a mogaill féin
bhaineadh do Chloinn Néill go nua;
is tric roighne na bhfear bhfial
go leabhaidh na Niall a-nuas.

An rogha fá deireadh díbh
's é thug gan mo bhrígh an sgéal:
do sgar riom mo leathchuing rúin,
a phaidrín do dhúisg mo dhéar.

**Is briste mo chridhe im chlí,
agus bídh nó go dtí m'éag,
ar éis an abhradh dhuibh úir,
a phaidrín do dhúisg mo dhéar.
A phaidrín.**

**Muire mháthair, muime an Ríogh,
go robh 'gam dhíon ar gach séad,
is a Mac do chruthuigh gach dúil,
a phaidrín do dhúisg mo dhéar.
A phaidrín.**

Thou Rosary That Has Waked My Tear

For want of one man all lonely am I after him, without sport, without kindly talk, without mirth, without cheer to show.

Without one mind to whom my mind draweth of the stock of MacNeill since young Neil is gone, ladies lack mirth and joy; I am without hope of gladness in song.

Sad is the state of smooth-soiled Gigha; Dún Suibhne I see without music, that greensward of a stronghold of generous men; the sorrow of the MacNeills is known to them.

Cause of our joyous mirth in turn, to which we were wont to go in stately wise, while now, alas! I endure not to view it from each height.

If thou, Son of the living god, hast made a breach upon the cluster of three nuts, true it is that Thou hast taken our choice hostage; Thou hast plucked the greatest of the three.

From Clann Neill hath been newly plucked the topmost nut of their cluster; often do the choicest of the generous men come down to the MacNeills' last bed.

The latest, choicest of them, it is that tale of him that hath sapped my strength; my loved yokefellow hath parted from me, thou rosary that hast waked my tear.

My heart is broken within my body, and will be so until my death, left behind him of the dark fresh eyelash, thou rosary that hast waked my tear.

Mary Mother, who did nurse the King, may she guard me on every path, and her Son who created each creature, thou rosary that hast waked my tear.

15 Thig Trì Nithean gun Iarraidh

Nighean Fhir na Rèilig (c. 1700)

Nam faicinn thu tighinn,
'S fios dhomh gur tusa bhiodh ann,
Gun èireadh mo chridhe
Mar aiteal na grèin' thar nam beann;
'S gun tugainn mo bhriathrar,
Gach gaoisdean tha liath na mo cheann,
Gum fàsadh iad buidhe,
Mar dhìthein am bruthaich nan allt!

Cha b' ann airson beartais,
No idir ro-phailteas na sprèidh,
Cha b' fhear de shìol bhodach

Bha m' osnaich cho trom à dhèidh,
Ach mac an duin'-uasail
Fhuair buaidh air an dùthaich gu lèir –
Ged a bhitheamaid falamh,
Tha caraid a chitheadh oirnn feum.

Mur tig thu fhèin tuilleadh,
Gur aithne dhomh mhalairt a th' ann:
Nach eil mi cho beartach
Ri cailin an achaidh ud thall;
Cha tugainn mo mhisneachd,
Mo ghliocas is grinneas mo làimh,
Air buaile chrodh ballach
Is cailin gun iùl air an ceann.

Ma chaidh thu orm seachad,
Gur taitneach, neo-thuisleach mo chliù:
Cha d' rinn mi riut comann,
'S cha d' laigh mi leat riamh ann an cùil;
Chan fhairichinn aithreachd
Do dhuine chuir ad air a chrùn,
On tha mi cho beachdail
'S gun smachdaich mi gaol nach fiù.

Bu lughaid mo thàmailt
Nam b' airidh ni b' fheàrr a bhiodh ann
Ach dubh-chail' a bhuachair
Nuair ghlacas i buarach na làimh;
Nuair thig an droch earrach
'S a chaillear an nì anns a' ghleann,
Bitheas is' air an t-siulaid,
Gun tuille dhe bunaltas ann.

Esan da freagairt:
'S truagh nach robh mi 's mo leannan
Sa chrannaig air stiùireadh le gaoith,
No 'm bùthaig bhig bharraich
Aig iomall a' ghleannain leinn fhìn;
No 'n Lochlainn an daraich
Ri taobh na mara fo thuinn,
Gun chuimhn' air a' chailin
A dh'fhàg mi air aire chruidh-laoigh.

Three Things Come Without Asking

If I saw you coming
and knew it was indeed you,
my heart would rise up
like a flash of the sun across the mountains.
Every grey hair in my head, I swear,
would become yellow
like the flower on the bank of the stream.

It was not for riches
nor at all for the abundance of cattle –
it was not for a man of peasant stock
I sighed so heavily after,
but a gentleman's son
who gained authority in the whole of the land:
even if we were poor,
there is a friend who'd see a place for us.

But if you never come,
well I do not know what bargain has been made:
it is because I am not as wealthy
as the lass with those pastures there.
Yet I would not give my courage
and my good sense and the skill of my hands
for any fold of dappled cattle
and an improvident girl to manage them.

If you have passed me by,
fragrant and unspoilt is my name:
I had no relationship with you
nor did I ever lie with you in a hidden place.
I'd feel no kinship
with anyone who aspired to a crown,
since I am so assured
I can control a love that is worth nothing.
My hurt would be less
if it were a better one in [my] place –
but a wench of the cattle dung
handling a spancel for the cows!
When a bad spring comes
and the cattle die in the glen,
she'll be quite without use
and her constancy no more found.

He answering her
Alas that I and my lover
are not in a boat steered by the wind
or in a little booth of birch
at the edge of the glen by ourselves,
or in Norway of the oakwood,
beside the sea and its waves,
without memory of the girl
who left me in charge of the milch-cows.

16 Fuar Leam an Oidhche-se dh'Aodh

Eochaidh Ó hEoghasa (c.1560–1612)

Saoth linn, do loit ar meanmain,
Learg thais a thaoibh míndealbhaigh
'Gá meilt i ngruamoidhche ghairbh
I mbeirt fhuarthoirfe iairn.

Bos tláith na dtachar neamhthláth
Síon oighridh dá fuaighealtáth
Re crann rionnfhuar gcaol gceise,
lonnfhuar d'Aodh san oidhcheise.

Nárab aithreach leis ná leam
A thuras timchioll Éireann,
Go ndeach tharuinn, ná tí m'olc,
An ní fá ngabhuim guasocht.

Dá dtí ris an toisg do thriall
Do chur chuarta chraoi Mhaicniadh –
Ní tháirthearnar séad mar soin –
Créad acht snáithghearradh saoghoil?

Líonaid re hucht na n-ánroth
Bruaigh ísle na n-uaránshroth,
Cluana sgor fá sgingbheirt reoidh
Dá gcor tar ingheilt d'aimhdheoin.

Folchar a gciomhsa cheana,
Nach léir do lucht foirgneamha
Bruaigh easgadh na ngrianshroth nglan –
Seasgadh fianbhoth ní féadtar.

Eagail dó, díochra an anbhuain,
Caill eachraidh is aradhshluaigh,
Sul deachar tar síoth-laoi siar
Do chreachadh míonchraoi Mhaicniadh.

Ní hé budh uireasbhaidh linn
A thuras an tráth smuainim,
Lór do chor chuarta ar gcridhe
Gomh fhuachta na haimsire.

Gidheadh is adhbhar téighthe
Dá ghnúis shuaithnidh shoiléirthe
Slios gach múir ghorm-shaothraigh ghil
'Na dhlúimh thonn-ghaothmhair theintigh.

Téighfidh teannál an adhnaidh
Sging reoidh an ruisg shocarghlain;
Geimhle chuisne a chorrghlac ndonn
Donnbhrat luisne ros leaghonn.

Seachnóin Mhumhan na múr ngeal
Iomdha ó airgtheoir fhuinn Ghaoidheal
Cúirte bruachnochta i mbeirt smóil
Ag ceilt fhuardhochta an aeóir.

Iomdha ó chuairt Aoidh Mhéig Uidhir,
Feadh iarthair fhóid fhionnfhuinidh,
Cúirt 'na doighir – ní díoth nuadh –
Críoch gan oighir gan iarmhua.

Ode to the Maguire

Large, large affliction unto me and mine it is,
That one of his majestic bearing, his fair, stately form,
Should thus be tortured and o'erborne – that this unsparing storm
Should wreak its wrath on head like this!

That his great hand, so often the avenger of the oppressed,
Should this chill, churlish night, perchance, be paralysed by frost –
While through some icicle-hung thicket-as one lorn and lost –
He walks and wanders without rest.

The tempest-driven torrent deluges the mead,
It overflows the low banks of the rivulets and ponds –
The lawns and pasture-grounds lie locked in icy bonds
So that the cattle cannot feed.

The pale bright margins of the streams are seen by none,
Rushes and sweeps along the untameable flood on every side –
It penetrates and fills the cottagers' dwellings far and wide –
Water and land are blent in one.

Through some dark wood, 'mid bones of monsters, Hugh now strays,
As he confronts the storm with anguished heart, but manly brow –
O, what a sword-wound to that tender heart of his were now
A backward glance at peaceful days.

But other thoughts are his – thoughts that can still inspire
With joy and onward-bounding hope the bosom of MacNee –
Thoughts of his warriors charging like bright billows of the sea,
Borne on the wind's wings, flashing fire!

And though frost glaze tonight the clear dew of his eyes,
And white ice-gauntlets glove his noble fine fair fingers o'er,
A warm dress is to him that lightning-garb he ever wore,
The lightning of the soul, not skies.

*Avran**

Hugh marched forth to the fight – I grieved to see him so depart;
And lo! tonight he wanders frozen, rain-drenched, sad, betrayed –
But the memory of the limewhite mansions his right hand hath laid
In ashes, warms the hero's heart.

**Avran*: conclusion

18 A Mhic Dhonnchaidh Inbhir Abha

Màiri Chamshron (c.1700)

Thèid mi ann mun òdhraich t' anart,
Bidh mi leat an cùirt nan aingeal;
'S fheàrr bhith leat na 'n seo air m' aineol,
Fhir bu chaoine guth na 'n cainneal.

Thug thu ginidh air mo bhrògan,
Còig dhiubh air mo bhreacan pòsaidh;
Cha d'fhuair mo leithid a bha beò e –
Saoil am b' iongnadh mi bhith brònach?

Son of Duncan of Inverawe

I will go there before your shroud has discoloured,
I will be with you in the court of angels;
I would rather be with you than a stranger here,
Man whose voice was sweeter than cinnamon.

You paid a guinea for my shoes,
five guineas on my wedding outfit;
outfit no-one alive like me got such –
is it any wonder that I am sad?

19 Clann Ghriogair air Fògradh

Gun Urrainn (c.1700)

'S ann a rinn sibh 'n t-sidheann anmoch
Anns a' ghleann am bi 'n ceathach.

Dh'fhàg sibh 'n t-Eòin bòidheach
Air a' mhòintich 'na laighe,

'Na starsnaich air fèithe
An dèidh a reubadh le claidheamh.

'S ann a thog sibh ghreigh dhùbhghorm
O lùban na h-abhann.

Ann am Bothan na Dìge
Ghabh sibh dìon air an rathad;

Far an d'fhàg sibh mo bhiodag
Agus crios mo bhuilg-shaighead.

Gur i saighead na h-àraich
Seo thàrmaich am leathar.

Chaidh saighead am shliasaid,
Crann fiar air dhroch shnaidheadh.

Gun seachnadh Rìgh nan Dùl sibh
O fhùdar caol neimhe,

O shradagan teine,
O pheileir 's o shaighid,

O sgian na rinn caoile,
'S o fhaobhar geur claidhimh.

'S ann bha bhuidheann gun chòmhradh
Didòmhnaich 'm bràighe bhaile.

Is cha dèan mi gàir èibhinn
An àm èirigh no laighe.

'S beag an t-iongnadh dhomh fèin siud,
'S mi bhith 'n dèidh mo luchd-taighe.

Pursuit of Clan Gregor

It was a late foray you made in the Misty Glen,
you left Handsome John lying on the moor,
acting as a threshold to a bog, hacked by a sword.
You took the dark-grey stud of horses from the windings of the river;
at the Dyke you took shelter on your way,
and there you left my dirk, and the baldric for my arrow-quiver.
This arrow from the battlefield has lodged in my hide:
an arrow penetrated my thigh, a crooked ill-fashioned shaft.
May the King of the Elements save you from slim bullet and venomous powder,
from sparks of fire from bullet and from arrow,
from sharp-pointed knife, and from keen edge of sword.

The company above the village on Sunday was not a talkative one,
and I shall not laugh merrily when I rise or when I go to rest.
Little wonder: I am left alive when the folk of my house are dead.

21 Is Mairg nár Chrean le Maitheas Saoghalta

Dáibhí Ó Bruadair (1625–1698)

Is tartmhar mo thasc ag treabhadh im aonarsa
le harm nár chleachtas feacht ba mhéithe mé;
d'atadar m'ailt de reath na crélainne
is do mharta' an feac ar fad mo mhéireanna.

A Athair na bhfeart do cheap na céidnithe,
talamh is neamh is reanna is réithleanna,
earrach is teaspach, tartha is téachtuisce,
t'fheargain cas is freagair m'éagnachsa.

Woe to that Man who Leaves on his Vagaries

It's a thirsty task, ploughing this lonely furrow,
with a weapon I never employed when I was rich:
this sword-play into the earth has swelled my ankles
and the shaft has martyred my fingers totally.

Father of Miracles, Who madest the first things
– Earth and Heaven and constellations and stars,
Spring and warmth, fruit and freezing water –
avert Thy wrath and answer my lamentation!

22 Dónall Óg

Gan Ainm (c.1700)

Och, ochón! agus ní le hocras,
Uireasa bí, dí na codlata
Fá ndear domh-sa bheith tanaí triuchalga
Ach grá fir óig is é threoigh go follas mé.

Is moch ar maidin do chonnac-sa an t-óigfhear
Ar muin chapaill ag gabháil an bhóthair,
Níor dhruid sé liom is níor chuir ná streo orm,
Is ar mo chasadh abhaile dhom sea ghoileas mo dhóthain.

Nuair théim-se féin go Tobar an Uaignis
Suím síos ag déanamh buartha,
Nuair chím an saol is ná feicim mo bhuachaill,
Go raibh scáil an ómair i mbarr a ghruanna.

Siúd é an Domhnach do thugas grá duit,
An Domhnach díreach roimh Domhnach Cásca,
Is mise ar mo ghlúinibh ag léamh na Páise,
Sea bhí mo dhá shúil ag síor-thabhairt an ghrá dhuit.

Dúirt mo mháithrín liom gan labhairt leat
Inniu ná amárach ná Dia Domhnaigh.
Is olc an tráth do thug sí rabhadh dom
'S é dúnadh an dorais é i ndiaidh na foghla.

O a dhe, a mháithrín, tabhair mé féin dó.
Is tabhair a bhfuil agat den tsaol go léir dó;
Eirigh féin ag iarraidh déirce,
Agus ná gabh siar ná aniar ar m'éileamh.

Tá mo chroíse chomh dubh le bairne
Nó le gual dubh a bheadh i gceárta,
Nó le bonn bróige ar hallaí bána,
Is tá lionn dubh mór os cionn mo gháire.

Do bhanais soir dhíom, is do bhanais siar dhíom,
Do bhanais romham is do bhanais im' dhiaidh dhíom,
Do bhanais gealach is do bhanais grian dhíom,
'S is ró-mhór m'eagla gur bhanais Dia dhíom.

Dónal Óg

And, oh, it's not hunger or lack of food
and drink or sleep that has me thin
and worn but the love of a young man
has left me wasted.

Early this morning I saw him
going the road on horseback;
he never came near me and asked me for nothing
and when I came home I cried my eyes out.

When I go down and sit by the Well of Loneliness
I sit there nursing my trouble,
when I see the whole world without my boy
and the shadow of amber high in his cheeks.

That was the Sunday I gave you my love,
the last Sunday before Easter,
I was on my knees reading the Passion
and my eyes never stopped reciting their love to you.

My mother told me not to speak to you
today or tomorrow or Sunday;
it was too late for warnings,
like shutting the door when the thief is gone.

And yes, mother, give me to him,
give him all you have in the world,
go out in the streets and beg,
only don't deny me what I ask.

My heart is black as the sloe,
as black as coal in a dark forge
or the sole of a shoe in white halls,
and there's a black cloud over my laugh.

You took the east from me and you took the west from me,
you took before me and you took behind me,
you took the moon and the sun from me,
and I'm greatly afraid, you took God from me.

25 Alasdair à Gleanna Garadh

Sìleas na Ceapaich (1660-1729)

Nam b' ionann duitse 's do Dhòmhnall
An uair a chuir e 'n long air muir,
Cha tigeadh tu dhachaigh gu bràth
Gun fhios dè 'm fàth às 'n do chuir;
Nuair a chunnacas air an tràigh sibh
A bhith gur fàgail air faondradh,
Thuit ar cridheachan fo mhulad:
'S lèir a bhuil – cha robh sibh saogh'lach.

Bu tu 'n lasair dhearg gan losgadh,
Bu tu sgoltadh iad gu 'n sàiltibh,
Bu tu curaidh cur a' chatha,
Bu tu 'n laoch gun athadh làimhe;
Bu tu 'm bradan anns an fhìor-uisg',
Fìreun air an eunlaith 's àirde,
Bu tu 'n leòmhann thar gach beathach,
Bu tu damh leathann na cràice.

Bu tu 'n loch nach fhaodte thaomadh,
Bu tu tobar faoilidh na slàinte,
Bu tu Beinn Nibheis thar gach aonach,
Bu tu chreag nach fhaodte theàrnadh;
Bu tu clach-uachdair a' chaisteil,
Bu tu leac leathann na sràide,
Bu tu leug lòghmhor nam buadhan,
Bu tu clach uasal an fhàinne.

Bu tu 'n t-iubhar thar gach coillidh,
Bu tu 'n darach daingeann làidir,
Bu tu 'n cuileann 's bu tu 'n draigheann,
Bu tu 'n t-abhall molach blàthmhor;
Cha robh do dhàimh ris a' chritheann
No do dhligheadh ris an fheàrna;
Cha robh bheag ionnad den leamhan;
Bu tu leannan nam ban àlainn.

Bu tu cèile na mnà prìseil,
'S oil leam fhèin da dìth an dràst thu;
Ged nach ionann domhsa 's dhise,
'S goirt a fhuair mise mo chàradh;
H-uile bean a bhios gun chèile,
Guidheadh i Mac Dè na àite,
O 's E 's urra bhith ga còmhnadh
Anns gach bròn a chuireas càs oirr'.

Guidheam t' anam a bhith sàbhailt
On a chàireadh anns an ùir thu;
Guidheam sonas air na dh'fhàg thu
Ann ad àros 's ann ad dhùthaich:
Gum faic mi do mhac ad àite
Ann an saidhbhreas 's ann an cùram:
Alasdair à Gleanna Garadh,
Thug thu 'n-diugh gal air mo shùilibh.

Alasdair of Glengarry

If you were in the same situation as Donald was when he put the boat to sea, you would never have come home without knowing why he launched it. When you were seen on the strand, left alone in the lurch our hearts fell into sorrow. The outcome is clear: you were not long-lived.

You were a red torch to burn them, you would cleave them to the heels, you were a hero for waging battle, you were a champion whose arm never flinched. You were the salmon in fresh water, the eagle in the highest flock, you were the lion above all beasts, you were the stout antlered stag.

You were an undrainable loch, you were the liberal fount of health; you were Ben Nevis above every moor, you were an unscalable crag. You were the top-stone of the castle, you were the broad flag of the street, you were a priceless gem, you were the jewel in the ring.

You were the yew above every forest, you were the strong steadfast oak, you were the holly and the black-thorn, you were the apple-tree, rough-barked and many-flowered. You had no kinship with the aspen, owed no bonds to the alder; there was none of the lime-tree in you; you were the darling of beautiful women.

You were the husband of an invaluable wife, and it grieves me that she is now without you: though it is not the same for me as for her, I have myself suffered a bitter fortune. Let every wife who is without a husband pray to have the Son of God in his place, for He it is who can aid her in every sorrow which afflicts her.

I pray that your soul may be saved, now that you have been buried in the clay. I pray for happiness for those you have left, in your home and in your lands. May I see your son in your place, in wealth and responsibility. Alasdair of Glengarry, you have caused me to shed tears today.

26 Mo Rùn Geal Òg

NicFhearghais (1750)

Bu tu 'm fear slinneanach, leathann,
Bu chaoile meadhan 's bu dealbhaich;
Cha bu tàillear gun eòlas
Dhèanadh còta math geàrr dhut,
No dhèanadh dhut triubhais
Gun bhith cumhang no gann dut:
Mar gheala-bhradain do chosan
Le d' gheàrr-osan mu d' chalpa,
Mo rùn geal òg.

Bu tu pòitear na dibhe
'N àm suidhe 's taigh-òsda:
Ge b' e dh'òladh, 's tu phàigheadh,
Ged thuiteadh càch mu na bòrdaibh;
Bhith air mhisg, chan e b' fhiù leat –
Cha do dh'ionnsaich thu òg e –
'S cha d' iarr thu riamh cùis
Le tè air cùl do mhnà-pòsda:
Mo rùn geal òg.

'S ioma baintighearna phriseil,
Len sìoda 's len sròlaibh,
Dan robh mis' am chùis-fharmaid
Chionn gun tairgeadh tu pòg dhomh;
Ged a bhithinn cho sealbhach
'S gum bu leam airgead Hanòbhair,
Bheirinn cnag anns na h-àithntean
Nan cumadh càch sinn bho phòsadh:
Mo rùn geal òg.

'S iomadh bean a tha brònach
Eadar Tròndairnis 's Slèite,
Agus tè tha na bantraich,
Nach d' fhuair samhla dam chèile;
Bha mise làn sòlais
Fhad 's bu bheò sinn le chèile,
Ach a-nis bhon a dh'fhalbh thu,
Cha chùis-fharmaid mi fèin daibh:
Mo rùn geal òg.

My Fair Young Love

Thick-set and broad-shouldered,
slim-waisted and shapely;
no ignorant tailor
could make you a short-coat,
or make for you trews
that fitted exactly:
legs with sheen of bright salmon
and short-hose round the calves,
my fair young love.

A drinker of liquor
in the inn when they sat there,
whoever drank, 'twas you settled
though they flopped by the tables;
you had no wish to be drunken,
when young did not learn that,
never had an affair
behind your wedded wife's back,
my fair young love.

Many ladies of note,
in their silk and their satin,
have looked at me in some envy
for the kisses you gave me.
Though I were endowed
with the wealth of Hanover
I'd defy the Commandments
had they kept us from marrying,
my fair young love

Many women are sorrowing
From Trotternish to Sleat,
there's many a widow
who had never one like you.
I was buoyed up by gladness
while our lives were together,
but now since you have gone
I am no cause of envy,
my fair young love.

29 Cead Deireannach nam Beann

Donnchadh Bàn Mac an t-Saoir (1724–1812)

Fhuair mi greis ann àrach
Air àirighnean a b' aithne dhomh,
Ri cluiche 's mire 's mànran
'S bhith 'n coibhneas blàth nan caileagan;
Bu chùis an aghaidh nàdair
Gum maireadh sin an dràst' ann,
'S e b' èiginn bhith gam fàgail
Nuair thàinig tràth dhuinn dealachadh.

Bha mi 'n-dè san aonach
'S bha smaointean mòr air m' aire-sa:
Nach robh 'n luchd-gaoil a b' àbhaist
Bhith siubhal fàsaich mar rium ann;
'S a' bheinn as beag a shaoil mi
Gun dèanadh ise caochladh,
On tha i nis fo chaoraibh,
'S ann thug an saoghal car asam.

Nuair sheall mi air gach taobh dhìom

Chan fhaodainn gun bhith smalanach,
On theirig coill is fraoch ann,
'S na daoine bh' ann, cha mhaireann iad;
Chan eil fiadh ra shealg ann,
Chan eil eun no earb ann,
Am beagan nach eil marbh dhiubh,
'S e rinn iad falbh gu baileach às.

Mo shoraidh leis na frìthean,
O 's mìorbhailteach na beannan iad,
Le biolair uaine 's fìor-uisg',
Deoch uasal rìomhach cheanalta;
Na blàran a tha prìseil,
'S na fàsaichean tha lìonmhor,
O 's àit a leig mi dhìom iad,
Gu bràth mo mhìle beannachd leò.

Final Farewell to the Bens

I earned my living for a time
at shielings that I knew full well,
with frolic, fun, flirtation,
enjoying maidens' tender fellowship;
'twere contrary to nature
that this should still obtain there;
we had perforce to leave them,
when the time arrived to separate.

Yesterday I was on the moor,
and grave reflections haunted me:
that absent were the well-loved friends
who used to roam the waste with me;
since the mountain, which I little thought
would suffer transformation,
has now become a sheep-run,
the world, indeed, has cheated me.
As I gazed on every side of me
I could not but be sorrowful,
for wood and heather have run out,
nor live the men who flourished there;
there's not a deer to hunt there,
there's not a bird or roe there,
and the few that have not died out
have departed from it utterly.

Farewell to the deer forests –
O! they are wondrous hill-country,
with green cress and spring water,
a noble, royal, pleasant drink;
to the moor plains which are well beloved,
and the pastures which are plentiful,
as these are parts of which I've taken leave,
my thousand blessings aye be theirs.

30 The Blackthorn Bush

Gan Ainm (c.1800)

This extract from a macaronic version of this song reflects how some communities responded to the massive shift from Irish to English in 19th-century Ireland. The English verses here are folk adaptations of the original Irish song, blending translation, phrases in Irish and elements of the style and content of the Anglo-Irish ballad tradition. Some folk translations of this kind have survived in areas where the language has died. (This version was recorded by Ewan Mac Coll and Peggy Seeger in 1964 from the singing of Joe Heaney.)

I got a 'féirín' on a fair-day from a handsome young man;
and a hundred sweet kisses from my own darling John;
I'll go roving all day till the evening comes on,
I'll be shaded by the blossoms early of the Droighneán Donn.

Síleann céad ban gur leo féin mé nuair a ólaim leann;
téann dhá dtrian síos díom nuair a smaoiním ar a gcómhrá liom.
Sneachta séidte a bheith dhá shíorchur ó Shliabh Uí Fhloinn
'S go bhfuil mo ghrá mar bhlath na n-airní ag gabháil an droighneán donn.

Dhá mbeinn i mo bhádóir nach deas a shnámhfainn an fharraige anonn;
Dhá mbeinn im' fhaoileán is deas a d'éireoinn ar bharr na dtonn
Bheinn ag éalú le mo chéadsearc 's ag fáisceadh a coim
Ach an lá nach bhféadfainn bean a bhréagadh níl báire liom.

I wish I had a small boat on the ocean to roam,
I would follow my true love where e'er he would go;
I would rather have my true love to roll, sport and play
than all the gold and silver by land or by sea.

31 An Bonnán Buí

Cathal Buí Mac Giolla Ghunna (1680-1756)

bhíodh sé choíche ag síoról na dí,
agus deir na daoine go mbím mar sin seal,
is níl deor dá bhfaighead nach ligfead síos
ar eagla go bhfaighinnse bás den tart.

Dúirt mo stór liom ligean den ól
nó nach mbeinnse beo ach seal beag gearr,
ach dúirt mé léi go dtug sí bréag
is gurbh fhaide mo shaolsa an deoch úd a fháil;
nach bhfaca sibh éan an phíobáin réidh
a chuaigh a dh'éag den tart ar ball? –
a chomharsain chléibh, fliuchaidh bhur mbéal,
óir chan fhaigheann sibh braon i ndiaidh bhur mbáis.

The Yellow Bittern

When he crosses the stream there and wings o'er the sea,
Then a fear comes to me he may fail in his flight –
Well, the milk and the ale are drunk every drop,
And a dram won't stop our thirst this night.

32 Bothan Airigh am Bràigh Raithneach

Gun Urrainn (c.1800)

Mo chriosan 's mo chìre
Is mo stìomag chaol-cheangail,
Mo làmhainne bòidheach
'S dèis òir air am barraibh,

Mo sporan donn iallach,
Mar ri sgian nan cas ainneamh.

Thig mo chrios à Dùn Eideann
Is mo bhrèid à Dùn Chailleann.

Cuime 'm biomaid gun eudail
Agus sprèidh aig na Gallaibh?

Gheibh sinn crodh às a' Mhaorainn
Agus caoraich à Gallaibh.

'S ann a bhios sinn gan àrach
Air àirigh 'm Bràigh Raithneach,

Ann am bothan an t-sùgraidh,
'S gur e bu dùnadh dha barrach.

Bhiodh a' chuthag 's an smùdan
A' gabhail ciùil duinn air chrannaibh;

Bhiodh an damh donn sa bhùireadh
Gar dùsgadh sa mhadainn.

A Shieling in Brae Rannoch

My girdle and my comb
And my finely-knotted headband,

My beautiful gloves
With golden tips on the ends of the fingers,

My brown laced purse
And a knife with a rarely wrought handle.

My belt will come from Edinburgh
And my kerchief from Dunkeld.
Why would we be without treasure
While the Lowlanders have livestock?

We will get cattle from the Mearns
And sheep from Caithness.

And we will rear them
On a shieling in Brae Rannoch,

In the bothy of pleasure,
Closed only with brushwood.

The cuckoo and the ringdove would
Make music for us in the trees;

And the brown stag with its roaring
Would waken us in the morning.

35 Is Trom Leam an Airigh

Rob Donn MacAoidh (1714-1778)

Ach labhair i gu fàiteagach, àilgheasach rium:
'Chan fhàir thu bhith làimh rium do chàradh mo chinn;
Tha sianar gam iarraidh o bhliadhna de thìm,
'S cha b' àraidh le càch thu thoirt bàrr os an cinn.
Ha, ha, hà! An d' fhàs thu gu tinn?
'N e 'n gaol a bheir bàs ort? Gum pàigh thu da chinn!'

Ach cionnas bheir mi fuath dhut, ged dh'fhuaraich thu rium?
Nuair as feargaich' mo sheanchas mu t' ainm air do chùl,
Thig t' ìomhaigh le h-annsachd na samhla nam ùidh:
Saoilidh mi 'n sin gun dèan an gaol sin an tùrn,
'S thèid air a ràth, gun dh'fhàs e às ùr,
Is fàsaidh e 'n tràth sin cho àrda ri tùr.

The Sheiling is a Sad Place for Me

But she spoke very disdainfully, superciliously to me
'You don't deserve to be beside me, stroking my head.
Six men have been seeking me since the year of your
  courtship
And the others would hardly expect you to surpass them.
Ha! Ha! Ha! Are you deranged?
If it's love that will cause your death, you are going to pay
  for it.'

But how can I hate you, even though you have grown so
  cold to me?
Whenever I disparage your name behind your back
Your image floats with its fascination as an embodiment of
  my dreams,
So that I will conceive love to be that which will never alter,
And this is proved as it wells up again
And it grows then as high as a tower.

37 Suantraí dá Mhac Tabhartha

Eoghan Rua Ó Súilleabháin (1748-784)

Do gheobhair sleá Achaill ba chalma i ngleo,
Is craoiseach Fhinn gan mhoill id' dhóid,
Éide Chonaill dob ursa le treoin,
Is sciath gheal Naois ó Chraobh na sló.
  Seóthó srl

Do gheobhair long le stiúr fá sheol,
Is corn glan cumtha, cúinneach óir,
Cruit Orphéus fá théadaibh ceoil,
Do spreagfadh na béithe id' dhéidh gan smól.
  Seóthó srl

Do gheobhaidh tú rí-bhean chaoin-tais mhodhúil
'Na mbeidh lasadh 'na gnaoi tré lí mar rós,
A samhail de mhnaoi thug mac Priam 's a shló
Ar faiche na Traoi chuir mílte ar feo.
  Seóthó, srl

Dob fhearra dhuit cácaí fáiscfi as beoir,
Nó dá n-abrainn árthaí lán d'fhíon leo,
Banaltra bhláth bhinn bháin-chíoch óg
Ná duanaireacht ghliogair ó fhile dem' shórt.
  Seóthó srl
Do gheobhaidh saill uaim, fíon is beoir
'S éadach greanta ba mhaise do threoin;
Ach ó chím do bhuime chúm sa ród
Ní gheallfad uaim duit duais níos mó.
  Seóthó, srl

Lullaby to his Illegitimate Son

The javelin of mighty Achilles you'll have
And Finn's own spear will be put in your hand,
The armour of Conall, pillar of the brave,
And the bright shield of Naoise of the Red Branch.
  Hush, my love, etc.

You will have a ship under sail to steer,
And a bright-gold, shapely, four-sided drinking horn,

The harp of Orpheus, strung for playing
To make beautiful women fall in love with you.
Hush, my love, etc.

You shall have a gentle modest queen
Whose pale cheek will glow like a rose from within,
Such a woman as was brought by the son of Priam
To the field of Troy where thousands were slain.
Hush, my love, etc.

Better by far for you cakes squeezed from beer,
Accompanied by vessels filled with wine,
And a delicate, sweet-voiced, white-breasted nurse
Than the gabbling rhyme of a poet like me.
Hush, my love, etc.

You will have bacon, wine and beer
And elegant clothes that would honour a hero;
But I see your mother coming the road
And now I will promise no more rewards.
Hush, my love, etc.

38 Cúirt an Mheán Oíche (sliocht)

Brian Merriman (1745-1805)

An bhfuil stuaire beo ná feofadh liath
Ag cuail dá shórt bheith pósta riamh,
Nár chuardaigh fós fá dhó le bliain
Cé buachaill óg í, feoil, nó iasc?
'S an feoiteach fuar so suas léi sínte
Dreoite duairc, gan bhua gan bhíogadh.
Ó! Cár mhuar di bualadh bríomhar
Ar nós an diabhail dhá uair gach oíche!
Ní dóch go dtuigir gurb ise ba chiontach,
Ná fós go gclisfeadh ar laige le tamhandacht
An maighre mascalach carthanach ciúintais
– Is deimhin go bhfaca sí a mhalairt de mhúineadh!
Ní labharfadh focal dá mb'obair an oíche
Is thabharfadh cothrom do stollaire bríomhar,
Go brách ar siúl nár dhiúltaigh riamh é
Ar chnámh a cúil 's a súile iata.
Ní thabharfadh preab le stailc mhíchuíosach,
Fogha mar chat ná sraic ná scríob air,
Acht í go léir 'na slaod comh-sínte,
Taobh ar thaobh 's a géag 'na thimpeall,
Ó scéal go scéal ag bréagadh a smaointe,
Béal ar bhéal 's ag méaraíocht síos air.
Is minic do chuir sí a cos taobh 'nonn de
Is chuimil a brush ó chrios go glún de,
Sciobadh an phluid 's an chuilt dá ghúnga
Ag spriongar 's ag sult le moirt gan súchas.
Níor chabhair dhi cigilt ná cuimilt ná fáscadh,
Fogha dá huillinn, dá hingin ná a sála;
Is nár dom aithris mar chaitheadh sí an oíche
Ag fáscadh an chnaiste 's ag searradh 's ag síneadh,
Ag feacadh na ngéag 's an t-éadach fúithi,
A ballaibh go léir 's a déid ar lúthchrith,
Go loinnir an lae gan néall do dhubhadh uirthi
Ag imirt ó thaobh go taobh 's ag ionfairt.

The Midnight Court (excerpt)

'Is there living a girl who could grow fat
Tied to a travelling corpse like that
Who twice a year wouldn't find a wish
To see what was she, flesh or fish,
But dragged the clothes about his head
Like a wintry wind to a woman in bed?

'Now was it too much to expect as right
A little attention once a night?'
From all I know she was never accounted
A woman too modest to be mounted.
Gentle, good-humoured and Godfearing,
Why should we think she'd deny her rearing?
Whatever the lengths his fancy ran,
She wouldn't take fright from a mettlesome man.

It wasn't her fault if things went wrong,
She closed her eyes and held her tongue;
She was no ignorant girl from school
To whine for her mother and play the fool
But a competent bedmate smooth and warm
Who cushioned him like a sheaf of corn;
Line by line she bade him linger
With gummy lips and a groping finger,
Gripping his thighs in a wild embrace,
Rubbing her brush from knee to waist,
Stripping him bare to the cold night air,
Everything done with love and care.
But she'd nothing to show for all her labour;
There wasn't a jump in the old deceiver,
And all I could say would give no notion
Of that poor distracted girl's emotion,
Her knees cocked up and the bedposts shaking,
Chattering teeth and sinews aching,
While she sobbed and tossed through a joyless night
And gave it up with the morning light.'

Note: The poet sets out alone on a summer morning and encounters a fearsome vision of a woman. She drags him through the mud to Monmoy Hill where a court is sitting, presided over by Aoibheal, a beautiful fairy queen.

A young woman there tells the court of her troubles: that she is without a mate because of the refusal of the young men of the country to marry.

Up jumps an old man to answer the young woman. He blames the dissolute life of young women for the predicament in which they find themselves. He recounts the circumstances of his own marriage, at the time of which, and unknown to him, his bride was pregnant by another. (In spite of this cuckoldry, he later praises bastards highly as part of his plea to Aoibheal to end the institution of marriage.)

The young woman again takes the stand mocking the old man's inability to satisfy his young wife. She advocates forcing young men to marry, with the clergy not being exempt from that edict.

Aoibheal issues her judgement on the issues brought before the court. She foretells that priests soon will be allowed to marry and she gives permission for the persecution of recalcitrant bachelors. The poet finds to his horror that he is the first to face the music.

42 Nuair Bha Mi Òg

Màiri Mhòr nan Òran (1821-1898)

Bhiodh òigridh ghreannmhor ri ceòl is dannsa,
Ach dh'fhalbh an t-àm sin 's tha 'n gleann fo bhròn;
Bha 'n tobht' aig Anndra 's e làn de dh'fheanntaig
Toirt na mo chuimhne nuair bha mi òg.

An uair a dhìrich mu gual 'an t-Sìthein,
Gun d'leig mi sgìths dhiom air bruaich an lòin;

Bha buadhan m' inntinn a' triall le sìnteig
   Is sùil mo chinn faicinn loinn gach pòir;
Bha 'n t-sòbhrach mhìn-bhuidh' 's am beàrnan-brìghde,
   An cluaran rìoghail is lus an òir,
'S gach bileag aoibhneach fo bhraon na h-oidhche,
   Toirt na mo chuimhne nuair bha mi òg.

Nuair chuir mi cùl ris an eilean chùbhraidh
'S a ghabh mi iùbhrach na smùid gun seòl,
Nuair shèid i 'n dùdach 's a shìn an ùspairt,
'S a thog i cùrsa o Thìr a' Cheò,
Mo chridhe brùite 's na deòir lem shùilean
A' falbh gu dùthaich gun sùrd, gun cheòl,
Far nach faic mi cluaran no neòinean guanach
No fraoch no luachair air bruaich no lòn.

Nuair chuir mi cuairt air gach gleann is cruachan,
   Far 'n robh mi suaimhneach a' cuallach bhò,
Le òigridh ghuanach tha nis air fuadach,
   De shliochd na tuath bha gun uaill, gun ghò –
Na raoin 's na cluaintean fo fhraoch is luachair,
   Far 'n tric na bhuaineadh leam sguab is dlò,
'S nam faicinn sluagh agus taighean suas annt',
   Gum fàsainn suaimhneach mar bha mi òg.

When I Was Young

And sunny youth fell to songs and dancing,
those days are gone now and sad the glen;
while Andrew's house with its rugs of nettles
brought back to mind days when I was young.

The time I climbed up the Sithean's shoulder,
I took my ease on the small stream's bank:
my thoughts went leaping in a blaze of wonder,
my eye could see every grain's true worth;
Each yellow primrose and dandelion
the royal thistle and the golden bloom,
each joyous leaf under dew at evening
brought back to mind days when I was young.

When I left behind me that fragrant island,
and took the smoke-tailed sail-less ship,
when she blew her horn and surged in uproar
and set her course from the Land of Mist;
my heart was crushed and the tears were flowing,
going to a place lacking joy or song,
where I'll see no thistle or giddy daisy,
no heath or rushes on bank or lawn.

When I paid a visit to each glen and hill-top,
where I'd herded cattle with tranquil mind,
with carefree youngsters who're now in exile,
a sturdy breed without pride or guile.
Each field and pasture's now heath and rushes,
where my sickle swept and I gathered sheaves;
could I see people and houses built there,
the peace would come back I knew when young.

46 Máire Ní Eidhin
Antoin Ó Raifteirí (1779-1835)

Shiúil mé Sasana is an Fhrainc le chéile,
An Spáinn, an Ghréig is ar ais arís,
Ó bhruach Loch Gréine go Béal na Céibhe
Is ní fhaca mé féirín ar bith mar í.
Dá mbeinnse pósta le bláth na hóige
Trí Loch an Tóraic a leanfainn í,
Cuanta 's cóstaí go siúlfainn is bóithre
I ndiaidh na seoidmhná atá i mBaile Uí Laí.

Sí Máire Ní Eidhin an stáidbhean bhéasach
Ba deise méin agus b'áille gnaoi,
Dhá chéad cléireach is a gcur le chéile
Agus trian dá tréithe ní fhéadfadh scríobh;

Bhuail sí Déirdre le breáthacht is Vénus,
Is dá n-abrainn Hélen le'r scriosadh an Traoi –
Ach scoth ban Éireann as ucht an méid sin
An pabhsae gléigeal atá i mBaile Uí Laí.

A réaltann an tsolais is a ghrian an fhómhair,
A chúileann ómra is a chuid den tsaol,
An ngluaisfeá liomsa faoi chomhair an Domhnaigh
Nó go ndéanfaimid comhairle cá mbeidh ár suí?
Níor mhór liom ceol duit gach oíche Dhomhnaigh,
Puins ar bord is, dá n-ólfá, fíon:
Is a Rí na Glóire, go dtriomaí an bóthar
Go bhfaighe mé an t-eolas go Baile Uí Laí.

The Lass from Bally-na-Lee

I've walked in my time
   Across England and France,
From Spain to Greece
   And back by sea;
Met many a maid
   At many a dance,
But none had an airy
   Grace like she.
If I had the power
   And the flower of youth,
I'd find her out
   Wherever she'd be,
I'd comb all the coasts
   From Cork to Beirut,
To live with this gem
   From Bally-na-Lee.

Mary Egan
   Is a bred lass,
With the looks and grace
   Of the queen of a tribe;
Looks, two hundred scholars
   En masse,
Or the pick of the poets
   Could never describe.

Venus and Deirdre
   Were no more grand,
Nor Helen, who launched
   The ships in the sea,
She's the brightest blossom
   Of all Ireland,
This fabulous flower
   From Bally-na-Lee

My star of light,
  My autumn sun,
My curly head,
  My summer sky,
In Sunday's shadow
  Let's rise and run
And arrange the place
  Where we shall lie.
All I ask is to sing
  To you each Sunday night,
With drink on the table
  And you on my knee –
Dear God high in Heaven,
  Who gives and takes sight,
Allow me this pleasure
  In Bally-na-Lee

49 Bean Dubh a' Caoidh a Fìr a Chaidh a Mharbhadh leis a' Phoileas

Donnchadh MacDhunLèibhe (1877-1964)

Air m' fhear-cèile 'n sin na shìneadh,
Nuair a thig mo mhic gu ìre,
  Baba Inkòsi Sikelele, Baba Inkòsi Sikelele.

An èirig dhuinn airson ar dòrainn,
Latha rèidh a ghearradh sgòrnan;
  Baba Inkòsi Sikelele, Baba Inkòsi Sikelele.

Ghearradh sgòrnan nam fear fuileach,
Fuil mum dhòrnaibh suas gu uilinn,
  Baba Inkòsi Sikelele, Baba Inkòsi Sikelele.

A bhith gan reubadh is gam pianadh
Is deagh fhaobhar air mo sgian-sa.
  Baba Inkòsi Sikelele, Baba Inkòsi Sikelele.

Thoir latha dhuinn gu saor a' pàigheadh
Fhir is mhnathan agus phàistean
  Baba Inkòsi Sikelele, Baba Inkòsi Sikelele.

An luchd ghil a bhuail ar daoine;
Cuairt mun amhaichean den caolain.
  Baba Inkòsi Sikelele, Baba Inkòsi Sikelele.

Cuairt den caolain 'n àite chneapan,
Is siridh mi 'n sin taobh do leapach,
  Baba Inkòsi Sikelele, Baba Inkòsi Sikelele.

Na fiachan uile air an dìoladh,
Fhir 's a ghràidh, 's tu 'n sin ad shìneadh.
  Baba Inkòsi Sikelele, Baba Inkòsi Sikelele.

A Black Woman Mourns her Husband Killed by the Police

For my husband lying before me,
When my sons have come of age,
  Baba Inkòsi Sikelele, Baba Inkòsi Sikelele.

In compensation for our grief,
Some perfect day for cutting throats,
  Baba Inkòsi Sikelele, Baba Inkòsi Sikelele.

For cutting throats of bloody men,
Blood on my fists up to the elbow,
  Baba Inkòsi Sikelele, Baba Inkòsi Sikelele.

For tearing them and torturing them
With a good blade upon my knife:
  Baba Inkòsi Sikelele, Baba Inkòsi Sikelele.

Give us a day to pay back freely
The men, the women and the children
  Baba Inkòsi Sikelele, Baba Inkòsi Sikelele.

Of the white folk who struck our people
With a turn of their guts around their necks –
  Baba Inkòsi Sikelele, Baba Inkòsi Sikelele.

A turn of their guts instead of beads,
And then I'll seek the side of your bed,
  Baba Inkòsi Sikelele, Baba Inkòsi Sikelele.
All the debts having been paid,
Beloved husband, who's lying before me.
  Baba Inkòsi Sikelele, Baba Inkòsi Sikelele.

52 Circeabost: An Ceann a Deas 2000

Domhnall MacAmhlaigh (b. 1930)

'S a-null air gàrradh na Buaile Ruaidhe,
suas ris a' ghàrradh-cùil chun na cachleith;
's an crodh a' tional le ruathar
ag èigheach duan an eadraidh,
a' dian-putadh a chèile gu crò;
's eadar thu 's leus an fheasgair
an anail ag èirigh na neul . . .
's a' sìolthadh na sgleò . . .

An-diugh a' cromadh à mullach Thotarail,
talamh eòlais fo mo chasan,
bloighean de dh'iomairt na h-oidhche
tighinn gu m' inntinn,
chì mi iathadh a' bhaile:
Leathad na Calltanaich 's an Leas Iosal,
an Creaga Ruadh is Sàil a' Chreagan,
sìos an Leathad Mòr gu làrach na h-Eaglais
a thog sean-seanair mo sheanar,
's a-nall chun na Ceàrdaich
far na shaothraich a shean-seanair eile
an dà dhùn luathadh tha am follais
fhathast an dèidh dà cheud bliadhna –
a' filleadh an ama dh'fhalbh am broinn mo bheatha.

'S ag èisdeachd ri agallamh mo dhaoine
's a ghlòir na mo chluais 's na mo chridhe,
cha bu dligheach dhomh àicheadh
gu bheil mo dhàimh ris an dùthaich s'
(a dheilbh dhomh m' fheist is mo shaorsa)
cho dlùth ris a' bhàrnaich air a' charragh,
ris a' bhuidhean air na clachan;
mo fhreumh an sàs cho righinn
na h-ùir ris an lus con-chulainn,
ri bun a' charra-meille;
cho glèidhte na liosan cearbach

ri lus na fraing is ris an ailleann;
('s a dh'aindeoin aomadh is tearbadh)
cho gnàthach na còmhdach
ris a' chearban, 's ris an t-seòbhraich …

Kirkibost: The South End 2000

And over the wall of the Red Fold
and up along the boundary to the entrance,
with the cattle gathering in a rush,
roaring their milking-time song,
nudging each other hard to the fold;
and against the evening light their breath
rising in a cloud … dispersing in a veil …

Today descending from Totaral summit,
familiar ground beneath my feet,
snatches of the night's adventure
coming to my mind,
I can see the layout of the village:
Hazelwood Brae and the Lower Enclosure,
the Red Homestead and the Heel of the Hillock,
down the Great Slope to the site of the Church
built by my grandfather's great-grandfather,
and along the path to the Smithy
where his other great-grandfather toiled,
piling the twin heaps of ash visible
still after two hundred years,
enfolding the time past into my life.

And listening to my people's colloquy,
its eloquence sounding in my ears and my heart,
it would be unthinkable to deny
that my attachment to this land
(that devised my tether and my freedom)
is as fast as the limpet on the rock,
as the lichen on its stones;
my roots are set as unyieldingly
in its soil as the roots of the meadow-sweet,
as the wild liquorice tubers;
are as protected in its gapped enclosures
as the tansy and the elecampane;
(in-spite of compromise and separation)
as native to its ground cover
as the buttercup and the primrose.

54 An Tuagh

Fearghas MacFhionnlaigh (b. 1948)

thàinig e oirbh
is sibh nur dìollaid
mar iolair air creig
mar leòmhainn na chrùban

thàinig e oirbh
le lanns is sgiath is clogaid is dos
is each is armachd is tàirneanach is fallas
is sitheadh is duslach is ràiteachas is bàs

thàinig e oirbh

ach a chlisge
le gluasad luath
le gradghluasad cruinn
le deasghluasad pongail
le snasghluasad brìoghmhor
san robh an sàs ar n-eachdraidh gu lèir

bhoillsg stàilinn
ur tuaigh sa ghrèin
is thuit briosgbhuille
a' sgoltadh clogaid
is claiginn

a' deargadh
Goliat earraidich
air raon uaine

ach bhriseadh ur làmhag, a Rìgh
is tha t'èile fhathast a dhìth oirnn

The Axe

he came at you
poised in your saddle
like an eagle on a crag
like a crouching lion

he came at you
with lance and shield and helmet and plume
and horse and armour and thunder and sweat
and impetus and dust and invective and death

he came at you

but instantly
with an agile movement
with a neat sudden movement
with a precisely executed movement
with an elegant energetic movement
on which our entire history hinged

the steel of your axe
blazed in the sun
and like a blur the blow fell
splitting helmet
and skull

displaying
an errant Goliath
red on green field

but your axe was broken, O King
And another we have yet to find

55 na thàinig anns a' churach ud

Aonghas Dubh MacNeacail (b. 1942)

chaidh cumhachd fios
air feadh na tìr

sgaoil duilleach fios
air feadh gach tìr

's ged a chaillte
bàrr nan leus,
anns a' cheathach liath
a dh'fhàg lasair dhubh
nan ìmpireachd,
bha luchd a' phòir
na shruth fo ghrunnd

chùm snàithleanan
de shileadh fann
siùbhlachd a' ghuth
tro uaimh a' chràidh,
sheinn an guth nach trèig
grian nan altramas
do bhlàth nan leus

an do chunntais thu,
a cholmain dàin,
na do long sheang sheice,
na làithean loma
a thigeadh oirnn
bhon a sheòl thu
thar na maoile,
le do leabhar mòr grèise
suaint nad chànan,
sgiath do-shàthte
an aghaidh lom-sgrìob

's ged a dh'fhalbh an cìobair,
ged a dh'fhalbh an treabhaiche,
dh'fhuirich an tobhta, na cochall
a' feitheamh an t-sìl

agus seall, ann an seo, eadar
coille beithe 's cuan a' bhradain,
a' chlach 's a' ghlainne
'g èirigh mar na blàthan ùra,
solas òrach na h-ath-bhliadhna,
dùn an dòchais, dùn a' gheallaidh

all that came in that one coracle

the power of knowledge
went through the land

the leaves of knowledge
through every land

and though the light
had lost its peak,
in the grey mist trail
of the black black flame
of empire states,
the seed's cargo
flowed underground

the smallest threads
of flowing veins
kept the fluid voice
through a cave of pain,
the unquenchable voice
sang a nursing sun
for the bloom of light

and did you count,
bold dove,
in your slender ship of skin,
the leanest days
that fell on us
since you sailed out
across the moil, with
your great embroidered book
wrapped in your language,
impenetrable shield
against devastation

and though the shepherd went,
though the ploughman left,
this ruin remained, like a husk
awaiting its seed

and see, over here, between
birch wood and salmon sea,
all the glass and stone
rising like new blossoms,
the golden light of next year,
fort of hopes, fort of promise

56 Dè a Thug Ort Sgrìobhadh sa Ghàidhlig?

Uilleam Nèill (b.1922)

Chan abrainn gu robh daoin' agam
cho uasal ris na Cinneidich,
ach luchd na speala an Cùl Shian:
Moireasdan, Ceallach, Nèill is Odhar
a' glaodh gu h-àrd nam chuislean-sa.
B' e *hungert helant ghaists* a bh' annta
mus robh Albais nar measg-ne,
Gàidhlig aig gach fear is tè dhiubh –
is mairg gun do dh'fhairtlich sin
air Raibeart san aon dùthaich seo.

O, horò, nach mi tha bàidheil
bhith nam fhuigheal de na Gàidheil dheasach;
Gàidhlig bhlasta Bhaltair Chinneide
eadar Reachrainn agus Manainn,
eadar Dail Ruigh is Cinn Tìre,
is Creag Ealasaid mar usgar
chnapa 'n targaid dùthaich Ualraig,
Bhruis is Aonghais is nan Dùghallach,
dùthaich Bhluchbhard agus Chian,
Rabbie is *the Hielant Captain.*
Is ma bhios feadhainn a' gearan
gun do sgrìobh mi cus sa Ghàidhlig,
b' e Cinneide a nochd an ròd dhomh
le sic eloquence, mo thruaighe,
as they in Erschry use, mo thogair –
is set my thraward appetyte.

Ro fhadalach a-nis bhith toinneamh
teanga bhorb gu blas-chainnt Lunnainn,
but blabberand wi my Carrick lippis
Erchse and brybour I maun bide,
sawsy in saffron back and syde.

What Compelled You to Write in Gaelic?

I would not say I came from people
as lordly as the Kennedies,
but from farmhands in Culzean:
Morrison, Kellie, Neill and Orr
crying aloud in my veins –
'hungry highland ghosts' they were,
before braid Scots came in among us
every man and woman had Gaelic:
a pity that it was denied
to Robert there in that same country.

O horo am I not joyful
to be a relic of the southern Gaels
warm Gaelic of Walter Kennedy
between Rathlinn and the Isle of Man,
between (St John's town of) Dalry and Kintyre
and Ailsa Craig like the jewel
on the boss of the shield of the land of Kennedy
of Bruce, of Angus (of Islay) and the MacDowalls,
the land of Bluchbard and Cian
Rabbie and the Highland Captain
and if some should complain
that I write too much in Gaelic,
it was Kennedy showed me the way;
with *sic eloquence*, alas,
as they in Erschry use, my pleasure,
is set my thraward appetyte.

Too late now to be twisting
a rough tongue to London's accent,
but blabbering with my Carrick lips,
Gaelic and villain I must bide,
saucy in saffron, back and side.

57 An Turas

Ruaraidh MacThòmais (b. 1921)

Fuil a' chruinn, fuil a' chruinn,
fuil a sgamhain air a' chrann,
dubh, dubh tha fuil a sgamhain,
dubh a' mhadainn air a' bheinn.
Dearg, dearg, dearg, dearg,
dearg air mo chridhe clis,
Thusa rinn fìon dhen an uisge,
dean uisge den fhìon a-nis.

A' chnuimh a tha ag ithe na feòla
a' bòcadh, 's a' chnuimh
a tha a sàs ann an cridhe an ubhail,
an cridhe tha spioladh nan cnàmh,
a' chnuimh aig bun na craoibh'
anns an t-seann ghàrradh.

Snagardaich gun sgur 'na mo cheann
ged tha deich bliadhn' ann bho dh'fhàg mi 'n gàrradh.
Ma shreapas mi gu mullach a' chran sin,
air a' ghèig as àirde
ruigidh mi air an ubhal,
's nuair a thuiteas mi
falbhaidh an snagardaich seo;
bheir Dia asam e leis an aon ghlamhadh.

'Cha bhi mi, ghràidh, a' buntainn dha,
cha bhi mi gabhail deur dheth.'

Nuair bhios mi leam fhìn
bidh mi gabhail drama;
cha bhi duine chì
mar lìonas mi 'ghlainne.
Nuair bhios mi leam fhìn
bidh mi gabhail drama.

Nuair thuirt thu a chaoidh, a chaoidh,
is beag a bha dh'fhios againn far a robh 'n fhoill,
is beag a bha 'bhrath againn far a robh 'n fhadal,
an gaol fon a' chadal 's an gràdh fon a' choill.

Nuair thuirt mi gu bràth,
cha b' e a' bhinn sin idir a bha 'nam inntinn,
cha do shaoil mi gur h-e 'n dàn seo a bha san dàn.

Nuair a thuirt sinn gu sìorraidh,
cha do dh'fhidir sinn an eaglais againn a' tuiteam 'na broinn
's gun Dia innt'.

A' tilleadh a dh'Eilean Leòdhais,
mo chridhe làn leis an toileachas,
smaoinich mi air a' chiad shealladh sin
de na h-Eileanan Mòra,
a' Phàirc 's a' Chàbag a' nochdadh,
is beul Loch Ratharnais,
An Rubha 's a' Ghearra Chruaidh,
ach chaill mi iad anns a' bhàr,
bha mi cho làn toileachais.

An t-seachdain ud aig an taigh
cha do dh'fhuaraich mi,
mi dha mo dhalladh bho mhoch gu dubh –
chan fhaca mi Beanntan Bharbhais an turas seo –
bha mi cho toilichte ri cù air a shitig fhèin.

Agus an là dh'fhalbh mi
bha mi leis a' chiaralas;
ghabh mi tè mhòr as a *Royal*,
's ma fhuair mi air bòrd, chaidil mi;
cha robh fhios 'am dè chanainn
nuair a chunna mi cidhe Ullapol.

A! Thighearna,
cuin a chì mi thu rithist, a Shliabh Shioin?

Mus do dh'fhàs an pàipear cruaidh seo air na meuran agam
leughainn na sanasan beaga
air madainn earraich
agus air oirean a' chonaltraidh;
'se tha dhìth orm *braille* nas gairbhe.

Gun a bhith 'g iarraidh a' chòrr ach a' cur charan,
a' tilleadh chon an aon stans,
a' cur mo shròin air a' bhloigh sin dhe m' eachdraidh,
mar gum b' e cù a bh' annam
ag iarraidh gu a sgeith fhèin.

A' dùsgadh sa mhadainn

le cnuimh dhearg 'na mo sgòrnan
chuir mi dh'iarraidh an doctair -
bha a rud air a dhol seachad air mo sgoileireachd.

Thàinig e.
Bha aodach soiller air is brògan canbhais,
guth cruaidh sgairteil aige,
is fo achlais bha *Orain Iain Mhic Fhearchair.*

Is thuirt mi ris, cho socair 's b' urra mi:
'Nach doir thu chnuimh sin às a sgòrnan agam
mus dig at ann' –
thuigeadh fear-leughaidh leth-fhacal, bha mi 'n dùil.

Cha duirt e càil rium ach
'Chan ann anns a sgòrnan agad a tha 'chnuimh,'
agus thoisich e leughadh às a leabhar

(... Gur e 'n ceann as treas cas dhaibh,
Lom-làn mheall agus chnapa,
Gach aon bhall dam bi aca
Goid an neart uath' gun fhios ...).

'Coma leat dhan a sin,' thuirt mi,
''Sann 'na mo sgòrnan a tha i,
agus tha fios agam co às a thàinig i,
às an ubhal a bha gu h-ard a staidhre ... ,'
ach leis an fhìrinn innse cha robh cuimhn' 'am
'n e staidhre ann a Fairfields,
no ann an Ibrox, no ann a Singapore.
Aon rud bha mi cinnteach às,
cha b' ann à Leodhas a bha i,
oir cha robh staidhr' againn.

A Dhia! dè math a bhith bruidhinn ri doctair,
bu cho math dhomh cur a dh'iarraidh an t-sagairt.

'S mura h-eil mi air mo mhealladh
thàinig an sagart cuideachd,
is thairg e dhomh an t-abhlan coisrigte;
Eireannach a bh' ann, cha robh Gàidhlig aige;
chuala mi e ag ràdh rudeigin mu *wafer*

's thuirt mi ris - Thighearna, 'n teas a bha sin! –
'Coma leat dheth, 'se ice-cream tha dhìth orm.'

Tha 'ghaoth ag eirigh;
nan togadh i às a seo mi
sheòlainn tarsainn air Cluaidh,
os cionn Leòdhais is Inis Tìle,
air sruthan na h-iarmailt:
bhithinn toilichte gu leor a-muigh a sin
a' cur charan air an talamh,
'sa' deanamh mothar riutha 'n dràst 's a-rithist
iad a ghleidheil na Sàbaid
's a bhith cuimhneachail orms' ann a sheo.

Na ròidean a' coiseachd chon na mara,
's na cnuic a' cur charan air na taighean,
beagan de cheò an t-samhraidh ann
's an fheamainn a' plubail anns an làn,
an Cruthaidhear san taigh-choinneimh a-nochd -
an creideamh slàn.

Co ris a tha E a' cumail coinneimh?

Mus do thòisich am feur ag at
aig na h-altan,
mus dàinig an niosgaid
air stoc na cuiseige,
mun do bhrùchd an aillse
air an langadar,
bha sinn le chèile san taigh-choinneimh,
's rinn sinn an t-altachadh aig a' bhòrd.
Càite bheil Bòrd an Tighearna an-diugh?

Mus do dh'eubhadh an t-sìth,
mus do rinneadh sginean is forcaichean às na claidheamhan,
mus do rinn iad bothan dhen destroyer,
mus dug iad an copan seo ri òl dhomh,
bha Thusa ann.

Ach a bheil Thu ann a-nis?

The Journey

Blood of the cross, blood of the cross,
blood from the lungs on the cross,
black, black is the lung's blood,
black the morning on the mount.
Stamp red, stamp red,
stamp on my fickle heart,
Thou who madest wine of water,
make water of wine now.

The grub that consumes the flesh
swells, as the grub
that attacks the heart of the apple,
the heart that picks at the bones,
the grub at the tree's base
in the old garden.

A continual tapping in my head
though it's ten years since I left the yard.
If I climb to the top of that crane,
on the highest branch
I shall reach the apple,
and when I fall
this tapping will stop;
God will pluck it out of me at a bite.

'My dear, I never touch it,
I never take a drop.'

When I'm on my own
I like to have a dram;
nobody can see
the glass is to the brim.
When I'm on my own
I like to have a dram.

When you said for ever more
we little knew where deceit lay,
we didn't think at all of the day
that love would sleep and bliss be a bore.

When I said till Doom,
that wasn't the judgement I had in mind,
I didn't think *that* fate was fated for us.

When we said for everlasting
we didn't notice that our church was falling in
and that God was past it.

Returning to Lewis,
my heart full with pleasure,
I thought of that first sight
of the Shiant Islands,
Park and Kebbock Head appearing,
and the mouth of Loch Ranish,
Point and the Castle Grounds,
but I missed them in the Bar,
I was so full of joy.

That week at home
there was no time to get sober,
I was plastered from dawn to dusk –
I never saw the Barvas Hills this time –
I was as happy as a dog on its own dump.

And the day I left,
what homesickness!
I took a burst in the Royal,
and if I got aboard I must have slept;
didn't know what to say
when Ullapool Pier came in sight.

Lord God,
when will I see you again, Mount Sion?

Before this rough paper grew on my fingers
I could read the tiny signals
on a Spring morning,
and on the margins of conversation;
I need a bolder braille.

Wishing only to keep going round in circles,
coming back to the same spot,
sniffing at that fragment of my history,
as though I were a dog
drawn to its own vomit.

Waking in the morning,
a red grub in my gullet,
I sent for the doctor –
the thing had got beyond me.

He came.
He wore light-coloured clothes and sandshoes,
had a loud harsh voice
and carried *The Songs of John MacCodrum* in his oxter.
And I said to him as quietly as I could:
'Would you take that grub out of my gullet
before inflammation starts' –
I thought a man of skill would understand.

All he said was
'The grub is not in your gullet,'
and he began to read from his book
(... the head is their third foot,
full of swellings and lumps,
each member that they have
stealing their strength from them unawares ...).

'Cut that out,' I said,
'It *is* in my gullet,
and I know where it came from,
from the apple at the top of the stairs ... ,'
but to tell the truth I couldn't remember
whether it was a stair at Fairfields,
or in Ibrox, or Singapore.
One thing I knew for certain
it wasn't in Lewis,
for we didn't have a stair.

God! What's the good of talking to a doctor,
I might as well send for the priest.

And if I'm not mistaken
the priest came too,
and offered me extreme unction;
an Irishman he was, but English-speaking;
I heard him mention 'wafer'
and said to him – God! What heat! –
'Forget it, it's ice-cream I want.'

The wind is rising;
if only it lifted me from here
I'd sail over the Clyde,
over Lewis and Iceland,
on the air currents;
I'd be happy enough out there
orbiting the earth,
and bawling at them now and then
to observe the Sabbath
and to be mindful of Me here.
The roads walking to the sea,
and the hills twisting round the houses,
a little summer haze
and the seaweed bubbling at high tide,
the Creator in the meeting-house tonight –
the faith whole.

With whom is He meeting?

Before the grass began to swell
at the joints,
before the boil appeared on the docken stem,
before the tumour swelled
on the tangle,
we were together in the meeting-house,
and said grace at the table.

Where is the Lord's table now?

Before peace was declared,
before the swords were turned into knives and forks,
before they made a *bothan* out of the destroyer,
before they gave me this cup to drink,
You were there.

But are You there now?

58 **Bisearta**
Deòrsa mac Iain Deòrsa (1915–1984)

An t-Olc 'na chridhe 's 'na chuisle,
Chì mi 'na bhuillean a' sìoladh 's a' leum e.
Tha 'n dreòs 'na oillt air fàire,
'Na fhàinne ròis is òir am bun nan speuran,
A' breugnachadh 's ag àicheadh
Le 'shoillse sèimhe àrsaidh àrd nan reultan.

Bizerta

I see Evil as a pulse
And a heart declining and leaping in throbs.
The blaze, a horror on the skyline,
A ring of rose and gold at the foot of the sky,
Belies and denies
With its light the ancient high tranquillity of the stars.

59 **Nuair Dh'iathas Ceò an Fheasgair Dlùth**
Murchadh MacIlleMhoire (1884-1965)

Bheil cuimhn' agad nuair bha sinn saor
'S air feadh nan raon gun leòn,
A' buachailleachd a' chruidh 's nan laogh,
Gun smaoin air maoin no stòr?
Tha cuimhneachan air àm a dh'aom
Gam dhèanamh aotrom beò;
Coinnichidh mi an gleann an fhraoich
Mo ghaol, mo rìbhinn òg.

Tha bàt' na smùid don chala dlùth
'S gach ròp is stiùir air dòigh,
'S nuair ruigeas i leam tìr mo rùin
San robh mi 'n tùs mo lò,
San anmoch chiùin nuair bhios gach flùr
'S an canach ùr nan glòir,
Coinnichidh mi an gleann an fhraoich
Mo ghaol, mo rìbhinn òg.

When the Evening Mist Surrounds Us

Do you remember us, free and innocently herding cattle
in the pasture with no thought of money or wealth?
Memories of that time lighten my spirit,
so I shall meet in the heather glen
my love, my young maiden.

The steamship nears the harbour,
all ropes and gear in readiness;
when I reach that beloved childhood country,
when flowers and fresh cotton-sedge display their glory in the calm of evening,
I shall meet in the heather glen
my love, my young maiden.

60 **Dán do Scáthach**
Colm Breathnach (b. 1961)

mar oilithreach chun do theampaill thánag
is mé ag foghlaim gaisce
san áit inar thit céad fear romham
níos fearr faoi chéad ná mé
níor chuala ach ceol na bpíob

nuair a léimeas thar do dhroichead
is nuair a réabas do bhaile poirt

ceol síoraí na bpíob
ag leagan urláir faoi mo chroí

an t-oileán glé gurb é tusa é
a chuir sciatháin le mo mhian

do bheanna mórtasacha ag éirí is ag ísliú
i gcónaí faoi gach gníomh a chuirim i gcrích

is cuma anois nó cuid díom tú
cé ná faca do shúile riamh
bhraitheasa do chroí ag bualadh

i siansán uafar na bpíob mór
is i nglórtha na ngaiscíoch a thit romham
faoi bhuillí fíochmhara ghile do chnis
sa tseomra dorcha os cionn na mara

oileán fairsing oscailte tú
a iompraím thart liom
im chroí ceilteach

A Poem to Scáthach

a pilgrim come to your temple
to learn warrior feats
where a hundred fell before me
a hundred times bolder than me
all I heard was the pipes wailing
as I vaulted your bridge
and breached your haven
the pipes eternal chant
grounding my heart

you are a bright island
settings wings to my desire
your proud peaks rise and fall
beneath my every feat one and all
almost a part of me
though I never saw your eyes
I felt your heart beat

in the fearful whine of the war-pipes
in the calls of the warriors who fell before me
beneath the fierce bright strokes of your skin
in the dark chamber above the ocean

a wide open island
borne
in my reserved heart

62 **Focaldeoch**
I gcuimhne Iain Mhic a' Ghobhainn
Louis de Paor (b. 1961)

Ag teacht thar reilig Uachtair Aird
bhí a chuimhne chosnocht á réabadh

ag clocha a sciobadh ó Theach na mBocht,
bhí sruthán buí an phailin
ag déanamh meala ar uaigh de Bhailís
is eascoin aibhléise ag glinniúint ar bhais
mo chomrádaí, a chroí is a chraiceann
breicneach scoilte mar mhias athláimhe.

Lá brothaill, adúirt sé, i dtigh comharsan,
dhein cnaipe domlais dá chroí ina bhéal
nuair a chonaic frithchaitheamh a amhrais féin
chomh soiléir le teastas báis
ar aghaidh na mná cneasta
ar eitigh sé muga leamhnachta as a láimh.

Tá mo scornach ata le tart
ag triall arís ar bhothán tite a dháin
go bhfaighead i measc na ngréithre briste
blas éigin den uaisleacht chráite
ná maireann sa tsaol níos mó,
an soiscéal de réir Iain
a leigheasfadh íota mo chroí.

Gospel
I.M. Iain Crichton Smith

As we passed the cemetery at Oughterard
a yellow stream of pollen
honeyed the headstone of Colm Wallace,
his barefoot memories were gashed
by stones stolen from the ruins of the Poorhouse,
electric eels glittered in his hands
heart and freckled skin
cracking like second-hand crockery.

On a sweltering day in a neighbour's house,
he said, his heart turned to gall in his mouth
when he saw his own uncertainty reflected
clear as a death-certificate on the woman's face
when he refused kindness from her hands.

My throat is swollen with thirst
as I make my way again
to the tumbled down cottage of his poem
hoping to find there among the broken crockery
a taste of the hurt and gentleness
that is no longer in the world,
the gospel according to Iain
that might relieve my raging heart.

63 Hallaig
Somhairle MacGill-Eain (1911–1996)

na fir 'nan laighe air an lèanaig
aig ceann gach taighe a bh' ann,
na h-igheanan 'nan coille bheithe,
dìreach an druim, crom an ceann.

Eadar an Leac is na Feàrnaibh
tha 'n rathad mòr fo chòinnich chiùin,
's na h-igheanan 'nam badan sàmhach
a' dol a Chlachan mar o thus.

Agus a' tilleadh às a' Chlachan,
à Suidhisnis 's à tìr nam beò;
a chuile tè òg uallach,
gun bhristeadh cridhe an sgeòil.

O Allt na Feàrnaibh gus an fhaoilinn
tha soilleir an dìomhaireachd nam beann
chan eil ach coimhthional nan nighean
a' cumail na coiseachd gun cheann.

a' tilleadh a Hallaig anns an fheasgar,
anns a' chamhanaich bhalbh bheò,
a' lìonadh nan leathadan casa,
an gàireachdaich 'nam chluais 'na ceò,

's am bòidhche 'na sgleò air mo chridhe
mun tig an ciaradh air na caoil,
's nuair theàrnas grian air cùl Dhùn Cana
thig peileir dian à gunna Ghaoil;

's buailear am fiadh a tha 'na thuaineal
a' snòtach nan làraichean feòir;
thig reothadh air a shùl sa choille:
chan fhaighear lorg air fhuil rim bheò.

Hallaig

the men lying on the green
at the end of every house that was,
the girls a wood of birches,
straight their backs, bent their heads.

Between the Leac and Fearns
the road is under mild moss
and the girls in silent bands
go to Clachan as in the beginning.

And return from Clachan,
from Suisnish and the land of the living;
Each one young and light stepping,
without the heartbreak of the tale.

From the Burn of Fearns to the raised beach
that is clear in the mystery of the hills,
there is only the congregation of the girls
keeping up the endless walk,

coming back to Hallaig in the evening,
in the dumb living twilight,
filling the steep slopes,
their laughter in my ears a mist,

and their beauty a film on my heart
before the dimness comes on the kyles,
and when the sun goes down behind Dun Cana
a vehement bullet will come from the gun of Love;

and will strike the deer that goes dizzily,
sniffing at the grass-grown ruined homes;
his eye will freeze in the wood;
his blood will not be traced while I live.

66 Loch na Craoibhe

Diarmaid Ó Doibhlin (b.1942)

Níl feidhm leo feasta mar ionaid
Níl feidhm ach mar ábhar machnaimh
Mar shamhailt don té istigh cois tine oíche gheimhridh
Ag iompú leathanaigh a chine
Agus stoirm na tíre ag riastradh taobh amuigh.
Fág iad mar atá, impím ort,
Fág faoi na scológa coimhthíocha
Nach bhfeiceann choíche marclaigh ná slua,
Nach gcluineann choíche claisceadal na dtéad úr,
Nach mbraitheann choíche uaigneas san fhuarlach seo.

Fág iad mar atá,
Níl ann ach scéal ag seanmhná,
Go mbíonn a gcuid féin ag locha.

Crew Lough

They serve no purpose now,
Have no use whatever anymore
But only to flutter across the page
I read on a stiff winter's night.
Turning the sad pages of my people's story
While the storm outside rages on.

Leave it and them, I say,
Leave it with the farmer who bolts tight the gate,
Who has never seen a cavalcade or hosting,
Who never hears the tune of the clean harp,
And in these low margins
Feels no otherworld, no haunting.

Leave them as they are I say,
It is after all only an old woman's tale
That loughs in due course claim back their very own.

67 Liadhain

Gabriel Rosenstock (b.1949)

Is í na gaotha í
an mhuir mheann –

An uile ní a chorraíonn
is nach gcorraíonn

Athrú i lár séasúir í
is í na ceithre ráithe í

Lá agus oíche is ea í
oíche agus lá

Codail anois, codail! Codail, a Liadhain
ar d'adhartán caonaigh, codail go caoin . . .

Dá bhféadfainn do thumfainn amach id shuan
d'fhonn bheith i do thaibhreamhsa, a ghile, go buan.
I gcoim na foraoise is míshuaimhneach don torc
Ach codail, is ná bíodh imní ort.

Féach! Liadhain sa linn
is í ag snámh ar a droim
mirabile visu –
sí an ghealach í
stoirm réaltaí
A Chríost ná tar i m'aice
A Mhuir Ógh, iompaigh do shúil.

Chun Dé
ní théann
mo phaidreacha
níos mó
Liadhain Liadhain
ar bharr mo theanga.

A cruth sa scamall
a gáire san aiteall
dathanna a hanama is ea
an bogha síne

Rógheal í mo chumann
mé im ghráinneog
a dhúisíonn maidin earraigh róluath
goineann an solas mo shúile

Tormán easa i gcéin
ní stadann
scíth ní ghlacann
mo dhála féin
cúr mo bhriathra
san aer

Blais de.

'Liadhain! Liadhain!' ag an abhainn dhubh
'Liadhain!' an chuach sa ghleann
an maighre méith scairteann 'Liadhain!'
'Liadhain! Liadhain!' ag an eilit sheang.

Cíorann leoithní a folt án drúchtmhar
Mé in éad leis ma dúile . . .

Ach do shéid ina anfa oighreata
Leagadh daracha
Reoigh an scol i ngob an loin
Bhúir tonnta uile Éireann

Níor liom mé féin níos mó
Níor liomsa Liadhain ná a háineas
Nocht Críost a chréachtaí –
Ar mo shonsa, leis, a céasadh É.

Ar leac seo m'urnaithe a chaillfear Liadhain
Is mise i gcríochaibh aineoil

A Dhé! Tabhair le chéile arís sinn
Naisc sinn – achainím ort – ar feadh aon oíche amháin
I bParthas róshoilseach na naomh.

Liadhain

She is all winds,
the middle of all seas –

Everything that moves

and does not.

She is a change in season,
All the months of the year.

She is day and night,
night and day.

Sleep now, sleep! Sleep, Liadhain,
On your mossy pillow, sleep easy . . .

If I could, I would dive far into your sleep,
to be forever, bright one, part of your dream.
In the middle of the forest, the boar is restless,
but sleep now, easy in yourself.

Look! Liadhain in the pool,
swimming on her back.
Mirabile visu –
She is moon,
a star-filled storm.
Christ, do not approach me.
Virgin Mary, avert your eye.

My prayers
don't go
anymore
to God.
Liadhain, Liadhain,
on the tip of my tongue.

Her shape in the clouds,
her laugh between showers,
the rainbow
her soul's colours.

My beloved is dazzling.
I'm like a hedgehog
waking too early on a spring morning.
Light hurts my eyes.

A waterfall thunders far off
without pause.
There's no relief
from the way things are.
My words are foam
in the air.

Taste it.

'Liadhain! Liadhain!' murmurs the dark river,
'Liadhain!' calls the cuckoo in the valley.
The plump salmon shouts out 'Liadhain'
'Liadhain! Liadhain!' cries the slender doe.

Breezes comb her dewy hair.
I am envious of the elements.

But an icy blast rose,
uprooting the oaks.
The blackbird's whistle froze in its beak.
All the waves of Ireland wailed.

My own self I had lost,
lost Liadhain and her merrymaking.
Christ bared his wounds –
for me, also, He was crucified.

On this, my slab of supplication, Liadhain will perish,
and I in unknown territories.

Dear God! Bring us together again.
Couple us – I beg you – for just one night
in the splendid Paradise of saints.

70 **Paddy**

Gearóid Mac Lochlainn (b.1966)
(i ndilchuimhne)

Londain thall. Súil na himpireachta.
Seanbhitseach sheargtha na gcíoch searbh.
Seanbhitseach na súl seachantach,
na sciathán leathair
a eitlíonn go réidh i mbolg dubh an *underground.*
Seanbhitseach starrfhiaclach
ag súmaireacht ar fhuil an deoraí
faoi ghealacha reonacha
Ríle, ríle, ráinne.
Seanbhitseach glic ag an choirnéal i Sóhó
a bhfuil a fhios aici "*What ya want. What ya need.*"
Cathair na mbréag. Cathair an chumha.
Cathair chruálach ag creimeadh croí Éireannaigh
croí Iamácaigh, croí Indiaigh,
croí Giúdaigh, croí Albánaigh.

Triop treap triopaití treap.
Seanbhitseach shnoite ina luí ag fanacht
faoin droichead i gcathair chairtchláir.

Triop treap triopití treap.
Seanbhitseach shnoite a chreim do chroí Feirsteach
amach
gur fágadh thú i do phuipéad. *Pinnochio* teipthe
gan píobaire teallaigh,
ag luascadh ó shíleáil sreangaithe amach sa deireadh.
Plúchta. Múchta.
D'amhrán gafa go deo i do scornach
gléasta i do chulaith ghorm is goirme.

Taibhsíonn tú i gcuan m'aigne anocht arís,
Stánaim gan deor i lonta dubha do chuid súl,
scáth spíonta i do shuí os mo chomhair ag an tábla sa
chistin,
mé ag éisteacht le víbeanna maithe ag preabarnach,
ag stealladh, ag doirteadh ina thonnta dorcha rithime ó
shúile dubha
na *speakers* ar mo *ghetto blaster,*
an Sliabh Dubh lasmuigh den fhuinneog
faoi fhial fearthainne
ag déanamh faire foighneach ar chathair bhriste Bhéal
Feirste.

Cuirim C.D. ar siúl, ag bleaisteáil víbeanna
a chuireann na cupáin ag rocáil ar an tseilf.

Ardaithe i ndilchuimhne
duitse, domhsa.
Briathra binne, beachta, cinnte
don neamdhuine ina luí i ndoras siopa i Londain thall,
Linton Kwesi Johnson ag ceol fírinne,
a scaoileann sealán na croiche,
a shuaimhníonn an oíche seo,
a thugann bomaite eile beatha duitse, a Phadaí,
i dteach slán na cuimhne.

– Inglan is a bitch
dere's no escapin' it

Paddy

London. Eye of the empire.
Old withered bitter-titted-bitch.
Bat-winged-bitch which flits in the whale-belly
underground.
Wide-boy-bitch on Soho corner who
knows 'What ya want. Got what ya need.'
Fanged–bitch sucking exile blood
under neon-moons.
City of remorse.
Cruel city gnawing the heart-strings
of Irish, Jamaican, Jew, Scot.

Trip-trap-trippity-trap.

Haggard-old-bitch
slupping out of the Thames
to trawl beneath the bridge in cardboard-city.

Trip-trap-trippity-trap.

Mean-old-bitch who munched out your Belfast heart,
left you a puppet. Pinnochioed;
suspended, finally strung out.
Your swan song stilled.
Dressed in your newest and bluest of blue suits.

Tonight you drift again
into the mind's harbour,
a parched dust-devil.

I stare deep into your blackbird-eyes
across the kitchen table,
the room
immersed in dark waves of rhythm
that roll and lash
from the black-eye-speakers
on the ghetto-blaster.
The Black mountain looms outside the window
under a dark veil of rain,
keeps patient vigil on Béal Feirste cois cuain.

I turn up the volume, pump it,
till it sets the cups jitterbugging on the shelf,
till the bind in me unravels.
I let it out,
soft sure words for the corpses washed up
in shopfronts. In London.
Linton Kwesi Johnson sings it true,
looses the noose,
soothes and smoothes away the night
and suddenly, Paddy, you catch your breath
in the safe-house of memory

– Inglan is a bitch
dere's no escapin' it
Inglan is a bitch fi true
a noh lie me a tell a true
Inglan is a bitch.

71 Dubh

Nuala Ní Dhomhnaill (b.1952)
ar thitim Shrebenice, 11ú Iúil, 1995

Tá na poiliticeoirí ar sciobaidh
is iad ag baint an gcos is na n-eireaball dá chéile
ag iarraidh a chur ina luí orainn
nach fada go mbeidh gach dubh ina gheal.

Is an té a leomhfadh a mhisneach dó
nó a chredifeadh an méid a deireann siad
níor mhiste dó b'fhéidir an cheist a chur
ab ann ab amhlaidh a chiallaíonn sé seo anois
nach mbeidh ins gach dubhthréimhse ach seal?

Ach ní dhéanfadsa
Mar táimse dubh.
Tá mo chroí dubh
is m'intinn dubh.
Tá m'amharc ar feadh raon mo radhairce dubh.
Tá an dubh istigh is amuigh agam díbh.

Mar gach píosa guail nó sméar nó airne,
gach deamhan nó diabhal nó daradaol,
gach cleite fiaigh mhara nó íochtar bonn bróige
gach uaimh nó cabha nó poll tóine
gach duibheagán doimhin a shlogann ár ndóchas
táim dubh dubh dubh.

Mar tá Srebenice, cathair an airgid,
'Argentaría' na Laidine,
bán.

Black

on the fall of Srebenica, 11 July, 1995

The politicians are scuffling about
biting the legs off each other
trying to persuade us
to look on the bright side.

Anyone who might be inclined
to take them at their word
would do well, maybe, to ask
why they think it goes without saying
that every cloud has a silver lining.

I myself won't be the one.
For I'm black.
My heart is black and my mind is black.
Everything that falls into my field of vision is black.
I'm full of black rage.

There's a black mark against all your names.

Like each and every lump of coal, every blackberry and sloe
Every grave and cave and arsehole,
Every bottomless pit in which we lose all hope,
I'm black as black can be.

Now that Srebenica, that silver city –
'Argentaria', as the Romans called it –
is blank.

72 Amhrán Mhis ag Grianstad an Gheimhridh

Biddy Jenkinson (b. 1949)

Maidin in ainnise in iubhar na cille
bláth seaca ar mo shúile
stualeirg mo dhroma
ar cnagadh
ar an stoc reoite,
mo mhásaí maoldearga
ag táth fúthu
in uanán buinní biolair,
chasas soir
is phóg gealán mo shúile
ag leá oighir iontu.

Lígh méar fhada gréine cuar mo bhéil
is shlíoc mo ghruanna,
neadaigh im leicne.

Bhraitheas an dúléan ag leá im chroí
an gile ag nochtadh cneá isteach go braon
is an dubh ag rith uaim.
Shíneas uaim mo lámha chuig an ngrian
a dheargaigh néalta
a thug suntas
do gach lóipín sneachta gur las sé,
gur tháth tír is aer in aon mhuir solais
mar ar chuir mo chroí chun cuain.

Sa dúluachair,
i bputóga dubha gach bliana,
mar chúiteamh comaoine,
ceapaim an ghrian
i gcuaschomhlaí mo chroí
is teilgim í sna harda
le hurchar ceoil
de bhéala éin an earraigh.

Song of Mis at the Winter Solstice

One morning, grief-struck in the chapel yew,
frost-flowers on my eyes,
spine in locked spasm
hammering
on frozen tree trunk,
my red-raw buttocks
discharging
a froth, a scutter of watercress,
I turned to the east
and a gleam of sunlight kissed my eyes,
a glitter of sunlight melted the ice in my look.

A long finger of light traced
the curve of my lips,
stroked my raw cheekbones,
rested on my cheek.

I felt the black grief thaw in my heart,
brightness lancing the poisoned wound,
the dark running out of me;
I stretched my hands out to the sun
as it reddened the clouds,
as it picked out, lit up flake after flake of snow
until earth and air became a sea of light
that carried my heart to harbour.

In the deep of every winter since,
in the dark entrails of the year,
in return for this grace and favour
I set the sun up in my heart,
I lance it high into the bowl of air and light
on a bolt of music,
that the birds may follow it into the mouth of spring.

73 An Scáthán

Mícheál Davitt (b. 1950)
i gcuimhne m'athar

Ag maisiú an tseomra chodlata dó
d'ardaigh sé an scáthán anuas
gan lámh chúnta a iarraidh;
ar ball d'iompaigh dath na cré air,
an oíche sin phléasc a chroí.

Mar a chuirfí de gheasa orm
thugas faoin jab a chríochnú
an folús macallach a pháipéarú,
an fhuinneog ard a phéinteáil,
an doras marbhlainne
a scríobadh. Nuair a rugas ar an scáthán
sceimhlíos. Bhraitheas é ag análú tríd.
Chuala é ag rá i gcogar téiglí:
I'll give you a hand here.

Is d'ardaíomar an scáthán thar n-ais in airde
os cionn an tinteáin,
m'athair á choinneáil
fad a dheineas-sa é a dhaingniú
le dhá thairne.

The Mirror

in memory of my father

While he was decorating the bedroom
he had taken down the mirror
without asking for help;
soon he turned the colour of terra-cotta
and his heart broke that night.

There was nothing for it
but to set about finshing the job,
papering over the cracks,
painting the high window,
stripping the door, like the door of a crypt.
When I took hold of the mirror
I had a fright. I imagined him breathing through it.

I heard him say a reassuring whisper:
I'll give you a hand here.

And we lifted the mirror back in position
above the fireplace,
my father holding it steady
while I drove home
the two nails.

74 An Loingeas (sliocht)
Alan Titley (b. 1957)

Ba mhór eadrainne agus Fearghus Mór mac Eirc a shín a radharc thar sáile óna dhún suáilceach gur tháinig a ríocht i dtír lastoir de chaolas Íle. Chonaic sé uaidh a fhlaitheas gan chríoch a raibh na lasracha uaidh ag lonradh ina aigne. Maidir liomsa, bhí an phian ag screadach trín pholl i mo chroí agus mé ag tabhairt cúl le hÉirinn.

Suibhne ina shuí thuas ar Charraig Alastair, áitreabh d'fhaoileáin, fuar dá haíonna. Fliuch ár leabana, beag a shíleamar gur charraig nó gur aistear naofa a bhí fúinn. Trua ár gcoinne-ne, dís chorr chrualoirgneacha, gealt ar eite agus file ar a theicheadh. Trua ár dturas-sa, cian ónár n-eolas-sa an chríoch gur ránamar.

The Ship Sailing (excerpt)

Much was the difference between us and Great Fergus son of Eirc who stretched his sight across the sound from his fast fort and settled his kingdom just east of Islay. He saw his weal without end whose fires of fame flamed in his head. As for me, the pain scoured a hole in my heart as our ship slewed its stern from Ireland.

Mad Sweeney astride the big berg of Ailsa Craig, home for seagulls, cold for guests. Wet our beds were, little thought we gave to rock nor wished a holy way we wended. Sad our plight, two sharpshinned herons, a flying madman and a fleeing poet. Sad our going, kept from our kenning the kingdom we came.

80 An Charraig (sliocht)
Mícheál Ó Conghaile (b. 1962)

D'aithneofá go bhfaca an charraig an uile mhíle ní ó chúil uile a cinn. Níor ghá di breathnú fiú. Chonaic i ngan fhios an dúiche uile máguaird. Amach os a comhair Machairí droimleathana. Cnocáin bheaga ghlasa. Bánta aerach bána aerach bána, claíocha biorracha is mantacha. Bearnaí. Aillteachaí. Clochair. Sclaigeanna is scailpeanna. Leacrachaí loma. Leacrachaí fada fadálacha. Is cótaí de chaonach liath fáiscthe anuas ar chuid acu . . .

Agus garrantaí. An draoi acu. Iad cearnógach, ciorclach agus triantánach. Tuilleadh garrantaí éagruthacha. Cosáin aistreánacha. Portaigh bhoga riascacha. Srutháin chasta leath-éalaithe as amharc. Gleannta doimhne ag síneadh agus ag síneadh uathu níos faide i gcéin . . . Agus níos íochtaraí síos - cuanta leathana: crompáin chúnga: caltaí: céibheanna clochach lámhdhéanta, tránna geala fairsinge, sáinnithe cúngaithe scaití ag na taoillte tuile. Farraigí imirceacha . . . Cheapfá gur sheanmháthair uasal chríonna í an charraig díobh go léir. Seanmháthair chiúin thostach, nár thug mórán airde ar a gairm, déarfá . . . ach a bhí ann i gcónaí, mar sin féin, ar nós aosach máchaileach i gcathaoir rothaí. Níor lig as amharc iad. Aingeal coimhdeachta cianradharcach. Í cúthail, b'fhéidir leathbhodhar fiú. Mar a bheadh ag míogarnach léi ansin . . .
Ba é saol é. A mhalairt eile níor chleacht a cnámh droma neamhaclaí stadaithe

The Rock (excerpt)

You sensed from the whole angry-looking precipice of its head that the rock had seen all things. It didn't have to look even. It just saw – unknown to the countryside around – all that lay ahead. Broad-backed fields. Small green hillocks. Good open grassland. Gapped, reedy boundaries. Openings. Cliffs. Strong ridges. Clefts and fissures. Bare slabs of rock. Long flat areas of stone. Some coated in mildew . . . And gardens. Loads of them. Shaped in squares, circles or triangles. Others irregular in shape. Rough-hewn paths. Soft damp bogs. Curving streams half-hidden from view. Deep glens stretching away wayout into the distance . . . And lower down, wide harbours, narrow creeks, straits, man-made quays, bright wide beaches, sometimes boxed in by the turning tide. The free, migrant ocean . . .

You'd think the rock was the wise old grandmother of them all. A quiet, taciturn grandmother who didn't pay much heed to her charge, you might say . . . but who was always there, all the same, like a seasoned old-timer in a rocking chair. It didn't let them out of its sight. Like a guardian angel watching from a distance. Reserved, and maybe even half-deaf. Looking like she was just dozing away there . . .

That was its life. That was all its locked ridged backbone had ever known.

81 Mairbhní ar Oileán Tréigthe
Tomás Mac Síomóin (b. 1938)

Ach má taoi ag déanamh cré sa chill,
A Chriomhthannaigh an oileáin,
Gad do ghinealaigh fós níor bhris
Ó chuiris cor id dhán,

Ó d'íocais deachú an fhocail led nós,
Ó bhreacais caint do dhaoine ar phár,
Strapann do nae fós fál na toinne
Idir Muir na mBeo is Muir na Scál.

Tá mise fós ar mo mharana ag faire
Is ó bhuanaigh do dhán a ndáil
Tá sluainte na marbh ag siúl go socair
Ar bhealaí an oileáin.

Is cluintear gáire mná le gaoth
Ag bearnú thost an bháis
Is cluintear gáir an choiligh arís
Ag baint macallaí as an ard.

Meditation on a Deserted Island

Though you are making graveyard clay,

O'Crohan, islandman,
The thread of your blood has yet to break
Since you put that twist in your fate

And paid the homage of the word to your ways,
Speckled parchment with your people's speech,
Your boat still breasts the rising wave
Between the Sea of Shadow and the Sea of the Living.

As I ponder, watchful still,
Your word brings back to life
The host of the dead I see walking there
Along the island roads.

A woman's laughter on the wind
Pierces death's numb silence;
Once again the village cock
Wake echoes on the mountain.

86 Dha Pàdraig, Bràthair Mo Mhàthar

Maoilios M. Caimbeul (b.1944)

Seo a' chùil
ged nach eil ann ach turas
eadar na sgalan:
's ged a thilleas mi, ged a thilleas mi
a-rithist, chan ann gus faicinn.
Ach tillidh mi gun teagamh
agus bidh an seann àite
na phàirt dhiom, agus mise dhen t-seann àite,
agus bidh an ròs dubh agus an ròs dearg fo shìth.

Na làithean fada samhraidh –
bha iad iongantach
nauir a bha am bodach beò.
Bha na dearcan cho dearg air a' chaorann
agus na h-oghaichean anns an fheur.
Tha a' ghaoth cho tioram,
nuair a ràcas sinn e
cha bhi e fada –
ach na dìochuimhnich an crogan uisge,
tha e teth anns an fheur.

Tha Seonaidh Ruadh agus Aonghas Ros
a' tional air lotaichean eile.
Tha iad a' tional mus tig an t-Sàbaid,
agus sàmhchair.

Tha a sheusan aig a h-uile nì,
seusan fuachd agus teas,
seusan abachaidh agus seargaidh,
agus tha àm agus aman ann.
Eadar trì 's a ceithir a h-uile latha
chuirinn am prosbaig taobh Gheàrrloch
far am biodh am bàta dol seachad –
luchd-turais eile, turasan eile,
gach fear le a chuimhne
agus a ròsan dubh agus dearg.

Bu tusa mo ròs dearg
mus do thuit uisge
nan leth-cheud geamhradh air mo cheann,
's mus do thrus mi am mìle caora
's mus tuirt mi 'Caora bheag, caora bheag'
ris a' pheata uain.
Bu tusa mo ròs dearg
uaireigin, uaireigin,
ach a-nise tha mise agus an ròs dubh
agus cha bhris thusa talamh
na h-aon chill rium.

Chan eil ann ach turas
eadar imir is iodhlann,
agus cuimhnichidh mi do làmhan
agus guth na h-ùmhlachd aig àm leabhair
agus gu robh thu creidsinn,
agus cuimhnichidh mi àm a' bhidh –
mar a ghabh thu an t-aran,
mar a dh'òl thu fìon do bheatha,
agus bidh mo dhòchas
air a mheasgadh
annsan a dh'ith an t-aran
uair eile
agus bidh sìth anns an fhlùr
agus anns an talamh.
Cha bhi an siubhal fada.

Uncle Peter

This is the cul-de-sac
although there is but a trip
between the squalls;
and though I return, though I return
again, it will not be to see.
But sure, I will return
and the old place
will be a part of me, and I of the old place,
and the black rose and the red rose will be at peace.

The long summer days –
they were great
when the old man was alive.
The rowan berries so red
and the youngsters in the hay.
The wind is so dry,
when we turn it
it will not be long –
but don't forget the water jar,
it is hot in the hay.
Seonaidh Ruadh and Aonghas Ros
gather on other crofts.
They gather before the Sabbath comes,
and silence.

Everything has its season,
a season of cold and heat,
of ripening and withering,
and there is a time and there are times.
Every day between three and four
I would look with the binoculars across to Gairloch
where a boat would be passing –
other travellers, other journeys,
each with his memory
and the black and the red rose.

You were my red rose once

before the rain
of fifty winters fell on my head,
and before I gathered the thousand sheep
and said 'caora bheag, caora bheag'
to the pet lamb.
You were my red rose
sometime, sometime,
but now there is me and the black rose
and you will not break the earth
of the same churchyard as me.

There is but a journey
between ridge and stackyard,
and I will remember your hands
and the voice of obedience at family worship
and that you believed,
and I will remember mealtime –
how you accepted bread
and drank the wine of life,
and my hope
will be bound
with Him who ate the bread
another time
and there will be peace in the flower
and in the earth.
The journey won't take long.

87 Tioram air Tìr

Tormod Caimbeul (b. 1942)
Mar Chuimhneachan air Murchadh Chaluim

An e làraidh no bhana
a thill leoth' a-null?
'S dòch' gur e Seòras
no carbaid le Ròigean –
dè 'n còrr a bhiodh ann?

Ach bhuannaich iad baile
dh'aindeoin ùpraid cinn!
Aig àm dol a chadal,
am fear nach d'fhuair leabaidh,
bu mhath leis a' bheing.

O, fàg iad nan cadal
's thoir maitheanas dhaibh –
feuch gun taisg thu an teine,
dùin gu socrach an doras,
tha na gaisgich fo rùm.

Back On Dry Land

Was it a lorry or a van that brought them back? Perhaps it was Seòras or one of Ròigean's vehicles – what else would it be?

But they made it home, in spite of the turmoil in their heads! And when the time came to sleep, anyone who did not get a bed was happy with a bench.

Oh, leave them resting and forgive them. Remember to dampen down the fire. Shut the door quietly – the heroes are asleep.

88 An Ataireachd Ard

Dòmhnall MacIomhair (1857-1935)

Ach chunnaic mis' uair
'M bu chuannar beathail an t-àit',
Le òigridh gun ghruaim
Bha uasal modhail nan càil,
Le màthraichean suairc
Làn uaill nan companaich gràidh,
Le caoraich is buar
Air ghluas'd moch-mhadainn nan tràth.

Ag amharc mun cuairt,
Cha dual dhomh gun a bhith 'm pràmh:
Chan fhaic mi an tuath
Dom b' shuaicheant' carthannas tlàth –
Nam fògarraich thruagh,
Chaidh 'm fuadach thairis air sàl,
'S cha chluinn iad gu buan
Mòr-fhuaim na h-ataireachd àird.

Fir-sgiùrsaidh an t-sluaigh,
Cha bhuan iad bharrachd air càch –
Bu chridheil an uaill
Gar ruagadh mach gun chion-fàth,
Ach sannt agus cruas,
An duais tha aca mu thràth –
Mòr-dhiomb is droch luaidh
An uaigh le mallachd nan àl.

Ach siùbhlaidh mi uat,
Cha ghluais mi tuilleadh nad dhàil:
Tha m' aois is mo shnuadh
Toirt luaidh air giorrad mo là;
An àm dhomh bhith suaint'
Am fuachd 's an cadal a' bhàis,
Mo leabaidh dèan suas
Ri fuaim na h-ataireachd àird.

The Sea's Lofty Roar

But I've seen an age
When the place was both snug and alive,
With youngsters unbowed
Whose manner was proud but polite,
Their mothers serene
Well pleased with their partners in life
With sheep and with cows
Setting out at the morning's first light.

But looking around
My spirits are bound to be low:
I don't see the tenants
Whose warm generosity flowed –
As exiles in misery
They've been driven away from our shores
And they'll never now hear
The great sound of the sea's lofty roar.

Those who've wielded the lash
Won't outlast the folk they have cleared –
Lusting for glory

They drove us out for no reason
  But power and desire;
The prize they've won for their deed
  Is disgust and ill fame,

The grave with the curse of the seed.
  But I must go away,
I can't stay with you any more:
  My age and appearance
Reveal that I've not far to go;
  When I'm finally seized
By the sleep of perpetual cold,
  In my bed lay me down
To the sound of the sea's lofty roar.

89 Motor-Boat Heidhsgeir

Dòmhnall Ruadh Chorùna. (1887-1967)

Copar agus cruaidhe fuaigheilte gu rèidh,
Cnòintean air an uachdar gus nach gluais 's nach gèill,
Peatarail gun sòradh, fuaim a bòrd gu treun,
Bataraidh ga suathadh 's sradag uaine leum.

Ach thug mise bòidean nach seòlainn gu bràth
'S nach dèanainn a' bhòidse leis na seòid a bha,
Ged a bha iad eòlach 's a Chlann Dòmhnaill àd –
Cha robh leud mo bhròige dhen chuairt-bheòil am bàrr.

The Heisgeir Motor-Boat

Copper and steel amalgamated smoothly,
With nuts on their surface so they'll not shift or yield,
Petrol unstinting, her boards vibrating loudly,
Battery brought to life with green spark leaping.

But I have made a promise not to sail again
Or make the voyage with the heroes of the day –
Despite their experience and for all they were MacDonalds,
Not the width of my shoe of the gunwale-board was
  showing.

91 Màiri Iain Mhurch' Chaluim

Anna C. Frater (b.1967)
Mo sheanmhair, a chaill a h-athair air an Iolaire, *oidhche na Bliadhn' Ùir, 1919*

Chàirich iad a' chreag
agus dh'fhàg sin toll.
Chruadhaich an sàl ur beatha
agus chùm e am pian ùr;
agus dh'fhuirich e nur sùilean
cho goirt 's a bha e riamh;
agus tha pian na caillich
cho geur ri pian na nighinn,
agus tha ur cridhe
a' briseadh às ùr
a' cuimhneachadh ur h-athar.

'. . . oir bha athair agam . . .'

Mairi Iain Mhurch' Chaluim

My grandmother, who lost her father on the Iolaire, *New Year's night, 1919*

They buried the rock
and that left a hole;
the salt hardened your life
and kept the pain fresh;
and it stayed in your eyes
as stinging as it ever was;
and the old woman's pain is
as keen as the girl's,
and your heart breaks anew
remembering your father.

'. . . because I had a father . . .'

95 Chunnaic Mi Uam a' Bheinn

Murchadh MacPhàrlain (1901-1982)

O bheinn mo chridhe, nad bhàrr
'S tric a bha, cha bhi tuilleadh mi chaoidh:
Dh'fhàs mo shìnteag 's mo shearrag cho geàrr –
'S innis mhilis na cuimhn' an-dè;
A-màireach, chan aithne dhomh e,
Mi mar sheillean deocadh mil anns gach blàth
Measg nan latha a dh'fhàg mi am dhèidh.

Mo sheann chù-bheinne na shrann
Dh'fhàg mis' air an staran sa ghrèin,
Cholg 'n-uiridh air peallach is fann,
Critheanach, mall a cheum;
Chas chlis a-nis tha bho fheum –
A thrusadh an casadh nam beann
A-chaoidh cha tèid mis' no e fhèin.

Chunnaic mise mo sheud sa bheinn,
'S cha tàrradh uaith' geàrr nan càrn –
Air an staran e nis air a shlinn,
Ri cùl gaoith 's aghaidh grèin' sa bhlàths:
Ann am broinn gach beatha tha bàs,
Mar an dèidh an latha tha 'n oidhch',
'S tha madainn nam beò cho geàrr.

Chunnaic mi uam a' bheinn –
An sealladh rinn tinn mo chrìdh',
Coin thìm a' trusadh mo linn –
Eisd, cluinn orra sìos an gleann!
Chan fhad' gum bi 'n trusadh aig ceann:
Sìos san iar chaidh a' ghrian anns na tuinn,
Mean air mhean oirnn an oidhch' a' tighinn teann.

I Saw at a Distance the Hill

O hill of my heart, on your crest
Often I was, never again will I be;
My stride and my step have become so short,
And the sweet place of memory yesterday;
Tomorrow I knew it not;
I, like a bee sipping honey from blossom,
Amid the days I have left behind me.

My old dog snoring
I left on the path in the sun
The coat of yesterday now matted and weak,

Shaky, slow his step
His agile foot now useless;
To gather at the foot of the hill
Never will I or he go.

I saw my hero on the hill
And the mountain hare couldn't draw away from him,
Now stretched out on the path
Out of the wind in the warmth of the sun.
Inside every life there is death
As after day there is night,
And the morning of the living is so short.

I saw at a distance the hill,
The sight that made my heart sick;
Time's dogs gathering my generation –
Hark! Listen to them down the glen!
Soon the gathering will be done:
In the west sank the sun down into the waves,
Little by little night approaches us.

96 Christy Ring

Seán Ó Tuama (b. 1926)

bhí cnagadh is cleatar,
liútar-éatar,
fir á dtreascairt,
fuil ag sileadh –
's nuair rop trí cúil isteach
bhí seandéithe Éireann uile
ag stiúrú a chamáin.

Dúirt bean os cionn a choirp
tráth a bháis anabaidh:
'ba mhór an peaca é
an fear san a adhlacadh'.

Ní féidir liomsa fós
Christy Ring a adhlacadh . . .
Samhlaím é uaireanta
is é ar buanchoimeád,
sínte ar leac na honóra
i mBrú na Bóinne
is Aonghas Mac an Daghda á choimhdeacht
go dtí an leath-uair bheag gach geimhreadh
go soilsíonn ga gréine go hómósach
ar a chúntanós.

Ach ní fhéadfadh aoinne againne
a mhair faoi bhriocht ag Christy Ring
é leagadh uainn go buan faoi ghlas
i measc míorúiltí na seanmhiotas –
mar, ó na míorúiltí
chonaiceamar dáiríre
is a chúntanós faoi loinnir
formhór gach Domhnach
geimhreadh is samhradh
ar an bpáirc.

Christy Ring

through clash and crash
hue and cry
men were toppled
hot blood spurted
as he rammed in
three lethal goals
all the gods of ancient Ireland
lent his hurley* a guiding hand.

Looking at his corpse laid out,
the day of his untimely death,
a woman said:
'It would be a sin to bury such a man.'

I have not managed yet to bury Christy Ring . . .
Sometimes I imagine him
being venerated
in the care of the great god, Aengus,
on a slab at Newgrange
and at each winter solstice
for just one half an hour
a ray of sunshine
lighting up his countenance.

But no friend of his could think
of laying Christy Ring eternally to rest
locked in with ancient miracles –
for, oh, the miracles of the living flesh
we saw when his countenance lit up
Winter days and Summer days,
Sundays in and Sundays out,
on the playing pitch.

**stick used in hurling*

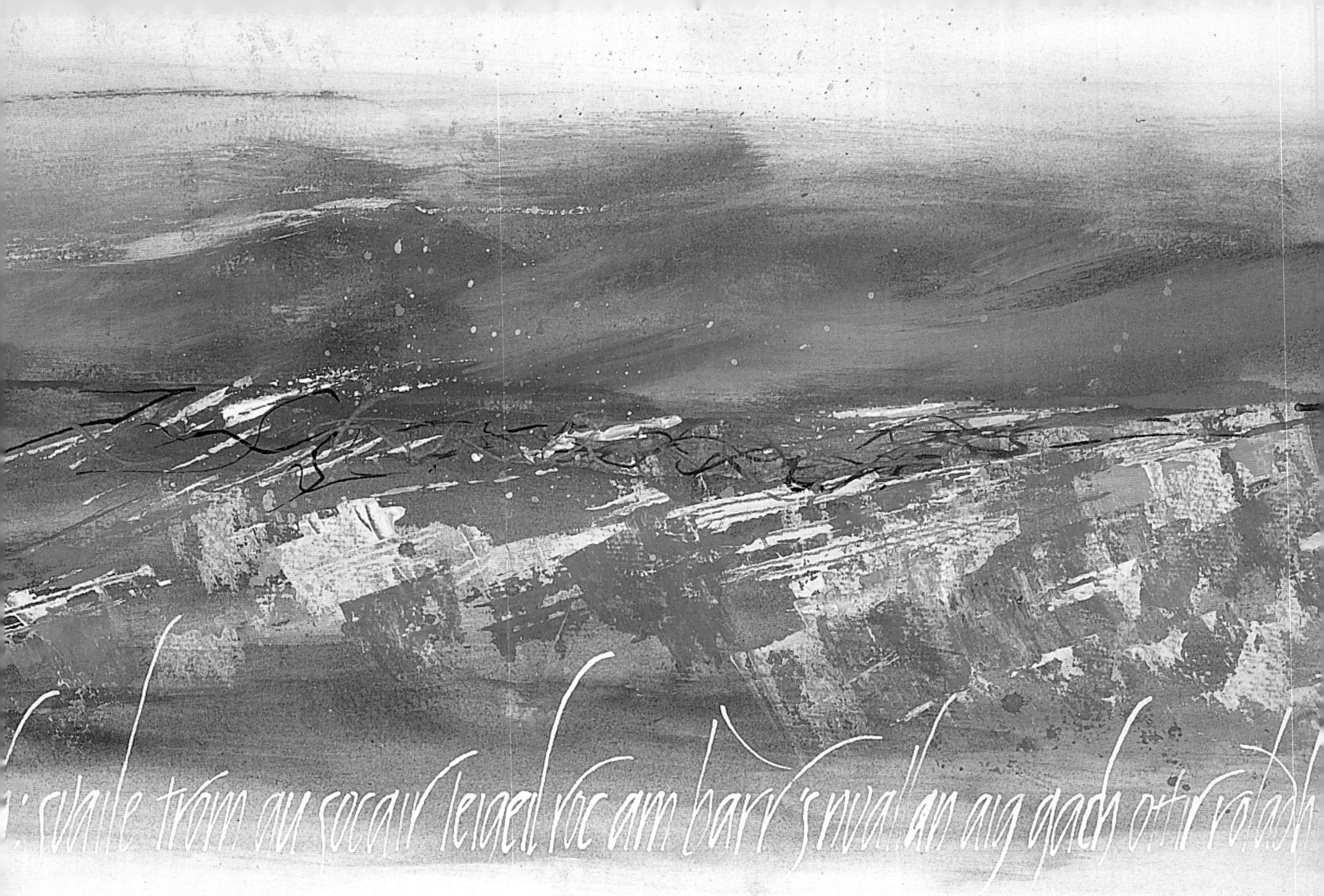

ALTERNATIVE SOURCES

It is not possible for even An Leabhar Mòr *to feature all of the longer, more epic poems. The following list gives alternative sources where the full text of all edited poems can be found in their entirety.*

1 **Amra Choluim Chille**
ANCIENT IRISH
The Bodleian Amra Choluimb Chille, Whitley Stokes, Revue Celtique 20 (1899) 31-55, 132-83, 248-89, 400-37; 21 (1900) 133-36 (corrections)
MODERN IRISH
Saoithiúlacht na Sean-Ghaeilge: Bunú an Traidisiúin, Stationery Office, Dublin 1978
ENGLISH TRANSLATION
New Oxford Book of Irish Verse (1986), Thomas Kinsella, Oxford

6 **Aithbe Damsa bés Mara:**
IRISH POEM AND ENGLISH TRANSLATION
Sages, Saints and Storytellers (1989), An Sagart, Maynooth, Co. Kildare, Ireland

14 **A' Chomhachag**
GAELIC POEM AND ENGLISH TRANSLATION
The Owl of Strone (1946), edited by John MacKechnie, Sgoil Eòlais na h-Alba

23 **Birlinn Chlann Raghnaill**
GAELIC
Sar Orain (1933), ed. A. MacLeod, An Comunn Gaidhealach, Glasgow
Alasdair Mac Mhaighstir Alasdair, Selected Poems (1996), edited by Derick S. Thomson, Scottish Academic Press for the Scottish Gaelic Texts Society.
ENGLISH TRANSLATION
Hugh MacDiarmid, Complete Poems (1978), Carcanet

27 **Oran do MhacLeòid Dhùn Bheagain**
GAELIC POEM AND ENGLISH TRANSLATION
Gair nan Clarsach, The Harp's Cry – An Anthology of Gaelic Poetry (1994), edited by Colm Ó Baoill, translated by Meg Bateman, Birlinn

28 **Crònan an Taibh**
GAELIC POEM AND ENGLISH TRANSLATION
Gaelic Songs of Mary Macleod (1982), edited by J. Carmichael Watson, Scottish Academic Press for the Scottish Gaelic Texts Society

38 **Cúirt an Mheán-Oíche**
IRISH
Cúirt an Mheán-Oíche (1982), edited by Liam P. Ó Murchu, Dublin
ENGLISH TRANSLATION
Kings, Lords & Commons (1st edition 1959), MacMillan

39 **Caoineadh Airt Uí Laoghaire**
IRISH POEM AND ENGLISH TRANSLATION
An Duanaire 1600-1900: Poems of the Dispossesed (1981), selected by Sean O'Tuama, translated by Thomas Kinsella, Dolmen Press

40 **Am Bàrd an Canada**
GAELIC POEM AND ENGLISH TRANSLATION
The Poetry of Scotland – Gaelic, Scots and English (1995), edited by Roderick Watson, Edinburgh University Press

41 **Turas Dhòmhnaill do Ghlaschu**
GAELIC
Clarsach an Doire – Gaelic Poems, Songs and Tales by Neil MacLeod (5th edition 1924), Alexander MacLaren & Sons, Glasgow
Translator – unknown

43 **Spiorad a' Charthannais**
GAELIC
Joni Buchanan, The Lewis Land Struggle – Na Gaisgich (1996), Acair, Isle of Lewis
ENGLISH
Translated by Prof. Donald E. Meek unpublished as yet. An earlier version available as above

45 **Fios thun a' Bhàird**
GAELIC POEM
Uilleam MacDhunlèibhe, Duain agus Oran, (1882), Archibald Sinclair, Glasgow
ENGLISH
The Celtic Garland of Gaelic Songs and Readings by 'Fionn' (3rd edition 1920), Alexander MacLaren & Sons, Glasgow

74 **An Loingeas**
IRISH EXCERPT
An Fear Dána, (1993), Alan Titley, An Clóchomhar, Dublin.
ENGLISH
Author's own – unpublished

80 **An Charraig**
IRISH EXCERPT
'An tAthair' in An Fear a Phléasc, (1997), Micheal Ó Conghaile, Cló Iar-Chonnachta. Indreabhán (lgh147-156)
ENGLISH TRANSLATION
Unpublished

94 **Coinneach Nèill**
GAELIC EXCERPT
Suathadh ri Iomadh Rubha (1973), Aonghas Caimbeul, Gairm Pubilications, Glasgow
ENGLISH TRANSLATION
Unpublished

97 **Cré na Cille**
IRISH EXTRACT AND ENGLISH TRANSLATION
Cre na Cille (1949) Máirtín Ó Cadhain, Sairseal agus Dill

98 **Bùth Dhòmhnaill 'IcLeòid**
GAELIC POEM AND ENGLISH TRANSLATION
An Tuil – Anthology of 20th-century Scottish Gaelic verse (1999) edited by Ronald Black, Polygon

The full text of edited poems can also be found on the Leabhar Mòr *website at* **www.leabharmor.net**

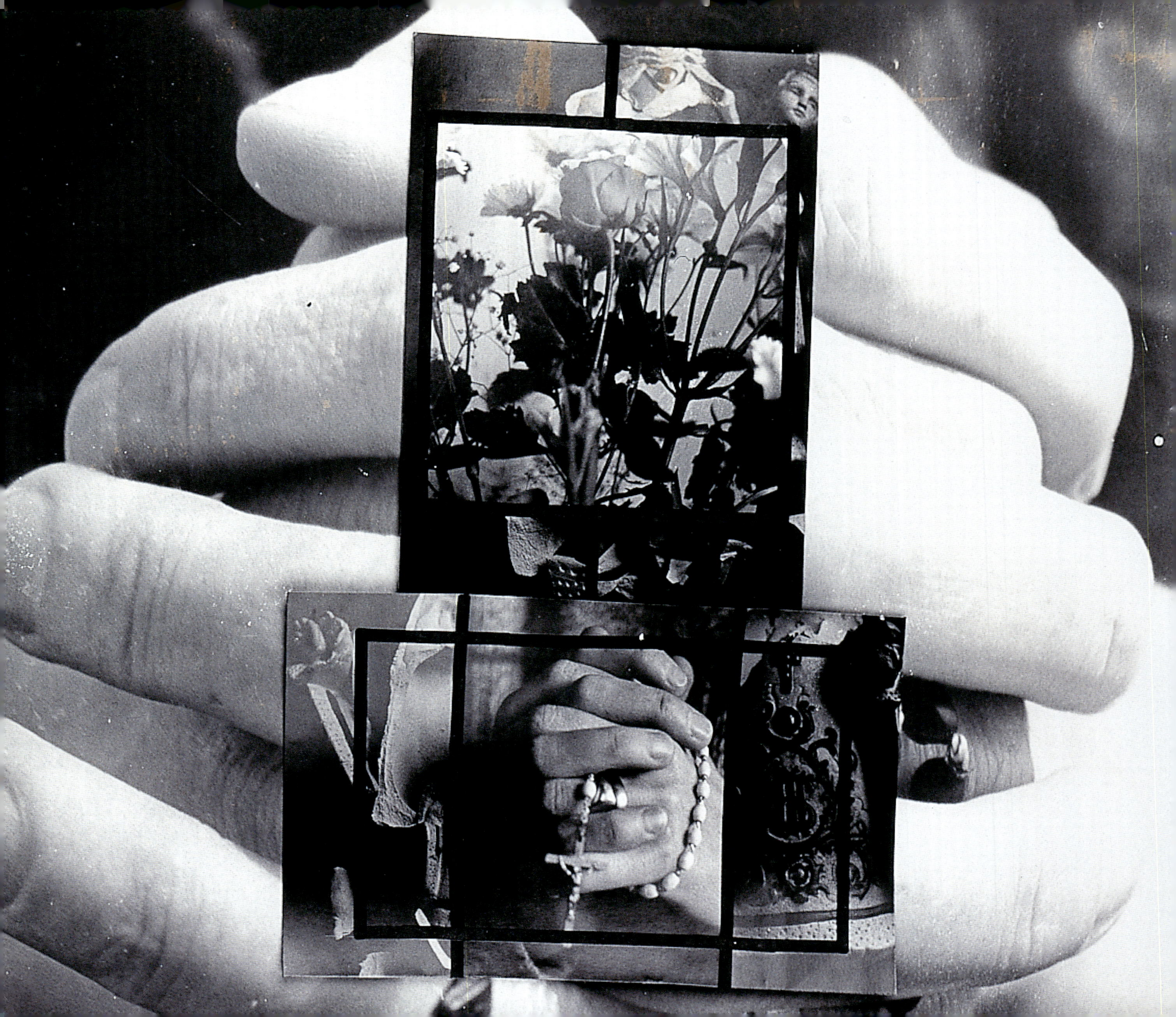

BIOGRAPHIES

1

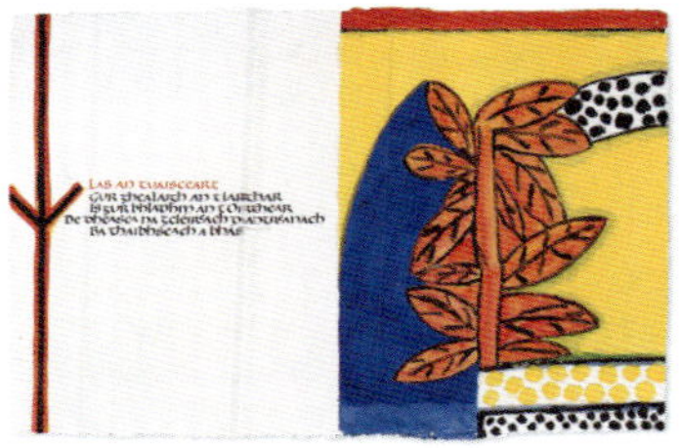

Dallán Forgaill

I mbarr a réime c.600. Glactar leis gurb é údar 'Amra Choluim Cille' é (curtha in eagar ag T. O'Beirne Crowe i 1871). Agus é ina Phríomhfhile creidtear gur chuir sé chun cinn cearta na bhfile chun flaithiúlacht a éileamh. Tá roinnt dréachta molta a cuirtear ina leith i gcló in *Irish Minstrelsy*, eag. Hardiman, 1831.

Dallán Forgaill

He flourished c.600, and is considered the likely author of 'Amra Choluim Chille', ed. T. O'Beirne Crowe, 1871. It is believed he formulated, as chief bard, the claim of bards to rights of hospitality. A number of eulogies attributed to him appear in *Irish Minstrelsy*, ed. Hardiman, 1831.

Uilleam Crozier *(Photo: Katherine Croun)*

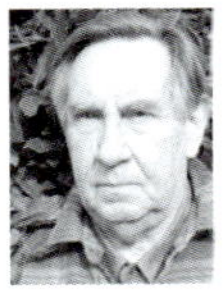

Rugadh Uilleam Crozier an Glaschu ann an 1930 agus cheumnaich e à Sgoil Ealain Ghlaschu far an robh e na oileanach o 1949 gu 1953. On uair sin tha e air a bhith a' fuireach, ag obair agus a' taisbeanadh ann an Lunnainn, am Baile Atha Cliath, am Paris agus am Malaga. O 1980 tha a thìde air a cur seachad an dà chuid eadar Corcaí an Iar, ann an Èirinn, agus Hampshire ann an Sasainn. Ann an 1991 chaidh a thaghadh mar bhall de Aosdana agus an 1994 choisinn e Bonn Òiran Oireachtais airson Peantadh. Tha filmichean aithriseach ann mu Chrozier a rinneadh le BBC Alba (1970) agus RTE (1993).

William Crozier

William Crozier was born in Glasgow in 1930 and is a graduate of Glasgow School of Art. Since then he has lived, worked and exhibited in London, Dublin, Paris and Malaga. In 1991 he was elected a member of *Aosdana* and in 1994 he was awarded the *Oireachtas* Gold Medal for Painting. There are documentary films on Crozier made by BBC Scotland (1970) and RTE (1993).

Dòmhnall Moireach

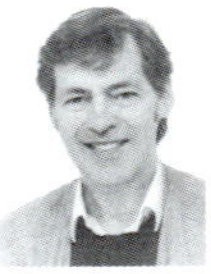

Rugadh Dòmhnall Moireach an Dùn Èideann ann an 1940. 'S i a' Ghàidhlig a' chainnt mhàthaireil. Ann an Colaiste na h-Ealain an Dùn Èideann, spèisealaich e ann an snas-sgrìobhaidh, a' ceumnachadh ann an 1962; agus às dèidh sin rinn e bliadhna de dh'obair iar-cheumnachais. Tha grunnan àiteachan-cleachdaidh agus ùghdarrasan cathaireach air cunnraidhean-obrach a thoirt dha. Bha e os cionn Roinn na h-Ealain ann an Colaiste Raibeairt Ghòrdain bho 1983-2000.

Donald Murray

Donald Murray, born in Edinburgh in 1940, is a native Gaelic speaker. At Edinburgh College of Art he specialised in calligraphy, graduating in 1962; a year of post-graduate work followed. Numerous institutions and civic authorities have commissioned his work. He was head of Art at Robert Gordon's College, Aberdeen from 1983 to 2000.

2

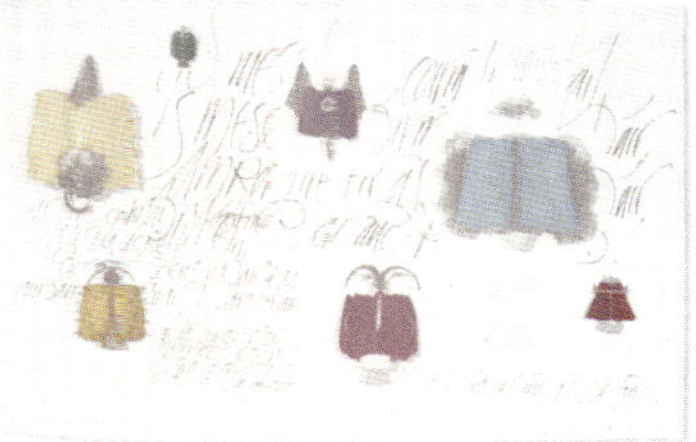

Gan Ainm

A Bé Find: dán i mbéal Midir, flaith de Thuatha Dé Danann, agus é ag mealladh Étaíne chun éaló leis chuig an sean-neamh phágánta; cuid, mar dhea, den tseanscéal *Tochmarc Étaíne* (féach Jeffrey Gantz, *Early Irish Myths and Sagas*, Penguin, 1981, lch.39). Ach creidtear nach mbaineann véarsaí 1 agus 7 ó thús leis an dán, a rinneadh c.900 mar mholadh ar neamh na Críostaíochta, agus ar cuireadh an dá rann sin mar bhreis leis.

Anon

'Lovely Lady': this poem purports to be addressed to the beautiful Étaín and to belong to a version of the tale *Tochmarc Étaíne* ('The Wooing of Étaín'), in the mythological cycle of early Gaelic tales (*Early Irish Myths and Sagas*, Gantz, 1981). A date around 900 has been suggested, but it is also thought that the first and last verses may be additions; that the original core of the poem was the five verses in the centre, a Christian picture of Heaven; and that the link to pagan mythology is therefore secondary.

Sonja Stringer *(Photo: Johann Delecour)*

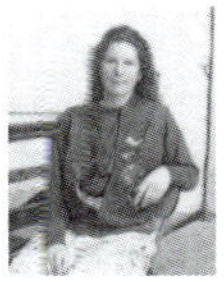

Chuir mi seachad a' chiad deich bliadhna dhem bheatha ann an Baile Atha Cliath agus tha dàimh nan daoine agus ceòlmhorachd a' chànain air fuireach còmhla rium. Tha 'suathadh' agus 'faicinn' nam puingean cudthromach dhòmhsa ann a bhith a' dèanamh ealain. Glè thric tha bàrdachd gam bhrosnachadh - tha bhith a' leughadh nam facal a' dùsgadh dath, faireachdainn agus cruth nam inntinn. Rinn mi Dealbhachadh Grinneis ann an Colaiste Rìoghail nan Ealan ann an Lunnainn agus Colaiste an Naoimh Mhàrtainn airson seachd bliadhna.

Sonja Stringer

The first ten years of my life were spent in Dublin, and the warmth of its people and the lyrical sense of language have stayed with me. Poems are often the inspiration, reading the text brings spontaneous colour texture and form. I studied Fine Art sculpture at London's Royal College of Art and Central St Martins.

Réiltín Murphy *(Photo: Ray Flynn)*

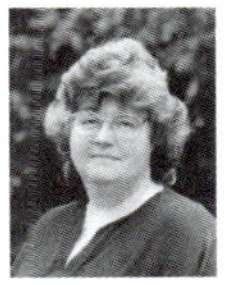

Is i mBaile Átha Cliath a rugadh Réiltín Murphy agus tá teastas sna Míndána aici ón gColáiste Náisiúnta Ealaíne is Deartha ansin. Tá céim aici i bPeannaireacht agus Leabharcheangal ón Roehampton Institute i Londain chomh maith le Máistreacht Ealaíne ón gColáiste Náisiúnta Ealaíne is Deartha. Chuir Réiltín taispeántais ar fáil go fairsing in Éirinn agus thar lear agus tá saothar léi le feiscint i Leabharlann Náisiúnta na nDearc-Ealaíon.

Réiltín Murphy

Born in Dublin, Réiltín Murphy has a diploma in Fine Art from the National College of Art and Design in Dublin, a BA in Calligraphy and Bookbinding from the Roehampton Institute in London and an MA from the National College of Art and Design in Dublin. Réiltín has exhibited widely in Ireland and abroad and is represented in the National Irish Visual Arts Library's collection.

3

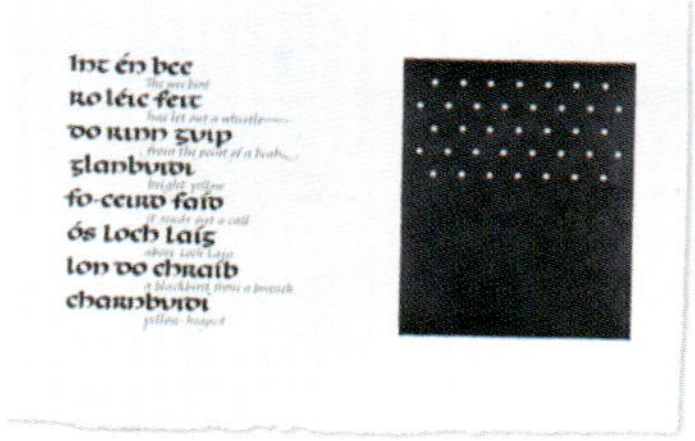

Gan Ainm

An Lon Dubh: níl sé seo againn ach ina shampla meadarachta i seantráchtas léannta, agus níl de fhianaise ann ach an t-ainm Loch Lao, a raibh mainistir Bheannchair, Co. an Dúin, lena thaobh. Síltear uaireanta, dá bharr sin, gurbh é manach sa mhainistir sin a chum an rann seo timpeall ar 1000 AD.

Anon

'Blackbird at Belfast Lough': this verse has been preserved only as an example in a medieval text on Gaelic metrics, so we have little to guide us as to its history or date, apart from the crucial mention of the placename Loch Laíg, Belfast Lough. This has led to speculation that it may be the work of a monk in the monastery of Bangor, Co. Down, anywhere within a century of 1000.

An t-Ollamh Jake Harvey DA; RSA *(Ph: Joe Rock)*

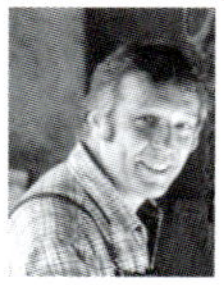

Ceannard Sgoil an Dealbhachaidh, Colaiste Ealain Dhùn Èideann. Tha a dhachaigh anns na Crìochan agus tha stiùidio aige an sin cuideachd. Obair-dealbhachaidh ann an cruinneachaidhean poblach agus prìobhaideach san Roinn Eòrpa, an Aimeireagaidh agus Iapan. Fhuair e barrantas airson *Cuimhneachan Ùisdein MhicDiarmaid* agus *Tools for the Shaman* (Taigh-Tasgaidh Hunterian). Tha e air a riochdachadh le Art First, Sràid Chorcaigh, Lunnainn.

Prof. Jake Harvey DA; RSA

Jake Harvey is head of the School of Sculpture at Edinburgh College of Art. He works from a studio in the Scottish Borders. Sculptures of his are in public and private collections in Europe, America and Japan. Commissions include the 'Hugh MacDiarmid Memorial' and 'Tools for the Shaman' (Hunterian Museum). The artist is represented by Art First, Cork St, London.

Dòmhnall Moireach/Donald Murray

4

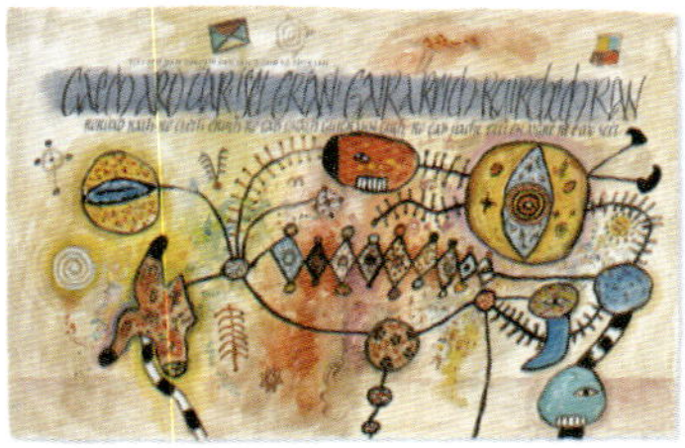

Gan Ainm

'Scél Lem Dúib': ceann eile nach bhfuil againn ach i dtráchtas léannta ón mheánaois, staidéar an iarraidh seo ar 'Amra Choluim Chille': chuir an scríobhaí an dán seo síos le ciall an fhocail *rian* (líne 8) a léiriú (uimh. 1 anseo, cuid 5, líne 14). Deir an scríobhaí céanna gurbh é Fionn mac Cumhaill a rinn an dán, rud nach bhfuil ina iontas.

Anon

'Brief Account': this brilliant little nature poem has been preserved only in a medieval scholarly text, where it is quoted as an example of the use of the word *rian* (line 8), 'the sea', in a commentary on the text of 'Amra Choluim Chille' (No. 1 here). There it is said that this poem is the work of Fionn mac Cumhaill, to whose followers nature poems are frequently attributed.

Alan Davie CBE; HRSA; RWA; DA (Edin); HONS D.LITT *(Photo: Iain Roy)*

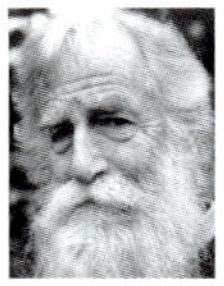

Rugadh e ann an 1920 ann an Inbhir Ghrainnse. Fhuair e fhoghlam ann an Colaiste Ealain Dhùn Èideann agus an dèidh sin rinn e Seirbheis Cogaidh anns a' Ghunnaireachd Rìoghail. Tha taisbeanaidhean air a bhith aige ann an Lunnainn, New York, Brazil, san Òlaind agus ann an Astràilia. Tha e cuideachd na neach-ciùil jazz agus na sheudair. Tha e air a bhith na òraidiche an dà chuid ann an Sgoil Ealain agus Ciùird agus an Colaiste Rìoghail nan Ealan ann an Lunnainn. Tha e a-nis a' fuireach is ag obair ann an Hertford agus sa Chòrn.

Alan Davie

Born in 1920 at Grangemouth, he studied at Edinburgh College of Art. He has exhibited extensively, notably in London, New York, Brazil, Holland and Australia. Davie is an accomplished jazz musician and jewellery maker. He has lectured at the Central School of Arts and Crafts and the Royal College of Art, both in London.

Louise Donaldson *(Photo: Tim Archbold)*

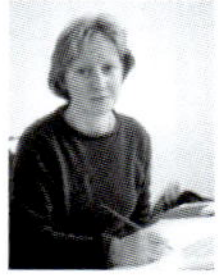

1980–81 Sgoil Ealain a' Chaisteil Nuaidh
1981–85 Colaiste Ealain Dhonnchaidh Iòrdanstain
BA (Àrd-ìre Le Urram) Prìomh Ìre Dealbhadh Grafaigeach
Iar cheumnachas an Dealbhadh Grafaigeach

Dh'obraich i an Dùn Èideann mar Dhealbhaiche Grafaigeach mus do ghluais i do Na Crìochan ann an 1989. Dh'obraich i an sin mar thaoitear foghlam inbhich ann an snas-sgrìobhadh.

1991–92 – Fhritheil i Institiut Roehampton, Lunnainn – Teisteanas le cliù ann an Snas-sgrìobhadh

1993 – Fhuair i tabhartas airgid airson Ciùird a chur air chois bhon SAC

Tha cuid dhe na barantais a bhuannaich i mar leanas:

Taighean-staile Ghleann Liobhait
Taigh-tasgaidh Rìoghail Alba
Comhairle Ealain na h-Alba
Riaghaltas na h-Alba

Louise Donaldson

Louise Donaldson studied at Newcastle School of Art and Duncan of Jordanstone College of Art. She worked in Edinburgh as a graphic designer before moving to the Borders in 1989. Donaldson worked in Adult Education as Tutor of Calligraphy. She got a Diploma in Calligraphy from Roehampton Institute, London. Her work includes commissions from Glenlivet Distilleries, Royal Scottish Museum, the Scottish Arts Council and the Scottish Executive.

5

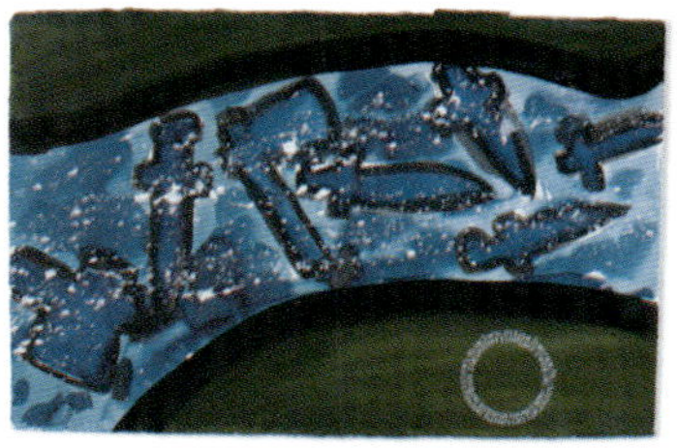

Gan Ainm

'Is Acher in Gáith In-Nocht': scoláire Gaelach, is cosúil, ag déanamh staidéir ar leabhar gramadaí Laidne uair éigin san naoú céad. D'éirigh sé bréan den obair agus de scríobh gluaiseanna seanGhaeilge san leabhar, d'amharc sé amach an fhuinneog agus scríobh an rann seo in imeall leathanaigh. Tugadh an lámhscríbhinn níos maille anonn chun na hEilbhéise agus tá sí le léamh fós i St Gallen.

Anon
'Since Tonight The Wind is High': this famous verse is written in the margin of a copy of a Latin grammar on which numerous Gaelic glosses were written in the ninth century. The manuscript is in St Gallen in Switzerland, but was probably written in Ireland, where the scribe takes a break from his study to tell us about the weather and the threat of Norse marauders.

Seòras Wyllie ARSA *(Photo: George Oliver)*

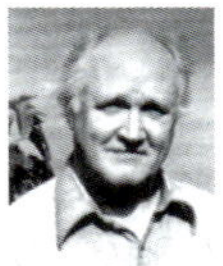

Rugadh Seòras Wyllie an 1921. Companach Stèidheachas Hand Hollow, New York. Tha ùidh aige an obair-ealain ath-thàrmaichte, coileanadh agus sgrìobhadh, agus thaisbean e am Breatainn, mòr-thìr na Roinn Eòrpa, an Aimeireagaidh agus anns na h-Innseachan. Air leth aithnichte airson *The Straw Locomotive, The Paper Boat, A Day Down a Goldmine, Spires* agus *Vent 2000*.

George Wyllie
Born in 1921, he has an honorary DLitt from Strathclyde University, and is a fellow of Hand Hollow Foundation, New York. Wylie is interested in regenerative artwork, performance and writing and has exhibited in the UK, mainland Europe, the USA and India. He is best known for *The Straw Locomotive, The Paper Boat, A Day Down a Goldmine, Spires* and now *Vent 2000*.

Tim O'Neill *(Photo: J Cox fsc)*

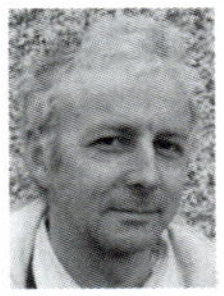

Tá Tim O'Neill ar dhuine des na peannairí is mó cáil in Éirinn agus múineann sé scríobh sa stíl Cheilteach. Tá léachtaí tugtha aige san Eoraip agus ins na Stáit Aontaithe ar lámhscríbhinní meánaoiseacha. Tá cur síos ar scríobhaithe meánaoiseacha foilsithe aige, chomh maith le heolaí ar script agus dearadh Ceilteach. I 1997 d'iarr British Airways air dearadh a chruthú sa stíl Cheilteach d'eití deiridh a n-aerloingis.

Tim O'Neill
Tim O'Neill is one of Ireland's best known calligraphers and is a teacher of Celtic style script. As an historian he has lectured on medieval manuscripts in Europe and the USA. He has published a study of medieval scribes and a guide to Celtic script and design. In 1997 British Airways commissioned him to design a Celtic-style tailfin for their aircraft.

6

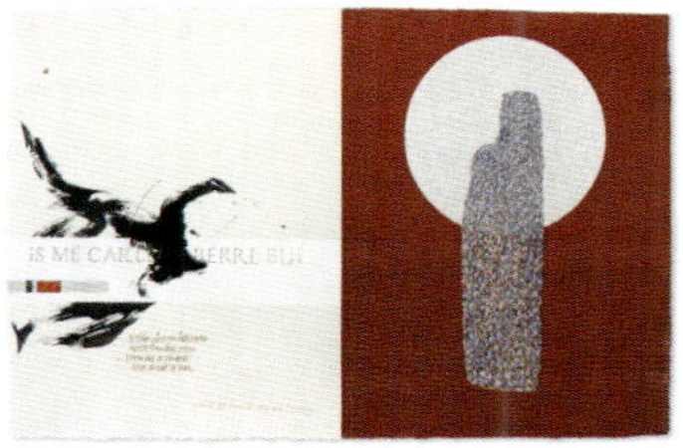

Gan Ainm
'Aithbe Damsa Bés Mara': ní aontaíonn na scoláirí i gcónaí fá dtaobh de dháta ná de théama an dáin seo. Baineann sé le Cailleach Bhéara, atá beo go fóill sa bhéaloideas, agus síltear uaireanta go mbaineann an dán le miotas na págántachta. Ach tá an bharúil eile ann, ar ndóigh, gur dán é a bhaineanns go domhain leis an Chríostaíocht, le cloí na ndraoithe agus na págántachta b'fhéidir, nó le fadhbanna na seanaoise. I gCo. Chorcaí atá Béara, ach ní fianaise ar bith é sin gur sa chontae sin a cumadh an dán; i dtimpeall 900, síltear, a rinneadh é.

Anon
'The Lament of the Old Woman of Beare': this poem has fascinated scholars for over a century. Some prefer to see it as an essentially pagan work, and its subject remains alive today in Gaelic oral tradition as *Cailleach Bhéara*; others see it as essentially a Christian composition. The most recent suggested date is c.900, and the placename links the subject, if not the poem, with Béara in the west of Co. Cork.

Bernadette Cotter *(Photo: Robert Rasmussen)*

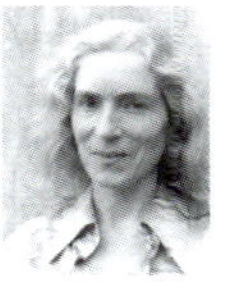

I mBeál Átha an Ghaorthaidh i gCo. Chorcaí a rugadh Bernadette Cotter i 1958 agus is ann a d'fhill sí chun cónaithe. Oileadh ina múinteoir í agus ansin chuaigh sí le péintéireacht sa Choláiste Náisiúnta Ealaíne is Deartha. Le tacaíocht ó scoláireacht Fulbright ghnóthaigh sí Máistreacht sa Dealbhóireacht ag an San Francisco Art Institute (1989). Ina saothar baineann Cotter leas as ealaín suiteála, léiriú agus, le deireanas, as meán na fístéipe. Tá taispeántais curtha ar siúl aici sna Stáit Aontaithe, i Hawaii, i Korea agus in Éirinn.

Bernadette Cotter
Bernadette Cotter was born in Ballingeary in County Cork in 1958. Trained as a teacher, she studied painting at the National College of Art and Design and completed a Masters in sculpture at the San Francisco Art Institute (1989), supported with a Fulbright scholarship. Cotter's art practice includes installation and performance, and, recently, the medium of video. She has exhibited in the USA, Hawaii, Korea and Ireland.

David McGrail

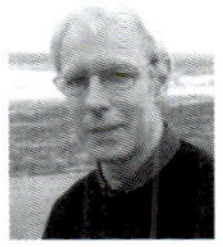

Maisitheoir agus dearthóir grafach gairmiúil is ea David McGrail. Tá spéis aige i bpeannaireacht agus baineann se úsáid as teicníochtaí traidisiúnta, ealaín chomhshaolach agus fealsúnacht an Oirthir agus an Iarthair. Cuireann sé ceardlanna cruthaitheacha sa bpeannaireacht agus sa dearadh ar siúl. Foilsíodh a shaothar in irisí agus cuireadh ar taispeáint é sna Stáit Aontaithe, i Sasana, sa Ghearmáin agus san Astráil. Tá sé le fáil fós i mbailiúcháin in Éirinn, i Sasana, sna Stáit Aontaithe agus i Hong Kong.

David McGrail
David McGrail is a professional graphic designer and illustrator. He has an interest in calligraphy and draws on traditional techniques, contemporary art, and philosophy from both East and West. His work has been published in journals and exhibited in the USA, England, Germany and Australia and is in collections in Ireland, England, the USA and Hong Kong.

7

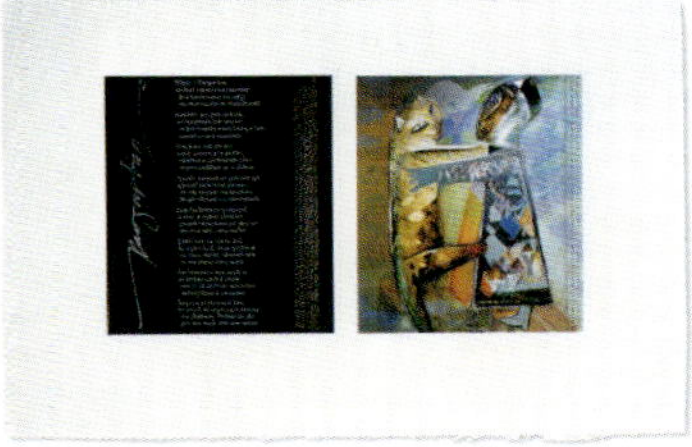

Gan Ainm
'Pangur Bán': scoláire eile ag scríobhadh filíochta ar imeall lámhscríbhinne, agus an leabhar féin lán den léann, den litríocht agus den réalteolaíocht. Tá an lámhscríbhinn seo i mainistir Naomh Póil, Unterdrauberg, Cairint na hOstaire, agus níl foinse eile againn don dán. Ainm Breatnaise atá ar an chat (ciallaíonn *Pangur* 'úcaire'), agus is dócha gur goirid i ndiaidh 800 a cumadh an dán. Tá daoine ann a ghlacann leis gur thaistil an scoláire Gaelach seo tríd an Bhreatain Bheag, go bhfuair sé an cat ansin agus go dtug leis é chun na Cairinte; ach ní mór a fhianaise sin.

Anon
'The Scholar and His Cat': as in the case of No. 5, this poem appears only in the margin of a scholarly manuscript, this time in the monastery of St Paul in Unterdrauberg, Carinthia, in Austria. The main text consists of learned discussion of literature, grammar and astronomy. A dating of the poem to the early ninth century appears to be widely accepted.

Sim Friseal *(Photo: Isabel McLeish)*
Rugadh e an 1950 agus cheumnaich e à Sgoil Ealain Ghray an Obar Dheathain an 1973. Ag

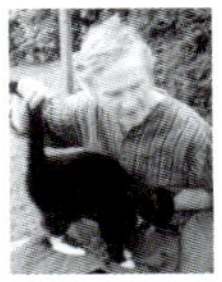

obair na neach-ealain, bha mòran thaisbeanaidhean aige, (Sarajevo, Paris, Lunnainn, Chicago) ann am peantadh agus clò-bhualadh, agus chithear an obair aige ann an gailearaidhean ealain Hull agus Obar Dheathain, am BBC agus Life Assurance. Tha e a-nis a' dealbhadh leabhraichean dha foillsichearan agus a' dèanamh dhealbh airson CD ROM agus làraich-lìn.

Simon Fraser
Born in 1950, Simon Fraser graduated from Grays, Aberdeen. Working as an artist, he has exhibited widely (Sarajevo, Paris, London, Chicago) in painting and printmaking. Collections of his work are in the art galleries of Hull and Aberdeen, the BBC and Life Assurance. He now produces books for publishers and designs for CD ROM and web.

Frances Breen *(Photo: Craig Mackay)*

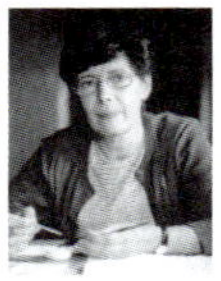

Is i Loch Garman a rugadh Frances Breen agus oibríonn sí in Éirinn agus san Ostair. Bhain sí céim amach mar dhearthóir grafach ón gColáiste Náisiúnta Ealaíne is Deartha. Ansin rinne sí sainstaidéar ar pheannaireacht, ag déanamh foghlaim ar litreoireacht agus ar leabharcheangal san Ostair agus sa Ghearmáin. Ta sí fostaithe mar oide cuartaíochta i Roinn na Dearc-Chumarsáide sa Choláiste Náisiúnta Ealaíne is Deartha, Baile Átha Cliath.

Frances Breen
Frances Breen was born in Wexford and lives and works in Austria and Ireland. She graduated in Graphic Design from the National College of Art and Design and then specialised in calligraphy, studying lettering and bookbinding in Austria and Germany. She is a guest tutor in the Department of Visual Communications at the National College of Art and Design in Dublin.

8

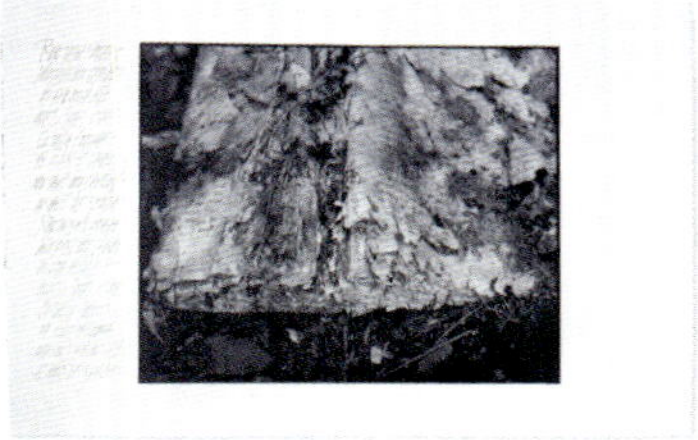

Gan Ainm
'Rop Tú Mo Baile': urnaí i bhfoirm dáin, le file gan ainm ag scríobhadh, is dócha, beagán i ndiaidh 1000. Tá dhá chóip di againn, i lamhscríbhinní i mBaile Átha Cliath.

Anon
'Fill My Horizon': this anonymous poem, in effect a prayer, probably dates from around 1000 or a little later. It exists in two manuscript copies, both preserved in Dublin, and has been used as the basis for the English-language hymn 'Be Thou My Vision', sung to the tune *Slane*.

Olwen Shone *(Photo: Norman MacLeod)*

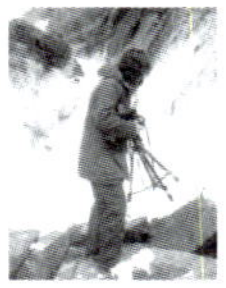

An dèidh ceumnachadh à Sgoil Ealain Ghlaschu, ghluais i a dh'Uibhist a Tuath sna h-Eileanan Siar far a bheil i a-nis a' fuireach agus ag obair na neach-ealain. Bidh i a' togail dhealbh le camara, a tha nam freagairt bàrdail dha na cumaidhean agus dha na pàtrain phearsanta a gheibhear anns an tìr seo. 'S e gu bheil an tìr seo cho fiadhaich agus air leth bho àitean eile, am prìomh nì a th' air cùl nan dealbh.

Olwen Shone
After graduating from Glasgow School of Art, she moved to the island of North Uist in the Western Isles. She makes pictures, through the medium of photography, which are a poetic response to the intimate forms and patterns to be found in this rural landscape. The wilderness and isolation within this landscape form the main source of inspiration for the photographs.

Frances Breen

9

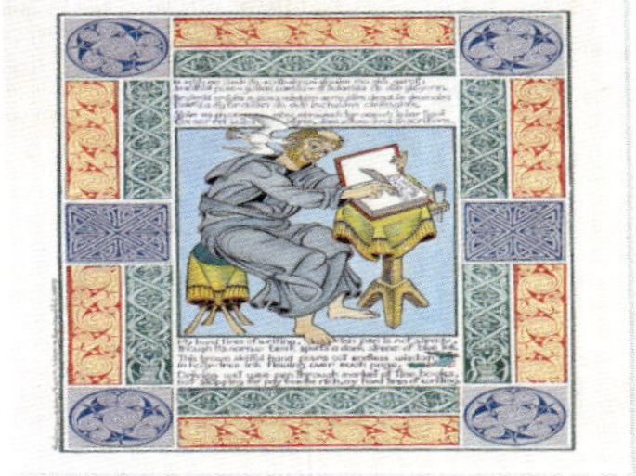

Gan Ainm
'Is Scíth Mo Chrob': de réir an aon fhoinse amháin atá againn don cheann seo, lámhscríbhinn (in Oxford anois) atá ina chnuasach mór d'ábhar a bhaineas le Colum Cille (c.521–597), b'é an naomh sin a chum é. Ach is léir ó theanga an dáin féin gur i dtrátha 1100 a rinneadh é.

Anon
'My Hand Is Weary With Writing': preserved only in a single manuscript, now in Oxford, this poem is there ascribed to Colum Cille (d.597), as is most of the content of the manuscript. But the form of its language shows clearly that this poem was composed round about 1100.

Alasdair Gray *(Photo: Alan Wylie)*

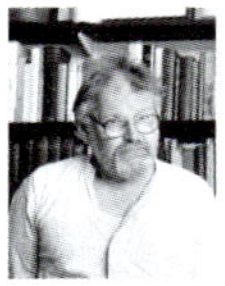

Rugadh e an Glaschu ann an 1934. Cheumnaich e à Sgoil Ealain Ghlaschu agus bha e a' teagaisg ealain pàirt-ùine gu 1962. Bha e a' peantadh sheallaidhean ann an taighean-cluiche Ghlaschu airson ùine ghoirid, agus tha grunnan thaisbeanaidhean air a bhith aige. Tha e air dealbhan-cluiche a sgrìobhadh airson telebhisean, rèidio agus taighean-cluiche. Chaidh a' chiad nobhail aige, *Lanark*, fhoillseachadh ann an 1981. 'S e sòisealach a th' ann a tha a' toirt taice do neo-eisimeileachd Alba agus an CND.

Alasdair Gray
Alasdair Gray was born in Glasgow in 1934. He graduated in Mural Painting from the City Art School and was a part-time art teacher till 1962. He had several exhibitions, and wrote plays for TV, radio and theatre. His first novel, *Lanark*, appeared in 1981.

10

Muireadhach Albanach
Ba de chlann Uí Dhálaigh é. Rugadh i gCo. na Mí é, de réir dealraimh. I mbarr a réime c.1220. Cumadh 'Éistidh riomsa a Mhuire mhór' agus é ar deoraíocht in Albain, áit ar chuir sé faoi ar deireadh. Tá 'M'anam do Sgar Riomsa A-raoir', marbhna ar a bhean, chomh maith le dánta cumasacha eile i gcló in *Irish Bardic Poetry* (eag. Osborn Bergin, 1970).

Muireadhach Albanach
Member of the Ó Dálaigh clan, he was probably born in Co. Meath, fl.1220. 'Éistidh riomsa a Mhuire mhór' was composed in exile in Scotland, his eventual adopted home. 'M'anam do Sgar Riomsa A-raoir', an elegy for his wife, and other powerful poems, appear in Bergin's *Irish Bardic Poetry* (1970).

Deirdre O'Mahony *(Photo: Stephen Douglas)*
I Luimneach is ea rugadh Deirdre O'Mahony

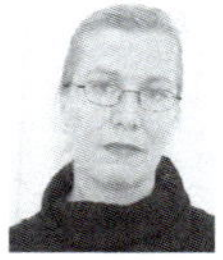

agus oileadh i gColáiste Réigiúnda na Gaillimhe agus ag St Martin's School of Art i Londain í. Bhí taispeántais aonair aici ins an Guinness Hopstore, in Ionad Ealaíne na Gaillimhe, Gailearaí Lukacs ag Ollscoil Fairfield sna Stáit Aontaithe, Gailearaí Context agus Gailearaí Ealaíne Chathair Luimní. Is léachtóir péintéireachta ag Institiúid Teicneolaíochta Ghaillimh-Mhaigh Eo í.

Deirdre O'Mahony

Deirdre O'Mahony was born in Limerick and studied at the Regional Technical College in Galway and St Martin's School of Art in London. She has had solo exhibitions in the Guinness Hopstore, Galway Arts Centre, the Lukacs Gallery at Fairfield University in the USA, Context Gallery and Limerick City Gallery of Art. She is a painting lecturer at the Galway-Mayo Institute of Technology.

Réiltín Murphy

11

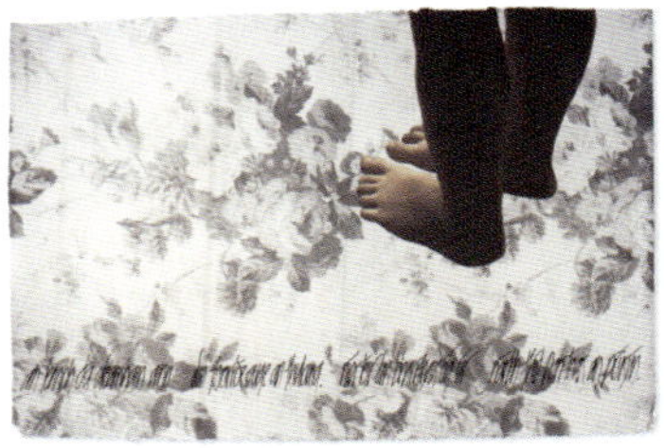

Gofraidh Fionn Ó Dálaigh

D'éag sé i 1387. Rugadh i gCo. Chorcaí de réir dealraimh. D'fhoghlaim a cheird i scoil filíochta de shliocht Mhic Craith. Meas air mar Phríomhfhile a linne agus mar shaineolaí ar chúrsaí gramadaí. File proifisiúnta ab ea é, agus adhmholtóir éifeachtach a raibh tuiscint mhaith aige ar pholaitíocht na tíre. Tá a chuid saothair foilsithe in *Díoghluim Dána*, eag. Lambert McKenna (1938).

Gofraidh Fionn Ó Dálaigh

Ó Dálaigh died in 1387. His probable birthplace was Co. Cork, and he was educated in a bardic school of the Mac Craith's. Considered chief poet of his time, he was a widely-cited grammatical authority and an astute political observer as well as a powerful eulogist. His work is collected in *Díoghluim Dána*, ed. Lambert McKenna (1938).

Moira Scott *(Photo: William W. Payne)*

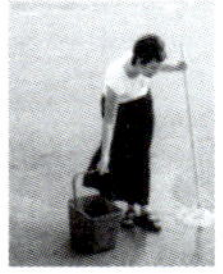

Rugadh i anns Na h-Innseachan a Deas, ann an 1959 agus bha i na h-oileanach an Colaiste Ealain Ghlaschu, 1976-81. An-diugh tha i ag obair an Obar Bhrothaig, Alba.

Taisbeanaidhean ùra thaghte:

Psychic Geography, VRC, Ionad Ealain Baile Dhùn Dè
Interior Spaces Still Lives, Ionad Ealain Siorrachd MhicIlleathain, Illinois, Aimeireagaidh
Ten Years On, Taisbeanadh Sgoilearachd Ealain Salvesen
Northern Ground, An Lanntair, Eilean Leòdhais
Works After a Trip to Alaska, Acadamh Rìoghail Alba.

Moira Scott

Moira Scott was born in South India in 1959 and studied at Glasgow School of Art. Scott currently works in Arbroath, Scotland. Selected recent exhibitions include: 'Psychic Geography', VRC, Dundee City Art Centre; 'Interior Spaces Still Lives', McLean County Arts Centre, Illinois, USA; 'Ten Years On', the Salvesen Art Scholarship Exhibition; 'Northern Ground', An Lanntair, Isle of Lewis; 'Works After a Trip to Alaska', Royal Scottish Academy.

Réiltín Murphy

12 Iseabail Ní Mheic Cailéin

Rinn Iseabail 'ní mheic Cailéin' (= nic Cailein) dà dhàn gaoil a tha ann an *Leabhar Deadhain*

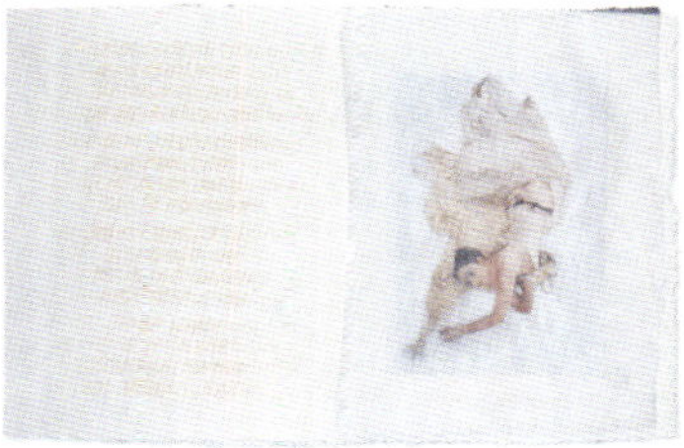

Liosa Mòir (1512-42). Tha dàn eile san leabhar, 'Èistibh a luchd an tighe-se', air a chur às leth 'Contissa Ergadien Issobell'. Faodaidh gur i a' Chontissa an aon tè ri 'ní mheic Cailéin'. Mura b' e màthair *agus* nighean iad, ma-thà, 's e as coltaiche gun robh Iseabail na nighinn aig Cailean air choreigin (Caimbeulach eile gun teagamh) 's gun do phòs i an Cailean Caimbeul a chaidh a dhèanamh na chiad 'Iarla Earra-Ghaidheal' an 1457

Iseabail Ní Mheic Cailéin

Iseabal 'Ní Mheic Cailéin' (= nic Cailein) composed two love poems which survive in 'The Book of the Dean of Lismore' (1512-42). Another poem in the book, 'Èistibh a luchd an tighe-se', is ascribed to 'Contissa Ergadien Issobell'. The Contissa may be the same lady as 'Ní Mhic Cailéin'. May also be mother and daughter, or possibly Isobel was the daughter of a man named Colin (another Campbell no doubt) and married the Colin Campbell who was made first Earl of Argyll in 1457.

Catherine Harper *(Photo: Amanda Stonham)*

Tá taispeántais curtha ar fáil go fairsing ag Catherine Harper in Éirinn, sa Ríocht Aontaithe agus sa tSeapáin, sa Rúis agus sna Stáit Aontaithe *inter alia*. Chomh maith le céim dochtúra ó Ollscoil Uladh tá Máistreacht agus Sparántacht Thaighde gnothaithe aici ó Goldsmiths College. Scrúdaíonn Harper ceisteanna gnéis, inscne, éadaigh agus léirithe tré úsáid a bhaint as íomhanna, téacs agus léiriú.

Catherine Harper

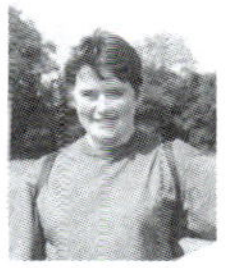

Catherine Harper has exhibited widely in Ireland, the UK and internationally, notably in Japan, Russia and the USA. Educated to PhD level at the University of Ulster, she has an MA and Doctoral research bursary from Goldsmiths College. Harper examines issues about sex and gender, clothing and performance in her visual, textual and performance practice.

Réiltín Murphy

13

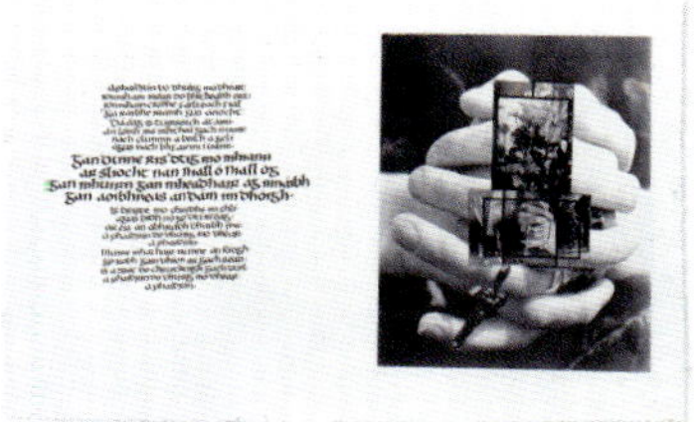

Aithbhreac inghean Coirceadail

Bha Aithbhreac inghean Coirceadail (Oighrig nighean Thorcaill) beò mun aon àm ri Iseabail (no an dà Iseabail). Ge b' e cò i, bha i pòsta aig Niall mac Thorcaill, a bha na cheann-cinnidh air Clann Nèill Ghiogha agus na chonastabal air Dùn Shuibhne ann an Cnapadal. Tha i ag innse dhuinn gun do dh'eug Niall na dhuine òg; bha seo eadar 1455, nuair a tha e air ainmeachadh mar chonastabal an Dùin, agus 1478, nuair a tha a mhac (am mac?) Maol Chaluim air ainmeachadh na cheann-cinnidh.

Aithbhreac inghean Coirceadail

Aithbhreac inghean Coirceadail (Africa daughter of Torquil) lived around the same time as Isobel (No. 12). She was married to Neil son of Torquil, who was chief of the MacNeils of Gigha and constable of Castle Sween in Knapdale. Neil died young; between 1455, when he is described as constable of the castle, and 1478, when his son (their son?) Malcolm is described as chief.

Kathleen O'Donnell

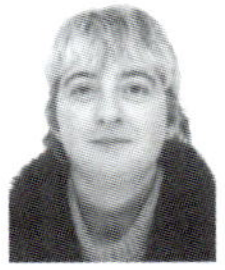

Is i Londain a rugadh Kathleen O'Donnell i 1968. Oileadh i gColáiste Ealaíne agus Deartha Crawford í. Bhain céim amach sna Míndána (Dealbhóireacht) ó Scoil Ealaíne Luimní agus i 1993 bhronn an University of Central England Máistreacht Ealaíne uirthi. Sa bhliain chéanna ghnóthaigh sí Duais Emma Jesse Phipps. Chuir Kathleen saothar ar taispeáint i 1987 don chéad uair. Taispeántais uaithi ó shin in Éirinn, i Sasana agus san Fhrainc.

Kathleen O'Donnell

Kathleen O'Donnell was born in London in 1968. Educated at Crawford College of Art, she graduated from Limerick School of Art in Fine Art (sculpture) and completed an MA from the University of Central England. She received the Emma Jesse Phipps Award in 1993, and has exhibited in Ireland, England and France.

Tim O'Neill

14

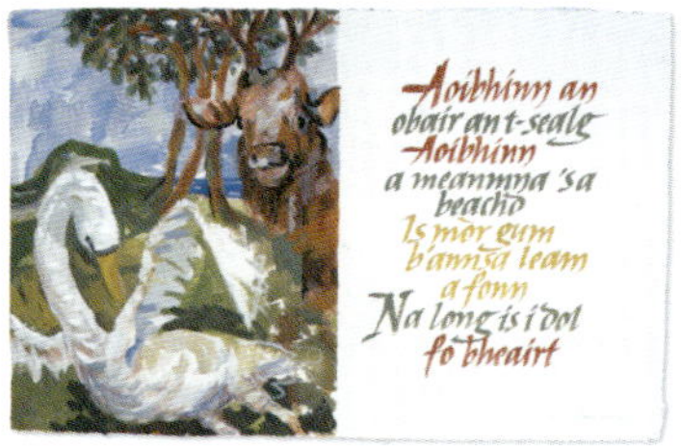

Dòmhnall Mac Fhionnlaigh nan Dàn

Theirear gur ann do Dhòmhnallaich Ghlinne Comhainn a bhuineadh Dòmhnall mac Fhionnlaigh nan Dàn (c.1540-c.1610), ach gun deach e mach air Mac 'ic Iain, agus ann an 'Òran na Comhachaig' - dàn fada no sreath dhàintean aig a bheil mòran ri ràdh rinn an-diugh mun àrainneachd, an aon bhàrdachd a dh'fhàg e – tha e glè mheasail air Clann Raghnaill na Ceapaich. Bha e na shealgair ainmeil a chaidh a dh'fhuireach fada bho dhaoine aig Creag Ghuanach faisg air ceann shuas Loch Trèig, agus tha mòran sgeulachdan ann mu dheidhinn.

Dòmhnall Mac Fhionnlaigh nan Dàn

Dòmhnall Mac Fhionnlaigh nan Dàn (Donald son of Finlay of the Poems, c.1540-c.1610) is said to have been a Glencoe MacDonald who fell out with his chief, and in 'The Owl of Strone' – a long poem or series of poems and the only verse he left - he shows great respect for the Keppoch MacDonalds. He was a celebrated hunter who went to live in isolation at Loch Treig, and there are many stories about him.

Diarmuid Delargy *(Photo: Catriona McLister)*

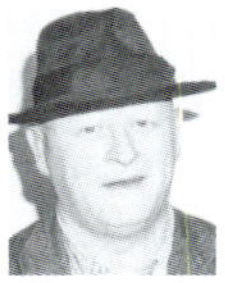

I mBéal Feirste a rugadh Diarmuid Delargy i 1958 agus bhain sé céim amach ins na Míndána in Ollscoil Uladh agus Máistreacht Ealaíne ón Slade School of Art. Le déanaí bhí Delargy ag obair ar sraith priontaí bunaithe ar shaothar Samuel Beckett agus ag obair i gcomhar le Paul Muldoon, file. Ball d'Aosdána é agus bhuaigh sé an Bonn Óir ag taispeántas an European Large Format Print i mBaile Átha Cliath i 1991.

Diarmuid Delargy

Diarmuid Delargy was born in Belfast in 1958 and graduated in Fine Art from the University of Ulster and with an MA from the Slade School of Art. Recently, Delargy has worked on a series of prints inspired by Samuel Beckett and also collaborated with poet Paul Muldoon. A member of Aosdána, he won the gold medal at the European Large Format Print Exhibition, Dublin (1991).

Dòmhnall Moireach/Donald Murray

15

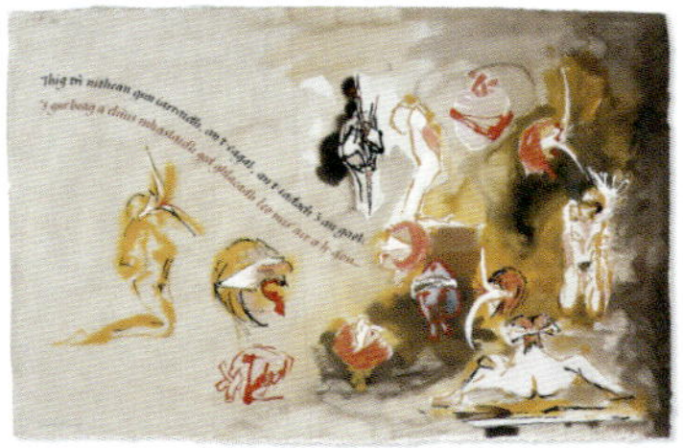

Nighean Fhir na Rèilig

Tha Iain MacCoinnich ag innse dhuinn ann an *Sàr Obair* (1841) gur i nighean Fhir na Rèilig a rinn 'Thig Trì Nithean gun Iarraidh'. Bha dithis nighean aig Alasdair Friseal (Fear na Rèilig 's Baran Mhon Itheig, 1610-94) 's a bhean Catrìona (nighean MhicCoinnich Shìldeig). B' i an tè a b' òige dhiubh Mairead, a dh'eug gun phòsadh am Mon Itheig, 1701. Rugadh an tè bu shine ro 1660 agus phòs i Sìm Friseal na Bruaiche ro 1678. Tha fios againn gun robh tè Barabal, bantrach na Bruaiche, na bana-bhàird mu 1720-40. 'S dòcha mar sin gur i a' Bharabal Fhriseal seo a rinn 'Thig Trì Nithean gun Iarraidh'.

Daughter of the Tacksman of Reelig

John Mackenzie tells us in *Sàr Obair* (1841) that the author of 'Thig Trì Nithean gun Iarraidh' was the daughter of the Tacksman of Reelig. Alexander Fraser (Tacksman of Reelig and Baron of Moniack, 1610-94) and his wife Katherine (daughter of MacKenzie of Shieldaig) had two daughters. The younger of them was Margaret, who died unmarried in Moniack in 1701. The elder had been born by 1660 and had married Simon Fraser of Bruiach by 1678. We know that a certain Barbara, Bruiach's widow, was a poet around 1720-40. Perhaps then it was this Barbara Fraser who made 'Thig Trì Nithean gun Iarraidh'?

Alice McCartney *(Photo: Sinead Devine)*

I nDoire Choilm Chille a rugadh Alice McCartney agus tá sí anois lonnaithe i mBeál Feirste. Ealaíontóir ilmhúinte í a chruthaíonn ealaín suiteála ag baint úsaid as dealbhóireacht, fuaim agus grianghrafadóireacht. Chaith sí blianta ag plé le healaín shóisialta – rud a d'fhág a rian ar a saothar. Is Oifigeach Oideachais í ag Gailearaí Ormeau Baths.

Alice McCartney

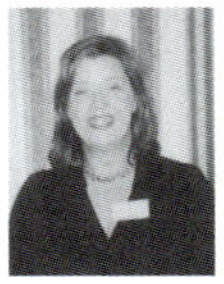

Artist Alice McCartney was born in Derry and currently lives and works in Belfast. This multi-disciplinary artist creates installations using sculpture, sound and photography. Much of her work is informed by the years she spent working in the area of socially engaged art. She is Education Officer at the Ormeau Baths Gallery.

Dòmhnall Moireach/Donald Murray

16

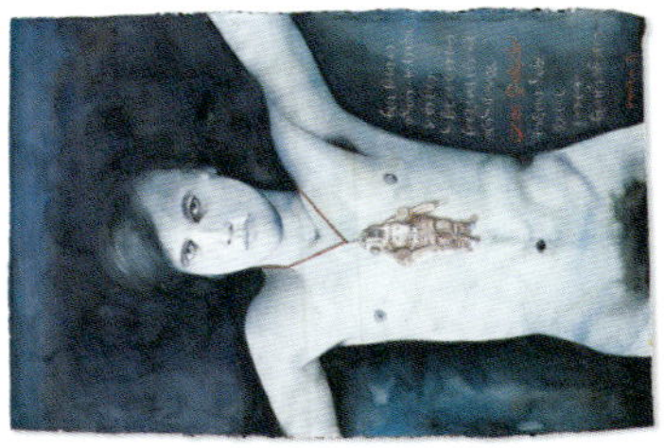

Eochaidh Ó hEoghasa

Rugadh c.1560 é, d'éag 1612. Bhí sé fostaithe mar Ollamh ag Clann Mhic Uidhir i bhFear Manach. Tá os cionn 50 dán leis a mhaireann agus is dánta molta do Chlann Mhic Uidhir timpeall a leath acu sin. Bhí an seanchóras Gaelach i mbarr a réime lena linn ach chonaic sé go raibh sé ag dul i léig. Féach James Carney, *The Irish Bardic Poet* (1967).

Eochaidh O'Hussey

Correctly written Eochaidh Ó hEódhasa, born c.1560, died 1612. Of more than fifty surviving poems, about half are to the Maguires of

Fermanagh, whose *ollamh* (chief poet) he was. Celebrant of the Gaelic order at its height, he also foresaw its fall. See James Carney, *The Irish Bardic Poet* (1967).

Iain Teàrlach Scott *(Photo: Frau Pöschl)*

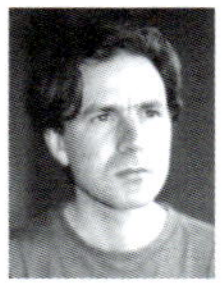

Is ann à Inbhir Ùige a tha Iain Teàrlach Scott. Tha e air ionnsachadh mu ealain agus peantadh agus air a bhith a' fuireach sa Ghearmailt. Tha e a' fuireach an-diugh ann am Baile-mòr New York. Tha an obair aige ann an taighean-tasgaidh ann am Breatainn, an Aimeireagaidh, sa Ghearmailt agus ann an Iapan. Chan eil e ach a' sireadh cruthachas na fhìor chumadh bhunaiteach; tha ùidh aige ann a bhith a' cur cruth – cumadh, dath, dianachd, mion-chunntas agus gaol.

Ian Charles Scott

Ian Charles Scott comes from Wick, and studied film and painting. He has lived in Germany, but is now in New York City. His work is in museums in the UK, the USA, Germany and Japan. He seeks creativity in its raw true form; he is concerned with figuration – shape, colour, intensity, detail and love.

Susan Leiper *(Photo: Julian Leiper)*

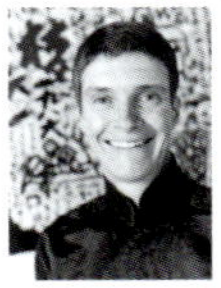

Rugadh i an 1955 agus 's e leabhraichean cnag cùrsa-beatha a beatha. Mar neach-deasachaidh tha i a' spèisealachadh ann an leabhraichean mu obair-ealain Sìonach agus 's i an t-ùghdar a th' air *Precious Cargo*. Mar shnas-sgrìobhadair bidh i a' gabhail bharantas airson leabhraichean a th' air a thighinn gu ìre fo bhuaidh a' mhodh Shìonaich. Chaidh a togail ann an Glaschu, tha i air a bhith ag obair an Hong Kong agus tha i a-nis a' fuireach an Dùn Èideann.

Susan Leiper

Susan Leiper was born in 1955 and books are the pivot of her career. She edits books on Chinese art and is the author of *Precious Cargo*. As a calligrapher she makes Chinese-inspired calligraphic books and works to commission. Susan now lives in Edinburgh.

17

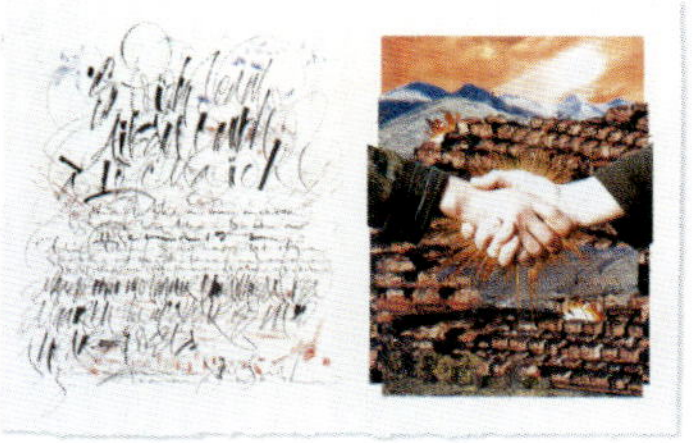

Tè de Chloinn Mhic Coinnich
Ailean Dubh à Lòchaidh

B' ann do Dhòmhnallaich Lunndaidh ann an Gleanna Garadh a bhuineadh Ailean Dubh. Ann an 1603 a ghabh e pàirt còmhla ri Garaich eile ann an ionnsaigh bhorb air dùthaich Chlann Choinnich, a dh'adhbhraich gun deach eaglais Chille Chrìosta san Eilean Dubh a chur na smàl air latha Sàbaid nuair a bha i làn luchd-adhraidh. Tha e coltach gun do dh'fhàg a mhì-chliù e tarraingeach do bhoireannaich, agus tha e ri thuigsinn bho fhacail 'Ailean Dubh à Lòchaidh' gur i tè de Chloinn Choinnich a rinn an t-òran.

Tè de Chloinn Mhic Coinnich

Black Allan was a MacDonald of Lundy in Glengarry. In 1603 he took part with other Glengarry men in a savage raid on MacKenzie territory which culminated in the burning of Kilchrist church on a Sunday while worshippers were inside. The words of 'Ailean Dubh à Lòchaidh' suggest that it was composed by a MacKenzie woman.

Seán Hillen *(Photo: Miriam Duffy)*

San Iúr i gCo. an Dúin a rugadh Seán Hillen agus tá cónaí anois air i mBaile Átha Cliath. Céimí é den London College of Printing agus Slade School. Baineann sé feidhm as meáin

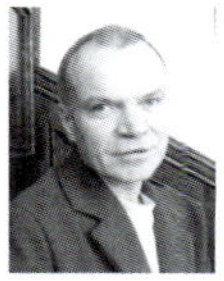

éagsúla agus tá cáil mhór ar a shaothar fóta-eagraithe faoin téama 'Troubles' agus ar an tsraith collage dar teideal 'Irelantis'. Chomh maith leis sin bíonn Hillen ag plé le dearadh stáitse, coimisiúin fistéipe popcheoil, dearadh grafach agus líondearadh.

Sean Hillen

Sean Hillen was born in Newry in Co. Down and is a graduate of the London College of Printing and the Slade School. He works in a variety of media and is well known for his photomontage works on the 'Troubles' and the collage series 'Irelantis'. Hillen has also been involved with stage set designs, pop video commissions and web and graphic design.

Anna Bowen *(Photo: Meyrah Gall)*

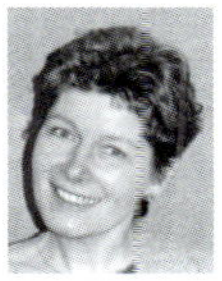

Dh'ionnsaich i mu shnas-sgrìobhadh ann an Sgoil Ealain agus Dealbhachaidh Reigate. HND (Dist). Duais Scrivners 1996. Air a taghadh mar làn bhall de *Letter Exchange*. Saorsannach de Chompanaidh *Livery Painter Stainers*. Ag obair làn-ùine mar shnas-sgrìobhadair air a ceann fhèin, agus a' teagasg pàirt-ùine. Tha an leabhar aice air Snas-sgrìobhaidh ga fhoillseachadh am-bliadhna. Am measg a taisbeanaidhean tha – 'Art in Action', Clò-bhualadairean Cider Dartington, Grinneas Wolsley, IPIDEC – Paris, Buidheann Ciùird Salon, Gailearaidh Ealain Alexander Llewellyn agus eile.

Ann Bowen

Ann Bowen studied calligraphy at Reigate School of Art & Design, and got a Scrivners Award in 1996. Bowen works full time as a freelance calligrapher, and teaches part time. Her book on callligraphy is published this year. Exhibitions include – 'Art in Action', Dartington Cider Press, Wosey Fine Arts, IPIDEC - Paris, Craft Salon Group, Alexander Llewellyn Art Gallery and others.

18

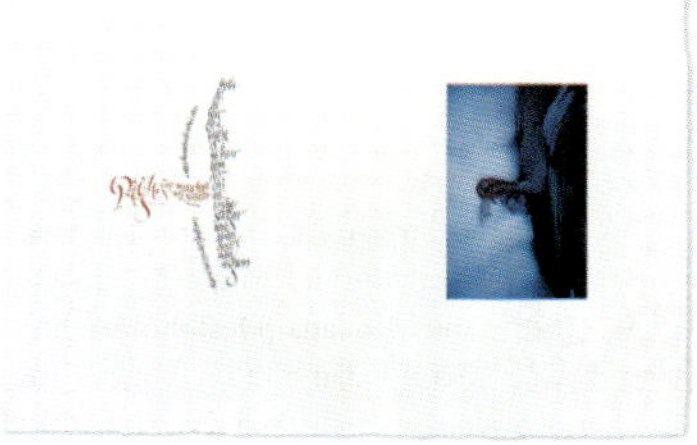

Màiri Chamshron

A rèir na sgeulachd bhuineadh Màiri Chamshron do theaghlach Challaird ann an Loch Abar 's bha Pàdraig (no, mar a chanadh daoine eile, Donnchadh) Caimbeul, oighre Inbhir Abha, ann an gaol rithe. Thug plàigh air falbh gach duine eile san taigh ach thug Pàdraig/Donnchadh oirre gabhail dhan mhuir, a h-aodach a thoirt dhith 's i fhèin a nighe. Thug e dhachaigh na bhreacan fhèin i, 's às dèidh a cumail trì mìosan ann am bothaig sa choille (no air Cruachan Beann) phòs e i. Chaidh Pàdraig a leòn am blàr Inbhir Lòchaidh, 1645, 's nuair a dh'eug e thug athair air Màiri 'Aba' Àrd Chatain a phòsadh.

Mary Cameron

According to the story Mary Cameron was of the Callart family in Lochaber and Peter (or Duncan) Campbell, younger of Inverawe, was in love with her. A plague carried off everyone else in the house but Peter/Duncan made her walk into the sea and wash herself. He brought her home in his own plaid, and after keeping her isolated for three months he married her. Peter was wounded at the battle of Inverlochy, 1645, and when he died his father forced Mary to marry the 'Prior' of Ardchattan.

Mary Kelly *(Photo: Mark Kelly)*

Ealaíontóir agus deántóir scannán is ea Mary Kelly. Céim Síceolaíochta is Fealsúnachta aici, chomh maith le Teastas sna Míndána agus Céim Scannánaíochta. Ní fada ó thaispeáin sí 'Eurofutures' ag an Royal Hibernian Academy,

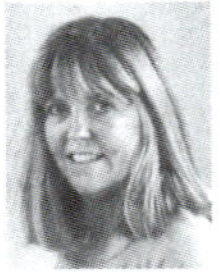

'Vacationland' ag Arthouse agus E.V.A. '98 – i gcomhar le Abigail O'Brien. Taispeánadh a cuid scannáin ag féilte éagsúla – ina measc Internazionale del Cinema in Chile, Féile Tai Wan agus N.Y.U. Tish School of the Arts in Cantor Film Center.

Mary Kelly

Artist and film maker Mary Kelly has a Psychology and Philosophy degree, fine art diploma and film degree. Recent exhibitions include 'Eurofutures' at Royal Hibernian Academy, 'Vacationland' at Arthouse and EVA '98, where she collaborated with Abigail O'Brien. Her films have been shown at festivals including Internazionale del Cinema in Chile, Tai Wan Festival and NYU Tish School of the Arts in Cantor Film Center

Susan Leiper

19

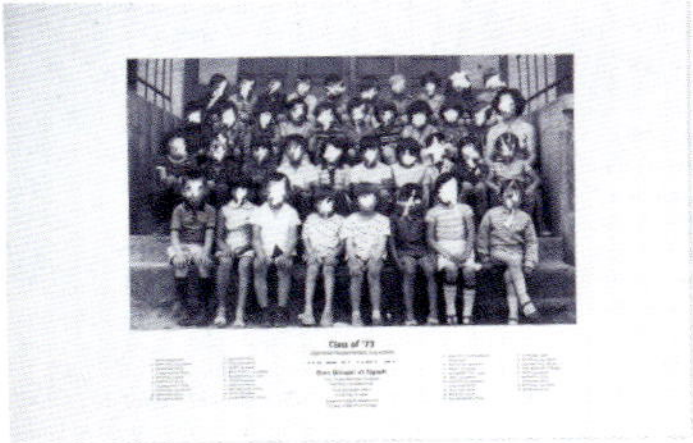

Gun Urrainn

Chan aithne dhuinn ainm na tè a rinn 'Clann Ghriogair air Fògradh' ach tha sgeulachd ann mu deidhinn. Às dèidh blàr Ghlinne Freòin (1603) bha na Griogaraich fon choill ach bha iomadach cinneadh bàidheil riutha 's an tè seo nam measg. Bha buidheann de Ghriogaraich am falach aice na fàrdaich nuair thàinig saighdearan air fàire. Chaidh i mach mar bu dual a thabhann deoch blàthaich dhaibh air an rathad mhòr 's nuair dh'fhaighnich iad am faca i Griogaraich sam bith thuirt i gum faca san leithid seo a dh'àite. Thog iad orra nan ruith air an tòir!

Anon

We do not know the name of the woman who made 'Clann Ghriogair air Fògradh' but there is a story about her. After the battle of Glen Fruin (1603) the MacGregors were outlawed but many were sympathetic to them, this woman included. She had a party of MacGregors concealed in her house when some soldiers approached. She went out to offer them a drink of buttermilk and when they asked if she had seen any MacGregors she sent them off in the wrong direction.

Anthony Haughey

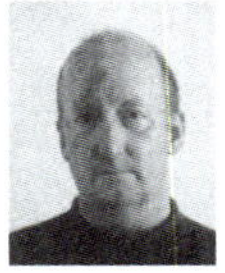

Is i dTuaisceart Éireann a rugadh Anthony Haughey in 1963 agus tá sé ag taispeáint a shaothair agus ag foilsiú ó thimpeall 1990 i leith. Ghnóthaigh sé duais an International Mosaique 2000 dá shraith 'Disputed Territory'. I mBaile Átha Cliath le gairid thaispeáin sé *Monitor* agus d'fhoilsigh sé leabhar ealaiontóireachta leis. Chuir sé 'Oh Europe' ar taispeáint ag an Nederlands Foto Instituut (Meán Fómhair 2001). I mí Feabhra 2002 cuirfear a shaothar ar taispeáint ag Bildmuseet – maraon le saothair Jeff Wall, Andreas Gursky agus Alan Sekula.

Anthony Haughey

Anthony Haughey was born in Northern Ireland in 1963. He has been exhibiting and publishing since the early '90s. He was the recipient of the International Mosaique Award 2000 for his series, 'Disputed Territory', and recently exhibited and published the artist's book *Monitor* in Dublin. He is currently exhibiting in 'Politics of Place'. Haughey is curated by Bildmuseet, Sweden.

Dòmhnall Addison *(Photo: Alan Young)*

'S e dealbhaiche grafaigeach a th' ann an Dòmhnall Addison. Tha e cuideachd na chlò-bhualadair agus bha e uair na àrd-òraidiche ann an Sgoil Ealain Ghray. Tha e an-dràsta ag obair ann an roinn-ealain ospadail.

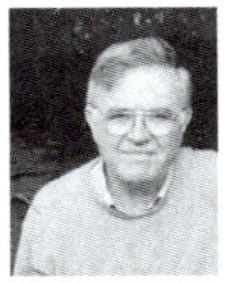

Donald Addison

Donald Addison, who lives in Aberdeen, is a graphic designer and printmaker and formerly a senior lecturer at Gray's School of Art. He is currently working in the field of Art for Hospitals.

20

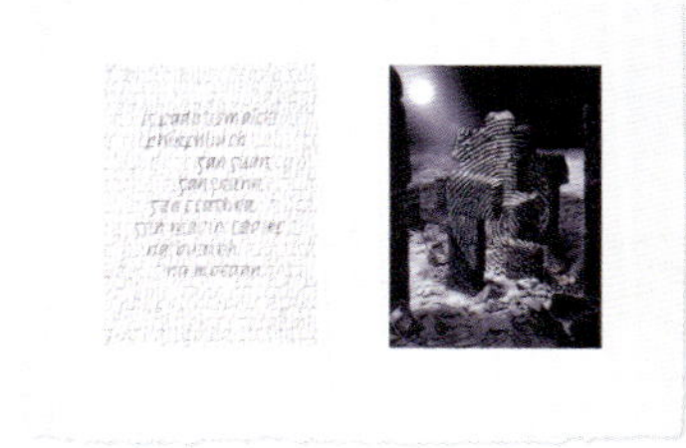

Aogán Ó Rathaille

Rugadh i Sliabh Luachra c.1670 é, d'éag 1729. Cumadh an dán seo tar éis dó dul i mbochtaineacht i gCorca Dhuibhne nuair a chaill a phátrún a thailte. Is é an foinse is údarásaí dá chuid saothair ná *Dánta Aodhagáin Uí Rathaille*, eag. Pádraig Ó Duinnín agus Tadhg Ó Donnchadha (1911).

Aogán Ó Rathaille

He was born at Sliabh Luachra c.1670, and died in 1729. This poem was written when he was reduced to poverty in Corca Dhuibhne after the fall of his patron. The chief contemporary source for his work is *Dánta Aodhagáin Uí Rathaille*, ed. Pádraig Ó Duinnín and Tadhg Ó Donnchadha (1911).

Calum Colvin *(Photo: Calum Colvin)*

Rugadh e an Glaschu an 1961 agus tha e na phroifeasair Dealbh-thogail Grinneis an Oilthigh Dhùn Dè. Gheibhear an obair aige ann am mòran chruinneachaidhean mar Taigh-tasgaidh a' Mhatropolatain, New York; Taigh-tasgaidh a' Ghrinneis, Houston; Taigh-tasgaidh Victoria agus Albert, Lunnainn agus anns a' Ghailearaidh Dhealbh Nàiseanta an Dùn Èideann.

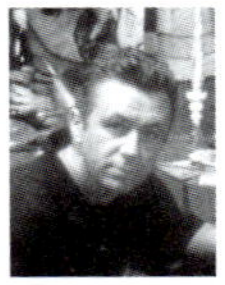

Calum Colvin

Born in Glasgow in 1961, Calum Colvin is Professor of Fine Art Photography at Dundee University. His work is held in numerous collections including the Metropolitan Museum of Modern Art, New York; the Museum of Fine Art, Houston; the Victoria and Albert Museum, London and the Scottish National Portrait Gallery, Edinburgh.

Réiltín Murphy

21

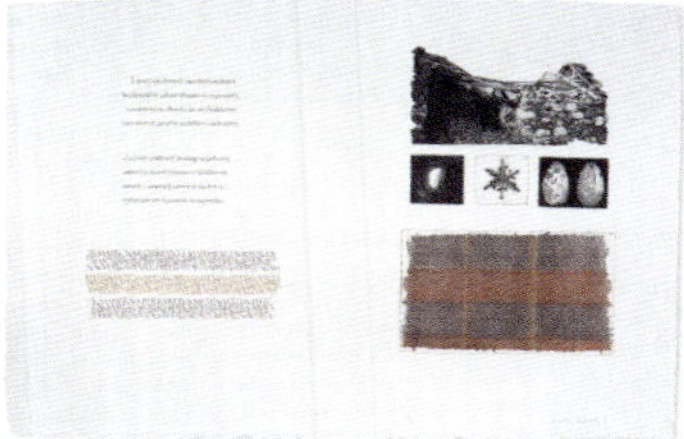

Dáibhí Ó Bruadair

Rugadh i gCo. Chorcaí é, c.1625, d'éag 1698. Tugann an dán is mó cáil uaidh, 'An Longbhriseadh', cuntas ar anchaoi na tíre tar éis Teitheadh na nIarlaí. Tá éadóchas agus dobrón na ndánta le brath go láidir in aistriúcháin Michael Hartnett (1985). Féach freisin *Duanaire Dháibhidh Uí Bhruadair*, eag. John C. Mac Erlean (1910-1917).

Dáibhí Ó Bruadair

He was born in Co. Cork, c.1625, and died in 1698. His most famous poem, 'An Longbhriseadh' ('The shipwreck') deplores the plight of the country after the flight of the Earls.

Michael Hartnett's translations (1985) are deeply moving. See also *Duanaire Dháibhidh Uí Bhruadair*, ed. John C. Mac Erlean (1910–17).

Silvana NicIlleathain *(Photo: Craig Mackay)*

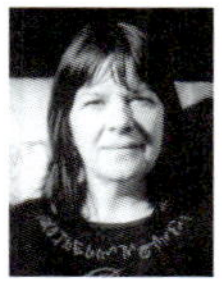

Rugadh i an Tobar na Màthar an 1953 agus bha i na h-oileanach ann an Colaiste Ealain Ghlaschu bho 1971–74. Fhritheil i clasaichean feasgair ann an dealbh-sgrìobhaidh ann an Colaiste Ealain Dhùn Èideann an 1977 agus mhisnich sin i gus am modh obrach sin a chumail a' dol. Mhair an ùidh sin chun an là an-diugh agus bhrosnaich e i gus dòighean ùra neo-thogsaigeach fheuchainn. 'S iad sin a chleachd i gus ìomhaighean a chruthachadh airson *an Leabhair Mhòir*.

Silvana McLean

Silvana McLean was born in Motherwell in 1953 and studied drawing and painting at Glasgow School of Art. Attending evening classes in etching at Edinburgh College of Art in 1977 kindled an interest in this medium which continues and embraces the developments in non-toxic etching methods which have been used to create the image for *An Leabhar Mòr*.

Frances Breen

22

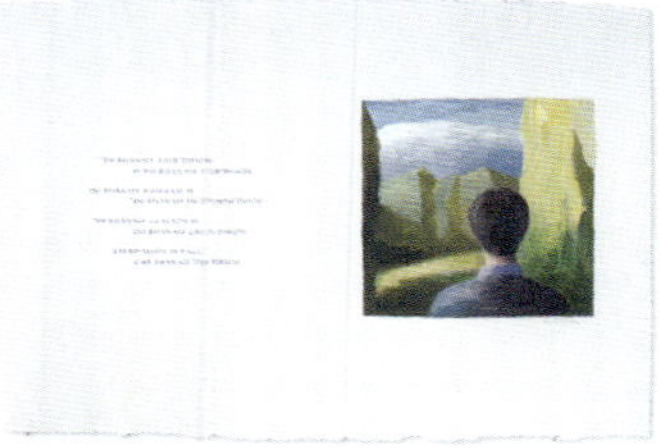

Gan Ainm

'Dónall Óg': ní minic is féidir dáta cruinn a chur le hamhrán grá, agus glactar leis de ghnáth gur san tseachtú nó san ochtú haois déag a rinneadh na cinn is cliúití dá bhfuil againn, na cinn atá le cluinstin i mbéal na ndaoine in gach cearn d'Éirinn. Is leis an chineál sin a bhaineas 'Dónall Óg' ach, de bhrí go bhfuil rann amháin ann (an rann deireanach anseo) a gheibhtear freisin in amhráin de chuid Gaeilge na hAlban (san amhrán *Fear a' Bhàta*, mar shampla), is féidir go bhfuil an t-amhrán seo níos sine ná an chuid eile. Síltear uaireanta gurab é ábhar an amhráin seo Dónall Óg Ó Dónaill, rí na nDálach, a fuair bás i 1258, ach ní móide ar bith é.

Anon

'Dónall Óg': this is one of a number of modern lovesongs, popular all over Ireland, but really undatable because lovesongs rarely contain references to current events. It is usually suggested that they date from the seventeenth or eighteenth century. Because this one, however, has at least one verse (the last one here) in common with a Scottish Gaelic song, its date may be earlier: it has even been suggested that Dónall Óg was a thirteenth-century Donegal chief.

Daibhidh Quinn *(Photo: Paula Corcoran)*

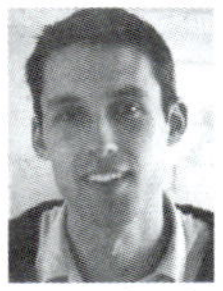

I 1970 sea rugadh David Quinn ealaíontóir, agus is i Sligeach a chaith sé a óige. Ghnóthaigh sé céim sna Míndána ón gColáiste Náisiúnta Ealaíne is Deartha i 1991 agus tá sé lonnaithe anois i gCo. Mhaigh Eo lena bhean agus ceathrar clainne. Tá saothar leis le feiscint i gcnuasaigh éagsúla – iad sin in Áras Nua-Ealaíne na hÉireann agus i bParlaimint na hEorpa ina measc.

David Quinn

David Quinn was born in 1970. He graduated in Fine Art from the National College of Art and Design and he now lives in Mayo with his wife and four children. His work is represented in various collections including the Irish Museum of Modern Art and the European Parliament.

Frances Breen

23

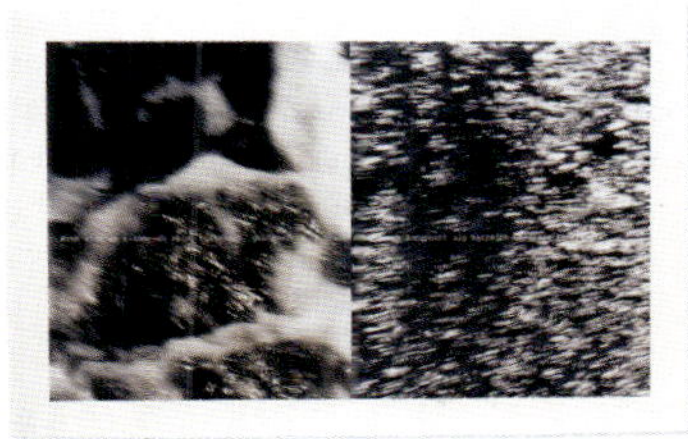

Alasdair Mac Mhaighstir Alasdair

B' e mac ministeir a bh' ann an Alasdair Mac Mhaighstir Alasdair (c.1698–c.1770) a rugadh an Dail Eildhe, am Mùideart. Chaidh oideachadh san lagh. Thug e greis na mhaighstir-sgoile 's greisean na bhàillidh, ach bha e riamh gnìomhach an cùis Rìgh Seumas. Bha e na chaiptean an rèiseamaid Mhic 'ic Ailein 1745–46. Dh'fhoillsich e faclair agus leabhar bàrdachd. Mhol e boireannaich is am Prionnsa Teàrlach agus dh'aoir e boireannaich is an Rìgh Deòrsa. B' e duine connspaideach a bh' ann, ach b' fhada a lean a bhuaidh air bàrdachd Ghàidhlig.

Alexander MacDonald

Alexander MacDonald (c.1698–c.1770) was a minister's son in Moidart. He received a legal training and spent a period as a schoolmaster and some time as a factor, but was consistently active in the Jacobite cause. He published a vocabulary and a book of verse. A controversial individual, he praised women and Prince Charles and satirised women and King George.

Anna Macleod *(Photo: Sue Williams)*

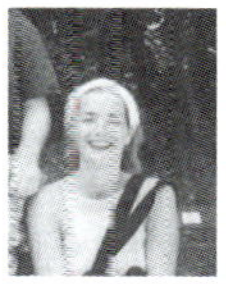

Albanach ó thús í Anna Macleod a bhfuil cónaí anois uirthi in Iarthar na hÉireann. Is minic a bhí a saothar ar taispeáint in Éirinn agus thar lear – agus bhí sé le feiscint ag Seastán na hÉireann ag Expo 2000 i Hanover. Ar na coimisiúin is déanaí atá aici tá Lough MacNean Sculpture Trail, Teach Custaim na Gaillimhe, 'Sculpture' ag Ceannannas Mór (2002) agus 'Site-ations/Snug Harbour' in Oileán Staten i Nua Eabhrac (2002).

Anna Macleod

Originally from Scotland, Anna Macleod lives in the West of Ireland. She has exhibited nationally and internationally, and contributed to the Irish Pavilion at EXPO 2000. Recent commissions and projects include Lough MacNean Sculpture Trail, Galway Customs House, 'Sculpture' at Kells (2002) and 'Site-ations/Snug Harbour' on Staten Island, New York (2002).

Frances Breen

24

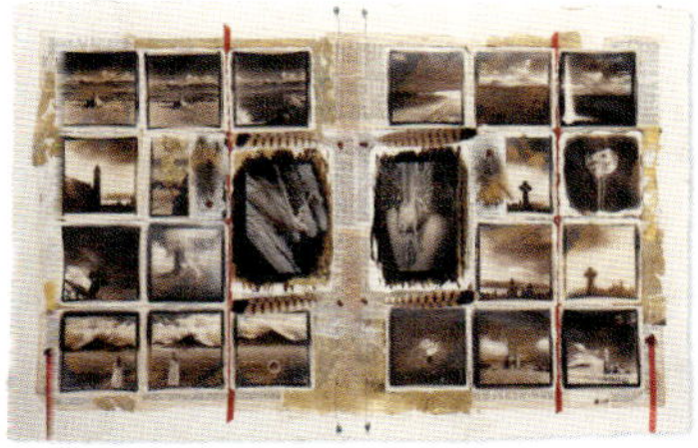

Séamas Dall Mac Cuarta

Rugadh c.1650, i gCo. Lú, meastar. D'éag 1733. File coinbhinseanach ab ea é, oilte ó thaobh ceardaíochta de. Tá iomrá ar an dán iontach 'Tithe Chorr an Chait' de bharr an réimse feirge agus dímheasa in aghaidh spríonlaitheachta a léirítear ann. Tá a shaothar ar fáil i *Séamas Dall Mac Cuarta; Dánta*, eag. Seán Ó Gallchóir (1971).

Séamas Dall Mac Cuarta

He was born in Co. Louth it is thought c.1650, and died in 1733. A technically accomplished and conventional poet whose brilliant occasional poem 'Tithe Chorr an Chait' is celebrated for its range of rage and contempt at meanness. His work is available in *Séamas Dall Mac Cuarta; Dánta*, ed. Seán O Gallchóir (1971).

Craig MacAoidh *(Photo: Craig Mackay)*

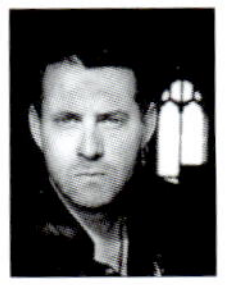

Thogadh Craig MacAoidh ann am Brùra, Cataibh, a tha a' coimhead a-mach dhan Chuan a Tuath agus dh'fhàg e an sgoil aig 15. Bha e ag obair ann an gnìomhachas na h-ola. B' e Albannach eile a chaidh a-mach air a cheann fhèin a bh' ann agus chaidh e a dh'ionnsachadh dealbh-thogail gu Oilthigh Napier ann an Dùn Èideann aig aois 25. Air ais air Ghaidhealtachd, tha e air mòran obrach ann an nòs an là an-diugh a dhèanamh a' dealbhadh riochdalachd a tha dorch, bruadarach, snasmhor, a' dùsgadh troimh-chèile agus bagradh os-nàdarrach.

Craig Mackay

Brought up in Brora, Sutherland, Craig MacKay left school at fifteen and worked in the oil industry. He later went off to study photography at Napier University, Edinburgh. Back in the Highlands he has produced a very contemporary body of work which typically constructs a dark, brooding but richly ornamented reality evoking noirish ironies and supernatural menace.

Réiltín Murphy

25

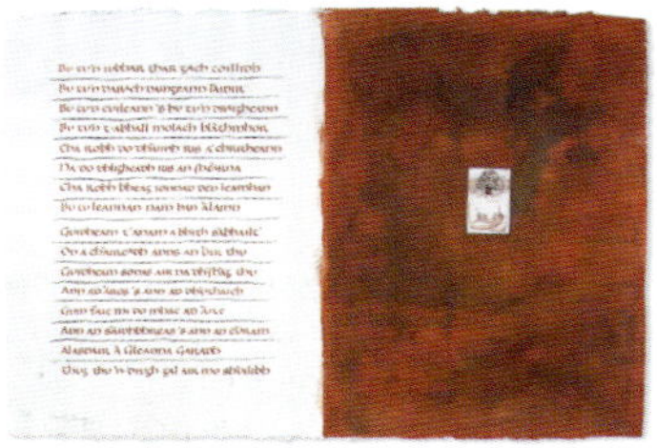

Sìleas na Ceapaich

B' i Sìleas na Ceapaich (c.1660-c.1729) nighean tighearna na Ceapaich an Loch Abar. Mu 1685 phòs i bàillidh, fear Alasdair Gòrdan, 's chaidh iad a thogail an teaghlaich fada bho dhùthaich a h-òige, gu siorrachd Bhainbh. Tha a cuid bhàrdachd a' nochdadh dhuinn bean-uasal chiallach, fhoghlaimte a bha comasach air àbhachdas agus mac-meanmna a chur an cèill. Tha i cuideachd na màthair-adhbhair air dà ruith chudthromach ann am bàrdachd na Gàidhlig – propaganda Seumasach agus laoidhean Caitligeach.

Sìleas na Ceapaich

Sìleas na Ceapaich (c.1660-c.1729) was a daughter of the chief of the MacDonalds of Keppoch in Lochaber. About 1685 she married, Alexander Gordon of Camdell, and went with him to Banffshire. Her poetry reveals a well-educated lady who was capable of expressing both humour and imagination. She is also the fountain-head of two important streams in Gaelic verse – Jacobite propaganda and Catholic hymns.

Rita Duffy *(Photo: Jim Maginn)*

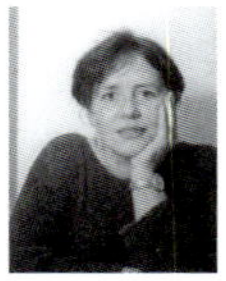

Tá Rita Duffy lonnaithe i mBéal Feirste agus an-chuid taispeántais uaithi go hidirnáisiúnta. Bhí mór-thaispeántais aonair aici i nGailearaí Ormeau Baths, Gailearaí Hugh Lane agus i Músaem na n-Ealaíon Chomhaimseartha i Zagreb. Tá saothar uaithi le fáil in an-chuid bailiúcháin phríobháideacha agus bailiúcháin phoiblí in Éirinn, sna Stáit Aontaithe, sa Ghearmáin agus san Ísiltír. Mar chuid d'Fhéile na Banríona i mBéal Feirste i 2001 chruthaigh sí saothar ealaíne poiblí ar Ilstórach Divis.

Rita Duffy

Belfast-based artist Rita Duffy has exhibited widely internationally. Major solo exhibitions have taken place at the Ormeau Baths Gallery, Hugh Lane Gallery and the Museum of Contemporary Art in Zagreb. Her work is represented in many public and private collections in Ireland, the USA, Germany and the Netherlands. As part of the 2001 Queens Belfast festival, she created a public artwork on Divis Tower Block.

Dòmhnall Moireach/Donald Murray

26

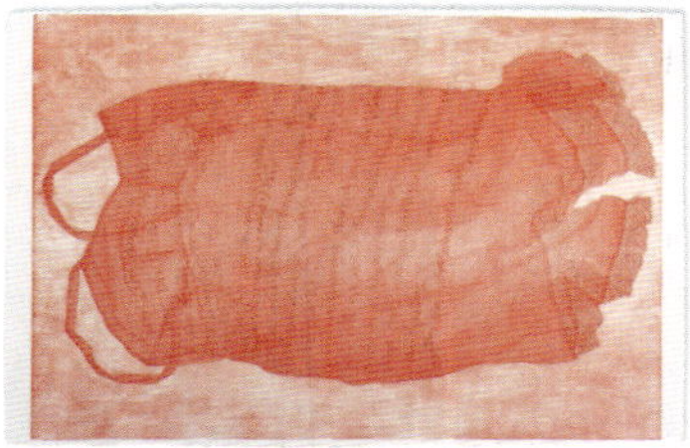

Cairistìona NicFhearghais

B' e nighean gobha à Cunndainn an Siorrachd Rois a bh' ann an Cairistìona NicFhearghais. Bha i pòsta aig Uilleam Siosal à Innis nan Ceann an Srath Ghlais. Chan eil Uilleam a' nochdadh idir an eachdraidhean nan Siosalach agus tha e coltach nach robh fearann aige, agus gu robh e air a mheas nach do phòs i fear a bha cho uasal rithe fhèin. A rèir sgeulachd air a bheil coltas na fìrinn, b' e trod a mhnà seach a bharail fhèin a thug air Uilleam gabhail ann an arm a' Phrionnsa 's a dhol gu bhàs an Cùl Lodair (1746). Tha facail 'Mo Rùn Geal Òg' a' nochdadh gu robh i moiteil às a cèile a-nis agus gu robh i air teiche gu tèarainteachd an Eilein Sgitheanaich.

Christiana Fergusson

Christiana Fergusson was a blacksmith's daughter from Ross-shire who married William Chisholm from Strathglass. It seems William was landless and that Christiana had married beneath herself. According to a story, it was his wife's scolding rather than his own judgement that made William join Prince Charlie's army and go to his death at Culloden (1746). The words of 'Mo Rùn Geal Òg' show that she was now proud of her husband and that she had fled to safety in Skye.

Oona Hyland *(Photo: Ian Joyce)*

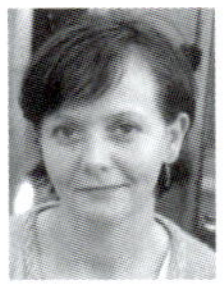

Oileadh Oona Hyland sa Slade School of Art agus bhain céim Mháistreachta amach ag Ollscoil na Banríona i mBéal Feirste. Chruthaigh sí leaca aolchloiche eitseálaithe don iarnród faoi thalamh i Lisbon. Faoi láthair tá sí ag déanamh deilbhe lasmuigh a cuirfear in Inis Oírr, in Árainn. Tá sí pósta le Ian Joyce agus tá ceathrar clainne orthu. Cónaíonn siad ar Chnoc Bealtaine, amach ó Ghort a' Choirce.

Oona Hyland

Oona Hyland studied at the Slade School of Art and completed an MA at Queen's University, Belfast. Her international experience includes creating etched limestone panels for the Lisbon underground. She is currently working on an outdoor sculpture commission for Inis Oírr, one of the Aran Islands.

Dòmhnall Moireach/Donald Murray

27

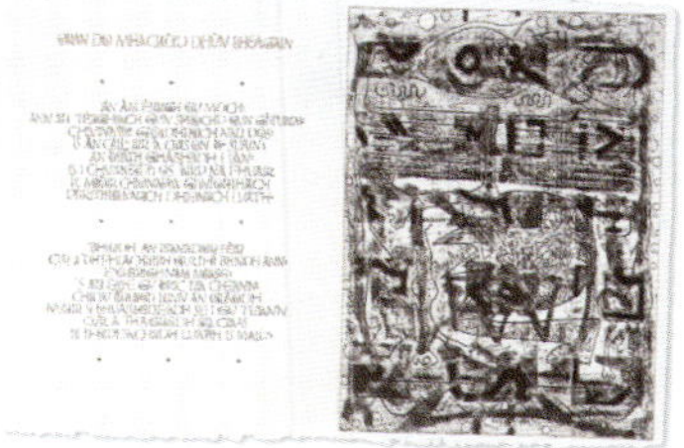

An Clàrsair Dall

B' e Ruairidh Mac Mhuirich (Moireasdan), an Clàrsair Dall (c.1656-1713/14), mac Iain Bhradhagair, tacadair a bha ainmeil fad is farsaing air son eirmseachd cainnte, sgoilearachd agus comas ciùil. Chaidh Ruairidh oideachadh air a' chlàrsaich an Èirinn. Còmhla ri bàird eile dhe sheòrsa, bhiodh e a' siubhal nan eilean 's a' chinn a tuath fo sgàth cinn-chinnidh (MacLeòid Dhùn Bheagain) a' cumail ceòl is dibhearsain ri uaislean na dùthcha. Thàinig an saoghal cofhurtail seo gu ceann ann an 1715, ach 's math a bha fios aig Ruairidh gur ann mar sin a bhitheadh.

The Blind Harper

Roderick Morison, the Blind Harper (c.1656–c.1713), was a son of John Morison of Bragar, a tacksman celebrated for his wit, scholarship and musical prowess. Roderick was trained in the harp in Ireland. He would travel the Islands and the North under the protection of a chiefly patron (MacLeod of Dunvegan) providing the nobility of the countryside with music and entertainment. This cosy world came to an end in 1715, but Roderick had seen the writing on the wall before then.

Seòras Mac a' Phearsain, ARSA 1987 *(Photo: John MacKinnon, Stornoway)*

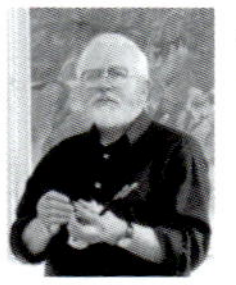

Rugadh e an Inbhir Sìn an, Cataibh an 1935, agus bha e na oileanach an Colaiste Ealain Dhun Èideann. Thug sgoilearachd shiùbhlach dha an cothrom obrachadh san Spàinn – agus rinn e trì cuairtean Albannach le Chòmhlan-cèilidh – mus deach e na neach-teagaisg ann an dealbhachd agus peantadh an an Colaiste Ealain Dhùn Èideann. Tha taisbeanaidhean air a bhith aige mar aon-neach agus ann am buidhnean. Tha e a-nis air a dhreuchd a leigeil dheth agus tha e a' fuireach agus ag obair na pheantair am Baile nam Feusgan.

George A. Macpherson ARSA

He was born in Sutherland, in 1935, and studied at Edinburgh College of Art. A travelling scholarship gave him working time in Spain, before he became a lecturer in drawing and painting at Edinburgh College of Art. He has shown work regularly in solo and group exhibitions. He now lives and works as a painter in Musselburgh.

Anna Bowen/Ann Bowen

28

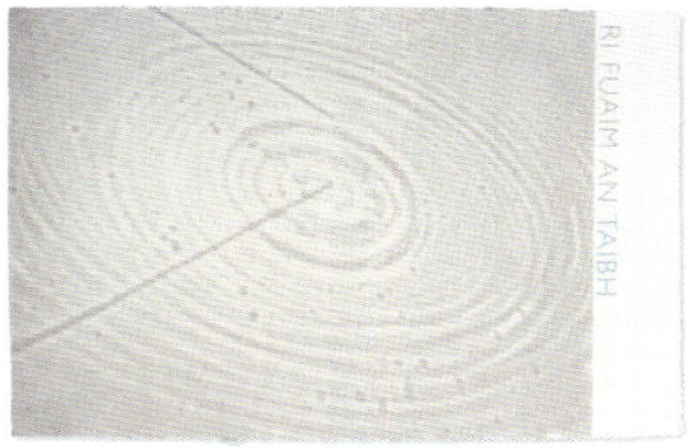

Màiri nighean Alasdair Ruaidh

Rugadh Màiri nighean Alasdair Ruaidh (c.1615–c.1707) an Roghadal sna Hearadh. Chaith i a beatha na banaltram aig na Leòdaich mhòra an Dùn Bheagain 's am Beàrnaraigh. Bha i na boireannach connspaideach a bhiodh a' trod ri bàird 's ri bana-bhàird. Bha i a' suathadh gach là ri filidhean a thug seachd bliadhna a' togail an ciùird ach dhèanadh i òrain mhòra mholaidh fada na b' fheàrr na iadsan agus chaidh a chur às a leth gun robh i na buidseach. Thug i greis fada mu dheas an Sgarba ga leigheas aig tobar Chille Mhoire.

Mary MacLeod

Mary MacLeod (c.1615–c.1707) was born at Rodel in Harris, and worked as a nurse for the MacLeods in Dunvegan and Berneray. She mingled on a daily basis with professional poets who had spent seven years learning their craft but her songs of praise were much better than theirs and she was accused of being a witch.

Ealasaid Ogilvie *(Photo: Robert Callender)*

Òraidiche ann an Colaiste Ealain Dhùn Èideann. Tha buaidh mhòr air a bhith aig Eilean Hiort agus a chrìochan (às an tàinig cuideachd a màthar) air a h-obair.

Am measg a cuid obrach o chionn ghoirid tha an 'Liquid Room', seallaidhean uisge a-staigh, a' toirt gu chèile ealain, ailtireachd agus saidheans ann an taigh-tasgaidh air abhainn Foirthe. Tha i a' fuireach an cladach Fhìobha còmhla ris an neach-ealain Raibeart Callander.

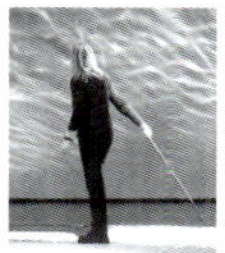

Elizabeth Ogilvie

Elizabeth Ogilvie is a lecturer at Edinburgh College of Art. One of the most compelling influences on her work has been the Island of St Kilda and its finite location. Recent works include the 'Liquid Room', a spectacular water installation; a fusion of art, architecture and science housed in a dockside warehouse on the Forth. She lives on the Fife coast with the artist, Robert Callendar.

Dòmhnall Addison/Donald Addison

29

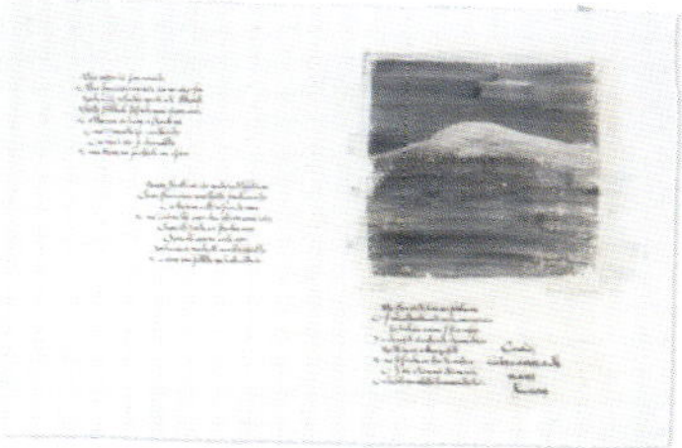

Donnchadh Bàn Mac an t-Saoir

Rugadh Donnchadh Bàn Mac an t-Saoir (1724–1812) an Gleann Urchaidh an Earra-Ghaidheal. Bha e na ghìomanach aig na Caimbeulaich am frìthean Ghleann Èite, Beinn Dòrain 's Gleann Lòchaidh, ach nuair thàinig a' chaora mhòr mu 1760 theich e fhèin agus 'Màiri Bhàn Òg' a Dhùn Èideann far na ghabh esan am Freiceadan a' Bhaile 's na dh'fhosgail ise taigh dhramaichean. B' e seo *hegira* na Gàidhlig. A' cleachdadh briathrachas mòr, mhol no dhì-mhol e dùthaich 's daoine mar bha dhìth, 's fhuair e air a bhàrdachd fhoil seachadh ged nach b' urrainn dha leughadh. Bha e na dhuine sunndach a choisinn meas agus gràdh nan Gaidheal uile.

Duncan Ban MacIntyre

Duncan Ban MacIntyre (1724–1812) was born in Glen Orchy in Argyll. He was a gamekeeper for the Campbells, but when the 'great sheep' came c.1760 he and 'Màiri Bhàn Òg' fled to Edinburgh where he joined the City Guard and she opened a dram-shop. Deploying a huge vocabulary, he praised or dispraised land and people as circumstances demanded, and had his verse published although he could not read.

Calum Aonghas MacAoidh *(Photo: Leila Angus)*

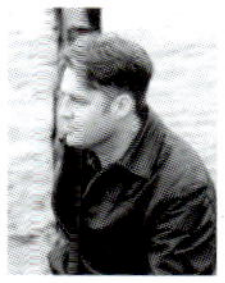

Rugadh e an 1964 ann an Eilean Leòdhais. Tha e pòsta le triùir chloinne agus tha iad mar theaghlach a' fuireach ann an Steòrnabhagh. Thogadh e ann am baile an Acha Mhòir agus cheumnaich e à Sgoil Ealain Ghlaschu an 1990 air cha bhith ag ionnsachadh mu Ghrinneas Dhealbh-thogail. Choisinn e sgoilearachd dhealbh-thogail Richard Hough an 1992, 's às dèidh sin còmhnaidheachdan ann an Èirinn agus sa Chuimrigh. Tha taisbeanaidhean air a bhith aige air feadh Bhreatainn agus tìr-mòr na Roinn Eòrpa. O chionn ghoirid thill e air ais a Leòdhas agus tha e ag obair mar riochdaire/stiùiriche telebhisean na Gàidhlig.

Calum Angus Mackay

He was brought up on Lewis and graduated from Glasgow School of Art having studied Fine Art Photography. He was awarded the Richard Hough Photography Scholarship, then took up residencies in both Ireland and Wales. Mackay has exhibited widely throughout UK and mainland Europe, and recently returned to Lewis working via the media as a Gaelic television producer/director.

Susan Leiper

30 **Gan Ainm**

'An Draighneán Donn': tugadh 'Rí na nAmhrán' ar an amhrán chliúiteach seo, amhrán grá a mhair beo i mbéaloideas gach cúige ón ochtú céad déag nó roimhe. Cuireadh i gcló é den chéad uair i 1789 agus creidtear, ón ainm *Sliabh Uí Fhloinn* atá san dara rann i bhfurmhór na leaganacha, gur i gConnachta a cumadh é: tá

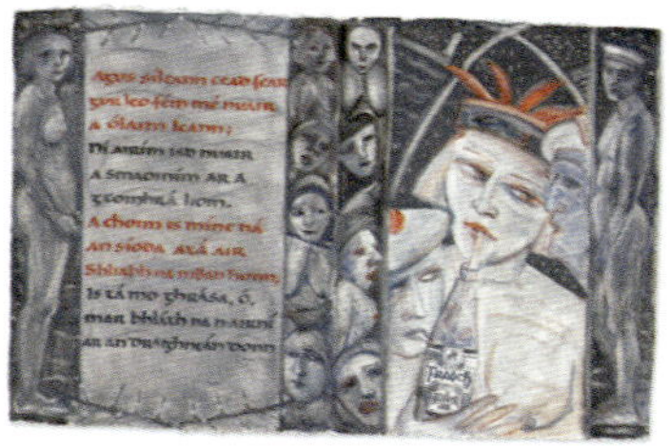

Sliabh Uí Fhloinn i bparóiste Chill Tulach i gCo. Ros Comáin.

Anon
'The Brown Blackthorn': another Irish lovesong, probably datable to the eighteenth century; it has been called 'Rí na nAmhrán', 'The King of Songs', and the first published version dates from 1789. The title, from the last line of the second English verse, is probably of no significance because it merely forms part of a simile for beauty. It has been argued that the placename in the second verse demonstrates that the song originated in Connacht.

Joyce W. Cairns RSA; RSW; MA (RCA) *(Photo: Robin Wilson)*

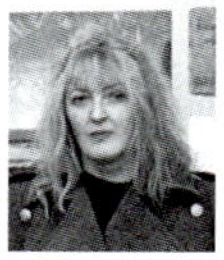

1966–71 Colaiste Ealain Ghray, Obar Dheathain. Teisteas agus Iar Theisteas, 1971–74 Colaiste Rìoghail Ealain, Lunnainn, 1974–75 Colaiste Ealain agus Dealbhadh, Gloucestershire, Caidreachas Cheltenham, 1975–76 Colaiste Goldsmith, Oilthigh Lunnainn ATC, 1976 Neach-teagaisg an Dealbhadh agus Peantadh, Sgoil Ealain Ghray.

Taisbeanaidhean an tòrr àiteachan, a' cosnadh mòran dhuaisean agus obair ann am mòran chruinneachaidhean poblach agus prìobhaideach am Breatainn 's thar chuan.

Joyce W. Cairns RSA; RSW; MA (RCA)
Joyce Cairns studied at Grays School of Art, and the Royal College of Art and Goldsmiths College in London. In 1976 she was appointed a lecturer in drawing and painting at Grays. She has exhibited widely, won numerous awards and has work in many public and private collections in the UK and abroad.

Dòmhnall Moireach/Donald Murray

31

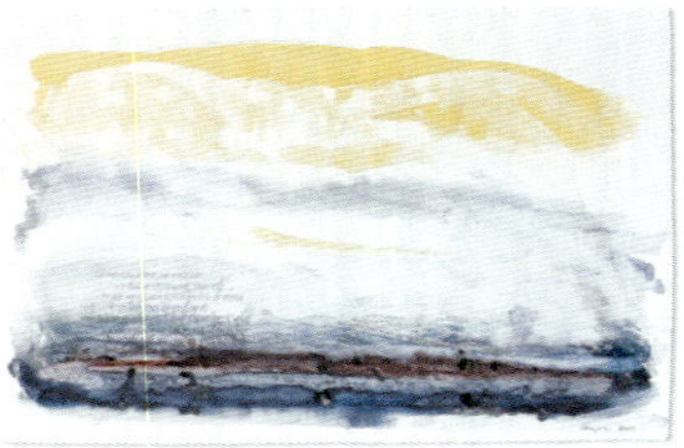

Cathal Buí Mac Giolla Ghunna
Rugadh i gCo. Fhear Manach é, meastar, c.1680. D'éag 1756. Clú agus cáil air i dtraidisiún an bhéaloideasa mar fhile ragairneach a chaith a shaol le cearrbhachas agus le hól. Is é 'An Bonnán Buí' an dán is clúití den 15 dhán a mhaireann – go mórmhór de bharr an ghrinn a bhaineann le dúil an fhile san ól. Féach *Cathal Buí: Amhráin*, eag. Breandán Ó Buachalla (1975).

Cathal Buí Mac Giolla Ghunna
Born probably in Fermanagh c.1680, he died in 1756, and has a considerable reputation in folk tradition as an archetypal rakish, gambling and drinking poet. The 'Bonnán Buí' is the most celebrated of his fifteen extant poems, chiefly for the humour of its horror at abstinence. See *Cathal Buí: Amhráin*, ed. Breandán Ó Buachalla (1975).

Eileen Ferguson *(Photo: Neal Greg)*
Albanach í Eileen Ferguson atá lonnaithe anois i gCo. Mhuineacháin. Eascraíonn a saothar péintéireachta ó thimpeallacht a sinsir. Ó bhronn Ollscoil Uladh Máistreacht Ealaíne sna Míndána uirthi (1989) tá taispeántais curtha ar fáil aici in

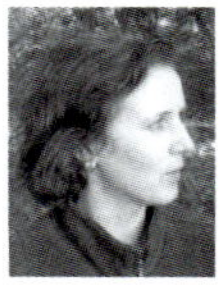

Éirinn, in Albain, i Sasana agus sna Stáit Aontaithe. Tá roinnt mhaith coimisiún curtha i grích aici agus bíonn sí gnóthach ag stiúrú ceardlanna agus scéimeanna cónaithe chomh maith le bheith ag feidhmiú mar chomhordaitheoir ealaíne d'oifig ealaíne Cho. Mhuineacháin.

Eileen Ferguson
Eileen Ferguson is a Scottish artist living in Co. Monaghan. Since graduating with an MA in Fine Art from the University of Ulster, she has exhibited in Ireland, Scotland, England and America. She has also completed several commissions and is active conducting workshops, residency schemes and working as arts co-ordinator for the Monaghan arts office.

David McGrail

32

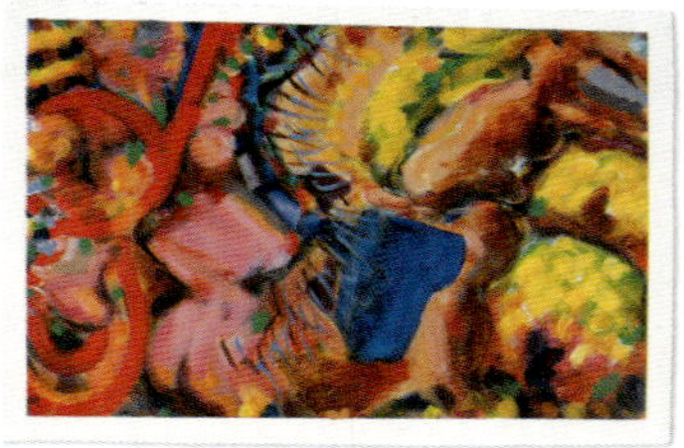

Gun Urrainn
A rèir na sgeulachd, rinn Raghnaid NicGriogair an Dùnain 'Bothan Àirigh am Bràigh Raithneach' do Dhòmhnall Camshron Bhlàr a' Chaorainn mu 1620. Chuir i a sùil ann, ach là dhe na làithean nach ann a nochd buidheann cheatharnach le Dòmhnall nam measg agus seann Raghnall, mac Alasdair na Ceapaich, air an ceann. Bha Raghnall ag iarraidh a pòsadh e fhèin! Dhiùlt i a-muigh 's a-mach e 's bha iad a' dol ga h-èigneachadh nuair a chuir cuideigin stad orra le na facail, 'An tè nach toir a roghainn à triùir, bheir i a deòin às a dhà dheug.' Thagh i Dòmhnall agus phòs iad.

Anon
'A shieling in Brae Rannoch': according to the story, Rachel MacGregor of Dunan made this poem for Donald Cameron of Blarachaorin about 1620. She had her eye on him, but one day a band of brigands appeared with Donald among them and old Ronald, son of Alexander of Keppoch, who wanted to marry her himself! She refused him and they were about to rape her when someone said, 'She who can't make up her mind out of three will find the one she wants in twelve.' She picked Donald and they were married.

Cóilín Moireach *(Photo: Michael Lieb, Skibbereen)*

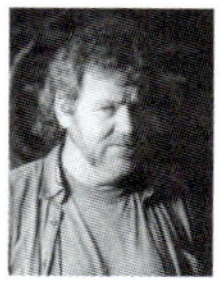

Priontálaí agus péintéir is ea Cóilín Moireach a chuir fé i mBéal an Dá Chab i gCo. Chorcaí. Cuireadh a shaothar ar taispeáint i mBeirlín, i Kraków, sa tSín agus sna Stáit Aontaithe, agus tá sé le fáil i measc an-chuid bailiúchán phoiblí. Le déanaí bhí taispeántais aonair uaidh in Iarsmalann Hunt i Luimneach agus i nGailearaí Hallward i mBaile Átha Cliath. Sheas sé d'Éirinn ag an Taispeáint Débhliantúil Priontaí san Ioruaidh i 1989 agus ag an 9ú British International Print Biennial.

Cóilín Murray
Cóilín Murray is a printmaker and painter living in Co. Cork. His work has been exhibited internationally in Berlin, Cracow, China and the USA and is included in many public collections. Recent solo shows have taken place at the Hunt Museum in Limerick and the Hallward Gallery in Dublin. He represented Ireland in the Print Biennial in Norway in 1989 and the 9th British International Print Biennial.

Frances Breen

33

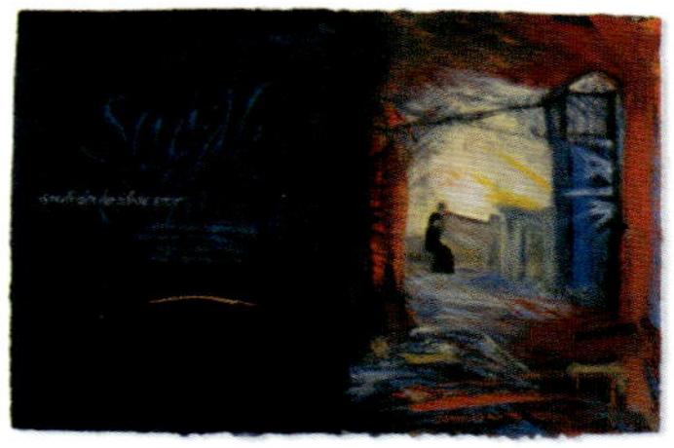

Niall Mòr MacMuireadhaigh

Bha Niall Mòr (c.1550-post 1613) air fear de Chlann Mhuirich a bha faisg air 600 bliadhna nam filidhean, nan seanchaidhean 's nan seirbheisich chatharra aig Iarlachan na Leamhnachd, Rìghrean nan Eilean agus Tighearnan Chlann Raghnaill. A rèir choltais bha fearann aig a sheanair an Cinn Tìre fhathast ann an 1541 agus thathas dhen bheachd gur e Niall Mòr a' chiad MhacMhuirich aig an robh gabhaltas tèarainte an Uibhist a Deas airson a sheirbheisean do Mhac 'ic Ailein. Chan eil ach ceithir dàin a chaidh a chur ri ainm, agus tha iad gu math eadar-dhealaichte o chèile.

Niall Mòr MacMuireadhaigh

Niall Mòr (c.1550-post 1613) was one of the MacMhúirichs who served for nearly six hundred years as poets, historians and civil servants to the Earls of Lennox, the Kings of the Isles and the chiefs of Clanranald. It has been suggested that Niall Mòr was the first MacMhúirich to have a secure holding in South Uist for his services to Clanranald. Only four poems have been ascribed to him and they are very different from each other.

Caitlín Ní Ghallchóir *(Photo: Eibhlín Ní Cholla)*

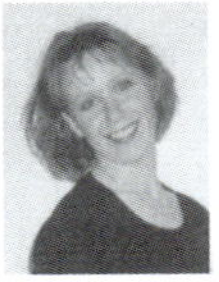

Tá cónaí ar Chaitlín Ní Ghallchóir i mBun-a-Leaca, Leitir Ceanainn, Co. Dhún na nGall. Péintéir agus maisitheoir a bhí inti ar dtús agus d'oibrigh sí í ngach aird den tír. Ar fhilleadh abhaile di d'fhreastail sí ar ranganna ealaíne agus rinne sí cúrsa sna míndána in Ollscoil Uladh i mBéal Feirste níos déanaí. Anois ó tá cónaí uirthi i nDún na nGall Thiar Thuaidh arís, deir sí go bhfuil '. . . gairbhe na tíre, an t-Aigéan Atlantach agus soineann agus doineann Dhún na nGall . . .' mar inspioráid aici.

Caitlín Gallagher

Caitlín Gallagher lives in Co. Donegal. She started painting as a painter and decorator and worked all around Ireland. Later, she attended art classes and completed a Fine Art Painting course at the University of Ulster at Belfast. Back in north-west Donegal Caitlín says she 'has the rugged landscape, Atlantic Ocean and Donegal weather' for inspiration.

David McGrail

34

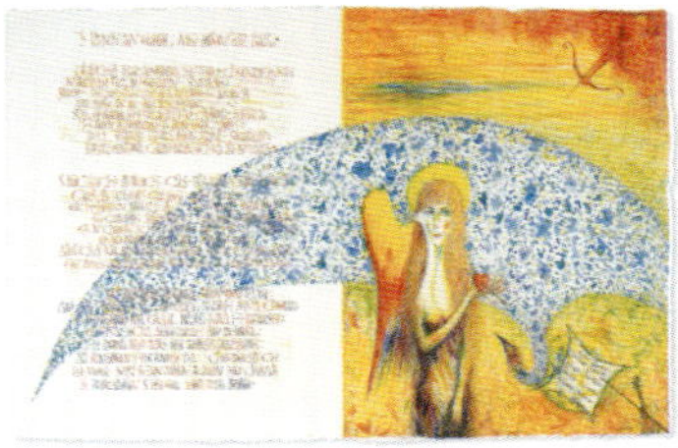

Uilleam Ros

Rugadh Uilleam Ros (1762-91) san Eilean Sgitheanach, dùthaich athar, 's thogadh e an Geàrrloch, dùthaich a mhàthar. Thugadh foghlam math dha 's tha an t-eòlas aige air ceòl ri aithneachadh na chuid òran. Chaidh e na cheannaiche-siubhail (mar athair roimhe) 's an uair sin na mhaighstir-sgoile. Do Mhòr Ros, a bha grunn bhliadhnachan na bu shine na e, thug e gaol ainmeil ris nach deach gabhail. Rinn e aoirean draosta cho math ri òrain ghaoil làn fèin-mhothachaidh. Dh'eug e leis a' chaitheimh is e fhathast na dhuine òg. Chuir e a' bhàrdachd aige ann an sgrìobhadh ach loisg e i, 's chaidh cuid dhith a chur ri chèile a-rithist bho bheul-aithris.

William Ross

William Ross (1762-91) was born in Skye and raised in Gairloch. He was given a good education and became a pedlar, like his father, then a schoolmaster. To Marion Ross, several years his senior, he gave unrequited love. He composed bawdy satires as well as love-songs full of self-awareness, dying of consumption when still a young man. He burned his poems but some were later restored from oral tradition.

Iòsaph Urie *(Photo: Neil Ramsay)*

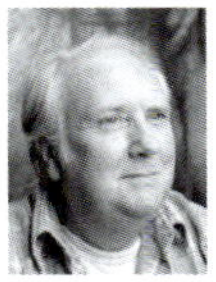

Rugadh e an Glaschu an 1947. Na oileanach an Colaiste Ealain Dhonnchaidh Iòrdanstain, Dùn Dè (1977-1981), Sgoiltean na h-Acadamh Rìoghail, Lunnainn (1981-84). Duaisean: Sgoilearachd Shiùbhlach Sheòrais MhicDhonnchaidh, Sgoilearachd Shiùbhlach Fhearchair MhicIlleRuaidh, Duais Vincent Harris, Duais DM Morgan, Duais J Van Bueren Wittman. Iomadh taisbeanadh buidhne agus aon-neach tro Bhreatainn. Cruinneachaidhean taghta: Gailearaidh Ealain Dhùn Dè, BBC (Alba), Ionad Ealain Baile Dhùn Èideann agus Cruinneachadh Companaidh Sir John Sainsbury.

Joseph Urie

Born in Glasgow in 1947, he studied at Duncan of Jordanstone College of Art, Dundee and the Royal Academy School, London. Awards received include the British Institute Prize, Farquhar Reid Major travelling scholarship, Vincent Harris Prize, D. M. Morgan Prize and the J. van Bueren Wittman Prize. He has exhibited in numerous group and solo shows. Selected collections are in Dundee Art Gallery, BBC (Scotland), Edinburgh City Arts Centre and Sir John Sainsbury Company Collection.

Anna Bowen/Ann Bowen

35 **Rob Donn MacAoidh**

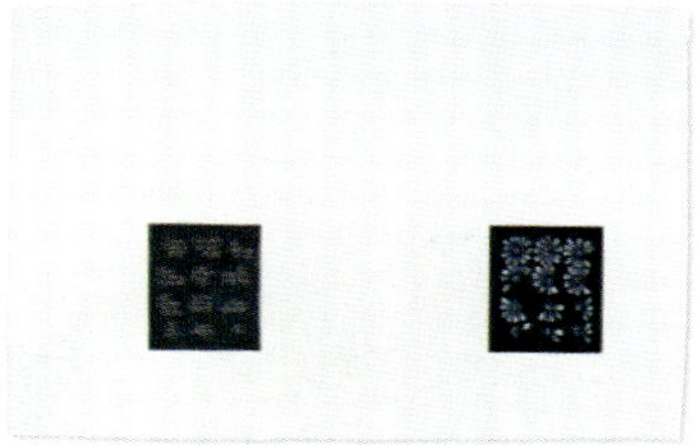

Rugadh Rob Donn (1714-78) aig Allt na Caillich ann an sgìre Dhiùranais an Dùthaich MhicAoidh. Thug e a bheatha ag obair le crodh – na bhuachaille, na ghille-cruidh, na dhròbhair – ach bha e a cheart cho furachail mu dhaoine. Chùm e muinntir na sgìre, àrd agus ìseal, fo smachd le amaladh breitheachail de dh'òrain molaidh 's de dh'aoirean. B' esan sùilean agus cluasan a' mhinisteir, ach bhruidhneadh e cainnt nan daoine, 's abair cainnt! Uairean drabasta, uairean ro onarach – 's uairean doirbh dhuinne a thuigsinn, oir cha do chaomhain e sinn bho Ghàidhlig amh na sgìre. Tha meas mòr air Rob Donn sa cheann a tuath gus an là an-diugh.

Rob Donn MacKay

Rob Donn (1714-78) was born in the parish of Durness. He spent his life working with cows but was just as attentive to people. He kept the people of the district, high and low, in control with a judicious mixture of songs of praise and satire. Sometimes raunchy, sometimes too honest – and sometimes hard for us to understand, for he did not spare us from the raw Gaelic of the district, Rob Donn is much esteemed in the north to this day.

Abigail O'Brien *(Photo: Mary Kelly)*

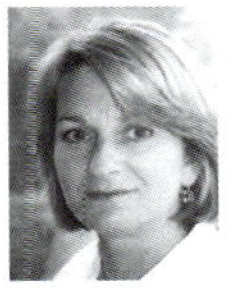

Tá an-chuid duaiseanna bainte amach ag saothar O'Brien. Saothar uaithi le fáil i mbailiúcháin phríobháideacha agus i mbailiúcháin phoiblí – ina measc siúd Áras Nua-Ealaíne na hÉireann i mBaile Átha Cliath agus bailiúchán Volpinum i Vín. Tá sí ag obair faoi láthair ar sraith dar téama Na Seacht Sacraimintí. Chuige seo baineann sí úsáid as meáin éagsúla– dealbhóireacht agus grianghrafadóireacht san áireamh - chun teaghlachas, deasghnátha coitianta agus deasghnátha fáis a iniúchadh.

Abigail O'Brien
O'Brien has won many awards for her work, which is in both private and public collections, including the Irish Museum of Modern Art in Dublin and the Volpinum collection in Vienna. She is currently producing a series of works with the theme of the Seven Sacraments. In this, she uses a variety of media including sculpture and photography.

Susan Leiper

36 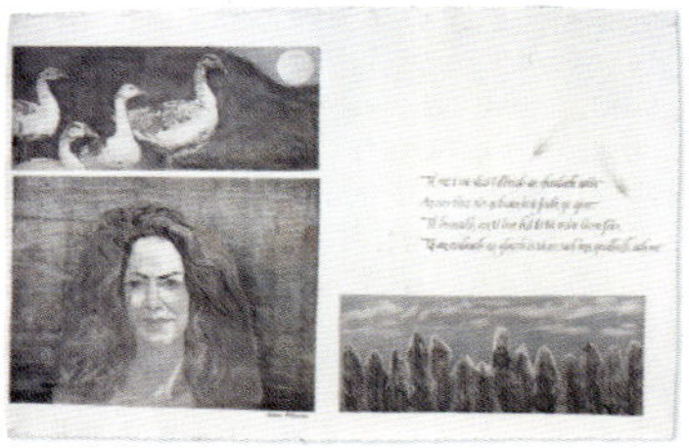

Gan Ainm
'Tá Mé I Mo Shuí': scríobhadh an t-amhrán grá seo síos i gCúige Uladh céad bliain ó shin, agus tá leaganacha go leor eile le fáil in Ultaibh agus i gConnachta. Is dócha gurab é oibriú an bhéaloidis a fhágann go minic roinnt véarsaí as amhrán mar seo gan snáithe téamúil le haithint tríothu. Ar ndóigh, níl fianaise dá laghad ann a chuirfeadh dáta ná áit chumtha leis an amhrán.

Anon
'Up All Night': taken from oral tradition in Ulster, this song is hard to pin down as to theme. There are various versions, some from Connacht, and we must accept that it is basically a love song, for the last line says so. But, doubtless due to the vagaries of the oral song tradition, our text is a fairly disjointed compilation of verses and we have no way of dating it.

Anndra MacMhoirein *(Photo: Cailean MacLean)*

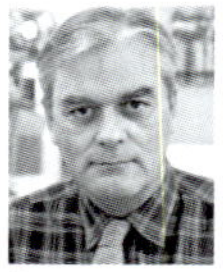

An dèidh foghlam fhaighinn ann an Colaiste Ealain Ghlaschu, tha e air a bhith a' fuireach sna h-Eileanan a' teagaisg agus a' peantadh o 1973. Tha e an-dràsta os cionn Roinn an Ealain ann an Àrd-sgoil Phort Rìgh agus tha a dhachaigh agus an stiùidio aige ann an Dùn Bheagain, san Eilean Sgitheanach. Tha taisbeanaidhean air a bhith aige ann an Dùn Èideann, Inbhir Nis, am Peairt agus ann am Baile Atha Cliath. Tha a chuid obrach ri a faicinn anns na cruinneachaidhean aig Comhairle nan Eilean Siar, Bòrd Slàinte Roinn a' Mhonaidh, Comhairle Baile Dhùn Èideann agus Oifis na h-Alba, a bharrachd air cruinneachaidhean prìobhaideach san Roinn Eòrpa agus ann an Aimeireagaidh.

Andrew McMorrine
After studying at Glasgow School of Art, he has lived in the Hebrides since 1973, teaching and painting. He is currently principal teacher of art at Portree High School and lives on Skye. He has exhibited in Edinburgh, Inverness, Perth and Dublin and has work in the collections of the Western Isles Council, Grampian Health Board, Edinburgh City Council and the Scottish Office as well as in private collections in Europe and the USA.

David McGrail

37 **Eoghan Rua Ó Súileabháin**
Rugadh i Sliabh Luachra i 1748 é, d'éag 1784. Liriceoir, aorthóir agus laoch an phobail, cluanaí ban, múinteoir scoile agus mairnéalach (faoi cheannas an Aimiréil Rodney). Tá urraim ag daoine fós dó i ngeall ar a ghaiscí agus a dhánta. Tá clú agus cáil ar a chuid aislingí. Is iad a dhánta ag moladh na mban a thuill clú dó. Féach *Amhráin Eoghain Rua Uí Shúilleabháin*, eag. Pádraig Ó Duinnín (1901).

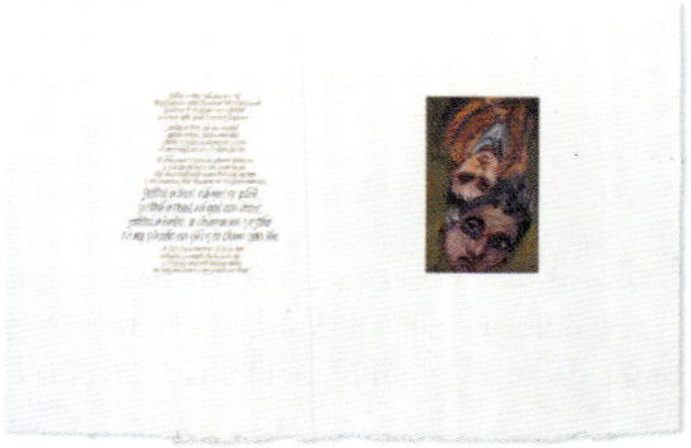

Owen Roe O'Sullivan
He was born at Sliabh Luachra in 1748, and died in 1784. Lyricist, satirist and folk-hero, philanderer, schoolteacher, sailor (under Admiral Rodney), he is still venerated for his exploits and poems. His aislings are considered atmospheric masterpieces; his poems in praise of women won him renown. See *Amhráin Eoghain Rua Uí Shúilleabháin*, ed. Pádraig Ó Duinnín (1901).

Steven Caimbeul

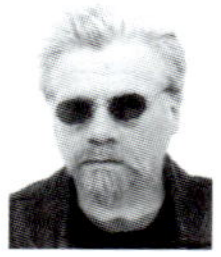

Am measg phroiseactan o chionn ghoirid tha taisbeanadh mòr air Bàrd-cùirte Alba, Edwin Morgan anns a' Ghailearaidh Dhealbh Nàiseanta an Dùn Èideann. O chionn greise tha e air a bhith ag ullachadh proiseact a bhios fhathast a' nochdadh ann an 2002 – 'Sùil air Ais' – agus chithear e sa Ghailearaidh Talbot Rice an Dun Èideann. Bidh m' obair a' cumail a' dol a' rannsachadh nan co-cheangal a th' eadar luchd-ealain anns an rìoghachd bhig ioma-chruthachail seo.

Steven Campbell
Recent projects include a large exhibition on Scotland's Poet Laureate, Edwin Morgan, at the National Portrait Gallery in Edinburgh. There is a planned show of major new works for 2002 at the Talbot Rice Gallery, Edinburgh. He wants to continue to explore the huge area of collaboration which exists among artists in 'this small but creatively diverse country'.

Réiltín Murphy

38 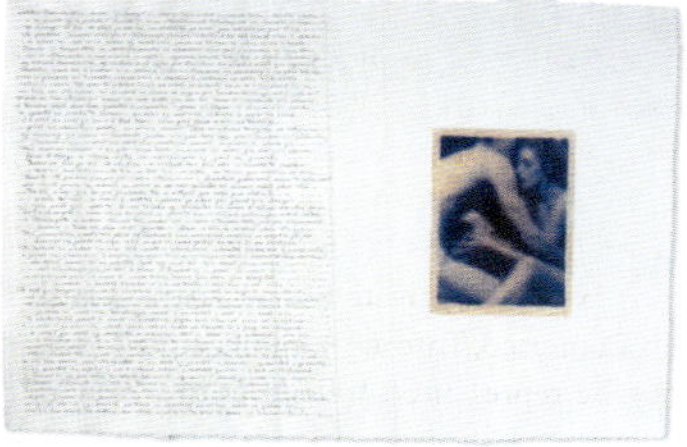

Brian Merriman
I gCo. an Chláir a rugadh c.1745. Cailleadh 1805. Taobh amuigh de mhionphíosa no dhó is cosúil nár chum sé ach an t-aon dán conspóideach amháin – 'Cúirt An Mheán Oíche', dán fada a mheall mórán aistritheoirí tríd na blianta síos, ina measc Frank O'Connor agus David Marcus. Féach *Cúirt An Mheon-Oíche*, eag. Liam Ó Murchú (1982).

Brian Merriman
Born c.1745 in Co. Clare, he died in 1805.
Apart from one or two slight pieces, he appears only to have written the controversial 'Cúirt An Mheán Oíche', a long poem which has attracted many translators over the years, including Frank O'Connor and David Marcus. See *Cúirt an Mheon-Oíche*, ed. Liam Ó Murchú (1982).

Shane Cullen *(Photo: Declan Barnes)*

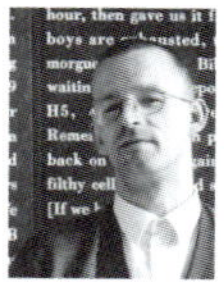

Rugadh Shane Cullen, ealaíontóir, i Longphort agus tá sé anois in a chónaí i mBaile Átha Cliath. Cuireadh a shaothar ar taispeáint ag go leor seónna aonair agus seónna oscailte in Éirinn agus thar lear. Taispeánadh a shraith 'Fragmens sur les Institutions Républicaines IV' ar fud na hEorpa, agus i San Francisco, Toronto agus Nua Eabhrac. I 1995 sheas sé ar son na hÉireann ag an Seastán Gaelach le linn Biennale na Veinéise. Fostaíodh mar ealaíontóir cónaitheach é i PS1 i Nua Eabhrac, san Fhrainc agus i mBudapest ag amanna éagsúla.

Shane Cullen

Shane Cullen is a Longford-born artist now based in Dublin. He has had many solo and group exhibitions nationally and internationally. His series of work 'Fragmens sur les Institutions Républicaines IV' has been exhibited throughout Europe, and in San Francisco, Toronto and New York. In 1995 he represented Ireland at the the Venice Biennale. He has completed artist residencies in PS1 in New York, France and Budapest.

Frances Breen

39

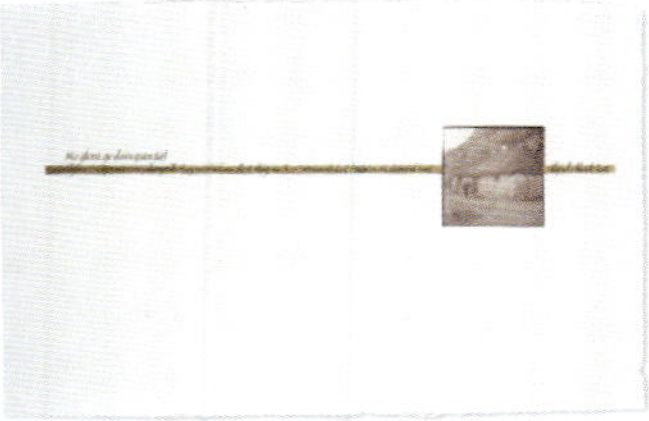

Eibhlín Dhubh Ní Chonaill

Is i gCiarraí a rugadh c.1743. Cailleadh 1800. Chum sí an marbhna iontach sin 'Caoineadh Airt Uí Laoghaire'. Cumadh an chéad chuid ar an láthair os cionn coirp a fir tar éis a dhúnmharú. Breacadh síos an téacs deiridh ón mbéaloideas na blianta ina dhiaidh sin. Féach *Caoineadh Airt Uí Laoghaire*, eag. Seán Ó Tuama (1961).

Eibhlín Dubh O Connell

Born in Kerry c.1743, she died in 1800. Composer of this extraordinary lament, the first part of which was extemporised over the fresh corpse of her murdered husband, the final text being taken down many years later from the oral tradition. See *Caoineadh Airt Uí Laoghaire*, ed. Seán Ó Tuama (1961).

Ceabhan MacIlleathain *(Photo: Martin Dobbin)*

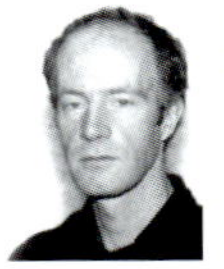

Rugadh e an 1966 an Obar Bhrothaig. Tha e air a bhith a' fuireach an Dùn Èideann airson còig bliadhna deug. Bha e ag obair còmhla ri Eideard Scott a' cleachdadh ìomhaighean na tìre mar mhodh air dealbh a thoirt air saoghal a' chinne daonna. 'S ann bhon bhunait sin a tha e air obair fhèin a thoirt air adhart, an urra anns a' bhitheantas ri na seann sgeulachdan Ceilteach. Tha an obair aige tric a' sealltainn na h-àbhaist ann an cruth neo-àbhaisteach.

Kevin MacLean

Born in Arbroath in 1966, he now lives in Edinburgh. MacLean worked collaboratively with Edward Scott using elements from the land to illustrate an anthropomorphic world. He developed his solo work from this starting point drawing mainly on Celtic myth and legend. His work frequently shows the ordinary in an out-of the-ordinary-way.

Louise Donaldson

40

Iain MacGillEathain

Rugadh Iain MacGillEathain, 'Bàrd Thighearna Chola' (1787–1848), sa Chaolas, an Tiriodh. Bha e na ghreusaiche. Rinn Tighearna Chola na bhàrd dha fhèin e, agus rinn e iomadh òran molaidh 's gàirdeachais dhan teaghlach aige, ach na latha-san cha robh tiotalan mar seo a' ciallachadh mòran, agus thug e Alba Nuadh air ann an 1819. Mar a dh'èirich do mhòran, bha an eilthireachd na mealladh dhuil dha, an toiseach co-dhiù. B' e dàin spioradail agus òrain aotrom bu mhotha a rinn e san t-saoghal ùr, ach tha caran de dh'inbhe laoidh nàiseanta aig 'A' Choille Ghruamach' am measg Gaidheil Cheap Bhreatainn, 's cha bheag an t-iongnadh.

John MacLean

John MacLean, 'The Laird of Coll's Bard' (1787–1848), was born in Tiree. The Laird of Coll made him his poet, and he composed many songs of praise and celebration for the family, but titles like this did not mean a great deal in his day, and he went to Nova Scotia in 1819. In the New World he composed mainly hymns and light songs, but his 'Coille Ghruamach' has something like anthemic status amongst Cape Breton Gaels.

Tarmod Seadha *(Photo: L. Szpak)*

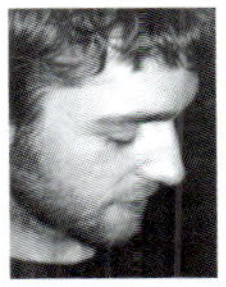

Àite-breith: Ulapul 1970, 1971–79 Corpach; 1979–88, Calanais
1993 – MA (Àrd-ìre Le Urram) Grinneas, Oilthigh agus Colaiste Ealain Dhùn Èideann
1994 – MPhil, Dùn Èideann
1996 – MFA (Peantadh), Dùn Èideann
1998–2002 – PhD, Colaiste Ealain Dhonnchaidh Iòrdanstain, Dùn Dè

Norman Shaw

Norman Shaw was born in Ullapool in 1970. He has an MA and MPhil from Edinburgh; and a PhD from Duncan of Jordanstone College in Dundee.

Réiltín Murphy

Niall MacLeòid

Rugadh Niall MacLeòid (1843–1924) an Gleann Dail san Eilean Sgitheanach, ach nuair a bha e 22 thug e Dùn Èideann air agus bha e an sin an còrr dhe bheatha, ag obair na mharsanta teatha. Bha a' bhàrdachd na fhuil – b' e 'Dòmhnall nan Òran' a chanadh iad ri athair, agus thathar ag ràdh gun robh bàrdachd a bhràthar, Iain Dubh, (a bha na mharaiche) na b' fhearr na dad a rinn Niall riamh. Chan eil fhios againn a bheil seo fìor. Bha Niall proifeiseanta gu chùl: ge b' e teatha no bàrdachd e, bheireadh e do dhaoine na bha dhìth orra, agus, eu-coltach ri bhràthair, bha de ghliocas aige a bhàrdachd (*Clàrsach an Doire*, 1883) a thoirt a-mach mar leabhar.

41

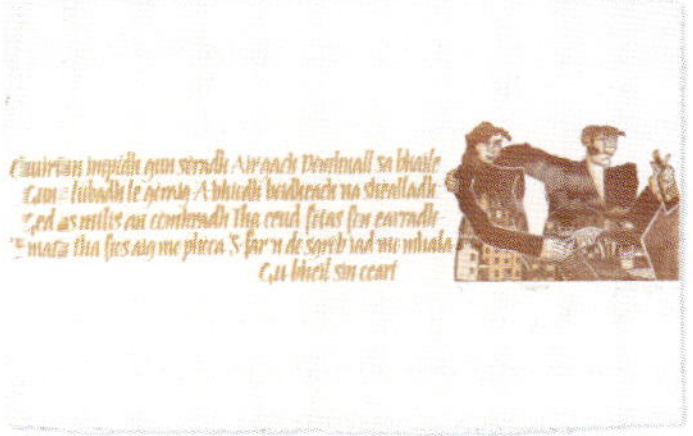

Neil MacLeod

Neil MacLeod (1843–1924) was born on Skye, but at twenty-two he went to Edinburgh and remained there the rest of his life, working as a tea merchant. Poetry was in his blood – his father's nickname was 'Donald of the Songs', and it is said that the poetry of his brother Iain Dubh (who was a seaman) was better than anything Neil had ever done. We do not know if this is true, but Neil had the wisdom to bring his poetry out as a book (*Clàrsach an Doire*, 1883).

Iain MacNaught *(Photo: John McNaught)*

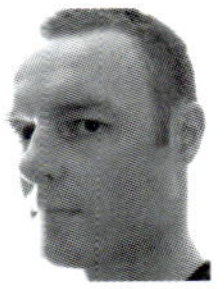

Rugadh Iain MacNaught an Glaschu an 1966. Thogadh e am Beinn na Fadhla agus san Eilean Sgitheanach, agus tha e a-nis a' fuireach an Cromba. Tha e a' spèisealachadh ann an clò-bhualadh cumach agus leabhraichean luchd-ealain. Tha na taisbeanaidhean aon-neach aige a' gabhail a-steach na leanas: 'The Argentina Debacle', 'Not Donald MacDonald' agus 'Mind Your Head' – tasglann de dh'Ospadal Chreig an Dùnain an Inbhir Nis

John McNaught

John McNaught was born in Glasgow in 1966.

He was brought up on Benbecula and Skye, and is now based in Cromarty. Specialising in relief printmaking and artists' books, his solo shows include: 'The Argentina Debacle', 'Not Donald MacDonald' and 'Mind Your Head' (an archive of Craig Dunain Psychiatric Hospital).

Louise Donaldson

42

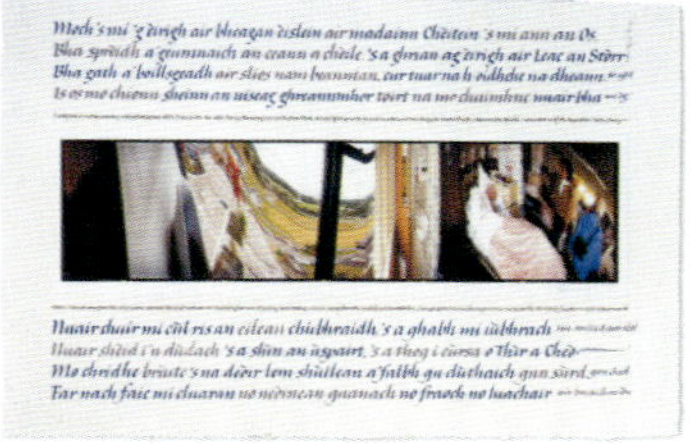

Màiri Mhòr nan Oran

B' e Dòmhnallach à Sgèabost san Eilean Sgitheanach a bh' ann am Màiri Mhòr nan Òran (1821-98). Phòs i Ìsaac Mac a' Phearsain à Inbhir Nis. Dh'eug esan an 1871, agus chaidh Màiri na searbhant. Ann an 1872 chaidh cur às a leth gun do ghoid i an t-aodach aig boireannach marbh nuair bha an tòrradh a' gabhail àite agus thugadh dhi dà fhichead là sa phrìosan. 'S e, na faclan fhèin, 'na dh'fhuiling mi de thàmailt / a thug mo bhàrdachd beò'. Ri linn aimhreit an fhearainn bha mòran Ghaidheal a' cur feum air barrachd brosnachaidh na bha Niall MacLeòid a' toirt dhaibh; fad còrr is fichead bliadhna b' e Màiri a thug dhaibh e, agus choisinn i meas agus gaol nan Sgitheanach.

Mary MacPherson

Màiri Mhòr nan Òran (1821-98) was born a MacDonald on Skye. She married Isaac MacPherson from Inverness. He died in 1871, and Mary became a servant. In 1872 she was accused of stealing a dead woman's clothes and was given forty days in prison. This was 'the humiliation I suffered/which brought my verse alive'. For over twenty years Mary provided her readers with strength during the land struggle, winning the love and respect of the people of Skye.

Stephen Lawson *(Photo: Stephen Lawson)*

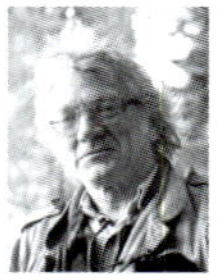

Rugadh e an Glaschu an 1942; thogadh e agus fhuair e fhoglam an Inbhir Nis. Dh'ionnsaich e mu dhealbhachadh ann an Colaiste Ealain Dhùn Èideann agus Oilthigh Cholorado, Boulder, Aimeireagaidh. Bho 1984, às dèidh trì bliadhna deug a' teagaisg dealbhachadh, tha e air obrachadh a' cleachdadh camarathan làmh-dhèante, anns a' bhitheantas a rèir na tire, an dà chuid an Alba 's an Aimeireagaidh. Tha an obair aige a' nochdadh ann an Cruinneachadh Nàiseanta nan Dealbh, Ionad Ealain Baile Dhùn Èideann, Kelvingrove, Inbhir Nis agus V&A, Lunnainn.

Stephen Lawson

Born in Glasgow in 1942, he was raised and schooled in Inverness. He studied sculpture at Edinburgh College of Art and Colorado University. Since 1984, after thirteen years teaching sculpture Lawson has worked using hand-made cameras, mostly via landscape, both in Scotland and the USA. He has had works in the National Photography Collection, Edinburgh City Art Centre, Kelvingrove, Inverness and the Victoria & Albert Museum, London.

Dòmhnall Moireach/Donald Murray

43

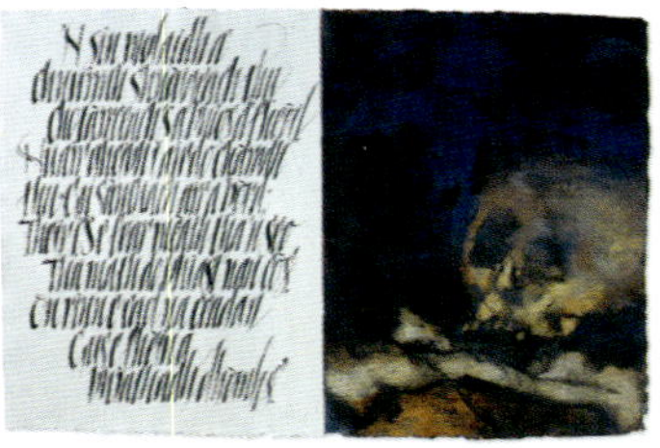

Iain Mac a' Ghobhainn

Rugadh Iain Mac a' Ghobhainn (Seonaidh Phàdraig, 1848-81) an Iarsiadar, Ùig, Eilean Leòdhais. Bha e còig bliadhna ag ionnsachadh leighis an Oilthigh Dhùn Èideann, ach ghabh e a' chaitheamh, agus thill e a chur seachad nan seachd bliadhna a bh' aige air fhàgail, aig an taigh. Rinn e oidhirp air mòran dhe na h-aon chuspairean bàrdail ri Uilleam MacDhunlèibhe (q.v.), ach bha aimhreit an fhearainn a' tachairt uile-thimcheall air, agus chuidich seo e gu fearg rianail a chur an cèill ann an cuid dhe na dàin as fhaide aige - mu 'Spiorad a' Charthannais' sgrìobh Ruaraidh MacThòmais gu bheil e na fhaochadh 'gun tàinig cridhe 's inntinn còmhla gu bàrdachd mhòr a dhèanamh mun do theirig an linn'.

John Smith

John Smith (Seonaidh Phàdraig, 1848-81) was born on Lewis. He studied medicine at Edinburgh University, but contracted consumption and returned home for his last seven years. The land-struggle was happening all around him, and this helped him express controlled passion in some of his longer poems. Of 'Spiorad a' Charthannais' Derick Thomson wrote that it is a relief 'that heart and mind combined to produce a great poem before the century was out'.

Hughie O'Donoghue *(Photo: Clare O' Donoghue)*

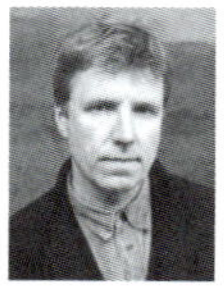

I Manchester a rugadh Hughie O'Donoghue i 1953. Déanann a phictiúir ollmhóra iniúchadh ar théamaí staire, cuimhne agus aitheanta agus táid ar fáil i músaem ar fud an domhain. Le déanaí bhí taispeántais aonair uaidh ag Gailearaí Rubicon (2001), sa Royal Hibernian Academy (1999) agus in Áras Nua-Ealaíne na hÉireann (1998/1999). B'é an chéad ealaíontóir cónaithe ag St John's College in Oxford é (2000).

Hughie O'Donoghue

Hughie O'Donoghue was born in Manchester in 1953. His monumentally scaled paintings explore themes of history, memory and identity and are represented in museums throughout the world. Recent individual exhibitions have taken place at the Rubicon Gallery, Royal Hibernian Academy and Irish Museum of Modern Art. The artist was the inaugural Resident Artist at St John's College in Oxford (2000).

Louise Donaldson

44

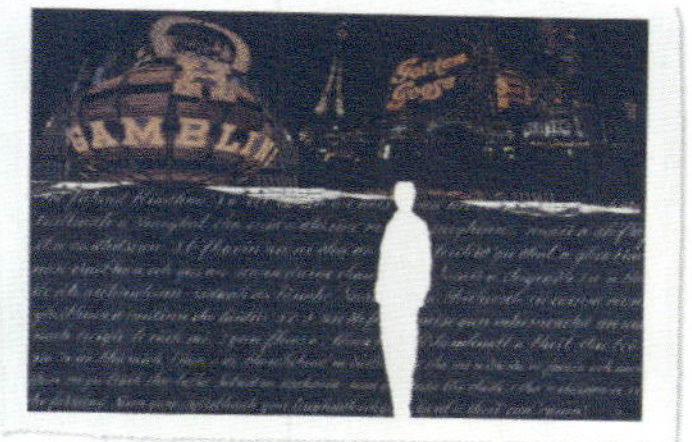

Dòmhnall Mac A' Ghobhainn (Dòmhnall mac Ailein)

B' e Dòmhnall mac Ailein a rinn 'Trì Fichead Bliadhna 's a Trì' ann am meadhan nan 1850an dha bhràthair, Aonghas, a bha air Dail ann an Nis fhàgail airson a dhol a dh'Aimeireagaidh còmhla ri dithis dhe thriùir mhac, Ailean agus Dòmhnall. Tha beul-aithris ag innse dhuinn gun robh bean Dhòmhnaill ga lorg aon là 's gun d' fhuair i e na shuidhe air an àth san t-sabhal, a' gal agus a' dèanamh an òrain seo - an aon òran as aithne dhuinn a rinn e riamh - agus fios aige nach biodh comhluadar tuilleadh eadar e fhèin 's a bhràthair seach nach robh sgrìobhadh aig fear seach fear. Chaidh Iain, am mac a dh'fhuirich aig an taigh, a bhàthadh. Rinn Dòmhnall Chràisgein, Bàrd Bharabhais, òran mun adhbhar-bròin - 'Òran Eathar Aonghais Chaluim Ruaidh'.

Donald Smith

He composed this poem in the mid-1850s for his brother, Angus, who left Dell for America with two of his three sons. Tradition has it that Donald's wife, looking for him one day found him sitting in the barn weeping as he composed this song knowing that his brother was beyond his reach because they were both illiterate. The son who stayed behind was drowned. Dòmhnall Chràisgein, the *Barvas Bàrd* composed a song about the tragedy – 'Òran Eathar Aonghais Chaluim Ruaidh'.

Noel Sheridan *(Photo: Anthony Hobbs, NCAD)*

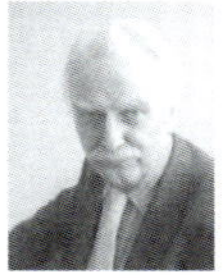

Ealaíontóir é Noel Sheridan a thaispeáin a shaothar in Éirinn agus thar lear ó na caogadaí déanacha ar aghaidh. Bhí taispeántas aige anois beag i nGailearaí an Royal Hibernian Academy i mBaile Átha Cliath – cuid de ag caitheamh súil siar ar a shaothar. Ní fada ó d'fhoilsigh The Four Courts Press *On Reflection* – leabhar bunaithe ar a shaothar.

Noel Sheridan

Noel Sheridan is an artist who has exhibited work in Ireland and overseas since the late 1950s. A recent exhibition has been a partial retrospective show at the Royal Hibernian Academy Gallery in Dublin. The Four Courts Press has recently published a book *On Reflection* based on his work.

Anna Bowen/Ann Bowen

45

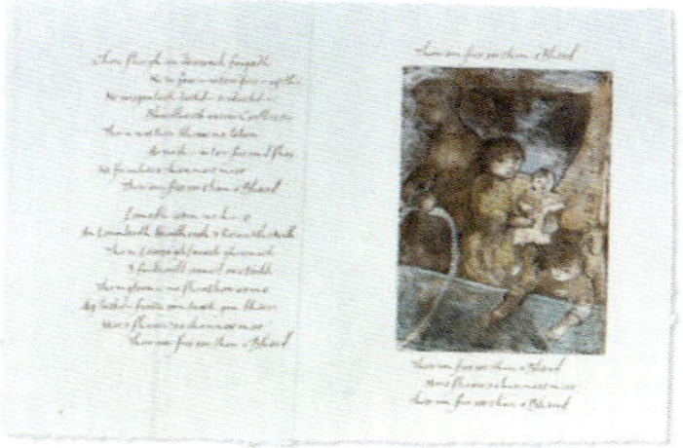

Uilleam MacDhunlèibhe

Rugadh Uilleam MacDhunlèibhe (1808-70) ann an Cill an Rubha an Ìle. Bha e na thàillear 's na dhuine fèin-ionnsaichte a bhiodh a' leughadh gun sgur. Chaidh e a dh'fhuireach a Thradeston an Glaschu. Cha robh e fhèin idir gaisgeil ach tha a bhàrdachd loma-làn ghaisgeach Gaidhealach. Bha e na nàiseantach Albannach agus bhiodh e a' dèanamh làn ròlaistean rannaigheachd mu bhlàir mhòra nan linntean a bh' ann. Tha neart nan liric agus geurad poileataigeach air am filleadh gu snasail ann an cuid dhe na dàin as giorra aige.

William Livingstone

William Livingstone (1808-70) was born on Islay. A tailor and a self-educated man who read constantly, he went to live in Glasgow. Livingstone was a Scottish nationalist and composed massive romances in verse about the great battles of the past. Some of his shorter poems are a perfect combination of lyric force and political acumen.

Anna Davis *(Photo: Richard Carter)*

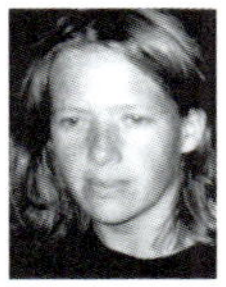

Cheumnaich Anna Davis ann an 1987 à Sgoil Ealain agus Dealbhaidh Ghray aig Prìomh-ìre ann an dealbhachd agus peantadh. Ann an 1990 ghluais i a dh'Uibhist a Tuath far an do rinn i a dachaigh airson deich bliadhna. Tha taisbeanaidhean air a bhith aice air feadh Alba – feadhainn dhen sin mar aon-neach. Tha a dachaigh a-nis an Dùn Èideann.

Anna Davis

Anna Davis graduated from Grays School of Art and Design with a first in Drawing and Painting. She moved to North Uist in 1990 where she continued to work as an artist. She has had solo exhibitions at An Lanntair, An Tuirean and Taigh Chearsabhagh Art Centre and various shows throughout Scotland. Davis now lives in Edinburgh.

Louise Donaldson

46

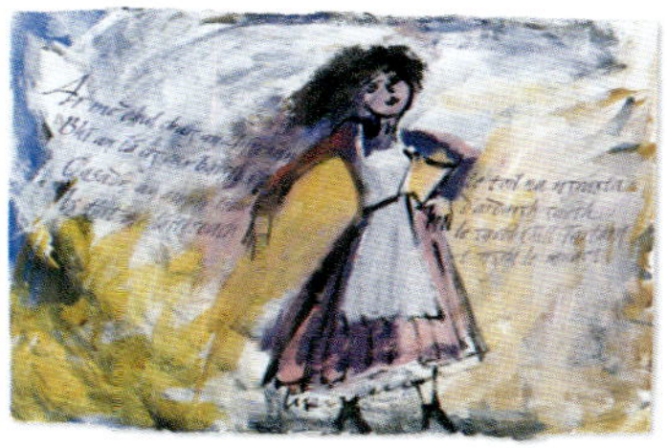

Antoin Ó Raifteirí

Antoine Ó Raifteraí a scríobhtar freisin. I gCo. Mhaigh Eo a rugadh 1779. Cailleadh 1835. Cliaraí fánach a raibh tuairimí polaitiúla radacaigh aige; Caitliceach díocasach agus file conspóideach a raibh an-tóir air, agus meas air i gcónaí. Tá sé ráite gurb é an dán corraitheach sin 'Eanach Dhúin' an saothar ab fhearr a dhein sé. Féach *Raifteaí: Amhráin agus Dánta*, eag. Ciarán Ó Coigligh (1987).

Anthony Raftery

(Also written Antoine Ó Raifteaí.) He was born in Co. Mayo in 1779, and died in 1835. A wandering minstrel of radical political views, he was fiercely Catholic, and a contentious popular poet cherished in folk memory. His lament 'Eanach Dhúin' is deeply moving, perhaps his finest poem. See *Raifteaí: Amhráin agus Dánta*, ed. Ciarán Ó Coigligh (1987).

Micheál Kane *(Photo: Alen MacWeeney)*

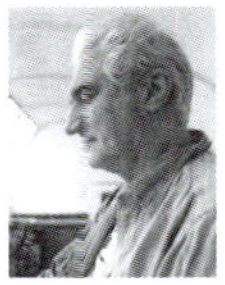

Chaith Michael Kane an chuid is mó dá shaol fásta i mBaile Átha Cliath - áit a rugadh é i 1935 – taobh amuigh de thréimhsí a chaith sé sa Spáinn, san Iodáil agus san Eilbhéis. D'fhreastail sé ar an gColáiste Náisiúnta Ealaíne is Deartha agus rinne sé staidéar ar conas priontaí a chruthú. Thaispeáin sé a shaothar don chéad uair ag Gailearaí Ritchie Hendriks i mBaile Átha Cliath i 1960 agus ó shin i leith is mó taispeántas aonair a chuir sé ar siúl i mBaile Átha Cliath, i Londain agus i Zurich. I 1995 bhí taispeántas aisbhreathnaitheach aige sa Royal Hibernian Academy.

Michael Kane

Born in Dublin in 1935, Michael Kane still lives there, with intervals spent in Spain, Italy and Switzerland. He attended the National College of Art and also studied printmaking. He has had many solo shows in Dublin, London, Zurich, including a retrospective at the Royal Hibernian Academy (1995); his first was at the Ritchie Hendriks Gallery in Dublin in 1960.

Frances Breen

47

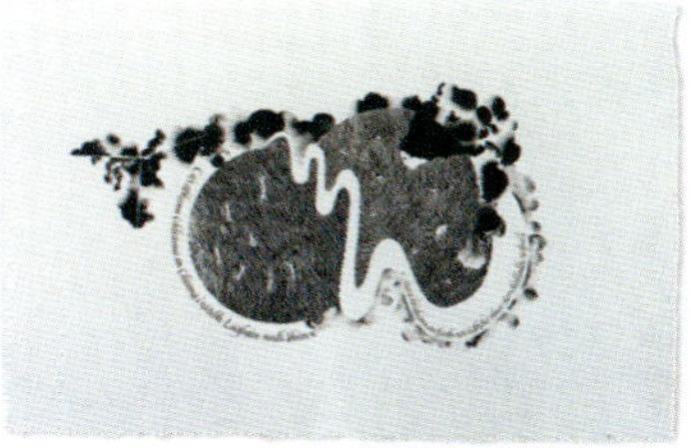

Máire Bhuí Ní Laoire

I gCo. Chorcaí a rugadh 1774. Cailleadh c.1849. Ní raibh léamh ná scríobh aici ach mhair a saothar i mbéaloideas Iarthair Chorcaí. Chum sí cánta grá, marbhnaí agus dánta diaga. Cáil fé leith don dán ornáideach sin 'Cath Chéim an Fhiaidh' agus don aisling 'Ar Leacain na Gréine'. Féach *Filíocht Mháire Bhuidhe Ní Laoghaire*, eag. Donncha Ó Donnchú (1931).

Máire Bhuí Ní Laoire

Born in Co. Cork in 1774, she died c.1849. She was illiterate, but her compositions survived in the folklore of West Cork. Maker of love poems, laments and religious poems, she is best known for the colourful 'Cath Chéim an Fhiaidh' and the aisling 'Ar Leacain na Gréine'. See *Filíocht Mháire Bhuidhe Ní Laoghaire*, ed. Donncha Ó Donnchú (1931).

Tom Fitzgerald *(Photo: Eoin Stephenson)*

Ó d'éirigh sé as oifig mar Cheann Roinn na

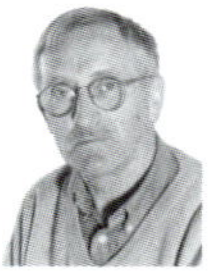

Dealbhóireachta i Scoil Ealaíne is Deartha Luimní sa bhliain 2000, chaith sé a chuid ama ag obair ar choimisiúin phoiblí agus ar chinn phríobháideacha. Ghlac sé páirt i roinnt mhaith taispeántas sa bhaile agus i gcéin agus tá saothar uaidh le feiceáil i mbailiúcháin fhiúntacha anseo in Éirinn. Deir an léirmheastóir Aidan Dunne ina thaobh (The Sunday Tribune, 1990): 'Dealbhóir cumasach ó Luimneach é Mac Gearailt, a chruthaigh stíl fhéitheogach ar leith dó féin'.

Tom Fitzgerald
Since retiring as head of the Sculpture department in Limerick School of Art and Design, he has devoted his time to public and private commissions. He has exhibited in many national and international shows and his work has been included in important public collections in Ireland. Critic Aidan Dunne has written: 'Fitzgerald is a formidable Limerick sculptor who has carved out a distinctive, muscular style for himself.'

David McGrail

48

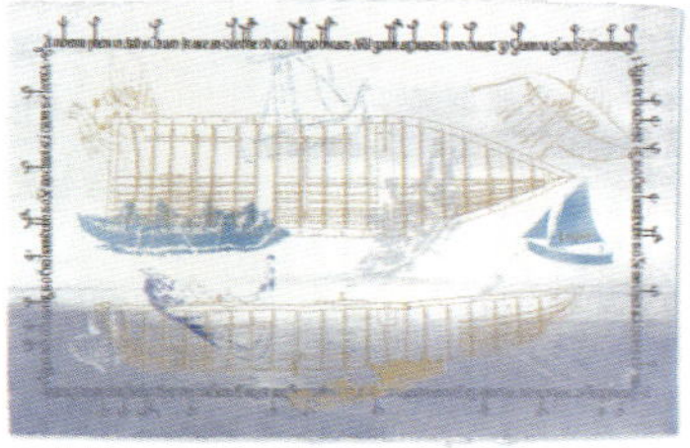

Eoin Mac Ambróis
Tugtar John McCambridge nó Iain Mac Ambróis freisin air. Rugadh i gCo. Aontroma, 1793. D'éag 1873. Is cosúil gurb é a chum 'Ard a' Chuain', a meastar a bheith ar cheann de na hamhráin Ghaeilge is deise dá bhfuil ann. Tá tréithe teangeolaíocha san amhrán seo a bhaineann le Gaeilge na hÉireann agus le Gàidhlig na hAlban araon.

John McCambridge
(Sometimes Iain Mac Ambróis.) He was born in Co. Antrim in 1793, and died in 1873. He is almost certainly the author of 'Ard a' Chuain', considered one of the finest songs in the language. The text contains some linguistic features which may be considered transitional between Irish Gaelic and Scottish Gaelic.

Brian Connolly *(Photo: Annette Hennessy)*

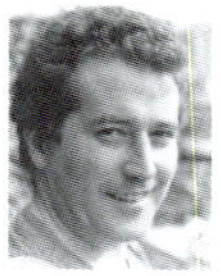

Ealaíontóir ilmheáin é Brian Connolly ó Thuaisceart na hÉireann. Tá baint ag a shaothar go minic le 'suíomh' nó le 'comhthéacs'. Cruthaíonn sé saothar déthoimhseach, ealaín suiteála, léirithe agus dealbhóireacht phoiblí. Tá taispeántais agus léirithe curtha ar fáil aige i bhfad i gcéin agus tá dealbhóireacht phoiblí cruthaithe aige in Éirinn agus san Iodáil. Eagraíonn se imeachtaí ealaíne idirnáisiúnta in Éirinn, i mBeirlín agus sa Pholainn. Fé láthair tá sé ina Chomhléachtóir ag Ollscoil Uladh i mBeál Féirste.

Brian Connolly
Brian Connolly is a Northern Irish multi-media artist whose works often relate to 'place' or 'context'. He creates 2D work, installation art, performance and public sculpture. The artist has exhibited and performed internationally and created public sculptures in Ireland and Italy. He is currently an associate lecturer at the University of Ulster at Belfast.

Tim O'Neill

Donnchadh MacDhunlèibhe *(with thanks to Mrs Helen Reynolds)*
B' e mac clachair à Raodal, Tòrrloisgt, Eilean Mhuile a bh' ann an Donnchadh MacDhunlèibhe (1877-1964). Chaidh a leòn an Cogadh nam Boer 1899-1902. Thill e a dh'Afraga

49

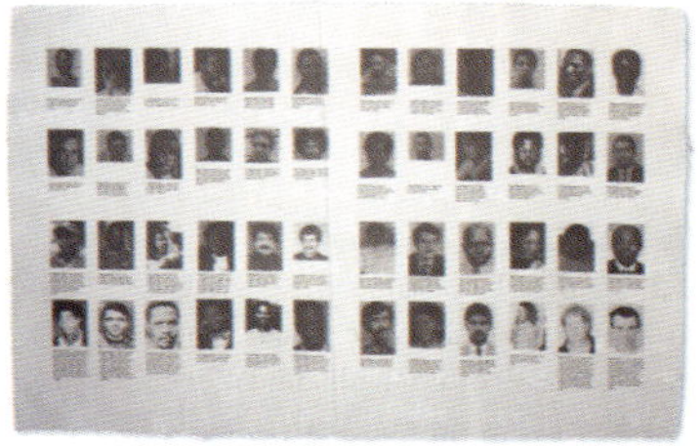

a Deas an 1903 a dh'obair na àrd-clachair 's bha e gu mòr an sàs ann a bhith a' togail ceann-chairtealan an riaghaltais ùir ann am Pretoria, an Afraga a Deas 1910-13. Bha beatha chofhurtail aige am measg a cho-Ghaidheal (cha do thill e dh'Alba riamh) ach o 1951 a-mach bha a bhàrdachd làn de dh'anshocair phoileataigeach agus cùram sòisealta.

Duncan Livingstone
Duncan Livingstone (1877-1964) was born on Mull. He was wounded in the Boer War but returned to South Africa in 1903 to work as a master mason and helped construct the headquarters of the new South African government in Pretoria. Livingstone enjoyed a comfortable life amongst his fellow-Gaels (he never returned to Scotland) but after 1951 his poetry was full of political anxiety and social concern.

Mick O'Kelly

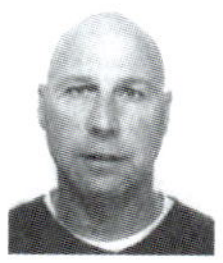

Cuireann Mick O'Kelly fé i mBaile Átha Cliath agus oibríonn go páirt-aimseartha sa Choláiste Náisiúnta Ealaíne is Deartha. Bhain sé céim amach mar dhealbhóir ón gcoláiste céanna agus bhain Máistreacht sna Míndána amach sa California Institute of the Arts. Chuir sé a shaothar ealaíne ar taispeáint in iarsmalanna agus i ngailearaithe i Frankfurt, Páras, Santa Monica agus i suímh neamhghnácha éagsúla.

Mick O'Kelly
Mick O'Kelly lives in Dublin and works part-time at the National College of Art and Design. He graduated in Sculpture from the National College of Art and Design and completed an MFA in the California Institute of the Arts. He has presented his artwork in museums and galleries in Frankfurt, Paris and Santa Monica as well as in non-conventional sites.

Dòmhnall Addison/Donald Addison

50

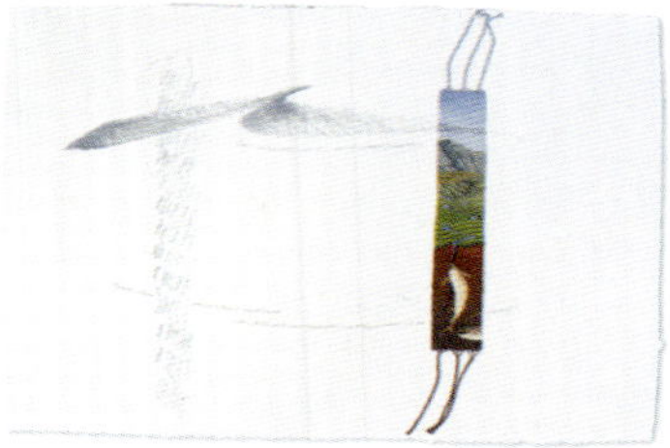

Màiri NicGumaraid *(Photo: Rod Huckbody)*

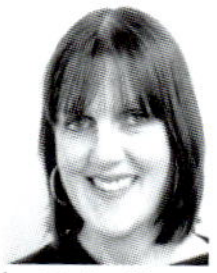

Rugadh Màiri NicGumaraid sa Mhàrt 1955 an Airidh a' Bhruaich an Sgìre nan Loch, Eilean Leòdhais, an tè a b' òige de thriùir chloinne. Tha dà leabhar bàrdachd aice foillsichte le Coiscéim ann am Baile Atha Cliath: *Eadar Mi 's a' Bhreug*, 1988 agus *Ruithmean 's Neo-Rannan*, 1997. Tha i a' fuireach ann am Baile Ailein ann an Leòdhas agus tha dithis chloinne aice.

Mary Montgomery
Mary Montgomery was born in March 1955 in Arivruaich, Lewis, the youngest of three children. She has had two books of poetry published by Coiscéim in Dublin: *Eadar Mi 's a' Bhreug*, 1988 and *Ruithmean 's Neo-Rannan*, 1997. She lives in Balallan in Lewis and has two children.

Joanne Breen (1960-2002) *(Photo: Frances Breen)*
Is i Loch Garman a rugadh an t-ealaíontóir taipéise Joanne Breen – iaroide sa Choláiste

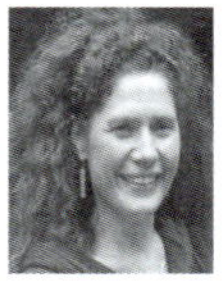

Náisiúnta Ealaíne is Deartha. Léiríonn a cuid saothair tionchar an duine agus an radhairc tíre ar a chéile ina h-áit dúchais, agus ins na hOileáin Siar in Albain. Ó 1990 i leith bíonn sí féin agus a deirfiúr, Frances Breen peannaire, ag obair as lámha a chéile ag léiriú fhilíocht agus amhrán na Gàidhlige agus na Gaeilge.

Joanne Breen

Born in Wexford, tapestry artist Joanne Breen studied and lectured at the National College of Art and Design in Dublin. Her work explores the traces and tracks left by man's interaction with the landscape. Since 1990 she and her sister, calligrapher Frances Breen, have collaborated on a series of works interpreting Scottish and Irish Gaelic poetry and song.

Frances Breen

51 

Morag NicGumaraid

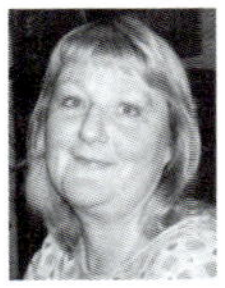

Rugadh i ann an 1950 ann an Ròdhag, An t-Eilean Sgitheanach. Fhuair i foghlam ann an Drochaid Bhatain, Port Rìgh agus Sgoil Ealain Ghlaschu. Ann an 1976 chaidh i na sgrìobhaiche còmhnaidheach gu Sabhal Mòr Ostaig, san Eilean Sgìtheanach. Tha i air a bhith air trì de Chuairtean bliadhnail nam Bàrd Albannach/Eireannach. Tha a bàrdachd air nochdadh ann an *Gairm, Sruth na Maoile* agus anns *A' Choille Chiar* - cruinneachadh còmhla ri a piuthar, Catrìona.

Morag Montgomery

Born in 1950 on Skye, she was educated at Vatten Bridge, Portree and Glasgow School of Art. In 1976 she became writer-in-residence at Sabhal Mor Ostaig, Skye. She has taken part in three of the Scottish-Irish annual Poets' Tours. Her poetry has appeared in *Gairm, Sruth na Maoile* and in *A' Choille Chiar* – a joint collection with her sister Catriona.

Eileen Coates *(Photo: Breege Moynihan)*

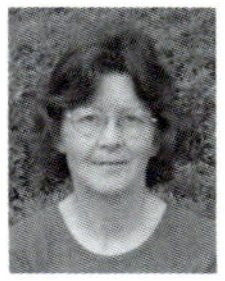

I Sasana i 1946 a rugadh Eileen Coates agus i 1978 d'aistrigh sí go hÉirinn. Chuaigh sí le criadóireacht ag Scoil Ealaíne is Deartha Luimní agus ghnóthaigh Máistreacht Ealaíne ón gColáiste Náisiúnta Ealaíne is Deartha. Ina saothar déanann sí iniúchadh ar chúrsaí ionannais, tomhais agus limistéir tré úsáid a bhaint as criadóireacht agus meáin mheasctha. Bhí taispeántais aonair aici i mBéal Feirste, i mBaile Átha Cliath agus i Luimneach chomh maith le taispeántais oscailte sa tSeapáin, san Astráil, sna Stáit Aontaithe, sa Ghearmáin agus in Albain agus Éirinn.

Eileen Coates

Born in England in 1946, Eileen Coates moved to Ireland in 1978. She studied Ceramics at Limerick School of Art and Design and received an MA from the National College of Art and Design. She explores repetition, scale and space using ceramics and mixed media. She has had solo exhibitions in Belfast, Dublin and Limerick and group exhibitions in Japan, Australia, USA, Germany, Scotland and Ireland.

Réiltín Murphy

52 **Domhnall MacAmhlaigh**

Àite-breith: Beàrnaraigh Leòdhais 21.05.30. Oideachadh: Àrd-sgoil Steòrnabhaigh;

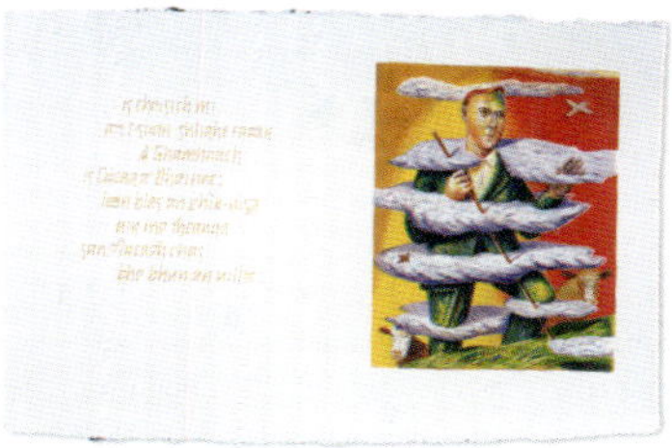

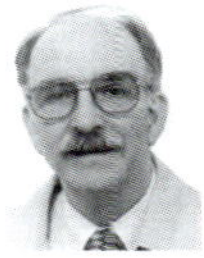

Oilthighean: Obar Dheathain (1949-53): Cambridge (1953-55). Ceuman: Ceiltis is Beurla, agus Ceiltis, Sean-Bheurla is Sean-Lochlannais; Iarcheum: Cànanachas. Dreuchdan: Oilthigh Dhùn Èideann (1958-60) agus (1963-67) Beurla is Cànanachas, Colàiste na Trìonòide, Baile Atha Chliath, (1960-63) Gaeilge agus Gàidhlig, Obar Dheathain (1967-91) Ceiltis, agus Ghlaschu (1991-96) Cathair na Ceiltis. Leabhraichean: *Seòbhrach as a' Chlaich*; (eag) *Nua-bhàrdachd Ghàidhlig*.

Donald MacAulay

Born in Bernera, Isle of Lewis in 1930, he was educated at the Nicolson Institute, Stornoway and thereafter at Aberdeen University and Cambridge. Since then he has worked at the universities of Edinburgh, Dublin, Aberdeen and held the chair of Celtic at Glasgow. He has published *Seòbhrach as a' Chlaich* and edited *Nua-bhàrdachd Ghàidhlig*.

Niall Mac a' Phearsain *(Photo: James McDonald)*

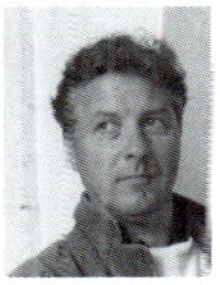

Rugadh e ann an Eilginn, Alba an 1954. Bha e na oileanach ann an Sgoil Ealain Ghlaschu (1974-78). Tha e air iomadh duais a chosnadh, nam measg Neach-ealain Òg Acadamh Rìoghail Alba, Prìomh Dhuais Lìg Rìoghail Thar Chuan agus Duais Alba Lunnainn Acadamh Rìoghail Alba. Tha taisbeanaidhean air a bhith aige ann an Glaschu, Lunnainn, Toronto, san t-Suain agus sa Bhruiseal. Tha taghadh de Chruinneachaidhean Poblach a' gabhail a-steach na leanas: Gailearaidhean Ealain agus Taighean-tasgaidh Ghlaschu, Comann Ealain Cho-aimsireil, Taigh-tasgaidh Nua-Ealain Ghlaschu, BBC.

Neil MacPherson

Born in Elgin in 1954, he studied at Glasgow School of Art. He has been the recipient of many awards including the Royal Scottish Academy Young Artist and the Royal Scottish Academy London Scottish Award, and has exhibited in Glasgow, London, Toronto, Sweden and Brussels. Selected public collections are in Glasgow Art Galleries and Museums, Contemporary Art Society, Museum of Modern Art, Glasgow, BBC.

Réiltín Murphy

53 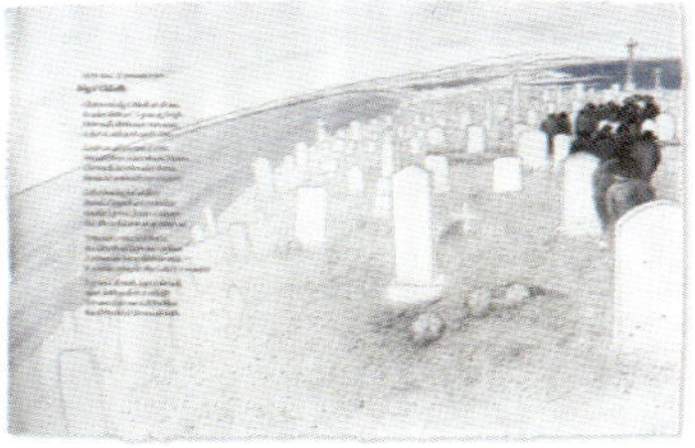

Iain Mac a' Ghobhainn *(Ph: The Gaelic Arts Agency)*

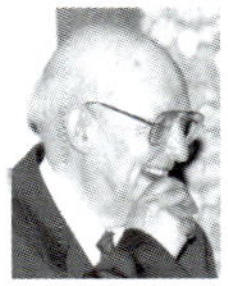

'S ann à Pabail, Eilean Leòdhais, a bha Iain Mac a' Ghobhainn (1928-98). Rugadh e ann an Glaschu agus 's e seòladair a bha na athair. Chaidh e a dh'Oilthigh Obar Dheathain 's bha e na thidsear Beurla san Òban mun deach e na sgrìobhadair làn-ùine ann an 1977. Na bhàrdachd tha gruaim spioradail a mhàthar a' cothachadh ris an àbhachdas aige fhèin – ann an dathan làidir samhlachail, mar eisimpleir. Mar sgrìobhadair dh'fhàg e lìonmhorachd de bhàrdachd, sgeulachdan goirid, nobhailean agus breithneachadh san dà chuid Gàidhlig agus Beurla.

Iain Crichton Smith
Iain Crichton Smith (1928–98) was born in Glasgow of Lewis parents – his father was a sailor. He was brought up in Bayble on the island of Lewis and educated at the Nicolson Institute, Stornoway and the University of Aberdeen. He taught English at Oban High School before becoming a full-time writer in 1977. His mother's spiritual gloom collides in his poetry with his own humour – in strong symbolic colours, for example. He was a prolific writer of poetry, short stories, novels and criticism in both Gaelic and English.

Frances Walker *(Photo: Don Addison)*

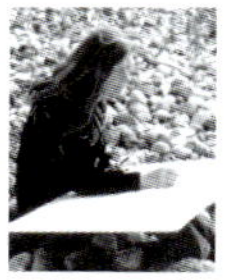

Rugadh i an Cathair Challdainn agus bha i na h-oileanach an Colaiste Ealain Dhùn Èideann. Tha i na ball dhen Acadamh Albannach Rìoghail, Comann Pheantairean Rìoghail Uisge-Dhathan Albannach agus Comann Luchd-Ealain Alba. Thug i dà bhliadhna gu leth na neach-teagaisg siùbhlach ealain ann an sgoiltean na Hearadh agus Uibhist a Tuath anns na h-Eileanan Siar. Thug i seachd bliadhna fichead mar neach-teagaisg ann an dealbhachd is peantadh ann an Sgoil Ealain Ghray an Obar Dheathain. Tha i a' fuireach 's ag obair an Obar Dheathain agus cuid dhen bhliadhna an Eilean Thiriodh.

Frances Walker
Born in Kirkcaldy, she studied at Edinburgh College of Art. She is a member of the Royal Scottish Academy, the Royal Scottish Society of Painters in Watercolours and the Society of Scottish Artists. Walker spent two years as a visiting teacher of art in Harris and North Uist, then twenty-seven years as a lecturer in drawing and painting at Grays School of Art, Aberdeen. She lives and works in Aberdeen and spends part of the year on the island of Tiree.

Dòmhnall Addison/Donald Addison

54

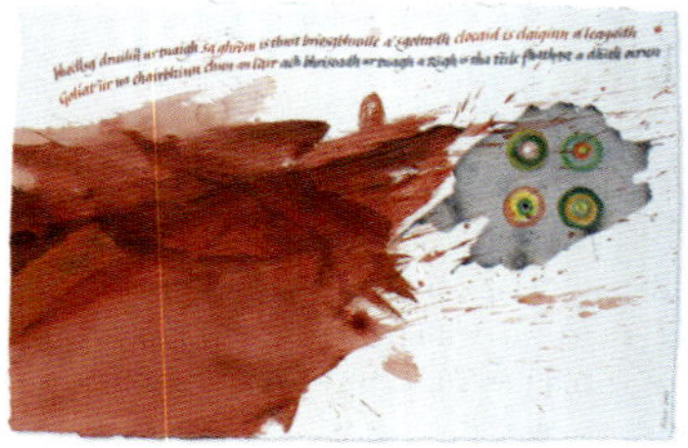

Fearghas MacFhionnlaigh *(Ph: Ciaran MacFhionnlaigh)*

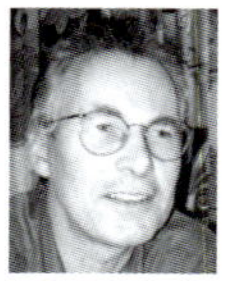

Rugadh Fearghas MacFhionnlaigh am Magh Leamhna, Siorrachd Dhun Breatainn, ann an 1948. Chaith e seachd bliadhna faisg air Toronto, Canada, nuair a bha e na bhalach. Thòisich e air Gàidhlig ionnsachadh, is e na dheugair. Tha e air gabhail ris an t-sealladh-saoghail nua-Chailbhineach Duitseach aig Van Til is Dooyeweerd. Tha e a' teagaisg ealain an Inbhir Nis.

Fearghas MacFhionnlaigh
Fearghas MacFhionnlaigh was born in Dunbartonshire, in 1948. When he was a boy he spent seven years near Toronto in Canada, and started learning Gaelic in his teens. He is committed to the Dutch neo-Calvinist world view of Van Til and Dooyeweerd. He teaches art in Inverness.

Katherine Boucher Beug *(Photo: John W. Lapsley)*

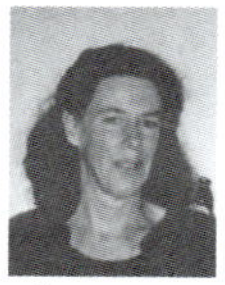

Bhain Katherine Boucher Beug Baitsiléireacht Ealaíne amach in Ollscoil Northwestern i 1969 agus lean sí leis an staidéar ar feadh dhá bhliain i Hamburg na Gearmáine. D'aistrigh sí go hÉirinn i 1971. Tá sí ag plé le péintéireacht, le priontáil, le líníocht agus ag cur leabhar ealaíontóireachta le chéile ó shin i leith. Chuir sí a cuid saothair ar taispeáint i seónna aonair agus seónna oscailte.

Katherine Boucher Beug
Katherine Boucher Beug received a BA from Northwestern University, Illinois in 1969. She went on to study for two years in Hamburg, Germany before moving to Ireland in 1971. Since then she has worked with painting, printmaking, drawing and making artist's books, and has exhibited her work in group and solo shows.

Dòmhnall Moireach/Donald Murray

55

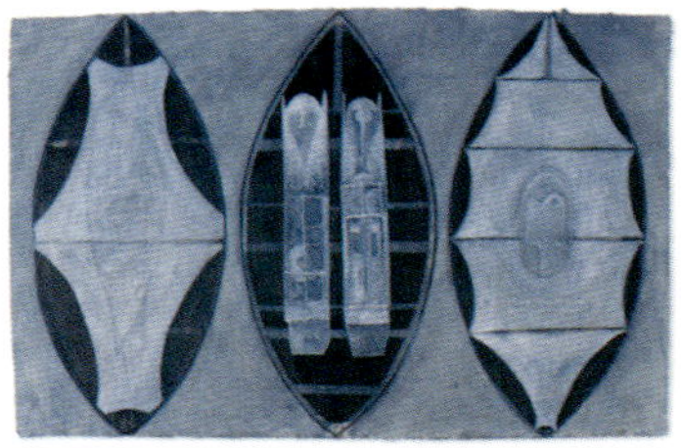

Aonghas Dubh MacNeacail *(Photo: Iain Smith)*

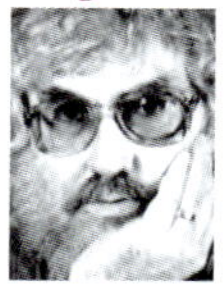

Sgitheanach: Bàrd an Gàidhlig 's am Beurla. Choisinn an cruinneachadh aige, *Oideachadh Ceart* (A Proper Schooling) Duais Sgrìobhaiche Albannach na Bliadhna an 1997. Tha a' bhàrdachd aige air a thoirt air feadh na Roinn Eòrpa, An Ear 's an Iar, bho Chearcall na h-Artaig chun na Mara Meadhan-thìrich, gu Aimeireagaidh a Tuath agus Iapan. (agus gach cùil is ceall de dh'Èirinn).

Aonghas Dubh MacNeacail
He is a Skyeman and a poet in Gaelic and English. His collection *Oideachadh Ceart (A Proper Schooling)* won the Scottish Writer of the Year Award in 1997. Poetry has taken him across Europe, East and West, from the Arctic Circle to the Mediterranean, to North America and Japan (and all corners of Ireland).

Uilleam MacIlleathain *(Photo: Colin Ruscoe)*

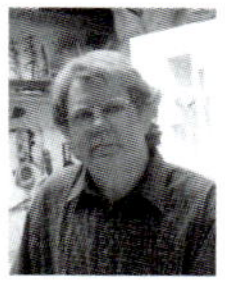

Rugadh e an Inbhir Nis an 1941 Taisbeanaidhean Aon-neach: Gailearaidh Nàiseanta Nua-Ealain an Alba, Taigh-tasgaidh Dakota a Tuath, Oilthigh MhicMhaighistir, Canada. Cruinneachaidhean Poblach: Taigh-tasgaidh Bhreatainn, Taigh-tasgaidh Fitzwilliam, Cambridge, Ionad Yale airson Ealain Bhreatainn, Aimeireagaidh, Gailearaidh Ealain Newfoundland agus Labrador, Taigh-tasgaidh Kelvingrove, Glaschu. Riochdaichte le Art First – Lunnainn agus New York.

Will Maclean
Born in Inverness in 1941, he has had solo exhibitions in the Scottish National Gallery of Modern Art, the Museum of North Dakota and McMaster University Canada. Public collections of his work are in the British Museum, the Fitzwilliam Museum, Cambridge, the Yale Centre for British Art, USA, the Art Gallery of Newfoundland and Labrador and Kelvingrove Museum, Glasgow. He is represented by Art First – London and New York.

Frances Breen

56

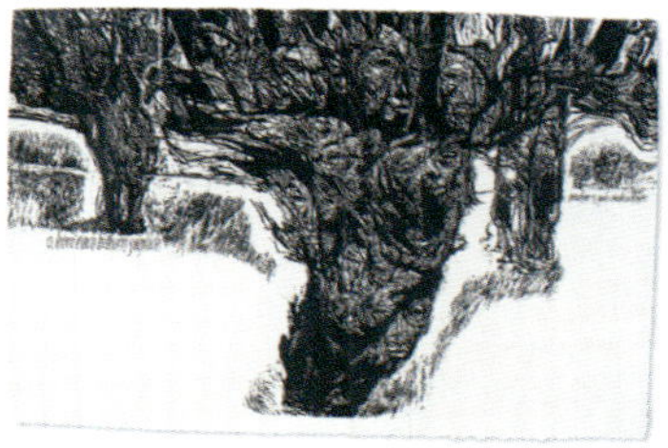

Uilleam Nèill *(Photo: Gordon Wright)*

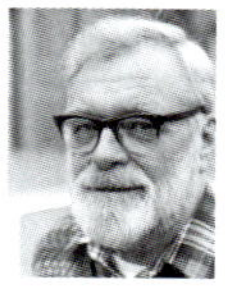

Ged a rugadh 's a thogadh mi ann am baile Phreastabhaig, thàinig a' chuid bu mhotha dhem shinnsrean à Carraig agus fhuair mi mo chiad Ghàidhlig bho sheann duine às an Àird. Thug mi air adhart i le bhith a' cur dragh air iomadh Gaidheal a thàinig a-steach a Dhùn Èideann. An dèidh sin rinn mi Ceum àrd-ìre le urram ann an Ceiltis an Dùn Èideann agus teisteanas neach-teagaisg an Cnoc Iòrdain.

William Neill

Born in Prestwick, most of his ancestors were from Carrick and he learned his first Gaelic from an old man in the Aird. He improved his knowledge by pestering incoming Gaels during a period in Edinburgh. Later Neill did an Honours Degree in Celtic and took a teacher's course in Jordanhill.

Stan Clementsmith *(Photo: Maureen Clementsmith)*

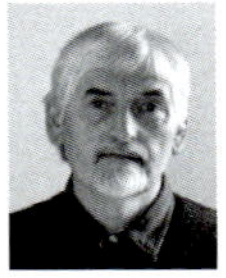

Cheumnaich e à Sgoil Ealain Ghlaschu (DA) an 1958 agus Colaiste Chnoc Iòrdain, 1960. Leig e dheth a dhreuchd ann an Sgoil Foghlam Lèirsinneach Dealbhaidh, Colaiste Dhonnchaidh Iòrdanstain, Oilthigh Dhùn Dè, san t-Samhain 2001. Ron sin bha e ag obair mar Neach-ealain Sgrùdaidh air Chòmhnaidheachd an Sgoil Ealain agus Dealbhaidh Kaywon, Korea a Deas agus mar Dhealbhaiche/Neach-ealain Grafaigeach ann an Colaiste Chnoc Iòrdain.

Stan Clementsmith

He graduated from Glasgow School of Art (DA) and Jordanhill College of Education. He was Designer in the Audio-Visual Unit, Jordanhill College of Education until 1969, then a full-time lecturer at the School of Design, DJC University of Dundee. Clementsmith was Research Artist in Residence at the Kaywon School of Art and Design in South Korea 1997. He retired from the university in September 2000.

Réiltín Murphy

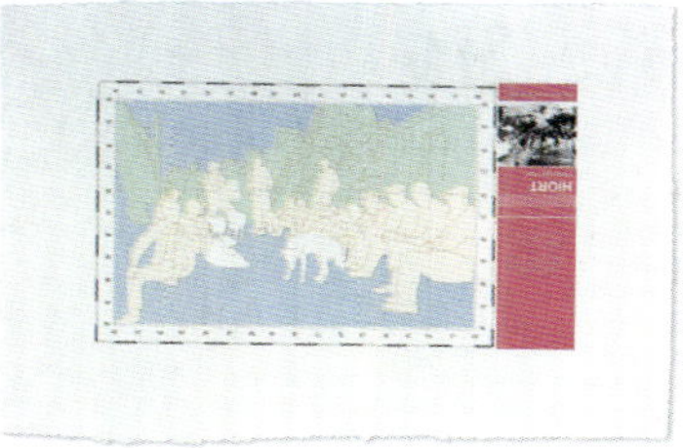

57 **Ruaraidh MacThòmais** *(Ph: Dòmhnall R. Thomson)*

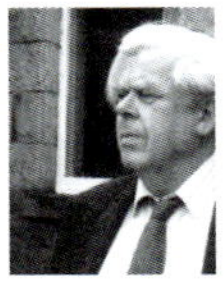

Rugadh Ruaraidh MacThòmais ann an 1921 ann an Steòrnabhagh, Eilean Leòdhais. Bha e a' teagaisg ann an Oilthighean Dhùn Èideann, Obar Dheathain agus Ghlaschu agus na Ollamh Ceiltis an Glaschu bho 1963 gu 1991. Tha e air seachd leabhraichean bàrdachd fhoillseachadh, nam measg a' Bhàrdachd Chruinnichte (*Creachadh na Clàrsaich*) agus an leabhar as ùire *Meall Garbh*; cuideachd mòran leabhraichean agus artaigilean air litreachas na Gàidhlig. Bha e a' deasachadh an ràitheachain *Gairm* bho 1952-2002.

Derick S. Thomson

Derick S. Thomson was born in 1921 in Stornoway, Lewis. He has taught at Edinburgh, Aberdeen and Glasgow Universities, serving as Professor of Celtic at Glasgow from 1963 to 1991. He has published seven poetry volumes, including the *Collected Poems* (*Creachadh na Clàrsaich*) and his latest *Meall Garbh*; also much on Gaelic literature. Editor of the quarterly *Gairm*.

Flòraidh NicCoinnich *(Photo: J Decker Forrest)*

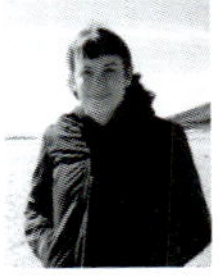

Rugadh i ann an Uibhist a Deas. Tha i air ceumnachadh o chionn ghoirid à Colaiste Ealain Ghlaschu, agus bhon Chùrsa Telebhisean Gàidhlig aig Sabhal Mòr Ostaig san Eilean Sgitheanach. Tha i ag obair an Glaschu na neach-cuideachaidh an Roinn na h-Ealain dha telebhisean. Tha an obair bho dheireadh a rinn i, nach gabh a cuingealachadh am broinn aon mhodh, a' sealltainn mar a tha i air a beò-ghlacadh leis a' cheangal a th' eadar daoine agus tìr.

Flòraidh MacKenzie

Born in South Uist, she is a recent graduate of the Glasgow School of Art and of the Gaelic Television course at Sabhal Mor Ostaig, Isle of Skye. She is currently working in Glasgow as an art department assistant for TV. Her most recent work, indefinable by any one medium, reflects her fascination with the relationships between people and the landscape.

David McGrail

58

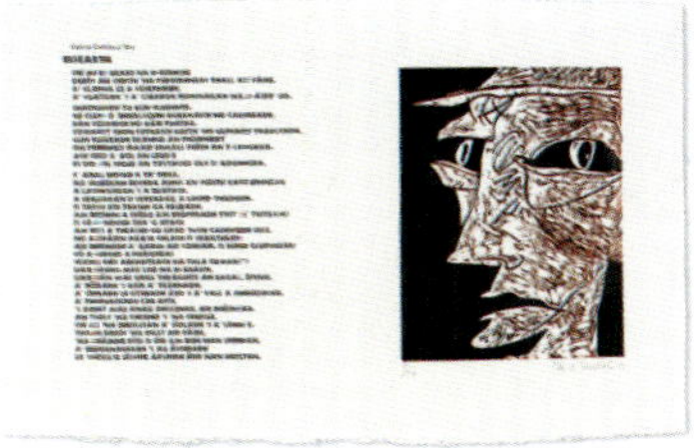

Deòrsa Mac Iain Deòrsa *(Photo: Gordon Wright)*

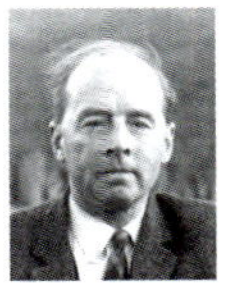

Rugadh Deòrsa Mac Iain Deòrsa (1915-84) ann an Elderslie ach thogadh e ann an Tairbeart Loch Fine. B' e athair an t-Urr. Iain MacDhùghaill Hay, a sgrìobh an nobhail iongantach sin, *Gillespie*. Bha gibht nan cànan aig Deòrsa 's thog e a' Ghàidhlig gu furasta. Fhuair e ceum bho Oilthigh Oxford 's bha e na nàiseantach Albannach. Bha e ann an Algeria agus sa Ghrèig fad an Dara Cogaidh agus is ann mu cheidhinn muinntir Afraga a Tuath – 's mu Chinn Tìre, muir agus tìr – a tha a' chuid as beartaiche dhen bhàrdachd aige. Às dèidh a' Chogaidh bha e a fuireach an Dùn Èideann ach bhris a shlàinte.

George Campbell Hay

George Campbell Hay (1915-84) was born in Elderslie but raised in Tarbert, Loch Fyne. George had the gift of languages and learned Gaelic easily. A graduate from Oxford University and a Scottish nationalist. He spent the Second World War in Algeria and Greece. The richest part of his verse is about the people of North Africa – and about Kintyre, land and sea.

Iain MacCullaich

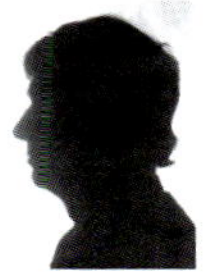

Rugadh Iain MacCullaich an Glaschu an 1935 agus bha e na oileanach ann an Colaiste Ealain Ghlaschu. Tha taisbeanaidhean nàiseanta agus eadar-nàiseanta air a bhith aige is a chuid obrach ann am mòran chruinneachaidhean poblach. Am measg nam barantas aige tha dealbhan dhen Ionad Eadailteach agus dhen Talla-ciùil Rìoghail an Glaschu. Bho 1994 tha e air a bhith na Chompanach Grinneis an Oilthigh Shrath Chluaidh.

Iain McCulloch

Iain McCulloch was born in Glasgow in 1935 and studied at Glasgow School of Art. He has exhibited extensively nationally and internationally, with works in many public collections. Among his commissions are paintings for the Italian Centre and Royal Concert Hall, Glasgow. Since 1994 he has been Fine Art fellow at Strathclyde University.

Dòmhnall Addison/Donald Addison

59

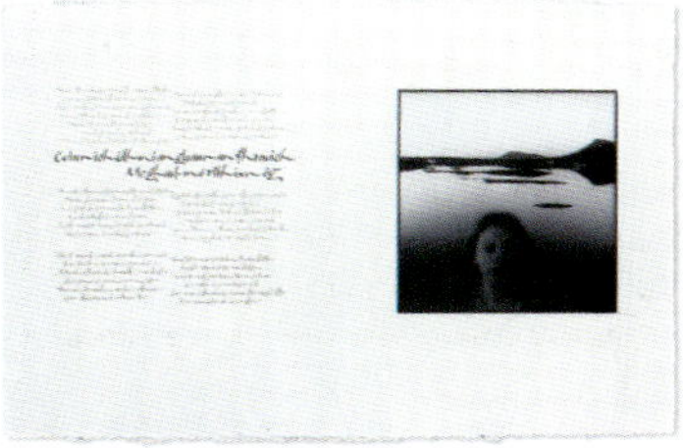

Murchadh MacIlleMhoire *(Photo: with thanks to Mr Donald Morrison)*

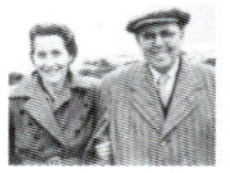

Rugadh Murchadh MacIlleMhoire (Murchadh a' Bhocs, 1884-1965) am Mullach an Tòil an Siadar Bharbhais an Leòdhas. Ann an 1903 chaidh e Steòrnabhagh a dh'ionnsachadh ciùird na fuineadaireachd agus ann an 1906 thug e Glaschu air. 'S e 'Bàrd Shiadair' a bh' aig daoine air, agus rinn e tòrr òran eile ann an Glaschu air an robh fèill mhòr nan latha. Sheòl e a dh'Ameireagaidh an 1911 agus rinn e a dhachaigh ann an Niagara Falls far an robh e beò am measg a cho-Ghaidheal; dh'fhan e na bhèicear. Thàinig a leabhar bàrdachd *Fear Siubhal nan Gleann* a-mach an Glaschu ann an 1923.

Murdo Morrison

Murdo Morrison (1884-1965) was born at Shader, on Lewis. In 1903 he went to Stornoway to learn the baking trade and in 1906 he left for Glasgow. People were already calling him 'the Shader Bard', and he composed many more songs in Glasgow. He sailed for America in 1911 and made his home in Niagara Falls where he lived amongst his fellow-Gaels. His book of poems *Fear Siubhal nan Gleann* was published in Glasgow in 1923.

Gus Wylie *(Photo: Gus Wylie)*

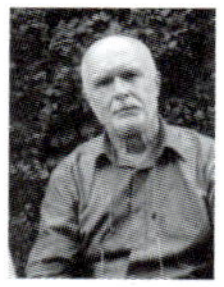

Ceum Ealantais (MA) an dà chuid ann an Grinneas Ealain (Peantadh) agus Dealbh-thogail bhon Cholaiste Rìoghail Ealain, còmhla ri Ollamhachd ann an Eachdraidh Chultarach. Bha e ag obair ann an Oilthigh Westminster agus an sin ann an Colaiste Rìoghail nan Ealan agus na Phroifeasair ann an Dealbh-thogail ann an Stèidheachd Rìoghail an Teicneòlais an New York. An-dràsta tha e a' teagaisg ann an Stèidheachd Lunnainn (Naidheachdas-dhealbh agus Fasan). Tha e cuideachd ag obair air dealbhan agus uisge-dhathan airson leabhar chloinne mu chuimhneachain òige ann am Fìobha an Ear aig àm an Dara Cogaidh.

Gus Wylie

He has a Masters degree (MA) in both Fine Art (painting) and Photography from the Royal College, London. He previously worked at the University of Westminster, the Royal College of Art, and was Professor of Photography at the Rochester Institute of Technology, New York. At present he teaches at the London Institute. He is also working on drawings and watercolours for an illustrated children's book of his childhood memories of East Fife during the Second World War.

Susan Leiper

60

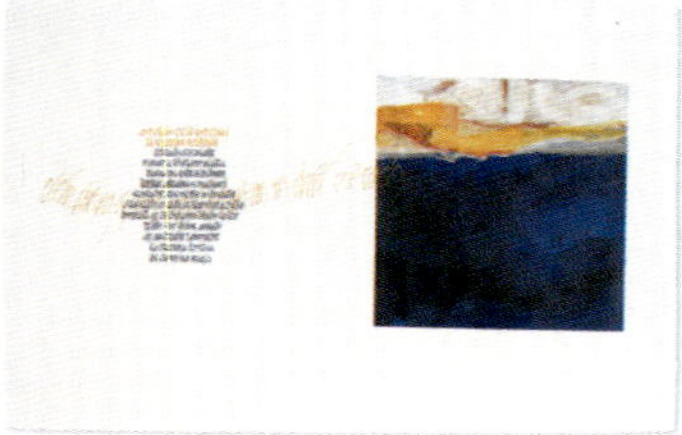

Colm Breathnach *(Photo: Mary Breathnach)*

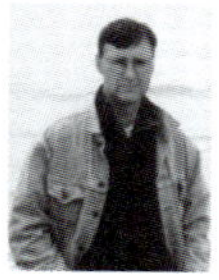

I gCorcaigh a rugadh é i 1961. Fuair oideachas i gColáiste Ollscoile Chorcaí. Cúig chnuasach dánta curtha amach aige, eadhon *Caintic an Bhalbháin* (1991), *An Fearann Breac* (1992), *Scáthach* (1994), *Croí agus Carraig* (1995) agus *An Fear Marbh* (1998). D'aistrigh sé *Katz und Maus* le Günter Grass go Gaeilge, i gcomhar le Andrea Nic Thaidhg.

Colm Breathnach

Born in Cork in 1961, he was educated at University College, Cork. He has published five collections of poetry: *Caintic an Bhalbháin* (1991), *An Fearann Breac* (1992), *Scáthach* (1994), *Croí agus Carraig* (1995) and *An Fear Marbh* (1998). He translated *Katz und Maus* by Günter Grass into Irish, with Andrea Nic Thaidhg.

Bridget Flannery *(Photo: Suzanna Crampton)*

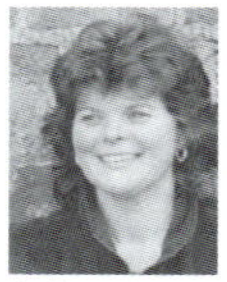

Rugadh Bridget Flannery i gCorcaigh sa bhliain 1959, agus rinne staidéar ag Coláiste Ealaíne agus Deartha Crawford i gCorcaigh ó 1977 gu 1981. Baineann sí úsáid as brait ábhar datha, péint, céir agus cóimheasctha chun a cuid pictiúr a chruthú. Tá tionchar nach beag ag tuath na hÉireann agus tuath Chríche Lochlann ar a cuid pictiúr. Cuireann sí a saothar ar taispeáint in Éirinn agus san Eoraip. Cónaíonn sí i gCeatharlach.

Bridget Flannery

Born in Cork in 1959, Bridget Flannery studied at the Crawford College of Art and Design, Cork. Her paintings are made using layers of pigments, paint, wax and collage and are rooted in the Irish and Scandinavian countryside. She exhibits in Ireland and Europe, and lives and works in Carlow.

Réiltín Murphy

61

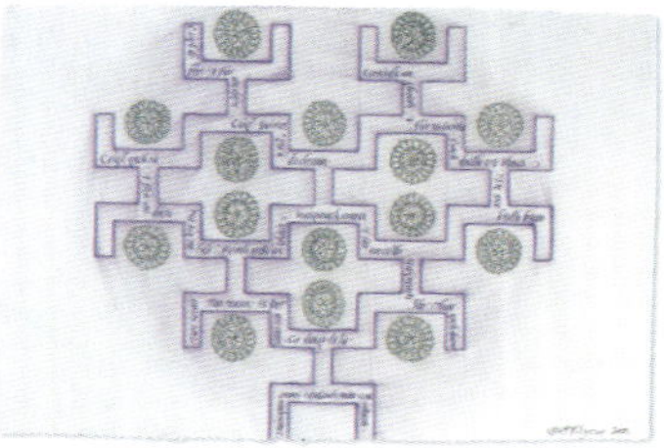

Máirtín Ó Direáin *(Photo: Bill Doyle)*

In Árainn a rugadh i 1910. Cailleadh 1988. Fuair oideachas sa cheantar. Bhí sé ag plé le drámaíocht ar dtús ach bhain cáil amach mar fhile. Cnuasaigh filíochta uaidh: *Coinnle Geala* (1942), *Dánta Aniar* (1943), *Rogha Dánta* (1949), *Ó Mórna agus Dánta Eile* (1957) agus *Ár Ré Dhearóil* (1963). Dar le mórán is é is mó a chuaigh i gcion ar fhorás fhilíocht Ghaeilge na linne seo.

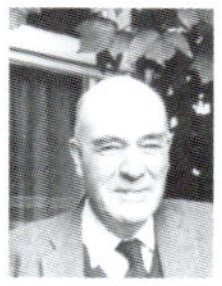

Máirtín Ó Direáin

Born in the Aran Islands in 1910, he died in 1988. He was educated locally and began in theatre, achieving fame as a poet. His collections are *Coinnle Geala* (1942), *Dánta Aniar* (1943), *Rogha Dánta* (1949), *Ó Mórna agus Dánta Eile* (1957), *Ár Ré Dhearóil* (1963). He is considered by many a seminal figure in the evolution of modern Irish poetry.

Scott Kilgour *(Photo: Greg Daniels)*

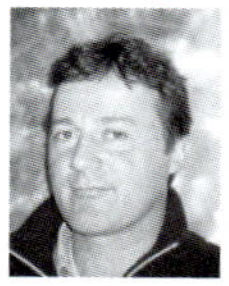

Rugadh e an Alba an 1960. Bha e an Sgoil Ealain Ghlaschu bho 1977-81. Ghluais e a New York an 1983 agus tha a dhachaigh an sin fhathast. Tha grunnan thaisbeanaidhean aon-neach air a bhith aige an sin agus air feadh Aimeireagaidh. Chuir e air adhart taisbeanadh 'Interspace' aig an G.S.A. mar phàirt de phrògram Baile Ailtireachd agus Dealbhaidh Bhreatainn an 1999.

Scott Kilgour

Born in Scotland in 1960, he attended Glasgow School of Art. He moved to New York in 1983 and currently lives there. Kilgour has had several one-man shows in New York and around the USA. He presented the 'Interspace' exhibition at the GSA as part of the UK City of Architecture and Design programme in 1999.

David McGrail

62 **Louis de Paor** *(Photo: Mike Shaughnessy)*

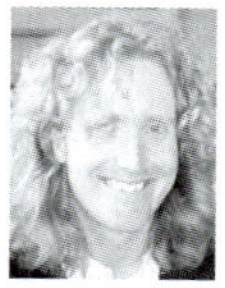

I gCorcaigh a rugadh 1961. Oilte i gColáiste Ollscoile Chorcaí. *Corcach agus Dánta Eile* (1999) an cnuasach is deireanaí dá chuid. Foilsíodh eagrán dátheangach de san Astráil mar *Cork and other Poems*. Chaith sé seal mar eagarthóir ar INNTI. I

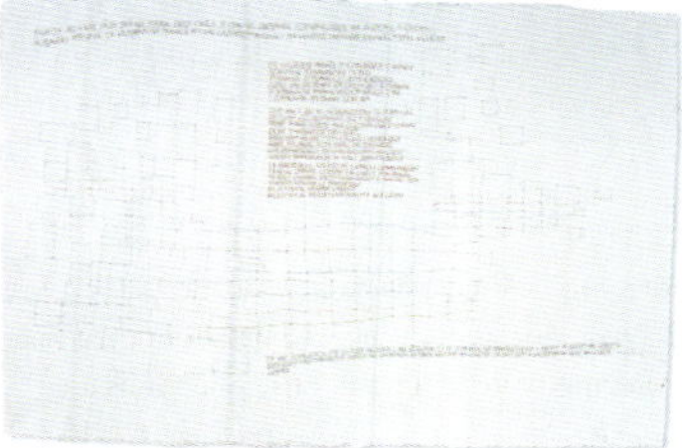

measc a chnuasaigh eile tá *Próca Solais is Luatha* (1988), *30 Dán* (1992) agus *Aimsir Bhreicneach / Freckled Weather* (1993).

Louis de Paor
Born in Cork in 1961, he was educated at University College, Cork. His most recent collection is *Corcach agus Dánta Eile* (1999), published in a bilingual edition in Australia as *Cork and Other Poems*. He is a former editor of INNTI. Among his other collections are *Próca Solais is Luatha* (1988), *30 Dán* (1992), *Aimsir Bhreicneach / Freckled Weather* (1993).

Helen O'Leary *(Photo: Eva O'Leary)*

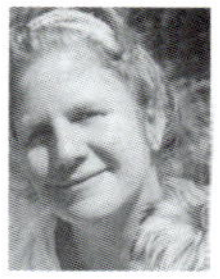

Is i Loch Garman a rugadh Helen O'Leary. Tá an-chuid duaiseanna gnóthaithe aici - Duais Pollock Krasner agus Duais Joan Mitchell do phéintéireacht san áireamh. Bhain sí céimeanna Baitsiléara agus Máistreachta amach ins na Míndána san Art Institute i Chicago. Chuir sí a saothar ar taispeáint go hidirnáisiúnta agus is Comhollamh Ealaíne anois í in Ollscoil Penn State sna Stáit Aontaithe.

Helen O'Leary
Helen O'Leary was born in Wexford. She has been a recipient of numerous awards, including the Pollock Krasner Award and the Joan Mitchell Award for painting. She graduated from the Art Institute in Chicago with Bachelor and Master degrees in Fine Art. She has exhibited internationally and is currently an associate professor of art at Penn State University in the USA.

Dòmhnall Moireach/Donald Murray

63

Somhairle MacGill-Eain *(Ph: The Gaelic Arts Agency)*

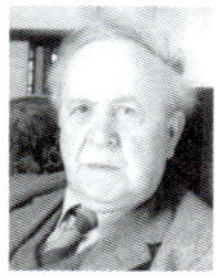

B' e mac tàilleir à Ratharsair a bh' ann an Somhairle MacGill-Eain (1911-96). Bha a cheann loma-làn dhe na seann òrain 's na searmonan a chuala e na òige. Eadar iad sin, poileataigs, agus gaol, nuair a bha e ann an Oilthigh Dhùn Èideann 1929-33 's a chaidh e na thidsear Beurla 1933-40, shruth bàrdachd Ghàidhlig a bha buileach ùr agus mìorbhaileach às eanchainn, gu sònraichte na *Dàin do Eimhir* agus *An Cuilithionn*. Chaidh a leòn aig El Alamein an 1942 ach thill e gu teagasg. Tha 'Hallaig' air aon dhen bheagan dhàn a rinn e an dèidh a' chogaidh.

Sorley MacLean
Sorley MacLean (1911-96) was born a tailor's son in Raasay. His head was full of the old songs and the sermons that he heard in his youth. He went to Edinburgh University and became an English teacher and wrote Gaelic poetry including *Poems to Eimhir* and *The Cuillin*. He was wounded at El Alamein in 1942 but returned to teaching. 'Hallaig' is one of the few poems he made after the war.

Dòmhnall Urchardan *(Photo: Alan Wylie)*
Rugadh Dòmhnall Urchardan am Bankfoot an

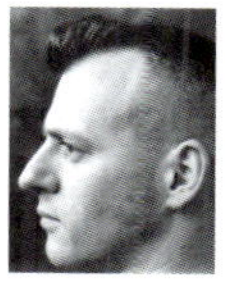

Siorrachd Pheairt ann an 1959 agus dh'ionnsaich e mu dhealbhachd agus peantadh an Colaiste Ealain Dhùn Èideann bho 1978-82. Tha e air obair a thaisbeanadh an Alba agus gu h-eadar-nàiseanta, agus tha e air grunnan dhuaisean a chosnadh - nam measg Mòr-dhuais Neach-Ealain bho Chomhairle Ealain na h-Alba ann an 1998 agus bho Phrògram Còmhnaidheachd Ealain an Taigh-tasgaidh Ealain Ùra na h-Èireann am Baile Atha Cliath. Tha e an-diugh a' fuireach agus ag obair an Dun Èideann.

Donald Urquhart
Donald Urquhart was born in Bankfoot, Perthshire in 1959 and studied drawing and painting at Edinburgh College of Art. He has exhibited widely both internationally and throughout Scotland and has numerous awards including a major Artist's Award from the Scottish Arts Council in 1998 and the artist's residency programme at the Irish Museum of Modern Art in Dublin. He works in Edinburgh.

Louise Donaldson

64

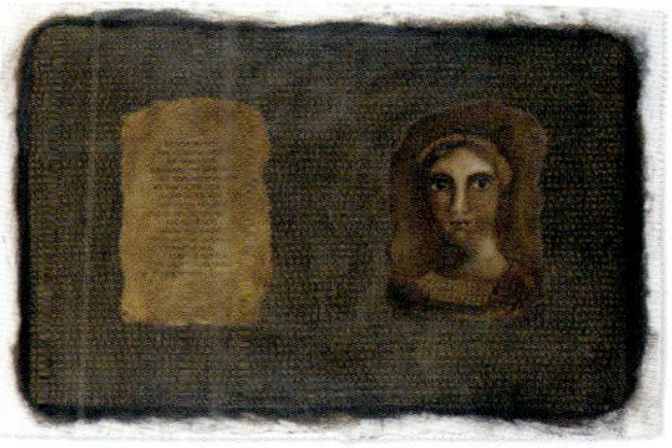

Máire Mhac an tSaoi *(Photo: Padraig Ó Flannabhra)*

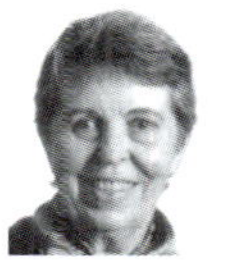

I mBaile Átha Cliath a rugadh i 1922. Fuair oideachas i gColáiste Ollscoile Bhaile Átha Cliath agus san Sorbonne. Ar na cnuasaigh uaithi tá *Margadh na Saoire* (1956), *Codladh an Ghaiscígh* (1973), *An Galar Dubhach* (1980), *An Cion go dtí Seo* (1987) agus *Shoa agus Dánta Eile*. Taighdeoir, gearrscéalaí agus eagarthóir í, chomh maith le bheith ina haistritheoir (go háirithe ar shaothar R.M. Rilke).

Máire Mhac an tSaoi
Born in Dublin in 1922, she was educated at University College, Dublin and the Sorbonne. Her collections include *Margadh na Saoire* (1956), *Codladh an Ghaiscígh* (1973), *An Galar Dubhach* (1980), *An Cion go dtí Seo* (1987) and *Shoa agus Dánta Eile*. She is also a researcher, short story writer, editor and translator (notably of R.M. Rilke).

Patricia Looby *(Photo: Austin McQuinn)*

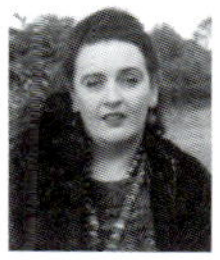

Is as Tiobraid Árann do Patricia Looby, ealaíontóir, agus tá a saothar á thaispeáint le fiche bliain anuas, in Éirinn agus thar lear. Is gearr ó bhí a céad mhór-thaispeántas aici - faoin teideal 'Harvester' – i nGailearaí Temple Bar (2001). Taispeánadh saothar léi go minic thar lear mar chuid de mhór-thaispeántais ealaíne na hÉireann – go háirithe in Amsterdam (1985), i Kraków (1993) agus in Aarhus na Danmhairge (1996).

Patricia Looby
Tipperary artist Patricia Looby has spent twenty years exhibiting in Ireland and abroad. In May 2001 she held her first solo exhibition in Dublin entitled 'Harvester', and it toured to Ennis and Clonmel. Her work has been part of several touring shows of Irish art including in Amsterdam (1985), Cracow (1993) and Aarhus in Denmark (1996).

Frances Breen

65 **Gréagóir Ó Dúill**
Rugadh i mBaile Átha Cliath é i 1946. Oideachas i mBéal Feirste, i mBaile Átha Cliath agus i Má Nuad. PhD. sa litríocht Angla-Éireannach aige. Foilsíodh ocht

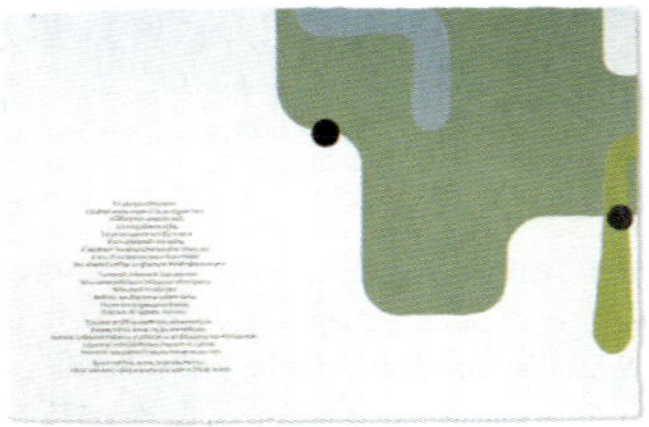

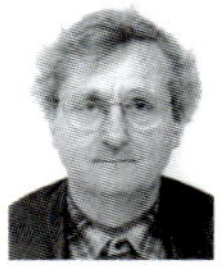

gcnuasach filíochta leis maraon lena *Rogha Dánta*, cnuasach gearrscéalta, beathaisnéis léirmheasa agus dhá dhíolaim - gan trácht ar léirmheasanna, ar shaothar critice, eagarthóireacht agus moltóireacht.

Gréagóir Ó Dúill

Born in Dublin in 1946, he was educated in Belfast, Dublin and Maynooth. He has a PhD in Anglo-Irish literature. Eight collections of poems and his selected poems, a collection of short stories, a critical biography and two anthologies have been accompanied by reviews, critical work, editing and adjudication.

Ronnie Hughes *(Photo: Eva Byrne)*

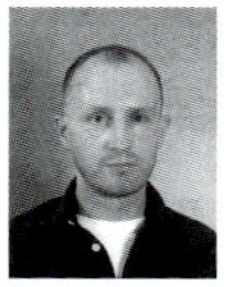

I mBéal Feirste a rugadh é sa bhliain 1965 agus tá cuid mhaith taispeántas aonair curtha de aige ar fud na hÉireann agus ghlac sé páirt i dtaispeántais oscailte ar fud an domhain leis. I measc na nduaiseanna a ghnóthaigh sé tá sealanna mar ealaíontóir cónaitheach i PS1, Nua Eabhrac (1990), Banff Arts Center i gCeanada (1994) agus Bemis Arts Center, Nebraska (1997). Tá a shaothar le fáil i mbailiúcháin an dá Chomhairle Ealaíon in Éirinn, in Áras Nua-Ealaíne na hÉireann agus i mbailiúcháin eile nach iad. I Sligeach a chuireann sé fé agus feidhmíonn Gailearaí Rubicon i mBaile Átha Cliath ar a shon.

Ronnie Hughes

Born in Belfast in 1965, Hughes has had numerous solo exhibitions throughout Ireland and has participated in group exhibitions worldwide. His awards include residencies at PS1, New York, Banff Arts Center, Canada and Bemis Arts Center, Nebraska. His work is held in many collections including both Irish Arts Councils and the Irish Museum of Modern Art.

Dòmhnall Moireach/Donald Murray

66

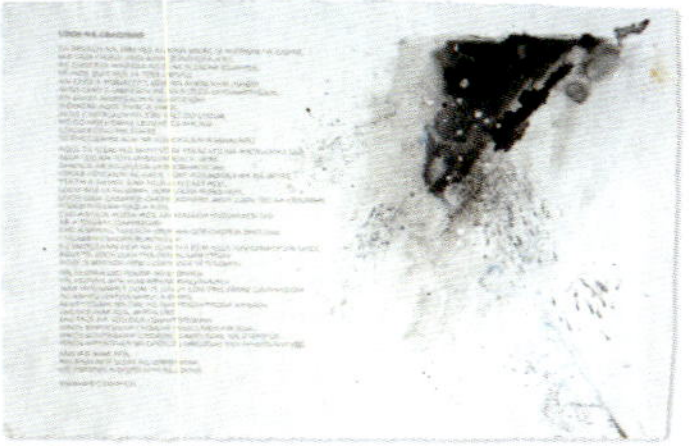

Diarmaid Ó Doibhlin

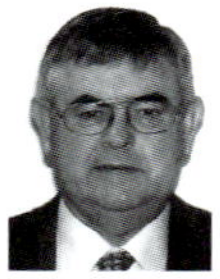

Rugadh Diarmaid Ó Doibhlin i nDeisceart Cho. Dhoire i 1942 agus fuair sé meánscolaíocht i gColáiste Phádraig, Ardmhacha, agus ollscolaíocht i gColáiste Phádraig, Maigh Nuad agus i gColáiste na hOllscoile, Baile Átha Cliath. D'fhoilsigh sé *Briseadh na Cora* in 1981 agus *Drumaí Móra* i 1997. Duaiseanna Oireachtais bainte aige. Tá sé ina léachtoir sinsireach le litríocht na Nua-Ghaeilge in Ollscoil Uladh i gCúil Raithin.

Diarmaid Ó Doibhlin

Diarmaid Ó Doibhlin was born in South Co. Derry in 1942 and was educated at St Patrick's College, Armagh, attending university at St Patrick's, Maynooth and University College Dublin. He published *Briseadh na Cora* in 1981 and *Drumaí Móra* in 1997. He has won prizes at the Oireachtas. He is a senior lecturer in modern Irish literature at the University of Ulster, Coleraine.

Marian Leabhan *(Photo: Colin Ruscoe)*

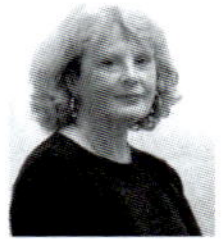

Rugadh Marian Leabhan ann an Dùn Èideann ann an 1944. Bha i ann an Colaiste Ealain Ghray, Obar Dheathain bho 1962-66. Choisinn i duais Noble Grossart/ *Scotland on Sunday* airson dealbhadh ann an 1998. Taisbeanaidhean Aon-neach:
An Tuireann, Port Rìgh
An Lanntair, Steòrnabhagh
Taigh Chearsabhagh, Uibhist a Tuath.
Cruinneachaidhean Poblach:
Taigh-tasgaidh agus Gailearaidh Ealain an Cathair Challdainn;
Gailearaidh Ealain Lillie, Muileann Dhaibhidh;
Dealbhadh ann an Ospadail.

Marian Leven

Marian Leven was born in Edinburgh in 1944. She studied at Grays School of Art, Aberdeen, and was the winner of the Noble Grossart/ *Scotland on Sunday* painting prize in 1998. She has had solo exhibitions at An Tuireann, Portree; An Lanntair, Stornoway and Taigh Chearsabhagh, North Uist. Public collections of her work are in Kirkcaldy Museum and Art Gallery; Lillie Art Gallery, Milngavie; and Paintings in Hospitals.

Dòmhnall Addison/Donald Addison

Gabriel Rosenstock *(Photo: Héilean Rosenstock)*

67

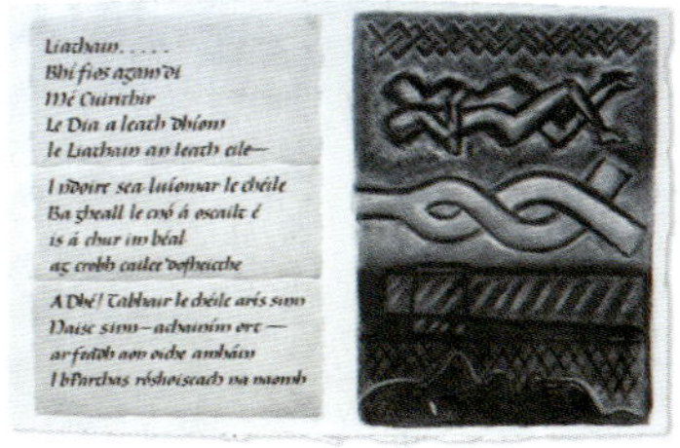

Is i gCill Fhionáin i gCo. Luimnigh a rugadh é i

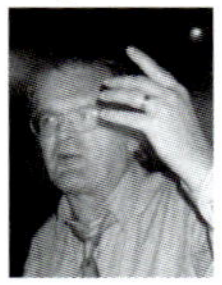

1949. B'é *Susanne sa Seomra Folctha* (1973) an chéad chnuasach uaidh agus tá sé ina údar / aistritheoir ar bhreis is céad leabhar ó shin. Bailiúchán de dhánta úrnua agus de dhánta roghnaithe is ea *Oráistí* (1991). Orthu siúd gur aistrigh sé a saothair tá Seamus Heaney, Georg Trakl agus Günter Grass. Tá sé oilte san foirm Haiku leis. Ball de Aosdána é.

Gabriel Rosenstock

Born in 1949 in Kilfinane, Co. Limerick, he is the author/translator of over one hundred books since his first collection *Susanne sa Seomra Folctha* (1973). *Oráistí* (1991) is a collection of new and selected poems. He has translated, among others, Séamus Heaney, Georg Trakl, Günter Grass, and is also a haikuist. Rosenstock is a member of Aosdána.

Uilleam Brotherston *(Photo: John K MacGregor)*

Rugadh Uilleam Brotherston an Dùn Èideann

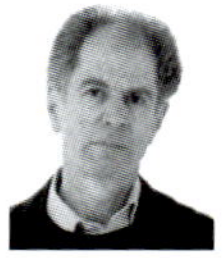

an 1943. An toiseach dh'ionnsaich e mu eachdraidh agus às dèidh sin, dealbhachadh. Bho 1971 tha e air a bhith a' teagaisg ann an Colaiste Ealain Dhùn Èideann agus a' dealbhachadh. Bidh e a' dèanamh ìomhaighean dealbhachaidh mar as trice a' cur cùis-bheachdan geomeatrach agus samhlaidhean de rudan faicsinneach an lùib a chèile, mar eisimpleir, cuspairean, innealachd, tìr-chumadh, cruthan. Tha na dealbhachaidhean aige gu math beag mar as trice, agus air an dèanamh de dh'umha.

William Brotherston

William Brotherston was born in Edinburgh in 1943. He first studied History and then Sculpture. Since 1971 he has been teaching at Edinburgh College of Art and making sculpture. He makes sculptural images typically combining geometric abstraction and references to visible things.

Dòmhnall Moireach/Donald Murray

68

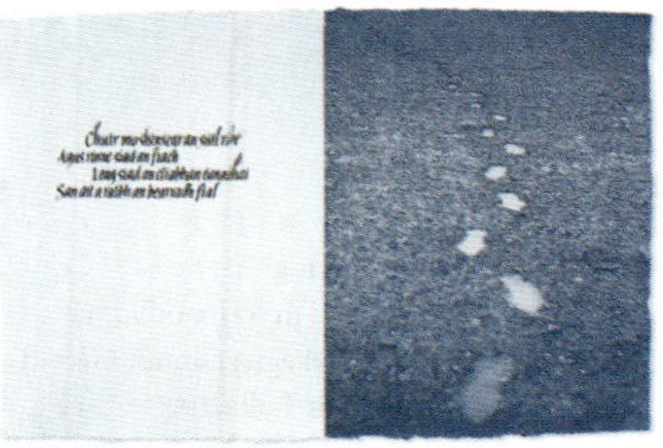

Seán Ó Curraoin

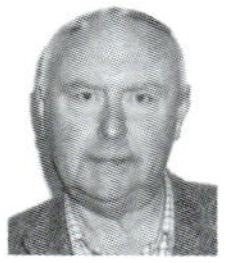

Is i mBearna i nGaeltacht Chonamara a rugadh é. M.A. i Litríocht na Gaeilge 1980. Foilseacháin: *Soilse ar na Dumhchannaí* (filíocht) 1985; *Beairtle* (filíocht) 1985; *Tinte Sionnaigh* (gearrscéalta) 1985; *De Ghlaschloch an Oileáin* (beathaisnéis a uncail Máirtín Ó Cadhain) 1987; *Iascairín Chloch na Cora* (scéalta agus seanchas ó Bhearna agus na Forbacha) 2000.

Seán Ó Curraoin

Born in Barna in the Connemara *Gaeltacht*, he graduated MA in Irish in 1980. His publications are *Soilse ar na Dumhchannaí* (poetry) 1985; *Beairtle* (poetry) 1985; *Tinte Sionnaigh* (short stories) 1985; *De Ghlaschloch an Oileáin* (a biography of his uncle Máirtin Ó Cadhain) 1987; *Iascairín Chloch na Cora* (stories and local lore from Barna and Furbo) 2000.

Eideard Summerton *(Photo: MinKyung Park)*

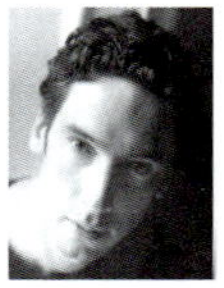

Tha an obair shoirbheachail a rinn Eideard Summerton o chionn ghoirid air a bhith air a taisbeanadh gu h-eadar-nàiseanta ann an cruth dhealbhan, deilbheadh, foillsichidhean luchd-ealain, suidheachaidhean a tha sònraichte a thaobh àite is fuaim, dealbh-thogail, irisean chairtean-phosta, co-obraichidhean agus tilgeadairean bhidiothan. Tha e an-dràsta na Òraidiche Grinneis an Oilthigh Dhùn Dè.

Edward Summerton

Edward Summerton's most recent and successful work has been exhibited internationally in the form of paintings, sculpture, artists' publications, site-specific and sound installations, photography, editions of postcards, collaborations and video projections. He is currently a Fine Art lecturer at the University of Dundee.

Louise Donaldson

69

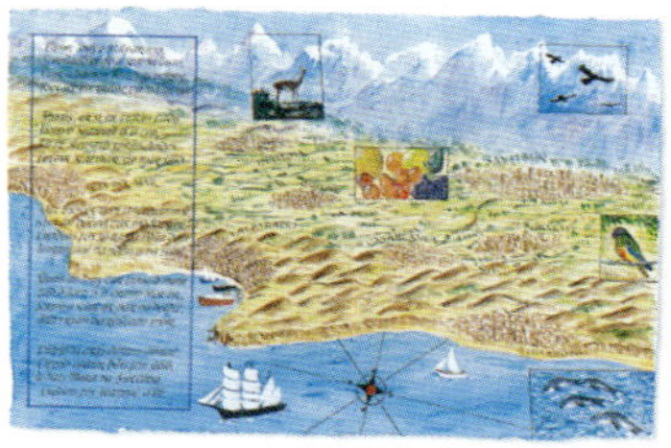

Pádraig de Brún *(Ph: with thanks to maire mhac an tSaoi)*

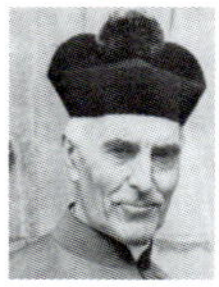

I dTiobraid Árann a rugadh 1889. Cailleadh 1960. Fuair oideachas i gColáiste Ollscoile Bhaile Átha Cliath, i bPáras, Göttingen agus san Róimh. Aistritheoir ar litríocht chlasaiceach na hEorpa – *Antigone* de chuid Sophocles (1926) agus *Athalie* le Racine san áireamh (1930). Rinne a neacht Máire Mhac an tSaoi eagarthóireacht iarbháis ar a dhán fada *Miserere* (1971). Dhein sé aistriúchán an-ábalta de Homer dar teideal *An Odaise* (1990).

Pádraig de Brún

Born in Tipperary in 1889, he died in 1960. He was educated at University College, Dublin; Paris; Göttingen and Rome. He was a translator of classical European literature, including Sophocles' *Antigone* (1926), and Racine's *Athalie* (1930). His long poem *Miserere* (1971) was posthumously edited by his niece Máire Mhac an tSaoi. He made a masterly translation of Homer, published as *An Odaise* (1990).

Tadhg McSweeney *(Photo: Catherine Ketch)*

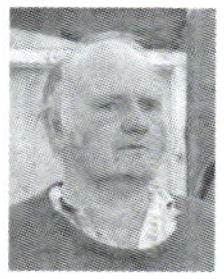

Rugadh Tadhg i 1936. Ealaíontóir féin-oilte é a bhaineann úsáid go mórmhór as ola agus meáin priontaí – ar nós liotagrafaíocht, eitseáil, scáthlán síoda, greanadóireacht adhmaid, priontáil nua-aoiseach – chomh maith le freascónna agus uiscedhathanna. Cé gur saothar fíortha a chruthaíonn sé, déanann sé iniúchadh ar limistéir theibí fós. Chaith sé tréimhsí ag obair agus ag taispeáint a shaothair sna Stáit Aontaithe, i Sasana, san Iodáil, sa Ghearmáin agus sa bhFrainc. Tá go leor portráidí agus roinnt freascónna cruthaithe aige.

Tadhg McSweeney

Tadhg McSweeney was born in 1936. A self-taught artist, he uses mainly oils and print media including lithography, etching, silk-screen, woodcuts, modern printing, in addition to fresco and watercolour. While his work is figurative, it also explores abstract dimensions. He has lived, worked and exhibited in the USA, England, Italy, Germany and France.

Frances Breen

70

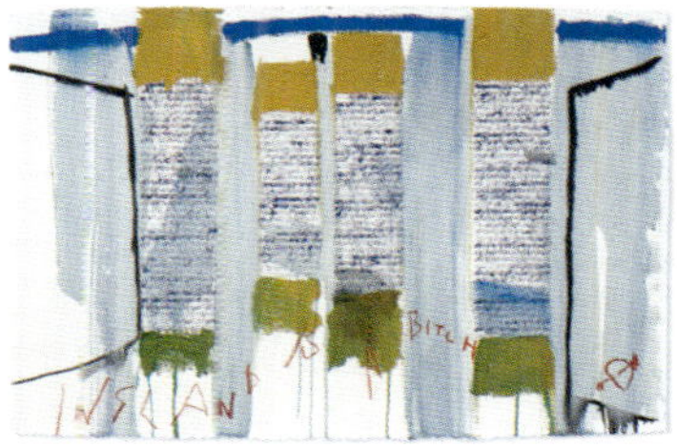

Gearóid Mac Lochlainn *(Ph: Gearoid MacLochlainn)*

I mBéal Feirste a rugadh i 1966. Tá dhá chnuasach dánta foilsithe aige: *Babylon Gaeilgeoir* (An Clochán 1998), *Na Scéalaithe* (Coiscéim 1999) agus cnuasach dátheangach *Sruth Teangacha/Stream Of Tongues* (Cló Iar-

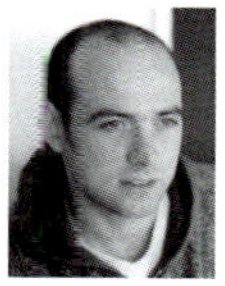

Chonnachta 2002). Ceithre dhlúthdhiosca de amhráin Ghaeilge do pháistí taifeadtha aige freisin (Outlet 1999).

Gearóid Mac Lochlainn

Born in Belfast in 1966, he has published two collections of poetry, *Babylon Gaeilgeoir* (1998), *Na Scéalaithe* (1999), and a bilingual collection, *Sruth Teangacha/Stream Of Tongues* (2002). He has also published four CDs of children's songs in Irish (1999).

Brian Maguire

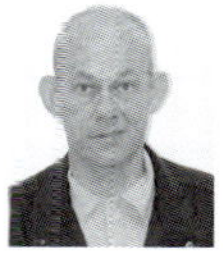

I 1951 i mBaile Átha Cliath sea rugadh Brian Maguire. Le déanaí tá taispeántais aonair curtha ar siúl aige i nGailearaí Kerlin, i nGailearaí Bardasach Crawford, i nGailearaí Bardasach Hugh Lane, sa Contemporary Art Museum i Houston agus i nGailearaí Ormeau Baths. Sheas sé d'Éire ag an XXIV Bienal de São Paulo agus chomhlíon sé dualgaisí ealaíontóra cónaithe i roinnt mhaith príosún in Éirinn. Ollamh leis na Mindána é sa Choláiste Náisiúnta Ealaíne is Deartha.

Brian Maguire

Brian Maguire was born in Dublin in 1951. Recent solo shows have taken place in the Kerlin Gallery, Crawford Municipal Gallery, Hugh Lane Municipal Gallery, Contemporary Art Museum in Houston and Ormeau Baths Gallery. The Irish representative at XXIV Bienal de São Paulo, he has completed Art Residencies in many Irish jails and is Professor of Fine Art at the National College of Art and Design.

Réiltín Murphy

71

Nuala Ní Dhomhnaill

I Lancashire, Sasana a rugadh í i 1952. Tógadh i nGaeltacht an Daingin agus in Aonach Urmhumhan í. Oileadh i gColáiste Ollscoile Chorcaí í. I measc a cuid bailiúchán tá *An Dealg Droighin* (1981), *Pharaoh's Daughter* (1990), *Feis*

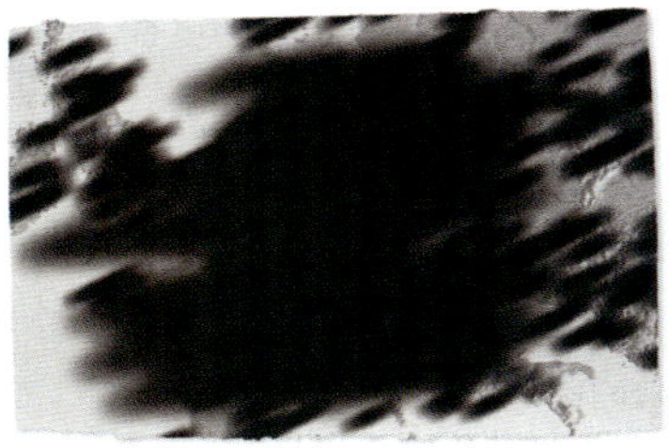

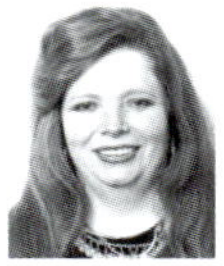

(1991) agus *Cead Aighnis* (1998). Drámadóir agus scríbhneoir scánnán freisin í. Tá cuid mhaith duaiseanna gnóthaithe aici. Bhronn Ollscoil Chathair Bhaile Átha Cliath D.Phil (honoris causa) uirthi i 1995. Ball de Aosdána í.

Nuala Ní Dhomhnaill

Born in Lancashire in 1952, she was brought up in Dingle Gaeltacht and Nenagh.
She was educated at University College, Cork and her collections include *An Dealg Droighin* (1981), *Pharaoh's Daughter* (1990), *Feis* (1991) and *Cead Aighnis* (1998). Also a playwright and screenwriter, she is the winner of many prizes, and was awarded a DPhil by Dublin City University in 1995. She is a member of Aosdána.

Frances Hegarty *(Photo: Charles Colquhoun)*

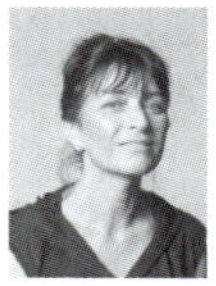

I dTeileann i gCo. Dhún na nGall a rugadh Frances Hegarty i 1946 agus cónaíonn sí anois i Sheffield. Is Ollamh le Míndána in Ollscoil Sheffield Hallam í. Cruthaíonn an t-ealaíontóir ilmhúinte seo ealaín suiteála tré úsáid a bhaint as ábhar fístéipe, fuaim, grianghrafadóireacht agus meáin digiteacha. Cuireann sí taispeántais ar siúl go hidirnáisiúnta i ngailearaithe agus i suímh ar leith - mór-thaispeántais suirbhéireachta cuid acu. Chuaigh sí i gcomhar leis an ealaíontóir Andrew Stones chun roinnt coimisiún phoiblí ar mhórchóir a chur i gcrích.

Frances Hegarty

Frances Hegarty was born in 1946 in Co. Donegal and currently is Professor of Fine Art at Sheffield Hallam University. This multi-disciplinary artist creates installations using video, sound, photography and digital media, and exhibits internationally in gallery and site specific contexts. She has collaborated with artist Andrew Stones on large scale public art projects.

Frances Breen

72

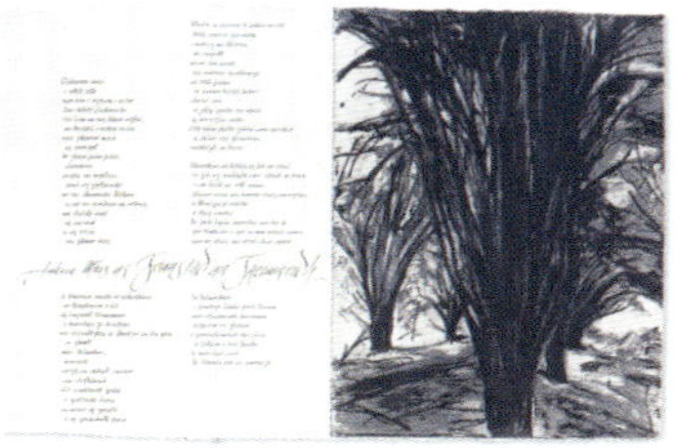

Biddy Jenkinson

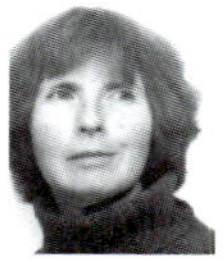

Ainm cleite. Ceithre chnuasach filíochta agus bailiúchán 'gáirscéalta' uaithi foilsithe ag Coiscéim, a d'fhoilsigh dán fada dá cuid, *Mis*, le deireanas. D'fhoilsigh Cló Ollscoil Chorcaí *Rogha Dánta*. Bíonn drámaí á scríobh aici.

Biddy Jenkinson

Biddy Jenkinson is her pen name. Coiscéim has published four collections of her poetry, a collection of short stories *An Grá Riabhach* and, recently, a long poem *Mis*. Cork University Press have published *Rogha Dánta*, selected by Seán Ó Tuama and Siobhán Ní Fhoghlú.

Geraldine O'Reilly

Tá céim sa bpéintéireacht ag Geraldine O'Reilly ón gColáiste Náisiúnta Ealaíne is Deartha agus lean sí den staidéar ag Hunter College i Nua Eabhrac. Suim ar leith aici i gcruthú priontaí. Is

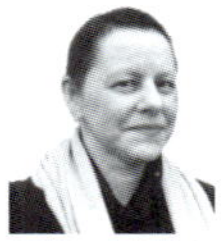

mó taispeántas aonair a chuir sí ar siúl – in áiteanna ar nós Ollscoil na Tasmáine, Context Gallery, Ionad Ealaíne Belltable, Gailearaí Temple Bar agus Ionad Ealaíne an Project. Chaith seal mar bhall chónaithe sa Tasmáin agus sa Banff Center i gCeanada.

Geraldine O'Reilly

A graduate in painting from the National College of Art and Design, Geraldine O'Reilly also studied at Hunter College in New York City and has a particular interest in printing. She has had many solo shows at venues including the University of Tasmania, Context Gallery, Belltable Arts Centre, Temple Bar Gallery and the Project Arts Centre. She has completed residencies in Tasmania and the Banff Center in Canada.

Frances Breen

73

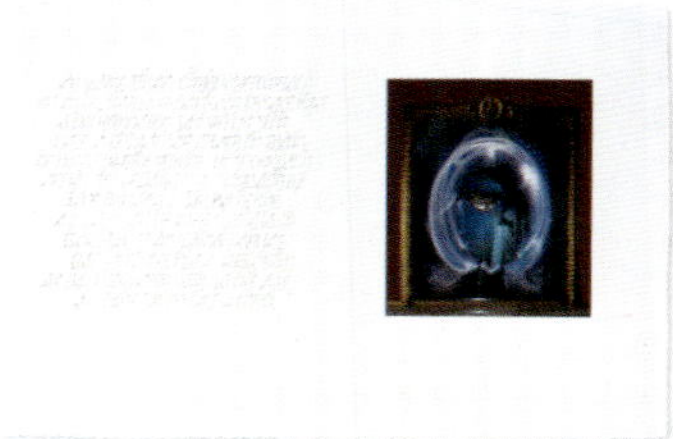

Micheál Davitt *(Photo: Moira Sweeney)*

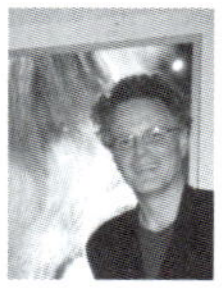

Rugadh i gCorcaigh i 1950 é. Bunaitheoir/eagarthóir na hirise filíochta cáiliúla INNTI ar feadh i bhfad. Ar na leabhair aige tá *Freacnairc Mhearcair/The Oomph of Quicksilver* (Cló Ollscoile Chorcaí, 2000) - rogha dánta as cúig chnuasach dánta leis, mar aon le haistriúcháin Bhéarla. Bronnadh Duais Litríochta an Bhuitléaraigh air i 1994. É ina bhall de Aosdána.

Michael Davitt

Born in Cork in 1950, he was the founder and editor for many years of the groundbreaking poetry journal INNTI. *Freacnairc Mhearcair/The Oomph of Quicksilver* (2000) is a selection from five previous collections along with English translations. He was awarded the Butler Prize for literature in 1994, and is a member of Aosdána.

Andrew Folan *(Photo: Roisin Kennedy)*

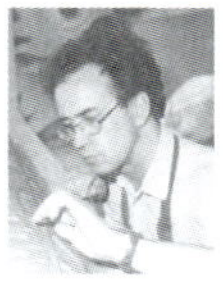

Priontálaí, dealbhóir agus ealaíontóir digiteach is ea Andrew Folan a bhfuil cónaí air i mBaile Átha Cliath. Sheas sé ar son na tíre i dtaispeántais idirnáisiúnta éagsúla. Cuireadh priontaí dealbhacha óna thaispeántas aonair 'Arterial Ink' ar taispeáint i mBaile Átha Cliath, i Londain, i bPáras agus i Stocalm. Fé láthair tá sraith grianghrafanna atá sintéisithe go digiteach idir lámhaibh aige.

Andrew Folan

Andrew Folan is a printer, sculptor and digital artist living in Dublin. He has represented Ireland in a number of international exhibitions. Sculptural print works from his recent solo exhibition 'Arterial Ink' were exhibited in Dublin, London, Paris and Stockholm. He is currently producing a series of digitally synthesised photographs.

Réiltín Murphy

74

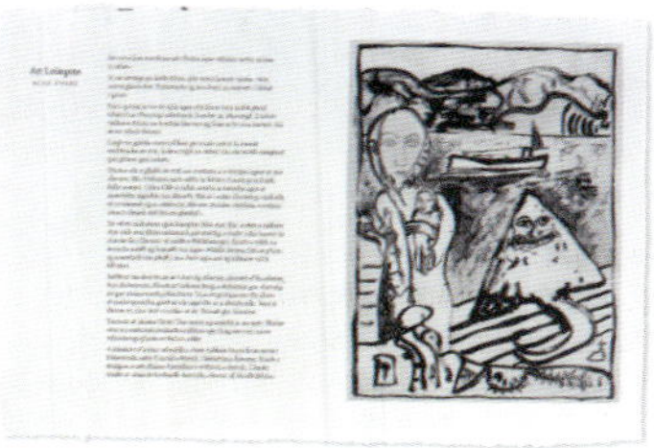

Alan Titley

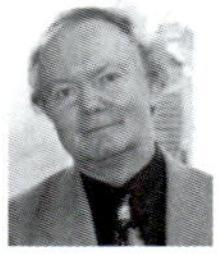

I gCorcaigh a rugadh 1947. Oilte i gColáiste Naoimh Phádraig i nDroim Chonrach. Úrscéalaí agus fear léinn. Ar a úrscéalta tá *Méirscrí na Treibhe* (1978), *Stiall Fhiall Feola* (1980) agus *An Fear Dána* - bunaithe ar shaol Mhuireadhaigh Albanaigh. Is imleabhar de ghearrscéalta *Eiriceachtaí agus Scéalta Eile* (1987).

Alan Titley

Born in Cork in 1947, he was educated at St Patrick's College, Drumcondra. Among his novels are *Méirscrí na Treibhe* (1978), *Stiall Fhial Feola* (1980) and *An Fear Dána* (1993), based on the life of Muireadhach Albanach. *Eiriceachtaí agus Scéalta Eile* (1987) is a volume of short stories.

Iain Bellany CBE

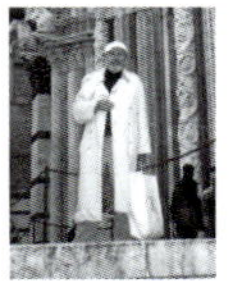

Rugadh e ann am Port Seaton, 1942. Buinidh e do theaghlach iasgairean. Aon dhe na peantairean Albannach as buadhaiche o àm a' chogaidh. Tha a dhealbhan ann an cruinneachaidhean prìomh thaighean-tasgaidh agus gailearaidhean ealain air feadh an t-saoghail, nam measg Gailearaidhean Nàiseanta na h-Alba, Gailearaidh Tate, Taigh-tasgaidh nan Nua-Ealan, New York agus Taigh-tasgaidh a' Mhatropolatain, New York.

John Bellany CBE

Born in Port Seaton in 1942, into a fishing family, he is one of the most influential Scottish painters since the war. His paintings are in the collections of major museums and art galleries throughout the world, including the National Galleries of Scotland, the Tate Gallery, the Museum of Modern Art, New York, and the Metropolitan Museum, New York.

Dòmhnall Addison/Donald Addison

75

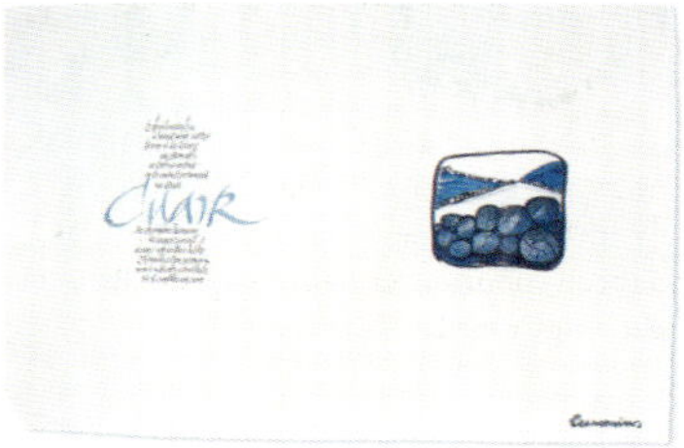

Áine Ní Ghlinn *(Photo: Louis Gunnigan)*

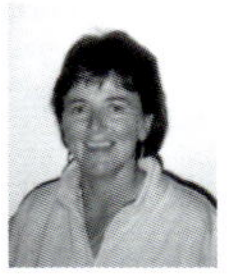

Rugadh i dTiobraid Árann í i 1955. Céim ollscoile aici ó Choláiste Ollscoile Bhaile Átha Cliath. Cnuasaigh: *An Chéim Bhriste* (Coiscéim, 1984), *Gairdín Pharthais* (Coiscéim, 1988), *Deora Nár Caoineadh/Unshed Tears* (Dedalus-Coiscéim, 1996); trí scéalta do pháistí: *Daifní Dineasár* (O' Brien Press), *An Leaba Sciathánach* (An Gúm) agus *Céard tá sa Bhosca?* (An Gúm). Is scríbhneoir í don dráma teilifíse *Ros na Rún* ar TG4.

Áine Ní Ghlinn

Born in Tipperary in 1955, she was educated at University College, Dublin. Her collections are *An Chéim Bhriste* (1984), *Gairdín Pharthais* (1988), *Deora Nár Caoineadh/Unshed Tears* (1996); three children's stories: *Daifní Dineasár, An Leaba Sciathánach* and *Céard tá sa Bhosca?* She writes also for TG4's drama series *Ros na Rún*.

Pauline Cummins *(Photo: Breeda Mooney)*

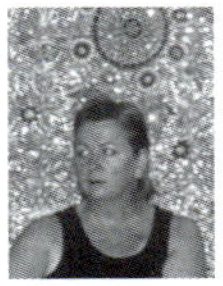

Oibríonn Pauline Cummins trí mheán an léirithe, na fístéipe agus suiteáil ghrianghrafach. Tá a saothar macnasach 'Inis t'Oírr'/'Aran Dance' (ar téip/sleamhnáin) mar chuid de bhailiúchán buan Áras Nua-Ealaíne na hÉireann i mBaile Átha Cliath. Taispeántais uaithi i gCeanada, sna Stáit Aontaithe, sa Ghearmáin, san Ísiltír agus sa Danmhairg. Oide fístéipe í sa Choláiste Náisiúnta Ealaíne is Deartha, Baile Átha Cliath.

Pauline Cummins

Pauline Cummins works in performance, video, and photographic installation. Her sensual slide/tape piece 'Inis t'Oírr'/'Aran Dance' is in the permanent collection of the Irish Museum of Modern Art in Dublin. She has exhibited in Canada, the USA, Germany, Holland, Denmark, and the Liverpool Tate, and is video tutor at the National College of Art and Design, Dublin.

Louise Donaldson

76

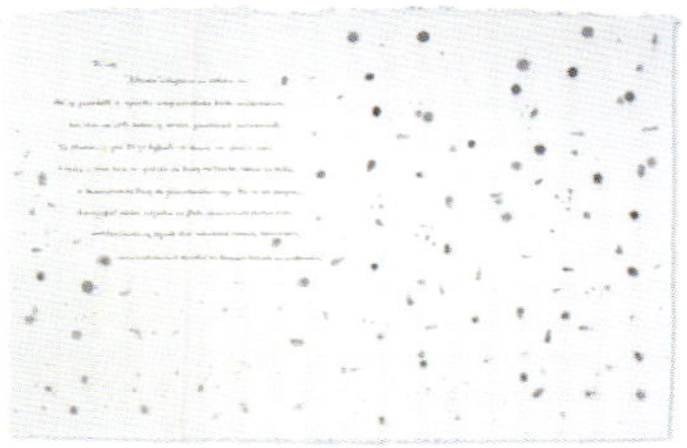

Pól Ó Muirí *(Photo: Irish Times)*

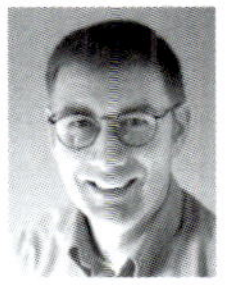

I mBéal Feirste i 1965 sea rugadh Pól Ó Muirí. D'fhreastail sé ar Ollscoil na Banríona ann, mar ar ghnóthaigh sé Baitsiléireacht Ealaíne (Onóracha) agus Céim Dochtúra sa Léann Cheilteach. Tá sé fostaithe mar iriseoir leis an *Irish Times* i mBaile Átha Cliath. Tá filíocht, gearrscéalta agus beathaisnéis foilsithe aige i nGaeilge agus i mBéarla.

Pól Ó Muirí

Pól Ó Muirí was born in Belfast in 1965 and graduated from Queen's University there with a BA and a PhD in Celtic Studies. He is a journalist with the *Irish Times*, Dublin, and has published poetry, short stories and a biography in Irish and English.

Fionnuala Ní Chiosáin

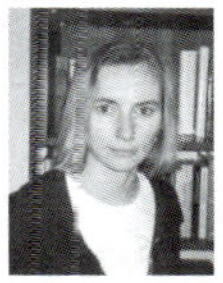

Is i mBaile Átha Cliath a rugadh Fionnuala Ní Chiosáin. Rinne sí staidéar ar na Míndána i St Martin's School of Art i Londain mar ar chónaigh sí ar feadh roinnt blianta. Tar éis bliain di i San Francisco d'fhill sí go Baile Átha Cliath d'fhonn stiúideo a bhunú ann. Roinnt mhaith taispeántais aonair uaithi i mBaile Átha Cliath agus i Nua Eabhrac agus bhí sí páirteach i dtaispeántais cscailte thar lear chomh maith. Feidhmíonn Gailearaí Kerlin ar a son.

Fionnuala Ní Chiosáin

Fionnuala Ni Chiosain was born in Dublin, and she studied fine art at St Martin's School of Art in London. After living in San Francisco for a year she returned to Dublin. She has had several solo exhibitions in Dublin and New York and been in group shows internationally. She is represented by the Kerlin Gallery.

Frances Breen

77

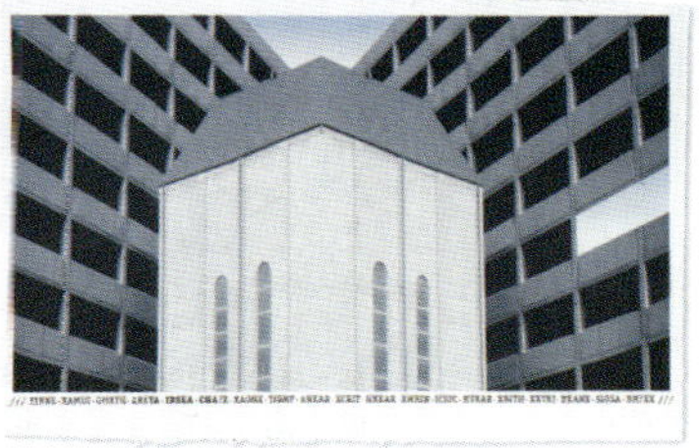

Liam Ó Muirthile *(Photo: Photocall Ireland)*

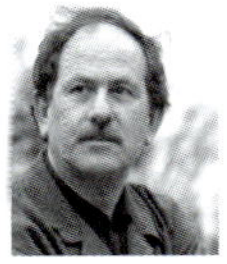

I gCorcaigh a rugadh 1950. Bhí baint aige le glúin INNTI i gC.Ó.C. Is iad a chnuasaigh filíochta *Tine Chnámh* (Sáirséal Ó Marcaigh), *Dialann Bóthair* (Gallery Press), *Walking Time agus*

Dánta Eile (Cló Iar-Chonnachta). Ar a chuid drámaí tá *Tine Chnámh* agus *Fear an Tae* (Cois Life) agus ar a chuid próis tá an t-úrscéal *Ar Bhruach na Laoi* (Comhar), agus *Gaothán* (Cois Life). Tá sé ina bhall de Aosdána.

Liam Ó Muirthile
Born in Cork in 1950, he was educated at University College Cork where he was associated with the poetry journal INNTI. His poetry collections are *Tine Chnámh, Dialann Bóthair* and *Walking Time agus Dánta Eile*. His plays include *Tine Chnámh* and *Fear an Tae*, and prose works the novel *Ar Bhruach na Laoi*, and *Gaothán*. He is a member of Aosdána.

Dùbhghlas Cocker *(Photo: John Hall)*

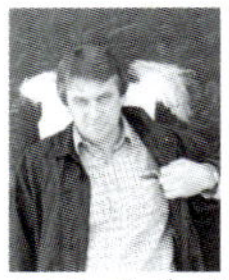

Rugadh e an Siorrachd Pheairt. Taisbeanaidhean Aon-neach: Gailearaidhean Ealain Obar Dheathain agus Pheairt; Gailearaidh Fruitmarket agus Talbot Rice, Dun Èideann; Artsite Bath; Air Gallery, Lunnainn. Taisbeanaidhean Bhuidhnean British Arts Show, Gailearaidh Serpentine; Ealain Albannach o 1900; Sculpture Symposium, Sarajevo; Transistors aig Taigh-tasgaidh Marioka Hashimoto, Iapan.

Riochdaichte ann an cruinneachaidhean poblach Breatannach agus thar chuan.

Doug Cocker
Doug Cocker was born in Perthshire. His one-man shows include Aberdeen & Perth Art Galleries; Fruitmarket & Talbot Rice, Edinburgh; Artsite Bath, Air Gallery, London. Group shows include British Art Show, Serpentine Gallery, 'Scottish Art since 1900', Sculpture Symposium Sarajevo, 'Transistors' at Morioka Hashimoto Museum, Japan.

Dòmhnall Addison/Donald Addison

78 **Seán Ó Ríordáin** *(Photo: Bill Doyle)*

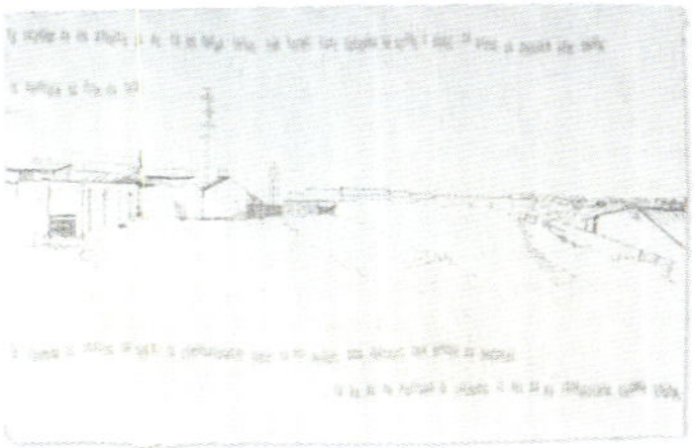

I gCo. Chorcaí a rugadh 1917. Cailleadh 1977.

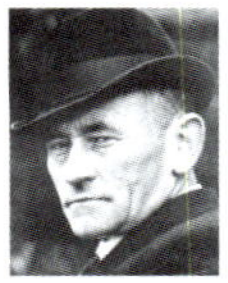

Cnuasaigh foilsithe: *Eireaball Spideoige* (1952), *Brosna* (1964), *Línte Liombó* (1971) agus *Tar Éis mo Bháis* (1979) – a foilsíodh i ndiaidh dó bás a fháil. I gcomhar le Séamas Ó Conghaile d'fhoilsigh sé *Rí na nUile* (1967) – nualeaganacha ar dhánta Sean-Ghaeilge. Tá a dhialann phearsanta (don tréimhse ó 1940 go dtí díreach sular cailleadh é) ar marthain i bhfoirm lámhscríbhinne.

Seán Ó Ríordáin
Born in Co. Cork in 1917, he died in 1977. His collections are *Eireaball Spideoige* (1952), *Brosna* (1964), *Línte Liombó* (1971) and *Tar Éis mo Bháis* (1979), published posthumously. With Séamus Ó Conghaile he published *Rí na nUile* (1967) – modern versions of Irish medieval poetry. His diary, surviving in manuscript from 1940 until just before his death, remains unpublished.

Aisling Ní Bheirn

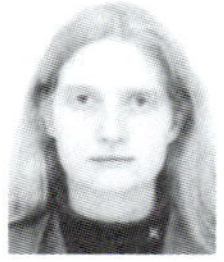

I mBéal Feirste atá Ní Bheirn lonnaithe agus oibríonn sí i Stiúideó Flaxart . Chuir sí a saothar ar taispeáint sa bhaile agus i gcéin. Ar na taispeántais aonair uaithi tá 'Temporary Provisions' ag Gailearaí Ormeau Baths (2001) agus 'Bureau', noctaithe i Halla an Chontae i nDún Laoghaire (1998). Fuair Ní Bheirn fós roinnt mhaith duaiseanna agus scoláireachtaí ó Chomhairle Ealaíon na hÉireann.

Aisling O'Beirn
This Belfast-based artist works in Flaxart Studios. She has exhibited in Ireland and abroad. Recent one-person exhibitions include the installation 'Temporary Provisions' at Ormeau Baths Gallery and 'Bureau' shown in Dun Laoghaire. O'Beirn has also received several awards and bursaries from the Arts Council of Northern Ireland and the Irish Arts Council.

Aisling Ní Bheirn/Aisling O'Beirn

79

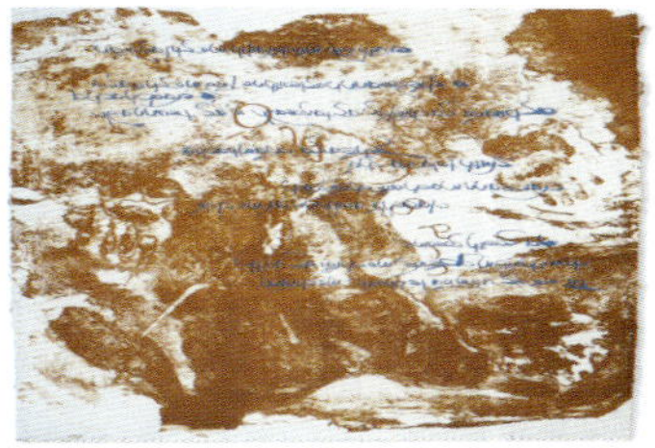

Cathal Ó Searcaigh

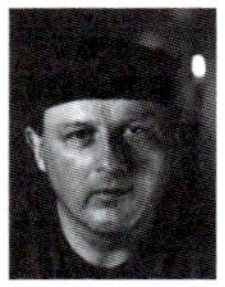

Rugadh i nDún na nGall i 1956 é. Oideachas i N.I.H.E., agus i Má Nuad. Go leor cnuasaigh foilsithe aige - ina measc *Súile Shuibhne* (1983); *Suibhne* (1987); *An Bealach 'na Bhaile* (1991); *Na Buachaillí Bána* (1996); *Out in the Open* (1998); *Ag Tnúth leis an tSolas; Rogha Dánta 1975-2000*. Drámaí foilsithe freisin aige - ina measc *Oíche Ghealaí i nGailílí*. É ina bhall de Aosdána.

Cathal Ó Searcaigh
Born in Co. Donegal in 1956, he was educated at the National Institute for Higher Education and Maynooth. His collections include *Súile Shuibhne* (1983); *Suibhne* (1987); *An Bealach 'na Bhaile* (1991); *Na Buachaillí Bána* (1996); *Out in the Open* (1998); *Ag Tnúth leis an tSolas* and *Rogha Dánta 1975-2000*. Plays include *Oíche Ghealaí i nGailílí*. He is a member of Aosdána.

Ian Joyce *(Photo: Olga Platilova)*

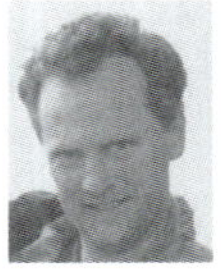

Ealaíontóir lán-aimseartha é Ian Joyce agus é ina stiúrthóir ar Chló Ceardlann na gCnoc Teoranta. Taispeánann sé a shaothar ealaíne go rialta thar lear – agus i Weimar na Gearmáine le cúpla bliain anuas. I 1994 chomhlíon sé coimisiún poiblí don amharclann i Leitir Ceanainn agus tá sé ag obair faoi láthair ar choimisiún don International Peace Centre in Inis Ceithleann. Tá sé pósta le Oona Hyland agus tá ceathrar clainne orthu. Cónaíonn siad ar Chnoc Bealtaine, amach ó Ghort a' Choirce.

Ian Joyce
Ian Joyce is a full-time artist and director of Cló Ceardlann na gCnoc Teoranta. He travels extensively with his arts projects, often to Germany. In 199_ he completed the public commission for the theatre in Letterkenny and has been working on a commission for the International Peace Centre in Enniskillen.

Réiltín Murphy

80

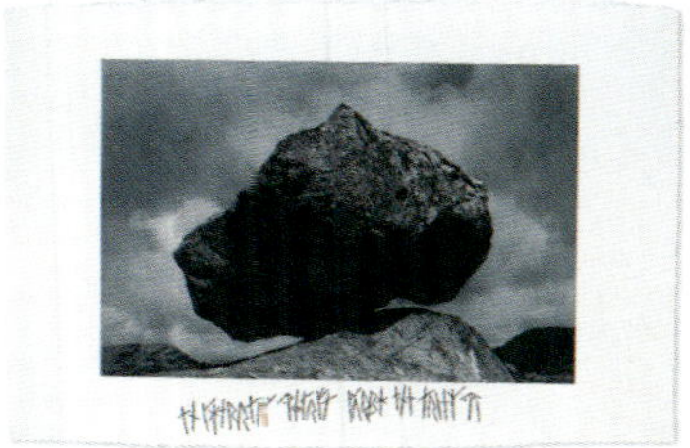

Micheál Ó Conghaile *(Photo: Clo Iar-Chonnachta)*

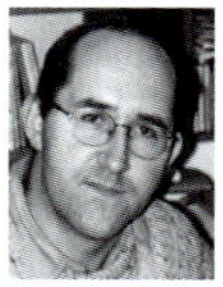

Is in Inis Treabhair a rugadh é i 1962 agus oileadh i gColáiste Ollscoile na Gaillimhe é. File, gearrscéalaí, úrscéalaí agus foilsitheoir é. I measc a chuid foilseachán tá *Mac an tSagairt* (1986), *Comhrá Caillí* (1987), *Conamara agus*

Árainn 1880–1980, *Gnéithe d'Amhráin Chonamara ár Linne* (1993), *An Fear a Phléasc* (1997), *Sna Fir* (1999). Ball de Aosdána é.

Mícheál Ó Conghaile
Born in Inis Treabhair in 1962, he was educated at University College, Galway. He is a poet, short story writer, novelist and publisher. Among his publications are *Mac an tSagairt* (1986), *Comhrá Caillí* (1987), *Conamara agus Árainn 1880–1980*, *Gnéithe d'Amhráin Chonamara ár Linne* (1993), *An Fear a Phléasc* (1997), *Sna Fir* (1999). He is a member of Aosdána.

Steve Dilworth *(Photo: Beka Dilworth)*

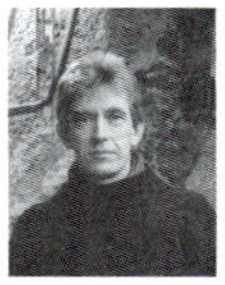

Rugadh e an 1949 ann an Kingston-upon-Hull. Tha a dhachaigh agus an obair aige an-diugh anns na Hearadh. Tha e riochdaichte le Gailearaidh Hart, Lunnainn.

Steve Dilworth
Born in Kingston-upon-Hull in 1949, he lives and works on the Isle of Harris. He is represented by Hart Gallery, London.

Susan Leiper

81

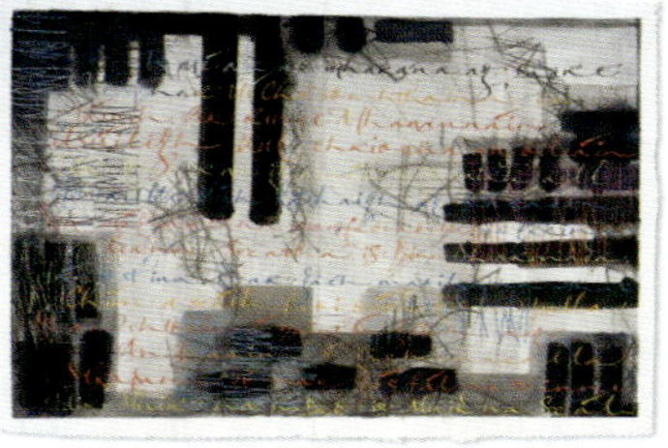

Tomás Mac Síomóin
Rugadh i mBaile Átha Cliath, 1938. Dochtúireacht ó Cornell (N.Y.). Chaith tréimhsí sna Stáit Aontaithe agus in Éirinn ag obair mar bhitheolaí agus mar iriseoir. Iareagarthóir ar na foilseacháin

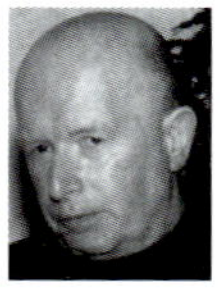

Ghaeilge *Anois* (nuachtán) agus *Comhar* (iris). Ceithre chnuasach filíochta uaidh go dtí seo chomh maith le gearrscéalta, altanna srl. i bhfoilseacháin éagsúla. É ag scríobh anois i mBarcelona, mar a bhfuil cónaí air.

Tomás Mac Síomóin
Born in Dublin in 1938. He has a doctorate from Cornell. He has had periods in USA and Ireland working as a biologist and journalist. A former editor of Irish-language publications, *Anois* and *Comhar*, he has had four collections of poetry published to date plus short stories and articles. He currently lives and writes in Barcelona.

Mary Avril Gillan *(Photo: John Gerrard)*

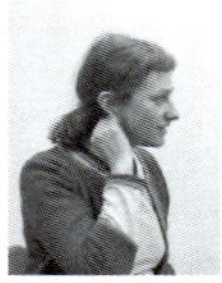

Tar éis a céad taispeántas aonair 'Nostalgia for Industry' ag Gailearaí Rubicon lean Mary Avril Gillan le roinnt mhaith taispeántas aonair – ina measc 'Virtual Belonging' ag Gailearaí Temple Bar agus an-chuid taispeántas oscailte sa bhaile agus i gcéin. Bronnadh Duais Dermot Larkin uirthi de bharr foirfeachta in oideachas ealaíne agus is céimí den Choláiste Náisiúnta Ealaíne is Deartha agus de Choláiste na Tríonóide í. Feidhmíonn Gailearaí Rubicon ar a son.

Mary Avril Gillan
Mary Avril Gillan's first solo show 'Nostalgia for Industry' at the Rubicon Gallery has been followed by several solo shows including 'Virtual Belonging' at the Temple Bar Gallery and many group shows in Ireland and internationally. A recipient of the Dermot Larkin award for excellence in art education and a graduate of the National College of Art and Design and Trinity College Dublin, she is represented by the Rubicon Gallery Dublin.

Anna Bowen

82

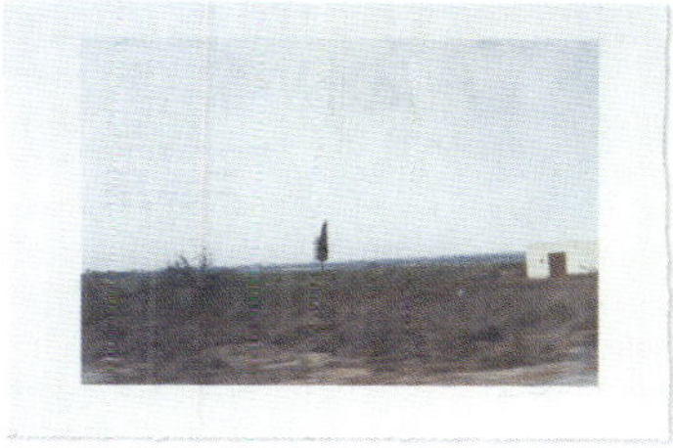

Caitlín Maude (1941–82) *(Photo: with thanks to Cathal Ó Luain)*

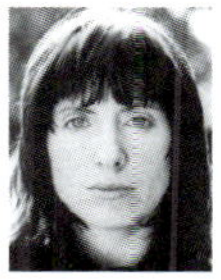

Ba as Ros Muc, i nGaeltacht Chonamara, do Chaitlín, file, drámadóir, ceoltóir. Bhí sí gníomhach i gcónaí i gcur chun cinn na Gaeilge agus na Gaeltachta. Chuir Gael Linn amach cnuasach dá cuid amhránaíochta agus léamh filíochta i 1975. Cruinníodh a cuid dánta san leabhar *Caitlín Maude, Dánta* i 1984. Cuireadh a cuid próis, agus dráma, *Lasair Coille* (comhúdar Mícheál Ó hAirtnéide), i gcló mar *Caitlín Maude, Drámaíocht agus Prós* i 1988.

Caitlín Maude (1941–82)
Caitlín (1941–82) a poet, dramatist and singer, was from Connemara. Caitlín was active in promoting Irish and the Gaeltacht. A collection of her singing with readings of her poems was issued in 1975. Her poems were gathered in one volume *Caitlín Maude, Dánta* in 1984. Her prose writings and a play *Lasair Coille* (co-authored with Michael Hartnett) were published in 1988, as *Caitlín Maude, Drámaíocht agus Prós*.

Daphne Wright *(Photo: Peter Sorg)*

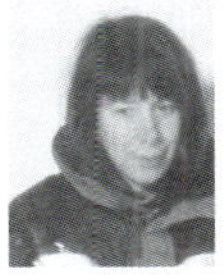

In Éirinn a rugadh Daphne Wright i 1963 agus tá cónaí anois uirthi i mBristol. D'fhoghlaim sí a ceird i Sligeach, i mBaile Átha Cliath agus i Newcastle. Bhí an chéad taispeántas aonair uaithi ag an Cornerhouse agus lean sí leo i nGailearaí Spacex, Gailearaí Aspex, Gailearaí Frith Street agus i nGailearaí Ealaíne Shligigh. Le déanaí bhí saothar léi mar chuid de thaispeántas nua-ealaíne na hÉireann ag PS1 i Nua Eabhrac agus ag Gailearaí Albright Knox i mBuffalo.

Daphne Wright
Born in Ireland in 1963, Daphne Wright currently lives in Bristol. She trained in Sligo, Dublin and Newcastle. Her first solo show at the Cornerhouse was followed by several one-person exhibitions including a major show at the Douglas Hyde Gallery. Recently her work was in an exhibition of new Irish art in New York and in Buffalo. She has won the Henry Moore Fellowship and the Paul Hamlyn Foundation Award.

Réiltín Murphy

83

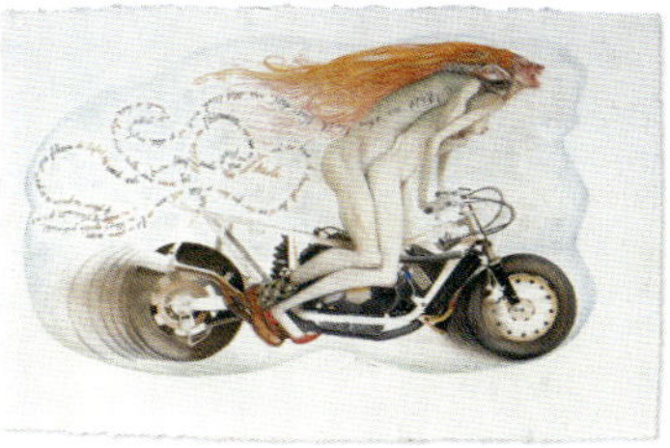

Pearse Hutchinson *(Photo: The Gallery Press)*

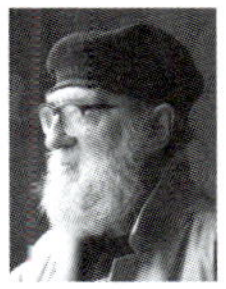

Is i nGlaschú a rugadh 1927. Oilte i gColáiste Ollscoile Bhaile Átha Cliath. Filíocht sa Bhéarla foilsithe aige leis. Aistritheoir ó Chatalóinis, ó Ghaeilge agus ó Galacio-Portaingéilis. Dhá chnuasach as Gaeilge uaidh: *Faoistin Bhacach* (1968) agus *Le Cead na Gréine* (1989). Roinnt mhaith eile as Béarla. D'aistrigh sé rogha dánta Gaeilge dá chuid féin faoin teideal *The Soul That Kissed The Body* (1990).

Pearse Hutchinson
Born in Glasgow in 1927, he was educated at

University College, Dublin. He is a poet in Irish and English, and a translator from Catalan, Irish, Galacio-Portuguese. There are two collections in Irish: *Faoistin Bhacach* (1968) and *Le Cead na Gréine* (1989) as well as many in English. *The Soul that Kissed the Body* (1990) is a selection of his Irish poems, translated by himself.

John Byrne *(Photo: Malcolm Maclean)*

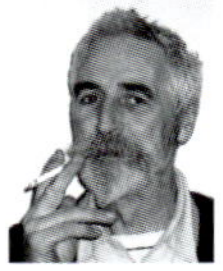

Rugadh e ann am Pàislig ann an 1940. Bha e ag obair mar ghille lice (preantas air dealbhachadh bhrat-ùrlair) mun deach e a Sgoil Ealain Ghlaschu (1958-64). 'S ann an 1968 a bha a' chiad taisbeanadh aon-neach aige ann an Lunnainn, fon ainm Patrick. Tha e na ùghdar air seachd dealbhan-cluiche, nam measg an triamh, *The Slab Boys*, dhen deach film a dhèanamh an 1987. Tha a chuid obrach ann an cruinneachaidhean air feadh an t-saoghail agus tha e a' fuireach air Ghaidhealtachd ann an Alba.

John Byrne

Born in Paisley in 1940, he worked as a colour mixer at A.F. Stoddard, the carpet manufacturer. He studied at Glasgow School of Art then worked as a graphic designer with STV, returning to A.F. Stoddard as a designer in 1966. He has written, designed and directed stage and screen presentations including *The Slab Boys* and *Tutti Frutti*.

84

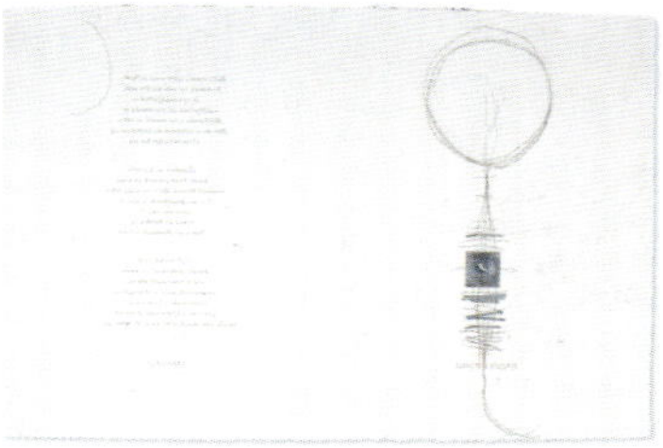

Meg Bateman *(Photo: Elsie Mitchell)*

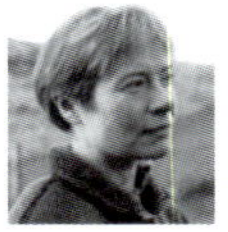

Rugadh Meg Bateman an Dun Èideann an 1959. Dh'ionnsaich i a' Ghàidhlig eadar oilthigh agus Uibhist a Deas. Rinn i teagasg seachd bliadhna an Oilthigh Obar Dheathain mus do thòisich i aig Sabhal Mòr Ostaig san Eilean Sgitheanach far a bheil i a' fuireach le a mac, Colm. Thug i a-mach dà chruinneachadh de bhàrdachd, *Òrain Ghaoil* (1990) agus *Aotromachd* (1997).

Meg Bateman

Meg Bateman was born in Edinburgh in 1959 and learned Gaelic at Aberdeen University and in South Uist. She taught at Aberdeen University before starting work at Sabhal Mòr Ostaig in Skye. She has published two collections, *Òrain Ghaoil* (1990) and *Aotromachd* (1997).

Màiri Killin *(Photo: Craig Mackay)*

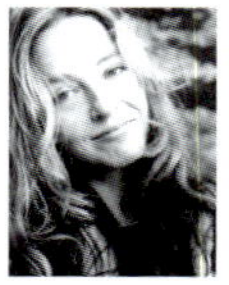

Tha Màiri Killin a' fuireach an I Chaluim Chille. Cheumnaich i à Sgoil Ealain Ghlaschu, agus tha buaidh aig arceòlas air a h-obair - 's e sin arceòlas ann an àrainneachd agus na cuimhneachain aice fhèin. Chaidh an obair airson an *Leabhair Mhòir* a chruthachadh air chòmhnaidheachd an Siorrachd Dhùn nan Gall còmhla ris an snas-sgrìobhadair, Frances Breen.

Mhairi Killin

Mhairi Killin lives on Iona. A graduate of Glasgow School of Art, her work is influenced by archaeology; that which is contained within her environment and within the landscape of personal memory. The piece of work for *Leabhar Mor* was created during a residency in Co. Donegal with calligrapher Frances Breen.

Frances Breen

85 **Ceabhan MacNèill** *(Photo: David Whyte)*

Rugadh is thogadh Ceabhan MacNèill ann an Leòdhas. Am measg nan leabhraichean aige tha: *Love*

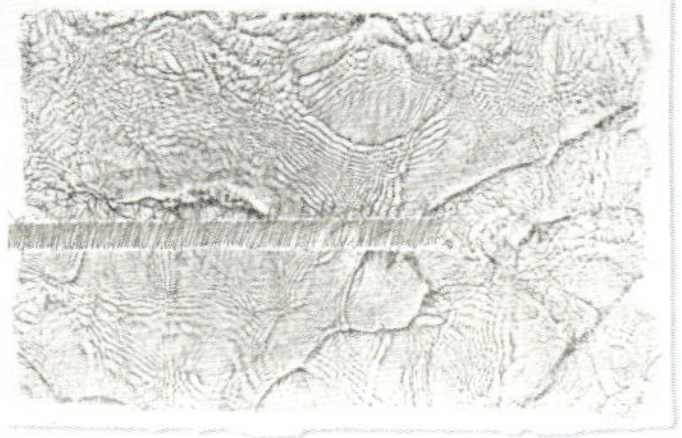

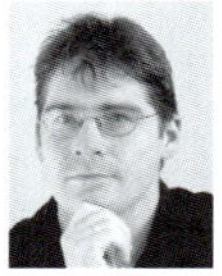

and Zen in the Outer Hebrides, A Little Borderless Village (eag.), *Wish I Was Here* (eag.), *Be Wise Be Otherwise, The Red Door* (eag.) agus *The Black Halo* (eag.). Am measg nan duaisean aige tha Duais Bàrdachd Eadar-Nàiseanta Tivoli Europa Giovani, Caidreachas Sgrìobhaidh Iain Mhic a' Ghobhainn (1999-2002) 's m.s.a.a. Tha e air a chuid bàrdachd aithris ann an iomadach dùthaich agus tha a bhàrdachd air a h-eadar-theangachadh gu dusan diofar chànan.

Kevin MacNeil

Kevin MacNeil was born on Lewis. Among his books are: *Love and Zen in the Outer Hebrides, A Little Borderless Village* (ed.), *Wish I Was Here* (ed.), *Be Wise Be Otherwise, The Red Door* (ed.) and *The Black Halo* (ed.). Among his prizes are: the Tivoli Europa Giovani International Poetry Prize, the Iain Crichton Smith Writing Fellowship, etc. His work has been translated into twelve languages.

Remco De Fouw *(Photo: Rachel Joynt)*

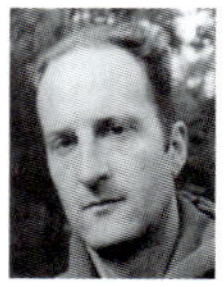

I mBaile Átha Cliath i 1962 a rugadh é. Ar na taispeántais aonair uaidh tá 'Reservoir' ag an Project Arts Centre (1994), 'Undercurrent' ag Gailearaithe Temple Bar (1997) agus 'Overflow' ag an Model Arts Centre (1998). Coimisiúin phoiblí: 'Quintessometry' ag Ospidéal Réigiúnach Phoirt Láirge, 'Satillites' ag Brú na Bóinne i nGráinseach Nua, 'In Touch' do Microsoft i mBaile Átha Cliath agus 'First Conundrum' ag an International Conference Centre i nDún Éideann.

Remco De Fouw

Born in 1962 in Dublin, his solo exhibitions include 'Reservoir' at the Project Arts Center (1994), 'Undercurrent' at Temple Bar Galleries (1997) and 'Overflow' at the Model Arts Center (1998). His public commissions include 'Quintessometry' at Waterford Regional Hospital, 'In Touch' for Microsoft in Dublin and 'First Conundrum' at Edinburgh International Conference Centre.

Réiltín Murphy

86

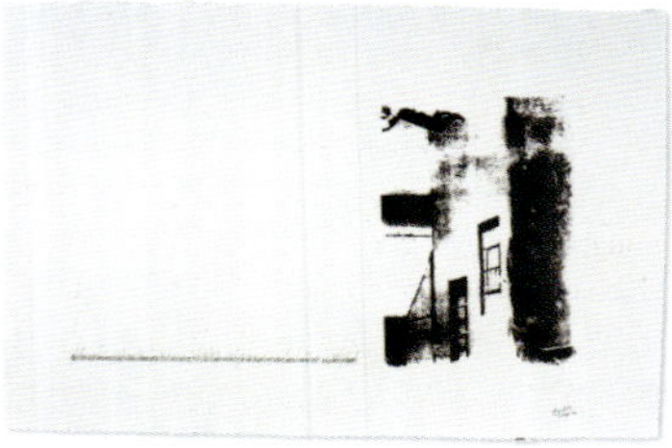

Maoilios M Caimbeul *(Photo: Tempest Photography)*

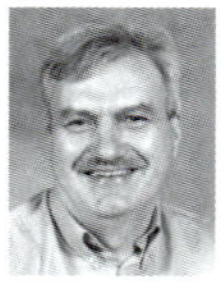

Rugadh Maoilios Caimbeul anns a' bhliadhna 1944 san Eilean Sgitheanach agus tha buntanas aige ris an eilean sin agus ri Leòdhas. Tha e air ceithir cruinneachaidhean bàrdachd fhoillseachadh a bharrachd air sgeulachdan do chloinn agus òigridh. Tha a bhàrdachd a' dèiligeadh ri gaol, poileataigs, cànan agus teagamhan mu chreideamh. Tha barrachd mu chreideamh anns a' bhàrdachd as ùire agus tha e nas bàidheile a thaobh ceistean creideimh.

Myles Campbell

Myles Campbell was born in 1944 in Skye. He has published four collections of verse and children's and teenage fiction. His poetry deals with love, politics, language and religious doubts. Religion is more to the fore in his most recent work where there is a mellowing.

Conor McFeely *(Photo: Pascale Steven)*

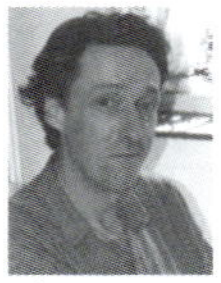

I nDoire Choilm Chille i 1958 is ea rugadh Conor McFeely agus idir 1977 agus 1980 lean sé leis na Míndána ag Kingston Polytechnic. Ealaín suiteála is mó a chruthaíonn sé. Taispeántais uaidh ar fud na hÉireann, sa Ríocht Aontaithe agus thar lear. Orthu siúd le déanaí tá 'Small Steps' a bhí ar turas sna Stáit Aontaithe agus in Éirinn (2000-2001) agus 'The British Art Show 5' a taispeánadh i nDún Éideann, i Southampton, i gCaerdydd agus i mBirmingham (2000-2001).

Conor McFeely

Conor McFeely was born in Derry in 1958 and studied Fine Art at Kingston Polytechnic. His work is mostly installation based. He has exhibited widely throughout Ireland, the UK and abroad. Recent exhibitions include 'Small Steps' that has toured the USA and Ireland and 'The British Art Show 5' that has been shown nationwide.

Réiltín Murphy

87

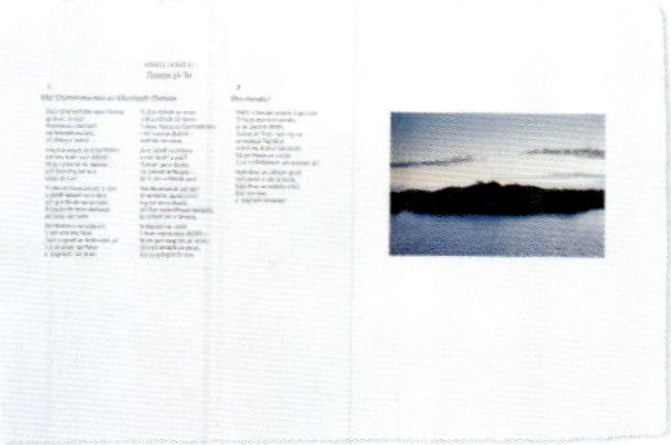

Tormod Caimbeul

'Nuair a rugadh mi ann an Dail-a-Dheas ann an 1942, bha gèile mhòr ann agus thug m'athair "Tormod a' Ghèile" orm. Theab na sgoiltean dhan deacha mi cur as dhomh 's bidh mi, gus an eà an diugh, a' dol lag agus air chrith a' cuimhneachadh

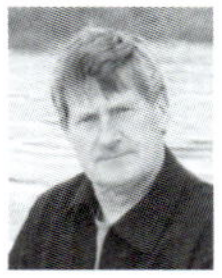

orra. Ach thuirt a' bhean-eiridinn rium an dè gu robh *am blood pressure* OK agus an fhuil fhèin cuideachd, 's chuir sin iongadh orm, duine a dh'òladh a' lèine. An dràsta tha mi a' sgrìobhadh leabhar ùpraideach – *Bourbonics* no *Turas an Eucoraich*. Nuair bhios e deiseal ann an 2042 thèid film a dheanamh dheth – starring Eli Wallach. Tha mi'n dòchas gum bi Eli beò gun uair sin – a-rèir choltais bidh mise.

Norman Campbell

'When I was born in South Dell in 1942 it was blowing a gale and my father called me "Tormod a' Ghèile". The schools I attended nearly finished me off and to this day I tremble and feel faint when I think about them. However, the nurse told me yesterday that my blood pressure is OK and that my blood is clear, which was surprising for someone who drinks like a fish. I am currently writing a riotous tome – *The Sinner's Progress*. When it is completed in 2042 a film will be made of it - starring Eli Wallach.'

Oliver Comerford

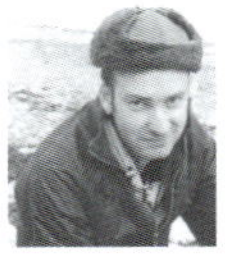

I mBaile Átha Cliath a rugadh Oliver Comerford i 1967 agus oileadh é sa Choláiste Náisiúnta Ealaíne is Deartha agus sa Chelsea College of Art and Design. Ghlac sé páirt in an-chuid seónna thar lear agus chuir sé taispeántais aonair ar siúl i nGailearaithe Hallward, Rubicon agus ag an Living Art Museum i Reykjavik. Bhí sé páirteach i gCeardlann na nEalaíontóirí ag Áras Nua-Ealaíne na hÉireann.

Oliver Comerford

Oliver Comerford was born in Dublin in 1967 and educated at the National College of Art and Design and Chelsea College of Art and Design. He has been included in many group shows internationally and has had one-person exhibitions in the Hallward Gallery, Rubicon Gallery and the Living Art Museum in Reykjavik. He was a resident in the Artists Work Programme at the Irish Museum of Modern Art.

Dòmhnall Addison/Donald Addison

88

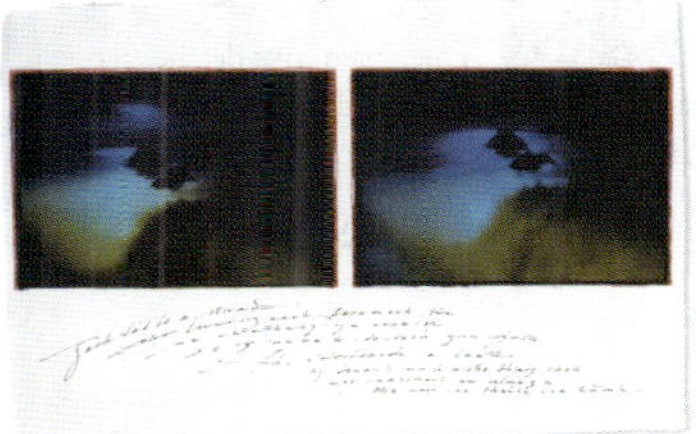

Dòmhnall MacIomhair

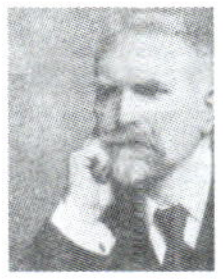

Rugadh Dòmhnall MacIomhair (1857-1935) an Crabhlasta, Ùig, Eilean Leòdhais. Bha athair, Iain mac Aonghais, na Mhaighstir-Sgoile Gàidhlig, dreuchd riatanach a chaidh a sguabadh air falbh ann an dearmad le Achd Foghlaim 1872. Chaidh Dòmhnall na mhaighstir-sgoile cuideachd agus thug e a bheatha a' nochdadh gun robh foghlam Gàidhlig a cheart cho riatanach ri foghlam Beurla. Bha e sia bliadhna fichead air ceann Sgoil Phabail san Rubha, tè dhe na sgoiltean a b' fheàrr sna h-Eileanan an Iar. Rinn e facail 'An Ataireachd Ard' airson Mòd 1905 à rud a chuala e uair aig bràthair athar, 'Chan eil nì an seo mar a bha ach ataireachd na mara air an tràigh.'

Donald MacIver

Donald Maciver (1857-1935) was born in Crowlista, Uig, Lewis. His father was a Gaelic schoolmaster, and Donald became a schoolmaster. For twenty-six years he was head of Bayble School in Point, one of the best schools in the Western Isles. He made the words of 'An Ataireachd Ard' out of something he once heard his uncle say, 'Nothing here is as it was except the surge of the sea upon the strand.'

Clare Langan *(Photo: Arran Lundy [age 3])*

Grianghrafadóir agus déantóir scannán í Clare Langan atá lonnaithe i mBaile Átha Cliath. Tar éis di

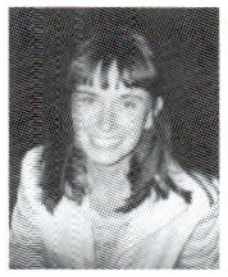

céim a fháil i nDealbhóireacht na Míndána ón gColáiste Náisiúnta Ealaíne is Deartha i 1989 chaith sí seal ag staidéar Scannánaíochta ag Ollscoil Nua Eabhrac i 1993. Luadh a hainm don Glen Dimplex Artists Award (2000) in Áras Nua-Ealaíne na hÉireann. Seasfaidh sí ar son na hÉireann ag an Biennale de São Paulo 2002 agus beidh taispeántas uaithi ag Biennale Léarphoill 2002.

Clare Langan

Clare Langan is a Dublin-based photographer and film-maker. Having graduated in Fine Art sculpture at the National College of Art and Design in 1989, she studied film at New York University in 1993. She was short-listed for the Glen Dimplex Artists Award at the Irish Museum of Modern Art. She is representing Ireland in the São Paulo Biennale 2002 and is exhibiting in the Liverpool Biennale 2002.

Frances Breen

89

Dòmhnall Ruadh Chorùna *(Photo: Comunn Eachdraidh Uibhist a Tuath)*

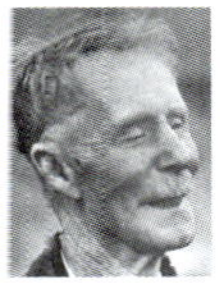

Rugadh Dòmhnall Ruadh Chorùna (1887-1967) am baile Chorùna air Cladach a' Bhaile Shear an Uibhist a Tuath. Chaidh e na chlachair, ach ann an cuid dhe na h-òrain as fheàrr aige tha sinn a' faicinn, a' cluinntinn, a' faireachdainn, agus fiù a' snotadh, oilt nan trainnsichean sa Chiad Chogadh Mhòr – cò ris a bha e coltach a bhith a' mèarrsadh gu aghaidh a' chath, no air do phuinnseanadh le gas, no air do chuartachadh le cuirp 's bloighean chuirp do cho-Ghaidheal. Bha e dèidheil air poitseadh agus tha samhla na seilge a' ruith na shnàithlean tro na h-òrain aige. Lean am fiorachas seo na bhàrdachd às dèidh a' chogaidh.

Donald MacDonald
Donald MacDonald (1887-1967) was born in the township of Corùna in Claddach Baleshare in North Uist. He became a mason, but in some of his best songs we see, hear, feel, even smell the horror of the trenches in the First World War. He was fond of poaching and the metaphor of the hunt runs in a thread through his verse. This realism remained in his poetry after the war.

Fiona R. Hutchison *(Photo: Brian Fishbacker)*

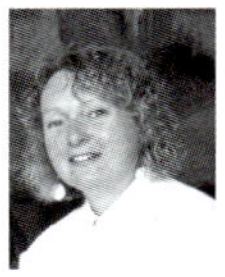

'S e neach-ealain a tha a' dèanamh grèis-bhrat agus peantadh a th' ann am Fiona Hutchison. Cheumnaich i à Colaiste Ealain Dhùn Èideann le urram sa phrìomh ìre agus le teisteas iar-cheumnachaidh. Bha i an dà chuid a' toirt a h-obrach phearsanta fhèin gu buil agus ag obair air proiseact coimhearsnachd, barantais agus a' gabhail pàirt ann an Co-chomhairlean Eadar-nàiseanta. Tha i air grunnan dhuaisean a chosnadh agus tha a cuid obrach a' nochdadh ann an cruinneachaidhean prìobhaideach agus poblach am Breatainn, an Aimeireagaidh is an Lithuania.

Fiona R. Hutchison
Fiona R Hutchison is an artist who works in tapestry and painting. Graduating from Edinburgh College of Art with a First Class Honours Degree and Postgraduate Diploma, she balanced producing her own work with working on a community project, commissions and contributing to international symposiums. She has won several awards and has work in private and public collections in the UK, USA and Lithuania.

Réiltin Murphy

90

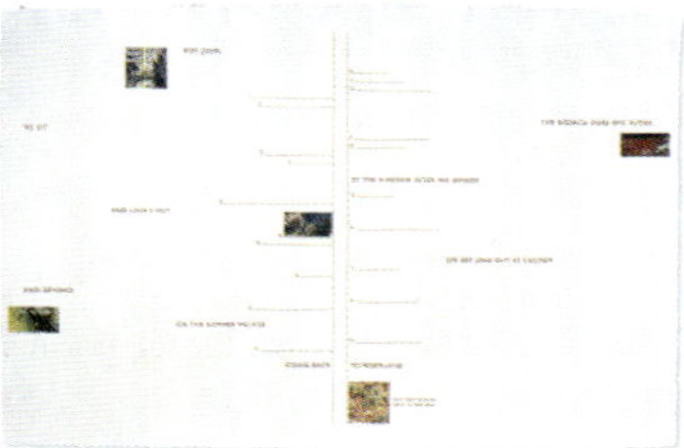

Rody Gorman

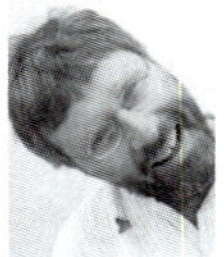

Rugadh e am Baile Atha Cliath 1960. Cruinneachaidhean bàrdachd: *Fax* (1996); *Cùis-Ghaoil* (1999); *Bealach Garbh* (1999); *Air a' Charbad fo Thalamh* (2000); *Faoi Shlí Cualann* (2002); *Gun Urra* (2002). Na sgrìobhadair aig Sabhal Mòr Ostaig 1998-2001. Sgrìobhadair Oilthigh Chorcaigh 2002.

Rody Gorman
Born in Dublin in 1960, his poetry collections are *Fax* (1996); *Cùis-Ghaoil* (1999); *Bealach Garbh* (1999); *Air a' Charbad fo Thalamh* (2000); *Faoi Shlí Cualann* (2002); *Gun Urra* (2002). He was an SAC writing fellow at Sabhal Mòr Ostaig and writer-in-residence at the University College Cork.

Alfred Graf *(Photo: Marlies Graf)*
Acadamh Grinneis Vienna (teisteanas ann am

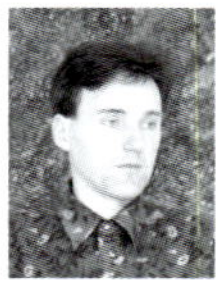

peantadh 1985); duaisean eadar-mheasgte, tabhartasan agus air thaigheadas thall thairis; taisbeanaidhean aon-neach agus buidhne anns an Ostair, an Alba, Sasainn, san Eilbheis, san Eadailt, san Fhraing, ann an Israel, sa Ghrèig, san Ungair, ann am Poblachd Chech, sa Phòlainn, ann an Èirinn, am Malta agus ann an Aimeireagaidh. Proiseactan: 'Fastentuecher für St Elisabeth', Vienna; 'Archipelago', Alba (le T. J. Cooper); 'Rhine' (le T. J. Cooper); Reiseskizzen, An Eadailt.

Alfred Graf
He studied at the Academy of Fine Arts Vienna and won diverse prizes. He now lives in Vienna and has had solo and group exhibitions in Austria, Scotland, England, Germany, Switzerland, Italy, France, Israel, Greece, Hungary, Czech Republic, Poland, Ireland, Malta and USA. Projects include 'Fastentucher für St Elisabeth', Vienna; 'Archipelago', Scotland; 'Rhine'; 'Reiseskizzen', Italy.

Dòmhnall Addison

91

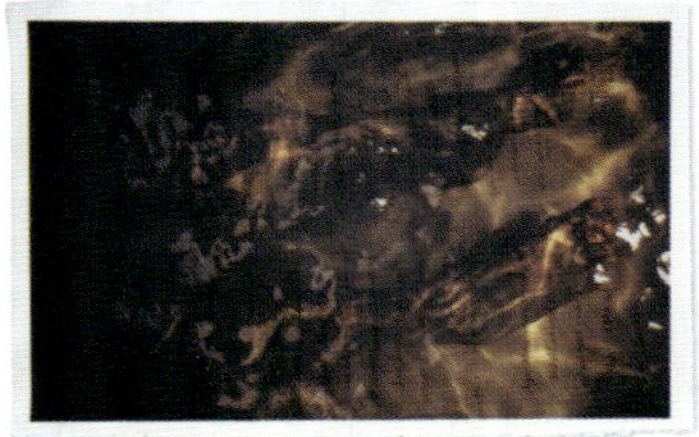

Anna C. Frater *(Photo: Angus Smith)*

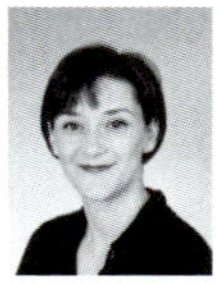

Rugadh mi ann an 1967 agus thogadh mi ann am Pabail Uarach ann an Leòdhas. An dèidh ceumnachadh an toiseach le Ceiltis agus Frangais le urram, agus an uair sin le Ph.D bho Oilthigh Ghlaschu, bha mi ag obair anns na meadhanan mus do thill mi a Leòdhas ann an 1999 mar òraidiche air Ceum Gàidhlig OGE ann an Colaisde a' Chaisteil.

Anne C. Frater
She was born in 1967 and brought up in Upper Bayble on the Isle of Lewis. After gaining an MA in Celtic and French, then a PhD in Celtic from Glasgow University, she worked in the media before returning to Lewis in 1999 as a lecturer on the UHI Gaelic Degree course based at Lews Castle College.

Alastair MacLennan *(Photo: Roger Côte)*

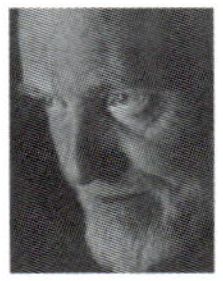

I mBlàr Athoill in Albain is ea rugadh Alastair MacLennan agus bhain se céimeanna amach ó Choláiste Ealaíne Duncan of Jordanstone i nDùn Dèagh i 1965 agus ón School of the Art Institute of Chicago i 1968. Ollamh le Míndána in Ollscoil Uladh é. Léiríonn sé 'ealaín ghníomhaithe' - léirithe agus ealaín suiteála i suímh éagsúla seachas i ngailearaithe. I 1997 sheas sé ar son na hÉireann san Biennale i Veinéis na hIodáile (1997).

Alastair MacLennan
Born in Blair Atholl in Scotland, Alastair MacLennan graduated from the Duncan of Jordanstone College of Art in Dundee and from the School of the Art Institute of Chicago. He is Professor of Fine Art at the University of Ulster. He stages 'actuations' which are performances and installations in both gallery and 'non gallery' spaces. He represented Ireland in the 1997 Venice Biennale.

Frances Breen

92

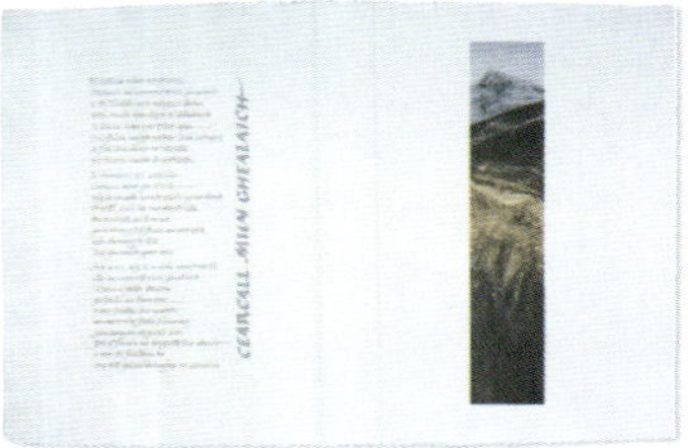

Catriona NicGumaraid

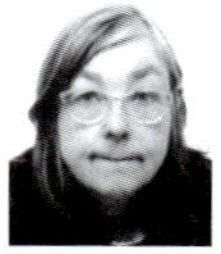

Tha i na bean-dachaigh, sgrìobhadair, neach-teagaisg agus craoladair. Rugadh Catrìona ann an Ròdhag san Eilean Sgitheanach an 1947. An dèidh dhi bhith an Oilthigh Ghlaschu b' i a' chiad sgrìobhaiche còmhnaidheachd ann an Sabhal Mòr Ostaig. Chan eil dràma no rosg (Beurla cuideachd) a thig suas ri ciad ghaol Catrìona: bàrdachd Ghàidhlig air a foillseachadh thar trì deicheadan, air a cruinneachadh anns *A' Choille Chiar* (1974, còmhla ri a piuthar, Morag) agus an *Rè na h-Oidhche* (1994).

Catriona Montgomery
Home-maker, writer, teacher, actor and broadcaster, Catriona was born in Roag, Skye in 1947. After Glasgow University she became first writer-in-residence at Sabhal Mòr Ostaig. Drama and prose (including English) fail to rival Catriona's first love: Gaelic poetry published over three decades, collected in *A' Choille Chiar* (1974, with sister Morag) and *Rè Na h-Oidhche* (1994).

Seumas Moireasdan *(Photo: Patterson copyright DC Thomson)*

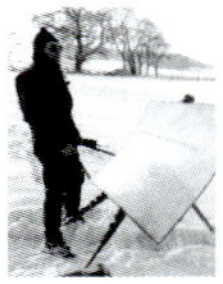

Rugadh e ann an 1932. Bha e a' teagaisg ann an Colaiste Ealain Dhonnchaidh Iòrdanstain, Dùn Dè, 1965-87 agus chaidh e na Cheannard Roinne ann an 1978. Tha taisbeanaidhean aon-neach air a bhith aige ann an Alba, Lunnainn, san Eadailt, sa Ghearmailt agus ann an Canada le mòran dhe chuid obrach ann an cruinneachaidhean prìobhaideach agus poblach ann am Breatainn agus thar chuan. Tha e air peantadh ann an àiteachan cho eadar-dhealaichte ri Afraga agus an t-Artaig.

James Morrison
Born in 1932, he taught at Duncan of Jordanstone College of Art and was made Head of Department in 1978. One man exhibitions include Scotland, London, Italy, Germany and Canada with many of his works in private and public collections both in the UK and overseas. He has painted in places as diverse as Africa and the High Arctic.

Dòmhnall Moireach/Donald Murray

93

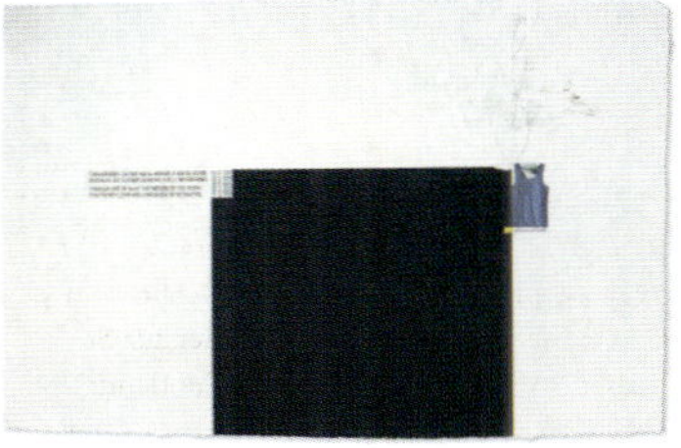

Crìsdean Whyte *(Photo: Ian Southern)*

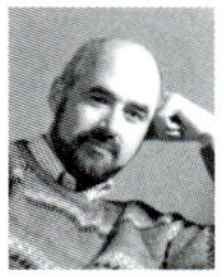

Rugadh Crìsdean Whyte ann an Glaschu ann an 1952. Fhuair e fhoghlam ann an Colaiste an Naoimh Aloysius agus an Colaiste Phembroke, Cambridge. Nochd *Uirsgeul* ann an 1991, *Bho Leabhar-Latha Maria Malibran* ann an 1995 agus *An Tràth Duilich* (1989-90). Thathas air a' bhàrdachd aige eadar-theangachadh gu Frangais, Catalanais, Croatianais, Eadailtis agus Albàinianais. Tha e cuideachd air ceithir nobhailean a sgrìobhadh sa Bheurla agus tha e an-dràsta ag obair air dhà eile agus air dealbh-chluich, *Elfra*.

Christopher Whyte
Born in Glasgow in 1952, he was educated at St Aloysius' College and at Pembroke College, Cambridge. Publications include *Uirsgeul* (1991), *Bho Leabhar-Latha Maria Malibran* (1995) and *An Tràth Duilich* (1989-90) His poems have been translated into French, Catalan, Croatian, Italian and Albanian. He is also the author of four working novels in English and is currently working on two more and on a play called *Elfra*.

Eilidh NicAlasdair *(Photo: Jane Reynolds)*

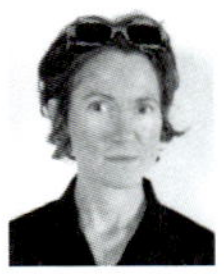

Rugadh i an Dùn Èideann an 1969. Cheumnaich i à Colaiste Ealain Dhonnchaidh Iòrdanstain, Dùn Dè an 1991. Dh'fhuirich i agus dh'obraich i airson mòran bhliadhnaichean san Fhraing agus san Eadailt, le taic bho iomadh sgcilearachd, duais, urras agus coimhearsnachd (a' gabhail a-steach Aimeireagaidh). Taisbeanaidhean Aon-neach, Alba agus Eadar-nàiseanta: 'La Langue de Bois', 'Stirrup-Cup', 'Chlorophyll Weddings' agus 'Bridal Drawings' An-dràsta an Dun Èideann. Riochdaichte le Art First, Lunnainn agus New York.

Helen MacAlister
Born in Edinburgh in 1969, she graduated from Duncan of Jordanstone College of Art. She has lived and worked for many years in France and Italy, supported by various scholarships, awards, sponsors and residencies (including USA). Solo exhibitions, Scotland and international include 'La Langue de Bois', 'Stirrup-Cup', 'Chlorophyll Weddings' and 'Bridal Drawings'. She is currently based in Edinburgh. Represented by Art First, London and New York.

Dòmhnall Addison/Donald Addison

94

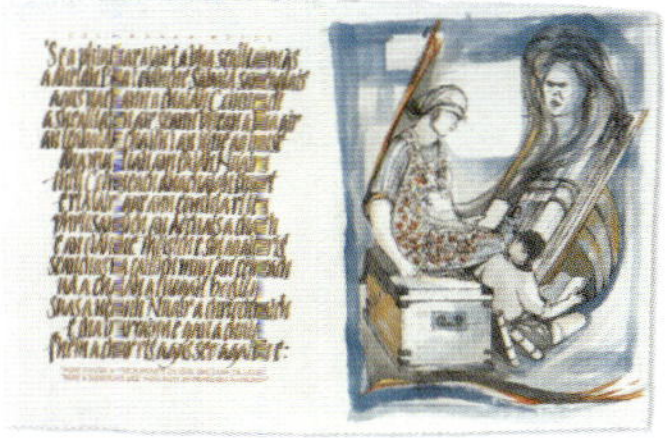

Aonghas Caimbeul *(Photo: Cuan Ard Press, Publishing & Media Services)*

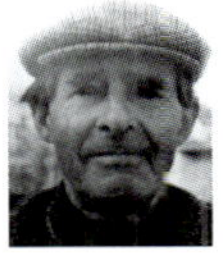

Rugadh Aonghas Caimbeul ('Am Puilean', 1903-82) an Suaineabost, Nis, Eilean Leòdhais. Bha beatha làn annais aige na fhear-bàta an Caolas na Hearadh, na fhear-criutha air gheataichean sòghmhor, na shaighdear a' cogadh ris na Pashtun – Gaidheil Afghanistan, mar a chanadh e fhèin – air a' Chrìoch an Iar thuath, agus na phrìosanach cogaidh sa Ghearmailt. Eadar siud uile, a bheachdan sònraichte air iomadh cuspair agus a thobar naidheachdan gun ghrunnd, chan iongnadh gu bheil eachdraidh a bheatha fhèin, *Suathadh ri Iomadh Rubha* (1973), air fear dhe na leabhraichean Gàidhlig as fheàrr a sgrìobhadh riamh. Is e na bhàrd cuideachd!

Angus Campbell
Angus Campbell (1903-82) was born in Swainbost, Lewis. He led an eventful life as a boatman in the Sound of Harris and worldwide. His independent views on many subjects and his bottomless well of anecdote led to an excellent autobiography *Suathadh ri Iomadh Rubha* (1973). And he was a poet too!

Domhnall Mac a' Ghobhainn *(Photo: Angus Smith)*

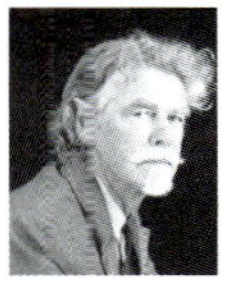

Rugadh e an Leòdhas an 1926. Fhuair e fhoghlam tràth an Sgoil Steòrnabhaigh. Bha e san Arm airson trì bliadhna gu leth – Na h-Innseachan, Sri Lanka, Singapore. Bha e an Sgoil Ealain Ghray an Obar Dheathain. Thug e a bheatha a' teagasg Ealain agus Dealbhaidh ann an baile Obar Dheathain agus anns na sgoiltean air tuath Leòdhais. Tha an ùidh a th' air a bhith aige fad' a bheatha anns na h-ealain lèirsinneach, ann an sgrìobhadh agus ceòl air a riochdachadh ann an dealbhachd/peantadh sluagh agus tìr Eilein Leòdhais.

Donald Smith
Born a Lewisman 1926, he was educated at Nicolson Institute, Stornoway, graduating from Grays School of Art, Aberdeen. He taught art and design in schools in Aberdeen and rural schools in Lewis and had a life-long interest in the visual arts, literature and music, expressed in drawing and painting the people and landscape of the Isle of Lewis.

Louise Donaldson

95

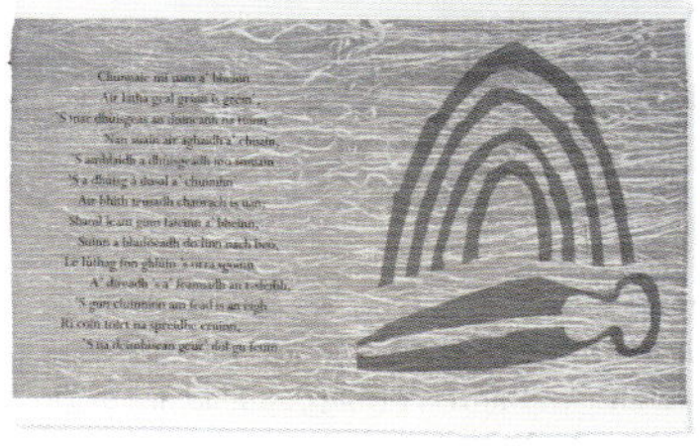

Murchadh MacPhàrlain *(Photo: Gus Wylie)*

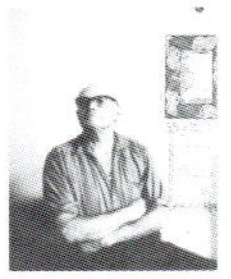

Rugadh Murchadh MacPhàrlain (1901-82) ann am Mealabost faisg air Steòrnabhagh. Bha e greis ag obair am Manitòba, ach thill e a Leòdhas an 1932 'cha mhòr cho bochd 's a dh'fhalbh mi, ach beagan na bu ghlice', mar a thuirt e fhèin, agus thug e an còrr dhe bheatha na chroitear am Mealabost. Tha boillsg mac-meanmnach agus blas air leth na bhàrdachd - ma bha 'bàrd liric' aig a' Ghàidhlig riamh, b' e Murchadh e. Bhiodh e fhèin a' dèanamh fhonn ùra 's gan cur ri na facail, agus anns na 60an 's na 70an air sgàth nan *hits* aige bha fèill mhòr air Murchadh mar leannan na h-òigridh 's nam meadhanan eleactronaigeach.

Murdo MacFarlane

Murdo MacFarlane (1901-82) was born in Melbost near Stornoway. He worked in Manitoba for a while, but returned to Lewis in 1932 and spent the rest of his life as a crofter in Melbost. His verse has an imaginative sparkle and a distinctive flavour and he set his words to new tunes which he composed himself.

Ceit Whiteford OBE *(Photo: Mairi S MacLeod)*

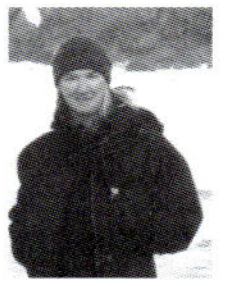

Rugadh Ceit Whiteford ann an Glaschu ann an 1952. Prìomh phroiseactan talmhainn air dealbhadh airson Calton Hill, Dun Èideann (1987), Venice Biennale (1990), Àrd Choimisean Breatannach, Nairobi (1994). Am measg nan dealbhan talmhainn o chionn ghoirid tha na h-obraichean aig Taigh Harewood, Leeds (2000) agus Mount Stewart, Eilean Bhòid (2001). Ann an 1997 fhuair i barantas bho Thaigh-tasgaidh na h-Alba an Dun Èideann airson grèis-bhrat brìgheil air Coire Bhreacain.

Kate Whiteford OBE

Born in 1952 in Glasgow, her major land projects include sculpture for Calton Hill, Edinburgh, the Venice Biennale and the British High Commission, Nairobi. Recent land drawings include works at Harewood House, Leeds and Mount Stuart, Isle of Bute. In 1997 her monumental Corryvreckan Tapestry was commissioned for the Museum of Scotland, Edinburgh.

Dòmhnall Addison

96

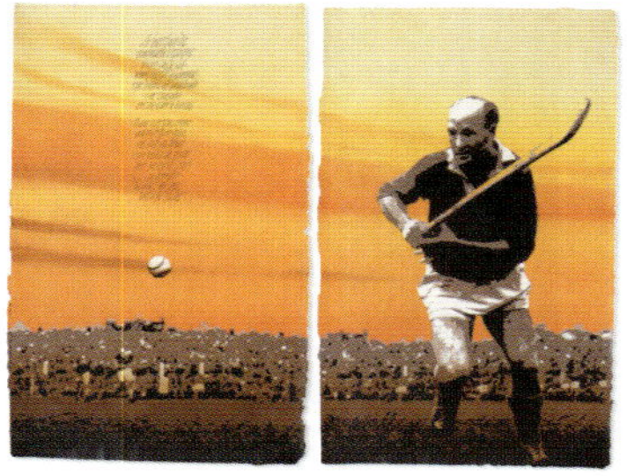

Seán Ó Tuama

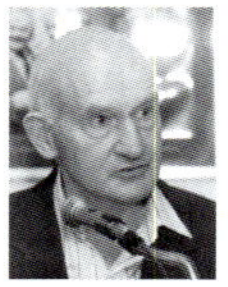

I gCorcaigh a rugadh 1926. Fuair oideachas i gColáiste Ollscoile Chorcaí. File, drámadóir, cnuasaire agus Ollamh le Gaeilge. Tionchar mór ag a thráchtas *An Grá in Amhráin na nDaoine* ar chúrsaí léinn. Cnuasaigh dánta: *Faoileán na Beatha* (1961), *An Saol Fó Thoinn* (1978) agus *An Bás i dTír na nÓg* (1988). Chuir eagar ar *An Duanaire 1600-1900: Poems Of The Dispossessed* (1981) i gcomhar le Thomas Kinsella.

Seán Ó Tuama

Born in Cork in 1926, he was educated at University College, Cork. *An Grá in Amhráin na nDaoine* is a key work of scholarship. *Faoileán na Beatha* (1961), *An Saol Fó Thoinn* (1978) and *An Bás i dTír na nÓg* (1988) are collections of poems. He edited, with Thomas Kinsella, *An Duanaire 1600-1900: Poems of the Dispossessed* (1981).

Robert Ballagh *(Photo: Derek Speirs/Report, Ireland)*

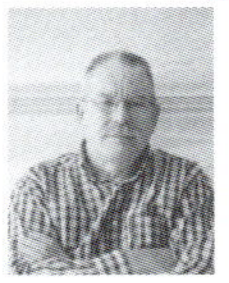

Ealaíontóir agus dearthóir é Robert Ballagh a bhfuil a shaothair ealaíne ar taispeáint i mbailiúcháin in Éirinn agus go hidirnáisiúnta. Tá dearaí uaidh le feiscint ar stampaí poist in Éirinn agus ar nótaí bainc do Bhanc Ceannais na hÉireann. Chruthaigh sé dearaí stáitse le haghaidh *Salome* le Wilde, *Endgame* le Beckett agus *Riverdance*. Ball de Aosdána agus é ina chomhalta den World Academy of Art and Science.

Robert Ballagh

Artist and designer Robert Ballagh's art works are represented in both Irish and international art collections. His designs have been used for Irish postage stamps and on banknotes for the Central Bank of Ireland. He has also created stage designs for Oscar Wilde's *Salome*, Samuel Beckett's *Endgame* and *Riverdance*. He is a member of Aosdána.

Frances Breen

97

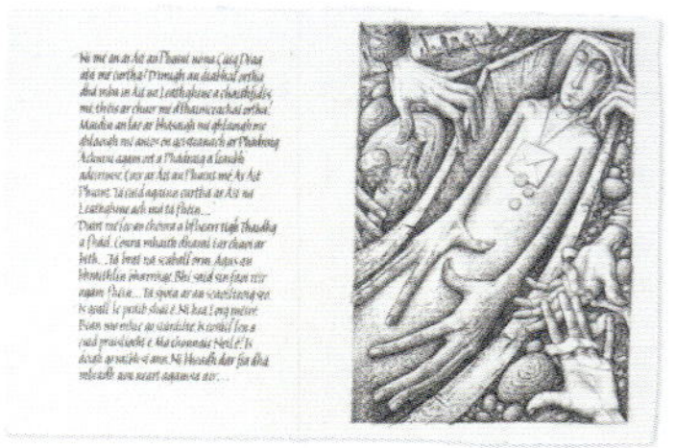

Máirtín Ó Cadhain *(Ph: RTE Archive – Stills Collection)*

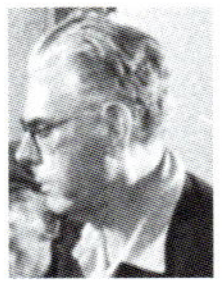

I gConamara a rugadh 1906. Cailleadh 1970. Úrscéalaí agus gearrscéalaí. Oilte i gColáiste Phádraig, Droim Chonrach. I measc a chnuasaigh scéalta tá *Cois Caoláire* (1953), *An tSraith ar Lár* (1967), *An tSraith dhá Tógáil* (1970) agus *An tSraith Tógtha* (1977, iarbháis). Úrscéal tábhachtach é *Cré na Cille* (1948). Níl an t-úrscéal *Athnuachan* foilsithe go dtí seo.

Martin O'Cadhain

Born in Connemara in 1906, he died in 1970. *Cois Caoláire* (1953), *An tSraith ar Lár* (1967), *An tSraith dhá Tógáil* (1970) and *An tSraith Tógtha* (1977, posthumous) are among his collections of stories. *Cré na Cille* (1948) is an important novel. The novel *Athnuachan* remains unpublished.

Iain Brady *(Photo: Jennifer Brady)*

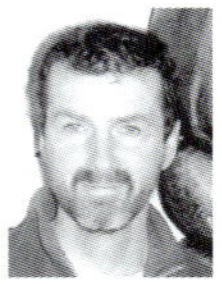

Thogadh mi air tuath, deas air Obar Dheathain agus dh'ionnsaich mi mu pheantadh ann an Sgoil Ealain Ghray. Às dèidh dhomh crìochnachadh sa cholaiste bha mi air a mo tharraing gu cumadh-tìre nan Innse Gall far a bheil mi air mo dhachaigh a dhèanamh anns na seachd bliadhna deug mu dheireadh. Seo far an d' fhuair mi mo chasan anns na h-ealain agus cuideachd far an do choinnich mi ri mo bhean. Tha mo thìde a-nis air a roinn eadar a bhith a' teagaisg pàirt-ùine agus a bhith ri ealain làn-thìde. Tha mòran thaisbeanaidhean air a bhith agam - aon-neach agus mar phàirt de bhuidhinn.

Ian Brady

'Brought up on a farm just south of Aberdeen I studied painting at Grays School of Art. After college I was drawn to the dramatic landscapes of the Outer Hebrides where I have lived for 17 years. I now split my time between being a part-time teacher and a full-time artist. I have exhibited widely with solo and group exhibitions.'

Louise Donaldson

98

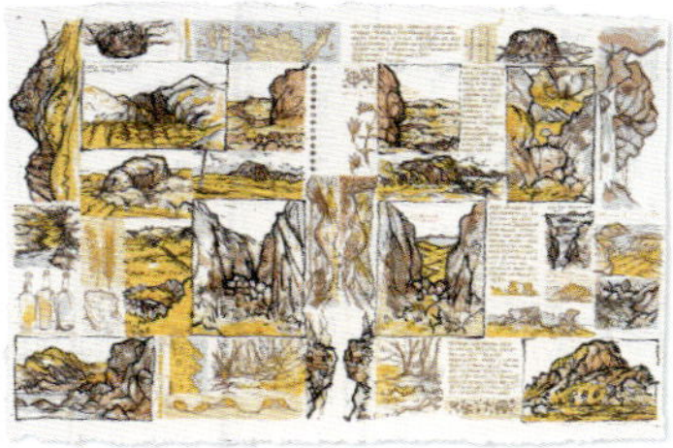

Dòmhnall Mac an t-Saoir *(Photo: Morag Cumming)*

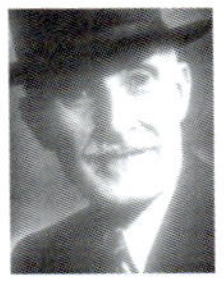

Rugadh Dòmhnall Mac an t-Saoir ('Dòmhnall Ruadh Phàislig', 1889-1964) ann an Snaoiseabhal an Uibhist a Deas. Bha e air a bhogadh ann an òrain agus sgeulachdan an eilein. Eadar an dà Chogadh Mhór chaidh e dh'fhuireach a Phàislig 's a dh'obair na bhreigire, ach sheachain e bàrdachd na h-ionndrain buileach. Tha e na Shomhairle gun fhoghlam oilthighe. 'S e sin, fhuair e facail, gnàthasan-cainnte agus cruthan na bàrdachd aige bho dhualchas Uibhist, a chuid bheachdan bho a cho-luchd-obrach air taobh Chluaidh, a chuspairean bho na pàipearan naidheachd - agus a chuid fealla-dhà bhuaithe fhéin!

Donald Macintyre

Donald Macintyre (1889-1964) was born in South Uist. Between the two World Wars he went to live in Paisley and worked as a bricklayer, but completely avoided the poetry of homesickness. He got the words, idioms and forms of his verse from Uist tradition, his opinions from his fellow-workers on Clydeside - and his sense of humour from himself!

Daibhidh Faithfull *(Photo: Graham Clark)*

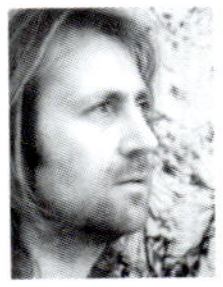

Nuair a bhios e a' cruthachadh leabhraichean luchd-ealain, ioma-sheòrsaichean no barantais, bidh e a' feuchainn ri modh bunaiteach agus rannsachail a ghleidheadh, a' cleachdadh chùrsan seann nòs agus ùr nodha. Tha proiseactan air sgrùdadh phalandroman fradharcach, tìr agus airgead, air miotasachd, làin, ailceamachd agus airgead sgaoilte, a ghabhail a-steach. O chionn ghoirid tha proiseactan air a bhith aige mar 'Sum of Parts' agus 'Glasgow's Art Fair' an lùib Gailearaidh Fruitmarket Dhùn Èideann, taisbeanaidhean aon-neach ann a Verona agus Lake Garda san Eadailt agus samhlaidhean o 'Là Fosglaidh Pàrlamaid na h-Alba'.

David Faithfull

Creating artist's books, he maintains a holistic and explorative approach, with both traditional and contemporary processes. Recent projects include 'Sum of Parts' and 'Glasgow's Art Fair' with Edinburgh's Fruitmarket Gallery, solo exhibitions in Italy and the 'Scottish Parliament's Opening Day' icons.

99

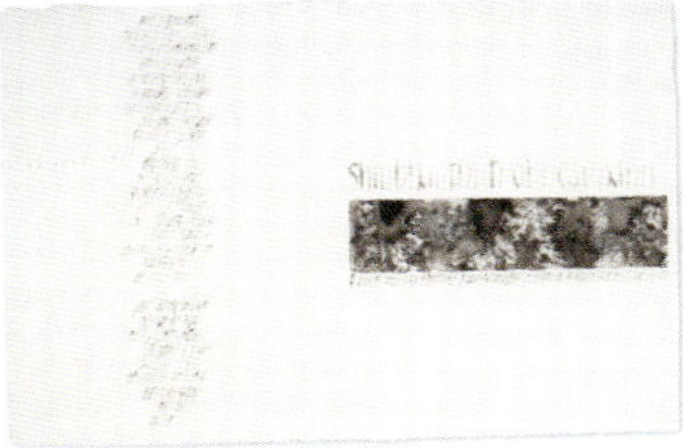

Iain Moireach *(Photo: Angus Smith)*

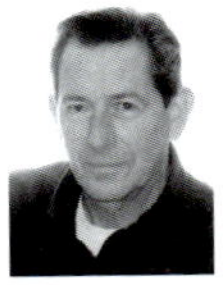

Rugadh e am Barabhas, Leòdhas an 1938. Sgrìobh e sgeulachdan, dràma, nobhailean, bàrdachd agus mòran stuth don òigridh, a thuilleadh air sgriobtan rèidio agus telebhisein. Na bheatha dhreuchdail agus na thìde fhèin, tha e an sàs ann an adhartachadh craoladh, foillseachadh agus foghlam nan Gaidheal, maille ri leasachadh cultarach, sòisealta agus coimhearsnachail.

John Murray

Born in Barvas, Lewis in 1938, he is the author of short stories, drama, novels, poetry and material for young readers as well as radio and television. He is actively involved in the advancement of Gaelic broadcasting, publishing and education as well as cultural, social and community development.

Sigrid Shone

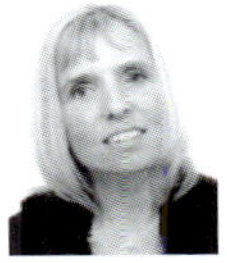

Bantanas làidir ri Gaidhealtachd na h-Alba. Bannan làidir teaghlaich agus eachdraidh a' toirt ceangal ri Srath Nabhair, Cataibh agus cultar na Gàidhlig. Cheumnaich i à Sgoil Dhealbhaidh agus Peantaidh Colaiste Ealain Dhùn Èideann, 1984. Na neach-ealain/clò-bhualadair aig Clò-bhualadairean Dhùn Èideann bho 1994. Taisbeanaichean air feadh Bhreatainn agus gu h-eadar-nàiseanta agus tha obair aice ann an cruinneachaichean ealain air feadh an t-saoghail.

Sigrid Shone

She originated from the Highlands and has strong family links with Strathnaver, Sutherland and Gaelic culture. She graduated in drawing and painting from Edinburgh College of Art, and has practised at Edinburgh Printmakers since 1994. Shone has exhibited widely in UK and internationally and has work in collections throughout the world.

Réiltín Murphy

100

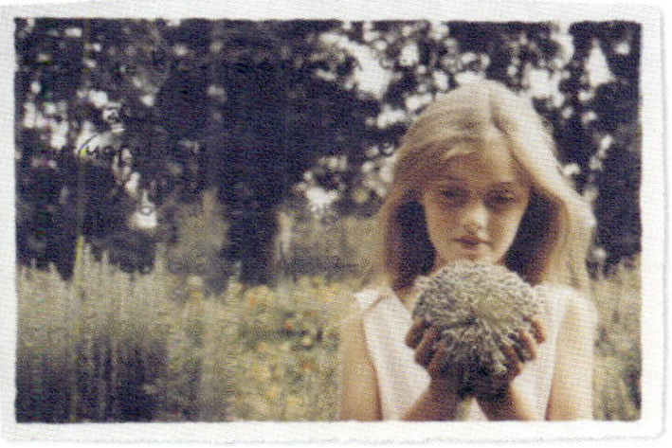

Micheál Ó hAirtnéide *(Photo: Bill Doyle)*

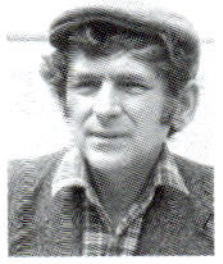

I Luimneach i 1941 is ea rugadh é. D'éag 1999. Dánta i mBéarla foilsithe faoin teideal *Collected Poems* (2001). An chéad chnuasach sa Ghaeilge *Cúlú Íde/The Retreat of Ita Cagney* (1975). Ina dhiaidh sin tháinig *Adharca Broic* (1978), *An Phurgóid* (1983) agus *Do Nuala; Foidhne Chrainn* (1984). Aistriúcháin ar shaothar Uí Bhruadair (1985), Ní Dhomhnaill (1986) agus Haicéid (1993), *inter alia*.

Michael Hartnett

Michael Hartnett was born in Limerick in 1941, and died in 1999. His poems in English are gathered in *Collected Poems* (2001). His first collection in Irish was *Cúlú Íde/The Retreat of Ita Cagney* (1975), followed by *Adharca Broic* (1978), *An Phurgóid* (1983) and *Do Nuala: Foidhne Chrainn* (1984). Hartnett has translated, among others, Ó Bruadair (1985), Ní Dhomhnaill (1986) and Haicéad (1993).

Alanna O'Kelly

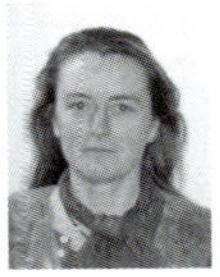

Tá Alanna O'Kelly lonnaithe i gCo. Loch Garman agus oibríonn sí trí mheán na fístéipe agus na fuaime, chomh maith le healaín suiteála agus léirithe a chur ar bun. Bhain céim amach ón gColáiste Náisiúnta Ealaíne is Deartha. Dhein staidéar fós i Helsinki agus ag an Slade School. Sheas sí d'Éirinn ag Biennale Internacional de São Paulo agus ghlac páirt i Documenta 8. Chaith seal ag obair san Iodáil, sa Ghearmáin, san Fhionnlainn agus sa Nigéir. Ball d'Aosdána í.

Alanna O'Kelly

Alanna O'Kelly is based in Co. Wexford and works with video, sound, installation and performance. She graduated from the National College of Art and Design and also studied in Helsinki, and at the Slade School. She has represented Ireland at the São Paulo Biennale and participated in Documenta 8. She has worked in Italy, Germany, Finland and Nigeria and is a member of Aosdána.

Réiltín Murphy

PROJECT TEAM BIOGRAPHIES

INTRODUCTORY TEXT AUTHORS

Calum MacGillEain *(Photo: Joanne Breen)*

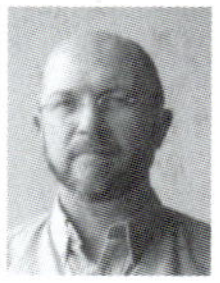

'S e Gaidheal à Glaschu a th' air a bhith a' fuireach sna Eileanan Siar bho 1975 a th' ann an Calum MacGillEain. 'S ann an sin a thog e a dhithis nighean brèagha. Ceumnaiche à Sgoil Ealain Gray an Obar-Dheathain is an Oilthigh Fhosgailte, tha e air a bhith roimhe na iasgair, na fhiosaiche-uisge, na leasaiche-ealain, na pheantair, na dhealbhadair-èibhinn, na dhealbhaiche-leabhair is na thidsear. Chuidich e le stèidheachadh Peacock Printmakers (Obar Dheathain 1974) is gailearaidh An Lanntair (Steòrnabhagh 1985). Na chùradair den taisbeanadh gluasadach 'Às an Fhearann' (1986–1990), co-chùradair Calanais (1995–1997) agus àireamh de thaisbeanaidhean gluasadach eile. Tha e an-dràst na Stiùiriche air Pròiseact nan Ealan.

Malcolm Maclean

Malcolm Maclean is a Glasgow Gael who has lived since 1975 in the Western Isles, where he helped raise two lovely daughters. A graduate of Gray's School of Art in Aberdeen and the Open University, his previous incarnations include fisherman, water-diviner, art therapist, painter, cartoonist, book designer and teacher. Helped found Peacock Printmakers (Aberdeen 1974) and An Lanntair art gallery (Stornoway 1985). Curator of the touring exhibition 'As an Fhearann' (1986-1990), co-curator of 'Calanais' (1995-1997), and various other touring exhibitions. He is currently Director of the Gaelic Arts Agency.

Theo Dorgan

Is file agus craoltóir raidio agus telifíse é Theo Dorgan. Trí leabhar filíochta foilsithe aige: *The*

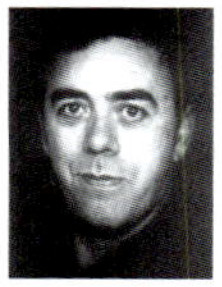

Ordinary House of Love (1991), *Rosa Mundi* (1995) agus *Sappho's Daughter* (1998). Tá sé ina eagarthóir ar *Irish Poetry Since Kavanagh* (1997), ina co-eagarthóir ar *Revising The Rising* (1991) agus, le Gene Lambert, ar *Leabhar Mor na hEireann/The Great Book of Ireland*. Tá a chuid saothair aistrithe go forleathan agus tá sé ina bhall de Aosdána.

Theo Dorgan

Theo Dorgan is a poet and broadcaster on radio and television. He is the author of *The Ordinary House of Love* (1991), *Rosa Mundi* (1995) and *Sappho's Daughter* (1998), editor of *Irish Poetry Since Kavanagh* (1997), co-editor of *Revising The Rising* (1991) and, with Gene Lambert, of *Leabhar Mór na hEireann/The Great Book of Ireland*. His work has been extensively translated and he is a member of Aosdána.

An t-Ollamh Donnchadh Mac a' Mhaoilein

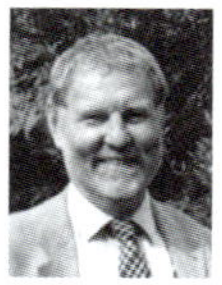

An t-Ollamh Donnchadh Mac A' Mhaoilein, MA, PhD, FRSA, HRSA, eachdraiche ealain, sgrùdair ealain agus stiùiriche gailearaidh, ùghdar air an leabhar dheimhinnte air ealain Alba, *Scottish Art 1460–1990*, cuideachd na ùghdar air iomadh leabhar, catalog, alt agus aiste eile air ealain eachdraidheil is co-aimsireach an Alba is san Roinn Eòrpa.

Professor Duncan MacMillan

Professor Duncan MacMillan, MA, PhD, FRSA, HRSA, art historian, art critic and gallery director, author of the definitive book on Scottish art, *Scottish Art 1460–1990*, also of many other books, catalogues, articles, essays etc. on Scottish and European art, historical and contemporary.

An t-Ollamh Colm Ó Baoill

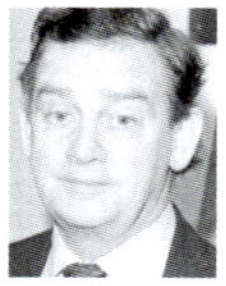

Rugadh i gcathair Ard Mhacha i 1938 agus hoileadh ansin agus in Ollscoil na Ríona, Béal Feirste. Tháinig sé go hAlbain i dtús i 1961 a dhéanamh staidéir ar canúintí Chinn Tíre agus Arann. Tugadh léachtóireacht le Ceiltis dó in Ollscoil Obar Dheathain i 1966, agus tá sé ansin go fóill.

Professor Colm Ó Baoill

Born in the city of Armagh in 1938 and educated there and at Queen's University, Belfast. Came to Scotland on short trips (first to Kintyre) to study Gaelic dialects between 1961 and 1965, and in 1966 was appointed as lecturer in Celtic in Aberdeen where he has remained ever since.

Raghnall MacilleDhuibh

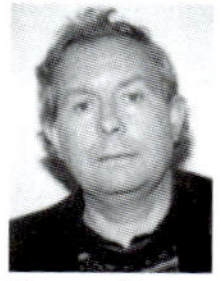

Rugadh Raghnall MacilleDhuibh an 1946 an Glaschu agus dh'ionnsaich e Gàidhlig san sgoil an sin. Thug e a-mach ceum oilthigh an Glaschu fo Ruaraidh MacThòmais agus chuir e air bhonn dha (1966–70) na cuairtean-reice a chaidh nam pàirt de dhleasnas tràth Chomhairle nan Leabhraichean Gàidhlig. Aig Institiúid Ard-Léinn Bhaile Àtha Cliath (1970–73) 's ann an Leabharlann Nàiseanta na h-Alba (1973–79) ghabh e ùidh an sgrùdadh làmh-sgrìobhainnean. Às dèidh greis a' teagaisg an oilthighean Ghlaschu 's Dhùn Èideann (1979–2001) tha e nis na sgrìobhadair 's na naidheachdair làn-ùine. Tha e na Dheasaiche Gàidhlig aig *An t-Albannach* agus *Am Pàipear* agus dheasaich e na duanairean *An Tuil* (1999) agus *An Lasair* (2001).

Ronald Black

Ronald Black was born in 1946 in Glasgow and learned Gaelic at school there. He studied under Derick Thomson at Glasgow University and pioneered for him (1966–70) the sales tours which became part of the early work of the early Gaelic Books Council. At the Dublin Institute of Advanced Studies (1970–73) and in the National Library of Scotland (1973–79) he developed an interest in the study of manuscripts. Following a period lecturing in Glasgow and Edinburgh universities (1979–2001) he is now a full-time writer and journalist. He is Gaelic Editor of *The Scotsman* and *Am Pàipear* and editor of the anthologies *An Tuil* (1999) and *An Lasair* (2001).

THE EDITORIAL TEAM

Malcolm MacLean

See above

Theo Dorgan

See above

Aodán Mac Póilin

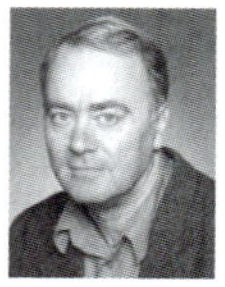

Born in Belfast, where he lives in an urban Irish-speaking community. Director of ULTACH Trust – a cross-community Irish language funding body. Active in a number of language, education, community relations and arts bodies, he has published translations of poetry and prose from Irish, and articles on literature and linguistic politics. Was Irish-language editor of the literary magazine *Krino*.

Aodán Mac Póilin

Rugadh i mBéal Feirste, agus cónaíonn i bpobal Gaeilge sa chathair. Ina Stiúrthóir ar Iontaobhas ULTACH, eagras maoinithe trasphobail. Gníomhach in eagrais a bhaineann le teanga, oideachas, caidreamh pobail agus na healaíona. D'fhoilsigh aistriúcháin ón Ghaeilge, idir fhilíocht agus phrós, agus altanna ar litríocht agus pholaitíocht teanga. Iar-eagarthóir Gaeilge ar an iris litríochta *Krino*.

Iain MacDhòmhnaill

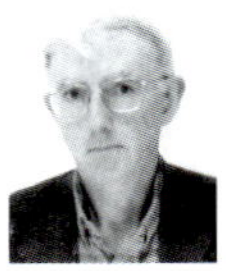

Tha Iain MacDhòmhnaill à Uibhist a Tuath, agus bha e air caochladh obraichean a dhèanamh an Uibhist, am Birmingham, an Glaschu is an Lunnainn mun deach e gu Comhairle nan Leabhraichean anns na 70an.

Ian MacDonald

Ian MacDonald is Director of the Gaelic Books Council, which has its office and Gaelic bookshop in Glasgow. He is from North Uist, and has worked at various jobs there and in Birmingham, Glasgow and London.

Aonghas Dubh MacNeacail

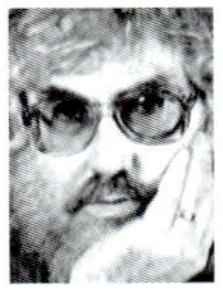

Sgitheanach: Bàrd an Gàidhlig 's am Beurla. Choisinn an cruinneachadh aige, *Oideachadh Ceart* (A Proper Schooling) Duais Sgrìobhaiche Albannach na Bliadhna an 1997. Tha a' bhàrdachd aige air a thoirt air feadh na Roinn Eòrpa, An Ear 's an Iar, bho Chearcall na h-Arctaig chun Mheadhan-thìreach, gu Aimeireagaidh a Tuath agus Iapan (agus gach cùil is ceall de dh'Èirinn).

Aonghas Dubh MacNeacail

Skyeman; Poet in Gaelic and English. His collection *Oideachadh Ceart* (A Proper Schooling) won the Scottish Writer of the Year Award in 1997. Poetry has taken him across Europe, East and West, from the Arctic Circle to the Mediterranean, to North America and Japan (and all corners of Ireland).

An t-Ollamh Uilleam MacIlleathain

Rugadh e an Inbhir Nis an 1941.
Taisbeanaidhean Aon-neach:
Gailearaidh Nàiseanta Nua-Ealain an Alba

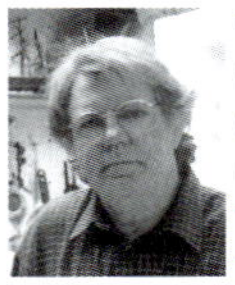

Taigh-tasgaidh Dakota a Tuath, Oilthigh MhicMhaighistir, Canada
Cruinneachaidhean Poblach:
Taigh-tasgaidh Bhreatainn
Taigh-tasgaidh Fitzwilliam, Cambridge
Ionad Yale airson Ealain Bhreatainn, Aimeireagaidh
Gailearaidh Ealain Newfoundland agus Labrador
Taigh-tasgaidh Khelvingrove, Glaschu

Riochdaichte le Art First – Lunnainn agus New York

Professor Will Maclean

Born Inverness, *1941*.
Solo exhibitions include:
Scottish National Gallery of Modern Art
Museum of North Dakota, McMaster University Canada
Public collections include:
British Museum
Fitzwilliam Museum, Cambridge
Yale Centre for British Art, USA
Art Gallery of Newfoundland and Labrador
Kelvingrove Museum, Glasgow

Represented by Art First – London and New York.

Frances Breen

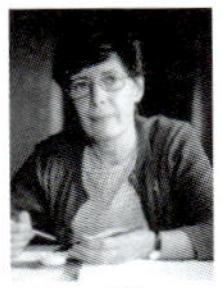

Is i Loch Garman a rugadh Frances Breen agus oibríonn sí in Éirinn agus san Ostair. Bhain sí céim amach mar dhearthóir grafach ón gColáiste Náisiúnta Ealaíne is Deartha. Ansin rinne sí sainstaidéar ar pheannaireacht, ag déanamh foghlaim ar litreoireacht agus ar leabharcheangal san Ostair agus sa Ghearmáin. Ta sí fostaithe mar oide cuartaíochta i Roinn na Dearc-Chumarsáide sa Choláiste Náisiúnta Ealaíne is Deartha, Baile Átha Cliath.

Frances Breen

Frances Breen was born in Wexford and lives and works in Austria and Ireland. She graduated in graphic design from the National College of Art and Design and then specialised in calligraphy, studying lettering and bookbinding in Austria and Germany. She is a guest tutor in the Department of Visual Communications at the National College of Art and Design in Dublin. Her creative collaborations with her tapestry artist sister, Joanne Breen, were the sustaining inspiration for *An Leabhar Mòr*.

Marisa Dhòmhnallach

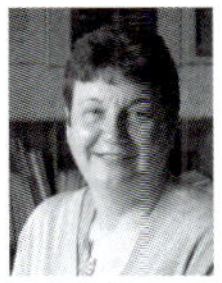

Rugadh, thogadh agus tha i fhathast a' fuireach ann am Pabail Uarach san Rubha an Eilean Leòdhais. Fhuair i foghlam ann an Colaiste Dhùn Creige mus do lean i cùrsa air àrd-ùrlar agus telebhisean. Tha i pòsta le triùir a theaghlach – Catriona, Donal agus Màiri Alice. Tha i air a bhith ag obair do Phròiseact nan Ealan o 1990 air iomadh pròiseact mar Fèisean nan Gàidheal, Ceòlas, Trèanadh airson nan Ealain's nam Meadhanan, Sgeulachdan agus obraichean eile dha mòr-fhèisean.

Marisa MacDonald

Born, brought up and still resides in Upper Bayble in Point on the Isle of Lewis. Educated at Duncraig Castle College before an acting career on stage and television. Married with three children – Catriona, Donal and Mairi Alice. Has worked with the Gaelic Arts Agency since 1990 on a wide range of arts projects such as Fèisean nan Gàidheal, Ceòlas, Arts & Media Training, Storytelling and other productions for major festivals.

THE VISUAL ARTS ADVISERS

Will Maclean

See above

Frances Breen

See above

Caoimhín Mac Giolla Léith

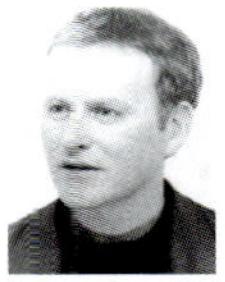

Is Leachtóir le Nua-Ghaeilge é Caoimhín Mac Giolla Leith sa Choláiste Ollscoile, Báile Átha Cliath. Is criticeoir agus eagraí taispeántas é freisin. Chuir sé eagar ar chnuasach aistí ar an bhfile Máirtín Ó Direán agus foilsíodh saothar leis i mórán irisí ealaíne *Artforum*, *Flash Art* agus *Modern Painters* ina measc.

Caoimhín Mac Giolla Léith

Caoimhín Mac Giolla Léith is a Lecturer in Modern Irish at University College Dublin and a critic and curator of contemporary art. His published works include an edited collection of essays on the poet Máirtín Ó Direáin and contributions to numerous art magazines including *Artforum*, *Flash Art* and *Modern Painters*.

Póilín Nic Cathmhaoil

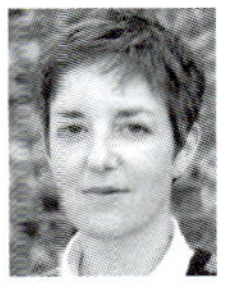

Rugadh Póilín Nic Cathmhaoil i mBéal Feirste. Tá céim onórach aici sna mínealaíona agus dioplóma iarchéime sa Bhainistíocht Chultúrtha. Bhí sí ina hOifigeach na nDearc-Ealaíon le Comhairle Ealaíon Thuaisceart Éireann ar feadh ocht mbliana. Tá taispeántais náisiúnta agus idirnáisiúnta eagraithe aici. Tá sí anois ag obair do Chumann Dhealbhóirí Éireann.

Paula Campbell

Paula Campbell was born in Belfast. She holds an honours degree in Fine Art and has a postgraduate diploma in Cultural Management. She was Visual Arts Officer with the Northern Ireland Arts Council for eight years and organised national and international exhibitions. She now works for the Sculptors Society of Ireland.

Oliver Dowling

Bhí Oliver Dowling ina Stiúrthóir ar Ghailearaí Oliver Dowling i mBaile Átha Cliath ó 1976 go

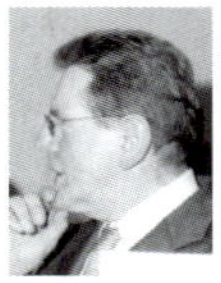

1995. Bhí sé mar bhall den fhoireann a d'eagraigh 'Imaginaire Irlandais' – féile ealaín na hÉireann a tionóladh sa bhFrainc i 1996 – agus roghnaigh sé saothar don taispeántas *'Shifting Ground'* – taispeántas d'ealaín na hÉireann le caoga bliain anuas – ag Áras Nua Ealaíne na hÉireann, Baile Átha Cliath 2000. Faoi láthair tá sé ag obair leis an Chomhairle Ealaíon agus é lonnaithe i mBaile Átha Cliath.

Oliver Dowling

Oliver Dowling was Director of the Oliver Dowling Gallery, Dublin, from 1976 to 1995. He was part of the organising team for 'Imaginaire Irlandais', the festival of Irish art in France 1996, and a selector for the exhibition 'Shifting Ground, 50 years of Irish Art', at the Irish Museum of Modern Art, Dublin 2000. He currently works with An Chomhairle Ealaíon/ The Arts Council. He lives in Dublin.

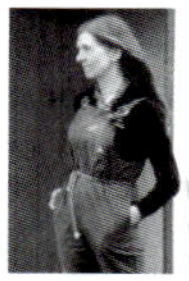

Frances Walker

Rugadh i an Cathair Challdainn agus bha i na h-oileanach an Colaiste Ealain Dhùn Èideann. Tha i na ball dhen Acadamh Albannach Rìoghail, Comann Pheantairean Rìoghail Uisge-Dhathan Albannach agus Comann Luchd-Ealain Alba. Thug i dà bhliadhna gu leth na neach-teagaisg siùbhlach ealain ann an sgoiltean na Hearadh agus Uibhist a Tuath anns na h-Eileanan Siar. Thug i seachd bliadhna fichead mar neach-teagaisg ann an dealbhachd is peantadh ann an Sgoil Ealain Ghray an Obar Dheathain. Tha i a' fuireach 's ag obair an Obar Dheathain agus cuid dhen bhliadhna an Eilean Thiriodh.

Frances Walker

Born: Kirkcaldy
Studied: Edinburgh College of Art
Member of: Royal Scottish Academy
Royal Scottish Society of Painters in Watercolours
Society of Scottish Artists

Two years as visiting teacher of art for all schools in Harris and North Uist, Western Isles. Then twenty-seven years as lecturer in drawing and painting at Grays School of Art, Aberdeen. Frances Walker lives and works in Aberdeen and part year also on the island of Tiree.

Ruairidh Moireach

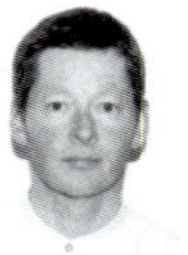

Tha Ruaraidh Moireach air a bhith na Stiùiriche air An Lanntair, Steòrnabhagh, bho dh'fhosgail an t-àite ann an 1985. 'S e Gaidheal a fhuair foghlam ealain ann an Sgoil Ealain Ghlaschu a th' ann. Tha e air iomadh taisbeanadh a leasachadh a chaidh air turas anns an rìoghachd seo agus gu h-eadar-nàiseanta. Tha e an-dràsta ag obair airson taigh-ealain mòr ùr a chruthachadh a ghabhas àite An Lanntair.

Roddy Murray

Roddy Murray has been Director of An Lanntair in Stornoway since it opened in 1985. A Fine Art graduate of Glasgow School of Art and a Gaelic speaker, he has curated several acclaimed exhibitions which have toured nationally and internationally. Presently involved in a major capital development for An Lanntair.

Artair MacBhatair

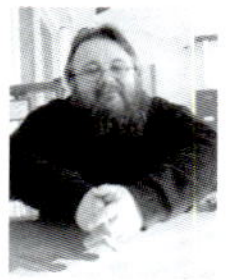

Rugadh e an Obar Dheathain. Fhuair e fhoghlam ann an Sgoil Ealain Ghray an Obar Dheathain. An-dràsta tha e na Cheannard air Roinn a' Cheumnachaidh, Sgoil Ghrinneis Oilthigh Dhùn Dè. Am measg a thaisbeanaidhean tha 'Singing for Dead Singers', còig taisbeanaidhean an Obar Dheathain agus leabhar nan cois anns a bheil seachdad 's a sia duilleagan.

Arthur Watson

1951 Born Aberdeen
1969-74 Grays School of Art
1974 Founded Peacock Printmakers
1990 Represented Scotland at the Venice Biennale
1996 School of Fine Art, University of Dundee, currently Head of Graduate Studies
2000 'Singing for Dead Singers': five exhibitions in Aberdeen, seventy-six-page publication

Pòl Liam Harrison

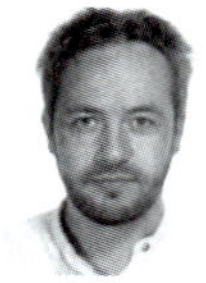

'S e neach-ealain iomadh-mheadhan proifeiseanta a tha am Pòl le eòlas spèisealta mu chlò-bhualadh agus modhan mar sin. 'S e an neach-cuideachaidh airson sgrùdadh/clò-bhualadh ealain ann an roinn foillseachaidh Sgoil a' Ghrinneis an Ionad Sgrùdaidh Lèirsinneach Oilthigh Dhùn Dè, far am bi e a' co-obrachadh le luchd-ealain agus luchd-sgrùdaidh air leabhraichean luchd-ealain a thoirt gu ìre. 'S e a tha sa cheart àm na riochdaire air proiseact an *Leabhair Mhòir* agus bidh e a' cur a chuid obrach fhèin, air a bheil fèill mhòr agus a th' air a taisbeanadh gu h-eadar-nàiseanta, air adhart cuideachd.

Paul Liam Harrison

Paul is a professional multimedia artist with specialist knowledge of printmaking and related techniques. He is the research assistant/artists printer based in the School of Fine Art publishing facility at the University of Dundee Visual Research Centre where he collaborates with artists and researchers on the conception and production of artists books and prints. He is currently engaged as production manager for the *Leabhar Mòr* project and pursues his own practice and research which is exhibited and recognised internationally.

Marian Lovett

Idir 1997 agus 2001 bhí Marian Lovett ina comhstiúrthóir ar an Artworking Projects and Commissions Agency i mBaile Atha Cliath, agus faoi láthair is í stiúrthóir an Temple Bar Gallery sa chathair. Agus í ina bainisteoir tionscnamh ag Artworking, d'eagraigh sí breith agus fás tionscnamh an *Leabhair Mhòir* in Eirinn o 1998 go 2001. Ise agus a comhleacaí Jenny Haughton (i gcomhairle le Proiseact nan Ealan) a cheap an córas a roghnaigh na healaíontóirí Eireannacha a bheadh páirteach san *Leabhar Mòr*. Cuireadh an córas céanna i bhfeidhm leis na healaíontóirí Albanacha a roghnú.

Marian Lovett

Marian Lovett was co-director of Artworking Projects and Commissions Agency (Dublin) from 1997 to 2001. She is now the director of Temple Bar Gallery in Dublin. As a project manager for Artworking she was closely involved with the *Leabhar Mòr* project from 1998 to 2001, administrating the earlier stages of the projects development in Ireland. Together with her work partner Jenny Haughton and in consultation with the Gaelic Arts Agency, she was instrumental in devising the complex selection process by which a representative group of Irish artists were selected for participation in the *Leabhar Mòr*. This process was replicated for the selection of the Scottish artists.

Jenny Haughton

Chuir Jenny Haughton tús i 1983 ar sraith de thaispeántais don Temple Bar Gallery & Studios, agus i 1987 roghnaíodh í mar Stiúrthóir ar Chumann Dealbhóirí na hEireann. I 1991 bhunaigh sí Artworking, a dhéanann comheagrú ar áit na hEireann sna Biennales agus ar fhorbairt na nua-ealaíne i measc an phobail.

Jenny Haughton

In 1983 Jenny Haughton founded Temple Bar Gallery & Studios and undertook a programme of exhibitions until she took up the position of Executive Director of the Sculptors Society of Ireland in 1987. In 1991 she founded Artworking which includes coordination of Ireland's participation in the Biennales and development of contemporary art projects in the public domain.

THE ADDITIONAL POETRY NOMINATORS

Seamus Heaney

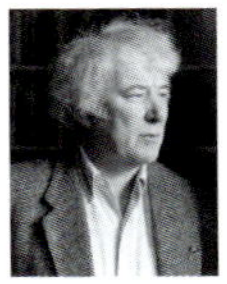

Rugadh i gCo. Dhoire, 1939. Oilte in Ollscoil na Banríona, Béal Feirste. Duais Litríochta Nobel bronnta air. Ar na cnuasaigh uaidh tá *Death of A Naturalist* (1966), *North* (1975), *FieldWork* (1979), *Sweeney Astray* (1983), *Station Island* (1984), *Seeing Things* (1991), *Electric Light* (2001). Ar na leabhair próis uaidh tá *The Government of The Tongue* (1988), *Finders Keepers, Selected Prose 1971–2001* (2002). Dráma uaidh: *The Cure at Troy*. Ina bhall de Aosdána.

Seamus Heaney

Born County Derry, 1939. Educated Q.U.B. Nobel Laureate in Literature. Among his collections: *Death of a Naturalist* (1966), *North* (1975), *FieldWork* (1979), *Sweeney Astray* (1983), *Station Island* (1984), *Seeing Things* (1991), *Electric Light* (2001). Among his prose books: *The Government of The Tongue* (1988) and *Finders Keepers: Selected Prose 1971–2001* (2002). Play, *The Cure At Troy*. Member of Aosdána.

Thomas Kinsella

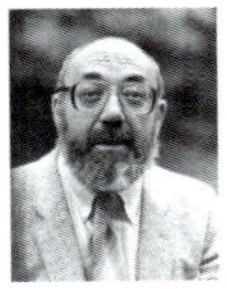

Rugadh i mBaile Átha Cliath, 1928. Oilte in Ollscoil na hÉireann, B.Á.C. D'aistrigh sé *Longes mac nUislenn* (1954) agus *An Táin* (1969). Cnuasaigh uaidh: *Poems* (1956), *Another September* (1958), *Downstream* (1962), *Nightwalker and Other Poems* (1968), *Notes From The Land of the Dead* (1972), *Blood and Family* (1988). Chuir sé eagar ar *An Duanaire 1600–1900: Poems of The Dispossessed* (1981), i gcomhar le Seán Ó Tuama.

Thomas Kinsella

Born Dublin 1928, educated U.C.D. Translation of *Longes mac nUislenn* (1954), *The Táin* (1969). Among his collections: *Poems* (1956), *Another September* (1958), *Downstream* (1962), *Nightwalker and Other Poems* (1968), *Notes from the Land Of the Dead* (1972), *Blood and Family* (1988). Edited, with Seán Ó Tuama, *An Duanaire 1600-1900: Poems of the Dispossessed* (1981).

John Montague

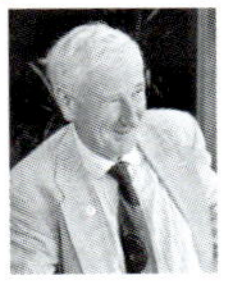

Rugadh i mBrooklyn 1929. Oilte i gColáiste na hOllscoile, B.Á.C. agus i Yale. An chéad Ollamh Filíochta Éireann. Cnuasaigh uaidh: *A Chosen Light* (1967), *Tides* (1970), *The Rough Field* (1972), *A Slow Dance* (1975), *Mount Eagle* (1988). *Collected Poems* curtha amach i 1995. *Death of a Chieftain* (cnuasach scéalta, 1964), *The Lost Notebook* (úrscéal gearr, 1987). Ball de Aosdána é.

John Montague

Born Brooklyn 1929, educated UCD, Yale. First Ireland Professor of Poetry. Among his collections: *A Chosen Light* (1967), *Tides* (1970), *The Rough Field* (1972), *A Slow Dance* (1975), *Mount Eagle* (1988). *Collected Poems* appeared in 1995. *Death of a Chieftain* (1964) is a collection of stories, *The Lost Notebook* (1987) a novella. Member of Aosdána.

Seumas MacEanraig (1919-2002)

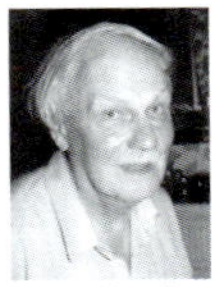

Rugadh e an 1919 ann an Blàr Gobharaidh, Siorrachd Pheairt. Chaidh oideachadh ann am Blàr Gobharaidh agus ann an Cambridge mus do thòisich e a sheirbeis mar oifigear fiosrachaidh san 51mh Roinn Ghàidhealaich ann an Afraga a Tuath agus san Eadailt. Bha e a' co-obrachadh le saighdearan neo-riaghailteach Tuscanach ann an 1944 agus chaidh a shònrachadh ann am pàipearan-airm an 1945. Chaidh e do Sgoil Eòlais na h-Alba a bha air a h-ùr stèidheachadh ann an 1952 mar fhear rannsachaidh agus leig e dheth a dhreuchd ann an 1988.

Hamish Henderson (1919-2002)

Born 1919, Blairgowrie, Perthshire. He was educated in Blairgowrie and in Cambridge before serving as an intelligence officer with the 51st Highland Division in North Africa and Italy. He liaised with Tuscan partisans in 1944 and was mentioned in dispatches in 1945. He joined the newly founded School of Scottish Studies in Edinburgh in 1952 as a research fellow and retired in 1988.

An t-Ollamh Iain MacAonghuis

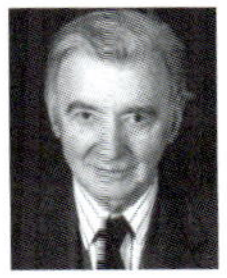

Àite breith, Ùig Leòdhais 1930; aig aois ochd bliadhna ghluaiseadh a Ratharsair; sgoil-mhòr am Port Rìgh agus foghlam an dèidh sin an Oilthigh Dhùn Èideann. O 1953 a' cruinneachadh à beul-aithris na Gàidhlig do Sgoil Eòlais na h-Alba agus a' sgrìobhadh mu chaochladh chuspairean Gaidhealach. Na bhall de dh'Oilthigh Dhùn Èideann, 1958–93; a-nis na chompanach urramach.

Dr John MacInnes

Born Uig, Isle of Lewis; moved to Raasay aged eight and spent his formative years there. After secondary education in Portree, studied English, Philosophy and Celtic at the University of Edinburgh. From 1953 onwards recorded Gaelic oral tradition for the University's School of Scottish Studies on various aspects of Gaelic culture. Member of university staff 1958–93; now honorary fellow.

Alasdair MacLeòid

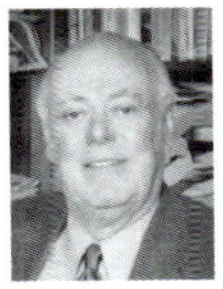

Rugadh e ann am Battleford a Tuath, Saskatchewan ann an 1936 agus thogadh e am measg teaghlach a chàirdean an Ceap Breatann, Alba Nuadh. Fhuair e foghlam ann an Colaiste Luchd-teagaisg Alba Nuadh, St Francis Xavier, Oilthigh New Brunswick agus Notre Dame. Tha e cuideachd air a bhith a' teagaisg sgrìobhadh cruthachail ann an Oilthigh Indiana. Ann an 1999 dh'fhoillsich e a' chiad nobhail aige, *No Great Mischief*, a choisinn àrd-dhuais.

Alistair MacLeod

He was born in North Battleford, Saskatchewan in 1936 and raised among an extended family in Cape Breton, Nova Scotia. He studied at the Nova Scotia Teachers College, St Francis Xavier, the University of New Brunswick and Notre Dame. He has also taught creative writing at the University of Indiana. In 1999 he published his first novel, the award-winning *No Great Mischief*.

THE BACK-UP TEAM

Marisa MacDonald

See above

Màiri S. NicLeòid

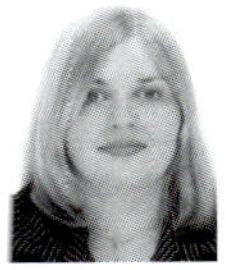

Rugadh i an 1969, ann an Eilean Leòdhais. Fhuair i foghlam an Sgoil Phabail san Rubha agus an Sgoil MhicNeacail, ann an Steòrnabhagh. BSc Eaconamas Fearainn agus PGCE. Bha i ag obair ann an Roinn na Gàidhlig aig a' BhBC airson grunnan bhliadhnachan. Thill i a Leòdhas ann an 1997 agus tha i air a bhith ag obair do Phroiseact nan Ealan on uair sin.

Mairi S. Macleod

Born 1969, Isle of Lewis. Educated at Bayble School, Point and The Nicolson Institute, Stornoway. BSc Land Economics and PGCE. Worked for the BBC Gaelic department, Glasgow for several years. Returned to Lewis in 1997 and has been working for the Gaelic Arts Agency since her return.

Domhnall Ruadh

'S e sgrìobhadair, actair, stiùiriche fhilmichean is craoladair sgileil a th' ann an Dòmhnall a tha a-nise stèidhichte ann an Nis, Leòdhas, àite àraich. Ball-stèidheachaidh den chompanaidh-cluiche Gàidhlig, Fir Chlis, ùghdar na deilbh-cluiche stèidhdse gluasadaich, *Craobh Nan Ubhal* is na comaig, *Smathsin,* B' ann ris a bha co-obrachadh nam bàrd agus a' chiad cho-òrdanachadh den *Leabhar Mòr* an urra.

Donald Smith

Donald is an accomplished writer, actor, film director and broadcaster who is now based in his native Ness, Isle of Lewis. A founding member of the Gaelic theatre company Fir Chlis, author of the touring stage play *Craobh Nan Ubhal* and the Gaelic comic *Smathsin*, he was responsible for the liaison with poets and the early co-ordination of the *Leabhar Mòr.*

Sine Chumberlidge

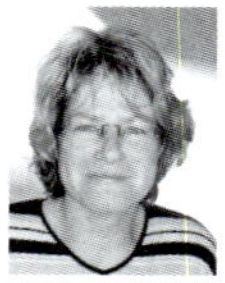

'S e rianaire proifeiseanta a th' ann an Sìne le eòlas air roinnean malairteach agus neo-mhalairteach. Tha iomadh seòrsa obrach air a bhith aice bho bhith a' ceannach bhròg gu bhith na manaidsear air siostaman inbheach. Thòisich i còmhla ris an VRC san Iuchar 2001, agus ron sin bha i na rianaire ann an Oilthigh an Naoimh Anndras.

Jane Cumberlidge

Jane Cumberlidge is a professional administrator with a background in both the commercial and non-commercial sectors. She has held a diverse range of jobs from footwear buyer to quality systems manager. Jane joined the Dundee Visual Research Centre (VCR) in July 2001 having previously been an administrator at the University of St Andrews.

Barabal NicColla

Cheumnaich Barabal NicColla, bha na Stiùiriche Ionad Sgrùdaidh Lèirsinneach Oilthigh Dhun Dè, à Sgoil Ealain an Naoimh Màrtainn. Tha i na sàr chlachair, agus dh'obraich i ann an ealain phoblach agus leagte, leasachadh meadhan agus ealain mus deach i dhan oilthigh a chuideachadh le togail buidheann ùr an VRC aig DCA. Tha i an diugh ag obair aig Còmhairle Ealain na h-Alba.

Babs McCool

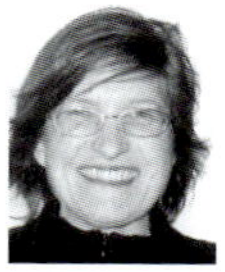

Babs McCool, former Director of the University of Dundee Visual Research Centre, is a graduate of St Martin's School of Art and a trained stonemason. She worked in public and applied art, media and arts development before joining the university to help build a new organisation, the VRC at DCA. She currently works with the Scottish Arts Council.

PROISEACT NAN EALAN – The Gaelic Arts Agency

Proiseact Nan Ealan

Thòisich Pròiseact Nan Ealan mar phròiseact rannsachaidh Chomhairle Ealain na h-Alba ann an 1987 agus an dèidh sin thàinig e gu bhith na bhuidheann-leasachaidh nàiseanta nan ealain Gàidhlig an Alba.

Chan e buidheann maoineachaidh a th' ann am PNE ach buidheann a tha a' dealbhachadh is a' leasachadh iomairtean ùra sna h-ealain Ghàidhlig. Tha am prògram leasachaidh ag amas air rannsachadh gnìomhach, leasachadh tàlant is pròiseactan suaicheanta. Far am bi seasmhachd aig pròiseactan dearbhaidh, thèid an stèidheachadh mar iomairtean air leth.

Tha na iomairtean a leanas air a bhith air an cur air chois: Fèisean nan Gàidheal; an sgoil shamhraidh, Ceòlas; an companaidh-cluiche, Tosg; cùirn-cuimhne nan Gaisgeach; pròiseact film anamanta nan sgoiltean, Dealbhan Beò; prògram trèidh nan ealaanan 's nam meadhanan, Sìol gu Bàrr; an t-sreath TBh ealain's ciùil, Tacsi agus co-obrachadh le Fèis Eadar-nàiseanta Dhùn Èideann is eile.

Tha PNE air na duaisean nàiseanta a leanas fhaighinn:Duais a' Bhùird Turasachd, Fòghnan na h-Alba airson Mòralachd ann an Turasachd Chultarach (taisbeanadh Cheòlais is Chalanais), sàr dhuais Dualchas Nàdair na h-Alba airson Ath-chruthachadh Àrainneachdail (Na Gaisgich) agus duaisean BAFTA na h-Alba is na Fèis Fhilm Ceiltich airson a' phrògram ealain is fèisdeis TBh as fheàrr (Tacsi)

Tha PNE stèidhichte sna h-Eileanan Siar ach a' gnìomhachadh air feadh na h-Alba is gu meudachail ann an com-pàirt ri buidhnean ealain Èireannach is Iomairt Cholm Cille, an iomairt eadar-dhùthchail a chaidh a stèidheachadh ann an 1997 gus na ceanglaichean eadar Gaidheil na h-Alba is na h-Èireann ath-nuadhachadh.

The Gaelic Arts Agency

Proiseact nan Ealan began as a Scottish Arts Council research project in 1987 and later became the national development agency for the Gaelic arts in Scotland.

PNE is not a funding agency but designs and develops new initiatives. The development programme is focused on action research, talent development and flagship projects. Where pilot projects prove to be sustainable they are established as independent entities.

Initiatives include Feisean nan Gaidheal; the Ceolas summer school; the Tosg theatre company; the Gaisgich memorial cairns; the Dealbhan Beo film-animation-in schools project; the Siol gu Barr arts & media training programme; the arts & music TV series Tacsi and collaborations with the Edinburgh International Festival and others.

National awards include the Scottish Tourist Board Thistle Award for Excellence in Cultural Tourism (Ceolas and the Calanais exhibition), the Scottish Natural Heritage Supreme Award for Environmental Regeneration (Na Gaisgeach), and the Scottish BAFTA and Celtic Film Festival Awards for best arts and entertainment TV programme (Tacsi).

PNE is based in the Western Isles but works throughout Scotland and increasingly in partnership with Irish arts organisations and Iomairt Cholm Cille, the inter-governmental initiative launched in 1997 to renew the links between Gaelic Scotland and Ireland.

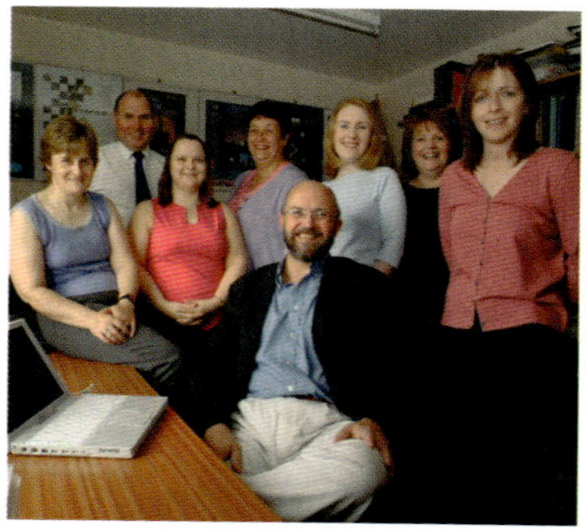

ARTISTS' MEDIA

Each artist, with a description of the media used and the name of the printmaker, is listed below. Print works without a specific printmaker credit were provided by the artist.

Poem	Artist	Media	Printmaker
1	William Crozier	Watercolour and acrylic	
2	Sonja Stringer	x 7 Colour screenprint	PH
3	Jake Harvey	Collage and graphite on paper	
4	Alan Davie	Gouache	
5	George Wyllie	Ink	
6	Bernadette Cotter	Acrylic paint and ink	
7	Simon Fraser	Digital print	
8	Olwen Shone	Photo print	
9	Alasdair Gray	Gouache, pen, ink and mixed media collage	
10	Deirdre O' Mahony	x 3 Colour screenprint	PH
11	Moira Scott	x 6 Colour screenprint	PH
12	Catherine Harper	Cibachrome print with acrylic and fabric	
13	Kathleen O' Donnell	Photo print	
14	Diarmuid Delargy	Watercolour and Gouache	
15	Alice McCartney	Watercolour and acrylic	
16	Ian Scott	Watercolour	
17	Sean Hillen	Digital print	
18	Mary Kelly	Photo print	
19	Anthony Haughey	Digital print	AH
20	Calum Colvin	Digital print	
21	Silvana Mclean	Photo etching	
22	David Quinn	Acrylic	
23	Anna MacLeod	Digital print	AH
24	Craig MacKay	Prints – gold selenium toned. Fibre based gelatine print. Gold and silver-leaf acrylic paint	
25	Rita Duffy	Watercolour, Gouache, pencil and ink	
26	Oona Hyland	Soft ground etching	
27	George A. Macpherson	Etching	AB
28	Elizabeth Ogilvie	x 5 Colour screenprint	
29	Calum Angus MacKay	Silver gelatine emulsion (liquid light) and acrylic varnish	
30	Joyce Cairns	Oils	
31	Eileen Ferguson	Watercolour, pencil and metallic ink	
32	Coilin Murray	Acrylic	
33	Caitlin Gallagher	Acrylic	
34	Joseph Urie	Watercolour, pen and coloured inks	
35	Abigail O'Brien	Digital print	
36	Andrew McMorrine	x 3 Plate etching (hand tinted)	
37	Steven Campbell	Acrylic	
38	Shane Cullen	Chromoscan heat transfer	
39	Kevin MacLean	Digital iris print	
40	Norman Shaw	Etching	PH & MH
41	John McNaught	Lino-cut relief print	JMN
42	Stephen Lawson	Digital print	
43	Hughie O' Donoghue	Acrylic	
44	Noel Sheridan	Digital print	
45	Anna Davis	Etching (hand tinted)	PH & AD
46	Michael Kane	Acrylic	
47	Tom Fitzgerald	Ink and watercolour	
48	Brian Connolly	Screenprint, metallic spraypaint and metallic ink	
49	Mick O' Kelly	Digital print	
50	Joanne Breen	Tapestry	
51	Eileen Coates	Ink and soft pastels	
52	Neil MacPherson	Acrylic	
53	Frances Walker	2 plate photo litho (hand tinted)	MM
54	Katherine Boucher Beug	Watercolour, acrylic and pencil	
55	Will MacLean	Pigment and acrylic medium	
56	Stan Clementsmith	Relief print	PH
57	Floraidh MacKenzie	x 8 Colour screenprint	PH
58	Ian McCulloch	x 2 Colour relief print	MW
59	Gus Wylie	Photo print	
60	Bridget Flannery	Watercolour, collage and acrylic	
61	Scott Kilgour	Colour pastel drawing	
62	Helen O' Leary	Pencil and colour pencil	
63	Donald Urquhart	Watercolour made using water collected from the waterfall, An Steall, at Hallaig	
64	Patricia Looby	Acrylic and collage	
65	Ronnie Hughes	Acrylic	
66	Marian Leven	Watercolour and acrylic medium	
67	William Brotherston	Charcoal and chalk	
68	Edward Summerton	Toray litho	PH
69	Tadhg McSweeney	Watercolour and acrylic	
70	Brian Maguire	Watercolour, acrylic, pen and ink	
71	Frances Hegarty	x 2 colour screenprint	
72	Geraldine O' Reilly	x 2 Plate etching	PH
73	Andrew Folan	photo print	

Poem	Artist	Media	Printmaker
74	John Bellany	Photo Polymer Gravure	MW
75	Pauline Cummins	Watercolour	
76	Fionnuala Ni Chiosain	Inkwash	
77	Doug Cocker	x 10 Colour screenprint	PH
78	Aisling O' Beirn	x 3 Colour screenprint	
79	Ian Joyce	Lithograph	
80	Steve Dilworth	Photo etching	
81	Mary Avril Gillan	Watercolour with drawing	
82	Daphne Wright	Digital print	AH
83	John Byrne	Watercolour and colour pencil	
84	Mhairi Killin	Woven wire and aluminium photographic image	
85	Remco De Fouw	Silver gelatine on emulsion coated paper (liquid light)	
86	Conor McFeely	Screenprint	
87	Oliver Comerford	Photograph	
88	Clare Langan	x 5 Colour screenprint	PH
89	Fiona Hutchison	Acrylic	
90	Alfred Graf	Watercolour and Screenprint	
91	Alastair McLennan	x 8 Colour screenprint	PH
92	James Morrison	x 7 Colour screenprint	PH
93	Helen MacAlister	x 8 Colour screenprint	PH
94	Donald Smith	Watercolour pen and ink	
95	Kate Whiteford	x 6 Colour screenprint	
96	Robert Ballagh	Oils	
97	Iain Brady	Drawing	
98	David Faithfull	x 8 Colour screenprint	PH
99	Sigrid Shone	Inkwash	
100	Alannah O' Kelly	Digital print	AH

AB	Alfons Bytautus
AD	Alexei Dilworth
AH	Anthony Hobbs
MD	Marty Dunne
PH	Paul Harrison
MH	Mark Hunter
MM	Mary Modeen
MW	Michael Waight

ACKNOWLEDGEMENTS

An Leabhar Mòr *has attracted a remarkable degree of goodwill and support from hundreds of people who, at different times and in multiple different ways, have all contributed to its creation. The key contributions by the poets, artists, calligraphers and the support team are all credited elsewhere. For me, the sustaining inspiration for the* Leabhar Mòr *has been the staff of the Gaelic Arts Agency, who have held the ring around this creative space for nearly three years They finally pulled all of the strands together, and without their multi-tasking, tenacity and heroic capacity for burning midnight oil, the* Leabhar Mòr *would simply not exist. We gratefully acknowledge the moral and practical support of the following individuals and apologise for any omissions.*

Anji MacLeod
Morag MacDonald
Donald S. MacLeod
Mairi MacLean
Domhnall Ruadh
Laura Macritchie
Moira Maclean
Carron McColl
Sandra Maciver
Nina Moir
Agnes Rennie
Iain MacAskill
John Angus MacKay
Donnie Munro
John Murphy
Margaret Bennett
Kenna Campbell
Jim Tough
Norman N. Gillies
Ciaran O Duibhin
Deirdre Davitt
Peadar O Flathartaigh
Michelle Ni Chroinin
Domhnall Angaidh MacLennan
Maolcholaim Scott
Mary Smith
Pat McAlastair
Eoghan O Conaill
Cian O Lionnain
Francis Brewis
Norman MacLeod
Norah Campbell
James Kerr
Helen Carey
Kieran Walsh
Peter Murray
Lorraine Comer
Tanya Kiang
Dorothy Walker
Anthony Hobbs
Alfons Bytautus
Michael Wright
Mark Hunter
Mary Modeen
Rebekah Dillworth
Alexe Dillworth
Marty Dunne
Peadar Cox
Nan S. Macleod
Alexina Graham
Norma Macleod
Donald John Maciver
Janet Macneil
John M. Macleod
Jo MacDonald
Kevin Anderson
Murray Grigor
Cassandra McGrogan
Seumas McGarvey
Conor Hammond
Alastair McCallum
Jane Carroll
Russell Kyle
Joe Woods
Hilary Robinson
Mairead Ni Einreachain
Mairin Murray
Patsy MacLean
Alex MacDonald
Sean McReamon
Muiris O Rochain
Harry Hughes
Brian Wilson
Joni Buchanan
Eamon O Cuiv
Dan Mulhall
Mark O Neill
Ellen McAdam
Victoria Hollowes
Stuart MacDonald
Anne Lorne Gillies
Anne Wallace
Margaret MacKelvie
Seonaidh A. Mac a'Phearsain
Sheila Murray
Joy Hatwood
Murray Forbes
Faith Liddell
Catherine Lockerbie
Ann Matheson
Robert Towers
Frank Devereaux
Eduard Delgado
Elisenda Belda
Annamari Laaksonen
Richard A. Wyndham
Samir R. Takla
Scottish Publishers Association
The People of Boolavogue

Canongate

Jamie Byng
David Graham
Judy Moir
Jim Hutcheson
Barrie Tullett
Charly Murray
Caroline Gorham
Colin McLear
Karen McCrossan
Nicola Wood
Michael Conway
Alison Rae
Tom Norton

COPYRIGHT PERMISSIONS

Various authors, publishers and Estates have generously given permission to use extracts from the following copyright works:

'Pangur Bán' translated by Gerard Murphy and reproduced by kind permission of Four Courts Press, Dublin and the author' s estate; 'A Bé Find' translated by Gabriel Rosenstock from *A Treasury of Irish Love*, Hippocrene Books, 'An Lon Dubh' with thanks to the Governing Board of the School of Celtic Studies of the Dublin Institute for Advanced Studies, translated by David Greene and Frank O'Connor and reprinted by permission of PFD on behalf of Frank O'Connor and David Greene © Frank O'Connor and David Greene; 'Is acher ingáith in-nocht' with thanks to the Governing Board of the School of Celtic Studies of the Dublin Institute for Advanced Studies, translated by David Green and Frank O'Connor and reprinted by permission of PFD on behalf of Frank O'Connor and David Greene © Frank O'Connor and David Greene; 'Aithbe damsa bés mara' translated by Donncha Ó hAodha le caoinchead saor ó An Sagart, An Daingean, Co. Chiarraí, Éire; 'Coinneach Neill' by Aonghas Caimbeul, with thanks to Donald John Campbell, Ness, Isle of Lewis; 'Bisearta' written and translated by George Campbell Hay from *Collected Poems and Songs of George Campbell Hay* (2000) edited by Michael Byrne, Edinburgh University Press, © the estate of George Campbell Hay; 'An Scáthán' written by Michael Davitt and translated by Paul Muldoon © Michael Davitt, Louis De Paor and Paul Muldoon, reproduced by permission of Cork University Press; 'Valparaiso' written by Pádraig de Brún, Fá thuairim Bhéarla Oiliféir Shinseoin Uí Ghógartaigh; 'Mo Rùn Geal Og' written by Cairstiona Fearghasdan and translated by Ruaraidh MacThòmais from *Gaelic Poetry in the Eighteenth Century* (1993) edited by Professor Derick Thomson, ASLS, reproduced with permission of the Association for Scottish Literary Studies; 'Amra Choluim Chille' composed by Dallán Forgaill with thanks to the Governing Board of the School of Celtic Studies of the Dublin Institute for Advanced Studies; 'Nár Mhéanar É' written and translated by Pearce Hutchinson, reproduced by kind permission of the author from *The Soul That Kissed the Body* (1990), The Gallery Press; 'Aig a' Chladh' written and translated by Iain Crichton Smith from *Collected Poems* (1992), Carcanet Press; 'Bùth Dhòmhnaill 'IcLeòid' written by Dòmhnall Mac an t-Saoir with thanks to Mrs Morag Cumming; 'Cead Deireannach nam Beann' written by Donnchadh Bàn Mac an t-Saoir, translated by Angus MacLeod and with thanks to Alasdair M. MacLeod; 'Birlinn Chlann Raghnaill' written by Alasdair Mac Mhaighistir Alasdair, translated by Hugh MacDiarmid from *Complete Poems* (1993–95), Carcanet Press; 'An On dubh bàite' written by Séamas Dall MacCuarta and translated by Thomas Kinsella with thanks to the Governing Board of the School of Celtic Studies of the Dublin Institute for Advanced Studies; 'Bean Dubh a' caoidh a Fir a chaidh a Mharbhadh leis a' Phoileas' written by Donnchadh MacDhunLéibhe with thanks to Mrs Helen Reynolds, translated by Raghnall MacIlle Dhuibh; 'Chunnaic Mi Uam a' Bheinn' written by Murdo MacFarlane with thanks to Angus Campbell Melbost; 'Hallaig' written and translated by Sorley MacLean from *From Wood to Ridge* (1989), Carcanet Press; 'An Bonnán Buí' composed by Cathal Buí MacGiolla Ghunna and translated by Thomas MacDonagh, with thanks to the Governing Board of the School of Celtic Studies of the Dublin Institute for Advanced Studies; 'An Ataireachd Ard' written by Domhnall MacIomhair with thanks to Mrs Lorna Steven; 'O ghrunnd na mara' written and translated by Kevin MacNeil from *Love and Zen in the Outer Hebrides* (1998), Canongate; 'An Turas' written and translated by Ruaraidh MacThòmais from *Creachadh na Clàrsaich* (1982), Gairm Publications; 'Cúirt an Mheán Oíche' written by Brian Merriman and translated by Frank O'Connor, reprinted by permission of Intercontinental Literary Agency; 'An Charraig' written by Micheál Ó Conghaile by kind permission of Cló Iar-Chonnachta; 'M'anam do sgar riomsa a-raoir' written by Muireadhach Albanach Ó Dálaigh and translated by Frank O'Connor, reprinted by permission of Intercontinental Literary Agency; 'Bí i do chrann' written by Máirtín Ó Direáin from *Tacar Dánta: Máirtín Ó Direáin* (1984) Irish copyright The Goldsmith Press Ltd; 'Dán do Lára' written and translated by Micheál Ó h-Airtnéide from *A Necklace of Wrens* (1987) by kind permission of the author and The Gallery Press; 'Fúar leam an oidhche-se si dh'Aodh' written by Eochaidh Ó hEoghasa, with thanks to the Governing Board of the School of Celtic Studies of the Dublin Institute for Advanced Studies; 'Tairseacha' written by Liam Ó Muirthile from *Walking Time agus Dante Eile* (Cló-Iar Chonnachta 2000); 'Feasgair Luain' written by William Ross and translated by Ruaraidh MacThómais from *Gaelic Poetry in the 18th Century* (1993), edited by Professor Derick Thomson, ASLS, reproduced with permission of the Association for Scottish Literary Studies; 'Liadhain' written by Gabriel Rosenstock and translated by Paddy Bushe, with thanks to *Poetry Ireland Review*; 'An Loingeas' written and translated by Alan Titley from *An Fear Dána* (Clóchomhar 1993); 'Dónall Óg' translated by Louis de Paor with thanks to the Governing Board of the School of Celtic Studies of the Dublin Institute for Advanced Studies; 'Ceist na Teangan' from *Pharaoh's Daughter* (1990) written by Nuala Ní Dhomhnaill, translated by Paul Muldoon and reprinted by kind permission of the author and the Gallery Press, Loughcrew.

SELECTED BIBLIOGRAPHY

Irish Poetry

Bolger, Dermot (ed.) (1986) *An Tonn Gheal*, Raven Arts Press.

Caerwyn Williams, J. E. and Ford, Patrick K. (1992), *The Irish Literary Tradition*, Cardiff.

Corkery, Daniel (1925, 1956) *The Hidden Ireland*, Dublin.

Davitt, Michael (ed.) (1993) *Sruth na Maoile*, Canongate.

de Paor, Louis and Ó Tuama, Seán (eds) (1991) *Coiscéim Na hAoise Seo*, Coiscéim.

Greene, David & O' Connor, Frank (1967) *A Golden Treasury of Irish Poetry* AD *600–1200*, London.

Henry, P. L. (1991) *Dánta Ban: Poems of Irish Women*, Mercier Press.

Hyde, Douglas (ed.) (1985) *The Songs of Connacht*, Irish Academic Press.

Kiberd, Declan and Fitzmaurice, Gabriel (eds) (1991) *An Crann Faoi Bláth*, Wolfhound Press.

Knott, Eleanor & Murphy, Gerard (1966) *Early Irish Literature*, London.

McReamoin, Sean (ed.) (1982) *The Pleasures of Gaelic Poetry*, Penguin.

Murphy, Gerard (1998, first published 1956) *Early Irish Lyrics*, Dublin.

Ó Conghaíle, Mícheál (ed.) (2000) *Rogha an Chéid*, Cló Iar Chonnachta.

Ó Dúill, Gréagóir (ed.) (2000) *Fearann Pinn*, Coiscéim.

Ó Tuama, Seán (ed.) (1981) *An Duanaire: Poems of the Dispossessed*, Thomas Kinsella (trans.), Dolmen Press.

— (ed.) (1968) *Nuabhéarsaíocht*, Sairseal & Dill.

Scottish Poetry

Black, Ronald (ed.) (1999, 2002) *An Tuil: Anthology of 20th-century Scottish Gaelic Verse*, Polygon, Edinburgh.

— (ed.) (2001) *An Lasair: Anthology of 18th-Century Scottish Gaelic Verse*, Birlinn, Edinburgh.

— (ed.) (2002) *Eilein na h-Òige: The Poems of Fr Allan McDonald*, Glasgow.

Byrne, Michel (ed.) (2000) *Collected Poems and Songs of George Campbell Hay*, 2 vols, Edinburgh.

Campbell, John Lorne (1933, 1984) *Highland Songs of the Forty-five*, Scottish Gaelic Texts Society, Edinburgh.

— Campbell, John Lorne and Collinson, F. (eds)(1969, 1977, 1981) *Hebridean Folks Songs* 3 vols, Oxford.

Campbell, Myles (1994), *A' Gabhail Ris*, Glasgow.

Crowe, Thomas Rain (ed.) (1997) *Writing the Wind: A Celtic Resurgence*, New Native Press, USA.

Gillies, William (ed.) (1985) *Ris a' Bhruthaich. The Criticism and Prose Writings of Sorley MacLean*, Stornoway.

Leodhais, Comunn Gaidhealach (ed.) (1982) *Eilean Fraoich*, Acair, Stornoway.

MacAulay, Donald (1967) *Seóbhrach as a' Chlaich*, Gairm Publications, Glasgow.

— (ed.) (1976), *Nua-Bhàrdachd Ghàidhlig: Scottish Gaelic Poems*, Canongate, Edinburgh.

Macaulay, Fred (ed.) (1995) *Dòmhnall Ruadh Chorùna*, North Uist.

MacCallum, Donald (1925) *Domhnullan: Dàn an Ceithir Earrannan*, Glasgow.

MacDonald, Thomas D. (1921) *An Dèidh a' Chogaidh*, Glasgow and Oban.

MacFhionnlaigh, Fearghas (1997) *Bogha-Frois san Oidhche*, Carberry.

Maclean, Sorley (1999) *O Choille gu Bearradh: From Wood to Ridge*, Manchester and Edinburgh.

— (2002) *Dàin do Eimhir agus Dàin Eile*, (ed. Whyte, Christopher) Glasgow.

MacMillan, Rev. Somerled (ed.) (1968) *Sporan Dhòmhnaill Gaelic Poems and Songs by the late Donald Macintyre*, Edinburgh.

MacNeacail, Aonghas (1996) *Oideachadh Ceart agus dàin eile: A Proper Schooling and other poems*, Edinburgh

MacNeil, Kevin (1998) *Love and Zen in the Outer Hebrides*, Canongate, Edinburgh

Montgomery, Mary (1997) *Ruithmean's Neo-Rannan*, Dublin.

Smith, Iain Crichton (1965) *Bìobuill is Sanasan-Reice*, Glasgow.

— (1992) *Collected Poems*, Carcanet, Manchester.

Thomson, Derick S. (1989, first published 1974) *An Introduction to Gaelic Poetry*, Edinburgh.

— (1982) *Creachadh na Clàrsaich/Plundering the Harp: Collected Poems 1940–1980*, Edinburgh.

— (1993) *Gaelic Poetry in the Eighteenth Century*, Aberdeen.

Watson, William J. (1937) *Scottish Verse from the Book of the Dean of Lismore*, Edinburgh.

Whyte, Christopher (ed.) (1991) *An Aghaidh na Sìorraidheachd: Ochdnar Bhàrd Gàidhlig/In the Face of Eternity: Eight Gaelic Poets*, Edinburgh.

— (1991) *Uirsgeul*, Glasgow.

Scottish Visual Arts

Gordon, Lindsay (ed.) (1995) *Calanais*, An Lanntair, Stornoway.

Hare, Bill (1992) *Contemporary Art in Scotland*, Sydney.

Macdonald, Murdo (2000) *Scottish Art*, London.

MacLean, Malcolm & Carrell, Christopher (eds) (1986) *As an Fhearann: Clearance, Conflict and Crofting*, An Lanntair & Mainstream, Edinburgh.

Macleod, Finlay (ed.) (1989) *Togail Tir/Marking Time*, Acair & An Lanntair, Stornoway.

MacMillan, Duncan (1990) *Symbols of Survival: Will Maclean*, Mainstream, Edinburgh.

— (2000) *Scottish Art 1460–2000*, Edinburgh.

— (2001) *Scottish Art in the Twentieth Century 1890–2001*, Edinburgh.

Patrizio, Andrew (1999) Contemporary Sculpture in Scotland, Sydney.

Irish Visual Arts

Arnold, Bruce, Walker, Dorothy, Dowling, Oliver, Ruane, Medb, Mac Giolla Léith, Caoimhín (2000) *Shifting Ground: Selected Works of Irish Art 1950–2000*, The Irish Museum of Modern Art.

Catto, Mike (1977) *Art in Ulster: 2*, Blackstaff Press, Belfast.

Fallon, Brian (1994) *Irish Art 1830–1990*, Appletree Press.

Kennedy, S. B. (1991) *Irish Art and Modernism 1880–1950*, Queen's University Press, Belfast.

Snoddy, Theo (1996) *Dictionary of Irish Artists, 20th Century*, Wolfhound Press, Dublin.

Strickland, Walter G. (1913) *A Dictionary of Irish Artists, 2 vols*, Maunsel & Co. Dublin.

Walker, Dorothy (1997) *Modern Art in Ireland*, The Lilliput Press.

Calligraphy

Andersch, Martin (1989) *Symbols – Signs – Letters. About Handwriting, Experimenting with Alphabets and the Interpretation of Texts*, Design Press, New York.

Backhouse, Janet (1981) *The Lindisfarne Gospels*, The British Library.

Brown, Michelle P. (1990) A *Guide to Western Historical Scripts from Antiquity to 1600,* The British Library.
— (1991) *Anglo-Saxon Manuscripts,* The British Library.
Brown, Peter (1980) *The Book of Kells*, London.
De Hamel, Christopher (1994) *A History of Illuminated Manuscripts,* Phaidon Press.
Haines, Susanne (1987) *The Calligraphers Project Book,* Collins.
Henry, Francoise (1974) *The Book of Kells*, Thames and Hudson.
Jackson, Donald (1981) *The Story of Writing,* Barrie & Jenkins.
Johnston, Edward (1971) *Writing and Illuminating and Lettering,* Pitman Publishing, London.
Knight, Stan (1998) *Historical Scripts from Classic Times to the Renaissance,* Oak Knoll Press, Newcastle.
Korger, Hildegard (1992) *Handbook of Type and Lettering,* TAB Books.
McGuinness, Dermot (1992) *Irish Type Design: A History of Printing Types in the Irish Character,* Irish Academic Press.
Massin, Henri (1970) *Letter and Image,* Van Nostrand Reinhold, New York.
Meehan, Bernard (1996) *The Book of Durrow,* Town House, Dublin.
Meyer, Hans (1977) *Die Schriftentwicklung. The Development of Writing. Le développment de l'écriture*, Graphis Press, Zürich.
Neugebauer, Friedrich (1980) *The Mystic Art of Written Forms. An Illustrated Handbook for Lettering,* Neugebauer Press, Salzburg.
Nordenfalk, Carl (1995) *Celtic and Anglo-Saxon Painting. Book Illumination in the British Isles 600–800,* George Braziller, New York.
O'Neill, Timothy (1984) *The Irish Hand. Scribes and their Manuscripts from the Earliest Times to the Seventeenth Century,* Dolmen Press, Portlaoise.
O' Regan, John (ed.) (1900–2002) *Work Series* (monographs on individual artists), Gandon Editions.
Pearce, Charles (1981) *The Little Manual of Calligraphy,* Collins.
Sullivan, Edward (1995) The Book of Kells, London.
UNESCO (1965) *The Art of Writing: An exhibition in fifty panels,* 65006015. Paris.
Zaczec, Iain (1997) *The Book of Kells: Art, Origins, History,* London.

Other

Crystal, David (2000) *Language Death,* Cambridge University Press.
McCoy, Gordon & Scott, Maolcholaim (ed.) (2000) *Aithne na nGael/Gaelic Identities,* Queen's University, Belfast.
Thomson, Derick S. (ed.)(1994) *The Companion to Gaelic Scotland,* Gairm Publication, Glasgow.

Poetry Ireland, the Scottish Gaelic Books Council and the magazine *Gairm* are reliable sources of further information on Gaelic poetry.

Websites of calligraphic interest

Historic: Irish: www.columcille.com
Irish Script On Screen: www.isos.dcu.ie
Irish in the Bodleian Library, Oxford: www.image.ox.ac.uk
International, in the British Library: www.bl.uk (go to collections, go to treasures).
Modern: Calligraphy Ring: www.studioarts.net/calligring/index
Calligraphy and Lettering Arts Society, UK: www.clas.co.uk
Irish calligrapher Denis Brown:
www.geocities.com/denisbrown72

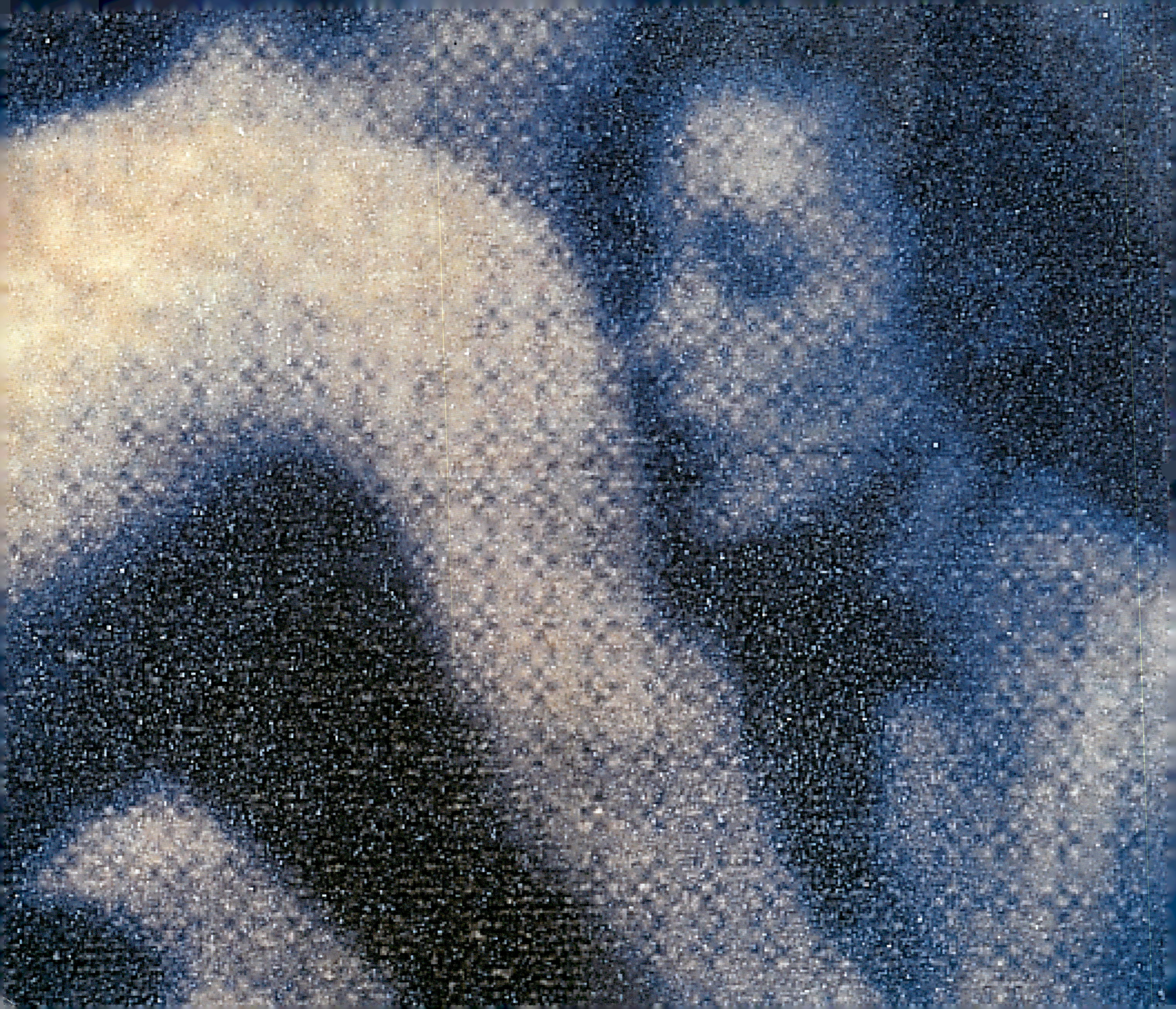

INDEX

The index consists of authors, artists, calligraphers, translators, and nominators, with details of their poems, artwork, translations, nominations and biographies. Page references to artwork are in bold type. Titles of poems in Scottish Gaelic (SG), Irish (Ir) and English are also entered. All poem titles are enclosed in single quotation marks and differentiated as follows: SG in bold, Ir in italics, English in plain text. The definite and indefinite articles in English are disregarded, but not inverted. Similarly, the definite article for SG and Ir – A', Am, An, Na – is disregarded, but not inverted.